SOCIO-INFORMATICS

Socio-Informatics

A Practice-Based Perspective on the Design and Use of IT Artifacts

EDITED BY

VOLKER WULF
VOLKMAR PIPEK
DAVE RANDALL
MARKUS ROHDE
KJELD SCHMIDT
GUNNAR STEVENS

OXFORD
UNIVERSITY PRESS

OXFORD
UNIVERSITY PRESS

Great Clarendon Street, Oxford, OX2 6DP,
United Kingdom

Oxford University Press is a department of the University of Oxford.
It furthers the University's objective of excellence in research, scholarship,
and education by publishing worldwide. Oxford is a registered trade mark of
Oxford University Press in the UK and in certain other countries

First Edition published in 2018

Published in the United States of America by Oxford University Press
198 Madison Avenue, New York, NY 10016, United States of America

British Library Cataloguing in Publication Data
Data available

Library of Congress Control Number: 2017949957

ISBN 978–0–19–873324–9

Preface

The editors of this book, despite some obvious differences, coalesce around a particular set of questions about design. The trajectory by which we arrived at the general positions expressed here varies, but it is not entirely accidental that all have played, and continue to play, roles at the University of Siegen in Germany. The reasons are complex but can be summed up as entailing both epistemological positioning and institutional commitments. All of the contributors to the book share a set of critical convictions about mainstream computing, and these have to do with an interdisciplinary stance (we could equally well gloss it as a "socio-technical" approach). In Germany, as elsewhere, this attitude manifested as explicitly opposing a rather traditional, and increasingly problematic, understanding of computer science, one which was also associated with conventional views of mainstream engineering and design methodologies.

The majority of the editorial team (Volker Wulf, Markus Rohde, Volkmar Pipek, and Gunnar Stevens) started their exploration into making computer sciences more relevant with respect to societal problems in the real world more than 20 years ago. They wanted to better understand the relationship between societal change, specifically on a micro level, and the design of meaningful IT artifacts in support of the actors involved. Or, to frame their interest in the concepts we promote in this book: they were interested in design-oriented investigations into the often complex interaction between social practices and IT artifacts implemented in their support.

Somewhat ambitiously, the aim was, and is, to establish a new research paradigm, but, and all the editors would agree on this, the road has been long (and winding). The interests and commitments of the core Siegen group have developed in a varied institutional context, which includes the University of Bonn; Fraunhofer FIT; the University of Oulu (Finland); Roskilde University (Denmark); the Hochschule Bonn-Rhein-Sieg; and—last but not least—the International Institute for Socio-Informatics (IISI) in Bonn. Kjeld Schmidt and Dave Randall, as more recently arrived fellow travelers, can trace similar institutional histories. Regardless, over time, we have been developing a set of theoretical, conceptual, and empirical commitments that we, somewhat in jest, like to call the Siegen School.

The concept of "practice" and, arguably, just as importantly, the idea of practice-based computing, has become core to these endeavors. We are grateful to colleagues and friends around the world for their intellectual (and other) support. In Siegen we owe much to Erhard Schüttpelz. Drawing on the strong local tradition in media studies, he worked out an ambitious program of grounding media research in ethnographical investigations of social practices. Erhard's turn to practices created additional grounding for an extremely fruitful interdisciplinary cooperation. Others have been equally influential. Mark Ackerman, Kari Kuutti, Gerhard Fischer, Peter Brödner, Batya Friedman, Ina Wagner, Liam Bannon, Susanne Bødker, Geoffrey Bowker, Wayne Lutters, Carla Simone, Antonella de Angeli, Irina Shklovski, Peter Tolmie, Myriam Lewkowicz, Gillian Hayes, Charlotte Lee, Peter Mambrey, Matthias Jarke, Austin Henderson, and Thomas Herrmann have generously supported our work. A design-oriented understanding of the concept of social practice, and the reflections upon it that we consider fundamental, is the result.

The evolving research paradigm described in this book is grounded in some twenty-five design interventions that we call design case studies. They took place in a variety of different fields of application and document our engagement with practitioners, typically over a period of years. Various collaborators have been influential in this process. They include, as well as contributors to the book, others such as Helge Kahler, Markus Won, Tim Reichling, Martin Stein, Thomas Ludwig, Nico Castelli, Rainer Wieching, Marén Schorch, Christian Reuter, Timo Jacobi, and Walter Schäfer.

We are also indebted to colleagues for administrative support. The administrative load is heavy, since long-term projects usually require external funding, and readers will know what administrative complexities follow on from that. Special thanks, then, to Marietta Krenzer-Gräb, Karin Ofterdinger, Monika Wagner, Rachel Schneider, Paulina Kühn, Roman Burbach, Christina Böhmer, and Julia Krämer, who have all, with astonishing grace and equanimity, dealt with our persistent failings.

Practice-based design research is an intellectual and emotional challenge. It is highly collaborative and requires a high, and sustained, degree of engagement. Somewhat guiltily, the editors can attest to the toll that these challenges can take on both colleagues and families. We, therefore, would like to express our deepest gratitude to our partners, children, families, and friends for having stood by us over all that time. This book is yours!

Finally, we would like to thank Dan Taber, our lector at Oxford University Press. He enthusiastically embraced the concept of this book and kindly accepted delays in our collaborative writing and editing process. While a first outline of this book was created in the stimulating environment of a Zimbabwean train, it took some 5 years to elaborate on this manuscript.

Siegen, Liverpool, and Copenhagen

Volker Wulf
Volkmar Pipek
Dave Randall
Markus Rohde
Kjeld Schmidt
Gunnar Stevens
April 2018

Contents

List of Contributors

Konstantin Aal
University of Siegen, Germany

Matthias Betz
University of Siegen, Germany

Julian Dax
University of Siegen, Germany

Tobias Dyrks
University of Siegen, Germany

Gillian R. Hayes
UC Irvine, CA, US

Jan Hess
University of Siegen, Germany

Nozomi Ikeya
Keio University, Tokyo, Japan

Timo Jakobi
University of Siegen, Germany

Kaori Kashimura
Hitachi, Ltd., Tokyo, Japan

Takafumi Kawasaki, Jr.
Hitachi, Ltd, Tokyo, Japan

Matthias Korn
University of Siegen, Germany

Charlotte P. Lee
University of Washington, Seattle, WA, USA

Claudia Müller
University of Siegen, Germany and International Institute for Socio-Informatics (IISI), Bonn

Bernhard Nett
University of Siegen, Germany

Corinna Ogonowski
University of Siegen, Germany

Volkmar Pipek
University of Siegen, Germany, and international Institute for Socio-Informatics (IISI), Bonn

Leonardo Ramirez
Fraunhofer IAO, Germany

Dave Randall
Unique Adequacy Ltd, Liverpool, UK, University of Siegen, Germany, and Keio University, Tokyo, Japan

Markus Rohde
University of Siegen, Germany and International Institute of Socio Informatics (IISI), Bonn

Kjeld Schmidt
Copenhagen Business School, Denmark, and University of Siegen, Germany

Kai Schubert
University of Siegen, Germany

Michael Spahn
SAP SE, Walldorf, Germany

Mary-Ann Sprenger
University of Siegen, Germany

Gunnar Stevens
University of Siegen, Germany

Thomas von Rekowski
University of Siegen, Germany

Ina Wagner
Vienna University of Technology, Austria, and University of Siegen

Lin Wan
University of Siegen, Germany

Anne Weibert
University of Siegen, Germany

Volker Wulf
University of Siegen, Germany, and Fraunhofer FIT

Fahri Yetim
FOM University of Applied Sciences, Essen, Germany

Introduction

Socio-Informatics—Practice Makes Perfect?

DAVE RANDALL, MARKUS ROHDE,
KJELD SCHMIDT, AND VOLKER WULF

The last 25 years have seen a small revolution in our approach to the understanding of new technology. It has become a founding assumption of computer-supported cooperative work (CSCW) and human–computer interaction (HCI) that in the future, if not already, most computer applications will be socially embedded, meaning that they will become infrastructures (in some sense) for the development of the social practices that they are designed to support. This will be true in an ever-increasing variety of domains and living conditions. Assuming that IT artifacts have to be understood in this sociotechnical way, traditional criteria for good design in computer science, such as performance, reliability, stability, or usability, arguably need to be supplemented by methods and perspectives that illuminate the way in which technology and social practice are mutually elaborating.

This is already underway. It has involved, inter alia, new methodologies for the investigation of patterns of use and the gathering of requirements (including ethnographic work, "living labs," etc.); new methodologies for design (methodologies that place flexibility and user involvement at the center), and new approaches to the product lifecycle (i.e., approaches that recognize the complex and long-term nature of the appropriation of technology by users and hence implicate a different understanding of evaluation). Nevertheless, these developments remain piecemeal. In our view, the field of human-centered computing—a field that has no precise definition but that foregrounds the practices of a number of different actors in order to better understand (and intervene in) the design process—has, to a considerable degree, been restricted in its development by a competition between theoretical perspectives largely founded in their disciplinary origins in sociology, psychology, and computing. The turn to "practice," which is, in large part ,what this book is about, exhibits a similar trend toward competing definitions, as we

Socio-Informatics, Volker Wulf, Volkmar Pipek, Dave Randall, Markus Rohde, Kjeld Schmidt, Gunnar Stevens (Eds). Published 2018 by Oxford University Press.

will see. The growth of a systematic and rigorous approach to practice- based in the broad domain of human-centered computing, we believe, requires new foundations, foundations that are distinct from their disciplinary origins while, perhaps, sensitizing us to a certain way of looking.

These foundations, we suggest, will be predicated on the resolution of a number of issues:

1. A clearer understanding of what we mean by the term "social practice" when taking a design-oriented perspective into account
2. A more nuanced view of the different ways in which processes of empirical investigation and the construction of IT artifacts may be linked to each other, allied to concepts for the design of IT artifacts that support (and challenge) certain practices in an innovative manner
3. A systematic approach to the design and use of technology that extends from early investigations into domains of practice, empirically grounded (and participatory) designs of IT artifacts, empirical studies into artifacts' long-term appropriation, and analysis of their developmental impact on existing social practices
4. A systematic view of the epistemological foundations of the context-specific nature of design-relevant knowledge and how these insights relate to problems of generalization, or, more humbly framed, of transferability across different domains of practice

Below, then, we make some brief remarks about how the "practice turn" can best be understood in relation to design. We can begin by observing that no sociologist or anthropologist working in the area would be especially surprised at the fact that investigation into the use of computer and other technologies often entails an appeal to some notion of "practice." It can, quite cogently, be argued that such a focus has been present in (and, in some views, foundational to) at least one strand of research in HCI and CSCW. That strand we can call, for convenience, the "situated" view (see Suchman 1986). It was, of course, and has been well attested to, a consistent theme of enquiry in the social sciences ever since the earliest days of anthropological interest in other cultures and, subsequently, in sociological work on and in a variety of subcultures (see Ortner 1984 for a useful overview). Sociological interest in the subgenre of "work" studies can be traced back at least to the work of Marx, to an interactionist school represented by the likes of Everett Hughes (1937, 1963), to Swedish and German work science (see Bannon et al. 2011 for a review), and to the "human relations" approach of the Tavistock school in the UK (see Trist and Bamforth 1951; Emery 1959; Trist 1990). It has arguably become something of an umbrella term, which can disguise various different shades of meaning (see Corradi et al. 2010 for a review of different traditions). More recently, and as a result of attempts to integrate theories of practice into our enquiries, there has been a resurgence in work that seeks to place "practice" as central to our interests in the design of complex, collaborative, computer systems (and, indeed, elsewhere). Exactly how we might conceptualize "practice" with respect to its relation to concepts such as "activity" or "action," and for what purposes, however, remains clouded by a number of difficulties, one of which has to do with the degree to which we might draw on the existing theoretical work to be found in the social sciences and, conversely, to what degree a new theoretical (or, at least, conceptual) lens might need to be ground(ed).

In this book, we seek to examine these themes both at a level of generality and in terms of practical application. Generality here refers to the problem of whether we can simply draw on existing frameworks for our understandings, what constitutes an appropriate level of conceptual analysis, and what methods are relevant to the examination of practice. To begin at the beginning, a large body of work over time has claimed to be dealing with the concept of practice. Outside of the context of human-centered computing, this is exemplified in the work of, for instance, Anthony Giddens (1984), Pierre Bourdieu (1977), Sherry Ortner (1984), Ted Schatzki et al. (2001), Andreas Reckwitz (2002), Davide Nicolini (2013), Shove et al. (2012), and others. The body of work that Shove and colleagues (2007, 2009, 2012) have produced emphasizes both that practices are connected and that they change. They make the point (in what they term a "slim-line" version of practice theory) that practices entail "the active integration of elements (materials, meanings, competences)" and that, as such, practices are "whatever actual and potential practitioners recognize as such" (see Shove et al. 2012, p. 82). In our view, this "slim-line" version—unlike some of the other offerings discussed here and elsewhere in the book—is empirically fruitful. Another consistent theme in the main sociological body of work is the possibility that an orientation to "practice" or "praxis" can unify otherwise disparate traditions in the social sciences. Of course, as Randall (in this book) points out, the interests of scholars such as these are primarily sociological (or anthropological), focusing on the constraints and affordances that produce both structure and agency.[1] The degree to which such interests are relevant to practice-based computing is arguable. Others, such as Schmidt (in this book), Wulf and his colleagues (Wulf et al. 2011; Wulf, Müller, et al. 2015; Wulf, Schmidt, et al. 2015), and Kuutti and Bannon (2014) have tried to turn this generic interest away from such abstract considerations and toward something more suited to human-centered computing interests. Nevertheless, we briefly examine such disciplinary interests here because they form a backdrop to our somewhat different approach. Initially, we focus on Reckwitz, largely because his work represents an attempt to provide a systematic analysis of "practice" and its distinctive consequences. On the face of it, as well, Reckwitz offers, in outline, a study program—one devoted to theory building in sociology.

Reckwitz (2002) builds on the work of the aforementioned social theorists, arguing first that the number of different theories that lay claim to the notion of practice are actually very diverse (in which respect, his argument is similar to that of Nicolini [2013]). He also argues (in our view, quite rightly) that, in some cases,

> one might even suspect that the "practice theorists" are hardly more than well-disguised successors to the time honoured sociological tradition of a theory of action as it was founded by Max Weber: After all, "practices" form structures of action which in some

[1] In passing, we should also note that some conception of "practice" has been in place at least since the middle ages. See the work by Schmidt (2014) for a detailed review.

> way are treated by all kinds of social theories stemming from the tradition of action theory. (Reckwitz 2002, p. 244)

He goes on, however, to dismiss that possibility, suggesting that the vocabulary of practice, when properly understood, does, in fact, confer something distinctive. It is important to note at this point that he is not arguing that new discoveries will result from this reorientation but rather that the practice view constitutes "new ways of seeing and analysing" that can help us resolve many of the classic dilemmas associated with the structure/agency debate in the social sciences (Reckwitz 2002, p. 246). His main argument is that this body of work, taken overall, constitutes a "culturalist" form of explanation. Culturalism here refers to the idea that human action makes little sense without reference to symbolic structures of meaning. He contrasts this (fairly obvious) idea with the assumptions behind the terms *homo economicus* and *homo sociologicus*. While we might accept for the purposes of discussion the basic contention that *homo economicus* entails, in the abstract, a model that is contingent on rational self-interest,[2] his description of *homo sociologicus* seems oddly thin. Here sociology, it is suggested, at least until the massed band of contemporary theorists arrived, was primarily concerned with the normative "glue" that holds societies together. Put very simply, these early models underplay—because of their insistence on the primacy of either rational self-interest or, conversely, normativity—the importance of "knowledge."[3] Reckwitz's position relies on what he sees as distinctive practice-oriented ways of viewing some classical sociological themes, or elements. These are the body, mind, things, language/discourse, and structure/process. In each instance, such concepts can be redrawn through the lens of "practice" and, more specifically, through the notion of "routine." There are things to take seriously here. Reckwitz is correct when he argues that a practice lens allows us to reorient the way we approach the matters he cites as being central to his concept of practice, such as materiality, discourse, routine, and process. These, without question, are germane to the kinds of design-related studies we might wish to undertake (although, cynically, we might say we already knew this). However, and we should be mindful of this, Reckwitz's primary concern is the reorientation of sociological theory. His argument consists largely in a set of oppositions to existing epistemologies in the social sciences (*homo economicus, homo sociologicus*). However, and for our design-related purposes, there are some significant lacunae to be addressed. If we are to cast practice approaches in our field as oppositional, then they will be in relation to something else, rather than social science theory. In HCI, those oppositions are better understood through a contrast with what Kuutti and Bannon (2014) call "dull-edge" HCI.

[2] Such a contention, in fact, does no justice to discussions by economists. Even a cursory reading of the neoclassical economics literature demonstrates that economists are only too aware of the role of knowledge in social life. Moreover, his all-embracing view of *homo economicus* pays no attention to the difference between "revealed preference" models and those that depend on assumptions about cognition (see Harper et al. 2016 for a review).

[3] While this may be broadly true, we should not forget the contributions of the late Durkheim (1915), Karl Mannheim (2013), and Berger and Luckmann (1991). Schutz (1967), an equally important figure in this tradition, is also, we feel, rather glossed over.

Kuutti and Bannon (2014) and Schmidt (2014; also in this book) draw on a variety of perspectives in order to elucidate what analysis of practice might mean in design-related contexts. Schmidt agrees with Reckwitz about one issue, although clearly not about others. That issue has to do with what is sometimes called neo-Cartesianism, and with new ways of maintaining the distinction between mind and body. For Schmidt also, following Wittgenstein, this distinction needs collapsing. However, let us remember that our interests here to not lie in sociology's theoretical moves—the problems of structure and agency are of no concern to us—but in whether a "theory of practice" has any explanatory value for HCI/CSCW purposes, or to be more specific, whether "better" design will result from these enquiries. While, as is apparent throughout this book, we very definitely subscribe to the view that conceptions of practice usefully orient our thinking about design, this is not at all the same thing as arguing that a "theory" of practice is necessary. Regardless, we need to understand more precisely what we might be talking about when we talk about "practice." For Reckwitz,

> a "practice" is a routinized type of behaviour which consists of several elements, interconnected to one other: forms of bodily activities, forms of mental activities, 'things' and their use, a background knowledge of investigating, of taking care of oneself or of others, etc.—forms so to speak a "block" whose existence necessarily depends on the existence and specific interconnectedness of these elements, and which cannot be reduced to any one of these single elements. Likewise, a practice represents a pattern which can be filled out by a multitude of single and often unique actions reproducing the practice (a certain way of consuming goods can be filled out by plenty of actual acts of consumption) in the form of understanding, know-how, states of emotion and motivational knowledge. (Reckwitz 2002, p. 249)

And,

> a practice is thus a routinized way in which bodies are moved, objects are handled, subjects are treated, things are described and the world is understood. (Reckwitz 2002, p. 250)

Now, we can have no objections to the idea that practice entails an understanding of the "doings," "usings," and knowledges that underpin our activities, nor to the idea that such activities are often regular and routine. The real question, for us, however, is whether such a characterization is adequate for the purposes we originally had when we embarked, with others, on the "ethnographic turn" many years ago (see, e.g., Brown and Duguid 1991; Hughes et al. 1992; Heath and Luff 1992; Schmidt and Bannon 1992; Hutchins 1995; Nardi 1996; Luff et al. 2000), a turn that, implicitly and explicitly, contained an appeal to work practice. Without delving into the differences between various perspectives that drew on this turn, there was a common acceptance that qualitative enquiries needed a focus (in some sense). Thus, while it is perfectly true that much of what we do can be characterized as routine, it is equally true both that we experience "troubles" in the course of everyday working life and that we sometimes have to identify ways of dealing with them. This, of course, was one of Garfinkel's (1967) concerns. Unlike conventional social science, which is largely predicated on the role of explanation, Garfinkel is concerned with *explication*—making things clearer. Explication can be thought of as spelling out, in detail, what it is that people are up to, how they make sense of the situations they find themselves in, and, in so doing, how they produce that situation in concert with others. Now, although we do not propose to engage in debates about the relevance of theory per se here, we should at least note the way in which, in those early days at least, the kinds of theory being deployed owed little to conventional sociologies. The reason for this lies in the fact that the design of any kind of technology is, by definition, an intervention in the world, an intervention usually aimed at making some kind of change. It follows from this that a need for change might usefully be identified by observing what we might call "problematic" situations. That is, although it is evidently the case that proceedings may often be routine, it is by no means true that they always are.

For Garfinkel, and other ethnomethodologists who sometimes characterize themselves as "Wittgensteinian sociologists," the processes of "endogenous rationality"—how people bring their reasoning to bear on situations—are very much their theme:

> A leading policy is to refuse serious consideration to the prevailing proposal that efficiency, efficacy, effectiveness, intelligibility, consistency, planfulness, typicality, uniformity, reproducibility of activities—i.e. that rational properties of practical activities—be assessed, recognised, categorised, described by using a rule or a standard obtained outside actual settings within which such properties are recognised, used, produced and talked about by settings' members. (Garfinkel 1967, p. 33)

That is, when confronted by normal, natural troubles in their working lives, simply having recourse to "routine" will not make the reasoning undertaken to resolve those troubles any clearer. Now, there are two main consequences of such a position. One is that it makes the investigation of rationality an empirical matter. The second is that the way in which we can be said to have knowledge through our wider cultural membership—what we used to call "socialization" or "learning"—is not a theme that we are particularly interested in. The focus, rather, is on "practical knowledge," "practical purposes," and "practical reasoning," and such interests stand in direct contrast to the disciplinary interests that so concern Reckwitz (see Knoblauch 2005). Attention to "practice" means, inter alia, attention to the way in which relevant knowledge in any given context is deployed in ways that are witnessable, that is, can be seen by all those involved in the action and by whom inferences about intentions and purposes can be drawn on a common-sense basis. Most tellingly, this common-sense basis is exactly what ethnographic observers are drawing upon to make their inferences about what is going on. This involves an orientation to rules. As Schmidt puts it, drawing on insights from Peter Winch,

> For an activity to be conceived of as an instance of a practice is predicated on its being a regularly recurrent activity. However, mere regularity is not a defining characteristic. The criterion of identity required for various activities to be considered regularly recurring (a type of activity) is that the activities in question are guided by the same body of rules. (Schmidt 2015, p. 104)

In keeping with what we have said above, these rules are understood and understandable by all members. How to apply them (and, indeed, whether to—because, in some circumstances, we may be confronted with a number of possibilities) is equally part of an ongoing decision-making process that may involve more than one person. We can, and typically do, then, draw entirely reasonable conclusions about what other people mean and what their intentions might be, drawing broadly on what we know in common. In addition, where we can see members deliberating over what to do, we can infer much about what their choices might be, and the reasons for any decision they make. If the reasons for such deliberations are not immediately apparent, they are likely to become so in fairly short order, not least because we can simply ask what they might be. On top of this, any mistakes we make about the intentions of others are usually quite easily repaired (see Garfinkel 1967). Enquiry into these emergent processes, into what can be identified as regularities, and into the reasons that people may have for doing what they do is, by definition, an empirical matter. Thus, Reckwitz is undoubtedly correct when he tells us that

> the knowledge that is a constitutive element of a practice is not only a way of understanding; it is—in connection with that—also a know-how and a certain way of wanting and feeling. Every practice contains a know-how knowledge of ethno-methods. Every practice implies a particular routinized mode of intentionality, i.e. of wanting or desiring certain things and avoiding others. (Reckwitz 2002, p. 254)

However, he is not telling us much about how this know-how is practically deployed. In sum, and we should stress that we are very much concerned with the "practice turn," we see a similarity with one of the pertinent questions that Reckwitz raises:

> Where does a certain vocabulary lead us? What are its effects? What are the effects of practice theory? There are two sorts of effects to be distinguished . . . a social-theoretical vocabulary is a heuristic device, a sensitizing "framework" for empirical research in the social sciences. It thus opens up a certain way of seeing and analysing social phenomena [and] vocabularies . . . [to] mould and change "our" self-understanding. Even without being applied in empirical research, social theories provide us with a certain way of defining our position as human beings in a social world, which inevitably implies a political and ethical dimension. (Reckwitz 2002, p. 257)

But we need to ask ourselves how such an argument can be translated into something that has a design relevance. What kinds of heuristic will serve our needs? What kind of intervention will be appropriate? How do we conceptualize our relationship to political and ethical problems? Against this background, Schüttpelz and Giessmann (2015), for instance, argue that IT infrastructures are cooperatively constructed and, at the same time, shape cooperative practices. Elaborating on this interdependency, they argue, should become the core paradigm of, in this case, media research. Reflections on how this might be done include those of Knoblauch (2005), who suggests that the answer to such questions lies in the idea of "focused ethnography," something he traces back to, at least, Glaser and Strauss (1967). Others (see Chapter 1) argue for a "grounded-design" approach.

Of course, some kind of intervention is quite clearly a large part of the human-centered computing agenda. This intervention is usually cast in relation to the design, introduction, and appropriation of IT artifacts. Such interventions depend on answering the "how" questions and, in very specific ways, some "why" questions. "Why" here is understood as very closely tied to the concept of "endogenous rationality" we have rehearsed above. Understanding this is largely a function of paying attention to certain kinds of concern. These may include identifying how it is that skillful practitioners actually and elegantly organize their activities in a particular order; how, in so doing, they sometimes need to pay heed to the activities of others around them (and sometimes do not); how tasks, learning activities, and various kinds of commitment are, in practice, allocated between people, and the bases on which that is done; what limits are placed on possible ways of doing things by the material environment in which people find themselves (and this, of course, means new technology as much as anything else); how, in their use of material artifacts, people sometimes find new and creative ways of accomplishing their tasks; what skills and knowledge, in practice, are used in order to do what needs/wants dictate should be done, and how these skills are distributed; understanding how rule-based routines have an important part to play in our activities; equally, understanding how we (sometimes) are beset by "troubles" which need resolution; and, finally, making sense of the ways in which normativity inflects (but does not impose upon) our decisions. Although it is obviously the case that rules, procedures, and other constructs affect our behaviors, it is equally true that our behaviors shift when and where we appropriate new technological forms. "Infrastructuring," a concept that seeks to explore the critical moments at which innovation and change may take place, is one conceptual resource for examining these emergent phenomena (Star and Ruhleder 1996; Pipek and Wulf 2009). The point here is that such analytic interests clearly have to orient to the opening up of design space. This means both examining the potential ways in which new artifacts can be brought to bear and looking at the way in which practices can be supported where they are discovered to be essential, and challenged where they pose problems for innovation. The marriage of the two is, quintessentially, what the term "sociotechnical" means.

One developing strategy for dealing with, and providing a focus for, the sociotechnical is to be found in the information systems community. There has been an extensive examination in this community, at least at the theoretical level, of the various ways in which technologies and practices interact with each other. We cannot do justice to the many variations on this theoretical theme, but we can make reference to the work of Wanda Orlikowski. She makes use of a "structuration" perspective (Giddens 1984) in order to show how practices are enactments of (i.e., producing and reproducing) structure but with the roles of material forces, and, specifically, technology, in view (see Jones and Karsten 2008). Orlikowski (1992) wants to argue that technology considered as "structure" is produced both out of its physical nature and out of human actions with it. Hence,

> technology is physically constructed by actors working in a given social context, and technology is socially constructed by actors through different meanings they attach to it and the various features they emphasize and use. (Orlikowski 1992, p. 406)

Later, she developed her position and focused much more clearly on the notion of practice as "situated," arguing that the "practice lens," as she terms it, constitutes "a means to examine how people, as they interact with a technology in their ongoing practices, enact structures which shape their emergent and situated use of that technology" (Orlikowski 2000, p. 408). Orlikowski proposed this lens to complement earlier structuration models of technology use (e.g., Orlikowski 1992; DeSanctis and Poole 1994), models that perhaps overemphasized the speed with which technologies become stable in use and underestimated the degree to which human actors can use them (or not) creatively. Another way of putting this, and one that has resonance for HCI and CSCW researchers, is that earlier models saw the stability of technological structures as being largely a function of their design (Stevens 2009). Now, among other things, Orlikowski (2000) argues that such perspectives were not adequate for understanding how complex, configurable, and networked technological ecologies might be appropriated by users of various kinds, nor did they adequately encompass the kinds of negotiation that might make their use legitimate or otherwise. Design, at least as traditionally imagined through some kind of "requirements" process, results in a particular kind of artifact. The material nature of the artifact, moreover, cannot explain either particular instances of use or why these instances become sedimented as regularities. That, inevitably, will be a function also of a whole gamut of factors, which might include the spatial and temporal configurations of work organization; the norms and interpretative schemes utilized; the experiences, skills, knowledge, properties, beliefs, conventions, and so on, brought to bear; the instructions given and enforced; and so on.

This diversion into information systems theory serves at least one function. It reminds us that if we cannot understand the uses of technology as being solely determined by the functionalities embedded in design, and if it is the case that transformations in use and appropriation take place over a period of time, then not only is a "practice" orientation implicated, but that orientation has a specific focus, in the way that Knoblauch (2005) suggests. Here, then, we say something about what that focus might look like. First, and most obviously, it is a focus with methodological features. Although it would be wrong to suggest that "practice" *necessarily* involves an ethnographic perspective (at least in the sense that most social scientists think about ethnography), it does, nevertheless, involve some kind of focus on in-situ behavior. If, as ethnographers insist, the behavior of people in any given context is a function of the way in which they construe that context, then a focused, or design-related, study of practice means paying attention to the way in which artifacts are used and the reasons why they are used in that way. Of course, this may be no simple matter, since they may be used in different ways by members in different circumstances; moreover, their use may evolve over time.

It follows that practice-based computing needs to accept the complexities that are entailed in recognizing the range of practices, the range of interests that inform practice, and the constraints (technical, institutional, etc.) under which practices are formed. What, then, might it look like? The paradigm of practice-based computing, of course, needs to align the understanding of social practices with the design of (innovative) IT artifacts in their support. Now, it is obvious that there will be some shift from designed-in functionality to patterns of actual use and that the practices that surround that use will shift. The question is, how do we identify these changes when they are likely to take place over a period of time—potentially a very considerable period of time? Extensive empirical and conceptual work of this kind can be turned again into design activities to (re-)develop or tailor these artifacts. We have tried to frame such an understanding of the design and use of IT artifacts by elaborating on the concept of infrastructuring (Pipek and Wulf 2009; also see Chapter 4). With regard to design methods, a practice perspective suggests the involvement of relevant actors and should therefore draw on methods that bring the endogenous rationalities of the practitioners to bear. To be clear, this does not entail any specific method but, rather, a commitment to a perspective. As such, methods that are associated with the participatory design community, with the ethnographic turn, with so-called living labs, and so on, are all germane (see Chapter 7). However, in any complex environment it is clear that IT artifacts should be designed with an understanding of the variability of practices in potential fields of application and their temporal evolution in mind. We believe that even small differences in social practices may, although not always, require differently designed IT artifacts in their support. So, techniques that support local appropriation practices (Stevens et al. 2010), and those that enable local actors to tailor IT artifacts to differences in the supported practices, need to be investigated and applied (Henderson and Kyng 1991; Lieberman et al. 2006; Wulf et al. 2008; also see Chapter 13).

Of course, and as should be obvious from the aforementioned, various theoretical perspectives have been brought to bear in an attempt to clarify what we might mean when we speak about "practice." In use, the word can be applied in a large number of different ways. We do not, at this stage, seek to stipulate the term but would make the following point, again somewhat in keeping with Reckwitz's observations about how a practice focus is distinct from a focus on more conventional social epistemologies. In a design-related context, we would argue, a practice focus entails rather more than a focus on interaction and its processual characteristics (e.g., whether this processual character is found in conversation and/or gesture) and rather more than an interest in specific technologies (which might, of course, get used in many different ways, depending on context). Although new technology has become a resource, as much as a topic, for analytic work, namely, the burgeoning interest in interaction design (see, e.g., Sharp 2003) and the use of video to support it, our point would be that "interaction" as a category is a subset of the category "practice." We can have many practices, some of which, but not all, involve interactions either with other people or with new forms of technology. "Practice," then, ought to provide a lens of a more inclusive character through which we can understand the complex, interwoven, and evolving interdependencies of purposes, rationalities, rules, procedures, technologies, and interactions. The findings that emanate from such analytic work will be the basis for what we now call "practice-based computing."

To explore the opportunities for practice-based computing, research frameworks such as grounded design (Rohde et al. 2017; also see Chapter 1), as mentioned above, have been developed. Here, it is proposed that we might conduct case studies where we reconstruct the social practices observed before and during the design and appropriation of innovative IT artifacts. These context-specific research endeavors are called "design case studies." The point here, according to these authors, is not only the investigation of practice at a particular moment, but to understand how practices change as new technologies are introduced—how they are appropriated. A better understanding of this dynamic interplay can and should inform the development of research infrastructures to enable IT design in practice. Such infrastructures are called PRAXLABS (see Chapter 10).

Another major issue inherent in the practice-oriented research paradigm is the situated nature of its findings. Traditionally, computer science believed in an epistemology of context-free findings. For the speed of a microprocessor, the formal correctness of a program's code, or the performance of an algorithm, the type of social context in which the IT artifacts were embedded was considered to be irrelevant. Rooted in a positivist intellectual tradition, computer science, therefore, believed in a broad/general validity and applicability of its findings. A standardization of test suites and test conditions helped to maintain this understanding. The assumptions underlying practice-based computing are, it goes without saying, in sharp contrast to the assumptions contained in more traditional approaches to computer science, as, in the latter, the social context of use has either been underplayed or completely ignored. All explorations of social practice, the related IT designs, and the IT artifact's appropriation are, by definition, highly context specific in their nature. However, newly designed IT artifacts can be, and are, transferred to other contexts of application. Their appropriation may, however, occur in a highly situated manner. Given these specifics, practice-based computing requires a new epistemological approach to acquire, document, and transfer insights. This requires solutions to a number of problems. These include our apparent inability to build a conceptual foundation that accommodates both the specificities we refer to and the need for findings to be represented at some appropriate degree of generality. Therefore, we believe that a practice-based research paradigm needs to engage in an explicit discussion of appropriate modes of knowledge and expertise within and beyond our research community (Ackerman et al. 2003, 2013).

A practice- based approach, we suggest, should also provide actors (researchers, practitioners, designers) with opportunities for self-reflection and learning. This means—a point that is often overlooked—that the work practices of IT design are just as investigable as the social practices of those actors for and with whom the IT artifacts are designed. Design outcomes are not, in fact, the result of some logical and highly structured process that leads inexorably to a "best" solution. They are influenced by the institutional setting, the engagement of the different practitioners involved, and, not least, the funding sources for the research. The outcome results from negotiations of various asymmetries of power and knowledge, and of different sets of values. It is not enough, however, simply to assert that this is the case. We arguably need a much more systematic approach to identify exactly how such matters ramify in design practice. That way, we will be able to question and develop our research and/though design practices. For a first example of an empirical investigation into our own design practices, see the article by Dachtera et al. (2014).

The Structure of the Book

The book is structured in the following way. Each part consists of at least one leading chapter that examines key conceptual and methodological issues and how these issues ramify in HCI/CSCW research, specifically in relation to the practice "turn." In turn, chapters follow that exemplify the themes that the lead chapter(s) enumerate.

In *Part I*, which is concerned with the conceptual issues that underpin "practice" and the ways in which the concept can be usefully deployed in pursuit of a computing agenda, Rohde, Korn, and Wulf, using the concept of "grounded design," develop arguments concerning appropriation and infrastructuring. They do so in order to provide practical proposals that have to do with the way in which design activities that pay attention to concrete practices, to the evolution of those practices in the context of changing infrastructures, and to the need to understand the way in which problems, breakdowns, and so on, as users perceive them might be a useful resource for design work. In relation to "grounded design," they elaborate the way in which the computer science agenda has been, and is being, transformed by a number of factors. Here, historically, a positivist paradigm dominated, one in which formal approaches to valid knowledge were developed independently of context of application and where quality criteria, as they point out, had to do with formal proofs, algorithmic efficiency, or structural elegancy. Understanding the practices of users is a first step, but a more systematic approach, they suggest, is needed. They situate their position with respect to design research, as it has become known, and argue that a similar positivism is in view in that paradigm. "Grounded design," as they term it, draws on case studies that entail three broad, iteratively connected activities. These are (largely) qualitative studies of technology use in a given context, capturing also practitioners' perspectives on potential innovation: the design of prototypical artifacts by some form of co-design or participatory process, and analysis of the appropriation of the artifact(s) in question over time. Documentation of this and other cases, it is argued, is the means by which a stable corpus can be built. Such a corpus is the foundation of comparative work. They further argue that there is little work that specifically shows how design results from the conceptualization of the sociotechnical as "infrastructure." Their chapter proposes a reworking of the notion to reflect the dynamic, design-conscious processes that occur through the design life cycle and that ought to inflect design with a more integrated view of design, evaluation, and appropriation over a longer period of time. In short, they argue for attention to "infrastructuring."

Schmidt (Chapter 2) looks at the concepts of practice and technique in some detail, outlining the major turning points in their historical evolution, and showing the need for their re-invigoration through a more systematic and rigorous conceptual examination. Schmidt makes the argument that the concept of practice has existed in different forms for centuries, although some version of this turn has been a central feature of design research in CSCW. He points out that the term "practice" is to be found in some 75% of papers published in this arena. He nevertheless argues that there is little agreement about how exactly the concept is to be used. A range of difficulties attend upon usage, not the least of which, he suggests, are to do with what criteria of sameness are to be adopted such that we can categorize something as a practice. Is "practice" to be thought of as just another word for "activity" or "action"? Evidently not, and Schmidt draws on a range of sources to demonstrate just how confused and diverse conceptualizations of "practice" have been. Their deployment in this chapter is designed to demonstrate that drawing on notions of "practice theory" do not take us very far in our attempts to provide an empirical and conceptual grounding for the work we do. Rather, our orientation should reflect an orientation to the normatively governed contingent activity of actors or members.

Schmidt, in Chapter 3, expands on his critique of "practice theory," drawing attention to the fact that this so-called theory is, in fact, no such thing. Rather, and as some of its proponents accept, it is a fairly loose agglomeration of otherwise quite eclectic ideas. Again, and this is a theme that recurs in this book, practice theories of whatever stripe have largely been deployed (successfully or otherwise) to solve some recalcitrant sociological problems, problems that can be summed up in relation to the subjectivism/objectivism or structure/agency debate that has bedeviled and entranced the social science disciplines since their inception. The critical question in relation to practice-based computing is what these theories might deliver for the kinds of purpose we have in mind. Although other contributors to this book do not entirely agree, Schmidt is adamant that the answer is very little, or nothing. The principle reason for this is that most, if not all, of the accounts on offer provide little in the way of attention to normative regularity.

Following this, in Chapter 4, Stevens and Pipek lay out some of the implications inherent in the move toward practice-based *computing*. That is, as an addition to the inspiration that ethnography and similar analytic stances provide, they argue for a more systematic understanding of the way in which practice and technology are interwoven, by focusing further on the concept of appropriation. In this chapter, they make the point that the concept of appropriation allows us to recognize and examine the sheer pace of change, provides for a sensitivity toward the open and creative ways in which people may use new technology, and, indeed, provides for reflection on the relationship between designer and user. Like Schmidt in Chapter 2, they point to the often confused and divergent ways in which we can think about "appropriation," tracing a history through participatory design, the cultural theories of de Certeau, and the orientation that activity theory brings, along with other traditions of usability. They suggest that a clearer focus on "appropriation work" can clarify some of the issues. As such, "appropriation work" is close to notions of tailorability and end-user development but encompasses both. The concept, they suggest, is particularly useful in respect to the way in which we might deal with a range of contingencies. These include the heterogeneity of users, use situations, and application contexts, and with dynamically evolving contexts. The concept has, as is clear in Chapter 4, a close relationship with that of "infrastructuring." In Chapter 5, Lee and Schmidt adopt a critical view of the concept of "infrastructure" and, more specifically, "information infrastructure," pointing again to the many different ways in which the concept has been deployed, including in the social studies of technology, in pursuit of an overarching view of "infrastructure" as a relational concept (Star and Ruhleder 1996) that helps us understand the way in which heterogeneous practices interrelate through technology and as a means to understand practices that are not in any strong sense "organized" through formal rules and procedures (Hanseth et al. 1996; Hanseth and Lundberg 2001). Their search for clarity leads them to argue that, regardless of the conceptual confusions that persist, the concept of "information infrastructure" as applied by, for instance, Hanseth et al. (1996) acts as a necessary and important corrective to the presumption that practices are necessarily spatially or organizationally bounded. In a wide-ranging critique of some of the problematic assumptions inherent in different conceptions, Lee and Schmidt argue that more recent conceptions like that of Ruhleder and Star (see also Star and Bowker 1995) place few, if any, limits on what we can usefully think of in infrastructural terms. Nevertheless, they continue that the concept of "information infrastructure" provides a "necessary corrective" to CSCW insofar as it provides an apparatus from which we can discern the ways in which technologies today may connect disparate practices.

In *Part II*, Randall (Chapter 6) discusses the various ways in which the evolution of "practice" as a suitable subject for investigation has, unsurprisingly, been accompanied by new methodological approaches such as the ethnographic turn. Nevertheless, this approach to qualitative investigation has not gone unchallenged. Different theoretical stances, time pressures, team pressures, new domains, and conceptual confusions have all led to the adoption of a variety of perspectives that are, to a greater or lesser degree, associated with the qualitative. Here, then, the concept of qualitative investigation are interrogated through an understanding of its purposes, limitations, and relationship to the design life cycle. Randall argues that there has been an ongoing confusion about the constitution of the ethnographic project—a confusion grounded in disciplinary pieties. Unlike those who argue, for instance, that approaches such as "grounded theory" are to be understood as methods, he proposes they be understood for their analytic conviction, one that, although ill defined, has to do with understanding practices from the point of view of those who engage in them rather than through the somewhat dubious lenses applied by various theoreticians. In this respect, and this is echoed in, for instance, Schmidt's argument in Chapters 2 and 3, we need to shift away from the disciplinary interests of anthropology, sociology, and psychology toward a genuine commitment to interdisciplinarity, in and through distinctive conceptual work.

Following this, in Chapter 7, Wagner presents a historical review of the role of participatory design in relation to the practice of design and discusses some of the challenges that participatory design continues to meet. Wagner looks at the participatory design movement as an example of "co-design." That is, how do we turn the insights into practice that we glean from our investigations into something that looks like useful design conclusions? She further makes the very strong point, one consistent with that made by the authors of Chapter 4, that the aim of participatory design ought to be that some user involvement should be central to all design projects but that issues around what kind of involvement and in what kind of context remain substantially unresolved. The complexities of stakeholder interests in large-scale projects is one such unresolved issue, as is the continuing debate about how one treats issues of power in the design context. She argues that participation as a concept and commitment has one of its origins in the historical and varied discourse on the complex notion of *civil society*, with its moral basis in ideas of self-organization, community, and solidarity, its utopian moments, and its notion of multiple (political, legal, social, and cultural) citizenship. Exploring these roots helps us, she suggests, think about challenges for participation in design. How can the "utopian moments" in a design project be driven forward, and how do we turn existing participatory design commitments into more systematic analyses—analyses that reflect complex organizational and discursive environments, increasingly heterogeneous communities, and cultural variation? The chapter reflects specifically on the role of the new media, with their potential for connecting, representing, and sharing.

Rohde and Wulf argue, in Chapter 8, for a certain systematicity in our handling of technical and organizational design problems, in their discussion of integrated organization and technology development (OTD). OTD was elaborated in the early nineties and applied to companies and social networks in several research and development projects. In a sympathetic critique of existing participatory frameworks, Rohde and Wulf suggest that dealing with outcomes of a longer period of time, and specifically with the emergence of unanticipated uses, requires a degree of methodological sophistication, especially in regard to the complex intertwining of organizational and technological development. OTD is characterized by the parallel development of workplace, organizational, and technical systems and implicates an analysis–development–evaluation–adaption cycle. In detail, the relevance of sociocultural concepts of social identity, social capital, and communities of practice are discussed. While the OTD framework focuses on workplace design and collaboration in more traditional organizations, these sociocultural concepts take processes of trust building, social identification, and community-based learning into account in a period where organizations and networks are being profoundly transformed. In respect of these issues, they look for a coherent way of linking OTD to concepts like appropriation and design case studies.

In Chapter 9, Gillian Hayes discusses the relationships between design, action, and practice. Here, she focuses specifically on action research and the way in which it entails an explicit commitment to solving a problem or meeting a challenge and, moreover, involves commitments to participation as well. She draws attention to the origins of action research through Dewey's pragmatism and the more explicit agenda of Kurt Lewin but ties this agenda more explicitly to practice and practice theory. One of the important consequences of such commitments is that research agendas become as much vehicles for reflection and learning as they are methods of collecting and analyzing data. "Doing" and "knowing," as she says, are more important than what is done or what is known. Again, and in keeping with much of what has been said in previous chapters, the focus is on practical participation within an ethical framework. That is, the transformation and improvement of human experience is an explicit objective, one that is not to be found in orthodox change-management strategies. Moreover, as Hayes argues, a practice-based view is inherent to action research because this type of research focuses on the "doings," "sayings," and "relatings" of people.

In Chapter 10, Ogonowski and colleagues present the PRAXLABS infrastructure, a specific approach to setting up a living-lab research agenda. The authors examine the challenges of designing in and for domestic environments in a comparative fashion, drawing on data from projects dealing with home entertainment, energy monitoring, and ambient assisted living. User needs, they argue, are likely to prove heterogeneous, depending on culture, family circumstance, the trajectory of domestic routines, and so on. They examine the idea of the "living lab" as a vehicle for accessing multicontextual user environments to understand their usage practices and for involving users in the design and evaluation of new IT artifacts. The approach has the purpose of providing a means for the sustained design and evaluation of artifacts in a more or less natural setting and incorporates elements of the ethnographic tradition, action research (see Chapter 8), and participatory design. They take the view that "method" here should be treated as a pragmatic business and, as such, use cultural probes, informal interviewing, diary studies, and other self-documentation methods, as well as observational methods, in the pursuit of data concerning the ordinary practices of householders.

In *Part III*, we provide a number of examples of what we have been termed here "design case studies." In Chapter 11, therefore, Müller and Wan look at a specific circumstance in design—that of the "unreliable witness." IT projects dealing with the care of the elderly, the authors argue, have for too long been "technology focused," meaning that too little attention has been paid to what the complex wants and needs of this population look like. Allied to this, there are significant methodological problems associated with understanding what these needs look like, not least because the population of formal and informal caregivers, elderly people, and their families is a heterogeneous one. Moreover, it is one where orthodox notions of agency and autonomy are somewhat problematized. Orthodox sociotechnical approaches assume that observation, interviewing, and so on, constitute adequate methods of enquiry. Witnesses (participants) can, it is assumed, be relied on to tell us, one way or another, what their needs and wants may be. In the case of the Alzheimer's patient, however, this is not always the case. Patients themselves are on a trajectory that means long-term involvement is impossible, and the population of elderly people who themselves might be caregivers is not necessarily very "tech-savvy," which means the envisaging of possible solutions is limited. Notions of "want" and "need," in addition, have to be filtered through a variety of familial and professional discourses. Here, they reflect on a methodological approach used to design a "location tracker" that aids care workers and family members to monitor Alzheimer's patients and the use of which depends on the normative and ideological framework in which such care takes place.

In Chapter 12, Weibert et al. present "come_NET," which is a sociotechnical solution to cope with issues that arose around problems of collaboration across a number of intercultural computer club houses in Germany. In 2012, the evolving network of come_IN computer clubs had seven nodes/clubs. Chapter 12 shows how the idea of connecting come_IN computer clubs, on a social as well as on technical level, was the main incentive for the establishment of come_NET: come_NET was designed as a means to deal with the spatial distribution of come_IN participants, by establishing a technical platform that would network the different computer club houses' online systems. The authors show how, in order to understand and meet the needs of the end users, they instituted participatory procedures predicated on the involvement of the participants throughout the development process to build up a platform especially for the computer clubs. Technically, come_NET is based on a PHP framework, providing an online community platform tailored to fit the demands of children and parents in come_IN computer clubs. Again, the chapter draws together many of the themes examined throughout the book, including the problem of designing in relation to societal needs, of participation and action research in a marginalized community, and how design case studies might be implemented in a networked context.

Spahn et al., in Chapter 13, look at the problem that many business users have of being unable to adapt the software they use to their individual needs and working practice. This, the authors suggest, is a particular problem for small and medium-sized enterprises that lack resources and expertise. Using the design case study approach, the authors present the development and evaluation of a prototypical environment that enables users to create enterprise widgets tailored to their personal information needs, without the users needing programming knowledge, by mashing up enterprise resources via a lightweight visual design technique. The authors of this chapter are particularly concerned with what they call the "data-centric" adaption problems that business users face. The authors' design phase consists of a prototypical environment that enables users to design widgets for the display of data. The prototype was deployed in three German SMEs, with a view to getting a better sense of usability and usefulness.

Kashimura et al. (Chapter 14) examine a case study in the construction of a large and complex power plant. Using an ethnographic approach, they detail the problems of coordination that arose across three different sites, and they reflect on the contingent relationship between their enquiries and the various possibilities in relation to design (both of the organizations involved and their technologies). Their case study demonstrates the particular difficulties that can arise when commercial interests are brought to bear on ethnographic work in a highly complex and distributed work setting. Although, unlike many other contributions to the book, theirs is not a study that draws on design case studies, it does throw up a range of issues having to do with choices about what one should focus on and where one should focus in highly complex environments where coordination and cooperation entail long chains of consequence and where difficulties in execution can be traced to many different factors. This in turn, in the real world, means that such enquiries often take place in advance even of decisions about what kind of technology might be invoked and what its scope might be.

In Chapter 15, Matthias Betz provides some reflections on how we might begin to make comparisons across more than one project, focusing on the way in which our understanding of possible design requirements might shift over time and after continued exposure to the appropriation practices, in this case, of firefighters. Two projects are examined: the Landmarke project and the Koordinator project that followed it. The grounded-design philosophy is put to the test here.

In *Part IV*, we reflect on the processes of learning raised by Hayes by examining the role of meta-research. A practice-based approach, the authors stress, needs to include some aspect of reflexivity. That is, reflecting on practice necessarily means reflecting upon one's own practices and on how they mesh, or otherwise, with those of the subjects of, and participants in, our research. The chapter draws on three different studies to make some salient points about the different ways in which reflexivity in each context is constituted. We finish with some concluding remarks concerning the future direction in which a "grounded" approach may take us.

References

Ackerman, M., Dachtera, J., Pipek, V., and Wulf, V. 2013. "Sharing knowledge and expertise: The CSCW view of knowledge management" *Computer Supported Cooperative Work* 22 (4–6): 531–73.

Ackerman, M., Pipek, V., and Wulf, V. (eds.). 2003. *Sharing Expertise: Beyond Knowledge Management.* Cambridge, MA: MIT Press.

Bannon, L., Schmidt, K., and Wagner, I. 2011. "Lest we forget." In *ECSCW'11*. Dordrecht: Springer, 213–32.

Berger, P. L., and Luckmann, T. 1991. *The Social Construction of Reality: A Treatise in the Sociology of Knowledge.* London: Penguin.

Bourdieu, P. 1977. *Outline of a Theory of Practice.* Vol. 16. Cambridge: Cambridge University Press.

Brown, J. S., and Duguid, P. 1991. "Organizational learning and communities-of-practice: Toward a unified view of working, learning, and innovation." *Organization Science* 2 (1): 40–57.

Corradi, G., Gherardi, S., and Verzelloni, L. 2010. "Through the practice lens: Where is the bandwagon of practice-based studies heading?" *Management Learning* 41 (3): 265–83.

Dachtera, J., Randall, D., and Wulf, V. 2014. "Research on research: Design research at the margins: Academia, industry and end-users." In *Proceedings of the ACM Conference on Computer Human Interaction.* New York: ACM, 713–22

DeSanctis, G., and Poole, M. S. 1994. "Capturing the complexity in advanced technology use: Adaptive structuration theory." *Organization Science* 5 (2): 121–47.

Durkheim, E. 1915. *The Elementary Forms of the Religious Life.* New York: Macmillan.

Emery, F. 1959. *Characteristics of Sociotechnical Systems.* London: Tavistock.

Garfinkel, H. 1967. *Studies in Ethnomethodology.* Englewood Cliffs: Prentice-Hall.

Giddens, A. 1984. *The Constitution of Society: Outline of the Theory of Structuration.* Oakland: University of California Press.

Glaser, B., and Strauss, A. 1967. *The Discovery of Grounded Theory: Strategies for Qualitative Research.* Chicago: Aldine.

Hanseth, O., and Lundberg, N. 2001. "Designing work oriented infrastructures." *Computer Supported Cooperative Work* 10 (3–4): 347–72.

Hanseth, O., Monteiro, E., and Hatling M. 1996. "Developing information infrastructure: The tension between standardization and flexibility." *Science, Technology, and Human Values* 21 (4): 407–26.

Harper, R., Randall, D., and Sharrock, W. 2016. *Choice.* Cambridge: Polity Press.

Heath, C., and Luff, P. 1992. "Collaboration and control: Crisis management and multimedia technology in London Underground line control rooms." *Computer Supported Cooperative Work* 1 (1): 69–94.

Henderson, A., and Kyng, M. 1991. "There's no place like home: Continuing design in use." In J. Greenbaum and M. Kyng, eds., *Design At Work: Cooperative Design of Computer Artefacts.* Hillsdale, NJ: Lawrence Erlbaum Associates, 219–40.

Hughes, E. C. 1937. "Institutional office and the person." *American Journal of Sociology* 43 (3): 404–13.

Hughes, E. C. 1963. "Professions." *Daedalus* 92 (4): 655–68.

Hutchins, E. 1995. *Cognition in the Wild.* Cambridge, MA: MIT Press.

Jones, M. R., and Karsten, H. 2008. "Giddens's structuration theory and information systems research." *MIS Quarterly* 32 (1): 127–57.

Knoblauch, H. 2005. "Focused ethnography." *Forum: Qualitative Social Research* 6 (3): 44.

Kuutti, K., and Bannon, L. J. 2014. "The turn to practice in HCI: Towards a research agenda." In *CHI'14*. New York: ACM, 3543–52.

Lieberman, H., Paterno, F., and Wulf, V. (eds.). 2006. *End User Development*. London: Springer.

Luff, P., Hindmarsh, J., and Heath, C. 2000. *Workplace Studies: Recovering Work Practice and Informing System Design*. Cambridge: Cambridge University Press.

Mannheim, K. 2013. *Ideology and Utopia*. Abingdon-on-Thames: Routledge.

Nardi, B. A. 1996. *Context and Consciousness: Activity Theory and Human-Computer Interaction*. Cambridge, MA: MIT Press.

Nicolini, D. 2013. *Practice Theory, Work, and Organization: An Introduction*. Oxford: Oxford University Press.

Orlikowski, W. J. 1992. "Learning from notes: Organizational issues in groupware implementation." In *CSCW'92*. New York: ACM, 362–9.

Orlikowski, W. J. 2000. "Using technology and constituting structures: A practice lens for studying technology in organizations." *Organization Science* 11 (4): 404–28.

Ortner, S. B. 1984. "Theory in anthropology since the sixties." *Comparative Studies in Society and History* 26 (1): 126–66.

Pipek, V. and Wulf, V. 2009. "Infrastructuring: Toward an integrated perspective on the design and use of information technology." *Journal of the Association for Information Systems* 10 (5): 447–73.

Reckwitz, A. 2002. "Toward a theory of social practices: A development in culturalist theorizing." *European Journal of Social Theory* 5 (2): 243–63.

Rohde, M., Brödner, P., Stevens, G., and Wulf, V. 2017. "Grounded design: A praxeological IS research perspective." *Journal of Information Technology* 32 (2): 163–79.

Schatzki, T. R., Knorr-Cetina, K., and Savigny, E von. 2001. *The Practice Turn in Contemporary Theory*. London: Routledge.

Schmidt, K. 2014. The concept of "practice": What's the point?" In *COOP'14*. Cham: Springer, 427–44.

Schmidt, K. 2015. "Practice must speak for itself: Remarks on the concept of practice." *Navigationen* 15 (1): 99–115.

Schmidt, K. and Bannon, L. 1992. "Taking CSCW seriously." *Computer Supported Cooperative Work* 1 (1–2): 7–40.

Schuettpelz, E., and Giessmann, S. 2015. "Medien der Kooperation." *Navigationen* 15 (1): 7–57.

Schutz, A. 1967. *The Phenomenology of the Social World*. Evanston: Northwestern University Press.

Sharp, H. 2003. *Interaction Design*. New York: John Wiley & Sons.

Shove, E., Pantzar, M., and Watson, M. 2012. *The Dynamics of Social Practice: Everyday Life and How It Changes*. London: Sage.

Shove, E., Trentmann, F., and Wilk, R. 2009. *Time, Consumption and Everyday Life: Practice, Materiality and Culture*. Oxford: Berg.

Shove, E., Watson, M., Hand, M., and Ingram, J. 2007. *The Design of Everyday Life*. Oxford: Berg.

Star, S. L., and Bowker, G. C. 1995. "Work and infrastructure." *Communications of the ACM* 38 (9): 41.

Star, S. L., and Ruhleder, K. 1996. "Steps toward an ecology of infrastructure: Design and access for large information spaces." *Information Systems Research* 7 (1): 111–34.

Stevens, G. 2009. *Understanding and Designing Appropriation Infrastructures: Artifacts as Boundary Objects in Continuous Software Development*. PhD thesis. Siegen: University of Siegen.

Stevens, G., Pipek, V., and Wulf, V. 2010. "Appropriation infrastructure: Mediating appropriation and production work." *Journal of Organizational and End User Computing* 22 (2): 58–81.

Suchman, L., 1986. *Plans and Situated Actions*. New York: Cambridge University Press.

Trist, E. 1990. *The Social Engagement of Social Science, Volume 1: A Tavistock Anthology: The Socio-Psychological Perspective*. Philadelphia: University of Pennsylvania Press.

Trist, E. L., and Bamforth, K. W. 1951. "Some social and psychological consequences of the long-wall method of coal-getting." *Human Relations* 4 (1): 3–38.

Wulf, V., Müller, C., Pipek, V., Randall, D., Rohde, M., and Stevens, G. 2015. "Practice-based computing: Empirically-grounded conceptualizations derived from design case studies." In V. Wulf, K. Schmidt, and D. Randall, eds., *Designing Socially Embedded Technologies in the Real-World.* London: Springer-Verlag London, 111–50.

Wulf, V., Pipek, V., and Won, M. 2008. "Component-based tailorability: Towards highly flexible software applications." *International Journal on Human-Computer Studies* 66 (1): 1–22.

Wulf, V., Rohde, M., Pipek, V., and Stevens, G. 2011. "Engaging with practices: Design case studies as a research framework in CSCW." In *CSCW'11*. New York: ACM, 505–12.

Wulf, V., Schmidt, K., and Randall, D. (eds.). 2015. *Designing Socially Embedded Technologies in the Real-World.* London: Springer-Verlag London.

Part I

Conceptual Foundations

1 Grounded Design

A Research Paradigm in Practice-Based Computing

GUNNAR STEVENS, MARKUS ROHDE,
MATTHIAS KORN, AND VOLKER WULF

1.1 Introduction

Computer science is a young but extremely successful academic discipline. It has developed into a discipline that nowadays has its organizational instantiations in almost every academic area. At one time, the hardware of mainframe computers needed to be run in specific (parts of) buildings, and interaction with machines was restricted by specific coding devices such as punch cards. However, computers today are radically different. They are mobile and ubiquitous and, along with this, a multiplicity of interaction techniques have been developed. Looking at the various fields of application, the origins of computer science were strongly related to scientific applications during the Second World War and the Cold War. In the business world, computing rose to importance in the already well-formalized world of bookkeeping and accounting. However, computing technologies today, as we all know, are on their way to supporting all aspects of life.

Given this fundamental transformation in the nature of computing and its high societal relevance to all aspects of life, we argue that the academic field of (applied) computer science needs to develop its epistemological paradigm and research methods accordingly. Originally emerging at the intersection between mathematics and electrical engineering, computer science has for a long time understood itself in terms of a structured science: applied computer science followed a positivistic paradigm, viewing itself as a formal discipline that creates generally valid knowledge, independently of the context of its application. In this tradition, quality criteria were established such as formal proofs, algorithmic efficiency, or structural elegancy. However, with the increasing societal relevance of applications, computer science arguably needs to define itself as a sociotechnical discipline that contributes to the solution of social problems in context. This is a process that, while underway,

Socio-Informatics, Volker Wulf, Volkmar Pipek, Dave Randall, Markus Rohde, Kjeld Schmidt, Gunnar Stevens (Eds). © Oxford University Press 2018. Published 2018 by Oxford University Press.

is a long way from completion. While computing relies on formal methods to transform users' input through a number of state transitions into certain outputs at the user interface, the products of this formal core of computing, as is argued throughout this book, are embedded in social practices. Therefore, the quality of formal techniques and their application is finally determined by their impacts on those practices. Since social problems and social practices are contingent on the particular context of their emergence, the knowledge derived from such a research paradigm will be local and context specific. Consequently, knowledge gained from the interactions between computing artifacts, and their impact on the social practices in the fields of their application, are context specific as well.

Ironically, the success of computing has meant that the question of the scope of the formalistic defined and positivistic applied discipline of computer science has become more pressing. Our position is that a design-oriented discipline of practice-based computing is needed, one where methods and techniques can deal with the context specificity of local knowledge more seriously.

In this chapter, we present an approach that outlines such practice-based computing by building on situated design knowledge and dealing with the interplay of the social and the technical. We relate our approach to recent nonpositivist discourses on design research, looking at the practices of design, their (technical) support, and the sharing of related knowledge—which from a different epistemological positioning is sometimes referred to as "design science."

The chapter's argument is structured as follows. We start with situating our argument within the state of the art of design research and describe the foundations and core principles of grounded design. We then introduce design case studies as a central approach in a grounded-design paradigm and argue for the transferability of the insights gained as their central quality criteria. We finally suggest building portfolios of design case studies that facilitate their comparison and allow for bottom-up concept building across cases. We close with a discussion and conclusion.

1.2 Design Research: State of the Art

Like computer science, research on design has its origins in the Cold War era. The increasing complexity of artifacts created in architecture and engineering required a better understanding of design processes and practices. Zimmerman et al. (2007) point to the importance of the military sector in this context, as the military demanded more predictable design methods for the engineering of battleships, airplanes, and rockets.

In his historical account, Bayazit (2004, p. 16) defines the newly emerging field as follows: "The objectives of design research are the study, research, and investigation of the artificial made by human beings, and the way these activities have been directed either in academic studies or manufacturing organizations." Pursuing this goal, the design-research community, like many other academic disciplines, is characterized by strong epistemological divides.

As with its origins in the 1960s, positivist perspectives dominated the newly emerging field of design research. Cross (2001) argues that the application of novel scientific and computational methods such as operations research and decision-making techniques was considered to offer considerable potential in dealing with pressing societal problems. In this sense, Buckminster Fuller (1969) called for a "design science revolution" that was based on science, technology, and rationalism, to overcome the human and environmental problems that he believed could not be solved by politics and economics alone. Simon (1969) popularized this concept in his book *The Science of the Artificial*. In defining design as an academic field and distinguishing it from others, Simon (1969, p. 114) suggests: "The natural sciences are concerned with how things are... design on the other hand is concerned with how things ought to be." In this sense, applied computer science should be considered a design discipline.

With regard to his positivist understanding of design science, Simon (1969) proposes scientific studies on how designers work and scientific methods to improve and rationalize their practices. To this end, he assumed that the understanding of the problem to be solved by an artifact is given, while knowledge relevant for problem solving is rather lacking. The practices of design, then, are construed around given (and to be invented) methods and techniques, a utility function, and the definition of constraints on their application. Based on this presumption, design is conceived mainly as the optimization process of an artifact.

This understanding of the field has been challenged and criticized for lacking practical validity. Following a nonpositivist epistemology, Rittel and Webber (1973) characterized design and planning problems as "wicked"—not suited to the application of scientific methods. Wicked problems imply that every solution is a "one-shot operation" that consequentially leaves "traces" that cannot be undone (Rittel and Webber 1973, p. 163). Every wicked problem is essentially unique. If so, there cannot be any general theory that determines the right design practice or outcome. In this sense, design is by its very nature theoretically underspecified. Still, this does not imply that design decisions are arbitrary. As a consequence, designers are confronted with the dilemma that "there is no right to be wrong," even if in such situations there is neither an ethically well-defined situation nor a sound theoretical base for differentiating "right" from "wrong."

Schön (1983) pointed out that design, in practice, is not a linear process. Adopting John Dewey's (1938) pragmatist theory of inquiry, Schön conceptualizes design as an inquiry process characterized by uncertainty, uniqueness, and conflict. Problems do not present themselves to the practitioner as a given but are constructed during the course of work. Design is understood to be a reflexive "conversation" with a given situation, characterized as "reflective practice" (Schön 1983). Therefore, he suggests developing "an epistemology of practice implicit in the artistic, intuitive processes that some practitioners do bring to situations of uncertainty, instability, uniqueness, and value conflict" (Schön 1983, p. 49). Such an epistemology is more ready to put trust in the abilities displayed by competent practitioners than the one of his positivist counterparts (see Table 1.1). In a nonpositivist understanding of design research, it is understood that the particular design communities have their own well-developed practices, which should not be swamped with techniques and methods derived from the sciences (and arts; Cross 2001).

To structure the field, Frayling (1993) introduced three different research categories: *research for design*, *research into design*, and *research through design*. While research *for*

Table 1.1 Comparing positivist and practice-based perspectives

Frame Categories	Positivist	Practice-Based
Paradigmatic position	Universalistic thinking: *"There is nothing new under the sun" (Plato)*	Evolutionary thinking: *"All the regularities of nature and of mind are regarded as products of growth" (Peirce)*
Concept of truth	Correspondence theory of truth: *True propositions map real phenomena*	Pragmatist theory of truth: *Propositions recognized as true if accepted by actors coping with the problem at hand*
Origin of cognition	Ontological realism Sensual experience *"The mind [initially is a] white paper, void of all characters, without any idea" (Locke)*	Methodological realism Conceptual percipience *"Our perceptual judgments are the first premises of all our reasoning" (Peirce)*
Relationships between cognition, the object of cognition, and human action	Facts are cognizable independently of cognitive process and their linguistic form Actions are *caused* by well-defined rules and concepts	Facts are interpreted and signified by interactively shared concepts Actions are *judged* by implicit rules and concepts
Method of knowledge development	Inductive and deductive *(Controlled experiments)*	Abductive *(Exploratory experiences)*
Method of design	Theory driven	Reflective practice
Representatives	Simon 1969	Schön 1983

design develops foundational insights to enable the creation of innovative artifacts, research *into* design investigates actual design practices. Research *through* design focuses on the activities of creating an artifact with regard to a specific societal condition, and documenting the process.

In the last few decades, actors with a design background have focused on design methods and techniques, and the concept of design thinking in particular has impacted the computing field (e.g., Winograd 1996; Binder et al. 2011). Two fields of applied computer science have specifically been discussing appropriate ways of adapting design-research methods: information systems (IS) and human computer interaction (HCI).[1] In the following, we want to critically discuss these approaches, mainly with regard to their epistemological stance and their treatment of the social ends for which IT artifacts should be created.

[1] Other fields of computing have applied individual methods from the field of design. For instance, the software engineering community has embraced Alexander's (1977) approach of design patterns for the reuse of software modules. However, these approaches were rather partial, limited to the appropriation of individual methods.

In the IS community, Hevner et al.'s (2004) influential paper has opened a debate on the understanding of the field and on legitimate and appropriate research methods, specifically addressing the relationship between design and behavioral research. The paper needs to be read against the background of structural problems in the IS field, specifically in the Anglo-Saxon community. In the mainstream, IS research had been understood as a field of mainly behavioral research, following a positivist research agenda. IS departments following such a paradigmatic positioning suffered from serious problems, such as reduced student enrolment and soft money inputs. Against this background, Hevner et al.'s work (2004) in the journal *MIS Quarterly* established an alternative paradigm for legitimate IS research.

Hevner et al. (2004) provide a holistic framework for IS research by reconciling a design perspective that attempts to ultimately determine the necessary functions of IT artifacts according to given requirements with a behavioral science perspective—a perspective that suggests one should explain and predict the ways in which artifacts are used. The authors advocate focusing on the properties of technical artifacts and propose a design (and research) process that, they suggest, leads to the emergence of such properties. While delivering useful and usable IT, design science should, according to Hevner et al. (2004), additionally lead to results that augment the scientific knowledge base for design.

Hevner et al.'s (2004) design concept stands in the tradition of Simon's (1969) work by assuming that there is an a priori well-defined problem, typically established by the business environment, to be solved by an innovative IT artifact. The utility of an IT artifact needs to be evaluated in relation to the problem being tackled. While the content of the design-related knowledge base is not too well specified, the authors speak about foundations and methodologies. Opportunities to extend the knowledge base should determine which research direction a design science project could take.

There is a certain alternative tradition in the IS community, predicated on nonpositivist approaches to design research (e.g., Baskerville et al. 2009; Goldkuhl and Lind 2010; Kuechler and Vaishnavi 2012). Arguably, the best known nonpositivist approach to design research in IS is Sein et al.'s (2011) action design research (ADR). ADR focuses on both the design of IT artifacts and the action that embeds these artifacts in use. It reflects the premise that IT artifacts are shaped by the organizational context during development and use and conceptualizes the research process as containing the inseparable and inherently interwoven activities of building the IT artifact, intervening in the organization, and evaluating it concurrently.

Zimmerman et al. (2007, 2010) have also spurred a discussion on the role of design research in HCI. This work needs to be read against the background of transformations in the HCI field; Bødker (2006) has called this the transition from second- to third-wave HCI. Due to the extension of (ubiquitous) computing toward application domains such as leisure, arts, or the home, design criteria such as emotionality became more relevant, supplementing traditional ones based on rationality (see, e.g., the discourse on "user experience"; e.g., McCarthy and Wright 2004). Zimmerman et al. (2007, 2010) also point to the fact that interaction designers play a much larger role in the software industry than they do in academia. Therefore, they suggest that the HCI community should more explicitly embrace research through design approaches. They suggest expanding and formalizing the research through a design approach, to better understand how knowledge, or theory, is generated from this type of research. For instance, they propose a model of how interaction designers should cooperate with engineers, anthropologists, and behavioral scientists in research through design projects. That is, they basically argue for modifying designers' practices to make them better suited to a traditional understanding of academic (even scientific) work.

Gaver has further contributed to the HCI community by means of research through design projects. With regard to the discussion brought up by Zimmerman et al. (2007, 2010), he strongly suggests resisting an endeavor of artificial academification of design research and practices:

> Overall, I suggest that the design research community should be wary of impulses towards convergence and standardisation, and instead take pride in its aptitude for exploring and speculating, particularizing and diversifying, and—especially—its ability to manifest the results in the form of new, conceptually rich artefacts. (Gaver 2012, p. 937)

In a similar vein, Cross (2001) had already suggested that design research should explicate and describe practitioners' competencies, rather than trying to supplant them.

In their alternative approach to generating knowledge from research through design, Gaver and Bowers (2012) and Bowers (2012) suggest constructing collections of selected artifacts that a designer or a group of designers have created. By annotating such collections in different manners, comparative perspectives can be established in a designer's oeuvre, leading to a set of transferable concepts and dimensions of knowledge derived from designed artifacts. The authors call these types of collections "annotated portfolios."

In addition, Gaver recognizes the openness and vagueness of using artifacts. In his considerations about cultural probes and breaching experiments, he points out that it is insufficient for design research just to design artifacts and then evaluate whether they have the intended effect. Instead, as artifacts intervene in existing practice in an open-ended manner, design research has to observe how people make sense of the artifact, in order to understand design from both a user and a practice perspective.

Höök and Löwgren (2012) also deal with the problem of transferring insights gained with regard to the design of IT artifacts. They formulate an approach that helps in the transferring of intermediate-level design knowledge. What the authors call "strong concepts" reside somewhere between particular instances of designed IT artifacts (from which they abstract) and generalized theories. Strong concepts are thought to carry a core design idea about the interactive capabilities of IT artifacts. These ideas cut across particular contexts of use and even application domains to inform future design processes. From the authors' perspective, strong concepts somehow emerge from practices of reflection, analysis, and articulation by the design researcher across a longer trajectory of design work covering a number of design instances.

With grounded design, we follow Gaver (2012) when he rejects an academically induced formalization of the designers' practices as suggested by Zimmerman et al. (2007, 2010).

We also agree with Gaver on the openness and vagueness of how artifacts are used and appropriated (also see Chapter 4). The problem, however, with Gaver and Bower's as well as Höök and Löwgren's proposals to transfer design-relevant insights is, arguably, their lack of concern for the interplay between the IT artifacts' design and the appropriation of the artifacts over long periods of time. This lack is partially grounded in a tradition long prevalent in the field of design. For instance, Cross (2001, p. 54) describes "designerly thinking" in the following way: "So design knowledge is of and about the artificial world and how to contribute to the creation and maintenance of that world." However, and in contrast, we believe that a practice-based paradigm needs to link the artificial world with the social. Even so, there seems to be a shift in design research to take phenomena of unintended use, practice breaching, and appropriation more seriously.

The IS discourse is more interested in making the evaluation of IT artifacts in social practice a legitimate element of design research. While Hevner et al. (2004) propose a basically positivist research program, Sein et al.'s (2011) paper moves paradigmatically in a more interesting direction. However, their approach does not fully embrace the particularities of social practices and the contingencies of an IT artifact's appropriation over a longer period of time.

1.3 Grounded Design: Foundations and Core Principles

In the following, we want to outline a research paradigm for applied computer science that is both design-centered and practice-oriented. Our work is in line with the nonpositivist perspectives proposed within the HCI and IS communities. Following the IS tradition, we believe that the quality of IT design is finally evaluated in its effectiveness in dealing with societally relevant problems. Following the R & D tradition, we believe that problem framing is an ongoing effort in a design effort. Only in the end is there a clear understanding of what the societally relevant problems are. Therefore, the study of an IT artifact's appropriation is an important element of the academic endeavor. To this end, an appropriate understanding of the concept of social practice is essential to our work (see Chapters 2 and 3).

Our perspective on social practices, inherently embracing our interaction with IT artifacts over time, is based on an understanding that our experienced reality is socially constructed (Berger and Luckmann 1966) rather than "discovered" in a world existing independently from us. Cognition evolves through neither deduction nor induction, but rather through the creative operations of abduction in concept formation and artifact appropriation (Peirce 1958–66).

We have developed a practice-based perspective for a number of reasons. First, it reflects the fact that cognition and knowledge are always mediated by language, while being embedded in social practices. Objective cognition or "truth," therefore, is not practically available. Second, the observation—and even more so, the shaping—of social practices is subject to "double hermeneutics": the process of gaining knowledge through concept formation is self-referential in the sense that it changes the social practice it refers to in the very moment it is performed; observing a social practice inevitably means to structure it. Third, it transcends the largely pointless sociological dispute over subjective acting versus objective structures in comprehending human action, and it simultaneously explains both the persistence as well as the dynamics of change in social practices. Fourth, it comprehends the functional properties of IT artifacts as a product of conceptualizing social practices, while the collective appropriation of the functions for effective practical use makes them a part of these practices. It thus informs design activities as interventions in organizational development rather than as the functional shaping of useful artifacts (e.g., Rohde et al. 2009; Wulf 2009; Stevens 2010; Rohde et al. 2013, 2017).

In a practice-based perspective, actions change the world, which is understood to be in a state of constant becoming. To perform desired changes, actions must figure out and be guided by purpose and knowledge (Goldkuhl 2012). Table 1.1 demonstrates basic features of the practice-based perspective as compared with the positivist perspective, according to the distinctive categories presented by Becker and Niehaves (2007).

The concept of practice is, in some respects, quite controversial. Schmidt describes in more detail (see Chapters 2 and 3) why that might be and takes issue with the notion of practice as "theory." While understanding and appreciating that view, we nevertheless feel that something of value can be taken from Reckwitz (2002) in particular. His perspective draws on social scientists such as Bourdieu (1977, 1992), Garfinkel (1984), Giddens (1984), and Mead (1934). While their conceptual work is not at all homogenous, Reckwitz (2002) identifies core principles of a school of practice-theoretical thinking. A social practice is understood to be a mainly routinized pattern of human action judged by implicit and explicit rules and norms. Practices are not only encompassed by mental and physical forms of activity but also greatly influenced by material objects, especially by tools, media, and their usage. A practice is grounded in background knowledge that is not entirely explicit and that contains emotional as well as motivational elements.

Following Reckwitz's (2002) elaboration, social practices can be argued to be the basic elements of sociological investigation and represent collective patterns of interaction that are reproduced in specific contexts. The situated enactment and reproduction of practices are of special interest from a design perspective. While collective patterns of interaction are routinized in some sense, concrete action is situated, and deviations from routine may be occasioned by a variety of factors. Challenging practices, in design-oriented variations of breaching experiments, can help to make implicit rules visible to uncover what counts, not just from deviation from the routine but also from the norms. Challenging practices in this manner is a source for the transformation of rules and routines.

With regard to the reproduction of practices, we assume that social systems emerge and reproduce themselves through continued sense-making, as well as through the mutually related and coordinated acting of their members. These processes of continuous action and interaction are based on developed routines, their context-specific enactment, and assumed expectations. The reproduction of practices goes along with a related perception of the world, common language usage, and shared identities.

We suggest taking the concept of practice as the foundation of design research (see Chapters 2 and 3). Social practices, in their interplay with IT artifacts, become the central object of our investigation. In particular, practice-oriented approaches to design research are concerned with action, change, and the interplay between knowledge, artifacts, and action (see Chapter 9). Accordingly, designing IT systems for effective use is seen as a multilayer intervention into social practices. Appropriation as the effect of these interventions can only be understood in a longer time perspective (Chapter 4). The practice perspective offers a thorough and adequate basis for studying these interventions (Wulf et al. 2011, 2015; Rohde et al. 2017).

1.4 Design Case Studies

Design case studies are the basic elements of our research approach. These studies allow us to understand the relationship between social practices and the design space for IT artifacts that are built to support these practices. The design of IT artifacts needs to take the given social practices into account. However, when these artifacts are rolled out "in the wild," the addressed practices typically undergo changes while appropriating the artifact. We need to understand the interaction between the IT design and the appropriation activities over a longer period of time (Pipek and Wulf 1999, 2009; Rohde et al. 2009; Wulf et al. 2011, 2015; Rohde et al. 2017; also see Chapter 4).

Therefore, design case studies typically involve three activities that, in part, build on each other (Wulf et al. 2011, 2015). Because actual design practices are reflective and iterative, these activities are treated as overlapping, interleaving, and recursive:

Context study: Empirical studies of a more or less ethnographic kind (see Chapter 6) offer microlevel descriptions of the social practices before (and during) design-oriented interventions take place. An analysis should particularly describe already-existing IT tools and media and their usage. It should also capture the practitioners' perspectives on potential developments in technological, organizational, and social dimensions.

Design study: Grounded in the context-study findings, an IT artifact is designed for and with the actors in the relevant field of practice, often using techniques associated with participatory design (see Greenbaum and Kyng 1992). The documentation of this activity should describe the resulting IT artifact, as well as the process of its emergence. This includes a description of the specific design process, the involved stakeholders, the applied design methods, and the emerging design concepts.

Appropriation study: The IT artifact is rolled out into the practice setting. Its appropriation and impact on social practices over a longer period of time is observed. We document the introduction, appropriation, and potential redesign of the IT artifact in its respective domain of practice. We are specifically interested in the transformative impact of certain functions and design options realized within the IT artifact.

This process is always a collaboration between researchers/designers and practitioners. Although there is a natural order of starting points with regard to the activities' temporal structure, the overall approach is reflective and, therefore, iterative. The activities are not strictly consecutive but are continuing: once an analysis of existing practices has started, it does not make sense to stop reflecting upon the trajectory of existing practice; rather, it continues throughout the design and the study of the artifact's appropriation. Once the design has started, it may be continued in several iterations, although the technology has already been introduced to potential future users.

With knowledge creation as the central goal for academic endeavor, the documentation of this process becomes essential. The documentation and analysis of design case studies is directed toward later comparison, concept building, and the transfer of insights to related, but never identical, domains of IT application. The activities described above may offer a potential perspective for structuring the data and, later on, creating a narrative.

Typically, a case is a "natural" unit to start working at and with: it is one set of connected activities of researchers and practitioners in one field of practice. There may be, however, difficulties of different types that make it impossible to maintain collaboration over the necessary time span of a design case study. There are basically two ways to deal with such a situation (Wulf et al. 2011, 2015):

- design case studies may shift over time from one field of practice to a related one (e.g., the context study may have been conducted in one field of practice, while the appropriation can only be observed in a similar, but different, field of practice)
- design case studies may need to be interrupted at a certain point of time, without covering design or appropriation phases (e.g., we may end up with only a study in a specific context); in this case, as the empirical study has, nevertheless, been conducted in a manner so as to explore design opportunities, the study is termed a "partial design case study"

In both cases, it is the (intended) research practice that defines the design case study. The need to work with incomplete or shifting design case studies may result from the practice under observation; it may also result from the resource structure of researchers.

1.5 Building Concepts by Comparative Analysis

What can we learn from a single case—beyond the simple validation or falsification of "design theories" (Gregor and Jones 2007)? This question cannot be answered by a positivistic epistemology that assumes a predefined and context-independent set of categories. For instance, Hevner et al. (2004) and Zimmerman (2007) assume that models and theories can be generated that describe the interaction of humans and IT artifacts in a reproducible, design-oriented manner. So, in this view, design practice applies (and empirically validates) a set of models and theories for creating innovative IT artifacts for specific contexts.

An alternative view was outlined by Peirce's considerations about abductive reasoning, suggesting building explanatory, sensitizing concepts from single-case observations. Here, abduction could be understood as reflecting on the practical reasoning, making sense of new, unknown situations, and making such reasoning explicit and criticizable (Oevermann

2001). While we do not believe in a deductive (nor, strictly speaking, inductive) paradigm in transferring design-relevant insights, we do assume an abductive emergence of new ideas within reflective design practice (see Chapter 3). Therefore, the context sensitivity and the complexity of individual design cases need to be preserved and documented—rather than abstracted. These specific experiences stimulate designers in an abductive manner to create new IT artifacts dealing with specific problems in new contexts.

The point of design case studies is to document individual incidents, analyze them in their highly contextualized nature, and build sensitizing concepts by aggregating and comparing. The nominal similarity between *grounded design* and abductive *grounded theory* (Reichertz 2007) is not accidental: grounded design can be understood as writing a "grounded theory" from design case studies by means of a comparative analysis of individual cases in their contextualized complexity. We believe that such an undertaking would be an appropriate means of supporting reflective practitioners and gaining design-related insights.

To identify analytic similarities within a collection of design case studies, we suggest creating bottom-up concepts by comparing individual cases. Concepts may relate to social practices in a given field of application, specific features of IT artifacts, or the fit between artifacts and practices and the artifact's appropriation over time. Such concepts make it possible to organize the documentation of design case studies.

By comparing two design case studies in the domain "IT for the aging society," we created the concept of *grown and constructed autonomies*, characterizing a specific feature of social practices (Wulf et al. 2015). This concept characterizes autonomy-related care situations by questioning given rationales in practices of caregiving. The concept sensitizes empirical analysis of, and IT design for, these practices by focusing on the sometimes neglected aspects of personhood on the part of older people, and how they are positioned in the sociocultural contexts of families and care homes. The concept of *grown and constructed autonomies* is an abstraction that emerged from a comparison of given care practices in two specific design case studies associated with an analysis of the related literature. In Chapter 15, Betz and Wulf create six conceptual dichotomies when comparing two consecutive design case studies in the domain of emergency response.

Appropriate documentation facilitates concept building across cases, and the transfer of such insights to multiple audiences (practitioners, education, society). Comparing documentation across individual cases yields insights that may be orthogonal to and transcend the focus of any single case. Through contrast and comparison, bottom-up concepts may emerge that from an analysis of a single case alone might appear tangential at best. However, such concepts may provide larger perspectives and societal relevance.

Design documentation has been a central concern in research through design (e.g., Bowers 2012; Dalsgaard and Halskov 2012; Gaver 2012; Gaver and Bowers 2012;). Yet, with grounded design, we argue for two issues that have so far been neglected in this body of work:

1. Design documentation needs to focus not on designed IT artifacts alone but on their embedding in a particular domain of practice
2. Design documentation needs to focus on longer-term developments in the appropriation of IT artifacts, and emergent practices of their use

The creation of bottom-up concepts offers opportunities for analyzing similarities across different studies and thus allows us to better navigate the complexity of larger collections of documentation. Put simply, they allow the establishment of a *corpus.*

1.6 Quality Criteria for Design Case Studies

On the one hand, the driving forces for grounded design are ever-changing and yet, to some extent, stable practices, and the related problems and developmental opportunities perceived by practitioners and designers. On the other hand, grounded design is stimulated by the emergence of new technologies in the broader field of computing. Against this background, grounded design finds innovative sociotechnical assemblages that are explored within design case studies.

So, the following question emerges: how does one judge the quality of a design case study and its documentation? Or, to frame it differently, what are good research practices in a grounded-design framework?

Design case studies are directed, on the one hand, toward the needs and desires of practitioners. From this point of view, satisfied actors whose practices have evolved toward a better quality of life are testimony to a successful project. On the other hand, these experiences and designs need to be documented and reflected on as part of the academic endeavor. Such a documentation is directed toward the preservation and transfer of insights gained while designing in practice. Documentation and reflection make up the core of the academic enterprise, thus distinguishing it from pure consultancy work by IT professionals. Traditionally, these documentations take place in the form of academic papers, which need to be directed to certain academic discourses that offer the required legitimation structures. Yet, a good academic analysis requires an in-depth engagement in practice. There can be considerable tensions between these two sets of quality criteria (Wulf et al. 2015).

Therefore, quality criteria for design case studies must relate to their different foci and activities: the study of social practices, the IT design (including the design process and designed IT artifact), and the appropriation of the IT artifact in use. These aspects require adequate documentation and analysis to facilitate knowledge gains. We elaborate on quality criteria for each aspect in the following.

Good design case studies are characterized by an in-depth understanding, and descriptions, of social practices in the field of application, with a specific focus on how these empirical findings may contribute to the design of IT artifacts. The quality of the understanding is not necessarily only related to the length of the empirical context study but also the complexity of the practices, and to the sensitivity and (field-specific) experience of the researchers and the (temporal) resources and willingness of the different practitioners to participate in the research endeavor. While IT design cannot be deduced directly from empirical data (Dourish 2006), these findings ground the IT design. Their quality is therefore essential for the research endeavor. A highly valuable genre of empirical analysis may also question the validity of a particular IT artifact or of a certain approach to the design of IT artifacts—for example, empirical insights into the inadequacy of certain IT artifacts for the practices of firefighters (Ramirez et al. 2012).

With regard to IT design, the central quality criterion is its fit with the social practices to be supported. It is not so much about high tech, then, but about high-value. A good example is Facebook: from the traditional applied computer science stance, Facebook just presents an ordinary distributed system. Still, with regard to social impact, Facebook and how it is appropriated present a very interesting design case (Rohde and Wulf 2011).

The quality of an artifact's appropriation needs to be investigated empirically for two reasons: first, to uncover what practices are affected by the design in the wild and, second, to reflect on and judge effects from the various standpoints of the stakeholder. For instance, from a user perspective, eco-feedback might be judged as being positive because it makes electricity consumption more visible—while from a society perspective, the technology is judged as a failure because it does not lead to the expected saving of electricity (Schwartz et al. 2013). In sum, the final evaluation is carried out in practice. However, an analysis of the design process itself and the resulting IT artifacts can additionally yield valuable insights.

With regard to the design process, it can consist of a long-term, highly participatory engagement, as, for instance, in the case of the design of navigation and communication support for firefighters (see Ramirez et al. 2012; also see Chapter 15). At the other extreme, it may just consist of selecting and tailoring an already-existing IT artifact. A longer-term design process can explore the design space systematically and reveal additional insights into the alignment of practices with specific design options.

With regard to the IT artifact, an obvious quality criterion is innovativeness—first with regard to the technological state of the art and, second, with regard to an artifact's specific configuration for a certain field of application. In any case, there is a trade-off between the potential impact of the technological innovation, and support for the relevant social practices. The point here is that a practice-based design paradigm takes this tension very seriously and seeks to find some balance in and through reflection with stakeholders. It is often technologically quite straightforward to realize an artifact that offers interesting opportunities to support practices. In the case of a sewage work company, we extended a given document management system with two rather simple tools to add metadata in a semiautomated manner. This way, the existing technical drawings could be searched much more efficiently when the street channels were to be maintained (Hinrichs et al. 2005). Additionally, the reuse of given (tailorable) artifacts in new contexts should be considered an important research direction, since it provides us with a better understanding of sociotechnical fit.

With regard to investigation into appropriation, high-quality research offers long-term, in-depth, and honest empirical observation of the way the use of artifacts changes the related social practice over time. In this sense, it does not matter whether the introduction of the IT artifact affords changes in social practice that were anticipated during IT design. We would argue that the most interesting results emerging in this phase are those associated with unanticipated appropriation moves (Orlikowski 1996; Pipek and Wulf 1999, 2009; also see Chapter 4).

A longer-term research approach is highly desirable, since practices do not evolve in an instant but rather need a longer period of time. It is highly desirable to describe how the changes in practices were brought about and how individual learning provides, in time, new collective insights and new artifact uses. To better understand appropriation, it is very important to document how the appropriation of the IT artifact has been supported by the research team.

As already indicated, the documentation and analysis of design case studies are directed not only toward comparison, concept building, and the transfer of insights to similar settings but, more ambitiously, toward related, but never identical, domains of application. Therefore, the analysis of design case studies in all three of the activities discussed in Section 1.4 needs grounding in, and a comparison with, related work. A practice-oriented paradigm needs particular emphasis when considering the state of the art. The aim is not to subsume the particular case under predefined categories but to understand not only the common issues but also the particularities of the case by comparing what we know from literature and other cases. Since all design case studies are deeply shaped by the social context they are happening in, it requires a sensitive description and treatment of the setting.

A practice-oriented design paradigm in academia favors in-depth exploration and cross-comparison. Insights are generated and validated by investigating into similar domains of practice as well as by introducing similar or even the same IT artifacts into different practices. Such an approach facilitates concept building through comparing and studying the fit of IT artifacts across similar settings or fields of practice. Of course, what is similar, and how it is to be construed (and by whom), are nontrivial problems.

A valuable design case study does not need to be equally well worked out with regard to all of the quality dimensions discussed above. There can be a myriad of reasons, often emerging from specificities in the field(s) of practice as well as from the ongoing design practice, for specific limitations (see Section 1.4). Most important is the coherence of the different research activities.

1.7 Sharing Knowledge in the Grounded-Design Paradigm

How can experiences gained in highly contextualized design case studies be made relevant and applicable beyond their specific setting? This question is closely related to the analytic issues associated with single-case studies but focuses more on how we can encourage the transferability of insights in a nonpositivist design-research paradigm. While IT designers gain their rich experience in practice, the question emerges of how to transfer these insights beyond individuals and their respective communities of practice. Structurally similar problems of transferring specific insights have already been widely discussed in knowledge management and, of more interest to us, knowledge sharing (Ackerman et al. 2002, 2013). To support knowledge sharing, these authors suggest that we need to focus on innovative and flexible assemblages of materials and actors (e.g., Pipek et al. 2012).

In sharing design-relevant knowledge, we can imagine different community structures and cross-community learning processes, for instance, (1) within the local context, sharing knowledge inside the design team working on the same project or among design teams working on related projects; (2) within the academic context, focusing on related cases but also working in the broader fields of human-centered computing or educating future design practitioners and researchers; and (3) within the commercial setting, between academic designers and IT designers or between academic designers and actors who want to apply given IT artifacts in different fields of application.

For each of these constellations of knowledge sharing, we need a different level of reflection, making the particular contexts and insights understandable. With regard to the audience, we need to cater for assemblages of appropriate materials and actors. For instance, in the academic context, the degree of explicitness is typically higher, on the assumption that the interpretations arrived at can and should be proofed and/or subjected to critique. In contrast, practitioners may be less theoretically or conceptually motivated but still desire a summary of lessons learned and how this knowledge could be applied to solve the problems at hand. While knowledge sharing in some of these constellations happens during the design process, in other cases it spans a longer period of time and may, therefore, require different approaches for documenting insights.

Practices of design-related knowledge sharing, and the forms of documentation that prove workable solutions, have not yet been investigated to any systematic degree in any of these constellations. So far, we have (to some degree) standardized formats to document knowledge within academic communities, but these formats are arguably singularly inappropriate for use in more commercial environments. In the field of human-centered computing, the academic practice of documenting insights mainly draws on conference and journal papers—describing aspects of the IT artifacts, the design process, and practice. While, for instance, the ACM Digital Library allows uploading additional material such as videos or source code, IT artifacts or additional empirical data are rarely made accessible. The link with the academic design practitioners is typically provided by the authors' published work. However, sharing design-related knowledge is, even within the community of researchers in the field of human-centered computing, not yet well understood or supported. Moreover, academic papers may not be the best means of communicating design-related insights—especially not for practitioners. Many aspects of knowledge sharing within other epistemic communities or cross-community linkages need further investigation. Overall, one may argue that the IT design community has not yet been very successful in knowledge sharing.

So, there is a considerable challenge in supporting knowledge sharing in the way we suggest. In discussing opportunities for knowledge building, Gaver (2012) and Gaver and Bowers (2012) suggest documenting IT artifacts created by a design studio, by means of a portfolio that compares and discusses individual instances. In addition, Gaver and his colleagues make use of YouTube to provide vignettes that show the appropriation of artifacts and illustrate possible futures for digital interior design.[2] Höök and Löwgren (2012) suggest synthesizing the core design idea behind a range of IT artifacts into a design concept through processes of reflection, analysis, and articulation. These steps, however,

[2] See "TheCuriousHome" Youtube channel: http://www.youtube.com/watch?v=5_XtGyCqqKM.

do not reflect the relationship with practices, and it is this relationship that we are most concerned with (see Chapter 4). Therefore, we need to find new ways of documenting design-relevant insights—thinking about the preservation of IT artifacts, empirical data, and their structuration in a new manner.

1.8 Building a Portfolio of Design Case Studies

We believe that collections of design case studies should be documented and presented in layered portfolios. The different layers would allow for different granularities of access to the basic materials and actors according to the type of audience that the insights are intended to be shared with. While the layers are based on the same basic design case, they need to be created specifically for different audiences—for example, academia, practitioners, and students in varying social arrangements. Such documentation is both a challenge and an extra burden for those working in this emerging (academic) design culture.

The most basic layer of portfolios should support the design work within the project team and document some of it. It should allow for the sharing of empirical (raw) data such as audio recordings and transcriptions of interviews, field notes, or field diaries, as well as analytic categories or coding schemes. It should document the design process to allow sharing of emerging technical designs such as scribbles, mock-ups, prototypes, and running system versions. Of special interest is the linkage between empirically analyzed practices, participatory design processes, resulting design ideas, and the appropriation of designed artifacts over time. The goal is to document the evolving analytic and creative work that leads to different aspects of a designed artifact.

One can consider good design practice to involve the sharing of such data within cross-disciplinary design teams, especially in the context of heterogeneous institutional interests, to shape a coherent project vision. However, this raises questions about the ownership, not just of the data, but also about the interpretation. In particular, single-case, abductive reasoning is often characterized by the fact that various interpretations are possible. This raises the following questions: who has the authority to deliver a final opinion, and how should one deal with conflicting interpretations?

Depending on the institutional divides and the degree of mutual trust within a design team, certain techniques of information hiding, for instance, in the sense of anonymization of sources or abstraction of insights, may need to be applied. IT companies, being part of the design team, may also hide some of their results because of issues relating to intellectual property rights and commercial product development.

At a next layer, it is beneficial to compare the results of different teams working in the framework of grounded design. Here, emerging bottom-up concepts may evolve into an additional dimension to navigate through design cases. We have conducted such comparative analysis so far in two ways:

1. We compared historical design case studies among themselves or with currently running ones; however, each historic design case study was at least represented by one member of the design team (Wulf et al. 2015; also see Chapter 15)

2. We compared across concurrently running projects; to this end, we set up workshops in which the different researchers explained what they did and which results they found most remarkable

Both approaches did not draw very much on design-relevant data documented in portfolios because we do not yet possess a rich and well-structured documentation of our design efforts. So, the analysis drew instead on the design team member's recollections, their articulation, some data and artifacts still at hand, and published papers. We believe that comparative analysis between design case studies could benefit from materials shared via the portfolios—specifically in the case where the design projects are not conducted concurrently and the members of the design teams are no longer available for face-to-face discussions.

In respect of academic communities, for the purpose of comparison, we need a richer description of social practices, design work, and the resulting IT artifacts that the format of conference or journal papers currently offers. Comparative conceptual work of the kind we advocate takes place only rarely, and academic conferences continue to consist of competition among concepts rather than the evolution of agreed frameworks. Given the current paper formats of top academic venues in the HCI and computer-supported cooperative work community (e.g., ACM–CHI or ECSCW), a design case study currently needs to be broken up in different parts to become publishable. Where a contextual study may contain detailed empirical work, conclude with some design concerns, include an analysis of the participatory design process focusing on procedural findings and artifact-oriented outcomes, or be a study of the artifact's evaluation and/or appropriation, it is difficult to provide in an adequate fashion a description of a case that incorporates all the possibly relevant facets. Individual academic papers are a poor vehicle for the systematic building of comparable cases.

With richer descriptions that reach beyond the typical academic article, design-related findings could become better accessible in a more profound and contextualized manner. For instance, the ability to play with a running system version could stimulate a comparative analysis that is much better than one that is merely based on viewing selected screenshots.

The current set of academic publication formats limits the possibilities of engaging in reflective meta-analysis and comparison across cases—as exemplified by the fact that very little that looks like a corpus is currently available to the HCI community. In publications, one dominant narrative derived from the analysis of documented empirical, design, and appropriation studies would arguably provide the necessary foundations. Deriving crosscutting insights may take place at the level of the research group or the community. The latter might show more resistance to such a radical form of openness, sharing, and possible vulnerability; the former may be more interested in deriving crosscutting insights.

Another major challenge in sharing design-related knowledge is crossing the divide between academia and practitioners. In the European context, research projects often enable (and sometimes require) the participation of IT companies and application partners inside the design team (see Wulf et al. 2015). Yet, differences in design practice, organizational goals, and value systems can pose a major challenge in conducting design research under these rather short-term funding schemes (see Dachtera et al. 2014). Co-constructing lightly structured collections of design materials as they accumulate during the project runtime helps maintain a common project repository. Such a repository can build a basis for co-creating representations of design-related insights that are geared toward practitioner audiences.

Transferring design-relevant insights is an even bigger challenge in those cases where practitioners have not been involved in the research project at all. Academic papers, with all their specificities of focus, may not be the best way to share knowledge in these instances. Transferring personnel or building regional networks of practice is one approach to knowledge sharing (Fischer et al. 2007), although without the conceptual foundations that would constitute a corpus, it is difficult to see how this can be done. As yet, beyond the local reach, we lack a clear understanding how the sharing of design-related knowledge could be best supported and which roles collections of well-documented design projects could play in that.

Collections of design case studies should, at least partly, be handled via specific computer applications. These support tools can allow us to link applications to handle qualitative data, such as MAXQDA, with repositories for code sharing, such as GitHub. To document design work and share it appropriately, additional functionality needs to be developed.

We suggest that such digitalized collections of design case studies be called *ePortfolios*. However, such ePortfolio applications, as and when they are developed, should allow for repositories that incorporate material forms as well, such as exhibits, manuals, or booklets. Bottom-up concepts could provide a potential navigation structure within ePortfolios. When selecting a concept, a description may be displayed together with links to the design case studies that the concept emerged from. From there, further links could offer access to the different layers of documentation that provide the basis for the concept's emergence.

Tools are required and need to be developed that support the creation of portfolios to document design case studies in adequate detail—adequate, that is, for the heterogeneous purposes we have described—and facilitate their comparison. Tools such as ePortfolio need to plug into grounded-design practices, which are highly heterogeneous and diverse. Such tools need to provide processes and scaffolds for the emergence of structures in the documentation—not precluding any form of design practice and design documentation over another. By variously enabling diverging practices of design and empirical work, these tools should be aimed at two objectives. First, they should facilitate collecting materials and documenting processes in as lightly structured manner as necessary for a particular design process. Second, to foster meta-analysis across cases, these tools should allow higher-order structuring of the design documentation, for instance, by flexibly allowing pathways through and interlinking of individual aspects in a body of materials. An interconnecting layer that rests on top of design documentation facilitates meta-analysis and post hoc structuring of heterogeneous materials.

Yet, no matter how well these tools are integrated into the design-research process, academics and designers still need to be motivated to do the additional work of sharing their data and designs. Making available raw data as well as outcomes needs to be seen, for instance, as directly analogous to publishing data sets that can be referenced, cited, and credited when reused and appropriated in other contexts (as is increasingly common in empirical research in the social sciences). Research valuation and career opportunities need to go along with such a change in design practices, for instance, considering the publication of data sets or case-study portfolios to be similar to research publication. Research standards (by funding bodies) would need to develop in that direction as well.

A similar issue concerns the perceived disutility of complex, long-term case studies within the academic community. The current academic culture is arguably driven by quantity of paper output as much as quality. Yet, sociotechnical design research is a risky endeavor, requires lots of maintenance work that is not directly related to the research outcomes, and takes a lot of time and resources. Other metrics, again, need to be developed that appreciate complex, long-term case studies, their rich documentation, and their potential meta-analysis and cross-comparison.

During such longer-term engagements in a particular domain of practice, problems will evolve, shift, change, vanish, or emerge. The exploration of a domain of practice becomes a journey with multiple different starting points, milestones, and, certainly, endings. In such an evolving context, the term "problem" needs to be rethought: to what degree can a set of problems be specified a priori? How much can they be identified in a context study? To what extent is the design-research process itself an exploration of a problem space? And how far can there ever be a definitive answer that can be distilled in just a few research papers?

A certain fluidity is necessary not only for the design-research process itself but also for the presentation and communication of its findings. Staying open to interpretation is an often-iterated mantra in design research (Sengers and Gaver 2006), but it should not be in the purview of the researcher–designer alone during the design process itself. Interpretation of takeaways should be afforded during and after the conclusion of a design process for practitioners (and for wider society where relevant) as well.

A challenge for longer-term engagement with a domain of practice is how to ensure the continuation of the design intervention after the funding of the research project runs out (see also Binder et al. 2011). The limited lifetime of research projects typically cuts short any longer-term study of an IT artifact's appropriation. Much worse, a limited time frame endangers the usefulness of the artifact for the domain if processes of embedding are not given enough time and care. While researchers are ethically accountable for their interventions in a field, it is not research funding's primary aim to cater for the practical adoption of a design innovation in a particular domain of practice. On an ethical basis, nevertheless, researchers are accountable for outcomes that extend beyond the lifetime of a project when and if participants from outside the academic environment are enlisted. To live up to such responsibilities, one approach is to build and nurture a community of practice extending beyond a single design project.

The vision of ePortfolios is to allow grounded design to put longer time spans to use by facilitating the comparison and contrast of not only different (but related) design case studies but also a succession of consecutive research projects. The ePortfolio should facilitate design-research trajectories that last longer than a single project's lifespan or the engagement of individual researchers, tackling difficult societal issues and concerns that are slow to change (see also Friedman et al. 2016). In this respect, the ePortfolio is a technique not only for grounding design in the past (practices) but also for shaping long(er)-term sociotechnical futures.

1.9 Conclusion

The grounded-design paradigm suggests an orientation of the computing field toward understanding the relationship between specific settings and wider conceptions of the domain more clearly. Understanding, and designing for, problem issues in work contexts as well as public issues in a wider societal context require procedures for establishing "boundary relevance." Just how far, that is, can the procedures we outline take us in terms of scoping and limiting possibilities? Grounded design, we argue, provides a sociotechnical approach for the solution of social issues in context. It builds on a practice-based and constructivist (rather than positivist) paradigm, seeking to study emerging and evolving practices of use over longer periods of time after new IT artifacts have been designed and introduced. In that sense, grounded design suggests a praxeological turn in the field of computing.

Two driving forces nurture such an approach: (1) supporting evolving practices and evolving social challenges and (2) developing new (basic) technological opportunities that may be employed to such ends. Grounded design explores new technological opportunities in the context of a certain domain of practice, as well as the challenges involved in studying the novel technology's fit with and impact on actual local practices over time.

By studying the appropriation of an IT artifact over time, grounded design is able to understand the transformation and fit between a (newly) designed artifact, certain practices, and the context of use (see Chapter 4). This leads to insights about user practices that degrade, change, or evolve in ways that are unexpected or surprising to the designer. Such insights about IT appropriation and changing practices of use are crucial for the (re-)design of IT artifacts. These are insights that often remain opaque with other approaches but fundamentally impact the design of future IT artifacts.

A key concern within a grounded-design paradigm is to ensure transferability of the rich yet local and context-specific design knowledge that emerges with such an approach. To ensure transferability, we propose conducting design case studies in various domains of practice. Design case studies, as we have suggested, consist of three interlocking activities appreciating the complexities of the field: (1) an empirical context study, (2) the participatory, experimental design of (digital) artifacts, and (3) the study of its appropriation.

We have argued that, when conducting design case studies, a key strategy for knowledge building and ensuring the transferability of insights is to facilitate the documentation of processes and outcomes and their button-up analysis in an abductive stance. Structured documentation of design case studies allows us to preserve, make accessible, and communicate knowledge for future research and design activities to other audiences, such as practitioners, or for education.

Fundamentally, with grounded design, we propose practice-based computing as an independent field beyond the theoretical and the positivistic computer science that fosters the comparison of local, situated, and context-specific insights documented in design case studies. We suggest that using a research infrastructure such as ePortfolio would allow for cross-comparison and meta-analysis of cases in various (potentially but not necessarily related) domains of practice. Through such cross-comparison, the ePortfolio would facilitate bottom-up concept building across cases. The emerging concepts would then provide a basis for navigating the empirical materials across cases and for drilling down to the empirically rich particulars. Thus, interlinking situated design knowledge through emerging concepts in an IT environment, such as ePortfolio, leads to the emergence of an experience and knowledge base for transferring insights to other domains of IT design and practice, as well as to other audiences.

Comparative analysis of this kind makes the research context and associated interventions in the field more understandable and improves their communicative quality. Portfolios of design case studies provide an additional layer of communication of knowledge that can be geared toward different audiences and that can relate directly to empirical and design materials.

From our point of view, a practice-based paradigm, such as grounded design, needs to be complemented with an approach to meta-research into its own design practices. Since grounded design explores and intervenes into the given social practices of its fields of application, this research practice needs to be documented and analyzed—at least in selected case studies. Meta-research strengthens researchers' self-reflectivity, and a comparative analysis may result in a better transferability of insights. Finally, meta-research can ground the design of IT tools in support of practice-based research, such as the ePortfolio (see Chapter 16).

Grounded design as a new paradigm for applied computer science comes with a normative positioning. It seeks to make the voices of practitioners heard and relevant to future developments. It engages in, broadly, the ethnography of often-invisible aspects of life and work, and the participatory design with and for practitioners, in order to improve certain practices. That is, grounded design engages with social and societal challenges on both small and large scales. Grounded design takes seriously computing's increasing societal relevance in all aspects of life.

References

Ackerman, M., Dachtera, J., Pipek, V., and Wulf, V. 2013. "Sharing knowledge and expertise: The CSCW view of knowledge management." *Computer Supported Cooperative Work* 22 (4–6): 531–73.

Ackerman, M., Pipek, V., and Wulf, V. (eds.). 2002. *Sharing Expertise: Beyond Knowledge Management*. Cambridge, MA: MIT Press.

Alexander, C. 1977. *A Pattern Language: Towns, Buildings, Construction*. Oxford: Oxford University Press.

Baskerville, R., Pries-Heje, J., and Venable, J. 2009. "Soft design science methodology." In *DESRIST'09*. New York: ACM, 9.

Bayazit, N. 2004. Investigating design: A review of 40 years of design research. *Design Issue* 20 (1): 16–29.

Becker, J., and Niehaves, B. 2007. "Epistemological perspectives on IS research: A framework for analysing and systematizing epistemological assumptions." *Information Systems Journal,* 17 (2): 197–214.

Berger, P. L., and Luckmann, T. 1966. *The Social Construction of Reality: A Treatise in the Sociology of Knowledge.* Garden City, NY: Anchor Books.

Binder, T., de Michelis, G., Ehn, P., Iacucci, G., Linde, P., and Wagner, I. (eds.). 2011. *Design Things.* Cambridge, MA: MIT Press.

Bødker, S. 2006. "When second wave HCI meets third wave challenges." In *NordiCHI'06.* ACM, 1–8.

Bourdieu, P. 1977. *Outline of a Theory of Practice.* Cambridge and New York: Cambridge University Press.

Bourdieu, P. 1992. *The Logic of Practice.* Cambridge: Polity Press.

Bowers, J. 2012. "The logic of annotated portfolios: Communicating the value of 'research through design.'" In *DIS'12.* New York: ACM, 68–77.

Cross, N. 2001. "Designerly ways of knowing: Design discipline versus design science." *Design Issues* 17 (3): 49–55.

Dachtera, J., Randall, D., and Wulf, V. 2014. "Research on research: Design research at the margins: Academia, industry and end-users." In *CHI'14.* New York: ACM, 713–22.

Dalsgaard, P., and Halskov, K. 2012. "Reflective design documentation." In *DIS'12.* New York: ACM, 428–37.

Dewey, J. 1938. *Logic: The Theory Of Inquiry.* New York: Henry Holt and Company.

Dourish, P. 2006. "Implications for design." In *CHI'06.* New York: ACM, 541–50.

Fischer, G., Rohde, M., and Wulf, V. 2007. "Community-based learning: The core competency of residential, research-based universities." *International Journal of Computer Supported Collaborative Learning* 2 (1): 9–40.

Frayling, C. 1993. "Research in art and design." *Royal College of Art Research Papers* 1 (1): 1–5.

Friedman, B., Nathan, L. P., and Yoo, D. 2016. "Multi-lifespan information system design in support of transitional justice: Evolving situated design principles for the long(er) term." *Interacting with Computers* 29 (1): 80–96.

Fuller, B. 1969. *Utopia or Oblivion.* New York:. Bantam Books.

Garfinkel, H. 1984. *Studies in Ethnomethodology.* Cambridge: Polity Press.

Gaver, W. 2012. "What should we expect from research through design?" In *CHI'12.* New York: ACM, 937–46.

Gaver, W., and Bowers, J. 2012. "Annotated portfolios." *Interactions* 19 (4): 40–9.

Giddens, A. 1984. *The Constitution of Society. Outline of the Theory of Structuration.* Cambridge: Polity Press.

Goldkuhl, G. 2012. "Pragmatism vs interpretivism in qualitative information systems research." *European Journal of Information Systems* 21 (2): 135–46.

Goldkuhl, G., and Lind, M. 2010. "A multi-grounded design research process." In *DESRIST'10.* Berlin/Heidelberg: Springer, 45–60.

Greenbaum, J., and Kyng, M. (eds.). 1992. *Design at Work: Cooperative Design of Computer Systems.* Hillsdale, NJ: Lawrence Erlbaum Associates.

Gregor, S., and Jones, D. 2007. "The anatomy of a design theory." *Journal of the Association for Information Systems* 8 (5): 312–323, 325–35.

Hevner, A. R., March, S. T., Park, J., and Ram, S. 2004. "Design science in information systems research." *MIS Quarterly* 28 (1): 75–105.

Hinrichs, J., Pipek, V., and Wulf, V. 2005. "Context grabbing: Assigning metadata in large document collections." In *ECSCW'05.* Dordrecht: Springer, 367–86.

Höök, K., and Löwgren, J. 2012. "Strong concepts: Intermediate-level knowledge in interaction design research." *ACM Transactions in Computer-Human Interactions* 19 (3): 23.

Kuechler, B., and Vaishnavi, V. 2012. "A framework for theory development in design science research: Multiple perspectives." *Journal of the Association for Information Systems* 13 (6): 395–423.

McCarthy, J., and Wright, P. 2004. *Technology As Experience*. Cambridge, MA: MIT Press.

Mead, G. H. 1934. *Mind, Self, and Society*, ed. C. W. Morris. Chicago: University of Chicago Press.

Oevermann, U. 2001. "Die Philosophie von Charles Sanders Peirce als Philosophie der Krise." In H.-J. Wagner, *Objektive Hermeneutik und Bildung des Subjekts*. Weilerswist: Velbrück Wissenschaft, 209–46.

Orlikowski, W. J. 1996. "Evolving with notes: Organizational change around groupware technology," in C. U. Ciborra, ed., *Groupware and Teamwork: Invisible Aid or Technical Hindrance?* Chichester: John Wiley & Sons, 23–60.

Peirce, C. S. 1958–66. "Lectures on pragmatism." In C. Hartshorne and P. Weiss, eds., *Collected Papers of Charles Sanders Peirce*. Vol. 5. Cambridge, MA: Harvard University Press, 141–212.

Pipek, V., and Wulf, V. 1999. "A groupware's life." In *ECSCW'99*. Dordrecht: Kluwer, 199–219.

Pipek, V., and Wulf, V. 2009. "Infrastructuring: Toward an integrated perspective on the design and use of information technology." *Journal of the Association for Information Systems* 10 (5): 447.

Pipek, V., Wulf, V., and Johri, V. 2012. "Bridging artifacts and actors: Expertise sharing in organizational ecosystems." *Computer Supported Cooperative Work* 21 (2–3): 261–82.

Ramirez, L., Betz, M., Dyrks, T., Scholz, M., Gerwinski, J., and Wulf, V. 2012. "Landmarke: An ad hoc deployable ubicomp infrastructure to support indoor navigation of firefighters." *Personal and Ubiquitous Computing* 16 (8): 1025–38.

Reckwitz, A. 2002. "Toward a theory of social practices: A development in culturalist theorizing." *European Journal of Social Theory* 5 (2): 243–63.

Reichertz, J. 2007. "Abduction: The logic of discovery of grounded theory." In A. Bryant and K. Charmaz, eds., *The SAGE Handbook of Grounded Theory*. London: Sage, 214–28.

Rittel, H. W. J., and Webber, M. M. 1973. "Dilemmas in a general theory of planning." *Policy Sciences* 4 (2): 155–69.

Rohde, M., Brödner, P., Stevens, G., Betz, M., and Wulf, V. 2017: "Grounded design: A praxeological IS research perspective." *Journal of Information Technology* 32 (2): 163–79.

Rohde, M., Brödner, P., Stevens, G., and Wulf, V. 2013. "Adjusting the paradigmatic shift: IS design as intervention in social practice." *International Reports on Socio-Informatics* 10 (1): 4–26.

Rohde, M., Stevens, G., Brödner, P., and Wulf, V. 2009. "Towards a paradigmatic shift in IS: Designing for social practice." In *DESRIST'09*. New York: ACM, 15.

Rohde, M., and Wulf, V. 2011. "Aktuelles Schlagwort: Sozio-Informatik." *Informatik-Spektrum* 34 (2): 210–13.

Schön, D. 1983. *The Reflective Practitioner*. London: Temple Smith.

Schwartz, T., Denef, S., Stevens, G., Ramirez, L., Wulf, V. 2013. Cultivating Energy Literacy—Results from a Longitudinal Living Lab Study of a Home Energy Management System. In CHI'13, ACM, New York, 1193–1202.

Sein, M. K., Henfridsson, O., Purao, S., Rossi, M., and Lindgren, R. 2011. "Action design research." *MIS Quarterly* 35 (1): 37–56.

Sengers, P., and Gaver, B. 2006. "Staying open to interpretation: Engaging multiple meanings in design and evaluation." In *DIS'06*. New York: ACM, 99–108.

Simon, H. A. 1969. *The Sciences of the Artificial*. Cambridge, MA: MIT Press.

Stevens, G. 2010. *Understanding and Designing Appropriation Infrastructures: Artifacts as Boundary Objects in the Continuous Software Development*. PhD thesis. Siegen: University of Siegen.

Winograd, T. (ed.). 1996. *Bringing Design to Software*. New York: ACM.

Wulf, V. 2009. "Theorien sozialer Praktiken als Elemente zur Fundierung der Wirtschaftsinformatik." In J. Becker, H. Kremar, and B. Niehaves, eds., *Wissenschaftstheorie und Gestaltungsorientierte Wirtschaftsinformatik*. Dordrecht: Springer, 211–24.

Wulf, V., Müller, C., Pipek, V., Randall, D., Rohde, M., and Stevens, G. 2015. "Practice-based computing: Empirically grounded conceptualizations derived from design case studies." In V. Wulf, K. Schmidt, and D. Randall (eds), *Designing Socially Embedded Technologies in the Real-World*. London: Springer-Verlage London, 111–50.

Wulf, V., Rohde, M., Pipek, V., and Stevens, G. 2011. "Engaging with practices: Design case studies as a research framework in CSCW." In *CSCW'11*. New York: ACM, 505–12.

Zimmerman, Z., Forlizzi, J., and Evenson, S. 2007. "Research through design as a method for interaction design research in HCI." In *CHI'07*. New York: ACM, 493–502.

Zimmerman, J., Stolterman, E., and Forlizzi, J. 2010. "An analysis and critique of research through design: Towards a formalization of a research approach." In *DIS'10*. New York: ACM, 310–19.

2 Practice and Technology*

On the Conceptual Foundations of Practice-Centered Computing

KJELD SCHMIDT

2.1 Practice-Centered Computing: The Conceptual Challenge

In the vast and widely ramified family of technologies, computing technologies occupy a very special place. Unlike other modern and, in important ways, science-based technologies such as nuclear energy or GPS navigation, computing technologies did not originate from a specific body of scientific theory.[1] Nor did they, like radio communication, develop in step with the development of a body of scientific theory. Nor do they have, as their core, a unified body of scientific theory. They rather evolved—organically, as it were—in response to an array of quite different and often urgent practical concerns. To be sure, their development depended critically upon a host of mathematical theories (Boolean algebra, symbolic logic, Shannon's information theory, recursive function theory, etc.), but they were not the result of the application of any specific body of theory, nor have they resulted in any.

As pointed out by the eminent historian of computing Michael Mahoney,[2]

> [When established as a discipline by 1970, computer science had taken] the form more of a family of loosely related research agendas than of a coherent general theory

* This chapter draws on arguments explored, sketched, and elaborated over several years, in a number of publications (Schmidt 2011a, 2011b, 2012a, 2012b, 2014a, 2014b, 2015a). The research has been supported by the Velux Foundation under the "Computational Artifacts" project (VELUX33295).

[1] The myth that computing technologies originated from a specific body of mathematical theory is common in accounts of the history of computer science (e.g., Davis 2000; Dyson 2012).

[2] A fine collection of Mahoney's papers, edited by Thomas Haigh, has recently become available (Mahoney 2011).

Socio-Informatics, Volker Wulf, Volkmar Pipek, Dave Randall, Markus Rohde, Kjeld Schmidt, Gunnar Stevens (Eds). © Oxford University Press 2018. Published 2018 by Oxford University Press.

> validated by empirical results. So far, no one mathematical model had proved adequate to the diversity of computing, and the different models were not related in any effective way. What mathematics one used depended on what questions one was asking, and for some questions no mathematics could account in theory for what computing was accomplishing in practice. (Mahoney 1992, p. 361)

That is, "the computer" was not, strictly speaking, "invented." As Mahoney puts it, "whereas other technologies may be said to have a nature of their own and thus to exercise some agency in their design, the computer has no such nature. Or, rather, its nature is protean" (Mahoney 2005, p. 122). However, the expression "protean nature" verges on being an oxymoron. The point is rather that "the computer" does not have a "nature" in the sense of a finite repertoire of dispositions. What we refer to by talking about "the computer" is a highly malleable technology. Computing technology is "protean" in the sense that the costs of construction and modification of software programs are drastically reduced, compared to those of previous machine technologies. According to Mahoney, therefore, there was a time, a rather long time, "when the question 'What is a computer, or what should it be?', had no clear-cut answer," and the computer and computing thus only acquired "their modern shape" in the course of an open-ended process that has lasted decades (Mahoney 1992, p. 349). And there is no reason why one should assume that the concept of "computing" has stabilized and solidified: the jury is still out, as the immense malleability of "the computer" or "computing" is being explored in all directions. In other words, it is confused to conceive of "the computer" as *a distinct* technology. Not only is "the computer" in front of me as I write this the result of the application of a host of technologies, from metallurgy, to semiconductor technology, to programming languages and operating systems; it can assume an endless range of very different incarnations. Computing is a protean technology, and what it develops into, and how, is determined by its *practical applications* in a far more radical sense than is the case with any other modern technology.

Let me briefly illustrate (summarizing Schmidt 2011a, Chapters 11 and 13; 2015b).

- Electronic digital computing technologies were initially developed in the mid-1940s to overcome the very practical problem that scientific and engineering calculations, with the demands of modern warfare and weapons development, had reached such a degree of complexity that they could no longer be carried out as a cooperative work effort based on advanced division of labor. The costs of planning and coordination of cooperative calculation work had simply become forbidding, a problem Turing dubbed "the human brake" (1945). The initial electronic digital computing technologies (Colossus, EDVAC, ENIAC, ACE, etc.), which were designed to overcome this problem by automating calculation work and hence eliminate the coordination task, were developed by or under the auspices of scientists deeply involved in organizing the mass-calculation work required in the war effort.
- Based on the initial technologies of electronic digital computing, the next major step in the development of computing technologies—interactive and collaborative computing technologies—was taken, shortly afterwards, in the early 1950s, to deal

with the related problem of managing real-time coordination of cooperative air-defense work in the age of nuclear weapons. Taking the practices and techniques of air defense developed under the Battle of Britain as the model but realizing that the coordination problem now was of a complexity far beyond what could be handled manually, the solution that was developed made it possible for the more than 2,000 operators distributed over the North American continent to perform the daunting task of monitoring the entire airspace as a large-scale cooperative work effort. The overall design of the Whirlwind prototype (operational as the SAGE system in 1958) was conceived of as a "semi-automatic" system in the sense that the task of identifying potential targets was done manually while the massive processes of data transmission and aggregation, target tracking, and coordination across sectors were performed automatically.

- The next major steps in the development of interactive and collaborative computing technologies were taken in the 1960s by computer technicians engaged in the cooperative work of developing and running time-sharing mainframe operating systems and, later, building computer network facilities (ARPAnet). To deal with their own very mundane problems of communication and coordination, the technicians devised ways of communicating with each other by exchanging files and "mail" messages via the shared networked facilities. The development of the World Wide Web, launched in 1990, followed a similar pattern. All this led to the technologies of distributed computing.
- And finally, as the cost of computing power was reduced exponentially with advances in semiconductor technology (for decades driven by practical applications other than computing, such as hearing aids, hand-held calculators, digital watches, etc.), computing facilities became sufficiently affordable for "personal computing" to become a realistic prospect. Initially conceived of as technologies to support "office work" (in the form of the Xerox Alto in 1973 and the Xerox Star in 1981), interactive computing underwent rapid development as innovative application programs building on and targeting various work practices and techniques (computer-aided design, spreadsheets, word processors, desk-top publishing) pushed the boundaries of computing, leading to modern technologies of interactive and collaborative computing.

In short, the crucial computing technologies were developed in intimate relation with work practices. However, the development of computing technologies in relation to practices was never pursued systematically and deliberately, in and through a systematic analysis of work practices for the purpose of developing such technologies—until, that is, the formation of Computer-Supported Cooperative Work (CSCW) as a research field, and, with that, the emergence of a practice-centered approach to the development of collaboration technologies (Schmidt and Bannon 2013). As Volker Wulf et al. have pointed out: "CSCW was the first research community in applied computer science which stressed the importance of an in-depth understanding of practices when designing ICT artefacts. From our point of view, this is the key achievement of the research field" (Wulf et al. 2011, p. 505).

A caveat is required here. CSCW of course always was (and is) a motley congregation, encompassing a variety of (often incompatible) research programs, and therefore not all CSCW researchers would subscribe to the practice-centered research program. In fact, while some prominent researchers have found it illusory (Grudin and Poltrock 2012), others have simply pretended it did not even exist (e.g., Olson and Olson 2003). Regardless of such overt or covert skepticism, the practice-centered approach to the development of collaboration technologies has been a crucial thread of CSCW even before the field was institutionalized in the form of regular conferences. In fact, the practice-centered research program was clearly articulated from the very beginning of CSCW.

In an article published at the first CSCW conference in 1986, Lucy Suchman and Randy Trigg outlined "a methodological and topical framework" for studying work practice, "a framework intended to capture the central activities and issues" and "represent them in a way that can inform the design of computer support": "To design technology that supports collaborative practices requires that we uncover the largely unarticulated detail of what people actually do when they work together" (Suchman and Trigg 1986, p. 221). This poses a specific challenge, because "those routine practices of which everyday activities are largely comprised, including the ubiquitous troubles, will generally be unremarkable to participants precisely because they are routine" (ibid., p. 223). The research program outlined by Suchman and Trigg in 1986 was quickly adopted and moved forward by a large number of researchers and was echoed by Bannon and Schmidt in a programmatic paper presented at the first European CSCW conferences (Bannon and Schmidt 1989). The research program soon resulted in a series of emblematic studies of work practices (Harper et al. 1991; Heath and Luff 1991, 1992; Harper and Hughes 1993; Suchman 1997) and has been thriving in the decades that have elapsed (for an overview, see Bannon and Schmidt 2013).

Unsurprisingly, then, the concept of "practice" has become a key concept. An indication of this development—albeit, admittedly, a very rough one—is that while the term "practice" in the mid-1980s only occurred in about 25% of papers in which the acronym CSCW also occurred, the frequency of use has increased steadily to the current level of about 75% (Schmidt 2014b). This indicator is, of course, crude but still, the terminological shift is significant. In other words, it has become common for CSCW researchers to conceive of their problems, observations, and findings in terms of "practices" (see, e.g., Luff et al. 2000).

However, although the concept of "practice" is now being used as a key concept in CSCW, it is, unsurprisingly, normally used in the ordinary sense. In everyday discourse, we will, for example, use expressions such as "Have you actually tried this procedure in practice?", "Does this actually work in practice?", "The new doctor bought the old doctor's practice," "He got his law degree but never practiced the law," "He stopped practicing the law when he turned 70," "What is standard practice here?", "He's practicing the 'La Bamba' riff again and again," "He's practicing using the new word processor," "He was a stranger to the practice of using knife and fork the European way," or "Engineering practice involves not only math and science but also administrative skills." In all such cases, the word "practice" is used in reference to the application of some general rule (theory, method, principle, representation, criterion, sign) under the vicissitudes of actually prevailing conditions; that is, to contingent activities performed under conditions of accountability or commitment to some norm that provides criteria for correct or incorrect conduct. In short, when behavior in ordinary discourse is described *as a practice,* it typically is characterized as normatively governed contingent activities.

There are sound reasons for why CSCW researchers would conceive of their problems, observations, and findings in terms of "practices." Computational artifacts incorporating collaboration technologies are, so to speak, designed to intervene, in some cases radically, in the cooperative effort by interposing mechanical regulation of workers' interactions. The design of such interventionist technologies cannot be based merely on a model of the application domain in the form of some idealized representation of prescribed procedures or relatively stable patterns of activity; rather, the design must also take into account the actual practice in which the system in question is to be integrated, its contingencies, variations, local circumstances, and so on. In the words of Lucy Suchman, "some amount of appropriation into local circumstances will always be required. The question is not whether that work will need to be done, but with what ease or difficulty" (2002, p. 139). Indeed, in the case of collaboration technologies, system rigidity may complicate coordination work unbearably and cause breakdowns. This insight is fundamental for CSCW.

In CSCW, the concept of "practice" is used, first of all, to be able to address and focus on the actual activities as unfolding contingently in the settings in which collaboration technologies may be used, in contrast to the ideal conditions or standard procedures typically presumed by engineers and managers. It is thus also typically used in preference to notions such as "task" and "performance" that imply some anterior analysis and decomposition of work activities, just as it is often preferred to vague and ineffectual gestures such as "use situation" or "context." Related to this, the concept is used in opposition to design paradigms in which new technologies are developed in laboratories, based on the experiences and predilections of the engineers and designers themselves. In the same vein, it is also used in opposition to an approach, prevalent in Human–Computer Interaction (HCI), that is committed to basing new technologies on models of (presumptively generic) human behavior derived from theories imported from cognitive or social psychology, from social linguistics, or from small-group sociology, as well as in opposition to approaches, prevalent in neighboring areas such as Computer-Supported Collaborative Learning (CSCL) or Group Decision Support Systems (GDSS), that are committed to building new technologies on (prescriptive) didactic theories and models, as in the case of CSCL, or, in the case of GDSS, (prescriptive) theories and models of presumptively efficient or effective decision making. Consequently, the concept is used to home in on the skills and competencies, etc., required of workers for them to be able to work according to plans, execute procedures, and make classifications and models work under actual and often varying conditions. That is, the concept of "practice" is generally used in opposition to transcendental constructs such as "'shared understanding," "shared goal," "shared knowledge," "shared situation awareness," or "tacit knowledge," which, putatively in order to "explain" the observable orderly conduct, already presume the existence and efficacy of that very order. In contrast to such occult constructs, the concept of "practice" is used to focus on the techniques and strategies through which cooperative work is ordinarily accomplished in an orderly way.

The use of the concept of "practice" in CSCW obviously has close affinity to the use of notions such as "situated action" and "articulation work." However, a motivation for the increased use of the notion of "practice" in CSCW may also have been that researchers have suspected or actually realized that some of the concepts that have served well in defining the focus and scope of CSCW have turned out to be less useful in actual empirical analysis.

On one hand, the notion of "situated action" (Suchman 1987) has been indispensable in creating a space for studying actual conduct in real-world settings, by rejecting, as confused, the assumption underlying cognitive science that action is nothing but the visible manifestation of the processing or execution of "plans" or "schemes" and by thus insisting on the categorial distinction between the action and its representation, between the landscape and the map. However, while it serves a crucial epistemological argument, "situated action" does not point to an observable occurrence, i.e., a phenomenon. It is rather a logical-grammatical category, the role of which in actual empirical investigation is restricted to that of a battle cry against cognitivism and similar strands of modern metaphysics: *Don't forget, the plan is not the action; action is inexorably situated!*

On the other hand, the notion of "articulation work," developed by Anselm Strauss and his colleagues (Strauss 1985; Strauss et al. 1985), has been very helpful for defining the focus and scope of CSCW (e.g., Bannon and Schmidt 1989; Schmidt and Bannon 1992) by emphasizing that, under conditions of division of labor, workers necessarily have to coordinate and mesh their individual activities. In doing so, the notion of "articulation work" identifies and highlights certain aspects of work activities ("a kind of supra-type of work in any division of labor," Strauss 1985, p. 8) that serve the function of coordinating and integrating the distributed activities. But again, while important for defining CSCW, the notion of "articulation work" is of limited benefit in empirical work. It does not point to a phenomenon but throws together certain abstract aspects of work activities, namely, activities, modalities, concerns, etc., that can be said to serve, in manifold ways, the *function* of coordinating and meshing individual contributions to a cooperative effort. In contrast, the concept of "practice," as it is ordinary used, does denote a phenomenon. It not only points to a regularly recurring activity, as actually unfolding, but also the skills and competencies required to perform the activity in an accountable manner under conditions of contingency, and it thus also points to the ways in which skills are acquired through learning and training; the ways in which techniques are adopted, acquired, adapted, and applied; and the ways in which performance standards are developed, negotiated, and brought to bear in actual situations.

In short, in CSCW the concept of "practice" has moved center stage because researchers, in a distributed process of learning from experience, have found that this concept, as we use it in ordinary language, somehow helps them express their research problems and empirical findings.

However, the concept of "practice" is also used to underpin the development of "theoretical constructs that can deepen our understanding *across work settings*" (Suchman and Trigg 1991, p. 65 [emphasis added]), that is, in order to be able to compare findings and transfer solutions from one domain to another or from one situation to the next. This then, in turn, raises the crucial question: How do we conceptualize the "local circumstances" and "work settings" into which the technology is to be integrated? Indeed, how do we compare "circumstances" and "settings"? How do we compare findings from one setting with those from another or even from one day to the next in the same setting? For the concept of "practice" to serve in this capacity requires that the *criterion of sameness* is clarified and specified: How do we determine which observed activities are instances of the same kind? When I am writing notes with a pencil and then, a moment later, make further notes on the same sheet using a ball pen, are these activities of the same kind or are they of different kinds? Or if my colleague and I are writing notes with a pencil, are we then engaged in the same kind of activity? If yes, in which sense? That is, are the concepts of "practice" and "technique" in fact coextensive?

Such questions have rarely been addressed. That this is untenable is clearly shown in the ambiguities and confusions that have accompanied reflections about the relationship between work practices and technology in CSCW. Bannon and Schmidt (1989), for instance, raised the issue that

> designing computer-based systems for cooperative work settings is like writing in water. By careful analysis and design, the information system may be designed to match the current social structure of the labor processes [i.e., work practices]. But this change of technology, in turn, induces a change of the social structure of the labor processes [or work practice]. This has been the bitter experience of a plethora of office automation projects and installations, designed to match the traditional allocation of tasks in the office. (Bannon and Schmidt 1989, p. 368)

In a similar vein, Suchman and Trigg argued that "our ways of working together and our technological systems" must be developed "simultaneously" (1991, p. 85):

> Because of the intimate relation between work and technology, the development of the artifacts with which people work and the development of their work practices go hand in hand. Available technologies afford certain resources and constraints on how the work gets done, and peoples' ways of working give the technologies their shape and significance. (Suchman and Trigg 1991, p. 65)

There is a sense—an important sense—in which these observations are true. The crucial question, however, is again this. What is it that changes, and what does not change? In which sense? According to which criteria does it make sense to say that the "social structure of the labor processes" or "our ways of working together" or "work practices" change (or do not change)? Indeed, how can we, *reasonably*, say of two observed activities or events that they are, or are not, instances of the same type? These are indeed crucial questions. But in using terms like "practice" in describing and discussing our findings, we, of course, presume that the observed activities or events are indeed, *somehow*, of the same type, that they are, in some *reasonably* specifiable sense, *practices* with their requisite technical complements. But how? What does that mean? What do the observed activities and events have in common that we can reasonably consider them of the same type? How do we distinguish one practice from another? And so on.[3]

[3] Even before any substantive answer to these crucial questions is in sight, the issue of how to identify observed activities as instances of the same kind is in risk of floundering, caught up as it is in the tumult in the

But these are questions that cannot be answered a priori, that is, prior to and isolated from the empirical research itself (for metaphysics will not help us). But as a first step, as a kind of preparatory exercise, clarification of the cornerstone concepts seems both necessary and useful. The aim of the present chapter is thus to attempt to clarify the concept of "practice" as it is ordinarily used and to explore the intimate and intricate relationship between the concept of "practice" and that of "technique" and, related to this, "technology."

Now, concepts are institutions. Our conceptual scheme—what Gilbert Ryle (1949, p. 8) called "the logical geography" of our concepts[4]—is the outcome of a process of selection, typically evolutionary (Austin 1956–7, p. 182). And as institutions, concepts have a history. The concepts of "practice" and "technique" are no exception: they in fact come with a suite of connotations and references that we can ignore only at our peril. In view of this, the present chapter attempts to clarify the concepts of "practice" and "technique" by what could be described as a two-pronged attack. The direct attack will be attempted in Section 2.3, where I will outline "the logical geography" of the two concepts as we typically use them today in ordinary discourse. First, however, in Section 2.2, I will sketch the major turning points in the historical evolution of the concepts of "practice" and "technique." The reason for taking a historical approach is not merely to describe where the concepts come from, the process of selection. It is rather that our ordinary concepts of "practice" and "technique" did not originate with some dictum from some more or less recent philosopher, be it a Karl Marx or a Martin Heidegger; they developed as integral elements in the evolution of modern technology, as tools for practitioners' and scholars' reflections on the role of technical knowledge in work. That is, it so happens that our ordinary concepts of "practice" and "technique" developed for the same kinds of problem as those now faced by practice-oriented computing. Section 2.2 will therefore outline not only the shifting uses of the terms by various scholars but will also, albeit in desperate brevity, sketch the *practical* contexts, the discourses, in which these shifts occurred.[5]

2.2 Conceptual Archeology

A significant motive for the development of our modern concepts of "practice" and "technique" has been the efforts—the efforts of generations of workers and engineers as

social sciences and their philosophy that goes under the name "practice theory." A critical inspection of "practice theory" is therefore required but does not belong here; it is offered in Chapter 3 of this volume.

[4] "To determine the logical geography of concepts is to reveal the logic of the propositions in which they are wielded, that is to say, to show with what other propositions they are consistent and inconsistent, what propositions follow from them and from what propositions they follow. The logical type or category to which a concept belongs is the set of ways in which it is logically legitimate to operate with it" (Ryle, 1949, p. 8).

[5] Over the last few of decades, a body of literature has emerged that has provided an account of the history of the conceptions of work and work practices from ancient Greece to the beginning of the Industrial Revolution in the late eighteenth century that is far more nuanced than what was previously taken to be the story (e.g., Whitney 1990; Hoven 1996; Long 2001; Cuomo 2007; Ehmer and Lis 2009; Lis and Soly 2012; Valleriani 2017). The sketch below is deeply indebted to this literature. —I am also indebted to the article "Praxis" by Alfred Schmidt (1974) for showing an historical approach to conceptual analysis.

well as managers and scholars—to express and reflect upon working knowledge and especially to reason about the *application of representations* of working knowledge *in work*. In other words, these concepts have, in important ways, been developed over centuries as an integral part of the efforts to articulate, ameliorate, and transmit working knowledge. An account of this process, even a cursory one, is, of course, entirely beyond the scope of the present chapter. But since the evolution of these concepts is intimately entwined with the development of work practices and productive techniques, there are good reasons for giving the origins of these concepts a moment's consideration.

The concepts of "technique" and "practice" emerged in ordinary Greek about 2,500 years ago and have evolved in a process that has been inordinately complex. In fact, in the course of that time, the meaning of the term "practice," to take the most vexing case, has been turned upside down and shifted about compared to the way in which it was used in ancient Greece and especially in the writings of Aristotle. As suggested above, "practice" is today normally used and understood as action unfolding in accountable relation to some kind of standard procedure, job description, textbook doctrine, or even in contrast to mere talk, in short: to "theory"—as in, "How does this work in practice?" But as pointed out by the French philosopher André Tosel,

> The relationship between theory and praxis is the outcome of a history that began quite differently. In ancient Greek thinking, theory and praxis are not juxtaposed as abstract science and concrete life, as were they two concepts that mutually imply each other of which the latter, the concept of praxis, signify the immediateness of reality. [...] The modern discourse inverts—concept by concept—the ancient issue and determination of the content of the concepts. (Tosel 2010, p. 2136)

This does not, of course, pose problems in ordinary discourse, where the historical distance separating these conceptual worlds typically is never bridged. The problem arises, however, because these otherwise separate conceptual worlds are fused if we, for scholarly purposes, try to clarify the concepts by invoking philosophical literature in which the diachronically separated conceptions coexist synchronically, much like fossils of dinosaurs and skeletons of ostriches might be on display next to each other in a natural history museum. The problem arises, that is, when the cordon separating these domains of discourse is breached and what would otherwise be relics are resuscitated and let loose in a completely different historical milieu. This has very much been the case in the modern literature on the concept of "practice" (e.g., Heidegger 1927, pp. 68 f., 193, 357 f.; Arendt 1958, pp. 13, 25, 97, 195 f.; Lefebvre 1966, Chapter 2; Lobkowics 1967; Schweizer 1971; Gadamer 1972, 1974; Dreyfus 1991; Nicolini 2012, pp. 25 ff.). A brief examination of the uses of the concepts of "technique" and "practice" in the Greek classics is called for.

2.2.1 Technē

The term "technique" is derived from Greek *technē*, which—related to the word for carpenter (*tekton*)—was originally and typically used as a reference to the skillfulness that was seen as a common property of the various handicrafts—carpentry, navigation, metallurgy, weaving—in spite of their being otherwise distinctly different. As always with words of ordinary language, *technē* was used flexibly, in a context-dependent way, sometimes simply as a shorthand way of referring to the various crafts in which the various skills were manifested, sometimes to characterize an activity as creative or artful, and sometimes even to characterize a method as crafty or cunning. The primary use of *technē* was, however, to denote a systematically acquired competence that in some specifiable sense is considered rational (Whitney 1990, p. 25, n. 7; Frede 2010, p. 2070).[6]

In the written record, the term *technē* appears as early as in the eighth century BCE (in Homer and in Hesiod), and later in the tragedies of the fifth century (in Sophocles and Aeschylus), in references to specific crafts but also, and remarkably, in the context of reflecting on the human condition in general and in particular the role of technical knowledge and artifacts in the existence and development of human kind.

However, the concept of *technē* was initially forged in the technical literature of ancient Greece, as means of expressing and reflecting upon working knowledge. It is in ancient Greece that the very issue of the *application of representations* of working knowledge *in work* first became serious, as a key issue in the actual improvement and transmission of working knowledge, because it was here, in the Greek city states, in a culture of strong democratic aspirations on the part of the working majority, that ordinary workers first acquired literate competencies and thus able to apply these for the purposes of making notes about experiences and observations and eventually for expressing and conveying generalized insights and methods, for their own use as well as for a wider readership. That is, in the case of ancient Greece, the issue of the production and application of representations of working knowledge in work was posed in a dramatically novel manner. On the one hand, written representations of working knowledge constituted a break with the oral tradition, in which technical knowledge is transmitted by speech and gesture and where it is difficult, if not impossible, independently of time and place, to fix and examine what is taken to be correct according to instructions, plans, recipes, etc., and thus also to make objective comparisons with actual conduct. On the other hand, it constituted a radical departure from what had been and still was the case in the despotic civilizations in Mesopotamia and Egypt, where literacy was the practical if not official monopoly of a caste of temple scribes or priests and where representations of working knowledge such as recipes accordingly typically were produced by scribal specialists, often not even for use *in* work but for other purposes such as glorification of the regime's accomplishments. The upshot is that we can see in ancient Greece the growth of a body of technical writing in areas such as medicine, town planning, architecture,

[6] For a systematic overview of the development of the concept of *technē* in ancient Greece, see the masterly study by Helmuth Schneider (1989) as well the meticulous philological analysis provided by Rudolf Löbl (1997, 2003, 2008). For broader historical accounts of the development of the understanding of technique and technology in the ancient world, see the studies by Elspeth Whitney (1990), Pamela Long (2001), and Serafina Cuomo (2005, 2007). On the organization of craft work in the ancient world, see the study by Alison Burford (1972).

navigation, and later, in the fourth century BCE, also optics, pneumatics, the construction of artillery, etc.[7]

The term *technē* was, to take the obvious example, used extensively in the Hippocratic corpus (the late fifth and early fourth century BCE) as part of the various efforts by the Hippocratic school to reflect upon the nature of medical work and defend its intellectual legitimacy against contemporary critics (cf. texts such as "On ancient medicine" and "On technē").[8] Closely related to this, the concept of *technē* became a key concept in the contemporaneous Sophistic movement. We unfortunately only have few surviving fragments of text from this tradition and must largely rely on Plato's quite hostile accounts; what seems clear, however, is that sophists such as Protagoras (486–411 BCE) worked professionally as educators to prepare Greek men for their civic duties as participants in the democratic life of the *polis* as jurors, councilors, etc. (Kerferd 1981). In reflecting upon this role, the sophists conceived of their work as one of cultivating the natural "virtues" of humans by teaching *technai* such as rhetoric. In the course of this, they developed a notion of *technē* as having a number of essential characteristics: A *technē* serves a useful purpose, has a specific function, and is performed by specialists who know how to apply the requisite means—methods and instruments—to meet the end; and it is essential that a *technē* can be taught and learned and thus, for the concept to make sense, that it is possible to say of an activity that it is performed correctly (or not) according to the principles and criteria of the *technē* in question (Heinimann 1961).

2.2.2 Praxis

The word "practice"[9] comes from the vernacular Greek noun *praxis* (vb.: *prattein*) which was used in a variety of ways to talk about doing, acting, passing through, or undertaking, but also bringing about, achieving, bringing to an end. In Homer and the tragedies, *praxis* is often also used in the sense of action with either a beneficial or an adverse outcome. Combined with *eu* ("good"), the composite term *eupraxia* was used for an action with an advantageous outcome, and in Socrates and Plato and their circle the form *eu prattein* was used in the sense of having success or luck in life: "to do well" or "to fare well." This usage was then extended from life in general to specific practices such as agriculture, medicine, and politics, where it then meant to perform some particular activity correctly and thereby with success. In Plato *praxis* is also used as a generic term for action in general, including speech, but also in the narrow sense of handicraft activity, in contrast to *logos* (Bien 1989, col. 1277 f.).

[7] On the uses of literacy in ancient Greece, see, e.g., the work by Lonie 1983; Wood 1988, pp. 163 ff.; Thomas 1992; Meißner 1999; Long 2001; Cuomo 2005, 2008; and Totelin 2009. On the key issue of literacy in the development of human practices and technologies, see the work of Jack Goody (1977, 1987), and for correctives, the works by Geoffrey Lloyd (1979, 2008), Roy Harris (1986, 1995, 2000), and David Olson (1994).

[8] The Hippocratic corpus is a collection of some seventy manuscripts on medical topics and is attributed to Hippocrates of Kos (*c.*460–*c.*370 BCE) and his students and followers (Hippokrates of Kos 1923).

[9] On the concept of *praxis* in ancient Greece, see, e.g., the works by Günther Bien (1968, 1989), André Tosel (2010), and Armin Wildfeuer (2011). (Cf. also Picht 1964; Rese 2003).

By contrast, in Aristotle[10] (384–322 BCE) the ordinary notion of *praxis* was transformed into a technical term, and a rather contrived one at that.[11] He introduced his transformed notion in a context where he was discussing the characteristics and qualities of distinctly different "forms of life" (*bioi*) in which human nature is realized. In contrast to lower life forms such as the "life of nutrition or growth" of plants and the "sentient life" of animals (*Nicomachean Ethics*, 1095 b–1098 a; cf. *Metaphysics*, 981 a–982 a), or the "life of pleasure" (a life "suitable for beasts," to which the "slavish" "mass of mankind" is devoted), he focused on the forms of life in which human reason (*logos*) is exercised:

- the *bios praktikē*, the life of the citizens of the *polis* among their fellow citizens, as that life, by virtue of the *polis*, transcends simple brutish necessity, a life the aim of which is "honor" (*timē*); "the activity of the practical virtues [*praktikon areton*] is exhibited in political or military affairs" (*Nic. Ethics*, 1177 b; cf. *Politics*, 1329 a)
- the *bios theōretikos*, the life of contemplation (*theōria*), also, of course, within the world of the *polis* but transcending it spiritually (*Nic. Ethics*, 1177 ab)[12]

The difference between these two forms of life can be summarized in saying that *theōria* strives to grasp that which is universal and unchanging, for the sake of knowledge, and is assessed on whether it is true or false. In contrast, *praxis* is engaged with the particular and variable; it is assessed on whether its purpose and motivation is virtuous and noble. That is, in Aristotle, *theōria* and *praxis* denote distinctly different forms of life that have no reciprocal or internal relationship. Accordingly, while "contemplative thinking" (*theoretikēs dianoias*) is concerned with "truth and falsity," "practical thinking" (*dianoia praktikē*) is concerned with "right and wrong," and its function (*ergon*) is the attainment of "truth in agreement with right desire." The source of praxis is desire and reasoning directed at some end (*prohairesis*), and it involves intuition and intellect as well as moral disposition (*hexis ēthikē*) (*Nic. Ethics*, 1139 a).

Now, since he argued that the use of the term *praxis* should be restricted to the domain of civic life, the question arises: where does *technē* fit into this scheme? After all, as Aristotle points out, everyone who makes something also does so "for an end"

[10] In the following I am using Jonathan Barnes' collection of Aristotle's works in English translation (Aristotélēs 1984). For purposes of readability, variations in the translations have been modestly and tacitly edited. For instance, the term *aretē*, which is sometimes translated as "virtue" and sometimes as "excellence," has here been rendered as "virtue." For key concepts such as *praxis*, *technē*, *poiēsis*, etc., I have in many places inserted (directly or in brackets) transliterations of the original Greek terms. In doing so, I have consulted the Perseus Digital Library (http://www.perseus.tufts.edu/hopper/), the Greek–English editions in the Loeb Classical Library, and Ursula Wolf's excellent new German translations of *Nicomachean Ethics* and *Metaphysics* (1994, 2006).

[11] As always, when a term in widespread use in ordinary language is adopted for use as a technical term, authors typically cannot dispense with using the term in its ordinary sense; hence, inconsistencies invariably arise. With respect to *praxis*, Aristotle is no exception, as he used the term occasionally in its various ordinary senses (for a systematic account, see Bien 1989).

[12] The word *theōria* originally referred to the observation of public ceremonies in honor of the gods: the experience of an uplifting spectacle.

(*Nic. Ethics*, 1139 a). This would lead us presume that the application of *technē* falls under the concept of *praxis*. Not so, Aristotle claimed. So, while Plato, in accordance with ordinary usage, talked about craft work (*technē*) as *praktikē* (e.g., *Statesman*, 258 de), Aristotle refuted this very notion, and to counter it, he postulated a categorical distinction between, on the one hand, *poiēsis* (making, producing) and, on the other, *praxis*, where the term *poiēsis* was used for activities in which *technē* is applied. This is an important and also puzzling claim, so I will dwell a bit on the key passage (*Nic. Ethics*, 1140 ab).

The passage begins by stating that "things made [*poieton*] and things done [*prakton*]," in contrast to the immutable objects of theoretical knowledge, have in common that they are "things that can be otherwise." But other than that, they are "different," the difference being that of the object and purpose of the activities of these two domains. Therefore, it is argued, also the reasoning involved is "different": "the reasoned disposition to act [*meta logou hexis praktikē*] is different from the reasoned disposition to make [*meta logou hexis poiētikē*]." And as if to leave no room for doubt, Aristotle states explicitly that the concepts of "making [*poiēsis*] and acting [*praxis*] are different" and "hence" that they "do not include each the other either; *praxis* is not *poiēsis* nor is *poiēsis praxis*" (*Nic. Ethics*, 1140 a). Having thus stipulated that *poiēsis* and *praxis* are categorially different, of separate conceptual regions, he goes on to state that *poiēsis* and *technē* are coextensive concepts:

> Now since building is [a *technē*] and is essentially a reasoned disposition to make [*logon poietikēs*], and there is neither any *technē* that is not such a disposition nor any such disposition that is not *technē*, *technē* is identical with a disposition to make, involving a true course of reasoning. (*Nic. Ethics*, 1140 a)

In short, *poiēsis* equals *technē*: "*Poiēsis* and *praxis* being different, *technē* must be a matter of *poiēsis*, not of *praxis*" (*Nic. Ethics*, 1140 a).

In this context, and in accordance with the conception of *technē* developed by the Hippocratic school and the sophists, Aristotle defines *technē* as an acquired and rational skill to bring about, under conditions of contingency, something that would not otherwise come to exist (by nature or necessity). First,

> All *technē* is concerned with coming into being, i.e. with contriving and considering how something may come into being which is capable of either being or not being, and whose origin is in the maker and not in the thing made. For *technē* is concerned neither with things that are, or come into being, by necessity, nor with things that do so in accordance with nature (since these have their origin in themselves). (*Nic. Ethics*, 1140 a)

Second, in exercising *technē*, the actor contains "chance," bringing contingent occurrences under control; thus, "in a sense chance and *technē* are concerned with the same objects." Third, he further specifies that in contrast to *technē*, namely, "a disposition concerned with making, involving a true course of reasoning," lack of *technē* [*atechnia*]" "is a disposition concerned with making, involving a false course of reasoning." That is, *technē* is rational in that it has a rationale.

On the other hand, *phronēsis* (the faculty of judgment required in exercising *praxis*) "is a true and reasoned disposition to act with regard to the things that are good or bad for man.[13] For while *poiēsis* has an end other than itself, *praxis* cannot; for good action [*eupraxis*] itself is its end" (*Nic. Ethics*, 1140 ab). This is a point that is spelled out when he states that "the activity of the practical virtues [*praktikon areton*] is exhibited in political or military affairs" (*Nic. Ethics*, 1177 b; cf. also *Politics*, 1325 a).

In Aristotle's philosophy, the concepts *poiēsis* and *praxis*, and by implication the capabilities required in exercising these forms of activity, *technē* and *phronēsis*, while distinctly different in terms of objects and ends, do have in common that they, in contrast to wisdom (*sophía*) and *theōria*, both are faced with and must cope with particular objects under conditions of contingency. On the one hand, both *technē* and *phronēsis* "are concerned with what can be otherwise" (*Nic. Ethics*, 1140 a; 1141 a), and on the other, "actions [*praxis*] and productions [*poiēsis*] are all concerned with the individual" (*Metaphysics*, 981 a).

That is, in Aristotle, the concepts of *phronēsis*/*praxis* and *technē*/*poiēsis* are positioned right at the center of his ubiquitous hierarchies of forms of life, knowledge, and socio-political status. On the one hand, *praxis* and *poiēsis* are superior to mere experience (*empeiria*): "art arises when from many notions gained by experience one universal judgement about a class of objects is produced" (*Metaphysics*, 981 a), and on the other, they are inferior to science (*epistēmē*), wisdom (*sophía*), and contemplation (*theōria*), the objects of which are immutable and universal.

It should be noted that Aristotle explicitly recognized the importance of experience in an ordinary line of work such as treating a patient. In the art of medicine, a man that has "the theory [*logoi*, concept] without the experience, and recognizes the universal but does not know the individual included in this" is likely "to fail to cure"; he is unlikely to be able to deal with the contingencies of the particular case (*Metaphysics*, 981 a). However, torn between, on the one hand, a striving for knowledge of the immutable and universal, and on the other hand, a redeeming curiosity in the rich multiplicity of the world of experience, that is, trapped in an insurmountable dichotomy of the universal and the particular, Aristotle's thinking exhibited great strain. So, having acknowledged the importance of experience for useful mundane purposes, he went on to apply the same dichotomy of the universal and the particular to his analysis of the role of experience:

> But yet we think that knowledge [*eidénai*] and understanding [*epaíein*] belong to *technē* rather than to [mere] experience [*empoeirias*], and we suppose artists [*technitas*] to be wiser [*sophía*] than men of [mere] experience [...]; and this because the former know the cause, but the latter do not. For men of [mere] experience know that the thing is so, but do not know why, while the others know the "why" and the cause. Hence we think also that the master-workers [*architechtones*] in each craft are more honorable and know in a truer sense and are wiser than the manual workers [*cheirotechnon*], because they know the causes of the things that are done (we think the manual workers are like certain lifeless things which act [*poiein*] indeed, but act without knowing what they do

[13] Aristotle uses *poiēsis* as well as *technē* in order not to confound the categories: *praxis* and *poiēsis* are classes or domains of contingent activity, while *phronēsis* and *technē* are the requisite rational faculties.

> [*poiei*], as fire burns, — but while the lifeless things perform each of their functions by a natural tendency, the laborers [*cheirotechnon*] perform them through habit [*phýsis*, natural disposition]); thus we view them as being wiser [*sofoterois*] not in virtue of being able to act [*praktikois*], but of having the theory [*logoi*] for themselves and knowing the causes. (*Metaphysics* 981 ab)

The (for us) remarkable statement that manual workers are "like certain lifeless things" that "act without knowing what they do, as fire burns" is not accidental, a slip of the pen; it expresses a view with deep roots in the thinking of the Socratic school. And it is this contempt of ordinary manual work, the work of carpenters and shoemakers and plowmen, that underlies Aristotle's distinction between *poiēsis* and *praxis*.

Aristotle's point by categorially separating *praxis* and *poiēsis* is that the domain of *technē* (*poiēsis*) is conceptually outside of that of domain of the civic life of the *polis* as such, *bios praktikē*:

> This [Aristotelian] concept of *praxis* separates what *praxis* in the modern sense unites: *bios praktikos* has nothing in common with technical action (*technē*) or productive making (*poiēsis*); it denotes the institutionalized, normatively regulated action, the ethical-political activity within the framework of the polis. *Praxis* was considered of higher value than *poiēsis* because it has its objective in itself. By contrast, *technē poietikē* is a teleological process, determined by its product, its object, or its use value; it is goal-directed and the audience of its products are the agents of praxis, humans who are complete humans, lords who by virtue of their power are liberated from work to live the good life, the free life of praxis. This free life of *praxis* finds its completion in the development of the ethical virtues in that exceptionally worthy form of life: political life. (Tosel 2010, p. 2137)

In fact, Aristotle's undertaking was in important ways an ideological one and should be understood as a continuation of the anti-democratic efforts of the Socratic tradition (Wood and Wood 1978; Wood 1988). The issue was this. Through a series of democratic reforms in the sixth and fifth centuries BCE, Athenian peasants and other commoners managed to establish a political-economic order in which they enjoyed full rights as citizens and were liberated of remnants of forced labor and similar forms of surplus extraction based on judicial or political power (Wood 1988; Ober 1998). More than that, to enable commoners to take part in political deliberations, act as judges, etc., those who participated in the performance of such civic responsibilities were compensated for their time and effort (as of 460 BCE). That is, in democratic Athens, the vast majority of citizens, the peasants and craftsmen, were able to exercise their civic rights to an extent unheard of elsewhere at that time (and, until quite recently, since). Although the political hegemony of the Athenian oligarchy was ultimately broken in the wake of the Peloponnesian War (431–404 BCE), with the fall of the Thirty Tyrants in 403, its adherents continued to offer intellectual resistance to the rule of the *demos*. As part of this opposition, Socrates and (after the trial and execution of Socrates in 399, partly for his association with the Thirty Tyrants), his followers such as Plato and Xenophon tried to counter the fundamentally democratic claim of the Sophistic movement, that any adult male could learn the techniques required to be an active participant of Athenian democracy, by arguing that such techniques were inadequate, since the requisite civic virtues could not be taught and learned and, hence, that government should be left to the select few who, free from the necessity of work, could be expected to have those qualities.

Aristotle developed the somewhat different argument that *bios praktikos* is a domain entirely different from that of *poiēsis*:

> Where then there is such a difference as that between soul and body, or between men and animals (as in the case of those whose business is to use their body, and who can do nothing better), the lower sort are by nature slaves, and it is better for them as for all inferiors that they should be under the rule of a master. For he who can be, and therefore is, another's and he who participates in rational principle enough to apprehend, but not to have, such a principle, is a slave by nature. Whereas the lower animals cannot even apprehend a principle; they obey their instincts. And indeed, the use made of slaves and of tame animals is not very different; for both with their bodies minister to the needs of life. (*Politics*, 1254 b)

That is, an ordinary manual worker may not be a slave in any legal or economic sense, but he might just as well have been since he, in order to survive and put bread and oil on the table, has to work for others or sell his wares in the marketplace. As Socrates is reported by Xenophon to have stated the point, in a rather crass manner:

> to be sure, the so-called *banausic*[14] occupations are scorned, and, naturally enough, held in low regard in our states. For they spoil the bodies of the workmen and the foremen, forcing them to sit still and stay indoors, and in some cases to spend the day at the fire. As their bodies become womanish their souls lose strength too. Moreover, these so-called *banausic* occupations leave no spare time for attention to one's friends and city, so that those who follow them are reputed bad at dealing with friends and bad defenders of their country. In some of the states, in fact, and especially in those reputed to be warlike, it is not even lawful for any of the citizens to work in the *banausic* occupations. (Xenophon, *Oeconomicus* § 4:2–3)

In accordance with this oligarchic stance, Aristotle asked in his *Politics*: "Is he only a true citizen who has a share of office, or is the mechanic [*banausous*] to be included?" (*Politics*, 1277 a). Granting that an argument *could* be made that those who are necessary for the

[14] The Greek term *banausikai* is often translated as "mechanical arts," and *banausous* similarly as "mechanic," but *banausikai* does not necessarily mean crafts in general, but only "certain crafts which were regarded as unworthy or degrading." In the Socratic tradition, the word was "strongly pejorative" and was "associated with philosophical and social attitudes which labeled certain occupations or activities, primarily but not exclusively those requiring physical, rather than mental, labor, as inferior and base. [...] The inferiority of the banausic arts is neither derived from their technological character nor their physicality alone but from the idea that those particular arts do not involve the soul in either its intellectual or its moral capacities but are practices *merely* to satisfy physical needs or pleasures" (Whitney 1990, pp. 27–30). — The word *banausous* (perhaps derived from *baūnos*, hearth or forge) only came in use after 460 BCE, its use a manifestation of rising oligarchic resentments against the increasing participation of artisans and laborers in the public affairs of Athens (Meier 1984, p. 83).

state should also be citizens, Aristotle nevertheless rejected the argument: "It must be admitted that we cannot consider all those to be citizens who are necessary to the existence of the state" (*Politics*, 1277 b). First of all, slaves were certainly necessary, in Aristotle's thinking: they are "living instruments."[15] And besides, many resident aliens are necessary for the state and they certainly cannot be citizens either. Anyway, and in general, "The necessary people [i.e., people providing necessary services for the wellbeing of the state] are either slaves who minister to the wants of individuals, or mechanics [*banausoi*] and laborers who are the servants of the community" (*Politics*, 1278 ab). And "The best form of state will not admit them [workers and foreigners] to citizenship." But if the artisans *were* to be admitted, as had unfortunately happened in Athens, "then our definition of the virtue of a citizen will not apply to every citizen nor to every free man as such, but only to those who are freed from necessary services," that is, have sufficient wealth to live a life of leisure. For "no man can practice virtue who is living the life of a mechanic [*bion banauson*] or laborer [*thetikon*]" (*Politics*, 1278 ab). Thus,

> in the state which is best governed and possesses men who are just absolutely, and not merely relatively, to the principle of the constitution, the citizens must not lead the life of mechanics [*banausoi bion*] or tradesmen, for such a life is ignoble, and inimical to virtue. Neither must they be husbandmen [*georgous*], since leisure is necessary both for the development of virtue and the performance of political duties. (*Politics*, 1328 b–1329 a)

To conclude, Aristotle's notion of *praxis*, that is, his attempt to appropriate the concept of *praxis* for the purpose of critiquing Athenian democracy, does not seem to have been widely accepted. There may be several reasons for this.

First, to most of Aristotle's contemporaries, his dichotomy of *praxis* and *poiēsis* would have been unconvincing, if not absurd. On the one hand, in support of the dichotomy, Aristotle postulated complete congruence between *poiēsis* and *technē* ("*technē* is *identical* with a disposition to make"). But in classical Greece, the concept of *technē* was not confined to the domain of production, neither in ordinary language nor in high literature and philosophy. It simply made no sense to say that affairs of governance, in political and military affairs, did not require mastery of various *technai* (such as, for instance, navigating navy vessels, auditing the accounts of the *polis*, or drafting and reviewing laws). On the other hand, the dichotomy was also predicated on the spurious argument that productive work, *poiēsis*, was defined by resulting in a distinct product—as opposed to *praxis*, which supposedly was undertaken only for the sake of *praxis* ("while *poiēsis* has an end other than itself, *praxis* cannot; for *eupraxis* itself is its end"). This argument is almost as sloppy

[15] "[I]nstruments are of various sorts; some are living, others lifeless; in the rudder, the pilot of a ship has a lifeless, in the look-out man, a living instrument; for in the arts the servant is a kind of instrument. [...] the instruments commonly so called are instruments of production [*organa poietika*], whilst a possession is an instrument of action [*ktema praktikon*]. [...] Further, as production [*poiēsis*] and action [*praxis*] are different in kind, and both require instruments, the instruments which they employ must likewise differ in kind. But life is action [*praxis*] and not production [*poiēsis*], and therefore the slave is the minister [*yperētes*: rower, instrument] of action [*praxis*]" (*Politics*, 1253 b–1254 a).

as Aristotle's argument for "natural slavery." It is tautology to say that "good action itself is its end," and one might just as well have objected, equally tautologically, that building a house that is "good" for people to live in or healing a wound "is itself its end." Or one might have objected that any political action anyway "has an end other than itself," in as much as political action is always embodied in particular decisions about particular measures (appointing officials, raising taxes, building roads, building navy vessels, and so on). In fact, as Aristotle points out himself, in another context, "military pursuits," while always "honorable," are not "the ultimate end of all thing" but "means to that end" (*Politics*, 1325 a). However, what Aristotle might have wanted to insinuate by this sloppy argument could have been that productive work, the application of the various *technai*, was the work of *specialists*, and that the outlook of specialists, their cognitive horizon, was parochial, in contrast to the concern for the *polis* as a whole expected of participants in the affairs of the *polis*. But this, in turn, begs the question: why should artisans and laborers not be able to act in the interest of the *polis*? In other words, if that was indeed his intention, he presumed what he labored to demonstrate: that commoners had no business in government. In sum, underlying Aristotle's dichotomy of *praxis* and *poiēsis* was his aristocratic prejudice, stated elsewhere, that there is no virtue or honor in being an artisan or laborer. But there is invariably a moral order to doing productive work that is not *essentially* distinct from the moral order of activities required of governance. Workers are under obligation to meet all sorts of norms and requirements (quality, schedule, reliability, economy, innovation, etc.) and workers of classic Athens evidently also took pride in their work (Burford 1972). The underlying aristocratic prejudice, while shared by the other members of the Socratic tradition and in general by the ideological residues of the oligarchy, was most certainly not widely shared among the majority of Athenians. The literary and archeological evidence is ample demonstration of this. That is, the thrust of Aristotle's argument would hardly have been acceptable to ordinary Athenians, had they been exposed to it, and later scientists and engineers who might have read Aristotle would hardly have found it sensible.

Second, the Aristotelian notion of *praxis*—the participation in the affairs of the *polis*, in governance and military affairs, as opposed to the domain of *poiēsis* or *technē*, the productive activities of medical doctors, peasants, artisans, and manual workers—anyway made little sense beyond the confines of the Athenian *polis* and the particular constellation of political forces prevalent there in the fifth and fourth centuries. It only made sense on the assumption that citizenship was an issue, as part of an argument against a form of government in which peasants and technicians enjoyed citizenship (cf. Meier 1984). In short, it only made sense as part of the oligarchic critique of democracy. When *that* particular context had become history, in the world of Hellenistic monarchies that emerged after Athens and its allies succumbed to Macedonian power, the Aristotelian dichotomy of *praxis* and *technē* also became ideologically irrelevant.

And third, with the advances of mathematics (e.g., Euclid, *c.*300 BCE, and Archimedes, *c.*287–212 BCE) and the application of mathematics in the articulation, application, and transmission of technical knowledge in areas such as mechanics, optics, pneumatics, and artillery (e.g., Ctesibios, *fl.* 285–222 BCE, Philo of Byzantium, *c.*280–220 BCE, and Hero of Alexandria, *c.*10–70 CE), Aristotle's very low regard of *technē* as a form of *epistēmē* would also have become problematic (see, e.g., Gille 1978a, pp. 243–320; Whitney 1990; Long 2001; Cuomo 2005, 2007). At about the same time, and possibly for related reasons, the notion of *theōria* as the domain of contemplation fell from its place in heaven, where it was replaced by explicitly theological notions, and became synonymous with, especially, mathematically articulated scientific and technical knowledge. In any event, the notion of praxis we find in later texts seems more in accord with the ordinary sense of praxis as it was used in the Greek world before Aristotle. We thus find that Hellenistic authors such as the linguist Dionysius Thrax (170–90 BCE) and the commentators on his *Grammatical Arts*[16] turned Aristotle's distinctions between *bion praktikē* and *theōretikos* and between *praxis* and *poiēsis* inside out by distinguishing between *productive arts* such as metalworking, shoemaking, and carpentry, which are characterized by the transformation of some matter into useful artifacts; *practical arts*, which are characterized by the use of instruments and machines in military affairs; and *theoretical arts* such as astronomy, geometry, and philosophy. In Elspeth Whitney's words, the "most striking aspect" of this work is the "emphasis on technology":

> The authors [...] have made use of Aristotelian categories but have redefined their content. [...] The practical arts [...] have partially or completely lost the ethical or social element of Aristotle's conception and reduced to physical actions, particularly actions using instruments or machines. (Whitney 1990, pp. 37 f.)

The trail ends about here. The linguistic divide between the Greek-speaking and the Latin-speaking worlds meant that the readership for Greek manuscripts in Western Europe anyway was small, and with decline of the Roman empire in the West and the Muslim ascendancy in the previous Hellenistic world, the Greek influence dwindled. The sophisticated terminology of the Greek classics was left behind. Thus, the Latin-speaking world did not adopt the Greek term *praxis*. It was, so to speak, taken out of circulation. However, almost a millennium after Aristotle, in the Middle Ages, when the surviving texts of the Greek classics slowly, drop by drop, began to become available in Western Europe, either as manuscripts or in the form of Arab commentaries, the term "praxis" entered into use again. While usage, until the Modern Era, was very much in flux (it was an imported word, after all, and for a long time the relevant texts by Aristotle were not or only partially available), it was often and perhaps generally used in ways quite different from that of the Greek classics.

First of all, the notions of *theōria* and *praxis* were adopted by scholastic authors for their own purposes, namely, in their ongoing debates about the nature of Christian theology, the central question being whether theology was contemplative (or speculative) or whether its teachings also were supposed to affect human conduct both in the external world and in the internal life of the will. Related to this, the notion of *praxis* was an object of contention in the debates in the late thirteenth and early fourteenth centuries between, on the one hand, Duns Scotus and his followers and, on the other, William of Ockham and his followers, with the Scotian camp reserving *praxis* for acts of the will, the very

[16] Only the Greek text seems available. (For a brief description, see Whitney 1990, pp. 37 f.)

willing to will to do what is good (or not), and the Ockham camp arguing that *praxis* involves advisory reason determining the means by which the ends are to be achieved (Kobusch 1989). The (for us) important thing to note is that the term *praxis,* in this tradition, from the very beginning, was used, generally, for voluntary human activities, acts of volition, as seen from the perspective of moral justification, and that Aristotle's separations (of *theōria* and *praxis* and of *praxis* and *poiēsis* as different domains of activity and knowledge) were not observed. Nor could they be, for the terms were now used in a theological discourse, that is, in a domain of discourse entirely different from the political-ideological one of Athens in the fourth century BCE. Contra Aristotle, the notions of *theōria* and *praxis* were now used as a *concept pair* referring to two aspects of the role of theology, whereas, for example, Thomas Aquinas went further, in that he presumed that *theory* and *practice* were concepts of the *same* category, in as much as he posited that theory "extends into practice."[17] The scholastic tradition of moral philosophy later fed into moral philosophy, in particular the strand that in the eighteenth century became known as "practical philosophy." However, in the complex history of the concepts of "practice," "technique," etc., this is a sideshow, for from around 1400 these terms became part of the terminology of artisans and engineers in their discourses about their work and technical knowledge.

In fact, we find the first traces of that usage already in the High Middle Ages, a century before Thomas Aquinas, in scholars with a keen interest in mundane technologies. Hugh of Saint Victor, for instance, wrote a treatise (*c.*1120) the very title of which, *Practical Geometry,* completely disregarded Aristotle's carefully constructed categorial separations. More to the point, a generation later, Domingo Gundisalvo, impressed by contemporary advances in mechanical technologies (such as the construction of water mills) and trying to assign them a proper place in the greater scheme of human knowledge in a treatise on the different bodies of knowledge, referred to engineering as "practical arts" ("*principia artium civilium practicarum,*" Gundisalvo *c.*1150, p. 234). And a century later, Robert Kilwardby, who was subsequently appointed as the Archbishop of Canterbury and a cardinal, openly attacked Aristotle's separation of *praxis* and *technē* by categorizing ethics and mechanics as "practical sciences" of the soul and the body, respectively (Kilwardby *c.*1250, §§ 347–57), and by pointing out that "practical sciences" such as mechanical arts are "speculative" (theoretical) and, conversely, that the speculative sciences such as arithmetic and geometry are not without *praxis*: "It seems therefore that every single science said to be speculative is also practical. It seems, therefore, that the speculative sciences are practical and the practical speculative" (Kilwardby *c.*1250, § 393 [English translation of this passage in Whitney 1990, p. 120]). Consonant with these conceptual shifts, the concept pair *theory* and *practice* was used to express and reason about the relationship between written representations of technical knowledge and its application under conditions of contingency already in the heydays of scholasticism. Thus, from the thirteenth century, "practical medicine" ("*practica,*" as opposed to "*medicina theorica*") became not only a topic of teaching but also generated a blossoming body of didactic literature (e.g., Riddle 1974; Demaitre 1975; Jacquart 1990). This notion of "practice" was, of course,

[17] "*Intellectus speculativus per extensionem fit practicus*" (*Summa Theologiae*, 1266–73 [quoted in Naus 1959]).

categorially distinct from that of Aristotle in that it now was used for actions that are held accountable with respect to a body of systematic secular knowledge, derived from experience and expressed in writing, a "theory" in the modern sense. As with Hugh's, Gundisalvo's, and Kilwardby's notion of "practical arts," this concept of "practice" upended Aristotle's categorial separation between the domains of *technē* (*poiēsis*) and *praxis*. In the following centuries, the term "practice," used in this new way, became a key part of the terminology of artisans and engineers, in their discourses about their work and the role of their technical knowledge.

2.2.3 The Construction of the Modern Concept of "Practice"

Der Maister sol auch kennen schreiben und lessen

Das Feuerwerkbuch (1420)

Pour éclairer la pratique

Académie Royale des Sciences (1761)

The Modern concept of "practice" was developed in the movement that unfolded in Western Europe in the Modern Era, from around 1400, and which resulted in the emergence of modern science and technology.[18]

With the early developments of a capitalist economy based on handicrafts ("mechanical arts") and the ensuing radical transformation of the organization of work and of the role of technical knowledge in work, together with the concomitant upheaval in the conception of work and technical knowledge, the issue of representations of working knowledge in work, which had first arisen with the use of writing in the various *technai*, now became one of acute practical import. What ensued was a veritable explosion of technical writing.[19]

The Italian historian Paolo Rossi has given a quite concise summary of this shift in his *Philosophy, Technology, and the Arts in the Early Modern Era* (1962):

> A new view of labor, of the function of technical knowledge, and of the significance of artificial processes through which nature was altered and transformed clearly makes its way into the work of artists and experimentalists of the fifteenth century and into the treatises of engineers and technicians of the sixteenth century. [...] The men who toiled in the workshops, in the arsenals, and in the studios, or those who had dropped their disdain of practice, considered the operations conducted on these premises a form of cognition. (Rossi 1962, pp. ix f.)

This "new view of labor, of the function of technical knowledge," was not just a change of workers' self-consciousness, or of their perceived status, but, more to the point, a critical conceptual aspect of the transformation of the organization of work and of "the function

[18] I will therefore call our ordinary concept of "practice" the "Modern concept of practice" (with a capital "M"). For literature on this movement, see the work by Zilsel 1942, Rossi 1962, Lefèvre 2004, Smith 2004, Ehmer and Lis 2009, Long 2011, and Lis and Soly 2012.

[19] If the expression "practice turn" (Schatzki et al. 2001) is to be applied to anything, this is it!

of technical knowledge" in work in the development of the emerging industrial forms of production. For the purposes of transforming the organization of work, it became crucial for merchants, mechanists, and scholars to reflect on and understand the actual role of practical reason and practical experience vis-à-vis the role of mathematics, physics, astronomy, etc. This process of reflection and inquiry played out, and is thus manifested, in the emergence of a vast body of literature in which the relationship between "theory" and "practice" was an organizing axis of argument.

It is, of course, a rather mixed bag of texts, addressing distinctly different topics and written for different audiences and from different motives. As Rossi puts it, this literature is "extraordinarily rich in treatises of a technical character, which at times were real manuals, and at times disconnected reflections on [the authors'] own work or procedures employed in the various arts" (Rossi 1962, p. 15). However, a few loose types can be distinguished.

First of all, a wealth of technical treatises were written by master artisans and scholars for didactic purposes and distributed as manuscript copies (e.g., Cennini *c.*1390; Alberti *c.*1450). They are typically texts written to give instruction and advice to their apprentices and other minions as well as to colleagues in guilds.[20] Thus, after 1400 there was, as the historian Bert Hall (1979) puts it, "a veritable flood of technical treatises; the written record becomes so rich that the historian is almost inundated with documents":

> Not all the authors of such works are known to us [...] but when we can discover an author's or copyist's name, it often reveals a practicing technical specialist. The quality of the anonymous texts is likewise sufficiently high to suggest 'professional' technicians as authors. [...] The quantitative change as well as the qualitative character of the surviving works argues quite strongly that men of the fifteenth century rather suddenly began to resort to pen and paper in a field where their fathers had been satisfied with memory and the spoken word. (Hall 1979)

A particularly interesting example is here the *Feuerwerkbuch* (1420), a "very popular" didactic manual for artillerymen, obviously written by a gunner, who insisted that the master gunner must also be literate, "*der Maister sol auch kennen schreiben und lesen*" (i.e., "The master gunner must also be able to write and read"), because of the large number of "pertinent elements which every gunner should know and which a master without writing cannot remember in his mind" (*Feuerwerkbuch* 1420 p. 16).[21]

From around 1530, this written tradition was augmented by the printed book, as such didactic texts began to be composed and published for the benefit of a wider readership (e.g., Dürer 1527). In the words of Hall again:

> From the 1530's onward there is a slow but steady increase in the number of printed books on technology, and by the latter third of the century, print had become a suitable

[20] For historical accounts of the dissemination of technical knowledge *among* artisans, see the work by Long 2001, Belfanti 2004, Hilaire-Pérez and Verna 2006, and Long 2011.

[21] On the *Feuerwerkbuch*, see Hall 1979; Crossgrove 1994, pp. 137 f.; and Long 2011, pp. 117–20.

> medium both for descriptive works and for presentation of technical innovations, as well as discussions of the significance of technology in general. This movement toward a fully public medium completed the transformation initiated with the shift toward manuscripts in the fifteenth century. Technology, which had once been nearly the exclusive possession of a particular craft group, was now being displayed and discussed before a wide audience of educated, but unspecialized readers. (Hall 1979)

The movement of artisans expressing and reasoning about their technical knowledge in writing soon widened to include studies of the work practices of artisans, written by outside scholars for the purpose of mediating their techniques and practices to other practitioners of the described technical professions and to the new technological public (e.g., Agricola 1556). Closely coupled to this movement, artisan-engineers and scholars began to develop mathematical representations of technical knowledge in an effort to develop a unified theory of motion (e.g., Monte 1577; Galilei 1594).[22]

An underlying and sometimes explicit theme in this literature was that, as Rossi puts it: the "actual union," "in reality," "between 'discourse' and 'practice,' 'speculation' and 'manufacture,' " "presented serious problems" (Rossi 1962, p. 61). To exemplify this observation, Rossi quotes the Italian military engineer Bonaiuto Lorini, who, in a treatise on fortifications (1596)[23], addressed the problem of the relation between the work of the "purely speculative mathematician" and that of the "practical mechanic":

> But before we proceed, it will be necessary to mention the difference that we find between the pure speculative Mathematician and the practical Mechanic[, namely, that] the demonstrations and proportions we find between lines on surfaces and imaginary bodies, abstracted from matter, do not respond so exquisitely when applied to material things; that is, the mental concepts of the Mathematician do not meet, nor are they subject to, the same impediments that, by nature, always accompany the materials [*materia*] with which the Mechanic operates. (Lorini 1596, pp. 171 f.)

For example, Lorini explained, we are "necessarily persuaded" by "the Mathematical demonstration" of what is normally referred to as "the law of the lever,"[24] namely, the principle "that it, for example, with a line whose distance from the fulcrum to the force equals four times the distance between the load and the fulcrum, is possible to lift the load with one fourth of the force," but, he added, "when we then experience this in matter, as we would do by using a beam as a lever, we should take into account the weight of such a lever as well." Similarly, "the very material itself could cause great difficulties, as would happen when we have to rotate material wheels around their axes, which could be

[22] For a historical analysis of Galilei's bridging technology and science, see Valeriani's study (2010). On the contribution of the practical methods of artisan-engineers to the rise of modern science, cf., e.g., Zilsel 1942; Rossi 2000; Freudenthal and McLaughlin 2009; and Long 2011.

[23] I am indebted to Elena Parmiggiani for providing me with a translation of Lorini's original Italian text (Lorini 1596, Fifth Book, Chapter 1, pp. 171 f.). The translation has been checked against the contemporaneous German translation (Lorini 1607, pp. 174–6).

[24] The lever principle is generally ascribed to Archimedes' *Quadrature of the Parabola* (Propositions 6–7).

obstructed if their own weight is unequally distributed; and again, if the wheels rest on axes that are out of true, or not concentric, all of which can bring difficulty to the motion." Thus, while "the pure Mathematician imagines them as having no weight, and as rotating around lines and indivisible points,"

> the judgment of the Mechanic, who must instruct and direct the executors of the work, consists for the greater part in knowing how to predict difficulties arising from the various materials that have to be used: and to be cautious in this in so far as one cannot make a certain rule out of those accidental difficulties. (Lorini 1596, p. 172)

In short, mathematical theory, for all its conceptual power, cannot encompass the multiplicity and contingency of the material world with which the mechanic has to cope. This insight was revolutionary.

Over time, systematic accounts of work practices of this kind developed into a great scientific research tradition, for which Agricola's study of work practices in the Bohemian metal trades (1556) is exemplary. This tradition culminated in the large-scale project launched by the French Academy of Science in 1675, undertaken at the government's request and with the express purpose of producing systematic descriptions of the work practices and techniques of the approximately 200 crafts and trades ("*arts et métiers*") then in existence in France, from bakeries to pin manufactures: "The king wished the Academy to work unceasingly upon a treatise on mechanics, in which theory and practice should be explained in a clear manner that could be grasped by everyone" (Académie Royale des Sciences 1729–34, p. 131). As expressed in the Academy's own *mémoire* from 1699, it had undertaken the task of "describing the crafts in their present condition," knowing full well that the task was "dry, thorny, and not at all dazzling." The eventual *Descriptions* were to "penetrate to the ultimate details, although it would often prove very difficult to acquire them from artisans or to explain them," but as a result, "an infinity of practices, full of spirit and inventiveness, but generally unknown, will be drawn from their shadows." The crafts would thereby be preserved for posterity, but in addition, "able men" who lacked the leisure to visit the artisans' workshops would be able to "work on the perfection" of these practices, just as the Academy itself would not fail to remark if something might usefully be amended (Académie Royale des Sciences 1702, pp. 117 f.).

The aim of all this, as stated in the Academy's preamble to the *Descriptions*, was not merely to "examine and describe in turn all operations of the mechanical arts" but also and equally "to contribute to their progress." The Academy expected that "new degrees of perfection of the arts" would be achieved when scholars undertake the effort of investigating and developing the "often ingenious operations performed by the artisan in his workshop; when they see by themselves the needs of the art, its limitations, the difficulties that prevent it from going further, the assistance that one could transfer from one art to another and which the worker is rarely expected to know." Subjecting work practices, which had slowly evolved from "obscurity," to systematic study and thus rationalizing them, would show competent workers a way to "overcome the obstacles that they have been unable to cross," ways to "invent new tools," etc. The point was, as it was proudly put, "*éclairer la pratique*"—that is, to explain/enlighten practice (Académie Royale des Sciences 1761, pp. xvi f.).

By 1757 only a few pieces of the accumulated analyses had been made publicly available (Peaucelle 2007). However, in 1751, Denis Diderot, together with Jean Le Rond d'Alembert, began publishing the famous *Encyclopédie, ou dictionnaire raisonné des sciences, des arts et des métiers* (1751–66) that on many topics covered much of the same ground. This was possible, in part, because many of the authors who contributed to the *Encyclopédie* had access to the reports of the Academy field researchers or were involved in both projects—but also because Diderot himself visited and interviewed craftsmen in their workshops as part of his editorial work. Anyway, the Academy eventually succeeded in getting the publication process organized and from 1761 to 1788 altogether eighty-one treatises (about one hundred volumes) were published under the title *Descriptions des arts et métiers*.

The reasons for the lack of visible progress for almost a century were, unsurprisingly, the enormity of the task. It of course involved extensive fieldwork in different lines of trade in different parts of the country. What is more, it involved the issue of developing standards for the analytic work so as to render it sufficiently systematic and accurate, as well as the issue of developing standardized and adequate verbal and graphical representations of work: its organization, procedures, methods, tools, and so on. Implicit in these issues, the project was faced with the fundamental problem of developing *written* representations of *orally* transmitted technical knowledge. As this challenge was expressed succinctly by Diderot and d'Alembert as they reflected on the experience with their own, partly overlapping, work on the *Encyclopédie*:

> The section on the mechanical arts required no fewer details and no less care [than the sections on the sciences and the fine arts]. Never, perhaps, has there been such an accumulation of difficulties, and, to conquer them, so little help from books. Too much has been written on the sciences; not enough has been written well on the mechanical arts. [...] Thus everything impelled us to go directly to the workers.
>
> We approached the most capable of them in Paris and in the realm. We took the trouble of going into their shops, of questioning them, of writing at their dictation, of developing their thoughts and of drawing therefrom the terms peculiar to their professions, of setting up tables of these terms and of working out definitions for them, of conversing with those from whom we obtained memoranda, and (an almost indispensable precaution) of correcting through long and frequent conversations with others what some of them imperfectly, obscurely, and sometimes unreliably had explained. There are some artisans who are also men of letters, and we would be able to cite them here; but their number would be very small. Most of those who engage in the mechanical arts have embraced them only by necessity and work only by instinct. Hardly a dozen among a thousand can be found who are in a position to express themselves with some clarity upon the instrument they use and the things they manufacture. We have seen some workers who have worked for forty years without knowing anything about their machines. With them, it was necessary to exercise the function in which Socrates gloried, the painful and delicate function of being midwife of the mind, *obstetrix animorum*.

> But there are some trades so unusual and some operations so subtle that unless one does the work oneself, unless one operates a machine with one's own hands, and sees the work being created under one's own eyes, it is difficult to speak of it with precision. Thus, several times we had to get possession of the machines, to construct them, and to put a hand to the work. It was necessary to become apprentices, so to speak, and to manufacture some poor objects ourselves in order to learn how to teach others the way good specimens are made. (Diderot and d'Alembert 1751a, p. xxxiv)

Although "dry, thorny, and not at all dazzling," this effort had huge impact: "there can be no doubt" that these scientific descriptions of arts and handicrafts at the time "exerted a potent influence in western Europe" (Cole and Watts 1952, p. 1). To take some prominent examples, it provided Adam Smith with an empirically grounded general conception of human work and of the division of labor (1776). This conception, in turn, inspired G. W. F. Hegel to conceive of work as the process of Man's "self-creation," as Karl Marx famously summarized it (1844a, pp. 404 f.; 1844b pp. 333 f.). On the other hand, it also provided the "proof of concept" for organizing mass-calculation work on the basis of advanced division of labor, and it thereby gave Charles Babbage strong impetus to engage in the development of mechanical computing (cf. Schmidt 2011a, pp. 279 ff.).

Not only that: The *Descriptions* provided an exemplar demonstrating to scholars that received practices were accessible to scholarly analysis and might be much improved by application of the insights, methods, etc., of the physical, chemical, mechanical, etc., sciences. Such systematic studies of work practices with a view to their rationalization were given the name "*technology*" by the contemporary German scholar Johann Beckmann (1777).[25] Referring to the *Descriptions des arts et métiers* and similar works as the "most esteemed general writings on technology" (p. 39), that is, the model of such research, he defined "technology" as follows:

> Technology is the science of the transformation of materials or the knowledge of handicrafts. Instead of merely instructing workers to follow the master worker's prescriptions and habits in order to fabricate a product, technology provides systematically ordered fundamental directives; how one for exactly these ends can find the means on the basis of true principles and reliable experiences, and how one can explain and exploit the phenomena occurring in the process of fabrication. (Beckmann 1777, p. 19)

Technology, he stated, provides "complete, systematic, and perspicuous explanations of all works, their outcomes, and their grounds" (p. 20). That is, he coined the term "technology" to characterize a category of technical knowledge that not only describes a

[25] Beckmann (1777, p. 20) mentioned that he suggested the term with some trepidation in 1772, namely, in a review of a book by a French upholsterer on the principles of this trade: "*Technologie oder Kenntnis der Handwerker*," or "technology or knowledge of the craftsman" (1772, p. 309; on Beckmann, cf. Exner 1878 and Beckert 1983).

technique in terms of what is to be done (e.g., recipes) but also provides a "theory" that explains the rationale of the technique, that is, why it works and thus under which circumstances it can be expected to work and work well.

Beckmann continued the tradition of technical writing that had evolved since around 1400 and, in particular, the paradigm established by the Academy in Paris and by the Encylopédistes. In fact, he even integrated it in his teaching, in that his students were taken to local workplaces: "One must have tried, without any preparation or instruction, to get acquainted with factories and manufactories to know how difficult it is" (p. a7). One of these students, Johann Poppe, continued this work and wrote the first systematically organized history of technology. Pointing out that the "stipulations and customs" that regulate handicraft "were often based on deficient or even non-existent principles" and were often influenced by "strong prejudices," Poppe emphasized the role of *technology*: "Different scholars that have obtained knowledge of several handicrafts have recently, by virtue of their sciences, already cleared away many things that obstructed the greater perfection of these trades" (Poppe 1807, p. 63), and referring explicitly to the *Descriptions*, he stated that

> The meticulous description of the arts and handicrafts that the Academy brought to light belongs to the greatest scholarly works of the 18th century. It engendered several works of a similar kind, to some extent very valuable works, not only in French but also in other languages. (Poppe 1807, pp. 91 f.)

In short, the Modern concepts of "technology" and "practice" were joined at the hip from birth, with technology conceived of as a systematic effort to investigate and transform the techniques applied in the practices of the useful arts.

2.2.4 The Heritage

Late in the sixteenth century, the autodidact French ceramist and inventor Bernard Palissy gave a series of lectures in Paris in which he argued strongly for the primacy of "practical" experience against speculative "theory." In a book published in 1580, based on these lectures, he advised his readers "to be wary of believing opinions of those who say and maintain that theory begets practice," that is, the intellectualist legend that "the thing that one wants to do must be imagined and pictured in one's mind, before laying hand to one's task." To underscore his critique of this intellectualist legend, he did not hold his contempt in check:

> I dare say, to confusion of those who hold such opinion, that they could not make a shoe, not even the heel of a boot, even if they had all the theory in the world. I would ask those who hold such opinion whether they, having studied fifty years in books on cosmography and navigation on the sea, and having maps of all regions and the chronometer, the compass and astronomical instruments, would undertake to sail a ship to all countries: as will a man who is expert and practical. They dare not place themselves in such danger, whatever theory they may have learned: and when they have long debated, they will be forced to admit that practice has begotten theory. (Palissy 1580a, pp. x–xii; 1580b, p. 26)

Francis Bacon, who may have heard Palissy's lectures in Paris, articulated the conceptual implication of the entire movement devoted to understanding ordinary work practices with a view to their rationalization and called for a reversal of the relationship between "theory" and "practice." Bacon rejected the notion, received from "the Ancients," that anything useful at all could be accomplished when men, in "mad effort and useless combination of forces," "endeavor by logic (which may be considered as a kind of athletic art) to strengthen the sinews of the understanding" (Bacon 1620, Preface). Thus, in explicit contradiction of Plato and Aristotle, Bacon argued that theory and practice are *equals*, so to speak, and he was thereby able to even conceive of *theorizing proved wrong in practice*: "sciences fair perhaps in theory, but in practice inefficient" (Bacon 1620, § II:xlv):

> Although the roads to human power and to human knowledge lie close together and are nearly the same, nevertheless, on account of the pernicious and inveterate habit of dwelling on abstractions it is safer to begin and raise the sciences from those foundations which have relation to practice, and to let the active part itself be as the seal which prints and determines the contemplative counterpart. (Bacon 1620, § II:iv)

In this revolutionary view, ordinary working practices and practical knowledge were no longer categorially separated from and inferior to scientific knowledge and philosophy. It was conceivable to "begin and raise the sciences from those foundations which have relation to practice." However, Bacon's "practice turn" was of course largely programmatic. Production at the time was craft-based and science immature: Galilei was in the early stages of his career when Bacon published his *Novum Organon* in 1620.

However, a century or so later, when Denis Diderot, together with Jean d'Alembert, edited the *Encyclopédie* (1751–66), the original "practice turn" was completed, and the new conception of science as grounded in practical experience that Bacon had vaguely sensed and promulgated could now become articulated most pointedly. Diderot thus wrote an article entitled "Arts," i.e., the *practical* crafts, arts, techniques, and sciences, for the first volume of the *Encyclopédie* in which he, following Bacon, flatly observed that "It is man's work [*l'industrie de l'homme*] applied to the products of nature," his effort to satisfy "his needs," "that has given birth to the sciences and the arts" (Diderot 1751a, pp. 265 f.; 1751b). He then went on to describe the relation between "theory" and "practice" as a reciprocal one:

> every art has its speculation and its practice [*pratique*]: the speculation is nothing but the idle knowledge of the rules of the art, the practical aspect is the habitual and unreflective application of the same rules. It is difficult, if not impossible, to develop the practice without speculation, and, reciprocally, to have a solid grasp of the speculation without the practice. There are in every art—with respect to the material, the instruments, and the operation—a multitude of circumstances which can only be learned in practice [*usage*]. It is for practice to present difficulties and pose phenomena, while it is for speculation to explain the phenomena and dissolve the difficulties; from which follows that hardly any but an artisan who masters reasoning that can talk well about his art. (Diderot 1751a, p. 266; 1751b)

To illustrate his argument, Diderot discussed the relationship between academic geometry and the practical geometry as exercised in workshops:

> Everyone will readily agree that there are few artists who can dispense with the elements of mathematics. However, a paradox, the truth of which is not immediately obvious, is that, in many situations, these elements would actually harm them if the precepts were not corrected in practice [*pratique*] by knowledge of a multitude of physical circumstances: knowledge of location, position, irregular forms, materials and their properties, elasticity, rigidity, friction, texture, durability, as well as the effects of air, water, cold, heat, dryness, etc. (Diderot 1751a, p. 271; 1751b)

For instance, Diderot argued, no lever exists "for which one could calculate all conditions." Among these conditions are a large number that are very important in practice:

> From this follows that a man who knows only intellectual [academic] geometry is usually rather incompetent and that an artist who knows only experimental geometry is very limited as a worker. But, in my opinion, experience shows us that it is easier for an artist to dispense with intellectual geometry than for any man to dispense with some experimental geometry. In spite of the calculus, the entire issue of friction has remained a matter for experimental and handicraft mathematics. [...] How many awful machines are not proposed daily by men who have deluded themselves that levers, wheels, pulleys, and cables perform in a machine as they do on paper and who have never taken part in manual work, and thus who never have known the difference in effect of one and the same machine in reality and as a plan? (Diderot 1751a, p. 271; 1751b)

The conceptual shift manifested in this text by the editor of the *Encyclopédie* articulated the insights that had been gained since 1400 by the movement of artisans and scholars concerned with the role of representations of technical knowledge in work. That is, it was eminently practical concerns that motivated the development of the Modern concept of practice, and the Modern concept of "practice" thus comes with a heavy baggage accumulated from its being deeply involved in the technical concerns at the heart of the Modern Era.

Let us summarize.

First, Aristotle's dogmatic separation of *praxis* and *poiēsis* has been dissolved in the Modern concept of "practice." It already made little sense outside of the very special context of the oligarchic critique of Greek democracy, and would make even less sense in a socio-economic context, like that of the Modern Era, in which the development of science is based on systematic production of practical experience and in which the development of production is increasingly based on systematic application of science and technology. The Modern concept of "practice" is not predominantly or exclusively referring to civic activities; it is rather modeled on mundane work and has been predominantly applied in discourses about technical knowledge in work.

Second, the Aristotelian separation of the *contemplative* life of *theōria* and *praxis* has been dissolved in the Modern concept of "practice." This conceptual shift is predicated on the development of a specifically Modern notion of *theory* understood as a body of (systematic, even formal) knowledge that is grounded in experience and applied in contingent action and thus also, and not least, on the new issues arising from the application of representations of technical knowledge in work.

In other words, the Modern concept of "practice" was developed in and for discourses focusing on (a) the acute issues of developing systematic or formal representations of such knowledge (theories, technologies, methods) from contingent action in settings of production or experimentation; and (b) the equally acute issues of applying such systematic or formal representations of knowledge in contingent action. In short, the Modern concept of "practice" conceives of action as guided by a "theory" in some strong sense. The "theory" provides the principles according to which actors assess what to do and how to do it, and whether what is done is done correctly.

From around 1400, the term "practice" slipped from the Latin of the scholastics into the vernacular (first French), where it again was used in the sense of the "practical application" of a body of knowledge, typically that of a profession, especially medicine (*Online Etymology Dictionary*), but eventually also in the wider sense of "actuality," in contrast to the mere notional (*Duden Herkunfswörterbuch*). Thus, in ordinary language, the term "practice" is also used in discourses where one cannot talk about a "theory" in the strong sense that actors point to a set of propositions based on systematically organized experience. But the concept of "practice" is left hanging in the air if actors are not able to express and agree about or, at least, recognize and acknowledge the principles according to which activities are held to account. (This will be developed in Section 2.3 and, in particular, in Chapter 3).

We leave the story of the development of the Modern concept of "practice" here, where it has become part of ordinary language with all its connotations of the skillful application of representations of technical knowledge in the construction of levers, machinery, etc., under the conditions offered by the material setting, the tools and instruments, the materials, and so forth. But before we can turn to an analysis of the concepts of "practice" and "technique" in ordinary language, we have to consider—briefly—the various more or less alternative uses of the term "practice" that exist in some specialized domains of discourse, in parallel universes as it were.

2.2.5 "Practice" in Moral Philosophy

As observed in passing in Section 2.2.2, the scholastic tradition revived Aristotle's terminology (albeit, for a time, only on the basis of fragments) and adopted it for its moral-philosophical discourses. In their doing so, the term *praxis*, which in Aristotle was reserved for the domain of *civic* actions, was now used for human action in general in so far as it was susceptible to moral judgment. At the same time, *theōria* was now used (sometimes rendered *speculation*), not to characterize a domain of action, but rather to characterize the moral teachings the Church derived from the scriptures. It is likely that these conceptual inversions, to use Tosel's expression, were influenced by the conceptual shifts that had already begun with the Hellenistic technical scholars and were picked up again, via Arab commentators, by Medieval scholars such as Domingo Gundisalvo and Robert Kilwardby. Be that as it may, what is important here is to note that the scholastic notion of "theory" is categorially different from that of "theory" as used in the Modern concept pair of "theory" and "practice": the notion of "theory" as exemplified in the application of geometry (theorems, techniques) to land surveying is, of course, not of the same category as normative notions such as, say, "Love thy neighbor."

The scholastic uses of "theory" and "practice" are mentioned here because they later fed into "practical philosophy." This, first, applies to German idealist philosophy in so far as it addresses issues of ethics, natural law, jurisprudence, politics, economics, and so on. Christian Wolff is the prime example of this strand. Deeply impressed by reading Chinese philosophical classics such as Confucius (then only recently translated) and realizing that China, though certainly not part of Christendom, had a highly sophisticated system of law and ethics, Wolff undertook to develop what was termed a "universal practical philosophy," a philosophy of ethics independent of Christian theology (Wolff 1726). Central to this philosophy, the concept of "practice" was understood as not merely dealing with the grounds of voluntary or involuntary action but also how something is to be done and how possible impediments can be overcome (Wolff 1738, *Prolegomena* §§ 2–3). While this notion of "practice" of course remained within the bounds defined by the scholastic tradition of moral philosophy (practice as acts of volition susceptible to moral judgment), it went beyond it at one important point, namely, in that his ambition was to construct a universal philosophy of ethics on the model of scientific theory.

Later in the eighteenth century, Immanuel Kant turned against Wolff's and similar attempts to establish ethics on the foundations of a "theory" in the strong sense of a body of knowledge based on experience, as it would open a backdoor to moral relativism. But in doing so, Kant indirectly demonstrated the strong gravitational pull exerted by the Modern concept of "practice." In an article entitled "On the common saying: That may be correct in theory, but it is of no use in practice," written in defense of his own writings on "practical philosophy," Kant gave an admirably concise definition of the Modern concept of "practice" as it, by then, had been developed in the course of four centuries:

> A sum of rules, even of practical rules, is called *theory* if those rules are thought as principles having a certain generality, so that abstraction is made from a multitude of conditions that yet have a necessary influence on their application. Conversely, not every doing is called *practice*, but only that effecting of an end which is thought as the observance of certain principles of procedure represented in their generality. (Kant 1793a, p. 127; 1793b, p. 279)

Here the two concepts "theory" and "practice" are conceived of as mutually constitutive: "practice" is the application of a set of "rules" derived from practical experience. This notion of "practice" is the Modern one. It is in complete accordance with the one we have found in Lorini, Palissy, Bacon, and Diderot and d'Alembert. But from the vantage point of the late eighteenth century and two centuries of scientific and technical advances, Kant did not leave it at that (1793a, pp. 127 f.; 1793b, pp. 279 f.):

First, in applying a theory or following the rules in action, the practitioner needs the faculty of judgment, "no matter how complete a theory may be." For while yet another rule could be added, this could "go on to infinity." Hence, "to a concept of the understanding, which contains a rule, must be added an act of judgment by which a practitioner distinguishes whether or not something is a case of the rule."

Second, echoing Palissy and Diderot, Kant pointed out that this means that there can be "theoreticians who can never in their lives become practical, because they are lacking in judgment."

Third, however, a theory may be deficient in some way: "But even where this natural talent [i.e., judgement] is present there can still be a deficiency in premises, that is, a theory can be incomplete and can, perhaps, be supplemented only by engaging in further experiments and experiences [...] In such cases it was not the fault of theory if it was of little use in practice, but rather of there having been *not enough theory*." Thus, again echoing Diderot,

> if an empirical engineer tried to disparage general mechanics, or an artilleryman the mathematical doctrine of ballistics, by saying that whereas the theory of it is nicely thought out it is not valid in practice since, when it comes to application, experience yields quite different results than theory, one would merely laugh at him (for, if the theory of friction were added to the first and the theory of the resistance of air to the second, hence if only still more theory were added, these would accord very well with experience). (Kant 1793a, p. 128; 1793b, p. 280)

Fourth, in this situation, Kant argued, the competent practitioner would have been able to cope anyway, as he "should have learned from experience," and he then added, harking back to the "Preliminary discourse" by Diderot and d'Alembert, that *this* practical competence "is true theory even if he is not in a position to state it himself and, as a teacher, set it forth systematically in general propositions, and so can make no claim to the title of theoretical physician, agriculturalist and the like" (Kant 1793a, p. 128; 1793b, p. 280).

That is, true to form, Kant not only summarized the Modern concept of "practice" as articulated by Bacon, Diderot, and others but went further in articulating it, arguing, first, that "theory," however complete and detailed, is nothing but a representation, a "sum of rules," and, second, that "theory," although it may be extended and enriched infinitely, anyway requires faculties of judgment to be applied in "practice" under whatever circumstances that may prevail.

Kant, however, was not in critical business to give the Modern concept of "practice" a nicely compact and elegant form; his business in this matter was to argue that the Modern concept of "practice" was *inappropriate for the purposes* of "practical philosophy":

> But in a theory that is based on the *concept of duty*, concern about the empty ideality of this concept ["theory"] quite disappears. For it would not be a duty to aim at a certain effect of our will if this effect were not also possible in experience (whether it be thought as completed or as always approaching completion) [...] For, to the scandal of philosophy, it is not uncommonly alleged of this theory that what may be correct in it is yet invalid in practice [...] This maxim ["That may be correct in theory, but it is of no use in practice"], which has become very common in our times, so full of talk and empty of deeds, does the greatest harm when it has to do with something moral (duties

> of virtue or duties of right). For here it is a matter of the canon of reason (in the practical), where the worth of practice rests entirely on its conformity with the theory underlying it, and all is lost if the empirical and hence contingent conditions of carrying out the law are made conditions of the law itself, so that a practice calculated with reference to an outcome probable in accordance with *previous* experience is given authority to control a self-sufficient theory. (Kant 1793a, p. 129; 1793b, p. 280)

In short, so strong was the gravitational field emanating from the Modern concept of "practice" by the end of the eighteenth century that Kant obviously felt he had to define the concept formally, and clarify it in some detail, in order to be able to evict the very same concept from his endeavors in "practical philosophy." And nonetheless, as the quoted passage shows, he was obviously stuck with the Modern notion of "theory and practice" as reciprocally constituted, all the while concerned with "theory" in the sense of an infallible "knowledge" of universal moral imperatives. Thus, since Kant, and "practical philosophy" in general, could not escape the gravitational field of the Modern notion of "theory and practice," an inexhaustible fountain of confusion had sprung.

2.2.6 "Practice *In Abstracto*"

Finally, and for the sake of propriety, it should be mentioned that the concept of "practice" has played a prominent role in the philosophy of the social sciences and politics of the twentieth century. A major reason—if not *the* reason—for this is that Marx, in manuscripts written 1845–6 but only published posthumously, used the term "praxis" to articulate his initial thinking about the guiding principle of his studies of human society as historically evolving (1845a, 1845b), the crucial point being that this principle does not seek to "explain practice from the idea but explains the formation of ideas from material practice" (Marx and Engels 1845–6a, p. 29; 1845–6b, p. 54).

Marx's reasons for giving heuristic priority to "practice" or "sensuous activity" (1845a, 1845b) were derived from, on the one hand, the work of the political economists, in particular, Adam Smith and his analysis of human work as a source of wealth,[26] and, on the other, from the works of the young G. W. F. Hegel, who, building on Smith's conception of work, developed a conception of history in which *work* is key to the development of humanity (1802–3, 1803–4, 1805–6, 1807). As Hegel later formulated this conception, referring to the classic Greek notion of *technē* (Sophocles):

> In man's *practical* approach to Nature, the latter is, for him, something immediate and external; and he himself is an external and therefore sensuous individual, although in relation to natural objects, he correctly regards himself as *end* [...] The practical approach to Nature is, in general, determined by appetite, which is self-seeking; need impels us to use Nature for our own advantage, to wear her out, to wear her down, in short, to annihilate her. [...] The necessities and the wit of man have found an endless variety of ways of using and mastering Nature.

[26] Adam Smith, in turn, drew heavily on the studies of manufactures reported in the *Descriptions* and the *Encyplopédie* (Peaucelle 2006, 2007).

Citing Sophocles' celebration of *technē* (in *Antigone*), he continued:

> Whatever force Nature develops and lets loose against man—cold, wild beasts, water, fire—he knows means to counter them; indeed, he takes these means from Nature and uses them against herself. The cunning of his reason enables him to preserve and maintain himself in face of the forces of Nature, by sheltering behind other products of Nature, and letting these suffer her destructive attacks. (Hegel 1830a, § 245; 1830b, § 245)

That is, what was meant by "practice" in Marx's early methodological considerations was a far cry from what the anemic notions of "praxis" in "practical philosophy" ("praxis" as acting in accordance with transcendental moral imperatives) or by the Left Hegelians ("praxis" as theoretical critique"). In contrast to such notions of "*practice in abstracto,*" what Marx and Engels had in mind was rather "sensuous" or "material practice." Humanity's ascent does not result from the application of some *theory* or as the realization of some *idea* but is rather to be understood as the cumulative but indeterminate outcome of the *ordinarily successful* activities of millions of individuals in the production and reproduction of their socially organized lives, and their transferring these experiences, their mundane innovations, to others as well as to the next generations (Engels and Marx 1845a, pp. 41, 98; 1845b, pp. 40, 93).

Although this heuristic later has been taken as a license to indulge in schematic speculation, the intention was the exact opposite: the heuristic was part of a call for empirically grounded studies of the complex totality of human activities (*Leitfaden* or "guiding principles," Marx 1859a, p. 100; 1859b, p. 262; cf. also, more emphatically, 1877a; 1877b; cf. also Korsch 1938, Chapter 3:1).

It should be noted and kept in mind, however, that when Marx, in these early methodological considerations, used the term "practice," he was (following Hegel) conceiving of the active expression of human social life *in totality*: "the 'total activity"' (1845–6a, p. 39; 1845–6b, p. 54). The unit of analysis he aimed at was not the "sensuous activities" of an individual or of some particular social entity but "the ensemble of the social relations," as he put it in his "Thesis on Feuerback" (1845 #6), or "individuals producing in society," as he put it when he in 1857, turning to his economic studies in earnest, again discussed the methodological issues (1857a, p. 21; 1857b, p. 17). This is also clear from the sole passage in his mature economic studies in which he used the term "practice."[27] Toward the end of *Grundrisse* (1857–8), he observed that technology and technical artifacts "are immediate organs of social practice":

> [Technical creations such as] machines, locomotives, railways, electric telegraphs, self-acting mules, etc. [...] are products of human industry; natural material transformed into organs of man's will over Nature, or of man's activity in Nature. They are *organs of the human mind which are created by the human hand,* the objectified power of knowledge. [Their level of development] shows the degree to which society's general science, *knowledge,* has become an *immediate productive force,* and hence the degree to which the conditions of the social life process itself have been brought under the control of the

[27] Apart from the trivial use of "in practice" in the sense of "in reality," of course.

> general intellect and remoulded according to it. It shows the degree to which the social productive forces are produced not merely in the form of knowledge but as immediate organs of social praxis, of the actual life process. (Marx 1857–8a, pp. 582 f.; 1857–8b, Vol. 28, p. 92)

That is, while Marx's notion of "praxis," as developed in his writings from 1845–6, built upon and was closely related to the historical movement in which the Modern concept of "practice" developed, the notion of "practice" expressed in these early writings is nevertheless *categorially different* in that his unit of analysis was not a class of work activities as defined or constituted by a "theory," by certain representations of technical knowledge applied in the work, but the aggregate "total activity" of human society or even human kind. There is no "sum of rules," no *theory*, in relation to which "total activity" or "social praxis" can be held to account. Thus, used for conceptualizing human effort in its totality, the notion of "practice" is flawed. Its apparent sense plays, like Hegel's reference to "man's practical approach to Nature," on the ambiguity of the notion "man" (*Mensch*), that is, on oscillating unaccountably between "man" as a species and as this or that individual worker.

It should thus be noted that as Marx's thinking evolved, the term "practice" largely disappeared from his writings, probably because he by then had broken out of philosophy and was engaged in the scientific work his early methodological remarks had pleaded for. Instead of philosophizing about "practice," his research became conceptualized by means of the more specific concepts of "productive forces," "relations of production," "production," "consumption," "division of labor," "cooperative work," "work piece," "tool," "machinery," and so on.[28] That is, what Marx did contribute to our understanding of practice and technique in the modern age is to be found elsewhere, especially in his solidly empirical accounts of the transformation of work in the course of the Industrial Revolution, especially in the analysis of the transformation of work with the introduction of automatic machinery (1867a, 1867b).

Now, in the wake of the posthumous publication of Marx's 1845–6 manuscripts, the concept of "practice" was catapulted to a prominent role in the philosophy of the social sciences and politics of the twentieth century. The outcome of all that is a sorry spectacle, however.

What I have in mind are, primarily, the ruinous intellectual effects of totalitarian movements such as Fascism, Nazism, Stalinism, Maoism, etc.[29] Put on the agenda of the

[28] It is here of some interest to note that the well-known "practice theorist" Davide Nicolini believes that the concept of "practice" had been ignored for centuries until Marx revived it: "Marx's version of materialism granted access to the citadel of science to a fundamental aspect of human existence, *praxis*, that for centuries had been previously ignored" (Nicolini 2012, p. 30). This is probably a sign of massive ignorance but, if so, a most convenient one, as he and other authors of that ilk then feel free to stipulate a meaning of the term "practice" that fits their purposes. (For a critical discussion of "practice theory," see Chapter 3).

[29] I used the concept "totalitarianism," not as a lazy invective, but as it has been developed by scholars such as Karl Korsch (1939), Hanna Arendt (1951), and Claude Lefort (1956, 1980, 1997, 1999), understanding by "totalitarianism" anti-democratic movements striving to overcome the economic, social, ideological, political, etc., multiplicity and discord characteristics of "civil society" in the modern age, by establishing a form of society in which (a) the existence of divisions in "the people" ("the proletariat," "the nation") is denied and apparent

philosophy of social science and politics by none other than Marx, the concept of "practice" was invariably caught up in this bloody maelstrom—most prominently, of course, in the form of Leninist "party theory." I am thinking of, for example and not least, Joseph Stalin's evacuating the notion of "theory and practice" of all content:

> Theory is the experience of the working-class movement in all countries taken in its general aspect. Of course, theory becomes aimless if it is not connected with revolutionary practice, just as practice gropes in the dark if its path is not illumined by revolutionary theory. But theory can become a tremendous force in the working-class movement if it is built up in indissoluble connection with revolutionary practice. [...] The 'theory' of spontaneity is a theory of opportunism, a theory of worshipping the spontaneity of the labour movement, a theory which actually repudiates the leading role of the vanguard of the working class, of the party of the working class. (Stalin 1924, pp. 28, 30)

Here, any trace of the contingency of practical action has vanished. Practice is reduced to "mere extension" of "theory"; the rest is "spontaneity." (For similar excretions, see Mao 1937). Since this kind of talk has been chewed over endlessly in most of the twentieth century, efforts to restore "philosophy of practice" are inescapably contaminated.

But I am here, also, thinking of the—bold, often grandiose, but ultimately futile—efforts by thinkers of the heterodox Marxist lineage (e.g., Labriola 1898; Sorel 1902, 1908; Lukács 1923; Gramsci 1929–35; Marcuse 1941; Merleau-Ponty 1946, 1947; Lukács 1948; Merleau-Ponty 1955; Sartre 1960, 1962; Lefebvre 1966) to construct, against the petrified doctrines of institutionalized Marxism, a "philosophy of practice" out of the methodological remarks Marx had made in 1844–6 in order to break out of philosophical theorizing altogether and engage in strictly scientific work. But in doing so, they and others of that lineage invariably relapsed into philosophical theorizing and, with that, the flawed notion of "practice" as "total activity" while *at the same time* presuming the Modern concept of "practice" as a specific type of action constituted and bounded by some "theory."[30]

But even that is not all. Recoiling in horror from the totalitarian repression and violence that dominated most of the twentieth century, scholars of various persuasions have been striving to construct an intellectual space—a mental *refugium*, as it were—in which modern technology, the alleged source of these violent excesses (and of our sundry miseries in general), has no place and where true humanity can somehow blossom. For

discords consequently attributed to conspiratorial efforts by alien forces that thus are to be liquidated; (b) the ubiquitous presence of party organs in all in all units of social life aims to dissolve the distinction between state and civil society and its myriad loci of power; and (c) "the party," the mythical embodiment of the mission of "the people," is vested with absolute and infallible knowledge of history and society. That is, in short, by virtue of its blanket denial of the fallibility of "theory" and the contingency of "practice," the very notion of *theorizing proved wrong in practice*, totalitarianism is a permutation of counter-enlightenment. — For accounts of the realities of totalitarianism, based on sources that have only recently become available for scholarly study, cf. the work by Stephen Kotkin (1995), Anne Applebaum (2003), and Timothy Snyder (2010).

[30] For less prominent examples of the sorry outcome of the efforts to construct a "philosophy of praxis" in the Marxist tradition, see, for example, the Yugoslavian *Praxis* journal (e.g., Bošnjak 1965; Grlić 1965; Vranički 1965) or the various Western contributions (e.g., Bernstein 1971; Arnason 1988; Kitching 1988).

this purpose, various attempts are made to *separate* "interaction" from "instrumental action" (Habermas 1968a, 1968b, 1988) and even to raise Aristotle's decrepit notional separation of *praxis* and *poiēsis* from the grave (Gadamer 1972, 1974).[31]

Be that as it may! Predicated on the observation that technology is an essentially human endeavor, the aim of practice-oriented computing is of an order completely different order from that of such philosophical discourses.

2.3 Conceptual Cartography

> To establish a practice, rules are not enough; one also needs examples. Our rules leave back doors open, and the practice must speak for itself
>
> Wittgenstein (1949–51, §139)

The point of the Modern concept of "practice" is to focus on the ways in which the competent actor in his or her action is taking the particular conditions into account while committed to and guided by the appropriate general principles ("theory," "rules"). The theory of, say, making bread, as expressed in cookbooks and handed-down recipes, summarizes the experience of generations in the form of general rules and principles. But in formulating rules and principles, one abstracts from a plethora of more or less accidental conditions and circumstances such as, for instance, the quality and age of the flour, the humidity and temperature of the air, and so on, which are nevertheless to be taken into account by the baker in action. On the other hand, not everything the baker does can be ascribed to the practices of baking bread. That he perhaps routinely drinks a cold beer while the dough is rising and another when the rolls are in the oven is not considered an element of this practice, however important it may be for his quality of life. The two concepts—"theory" and "practice"—are mutually constitutive.

The noun "practice" thus ordinarily means *normatively governed contingent activity*.

This much should be clear by now. When we ordinarily talk about "practices," we do that in types of discourse—"language games"—in which an activity is conceived of as an application of some general principles under conditions of contingency and in which the relationship between these general principles and the actually unfolding action is of central concern.

[31] What these fine scholars do not realize is that they, by reducing the concept of work to an ahistorical notion of "instrumental action" and thus conflating "technology" and historically specific social organization of work (e.g., slavery, capitalist production, etc.), fall into the Counter-Enlightenment trap exemplified by Heidegger when he appointed the fundamental stance of the Modern Era, the technological "machination" with its "calculation" and "planning," as the cause of the terror he himself had been an active party to. Note, for example, the characterization of the "essence of technology" he gave in a lecture in Bremen on 1 December 1949: "Agriculture is now a motorized food industry, in essence the same as the fabrication of corpses in gas chambers and extermination camps, the same as the blockade and starving of countries, the same as the fabrication of hydrogen bombs" (Heidegger 1949, p. 27).

2.3.1 "Practice"

However well established, the concept of "practice" can be tricky. Let us therefore explore this part of our conceptual scheme more systematically.

Let us start by observing that a given sequence of actions can be described in endless ways (Anscombe 1957, § 6 et passim). Saying that Peter is seated in a chair with his gaze directed at an open book in his hands is not the same as saying that he is *reading*. Nor is saying that Paul is moving horizontally in an upright position while alternately moving his left and right legs forward the same as saying that he is *taking a walk*. Saying that Mary routinely looks in people's mouths and asks them to cough and makes a series of similar recurring operations is not the same as saying that she is *practicing medicine*. To characterize a series of recurrent actions as instances of a certain practice is a quite specific characterization.

To take an example from Gilbert Ryle, a person's holding a pen in his right hand while moving it across a white surface, thereby leaving a curly blue line, can be described in endless ways: we may say that he is writing his name, testing a new fountain pen, practicing his signature, doodling, signing a letter of resignation, or signing a peace treaty.

> A statesman signing his surname to a peace-treaty is doing much more than inscribe the seven letters of his surname, but he is not doing many or any more things. He is bringing a war to a close by inscribing the seven letters of his surname. (Ryle 1968, p. 496)

When described as *a practice*, the given sequence of activity—moving a pen across a white surface while making a curly blue line—is described as *an instance of a particular class of action*, in this case, the institutionalized practice of signing treaties as specified in diplomatic protocol. When we describe a given action or sequence of actions as *a practice*, we thereby say that it is an instance of a class of activity defined by a set of norms. The statesman's writing his signature belongs to the class of action we call signing treaties. His writing his signature on another treaty document with another pen at some other occasion would be yet another instance of the same practice, as long as he is actually mandated to put his signature to the document and in general does so in accordance with diplomatic protocol. And other statesmen's writing their very different signatures with different pens on different treaty documents are as many instances of the practice of signing treaties. The criterion of an action's belonging to this particular practice is its being taken to be in accordance with the norms (conventions, procedures, rules) to which actors are committed in performing the action and in terms of which their action is deemed right, correct, timely, appropriate, legitimate, acceptable, and so on.

When categorizing a sequence of actions as instances of a practice, we are conceiving of these occurrences as constituted by the rules and principles to which actors are committed and by virtue of which they are accountable for their doings. The rules and principles to which actors are committed in their contingent activities provide the criterion of sameness that enables them (and observers) to determine not only what is deemed correct conduct but also what is being deemed activities of the same kind. One practice differs from another in so far as the rules and principles differ.

That practices are normatively constituted tends to elude "practice theorists." The snag is our distinction between "mere regularity" and "rule-following" (Wittgenstein 1937–44, VI, VII §§ 24 ff.; 1945–6, §§ 143–242)[32] or between "natural regularity" and "normative regularity" (Williams 2010). When we observe stable patterns or correlations (according to some criterion), what we find is *mere regularity*. But when we observe that actors from time to time make excuses for particular actions ("Sorry, my mistake!"), justify their actions ("Well, I had to do it this way because that part there was defective"), sanction the actions of colleagues ("You were supposed to deliver this part at my workstation by lunch," or "Great, thanks!"), instruct novices ("Be careful with this!"), or ask for guidance ("Where do I put this draft when I'm done?"), then we are observing something *other* than natural regularity in behavior; we are finding instances of *normative regularity*.

In our conceptual scheme, "practice" belongs to the web of *activity* concepts. A practice is something we *perform* or engage in; it has a temporal structure. However, "practice" should not simply be conflated with the concept of "activity." An activity has "genuine duration": it has a starting point and an end-point in time (Wittgenstein 1945–8, §§ 71–83). Our baker may begin preparing breakfast rolls on Friday morning at 03:00, place the hot rolls on the shelves in the shop at 05:00, and then go to bed. At this point, this particular sequence of activity ends, but not his practice of baking bread. A lawyer does not cease to practice the law when she is fast asleep. When we refer to a specific practice, we are referring to a specific *type* of activity, namely, activities as related by virtue of actors being committed to certain rules and principles.

When engaged in a practice (as a type of activity, as opposed to being part of a culture or a tradition or manifesting a custom), actors are confronted with the inexorability of action, in as much as avoidance or postponement of action may also have effects, which are perhaps unwanted. The practitioner does not have the privilege of an observer. In the course of action, the practitioner has to take for granted that things that look normal are, in fact, normal. Alfred Schütz (1953) dubbed this stance "the natural attitude." The practitioner is faced with "imposed relevances" that he or she has to cope with (Schütz 1947–51; Bittner 1973). Faced with the "urgencies" of his or her work, the practitioner has to "economize" any ambition that the effort be consistent, complete, etc. (Bourdieu 1980).

The concept of "practice" is located in a rather troubled part of the "geography of our conceptual scheme." It is, for instance, adjacent to the concept of "culture," but its grammar is distinctly different. "Culture" is not an activity category. One *performs* a practice, but one does not *perform* a culture or a tradition; one belongs to it, and one's behavior may exhibit traits typical of that culture or tradition ("customs"). In addition, the term "culture" is used in bewildering ways, encompassing prevalent or even normatively governed patterns of everyday conduct (e.g., dietary preferences, table manners) as well as various "ideological" phenomena (e.g., notions of virtue and duty, of what amounts to a "good life"), and even mythologies and cosmologies. By assimilating "practice" with

[32] See also Chapter 3.

"culture" or "tradition," the point of the Modern concept of "practice" is elided, namely, the point that not just any pattern of behavior is considered a practice but only one that is governed by a "theory" that has been abstracted from experience as a body of rules and principles and that the practice thus has a rationale. By assimilating "practice" with "culture" or "tradition," the essential relation of "practice" to "theory" is severed.

2.3.2 "Technique"

The relationship between the concept of "practice" and that of "technique" is a particularly tricky one. On one hand, the concept of "practice" is inextricably tied up with the concept of "technique" in as much as the mastery of a practice, *in practice*, presumes the mastery of a repertoire of *techniques*, that is, methods and procedures, routines and recipes, tools and their bodily counterparts, as well as also professional perception (Hanson 1958), that is, the (visual, auditory, tactile) ability to distinguish objects, states, and events that are known from experience to be of relevance for their effort.[33] But on the other hand, the concepts of "practice" and "technique" do not march in lockstep. First, there is (normally) no one-to-one mapping between a given practice and a particular technique. In fact, it is typically a criterion of mastery of a practice that the practitioner is able to select the appropriate technique in a given situation, in view of present constraints and exigencies. Second, techniques are *means*, they are *applied*; practices are types of *activity*, they are *performed*. We do not say that one *performs* a technique, we say that one *uses* or *applies* it; just as we do not say that one *uses* or *applies* a practice. That is, techniques are in a sense neutral with respect to the purposes for which they are applied: they are means to an end, and one technique may substitute for another, just like a specific technique may be applied in multiple practices. Techniques are, for example, routinely adopted for purposes different from the ones for which they were originally devised. In contrast, practices, as normatively governed, are defined in terms of the general principles to which actors are committed and from which the criteria of correctness are derived.

Now, there are techniques that are, so to speak, idiosyncratic of a particular individual. He or she may have a particular way of holding the pen when writing or of wielding a knife when cutting a leg of lamb. This is trivial. Similarly, a painter may have perfected a quite sophisticated technique for applying the oil paint with a brush, or a sculptor may have discovered and refined an inimitable way of "reading" the stone when using the chisel. And so on. Whether trivial or sophisticated, such techniques are expressions of the individual in question, as unalienable as is his or her voice. They are, if I may, beyond right and wrong. No issues of normative governance need arise here: this is just the way these individuals comport themselves.

Next, consider those techniques that are acquired through teaching and training. Here, further complications arise. First, learning to use a technique requires more than reading a set of instructions; it requires *training*, and it does so for the simple reason that it involves what could be called reconfiguring the body. Take, for example, what is required of a child to learn to write with a pencil or eat with knife and fork. Or take what is required of an

[33] Alfred Schütz suggested the term "typifications" for such distinctions (cf., e.g., Schütz 1953, 1957).

adult who has been trained in using pencils for writing, and knife and fork for eating, to learn to use a calligraphy brush for writing, and chopsticks for eating. It requires the building of a specific array of muscles, bones, tendons, ligament, and synapses. Whether an idiosyncratic technique or one in which the individual has been trained by parents or teachers, techniques are of the body.[34] For the very same reason, and as pointed out by Diderot and d'Alembert, while the trained actor should be able to demonstrate the technique for which his or her body has been configured, the same actor may not be able to articulate the technique in physiological terms, nor may he or she be able to articulate its rationale. Articulating the physiology or the rationale of a technique requires work, specialized work. Second, as pointed out by the French anthropologist Marcel Mauss in his 1934 lecture on "techniques of the body," because of the time and effort required for the configuration of the body, a technique of the body, when perfected, exhibits a certain inertia. Take for example "the technique of digging":

> The English troops I was with [in World War I] did not know how to use French spades, which forced us to change 8,000 spades a division when we relieved a French division, and vice versa. This plainly shows that a manual knack can only be learnt slowly. Every technique properly so-called has its own form. (Mauss 1936a; 1936b, p. 71).

More than that: being taught to use a technique is being taught to use a set of rules and principles. Mauss again:

> Previously we were taught to dive after having learnt to swim. And when we were learning to dive, we were taught to close our eyes and then to open them under water. Today the technique is the other way round. The whole training begins by getting the children used to keeping their eyes open under water. Thus, even before they can swim, particular care is taken to get the children to control their dangerous but instinctive ocular reflexes, before all else they are familiarised with the water, their fears are suppressed, a certain confidence is created, suspensions and movements are selected. Hence there is a technique of diving and a technique of education in diving which have been discovered in my day. (Mauss 1934a; 1934b, p. 71)

That is, there may also be a "theory" of a technique, that is, a set of general principles for how to use the body—perhaps extended with tools—effectively in an activity to which the actor is committed: there are criteria of correctness. Here the concept of "practice" and that of "technique" join up. When a technique of the body is not only a more or less perfected individual expression but is acquired through teaching (instruction and correction, coaching and training), the employment of the technique is governed by a set of general principles that provide criteria of correct or incorrect performance. Or rather, in so far as there exists a "theory" of the technique in question (a set of principles manifested in teaching and training), the technique might just as well be described as a practice (of swimming, say), or rather, as an integral part of the practice. Let us develop this a little further.

[34] But then, what else could they be?

As pointed out by Kant, "theory" is itself a rather manifold phenomenon. There is, crudely put, on the one hand, official or codified "theory" in the form of, say, the rules of arithmetic and geometry, norms of certified accounting, the codified ethos of medical or legal work, standard organizational procedures, etc.; but on the other hand, practitioners also master a repertoire of not-yet canonized routines and distinctions that are passed on through training, exercise, imitation, etc., typically in a primarily oral culture. That is, an adequate description of a given practice will provide not only a reconstruction of the repertoire of official ("academic") rules and principles but also the not-yet canonized routines and distinctions. But when the previously not-yet-canonized routines and distinctions *have been* described and their rationales accounted for, the analysis—potentially—enhances the validity, strength, and scope of the "theory" to which practitioners are now committed. Accordingly, an analysis of a practice may stand in a recursive relationship to that same practice. This should not come as a surprise by now, for as shown in Section 2.2.3, the Modern concept of "practice" was developed for exactly that purpose: as the conceptual underpinning of our intervening in our practices in order to rationalize them: "*éclairer la pratique*"—"explain/enlighten practice" (Académie Royale des Sciences 1761, pp. xvi f.).

That is, practices can be and are transformed through analysis and rationalization of techniques, in so far as the set of general principles defining the practice is amended (adjusted, extended, enriched). Practices evolve and are transformed as practitioners develop their "technical knowledge," that is, as "unofficial" methods, routines, etc. are explicated, clarified, rationalized, specified, enriched, and refined so as to take into account a wider repertoire of variations, routine troubles, etc. and thus become normative of the practice.

But there is more to it. The *form* of "technical knowledge" (Gille 1978b) changes not only when the methods, routines, etc., of a practice are analyzed and rationalized and the general principles to which actors are committed thereby are validated and enriched, but also and most importantly when scientific knowledge or science-based techniques (or "technology") are somehow incorporated in the techniques of a given practice. Archimedes' analysis of the "law of the lever" was perhaps the first instance of a scientific theory that became incorporated into ordinary practices. Mechanics of the early Modern Era applied it routinely to the problems they were faced with, and its correct application was defining the practice of mechanics. The other outstanding historical example is, of course, ballistics. In contrast, heat engines were for centuries built by skilled mechanics—until the theory of thermodynamics was developed to account for the transformation of forms of energy. Thus, a contemporary engineer building a turbojet engine will be applying the theory of thermodynamics, even if he or she may not be able to demonstrate the theory. In doing so, he or she may be using a Computer-Aided Engineering software package, by means of which thermodynamic and structural calculi are applied interactively.

This opens yet another complication for understanding and describing the ways in which new techniques and technologies may transform practices. For this opens a range of variations in the ways technical knowledge is acquired by practitioners and also in the ways it is present and employed in the course of performing the practice. Following Bertrand Gille (1978b), some (crude) distinctions may illustrate the point:

- techniques of the body that are idiosyncratic individual expressions, acquired and refined in a process of empirical trial and error
- techniques of the body that have been acquired through teaching and training and for which there are criteria of correctness (swimming, using a specific type of spade, eating with chopsticks, parallel parking)
- representations of technical knowledge, such as recipes or procedures, typically devised in a division of labor by technical specialists, acquired by workers through instruction and training, and present *in* work, if need be, as inscribed representation for direction or consultation in the course of the work activity; similarly, visual representations of the outcome of the work (drawings, part explosions, models), and graphical representations of the work process (checklists, assembly instructions, work schedules, task flows)
- science-based techniques in the form of metrics, formulas, calculi, etc., derived from science; connected to such techniques are also abacuses, tables, slide rulers, measurement and navigation instruments, charts, etc., devised by others, and applied by practitioners, routinely but competently, but perhaps without knowing or understanding the underlying science
- and finally, science-based techniques in the form of automatic machinery (timepieces, calculators, computational artifacts) that practitioners use routinely in order to apply—automatically—the schemes, formulas, calculi, etc., represented by the machinery in question

That is, division of labor introduces yet another complication. A work for which the general principles are expressed by some workers for other workers to comply with is, in important ways, a different practice compared to a work with the same outcome performed by an individual, simply because the governing general principles and representations of technical knowledge are differently distributed. Conversely, a practice in which the general principles of the involved techniques are, strictly speaking, techniques of the body would be considered different from one in which workers (also) rely on knowledge of technical principles expressed in written recipes, workflow representations, calculations, etc. In any event, whatever the achieved level of theoretical sophistication and rationalization, a practice is always, at bottom, realized through techniques of the body: wielding a hammer, holding a pen, using a keyboard.

2.4 Conclusion

The methodological upshot of all this is that we, when looking at an activity as an instance of a practice, identify it as constituted by a certain body of rules and principles, but at the very same time we look at the ways in which these rules, principles, associated skills and techniques (methods, tools), etc., are applied with respect to varying circumstances.

The point of the Modern concept of "practice" is to be able to focus on the unity of work. On the one hand, without accounting for the circumstances and the ways in which they are handled, our descriptions would amount to nothing but yet another representation of the "theory." On the other hand, when conceived of as a practice, work is not reduced to mere behavior or to mere execution of some already given task, but is taken to encompass:

- the inexorable ongoing handling of variations and contingencies
- anticipatory measures, such as devising methods, planning for probable contingencies, identifying tasks to be performed, preparing operations, and allocating or assuming responsibility
- activities of coordinating, aligning, evaluating, instructing, learning, training, etc.

When investigating a practice, we are thus focusing on how the practitioners determine the nature of the situation, how they select effective and efficient techniques (materials, implements, bodily postures, methods, etc.), determine deviations from what has been assumed in the rule formulations, deal with routine troubles, recover from breakdowns, etc., as well as the ways in which these capabilities (skills, techniques, etc.) are developed, transmitted, acquired, etc.

A description of a practice will be incomplete if it does not account for the circumstances and their variation, for typical sources of variation, and for typical patterns of variation (i.e., those occurrences on which the "theory" is silent, such as variations and defects in properties of materials, equipment, and tools; variations in environmental parameters such as temperature, humidity, etc.), just as it will be incomplete if it does not account for practitioners' strategies for handling these variations.

As a concept of normatively governed contingent activity, the concept of "practice" is used to focus on, and highlight, the (potentially troublesome) application of the abstract general principles ("theory") while acting under the varying and perhaps unforeseen conditions that inexorably characterize the contingent materiality of work. There is the theory of heart surgery and there is the practice; one learns to master the practice by practicing: by learning to use the available repertoire of techniques under varying conditions.

In sum, the concept of "practice," as developed over centuries in reflections on mundane work, does not lead to the mystifications inherent in notions like "shared goal" or "tacit knowledge" or to the infinite regress of rule-skepticism as exemplified by, say, "situated action." Work practices are rigorously observable. We can observe and determine the normative make-up of a practice ("rules" and "principles") when we, for example, observe that workers consult or discuss drawings or project plans, or give and receive instructions on how to undertake a certain line of activity, or justify their actions, with their justifications being accepted (or rejected), or correct themselves and accept corrections and sanctions with respect to their conduct, etc. It is a researchable program; it works not only in theory but also in practice.

References

Académie Royale des Sciences (1702). *Histoire de l'Académie royale des sciences, M.DC.XCIX [1699], avec les mémoires de mathématique & de physique, tirez des registres de cette Académie.* Vol. 1. Paris: Boudot.—Paris: Gabriel Martin etc., 1732.

Académie Royale des Sciences (1729–34). *Histoire de l'Académie royale des sciences depuis son etablissement en 1666 jusqu'en 1699.* Vol. 1–13. Paris: Compagnie des libraires.—Paris: Gabriel Martin, etc., 1732.

Académie Royale des Sciences (1761). Avertisement de l'Academie des Sciences de Paris. In Académie Royale des Sciences: *Descriptions des arts et métiers, faites ou approuvées par Messieurs de l'Académie royale des sciences de Paris.* Neuchatel: Société typographique, 1771, Vol. 1, pp. xvi–xix. (2nd ed.).

Agricola, Georgius [G. Bauer] (1556). *De Re Metallica.* Transl. from *De Re Metallica* (Froben: Basel). Transl. H. C. Hoover and L. H. Hoover. London: The Mining Magazine, 1912.—Dover Publications, New York, 1950.

Alberti, Leone Battista (*c.*1450). *On the Art of Building in Ten Books.* (Manuscript, Rome). Transl. from *De Re Aedificatoria.* Transl. J. Rykwert; N. Leach; and R. Tavernor. Cambridge, MA, and London: The MIT Press, 1988.

Anonymous (1420). *Das Feuerwerkbuch.* (Manuscript). München: Deutschen Technik, 1941. (Neudruck des Erstdruckes aus dem Jahre 1529).—["Hassenstein was a dedicated *Oberregierungsrat* in the NS regime, and his work should be used with extreme caution." (Hall, 1979, n. 12)].

Anscombe, Gertrude Elizabeth Margaret (1957). *Intention.* Cambridge: Basil Blackwell Publishers. (Second ed., 1963).—Cambridge, MA, and London: Harvard University Press, 2000 (Paperback ed.).

Applebaum, Anne (2003). *Gulag: A History of the Soviet Camps.* New York: Random House.—London: Penguin Books, 2004.

Archimedes (*c.*240 BCE). *Quadrature of the Parabola.* Transl. T. L. Heath. *The Works Of Archimedes.* Cambridge: Cambridge University Press, 1897, pp. 233–52.

Arendt, Hannah (1951). *The Origins of Totalitarianism.* San Diego, CA, etc.: Harcourt Brace & Co. (new ed., 1979).

Arendt, Hannah (1958). *The Human Condition.* Chicago, IL, and London: University of Chicago Press. (2nd ed., 1998).

Aristotélēs [Aristotle] (1984). *The Complete Works of Aristotle.* J. Barnes (ed.). Princeton, NJ: Princeton University Press, 1984. Vol. 1–2.

Aristotélēs [Aristoteles] (1994). *Metaphysik.* Hamburg: Rowolth. Transl. U. Wolf. Ed. U. Wolf.

Aristotélēs [Aristoteles] (2006). *Nikomachische Ethik.* Hamburg: Rowolth. Transl. U. Wolf. Ed. U. Wolf.

Arnason, Johann P. (1988). *Praxis und Interpretation: Sozialphilosophische Studien.* Frankfurt am Main: Suhrkamp.

Austin, John Longshaw (1956–57). A plea for excuses. (*Proceedings of the Aristotelian Society*, 29 October 1956). Text ed. by J. O. Urmson and G. J. Warnock. In J. L. Austin: *Philosophical Papers.* Oxford: Oxford University Press, 1979, pp. 175–204. (3rd ed.; 1st ed., 1961).

Bacon, Francis (1620). *The New Organon: Or True Directions Concerning the Interpretation of Nature.* Transl. from *Novum Organum, Sive Vera de Interpretatione Naturae.* Transl. J. Spedding; R. L. Ellis; and D. D. Heath. In F. Bacon: *The Works.* Boston: Taggard and Thompson, 1863.

Bannon, Liam J.; and Kjeld Schmidt (1989). CSCW: Four characters in search of a context. In P. Wilson; J. M. Bowers; and S. D. Benford (eds): *ECSCW'89: Proceedings of the 1st European*

Conference on Computer Supported Cooperative Work, 13–15 September 1989, Gatwick, London. London: Computer Sciences Company, pp. 358–72. <http://dl.eusset.eu/dspace/handle/20.500.12015/1870>

Bannon, Liam J.; and Kjeld Schmidt (eds) (2013). CSCW: The first quarter century. [Special theme of] *Computer Supported Cooperative Work (CSCW)*, Vol. 22, no. 4–6, August–December 2013, pp. 345–715.

Beckert, Manfred (1983). *Johann Beckmann*. Leipzig: B. G. Teubner.

Beckmann, Johann (1772). *Politisch-Oekonomische Bibliothek worinn von den neusten Büchern, welche die Naturgeschichte, Naturlehre und die Land- und Stadtwithschaft betreffen, zuverlässige und vollständige Nachrichten ertheilt werden.* Göttingen: Vandenhoeck und Ruprecht.

Beckmann, Johann (1777). *Anleitung zur Technologie, oder zur Kenntniß der Handwerke, Fabriken und Manufacturen, vornehmlich derer, welche mit der Landwirthschaft, Polizey und Cameralwissenschaft in nächster Verbindung stehn; nebst Beyträgen zur Kunstgeschichte.* Göttingen: Vandenhoeck und Ruprecht. (5th ed., 1802).

Belfanti, Carlo (2004). Guilds, patents, and the circulation of technical knowledge: Northern Italy during the early modern age. *Technology and Culture*. Vol. 45, no. 3, July 2004, pp. 569–89.

Bernstein, Richard J. (1971). *Praxis and Action: Contemporary Philosophies of Human Activity.* Philadelphia, PA: University of Pennsylvania Press.

Bien, Günther (1968). Das Theorie-Praxis-Problem und die politische Philosophie bei Platon und Aristoteles. *Philosophisches Jahrbuch*. Vol. 76, no. 1, 1968, pp. 264–314.

Bien, Günther (1989). Praxis, praktisch: I. Antike. In J. Ritter and K. Gründer (eds): *Historisches Wörterbuch der Philosophie*, Vol. 7. Basel: Schwabe Verlag, pp. 1277–86.

Bittner, Egon (1973). Objectivity and realism in sociology. In G. Psathas (ed.): *Phenomenological Sociology: Issues and Applications.* New York, NY, etc.: John Wiley & Sons, pp. 109–25.

Bošnjak, Branko (1965). Betrachtungen über die Praxis. *Praxis*. Vol. 1, no. 1, 1st quarter 1965, pp. 9–25. <http://www.marxists.org/subject/praxis/issue-01/grlic.htm>

Bourdieu, Pierre (1980). *Le sens pratique*. Paris: Les Éditions de Minuit.

Burford, Alison (1972). *Craftsmen in Greek and Roman Society.* London: Thames & Hudson.

Cennini, Cennino d'Andrea (*c.*1390). *The Craftman's Handbook.* (Manuscript, Padua). Transl. from *Il Libro dell'Arte.* Transl. D. V. Thompson, Jr, New Haven, CT, and London: Yale University Press, 1933.—New York: Dover, 1960.

Cole, Arthur H.; and George B. Watts (1952). *The Handicrafts of France as Recorded in the Descriptions des Arts et Métiers, 1761–1788.* Boston, MA: Baker Library, Harvard Graduate School of Business Administration.

Crossgrove, William (1994). *Die deutsche Sachliteratur.* Bern, etc.: Peter Lang.

Cuomo, Serafina (2005). *Ancient Mathematics.* London and New York, NY: Routledge.

Cuomo, Serafina (2007). *Technology and Culture in Greek and Roman Antiquity.* Cambridge: Cambridge University Press.

Cuomo, Serafina (2008). Ancient written sources for engineering and technology. In J. P. Oleson (ed.): *The Oxford Handbook of Engineering and Technology in the Classical World.* Oxford, etc.: Oxford University Press, pp. 15–34.

Davis, Martin (2000). *The Universal Computer: The Road from Leibniz to Turing.* New York, NY: W, W. Norton & Co.

Demaitre, Luke (1975). Theory and practice in medical education at the University of Montpellier in the thirteenth and fourteenth centuries. *Journal of the History of Medicine and Allied Sciences.* Vol. 30, no. 2, 1975, pp. 103–23.

Diderot, Denis (1751a). Art. (*Encyclopédie, ou dictionnaire raisonné des sciences, des arts et des métiers,* Paris). In D. Diderot: *Œeuvres.* Paris: Robert Laffont, 1994, Vol. 1 (*Philosophie*), pp. 265–76.

Diderot, Denis (1751b). Art. (*Encyclopédie, ou dictionnaire raisonné des sciences, des arts et des métiers*, Paris, 1751). Transl. N. S. Hoyt and T. Cassirer. In N. S. Hoyt and T. Cassirer: *The Encyclopedia: Selections: Diderot, d'Alembert and a Society of Men of Letters*. Indianapolis: Bobbs-Merrill, 1965. <http://hdl.handle.net/2027/spo.did2222.0000.139>

Diderot, Denis; and Jean Le Rond d'Alembert (1751a). Discourse préliminaires des editeurs. In D. Diderot and J. L. R. d'Alembert (eds): *Encyclopédie, ou dictionnaire raisonné des sciences, des arts et des métiers*, Vol. 1. Paris: Briasson, David, Le Breton & Durand, pp. i–xlv.

Diderot, Denis; and Jean Le Rond d'Alembert (1751b). Preliminary discourse. (Diderot and d'Alembert (eds): *Encyclopédie, ou dictionnaire raisonné des sciences, des arts et des métiers*. Paris: Briasson, David, Le Breton & Durand). Transl. from "Discourse préliminaire." Transl. R. N. Schwab and W. E. Rex. In D. Diderot and J. L. R. d'Alembert: *The Encyclopedia of Diderot & d'Alembert Collaborative Translation Project*. Ann Arbor, MI: Michigan Publishing, University of Michigan Library, 2009. <http://hdl.handle.net/2027/spo.did2222.0001.083>

Diderot, Denis; and Jean Le Rond d'Alembert (eds) (1751–66). *Encyclopédie, ou dictionnaire raisonné des sciences, des arts et des métiers*. Paris: Briasson, David, Le Breton & Durand. Ed. R. Morrissey.—Chicago, IL: ARTFL Encyclopédie Projet, University of Chicago, 2008. <http://encyclopedie.uchicago.edu>

Dionysius Thrax (*c*.100 BCE). *Scholia eis ten Dionysioy Grammatiken*. In I. Bekker (ed.): *Anecdota graeca*. Berlin: G. Reimer, 1816, Vol. 2, pp. 646–971.

Dreyfus, Hubert L. (1991). *Being-in-the World: A Commentary on Heidegger's Being and Time, Division I*. Cambridge, MA: The MIT Press.

Dürer, Albrecht (1527). *Etliche underricht, zu befestigung der Stett, Schloß und Flecken*. Nürnberg: Hieronymus Andreae.

Dyson, George (2012). *Turing's Cathedral: The Origins of the Digital Universe*. London: Allen Lane.

Ehmer, Josef; and Catharina Lis (eds) (2009). *The Idea of Work in Europe from Antiquity to Modern Times*. Farnham, England, and Burlington, VT: Ashgate.

Engels, Friedrich; and Karl Marx (1845a). *Die heilige Familie, oder kritik der kritischen Kritik: Gegen Bruno Bauer & Consorten*. (Literarische Anstalt: Frankfurt am Main). In K. Marx and F. Engels: *Werke*. Berlin: Dietz Verlag, 1962, Vol. 2, pp. 3–224.

Engels, Friedrich; and Karl Marx (1845b). *The Holy Family, or Critique of Critical Criticism: Against Bruno Bauer and Company*. (Literarische Anstalt: Frankfurt am Main). Transl. R. Dixon and C. Dutt. In K. Marx and F. Engels: *Collected Works*. London: Lawrence & Wishart, 2010, Vol. 4, pp. 5–211.

Exner, Wilhelm Franz (1878). *Johann Beckmann: Begründer der technologischen Wissenschaft*. Wien: Gerold.—Whitefish, Montana: Kessinger Pub Co, 2009.—[The reprint title contains a typo: *Johann Beckmann: Segründer der technologischen Wissenschaft*].

Frede, Dorothea (2010). Poiesis/techne. In H.-J. Sandkühler (ed.): *Enzyklopädie Philosophie*, Vol. 2. Hamburg: Felix Meiner Verlag, pp. 2069–71.

Freudenthal, Gideon; and Peter McLaughlin (eds) (2009). *The Social and Economic Roots of the Scientific Revolution: Texts by Boris Hessen and Henryk Grossmann*. Dordrecht: Springer.

Gadamer, Hans-Georg (1972). Hermeneutik als praktische Philosophie. (Riedel, Manfred (ed.): Rehabilitierung der Praktischen Philosophie, 1972).—In *Vernunft im Zeitalter der Wissenschaft: Aufsätze*. Frankfurt am Main: Suhrkamp, 1991, pp. 78–109.

Gadamer, Hans-Georg (1974). Was is Praxis? Die Bedingungen gesellschaftlicher Vernunft. (Universitas, 1974). In *Vernunft im Zeitalter der Wissenschaft: Aufsätze*. Frankfurt am Main: Suhrkamp, 1991, pp. 54–77.

Galilei, Galileo (1594). Delle Machine. (Manuscript, Padova, 1594). *Osiris*, Vol. 13, 1958, pp. 270–89. Ed. M. S. Drake.

Gille, Bertrand (1978a). *The History of Techniques. Volume I.: Techniques and Civilizations.* New York, NY, etc.: Gordon &. Breach Science Publishers, 1986. Transl. from *Histoire des techniques: Technique et civilisation; techniques et sciences*, Paris: Éditions Gallimard, 1978a. (2nd ed.; 1st ed. 1964). Transl. P. Southgate and T. Williamson.

Gille, Bertrand (1978b). Essay on technical knowledge. (B. Gille: *Histoire des techniques: Technique et civilisation; techniques et sciences.* Paris: Éditions Gallimard). Transl. from "Essai sur la conaissance technique." Transl. J. Brainch, et al. In B. Gille: *The History of Techniques. Volume II: Techniques and Sciences.* New York, NY, etc.: Gordon &. Breach Science Publishers, 1986, pp. 1136–85.

Goody, Jack (1977). *The Domestication of the Savage Mind.* Cambridge: Cambridge University Press.

Goody, Jack (1987). *The Interface Between the Written and the Oral.* Cambridge: Cambridge University Press.

Gramsci, Antonio (1929–35). *Prison Notebooks.* Transl. from *Quaderni del Carcere.* Transl. J. Buttigieg and A. Callari. Ed. J. Buttigieg. New York, NY: Columbia University Press, 2011.

Grlić, Danko (1965). Practice and dogma. *Praxis*, Vol. 1, no. 1, 1st quarter 1965, pp. 49–58. <http://www.marxists.org/subject/praxis/issue-01/grlic.htm>

Grudin, Jonathan; and Steven E. Poltrock (2012). Taxonomy and theory in Computer Supported Cooperative Work. In S. W. J. Kozlowski (ed.): *The Oxford Handbook of Organizational Psychology*, Vol. 2. Oxford: Oxford University Press, pp. 1323–48.

Gundisalvo, Domingo [D. Gundissalinus] (*c.*1150). *De divisione philosophiae/Über die Einteilung der Philosophie: Lateinisch/Deutsch.* Transl. A. Fidora and D. Werner. Ed. A. Fidora and D. Werner. Freiburg. etc.: Herder, 2007.

Habermas, Jürgen (1968a). Technik und Wissenschaft als "Ideologie." (Merkur, July-August 1968). In J. Habermas: *Technik und Wissenschaft als "Ideologie."* Frankfurt am Main: Suhrkamp, 1968, pp. 48–103.

Habermas, Jürgen (1968b). *Erkenntnis und Interesse.* Frankfurt am Main: Suhrkamp.

Habermas, Jürgen (1988). *Der philosophische Diskurs der Moderne: Zwölf Vorlesungen.* Frankfurt am Main: Suhrkamp.

Hall, Bert S. (1979). *Der Meister sol auch kennen schreiben und lesen*: Writings about technology ca. 1400–ca. 1600 AD and their cultural implications. In D. Schmand-Besserat (ed.): *Early Technologies, Vol. 3.* Malibu, CA: Undena Publications, pp. 47–58.—Address given at University of Texas, Austin. <http://web.archive.org/web/20020109075840/www.chass.utoronto.ca/~bhall/articles/meister1.htm>

Hanson, Norwood Russell (1958). *Patterns of Discovery: An Inquiry into the Conceptual Foundations of Science.* Cambridge: Cambridge University Press.

Harper, Richard H. R.; and John A. Hughes (1993). What a f—ing system! Send 'em all to the same place and then expect us to stop 'em hitting: Managing technology work in air traffic control. In G. Button (ed.): *Technology in Working Order: Studies of Work, Interaction, and Technology.* London and New York, NY: Routledge, pp. 127–44.

Harper, Richard H. R.; John A. Hughes; and Dan Z. Shapiro (1991). Harmonious working and CSCW: Computer technology and air traffic control. In J. M. Bowers and S. D. Benford (eds): *Studies in Computer Supported Cooperative Work: Theory, Practice and Design.* Amsterdam: North-Holland, pp. 225–34.

Harris, Roy (1986). *The Origin of Writing.* London: Duckworth.

Harris, Roy (1995). *Signs of Writing.* London and New York, NY: Routledge.

Harris, Roy (2000). *Rethinking Writing.* Bloomington, IL, and Indianapolis, IL: Indiana University Press.

Heath, Christian C.; and Paul Luff (1991). Collaborative activity and technological design: Task coordination in London Underground control rooms. In L. J. Bannon; M. Robinson; and K. Schmidt (eds): *ECSCW'91: Proceedings of the Second European Conference on Computer-Supported Cooperative Work, 24–27 September 1991, Amsterdam*. Dordrecht: Kluwer Academic Publishers, pp. 65–80.

Heath, Christian C.; and Paul Luff (1992). Collaboration and control: Crisis management and multimedia technology in London Underground control rooms. *Computer Supported Cooperative Work (CSCW)*. Vol. 1, no. 1–2, March 1992 [published September 1992], pp. 69–94.

Hegel, Georg Wilhelm Friedrich (1802–3). Über die wissenshaftlichen Behandlungsarten des Naturrechts, seine Stelle in der praktischen Philosophie und sein Verhäalnis zu den positiven Rechtswissenshaften. (*Kritisches Journal der Philosophie*, Tübingen). Text ed. by E. Moldenhauer and K. M. Michel. In G. W. F. Hegel: *Werke in zwanzig Bänden*. Frankfurt am Main: Suhrkamp, 1970, pp. 434–530.

Hegel, Georg Wilhelm Friedrich (1803–4). *Anhang zur Jenaer Realphilosophie. Ausarbeitungen zur Geistesphilosophie von 1803/04*. Ed. G. Göhler. In G. W. F. Hegel: *Frühe politische Systeme*. Frankfurt am Main: Verlag Ullstein, 1974, pp. 291–335.

Hegel, Georg Wilhelm Friedrich (1805–6). *Jenaer Realphilosophie. Die Vorlesungen von 1805/06. Philosophie des Geistes*. Ed. G. Göhler. In G. W. F. Hegel: *Frühe politische Systeme*. Frankfurt am Main: Verlag Ullstein, 1974, pp. 201–90.

Hegel, Georg Wilhelm Friedrich (1807). *Phänomenologie des Geistes*. (Joseph Anton Goebhardt: Bamberg und Würzburg). In G. W. F. Hegel: *Werke in zwanzig Bänden*. Ed. E. Moldenhauer and K. M. Michel. Frankfurt am Main: Suhrkamp Verlag, 1970.

Hegel, Georg Wilhelm Friedrich (1830a). *Enzyklopädie der philosophischen Wissenschaften im Grundrisse. Zweiter Teil. Die Naturphilosophie*. (Joseph Anton Goebhardt: Bamberg und Würzburg). Ed. E. Moldenhauer and K. M. Michel. In G. W. F. Hegel: *Werke in zwanzig Bänden*. Frankfurt am Main: Suhrkamp Verlag, 1970, Vol. 9.

Hegel, Georg Wilhelm Friedrich (1830b). *Hegel's Philosophy of Nature: Part II of th Encyclopedia of the Philosophical Sciences (1830)*. Oxford: Oxford University Press. Transl. from *Enzyklopädie der philosophischen Wissenschaften im Grundrisse. Zweiter Teil. Die Naturphilosophie*, Joseph Anton Goebhardt: Bamberg und Würzburg, 1830b. Transl. A. V. Miller. 1970 (2nd ed., 2004).

Heidegger, Martin (1927). *Sein und Zeit*. Tübingen: Max Niemeyer Verlag. (Revised ed., 1953).— Tübingen: Max Niemeyer Verlag, 1993.

Heidegger, Martin (1949). Das Ge-stell. (Lecture, Bremen, 1 December 1949). Ed. P. Jaeger. In M. Heidegger: *Gesamtausgabe. III. Abteilung: Unveröffentlichte Abhandlungen. Band 79: Bremer und Freiburger Vorträge*. Frankfurt am Main: Vittorio Klostermann 1994, pp. 5–77. (2nd ed., 2005).

Heinimann, Felix (1961). Eine Vorplatonische Theorie der τέχνη. *Museum helveticum: Schweizerische Zeitschrift für klassische Altertumswissenschaft*. Vol. 18, no. 3, 1961, pp. 105–30.

Hilaire-Pérez, Liliane; and Catherine Verna (2006). Dissemination of technical knowledge in the Middle Ages and the Early Modern Era: New approaches and methodological issues. *Technology and Culture*. Vol. 47, no. 3, July 2006, pp. 536–65.

Hippokrates of Kos [Hippocrates] (1923). *Hippocrates*. Transl. W. H. S. Jones. Ed. W. H. S. Jones. London: Heinemann, 1923. Vol. 1–4.

Hoven, Birgit van den (1996). *Work in Ancient and Medieval Thought: Ancient Philosophers, Medie Monks and Theologians and their Concept of Work, Occupations and Technology*. Amsterdam: J. C. Gieben.

Hugh of Saint Victor (*c.*1120). *Practical Geometry*. Transl. from *Practica Geometriae*. Transl. F. A. Houmann. Ed. F. A. Houmann. In Hugh of Saint Victor: *Practical Geometry [Practica Geometriae]. Attributed to Hugh of Saint Victor*. Milwaukee, WI: Marquette University Press, 1991.

Jacquart, Danielle (1990). Theory, everyday practice, and three fifteenth-century physicians. *Osiris*. Vol. 6, January 1990, pp. 140–60.

Kant, Immanuel (1793a). Über den Gemeinspruch: Das mag in der Theorie richtig sein, taugt aber nicht für die Praxis. (*Berlinische Monatsschrift*, September 1793). Text ed. by W. Weischedel. In I. Kant: *Werke in zwölf Bänden*. Frankfurt am Main: Suhrkamp Verlag, 1964, Vol. 11, pp. 125–72.

Kant, Immanuel (1793b). On the common saying: That may be correct in theory, but it is of no use in practice. (*Berlinische Monatsschrift*, September 1793). Transl. M. J. Gregor. Ed. M. J. Gregor. In M. J. Gregor (ed.): *Practical Philosophy*. Cambridge: Cambridge University Press, 1999, pp. 273–310.

Kerferd, George Briscoe (1981). *The Sophist Movement*. Cambridge: Cambridge University Press.

Kilwardby, Robert (*c*.1250). *De ortu scientiarum*. (Manuscript, Oxford, *c*.1250). Ed. A. G. Judy. Oxford: Oxford University Press, 1976.

Kitching, Gavin (1988). *Karl Marx and the Philosophy of Praxis*. London and New York, NY: Routledge.

Kobusch, Theo (1989). Praxis, praktisch: III. Mittelalter und frühe Neuzeit. In J. Ritter and K. Gründer (eds): *Historisches Wörterbuch der Philosophie*, Vol. 7. Basel: Schwabe Verlag, pp. 1287–95.

Korsch, Karl (1938). *Karl Marx*. London: Chapman & Hall. —New York, NY: Russell & Russell, 1963.

Korsch, Karl (1939). State and counter-revolution. *The Modern Quarterly*, Vol. 11, no. 2, Winter 1939, pp. 60–7.

Kotkin, Stephen (1995). *Magnetic Mountain: Stalinism as a Civilization*. Berkeley, CA: University of California Press. (Paperback ed., 1997).

Labriola, Antonio (1898). *Socialism and Philosophy*. Chicago, IL: Charles H. Kerr & Co., 1912. Transl. from *Discorrendo di socialismo e di filosofia. Lettere a G. Sorel*, Roma: Loescher, 1898. Transl. E. Untermann. (3rd ed.).

Lefebvre, Henri (1966). *The Sociology of Marx*. London: Allen Lane The Penguin Press, 1968. Transl. from *Sociologie de Marx*, Paris: Presses Universitaires de France, 1966. Transl. N. Guterman.

Lefèvre, Wolfgang (ed.) (2004). *Picturing Machines, 1400–1700*. Cambridge, MA, and London: The MIT Press.

Lefort, Claude (1956). Totalitarianism without Stalin. (*Socialisme ou Barbarie*, July–September 1956). Transl. from *Le totalitarisme sans Staline*. Transl. J. B. Thompson. Text ed. by J. B. Thompson. In C. Lefort: *The Political Forms of Modern Society: Bureaucracy, Democracy, Totalitarianism*. Cambridge, MA: MIT Press, 1986, pp. 52–88.

Lefort, Claude (1980). The logic of totalitarianism. (*Kontinent Skandinavia*, 1980). Transl. from *La logique totalitaire*. Transl. J. B. Thompson. Text ed. by J. B. Thompson. In C. Lefort: *The Political Forms of Modern Society: Bureaucracy, Democracy, Totalitarianism*. Cambridge, MA: MIT Press, 1986, pp. 273–91.

Lefort, Claude (1997). Überlegungen zum Begriff der totalen Herrschaft. In D. Ganzfried and S. Hefti (eds): *Hannah Arendt: Nach dem Totalitarismus*. Frankfurt am Main: Europäische Verlagsanstalt, pp. 31–53.

Lefort, Claude (1999). *Complications: Communism and the Dilemmas of Democracy*. New York, NY: Columbia University Press, 2007. Paris: Librarie Arthème Fayard, 1999. Transl. J. Bourg.

Lis, Catharina; and Hugo Soly (2012). *Worthy Efforts: Attitudes to Work and Workers in Pre-Industrial Europe*. Leiden and Boston, MA: Brill.

Lloyd, Geoffrey E. R. (1979). *Magic Reason and Experience: Studies in the Origin and Development of Greek Science*. Cambridge: Cambridge University Press.—London: Gerald Duckworth, 1999 (Paperback ed.).

Lloyd, Geoffrey E. R. (2008). Literacy in Greek and Chinese science: Some comparative issues. In H. Yunis (ed.): *Written Texts and the Rise of Literate Culture in Ancient Greece*. Cambridge: Cambridge University Press, pp. 122–38.

Lobkowics, Nicholas (1967). *Theory and Practice: History of a Concept from Aristotle to Marx*. Notre Dame, IN, and London: University of Notre Dame Press.

Löbl, Rudolf (1997). *TEXNH—Techne: Untersuchung zur Bedeutung dieses Wortes in der Zeit von Homer bis Aristoteles. Band I: Von Homer bis zu den Sophisten*. Würzburg: Königshausen & Neumann.

Löbl, Rudolf (2003). *TEXNH—Techne: Untersuchung zur Bedeutung dieses Wortes in der Zeit von Homer bis Aristoteles. Band II: Von den Sophisten bis zu Aristoteles*. Würzburg: Königshausen & Neumann.

Löbl, Rudolf (2008). *TEXNH—Techne: Untersuchungen zur Bedeutung dieses Wortes in der Zeit nach Aristoteles. Band III: Die Zeit des Hellenismus*. Würzburg: Königshausen & Neumann.

Long, Pamela O. (2001). *Openness, Secrecy, Authorship: Technical Arts and the Culture of Knowledge From Antiquity to the Renaissance*. Baltimore, MD, and London: Johns Hopkins University Press.

Long, Pamela O. (2011). *Artisan/Practitioners and the Rise of the New Sciences, 1400–1600*. Corvallis, OR: Oregon State University Press.

Lonie, Iain M. (1983). Literacy and the development of Hippocratic medicine. In F. Lasserre and P. Mudry (eds): *Formes de pensée dans la collection hippocratique: Actes du IVe Colloque International Hippocratique (Lausanne, 21–26 Septembre 1981)*. Geneve: Librairie Droz, pp. 145–61.

Lorini, Bonaiuto (1596). *Delle fortificationi di Buonaiuto Lorini, libri cinque: ne'quali si mostra con le piu facili regole la scienza con la pratica, di fortificare le città, & altri luoghi sopra diuersi siti [. . .]*. Venetia: Gio. Antonio Rampazetta. (2nd ed., 1609).

Lorini, Bonaiuto (1607). *Fünff Bücher von Vestung Bauwen*. Frankfurt am Main: De Bry. Transl. from *Delle fortificationi*, Venetia: Gio. Antonio Rampazetta, 1596. Transl. D. Wormbser.

Luff, Paul; Jon Hindmarsh; and Christian C. Heath (eds) (2000). *Workplace Studies: Recovering Work Practices and Informing System Design*. Cambridge: Cambridge University Press.

Lukács, György [G. Lukács] (1923). Geschichte und Klassenbewusstsein. (Malik-Verlag: Berlin). In G. Lukács: *Werke*. Darmstadt: Luchterhand, 1977, Vol. 2.

Lukács, György [G. Lukács] (1948). *Der junge Hegel: Über die Beziehungen von Dialektik und Ökonomie*. Zürich and Wien: Europa Verlag.

Mahoney, Michael S. (1992). Computers and mathematics: The search for a discipline of computer science. In J. Echeverria; A. Ibarra; and T. Mormann (eds): *The Space of Mathematics: Philosophical, Epistemological, and Historical Explorations*. Berlin and New York, NY: Walter de Gruyter, pp. 349–63.

Mahoney, Michael S. (2005). The histories of computing(s). *Interdisciplinary Science Reviews*. Vol. 30, no. 2, 2005, pp. 119–35.

Mahoney, Michael S. (2011). *Histories of Computing*. Cambridge, MA, and London: Harvard University Press.

Mao, Zedong (1937). On practice: On the relation between knowledge and practice, between knowing and doing. (Lecture, Yenan, July 1937). In *Selected Works of Mao Tse-tung. Volume I*. Peking: Foreign Languages Press 1965.

Marcuse, Herbert (1941). *Reason and Revolution: Hegel and the Rise of Social Theory*. Oxford: Oxford University Press.—London: Routledge & Kegan Paul, 1967 (2nd ed., 1955).

Marx, Karl (1844a). *Ökonomisch-philosophische Manuskripte (Zweite Wiedergabe)*. (Manuscript, Paris, June–August 1844). Ed. I. Taubert; I. Bauer; and B. Dohm. In K. Marx and F. Engels: *Gesamtausgabe (MEGA②)*. Berlin: Dietz Verlag, 1982, Vol. I/2, pp. 323–438.

Marx, Karl (1844b). *Economic and Philosophic Manuscripts of 1844*. (Manuscript, Paris, June–August 1844). Transl. M. Milligan and D. J. Struik. In K. Marx and F. Engels: *Collected Works* London: Lawrence & Wishart, 2010, Vol. 3 (*Karl Marx March 1843 – August 1844*), pp. 229–348.

Marx, Karl (1845a). *ad* Feuerbach [Thesen über Feuerbach]. (Manuscript, Bruxelles, Spring 1845). Ed. G. A. Bagaturija, *et al*. In K. Marx and F. Engels: *Gesamtausgabe (MEGA②)*. Berlin: Akademie Verlag 1998, vol. IV:3 (*Exzerpte und Notizen Sommer 1844 bis Anfang 1847*), pp. 19–21. – [Entry in Notebook from 1844–7].

Marx, Karl (1845b). Theses on Feuerbach. (Manuscript, Bruxelles, Spring 1845). Transl. W. Lough. In K. Marx and F. Engels: *Collected Works*. London: Lawrence & Wishart 2010, vol. 5 (*Marx and Engels 1845–47*), pp. 3–5.

Marx, Karl (1857a). Einleitung. (Manuscript, London, August 1857). Ed. V. K. Brušlinskij; L. R. Mis'kevič; and A. G. Syrov. In K. Marx and F. Engels: *Gesamtausgabe (MEGA②)*. Berlin: Dietz Verlag 1976–81, Vol. II/1.1 (*Ökonomische Manuskripte 1857/58*), pp. 17–45.

Marx, Karl (1857b). Introduction. (Manuscript, London, August 1857). Transl. from "Einleitung." Transl. V. Schnittke. In K. Marx and F. Engels: *Collected Works*. London: Lawrence & Wishart 2010, Vol. 28 (*Economic Manuscripts of 1857–58 (First Version of Capital): Outlines of the Critique of Political Economy*), pp. 17–48.

Marx, Karl (1857–8a). *Grundrisse der Kritik der politischen Ökonomie*. (Manuscript, October 1857–May 1858). Ed. V. K. Brušlinskij; L. R. Mis'kevič; and A. G. Syrov. In K. Marx and F. Engels: *Gesamtausgabe (MEGA②)*. Berlin: Dietz Verlag, 1976–1981, Vol. II/1, pp. 47–747.

Marx, Karl (1857–8b). *Economic Manuscripts of 1857–58 (First Version of Capital): Outlines of the Critique of Political Economy*. Transl. from *Grundrisse der Kritik der politischen Ökonomie* Transl. V. Schnittke. In K. Marx and F. Engels: *Collected Works*. London: Lawrence & Wishart, 2010, Vol. 28–29.

Marx, Karl (1859a). *Zur Kritik der politischen Ökonomie. Erstes Heft*. (Verlag von Franz Duncker: Berlin, 1859). In K. Marx and F. Engels: *Gesamtausgabe (MEGA②)*. Ed. L. R. Mis'kevič; I. Antonova; and L. L. Vasina. Berlin: Dietz Verlag, 1980, Vol. II/2 (*Ökonomische Manuskripte und Schriften 1858-1861*), pp. 95–245.

Marx, Karl (1859b). *A Contribution to the Critique of Political Economy. Part One*. Transl. from *Zur Kritik der politischen Ökonomie. Erstes Heft* (Verlag von Franz Duncker: Berlin, 1859). Transl. S. Rjazanskaja. In K. Marx and F. Engels: *Collected Works*. Ed. L. R. Mis'kevič. London: Lawrence & Wishart, 2010, Vol. 29, pp. 257–420.

Marx, Karl (1867a). *Das Kapital. Kritik der politischen Ökonomie. Erster Band. Buch I: Der Produktionsprocess des Kapitals*. (Verlag von Otto Meissner: Hamburg; 4th ed., 1890). Ed. F. Engels. In K. Marx and F. Engels: *Werke*. Berlin: Dietz Verlag, 1962, Vol. 23.

Marx, Karl (1867b). *Capital: A Critique of Political Economy. Book One: The Process of Production of Capital*. (Verlag von Otto Meissner: Hamburg; 4th ed., 1890). Transl. S. Moore and E. Aveling. Ed. F. Engels. In K. Marx and F. Engels: *Collected Works*. London: Lawrence & Wishart, 2010, Vol. 35.

Marx, Karl (1877a). *À la rédaction de l'Otečestvennyâ Zapiski*. (Draft letter, in French, October–November 1877). Ed. H. Schwab, et al. In K. Marx and F. Engels: *Gesamtausgabe (MEGA②)*. Berlin: Dietz Verlag 1985, Vol. I/25, pp. 112–17.

Marx, Karl (1877b). Letter to the editor of Otyecestvenniye Zapisky. (Draft letter, in French, October–November 1877). Transl. from *À la rédaction de l'Otečestvennyâ Zapiski*. Ed. B. Selman. In K. Marx and F. Engels: *Collected Works*. London: Lawrence and Wishart 2010, Vol. 24, pp. 196–201.

Marx, Karl; and Friedrich Engels (1845–6a). [Konvolut zo Feuerbach]. (Manuscript, Bruxelles, October 1845 – medio July 1846). Ed. U. Pagel; G. Hubmann; and C. Weckwerth. In K. Marx and F. Engels: *Gesamtausgabe (MEGA②)*. Berlin and Boston: De Gruyter 2017, vol. I:5 (*Deutsche Ideologie: Manuskripte und Drucke*), pp. 16–123.

Marx, Karl; and Friedrich Engels (1845–6b). *The German Ideology: Critique of Modern German Philosophy According to its Representatives Feuerbach, Bruno Bauer and Stirner, and of German Socialism According to Its Various Prophets.* (Manuscript, Bruxelles, November 1845–August 1846). Transl. C. Dutt; W. Lough; and C. P. Magill. Ed. R. Pascal. In K. Marx and F. Engels: *Collected Works*. London: Lawrence & Wishart, 2010, Vol. 5 (*Marx and Engels 1845–47*).

Mauss, Marcel (1934a). Les techniques du corps. (Lecture, Société de Psychologie, 17 May 1934). *Journal de Psychologie*, Vol. 32, no. 3–4, 1936, pp. 271–93.

Mauss, Marcel (1934b). Techniques of the body. (Lecture, Société de Psychologie, 17 May 1934). *Economy and Society*, Vol. 2, no. 1, 1973, pp. 70–88. Transl. B. Brewster.

Meißner, Burkhard (1999). *Die technologische Fachliteratur der Antike: Struktur, Überlieferung und Wirkung technischen Wissens in der Antike* (ca. *400. v. Chr.*–ca. *500 n. Chr.*). Berlin: Akademie Verlag.

Meier, Christian (1984). Arbeit, Politik, Identität: Neue Fragen im alten Athen? In *Chronik der Ludwig-Maximilians-Universität München 1983/84*. München: Ludwig-Maximilians-Universität, pp. 69–95. <http://epub.ub.uni-muenchen.de/13661/1/lmu_chronik_1983_84.pdf>

Merleau-Ponty, Maurice (1946). Marxism and philosophy. (*Revue internationale*, June–July 1946). Transl. from *Marxisme et philosophie*. Transl. H. L. Dreyfus and P. A. Dreyfus. In M. Merleau-Ponty: *Sense and Non-Sense*. Evanston, IL: Northwestern University Press, 1964, pp. 125–36.

Merleau-Ponty, Maurice (1947). *Humanism and Terror: The Communist Problem*. Boston, MA: Beacon Press, 1969. Transl. from *Humanisme et terreur: Essai sur la problème communiste*. Paris: Gallimard, 1947. Transl. J. O"Neill.—London and New York: Routledge, 2000 (2nd ed.).

Merleau-Ponty, Maurice (1955). *Les Aventures de la dialectique*. Paris: Gallimard.

Monte, Guidobaldo Del (1577). *Guidi Ubaldi e Marchionibus Montis mechanicorum liber*. (Hieronymous Concordia: Pesaro). In J. Renn and P. Damerow (eds): *Guidobaldo Del Monte's Mechanicorum Liber*. Berlin: Ed. Open Access, 2010.

Naus, John E. (1959). *The Nature of the Practical Intellect according to Saint Thomas Aquinas*. Roma: Libreria Editrice Dell' Universita Grecoriana.

Nicolini, Davide (2012). *Practice Theory, Work, and Organization: An Introduction*. Oxford: Oxford University Press.

Ober, Josiah (1998). *Political Dissent in Democratic Athens: Intellectual Critics of Popular Rule*. Princeton, NJ, and Oxford: Princeton University Press. (Paperback ed., 2002).

Olson, David R. (1994). *The World on Paper: The Conceptual and Cognitive Implications of Writing and Reading*. Cambridge: Cambridge University Press.

Olson, Gary M.; and Judith S. Olson (2003). Groupware and computer-supported cooperative work. In J. A. Jacko and A. Sears (eds): *The Human-Computer Interaction Handbook: Fundamentals, Evolving Technologies and Emerging Applications*. Mahwah, NJ: Lawrence Erlbaum Associates, pp. 583–95.

Palissy, Bernard (1580a). *Discours admirables de la nature des eaux et fontaines tant naturelles qu'artificielles, des metaux, des sels & salines, des pierres, des terres, du feu & des emaux*. Paris: Martin le Jeune. <http://gallica.bnf.fr>

Palissy, Bernard (1580b). *The Admirable Discourses of Bernard Palissy*. Urbana, IL: University of Illinois Press, 1957. Transl. from *Discours admirables de la nature des eaux et fontaines tant naturelles qu'artificielles, des metaux, des sels & salines, des pierres, des terres, du feu & des emaux*, Paris: Martin le Jeune, 1580b. Transl. A. La Rocque.

Peaucelle, Jean-Louis (2006). Adam Smith's use of multiple references for his pin making example. *The European Journal of the History of Economic Thought*. Vol. 13, no. 4, 2006, pp. 489–512.

Peaucelle, Jean-Louis (2007). *Adam Smith et la division du travail: La naissance d'une fausse idée*. Paris: L'Harmattan.

Picht, Georg (1964). Der Sinn der Unterscheidung von Theorie und Praxis in der griechischen Philosophie. (*Zeitschrift für Evangelische Ethik*). In G. Picht: *Wahrheit, Vernunft, Verantwortung: Philosophische Studien*. Stuttgart: Ernst Klett Verlag, 1969, pp. 108–40.

Plato (*c*.365–361 BCE). Statesman. In Plato: *The Complete Works of Plato (423–348 bc)*. Hastings: Delphi Classics, 2015.

Poppe, Johann Heinrich Moritz (1807). *Geschichte der Technologie seit der Wiederherstellung der Wissenschaften bis an das Ende des achtzehnten Jahrhundert: Erster Band*. Göttingen: Röwer.—Hildesheim, etc.: Georg Olms Verlag, 1999.

Rese, Friederike (2003). *Praxis und Logos bei Aristoteles: Handlung, Vernunft und Rede in Nikomachischer Ethik, Rhetorik und Politik*. Tübingen: Mohr Siebeck.

Riddle, John M. (1974). Theory and practice in medieval medicine. *Viator: Medieval and Renaissance Studies*. Vol. 5, 1974, pp. 157–84.

Rossi, Paolo (1962). *Philosophy, Technology, and the Arts in the Early Modern Era*. New York, etc.: Harper & Row, 1970. Transl. from *I filosofi e le macchine*, Milano: Feltrinelli Editiore, 1962. Transl. S. Attanasio. Ed. B. Nelson.

Rossi, Paolo (2000). *The Birth of Modern Science*. Oxford, etc.: Basil Blackwell Publishers, 2001. Transl. from *La nascita della scienza moderna in Europa*, Roma-Bari: Laterza, 2000. (1st ed. 1997). Transl. C. D. N. Ipsen.

Ryle, Gilbert (1949). *The Concept of Mind*. London: Hutchinson's University Library.

Ryle, Gilbert (1968). The thinking of thoughts: What is "le Penseur" doing? (*University Lectures*, University of Saskatchewan). In G. Ryle: *Collected Papers. Volume II: Collected Essays, 1929–1968*. London: Hutchinson & Co, 1971, pp. 480–96.

Sartre, Jean-Paul (1960). *Critique de la raison dialectique. Tome I: Théorie des ensembles pratiques*. Paris: Gallimard.

Sartre, Jean-Paul (1962). *Critique de la raison dialectique. Tome II: L'Intelligence de l'histoire*. (Manuscript, Paris, written 1958–62). Paris: Gallimard, 1985.

Schatzki, Theodore R.; Karin D. Knorr-Cetina; and Eike von Savigny (eds) (2001). *The Practice Turn in Contemporary Theory*. London and New York, NY: Routledge.

Schmidt, Alfred (1974). Praxis. In H.-G. Backhaus; H.-D. Bahr; and G. Brandt (eds): *Gesellschaft: Beiträge zur Marxschen Theorie*, Vol. 2. Frankfurt am Main: Suhrkamp, pp. 264–308.

Schmidt, Kjeld (2011a). *Cooperative Work and Coordinative Practices: Contributions to the Conceptual Foundations of Computer-Supported Cooperative Work (CSCW)*. London: Springer.

Schmidt, Kjeld (2011b). The concept of "work" in CSCW. *Computer Supported Cooperative Work (CSCW)*. Vol. 20, no. 4–5, October 2011, pp. 341–401.

Schmidt, Kjeld (2012a). The trouble with "tacit knowledge." *Computer Supported Cooperative Work (CSCW)*. Vol. 21, no. 2–3, June 2012, pp. 163–225.

Schmidt, Kjeld (2012b). Predicate or subject? Assorted notes on the metaphysical notion of "sharing." In *Workshop: Do We Really Need to Share to Cooperate?, COOP 2012: 9th International Conference on the Design of Cooperative System, 29 May–1 June 2012, Marseille*. <http://www.academia.edu/1785659/Predicate_or_subject_A_critique_of_the_notion_of_shared_awareness_>

Schmidt, Kjeld (2014a). Praksisanalyse. In S. Vikkelsø and P. Kjær (eds): *Klassisk og moderne organisationsteori*. København: Hans Reitzels Forlag, pp. 157–80.

Schmidt, Kjeld (2014b). The concept of "practice": What's the point? In C. Rossitto et al. (eds): *COOP 2014: Proceedings of the 11th International Conference on the Design of Cooperative Systems, 27–30 May 2014, Nice, France*. London: Springer, pp. 427–44.

Schmidt, Kjeld (2015a). "Practice must speak for itself": Remarks on the concept of practice. *Navigationen: Zeitschrift für Medien- und Kulturwissenschaften*. Vol. 15, no. 1, 2015, pp. 99–115. <http://dokumentix.ub.uni-siegen.de/opus/volltexte/2015/929/pdf/Navigationen_Medien_der_Kooperation.pdf>

Schmidt, Kjeld (2015b). Of humble origins: The practice roots of interactive and collaborative computing. *ZfM Online*, May 2015. <http://www.zfmedienwissenschaft.de/online/humble-origins>

Schmidt, Kjeld; and Liam J. Bannon (1992). Taking CSCW seriously: Supporting articulation work. *Computer Supported Cooperative Work (CSCW)*. Vol. 1, no. 1–2, March 1992 [published September 1992], pp. 7–40.

Schmidt, Kjeld; and Liam J. Bannon (2013). Constructing CSCW: The first quarter century. *Computer Supported Cooperative Work (CSCW)*. Vol. 22, no. 4–6, August–December 2013, pp. 345–72.

Schneider, Helmuth (1989). *Das Griechische Technikverständnis: Von den Epen Homers bis zu den Anfängen der technologischen Fachliteratur*. Darmstadt: Wissenschaftliche Buchgesellschaft.

Schütz, Alfred [A. Schutz] (1947–51). *Reflections on the Problem of Relevance*. (Manuscript). Ed. R. M. Zaner and L. Embree. In A. Schütz: *Collected Papers. Vol. V: Phenomenology and the Social Sciences*. Berlin: Springer-Verlag, 2011.

Schütz, Alfred [A. Schutz] (1953). Common-sense and scientific interpretations of human action. (*Philosophy and Phenomenological Research*, September 1953). Text ed. by M. Natanson. In A. Schutz: *Collected Papers. Vol. I. The Problem of Social Reality*. The Hague: Martinus Nijhoff, 1962, pp. 3–47.

Schütz, Alfred [A. Schutz] (1957). Equality and the meaning structure of the social world. Text ed. by A. Brodersen. In A. Schutz: *Collected Papers. Vol. II. Studies in Social Theory*. The Hague: Martinus Nijhoff, 1964, pp. 226–73.

Schweizer, Herbert (1971). *Zur Logik der Praxis: Die geschichtlichen Implikationen und die hermeneutische Reichweite der praktischen Philosophie des Aristoteles*. Freiburg - München: Verlag Karl Alber.

Smith, Pamela H. (2004). *The Body of the Artisan: Art and Experience in the Scientific Revolution*. Chicago, IL, and London: University of Chicago Press.

Snyder, Timothy (2010). *Bloodlands: Europe between Hitler and Stalin*. New York, NY: Basic Books.—London: Vintage, 2011 (Paperback ed.).

Sorel, Georges (1902). *Le matérialisme historique. Bulletin de la Société française de Philosophie* 2 (5). <http://classiques.uqac.ca/classiques/sorel_georges/decomposition_marxisme/texte_7/materialisme_historique.pdf>

Sorel, Georges (1908). *La décomposition du marxisme*. Paris: Éditions Marcel Rivière.

Stalin, Joseph (1924). *Foundations of Leninism*. Transl. from *Osnovy Leninizma* (Moskva). In J. Stalin: *Works*. Moscow: Foreign Languages Publishing House, 1953, Vol. 6, pp. 71–196.

Strauss, Anselm L. (1985). Work and the division of labor. *The Sociological Quarterly*. Vol. 26, no. 1, 1985, pp. 1–19.

Strauss, Anselm L.; Shizuko Y. Fagerhaugh; Barbara Suczek; and Carolyn L. Wiener (1985). *Social Organization of Medical Work*. Chicago, IL, and London: University of Chicago Press.

Suchman, Lucy A. (1987). *Plans and Situated Actions: The Problem of Human-Machine Communication*. Cambridge: Cambridge University Press.

Suchman, Lucy A. (1997). Centers of coordination: A case and some themes. In L. B. Resnick, et al. (eds): *Discourse, Tools, and Reasoning: Essays on Situated Cognition*. Berlín-Heidelberg: Springer, pp. 41–62.

Suchman, Lucy A. (2002). Practice-based design of information systems: Notes from the hyperdeveloped world. *The Information Society*. Vol. 18, no. 2, 2002, pp. 139–44.

Suchman, Lucy A.; and Randall H. Trigg (1986). A framework for studying research collaboration. In H. Krasner and I. Greif (eds): *CSCW'86: Proceedings. Conference on Computer-Supported Cooperative Work, 3–5 December 1986, Austin, Texas.* New York, NY: ACM Press, pp. 221–8.

Suchman, Lucy A.; and Randall H. Trigg (1991). Understanding practice: Video as a medium for reflection and design. In J. Greenbaum and M. Kyng (eds): *Design at Work: Cooperative Design of Computer Systems.* Hillsdale, NJ: Lawrence Erlbaum Associates, pp. 65–89.

Thomas, Rosalind (1992). *Literacy and Orality in Ancient Greece.* Cambridge: Cambridge University Press.

Tosel, André (2010). Praxis. In H.-J. Sandkühler (ed.): *Enzyklopädie Philosophie,* Vol. 2. Hamburg: Felix Meiner Verlag, pp. 2136–8.

Totelin, Laurence M. V. (2009). *Hippocratic Recipes: Oral and Written Transmission of Pharmacological Knowledge in Fifth-and Fourth-Century Greece.* Leiden and Boston, MA: Brill.

Turing, Alan M. (1945). Proposed electronic calculator (1945). (Report). In B. J. Copeland (ed.) *Alan Turing's Automatic Computing Engine: The Master Codebreaker's Struggle to Build the Modern Computer.* Oxford: Oxford University Press, 2005, pp. 369–454.—Written late 1945; submitted to the Executive Committee of the NPL February 1946 as "Report by Dr. A. M. Turing on Proposals for the Development of an Automatic Computing Engine (ACE)."

Valleriani, Matteo (2010). *Galileo Engineer.* Dordrecht, etc.: Springer.

Valleriani, Matteo (ed.) (2017). *The Structures of Practical Knowledge.* Cham, Switzerland, etc.: Springer.

Vranički, Predrag [P. Vranicki]. (1965). On the problem of practice. *Praxis* Vol. 1, no. 1, 1st quarter 1965, pp. 41–8. <http://www.marxists.org/subject/praxis/issue-01/vranicki.htm>

Whitney, Elspeth (1990). *Paradise Restored: The Mechanical Arts from Antiquity through the Thirteenth Century.* Philadelphia, PA: The American Philisophical Society.

Wildfeuer, Armin G. (2011). Praxis. In P. Kolmer, et al. (eds): *Neues Handbuch philosophischer Grundbegriffe in drei Bänden,* Vol. 2. Freiburg im Breisgau: Verlag Karl Alber, pp. 1774–804.

Williams, Meredith (2010). *Blind Obedience: Paradox and Learning in the Later Wittgenstein.* London and New York, NY: Routledge.

Wittgenstein, Ludwig (1937–44). *Remarks on the Foundations of Mathematics.* (Manuscript, 1937–44). Transl. from *Bemerkungen über die Grundlagen der der Mathematik.* Transl. G. E. M. Anscombe. Ed. G. H. von Wright; R. Rhees; and G. E. M. Anscombe. Oxford: Basil Blackwell Publishers, 1978. (Revised ed.; 1st ed. 1956).

Wittgenstein, Ludwig (1945–46). *Philosophical Investigations.* (Manuscript). Transl. from *Philosophische Untersuchungen.* Transl. G. E. M. Anscombe; P. M. S. Hacker; and J. Schulte. Ed. P. M. S. Hacker and J. Schulte. In L. Wittgenstein: *Philosophical Investigations.* Oxford: Basil Blackwell Publishers, 2009, pp. 1–181. (Revised 4th ed.).—[TS 227: Previously published as *Philosphical Investigations, Part 1*].

Wittgenstein, Ludwig (1945–48). *Zettel.* (Manuscript). Transl. G. E. M. Anscombe. Ed. G. E. M. Anscombe and G. H. von Wright. Oxford: Basil Blackwell Publishers, 1981. (2nd ed; 1st ed. 1967).

Wittgenstein, Ludwig (1949–51). *On Certainty.* (Manuscript). Transl. from *Über Gewissheit.* Transl. D. Paul and G. E. M. Anscombe. Ed. G. E. M. Anscombe and G. H. von Wright. Oxford: Basil Blackwell Publishers, 1975. (2nd ed.; 1st ed. 1969).

Wolff, Christian (1726). *Rede über die praktische Philosophie der Chinesen/Oratio de sinarum philosophia practica.* (Joh. B. Andreæ & Henr. Hort: Frankfurt am Main). Transl. M. Albrecht. Ed. M. Albrecht. Hamburg: Felix Meiner Verlag, 1985.

Wolff, Christian (1738). *Philosophia practica universalis: methodo scientifica pertractata. Theoriam complectens, qua omnis actionum humanarum differentia.* Vol. 1. Frankfurt am Main and Leipzig: Officina libraria Rengeriana.

Wood, Ellen Meiksins; and Neal Wood (1978). *Class Ideology and Ancient Political Theory: Socrates, Plato, and Aristotle in Social Context.* Oxford: Basil Blackwell Publishers.

Wood, Ellen Meiksins (1988). *Peasant-Citizen and Slave: The Foundations of Athenian Democracy.* London and New York, NY: Verso.

Wulf, Volker; Markus Rohde; Volkmar Pipek; and Gunnar Stevens (2011). Engaging with practices: Design case studies as a research framework in CSCW. In P. J. Hinds et al. (eds): *CSCW 2011: Proceedings of the ACM 2011 Conference on Computer Supported Cooperative Work, Hangzhou, China, 19–23 March 2011.* New York, NY: ACM Press, pp. 505–12.

Xenophon (*c.*362 BCE). *Oeconomicus.* Transl. E. C. Marchant. Ed. J. Henderson. In Xenophon: *Xenophon IV.* Cambridge, MA, and London: Harvard University Press, 2013, pp. 379–557. (Revised ed.; 1st ed., 1923).—Loeb Classical Library, Vol. 168.

Zilsel, Edgar (1942). The sociological roots of science. (*The American Journal of Sociology*). Text ed. by D. Raven; W. Krohn; and R. S. Cohen. In E. Zilsel: *The Social Origins of Modern Science.* Dordrecht, Boston, MA, and London: Kluwer Academic Publishers, 2003, pp. 7–21.

3 "Practice Theory"

A Critique

KJELD SCHMIDT

Areas of research such as Computer-Supported Cooperative Work (CSCW), Information Systems (IS), and Human–Computer Interaction (HCI) are, by virtue of their particular research questions, interdisciplinary: destined to bridge multiple academic disciplines, and they therefore, in a sense, must find their way beyond the conceptual and methodological sanctuaries of institutionalized conceptualizations. This is, of course, both taxing and troublesome. Researchers in such areas therefore face a constant temptation to take under consideration conceptual innovations or theories that might make it less taxing and troublesome to venture outside the disciplinary habitat. However, theories are not neutral constructs that can simply be adopted and applied—they come with serious, if implicit, assumptions and intellectual commitments. As always in theoretical affairs, it is advisable to proceed with caution.

In the case of practice-centered computing, so-called practice theory is obviously such a temptation (e.g., Schmidt 2002; Feldman and Orlikowski 2011; Schmidt 2011; Wulf et al. 2011; Kuutti and Bannon 2014) and should not be imported unexamined. The aim of this chapter is to subject this body of theory to critical scrutiny.[1]

3.1 "No Such a Thing"

First, and quite elementarily, the term "practice theory" does not refer to an actual research tradition in the normal sense of a line of research whose members conceive of their activities as contributing (in different ways) to a body of theory or knowledge, or even one that is identifiable by a history of interlocking debates as manifested in references. The term is rather used for a quite recent *post hoc construction* of a tradition. "Practice theory" is, as one of its advocates, Andreas Reckwitz (2002, p. 244), puts it,

[1] The research has been supported by the University of Siegen and by the Velux Foundation under the "Computational Artifacts" project (VELUX33295).

Socio-Informatics, Volker Wulf, Volkmar Pipek, Dave Randall, Markus Rohde, Kjeld Schmidt, Gunnar Stevens (Eds). © Oxford University Press 2018. Published 2018 by Oxford University Press.

an "ideal type," that is, an arbitrary construct.[2] The arbitrariness of the construct is obvious when one looks at which authors are included under the label, and which are excluded. Theodore Schatzki, in his book *Social Practices* (1996), enlists under the "practice theory" label especially Pierre Bourdieu and Anthony Giddens but also Michel Foucault as well as the postmodernist theorists Jean-François Lyotard, Charles Taylor, and, "to some extent," "post-Marxist" and post-structuralist philosophers such as Ernesto Laclau and Chantal Mouffe; he nevertheless draws extensively on Ludwig Wittgenstein but also calls in Martin Heidegger when not satisfied with Wittgenstein.[3] In a paper published shortly afterward (Schatzki 1997), the cast is more of less the same (with Heidegger reduced to a minor role and with the libertarian philosopher and psychoanalyst Cornelius Castoriadis thrown in). A few years later, in his introduction to the *Practice Turn* collection (2001), Schatzki again includes Bourdieu, Foucault, Giddens, Lyotard, and Taylor, and again with Wittgenstein as heavy-artillery support, but now also "the ethnomethodologists" (e.g., Lynch) and STS studies (e.g., Pickering). —Andreas Reckwitz (2002), who in this regard stays close to Schatzki, likewise includes Bourdieu, Giddens, Foucault, Garfinkel, and Taylor but then, surprisingly, adds Bruno Latour.[4]—On the other hand, Davide Nicolini (2012) expands the cast significantly by including—in addition to Bourdieu and Giddens—a wide variety of authors. He identifies among the roots of "practice theory" the work of Karl Marx, Friedrich Nietzsche, and Martin Heidegger, and (again) some peculiar reading of Wittgenstein, and he then goes on to include Jean Lave and others' work on the notion of "communities of practice," ethnomethodology, activity theory (from Lev Vygotskij to Yrjö Engeström), and Latour's "actor network theory." To render support for his account, he also, at various places, enlists authors as different as Merleau-Ponty and Michael Polanyi.

Apart from the general agreement among proponents of "practice theory" that Bourdieu, Giddens, and a few others are central figures, the picture that emerges is quite blurred. In fact, it is all over the place: On the one hand, it reads like an inventory of large parts of social thinking in the West since about 1845. That hardly supports a claim to a distinct tradition, let alone a "practice turn." On the other hand, it also it comes across

[2] An "ideal type" is an academic way of establishing a conceptual construct by positing, as defining, a selection of characteristics, the internal relations of which have not been explicated—a source of arbitrary concept construction.

[3] It is beyond the scope of this chapter to discuss it, but it should be mentioned, for the sake of clarity, that Schatzki's use of Wittgenstein is peculiar if not outright bizarre, something he himself seems to be aware of: "Wittgenstein abjured metaphysics, yet [!] his ideas on mind reflect a change in ontological proclivity. [...] [F]rom the vantage point afforded by historical distance, [Wittgenstein's] ideas can [?!] be seen as swimming in the emergent stream of process-metaphysical approaches to mind" (Schatzki 1996, p. 25). Schatzki's own characterization of his reading as "speculative interpolation" is apt (Schatzki 1996, pp. 25 ff.). However, it is here appropriate to observe that Wittgenstein's response to this urge always to go further was "The real discovery is the one that enables me to break off philosophizing when I want to" (1945–6, § 135). The reason for Schatzki's somersaults is that he is dissatisfied with Wittgenstein's analysis of normative regularity (or "rule-following") and therefore, midstream, calls on Martin Heidegger to serve as substitute philosophical underpinning (as pointed out by Baltzer 1997).

[4] Including Latour's work in "practice theory" is rather surprising since his work arguably could be seen as a systematic attempt to expel from social studies the concept of "practice" with its notion of human agency.

as an arbitrary construct in so far as a large number of scholarly works in which the concept of "practice" plays a key role is implicitly excluded. For example, why not include Marcel Mauss' reflections on "embodied techniques" (1934)? Or, in addition to Michael Polanyi, conservative thinkers such as Friedrich Hayek (1963, 1964, 1969)? Or Ludwig von Mises' "praxeology" (1949)? Or Alfred Schütz' notion of "natural attitude" and "relevance" (e.g., 1945, 1947–51, 1953)? Or Jean-Paul Sartre's *magnum opus* on "Practical Ensembles" (1960)? Or Gilbert Ryle's notion of "knowing how" and his discussion of "thick description" of human conduct (e.g., 1946, 1968)? Or Elizabeth Anscombe's analysis of the concept of "intentional action" (1957). Or Thomas Kuhn's notion of "paradigm" (1962)?

The simple but massive fact is that "practice theory" is not anything like a theory or school of thought. Rather, in the words of one of its principal advocates, Theodore Schatzki, "practice theory" is "a collection of accounts" that exhibit "considerable differences" (1996, p. 12). Or as he put it later, "there is no unified practice approach" (Schatzki 2001, p. 11; see also Reckwitz 2002, p. 244). In the words of another proponent, Davide Nicolini, "There is no such a thing as a unified practice theory"; the "approach" referred to by the term "practice theory" "does not stem from a single unified theory of practice but emerges instead from the coming together of several distinct scholarly traditions" that "comprise a complicated network of similarities and dissimilarities" (Nicolini 2012, pp. 8 f.). In short, even according to the leading proponents of "practice theory," what is proposed is not anything like a coherent body of conceptualizations. In his critical review essay, the prominent Wittgensteinian philosopher David Stern is less circumspect: "there are enormous differences between practice theorists"; in fact, " 'practice theorists' are an unusually diverse group," and there is even "considerable disagreement as to who is a practice theorist and how practice theory is to be understood" (Stern 2003, p. 186).

In short, there is no "practice theory" that practice-centered research in CSCW and related research areas could possible appropriate or build on. Or, to quote what Gertrude Stein once said of her hometown, Oakland, "there is no *there* there." There is merely a heterogeneous gathering of authors representing a motley crew of diverse conceptualizations and approaches.

3.2 And Yet, There Is Method to It

> Though this be madness, yet there is method in 't
>
> (Shakespeare, *Hamlet*, Act 2, Scene 2)

The fragmented picture notwithstanding, a common pattern of sorts can be distinguished in what is offered as "practice theory." First of all, as pointed out by Sherry Ortner in her review paper entitled "Theory in anthropology since the sixties" (1984), the movement toward focusing on "practices" can be largely seen as a "direct reaction to structuralism" that at the same time is striving to avoid "interactionism" (1984, pp. 144 ff.). And in fact, both Pierre Bourdieu (1972, 1980b) and Anthony Giddens (1979, 1984), on all accounts the founding figures, are quite explicit that they primarily strike at "objectivism" (structuralism, functionalism, Marxism) while keeping "subjectivism" (symbolic interactionism, phenomenology) in check. Later "practice theorists" such as Schatzki, Reckwitz, and Nicolini by and large take this battle order as given.

Underlying this axis of confrontation is the implicit assumption that a general "explanation" of "social order" is required and that "practice" in some shape or form is key to such an "explanation." Thus, the question to which "practice theory" is supposed to offer an answer is this: How can "social order" be explained so that, in particular, social structure and individual agency is somehow reconciled? That is, "practice theory" is to be seen as a scattering of attempts to develop a conceptualization that somehow "mediates" "objectivist" and "subjectivist" conceptualizations of social action. The different officially recognized "practice theorists" of course express such issues differently, but their different questions have the same overall architecture. For Bourdieu, to take the most notable example, the question is: "how can behaviour be regulated without being the product of obedience to rules?" (Bourdieu 1987, p. 65). More specifically, the "regularities" he wants to understand are patterns of behavior such as matrimonial preferences in pre-modern cultures, the predominant leisure activities or educational paths of working class versus middle class boys, etc., that is, regularities that "can be observed, thanks to statistics" because they are "the aggregate product of individual actions guided by the same constraints" (Bourdieu 1987, p. 65). In a similar vein, for Giddens, "The basic domain of study of the social sciences" is "practices ordered across space and time" and the challenge thus to understand "the continuity of practices that makes them distinctively 'the same' across space and time." Accordingly, the task for him is to explain the "reproduced social practices" while "resisting" "'normative' commitments" (Giddens, 1984, pp. 2–4, 17). For Ortner, the task for "a practice theory" is similarly to "explain [...] the genesis, reproduction, and change of form and meaning of a given social/cultural whole" (Ortner 1984, p. 149). And for Schatzki, finally, the job is to account for the "web of understanding and intelligibility" "underlying and connecting all the particulars populating the social world" "that establishes meanings and possibilities and thereby institutes agents while coordinating them with their milieus" (Schatzki 1996, p. 18).

Accordingly, what "practice theory" offers, or aims to offer, on Schatzki's view, is nothing short of "a general conception of social life" (Schatzki 1996, p. 12). This would make "practice theory" just another name for social theory. But in fact, it purports to offer even more than that, for in the words of Schatzki, "practice theory" encompasses "a collection of accounts that promote practices as *the* fundamental social phenomenon." The theorists he has singled out as the main representatives of "practice theory"

> agree that practices are not only pivotal objects of analysis in an account of contemporary Western society, but also *the* central social phenomenon by reference to which other social entities such as actions, institutions, and structures are to be understood. [Practice theorists] specify a particular type of entity, namely, practices, as *the* principal constitutive element in social life. [Practices are] *the* site

> where understanding is structured and intelligibility [...] articulated [...] (Schatzki 1996, pp. 11–12 [emphases added])

Schatzki's use of the definite article is noteworthy: "practices" are not only important or even fundamental "social phenomena" but are "*the* fundamental social phenomenon." To underscore that this is indeed the message, he repeats that practices are "*the* central social phenomenon." Indeed, on this view, practices are nothing less than "*the* site where understanding is structured and intelligibility articulated."

What kind of propositions are these? What status do they have? They are certainly not empirical, nor do they summarize findings from a body of empirical studies. Schatzki's propositions rather aim at expressing "a general conception of social life," that is, establishing a conceptual foundation *prior to* building a framework bottom-up from actual empirical studies, thereby providing social theorizing with an "ontological" or transcendental foundation. According to Schatzki,

> In social theory, [...] practice approaches promulgate a distinct social ontology: the social is a field of embodied, materially interwoven practices centrally organized around shared practical understandings. This conception contrasts with accounts that privilege individuals, (inter)actions, language, signifying systems, the life world, institutions/roles, structures, or systems in defining the social. These phenomena, say practice theorists, can only be analyzed via the field of practices. (Schatzki 2001, p. 12)

Similarly, in the words of Nicolini:

> Practice theories are fundamentally ontological projects in the sense that they attempt to provide a new vocabulary to describe the world and to populate the world with specific "units of analysis"; that is, practices. (Nicolini 2012, p. 9)

Schatzki and the various other authors who are typically categorized as "practice theorists" do not, in spite of the foundationalist discourse, ask the rather fundamental question: Is the notion of a "general conception of social life"—a Theory of Everything Social!—even intelligible? Does it even make sense to state that practices are "*the* fundamental social phenomenon"? Would it, to take an analogy, make sense to try to establish "a general conception" of, say, *materiality*, in contrast to the manifold conceptions developed in the various specialized natural sciences (from particle physics, to chemistry, to microbiology, to geology, to vertebrate zoology, to ecology), or, for that matter, would it make sense to say that, say, quarks are "*the* fundamental phenomenon" of materiality?

The point is that "practice theory," as initiated by Bourdieu and Giddens and today represented by, for example, Schatzki, Reckwitz, and Nicolini, is not an attempt to build a theory or conceptual framework through careful comparative analysis of studies, through cautious abstraction and reasoned generalization, but rather deals in metaphysical stipulation. The various theorists are united in proposing "ontologies," competing ones, of course, but ones that nevertheless have in common that "practice" is posited at the center of the (social) universe.

3.3 The Generative Scheme of "Practice Theory": The Case of Bourdieu

Given that the "practice theory" outlined by Pierre Bourdieu is emblematic of the fabled "practice turn," let us, for the sake of brevity, focus on his contribution.[5]

As noted, the question for Bourdieu is "how can behaviour be regulated without being the product of obedience to rules?" (Bourdieu 1987, p. 65). That is, Bourdieu rejects as a fallacy the notion of "following a rule" in the sense of "a rule that governs, directs, or orients behaviour," because this "presupposes that it is known and recognized, and can therefore be stated." Such a notion of practice, conceived of as normatively constituted, is not only rejected by Bourdieu but vehemently condemned as amounting to nothing less than "succumbing to the most elementary form of legalism, that variety of finalism which is perhaps the most widespread of the spontaneous theories of practice and which consists in proceeding as if practices had as their principle conscious obedience to consciously devised and sanctioned rules" (Bourdieu 1980a, pp. 67 f.; 1980b, pp. 39–40).[6] According to Bourdieu, practices "have as their principle not a set of conscious and constant rules, but practical *schemes, opaque to their possessors*, varying according to the logic of the situation, the almost invariably partial viewpoint which it imposes, etc." (1980a, p. 26; 1980b, p. 12 [emphasis added]).

In Bourdieu, that is, the source of social order is not rational practical conduct of which actors are aware in as much as they can offer justifications or accept sanctions, but "the deep-rooted schemes of the habitus" (1980a, p. 16; 1980b, p. 6), and, like Polanyi's notion of "tacit knowledge" (1958, 1966), the "schemes" are unknown and unknowable to actors (e.g., 1980a, pp. 26, 28 f., 90–2, 115 f., 122 f.; 1980b, pp. 12–14, 54 f., 68 f., 72 f.). This is foundational for Bourdieu. Social order is "the product of the age-old application of the same schemes of action and perception that, because they have never been constituted as explicit principles, can only produce an unwilled necessity that is therefore necessarily imperfect but also a little miraculous" (1980a, p. 28; 1980b, p. 13).

On this view, action is *either* performed in "conscious obedience to consciously devised and sanctioned rules," *or* it is the enacted manifestation of "schemes" that are "opaque to their possessors":

> The conditionings associated with a particular class of conditions of existence produce *habitus*, systems of durable and transposable *dispositions*, structured structures predisposed to function as structuring structures, that is, as generative and organizing principles of practices and representations that can be objectively adapted to their goal *without presupposing a conscious intentions or an express mastery of the operations*

[5] After all, according to Ortner, Bourdieu can be seen as having triggered the so-called practice turn: "An English translation of Bourdieu's book was published in 1978, and it was at about that time that the calls for a more practice-oriented approach became increasingly audible" (Ortner 1984, p. 145).

[6] Bourdieu's main theoretical work, *Le sens pratique* (1980), is rather hermetic, and its English translation (1980b) unfortunately even more so. In quoting this work I therefore have amended the translation extensively. All references to this work are to both editions.

> *necessary in order to attain them*; objectively "regulated" and "regular" without being in any way the product of obedience to rules, they can be collectively *orchestrated without being the product of the organizing action of a conductor*. (Bourdieu 1980a, pp. 88 f.; 1980b, p. 53 [emphasis added])

Accordingly, "practice" is not the central concept in Bourdieu's "theory of practice." To the contrary, and in spite of the ambition to overcome the duality of "objectivism" and "subjectivism," of structure and action, in Bourdieu's thinking, practices are structured *behind the backs of actors* by "the *habitus*," that is, by "an acquired system of generative schemes" (1980a, p. 92; 1980b, p. 55), that is, embodied schemes of action and perception and of thought and expression that are somehow "internalized" and that, in turn, are produced by the conditions of existence:

> A product of history, the *habitus produces practices, individual and collective*, and thus historical, that conform with the schemes generated by history; it ensures the active presence of past experiences that are deposited in each organism in the form of schemes of perception, thought and action and tend to guarantee, more reliably than all the formal rules and explicit norms, the conformity of practices and their constancy over time. [...] As an acquired system of generative schemes, the habitus makes possible the free production of all the thoughts, all the perceptions, and all the actions inherent in the particular conditions of its production — and only those. *Through the habitus, the structure of which it is the product governs practice*, not along the paths of a mechanical determinism, but within the constraints and limits initially set on its inventions. (Bourdieu, 1980a, pp. 91 f.; 1980b, pp. 54 f. [emphases added])

The "habitus," an "immanent law" "inscribed in bodies by identical histories," is "the precondition not only for the co-ordination of practices but also for practices of co-ordination" (Bourdieu 1980a, p. 98; 1980b, p. 59), and as such it is the source of social order:

> Practical sense, social necessity turned nature, converted into motor schemes and bodily automatisms, is what makes practices, in and through what makes them obscure to the eyes of their producers and indeed betrays the trans-subjective principles of their production, *sensible*, that is, informed by a common sense. It is because agents never know completely what they are doing that what they do has more sense than they know. (Bourdieu 1980a, p. 116 ; 1980b, p. 69)

Where structuralism and functionalism, according to Bourdieu, posit social "structure" as the generic explanation of the social order that manifests itself in practices, Bourdieu interjects a mediating agency, namely, the "habitus": "the structure" produces "schemes" that in turn constitute the "habitus" which then in turn "governs" "practice" and hence the observed regularity of behavior (Bourdieu 1980a, p. 98; 1980b, p. 59).

Now, what *are* these "schemes"? What do they consist *of*? How are they *produced*? How is their integrity or homology ensured across time and space (and bodies): are they somehow transmitted like a genetic code? How do they *work*? How do they, as "generative schemes," *generate* patterns of conduct? Are they *made* to work by some agency and, if so, *which* and *how*? Or are they a kind of automata that, once implemented ("internalized"), tick away, controlled by some code "inscribed" in the "scheme," and, if so, how do they—the "schemes"—manage to do so in such a flexible manner that the contingencies of the environment are—"miraculously"—taken into account and *social order* produced? But, and this is a big "but," might whatever agency or mechanism that makes the "schemes" work not just as well generate *random* behavior? Why not? Because the "schemes" are produced by "the structure"? Very well, but then we are surely going in circles.

And in fact, of course, "generative schemes," as well as the "system of generative schemes" Bourdieu calls "*habitus*," are not only hypothetical constructs. These "schemes" cannot be observed and described *independently* of their presumptive effects on behavioral regularities across time and space. They are nevertheless granted explanatory power over precisely the regularities of human behavior. Such explanations, predicated on constructs that cannot be inspected or described independently of what they are supposed to explain, are occult; they are in their architecture related to mythical thinking.[7] The circularity of the argument is a symptom of that. And in fact, Bourdieu later admitted to have been "keenly aware" "all along" of the "danger" of circular argumentation (Bourdieu and Wacquant 1992, p. 129). But as Karl Maton dryly comments, "vigilance is one thing, a conceptual means of avoiding the possibility of circularity is another" (Maton 2008, p. 64).

3.4 The Challenge of Normative Regularity

It is an underlying common theme in "practice theory" that it abjures the ordinary use of the term "practice," predicated on the Modern concept of "practice," by openly and sometimes even passionately evicting the notion of normative regularity from the account of the concept of "practice."

Bourdieu is quite direct, or simply reckless, in that he rejects the very notion of "a rule that governs, directs, or orients behaviour," because this "presupposes that it is known and recognized, and can therefore be stated" (Bourdieu 1980a, pp. 67 f.; 1980b, pp. 39–40) and instead stipulates that practices "have as their principle not a set of conscious and constant rules, but practical schemes, opaque to their possessors" (1980a, p. 26; 1980b, p. 12). In Bourdieu, then, the very notion of normative governance of behavior has been barred from "practice theory."

In contrast, Giddens uses the term "rules" quite happily, albeit in two different senses, as he makes a distinction between "formulated rules," that is, "codified interpretations of rules" on the one hand, and on the other hand, "rules as such" or "rules in general," of which "formulated rules" are merely "specific types" (Giddens 1984, pp. 21 f.). That is, "Most of the rules implicated in the production and reproduction of social practices are

[7] Bourdieu's argumentation has striking affinities with cognitivism (in this case, most likely that of Piagetian provenance; cf. Lizardo 2004). And as with cognitivist theorizing in general, where deus ex machina constructs such as "demons," "schemes," "frames," "plans," etc., have played roles functionally equivalent to that of "schemes" in Bourdieu, the circularity of the argument is unmistakable.

only tacitly grasped by actors: they know how to 'go on' " (1984, pp. 22 f.). What Giddens promulgates, then, is a notion of "rules" that are "tacitly grasped by actors," that is, "social rules expressed first and foremost in practical consciousness" and as such "not accessible" to "discursive consciousness," in short, "rules" that actors are unable to "access" and "formulate." We are, in other words, led to believe that actors generally act in accordance with "tacit" "social rules" that they nonetheless are unable to "formulate." On this view, actors act in accordance with "rules," but since they are unable to "access" and "formulate" these rules, they would also be unable to explain or justify their conduct with reference to "rules" or, for that matter, receive instructions or accept reprimands. In sum, when Giddens is talking about "the rules implicated in the production and reproduction of social practices," he is merely stating that actors generally somehow act in a regular manner. We are led in a circle again.

Schatzki's position on rule-following is more equivocal. His overall position is this:

> Whatever abilities to go on intelligibly out of which people nonverbally proceed likewise cannot be exhaustively formulated in words. [...] The abilities to go on nonverbally that are evidenced in both actions and judgments of intelligibility and correctness cannot be adequately reproduced in linguistic formulations. [...] Knowing how to act cannot be laid out in explicit formulations. [...] It is far better to renounce the idea that rules and meanings guide or determine language use and instead allow future reflection to be guided by the idea of unformulable understandings — wherever this may lead. From this perspective, rules and meanings are really only ex post facto attempts to recoup past usage. (Schatzki 1996, pp. 50 f.)

Schatzki goes on to stress that "To follow a rule is to use language, as it is normally used, in those domains of usage where significant regularity exist." Thus, "to say that language is rule governed is simply to say that it is regular" (1996, p. 216, n. 34). In short, like Giddens, he reduces rule-following to mere regularity, thereby dismissing any notion that an action can be erroneous, untimely, unsuccessful, failed, or a violation. On the other hand, however, in a later chapter in the same book, he says that "the entirety of a practice's organization is normative" in the sense of "oughtness or rightness":

> The understandings, rules, and teleoaffective structure that organize a practice specify how actions (including speech acts) ought to be carried out, understood, prompted, and responded to; what specifically and unequivocally should be done or said (when, where...); and which ends should be pursued, which projects, tasks, and actions carried out for that end, and which emotions possessed — when, that is, one is engaged in the practice. (ibid., p. 101)

He even articulates the methodological implication of the normative constitution of practices: "Evidence for a practice's organization is thus found in the presence and absence of corrective, remonstrative, and punishing behaviors and in the verbal and nonverbal injunctions, encouragements, and instructions whereby neophytes are brought into line" (ibid.). The contradiction seems to dissolve when he goes on to insist that normative organization of practices is based on "not fully formulable understandings of how to react and respond" and that even "more complex activities governed by explicit rules also are governed by unformulable understandings." But only apparently, for we are asked to accept that it is intelligible to say that practices may be "normatively" "organized" while "understandings of how to react and respond" are "not fully formulable" or "unformulable." How could a practice be *normatively organized* if actors are unable to justify their conduct?—Why would Schatzki get into such gross incoherence? He offers an answer of sorts when he adds that "Insistence on the omnipresence of rules threatens to obscure" "the unformulability of understandings" (ibid, pp. 102 f.). In "practice theory" commitment to the "tacit knowledge" mythology runs very deep indeed.

In short, "practice theory" offers accounts of the concept of practice in which the notion of normative regularity is either absent or outright rejected. This is quite remarkable, indeed, since Wittgenstein, according to Schatzki, is "the thinker who perhaps focused more intensely than anyone else on how practices carry understanding and intelligibility" and his work "harbors a seminal analysis of practices with significant implications for the constitution of the individual and the nature of sociality" (Schatzki 1996, pp. 12 f.), and since "practice theorists," in different ways but always at key points in their expositions, draw on Wittgenstein's investigation of normative regularity (or "rule-following") in their investigations (cf., e.g., Giddens 1979, pp. 4, 33–8, 41, 49 f. 67 f.; Bourdieu 1980a, pp. 43, 66 f.; 1980b, pp. 27, 39; Giddens 1984, pp. 18 f., 20 f.; Schatzki 1996, pp. 50 f, 101 ff., et passim; 1997; Reckwitz 2002).

That is, "practice theorists" have obviously felt that Wittgenstein's investigations into the normative regularity of our practices are somehow crucial and that they either support a rule-skepticist account of practices (as in Bourdieu) or that they fall short (as in Giddens and Schatzki). In my view, however, whatever their differences, the different varieties of "practice theory" break down right here: on the notion of the normative regularity of practices. In the remainder of this chapter, I will therefore examine the main issues where "practice theory" founders. In doing so, I will draw extensively on Wittgenstein's account of normative regularity—not in order to show that these theorists' readings of his work are flawed or even outrageous (which they are) but in order to overcome common conceptual puzzlements and bring out some conceptual observations and clarifications that crucially relevant for empirical studies of work practices.[8]

In their discussion of normative regularity, the different versions of "practice theory" make several interlaced but fatally flawed assumptions. (a) They presume that the identification and determination of their phenomenon, "practices," is unproblematic, as if "practices" somehow can be seen wandering about in the streets wearing placards

[8] I will be using P. M. S. Hacker and J. Schulte's revised translation of Wittgenstein's *Philosophical Investigations* (1945–6, published 2009) together with manuscripts MS 164 (1941–4b) and MS 124 (1941–4a, §§ 24 ff.), which are published as Parts VI and VII of the *Remarks on the Foundations of Mathematics* ([1937–44a, originally published in 1956 and revised in 1978), as they contain some very illuminating additional discussions of "rule-following."—Quotes from the English translation of *Remarks*... have been checked against the German manuscripts (MS 124 and MS 164) in the Bergen Electronic Edition of Wittgenstein's *Nachlass* (Wittgenstein 1998), and I have amended the translation (mostly modestly).—The following discussion is indebted to a range of outstanding Wittgensteinian studies (in particular Minar 1986; Williams 1999, 2010; Minar 2011). (For excellent introductions, see, e.g., Stern 2004; McGinn 2013).

saying, "I'm a practice," "I'm another practice," and so on. They simply, and utterly naively, ignore the fundamental methodological issue of *criteria of sameness*. (b) They are all, in different ways, committed to the mythology of "tacit knowledge" and, accordingly, trade in the transcendental notion that a "rule" should, or could, be "explicit" (or "exhaustive") in and of itself, that is: absolutely "explicit" (or "exhaustive"). The notion of normative regularity is thereby emptied of content and meaning, leaving us with a notion of "schemes" or "rules" that are inaccessible to or inexpressible by practitioners and thus with an account of regularity in which there is no room for "practitioners" explaining or justifying their actions with reference to "rules." (c) They thus assimilate "practice" with "recurrent behavior" or "routine" and confound the notion of "following a rule" with that of "mere regularity". (d) In accordance with these puzzlements, they confuse the concept of "rule" and that of "rule formulation" or "expression of a rule.".

3.4.1 The Problem of "Sameness"

> The use of the word "rule" and the use of the word "same" are interwoven.
>
> (Wittgenstein, 1945–6, *Philosophical Investigations* § 225)

It is a tacit presumption of "practice theory" that it is unproblematic and even trivial to identify practices and to determine whether or not a multitude of activities are instances of the same practice.

Addressing the issue of what constitutes social order, Bourdieu, for instance, proclaims that the "coherence without apparent intention and the unity without an immediately visible unifying principle of all the cultural realities [...] are the product of the age-old application of the same schemes of action and perception" (1980a, p. 28; 1980b, p. 13). "Coherence" of what? "Unity" of what? The "*same* schemes"? According to which criteria? He likewise uses expressions such as "the same schemes of perception and action," "the same schemes of thought," "the same habitus," "homologous habitus," and "homogeneity of habitus" (1980a, pp. 28 f., 93 f., 97 f.; 1980b, pp. 13 f., 55 f., 58)—without pausing for a moment to clarify or even consider what entitles him or any analyst to categorize activities, dispositions, thoughts, or schemes as so many instances of "the same."

Strikingly similar carefree language is found in Giddens when he, for example, talks about the "continuity of practices" that "makes [practices] distinctively "the same" across space and time" (1984, p. 3).[9] The later "practice theorists" continue this untroubled pattern. Davide Nicolini, for example, advocates "practice theory" on the ground that it supports comparing activities but does not disclose what the required criterion of sameness might be (Nicolini 2012, pp. 221 f.).

Alfred Reckwitz, however, has a little more to say about this. In "practice theory," he says, a "practice" is understood as a "routinized, oversubjective complex," "a routinized type of behaviour," "a way of" doing something, "a pattern," or "a type of behaving":

[9] As the quote shows, Giddens surpasses even Bourdieu in circular argumentation, by showing complete disregard for tautological propositions: "continuity of practices [...] makes them distinctively 'the same' across space and time."

> A "practice" (*Praktik*) is a routinized type of behaviour which consists of several elements, interconnected to one other: forms of bodily activities, forms of mental activities, "things" and their use, a background knowledge in the form of understanding, know-how, states of emotion and motivational knowledge. A practice — a way of cooking, of consuming, of working, of investigating, of taking care of oneself or of others, etc. — forms so to speak a "block" whose existence necessarily depends on the existence and specific interconnectedness of these elements, and which cannot be reduced to any one of these single elements. Likewise, a practice represents a pattern which can be filled out by a multitude of single and often unique actions reproducing the practice (a certain way of consuming goods can be filled out by plenty of actual acts of consumption). The single individual — as a bodily and mental agent — then acts as the "carrier" (*Träger*) of a practice [...]. Thus, she or he is not only a carrier of patterns of bodily behaviour, but also of certain routinized ways of understanding, knowing how and desiring [...] A practice is thus a routinized way in which bodies are moved, objects are handled, subjects are treated, things are described and the world is understood. To say that practices are "social practices" then is indeed a tautology: A practice is social, as it is a "type" of behaving and understanding that appears at different locales and at different points of time and is carried out by different body/minds. (Reckwitz 2002, pp. 249 f.)

It certainly makes sense to say that we use the term "a practice" to refer to a set of particular activities as being of the *same* "type" by invoking some more or less specific or explicit criteria for inclusion of those particular activities in the given "type." But no such criterion is given or suggested. When Reckwitz "invites us to regard agents as carriers of routinized, oversubjective complexes of bodily movements," etc., which criteria would be applied to determine which of the endless array of observable "bodily movements" are to be included in these "complexes"? On what grounds would "practice theory" determine that "behaving" that "appears at different locales and at different points of time and is carried out by different body/minds" is of *the same* "type"? What is the criterion for saying that *this* particular sequence of action is of the same "type" or is part of the same "routine" or "pattern" as *that* one? What is *the criterion of sameness*?—Is lying on one's knees praying some divinity for salvation of the same "type" as kowtowing before one's ruler pleading for promotion or as laying floors while praying tacitly that it soon be time to get up and go home? Why? Or why not?—The point is that we can categorize activities into "types" in endless ways: activities performed by the same person, by employees with the same firm, by people of the same occupation or profession, or by people of the same ethnicity; but also activities using the same tools, occurring in the same place or time period, involving the same bodily postures or movements, or having the same outcome; as well as activities in which people are serious or are having fun, in which actors perspire profusely or do not, and so on. But would any of these criteria be considered defining of "practices"? Why? Or why not?

Theoreticians may want to categorize activities into "types" as they please. But no, the criterion of "sameness" is internally related to the given research question. To an ergonomist, for example, the overriding concern is that of the effects on the human body of different postures and movements. From that perspective, the criterion of, say, *kneeling* is that both knees touch the ground and that most of the weight of the body is transferred to the knee caps, and the rationale of this is that prolonged kneeling may lead to musculoskeletal disorders, irrespective of whether the posture is assumed in the context of gardening or laying floors, for purposes of political or religious submission, or as a technique of torture. But for persons who assume these *ergonomically practically identical* bodily postures as a feature of their daily lives, kneeling is part of *categorially different types* of activity: different *practices*.

This is the crux of the matter. The problem of "sameness" is a vital practical issue for practitioners, and it is an issue they deal with routinely every day, as they recognize an activity as an instance of the practice they are engaged in or otherwise depend on, or for that matter, ignore it, disregard it, or even reject it, as the case may be: "Whether and how activity embodies this or that practice is a live issue for members" (Llewellyn and Spence 2009, p. 1421). It is a problem normally dealt with as a matter of routine, typically implicitly; but doubt may occasionally arise, of course, and then the issue of whether this or that act belongs to a given practice may become articulated and require negotiation.

Consequently, if we, as observers and analysts, are to understand a specific practice, we first of all have to understand how practitioners themselves determine what is considered part of that practice and what is not. If we did not do that, our findings would be as meaningless as those of a feckless ethnographer who, tasked with studying practices of expressing religious submission, would include floor layers and carpet fitters in his study. As observers and analysts of *practices*, we are in a situation comparable to that of practitioners themselves, in that we can—and indeed, *must*—employ the same criteria in identifying activities as instances of a given practice (cf. Winch 1958; Bittner 1965; Pitkin 1972).

An example. Two persons are facing each other over a chessboard, taking turns moving chessmen from square to square. What would make these moves part of the practice of playing chess? I suggest that we would consider the activity an instance of playing chess if we were to observe that the players have made arrangements to play a game and, as a matter of course, have gone through the appropriate steps such as, for instance, fetching the board, drawing lot, arranging the pieces; that their moves generally are in accordance with the official rules of chess, that it, should an apparently illegal move be made, would give rise to protests and justifications or excuses; and, of course, that there are indications (e.g., expressions of grief or glee) that the persons are playing to win and not merely making idle but formally legal moves. That is, we would say that the observed activity is an instance of the practice of playing chess if there is evidence that actors are committed to a set of rules, conventions, norms, etc. and have all the air of those who know what they are doing and why. And we would do so and be entitled to do so because those are the same criteria the players themselves would be employing as they recognize moves as legitimate, interesting, fateful, etc. and the very same criteria one of the players might apply by saying, for example, "Stop fooling around! We're playing chess, right?"—On the other hand, if the exquisite hand-carved wooden chessmen they have been using until this point are replaced by plastic pieces, they and we would still call the match an instance of the practice of playing chess, for the material substance of the chessmen is not normally defining of the practice of playing chess. This is how we ordinarily use the term "practice" and the criterion of determining inclusion. And the *criterion of sameness* is here, again, the same as the one employed by actors, namely, their being accountable in accordance with the rules of the game, with its very point: *playing to win.*

In short, for practitioners, the general principles to which they are committed in performing their activities and that provide the criteria of valid procedure and outcome also provide, at the very same time, the criteria of what counts as doing *the same* and for determining which activities and aspects are to be considered relevant.

"Practice theorists" set out to *explain* social order: the very regularity of human conduct. In doing so, by describing human conduct *as regular,* they have already attributed some orderliness according to some criterion of sameness. Moreover, in latching on to "practices" as the key to the explanation, "practice theorists" already, from the very beginning, *presume* the order they want to explain, namely, the fact that actors in their daily activities strive to conduct their affairs in an orderly manner and are able to "go on" in ways they take to be "*the same.*" In short, "practice theorists" *presume* from the outset the very same normative regularities we all, practitioners and observers alike, ordinarily characterize as *practices.*

3.4.2 Mere Regularity versus Normative Regularity

> 'When I say: "If you follow the rule, this *must* come out," that doesn't mean: it must, because it always has. Rather, that it comes out is one of my *foundations.*
> What must come out is a foundation of judgment, which I do not touch.'
>
> (Wittgenstein, 1937–44a, *Remarks*... VI § 46; 1941–4b, MS 164, p. 141)

For all practice-theoretical purposes, Bourdieu and later "practice theorists" disregard or even emphatically discard the distinction we in our daily lives make between *mere regularity* of behavior on the one hand (statistical correlations showing, say, differential suicide rates) and on the other the *normative regularity* of conduct that is exhibited in actors' acting in ways that actors explain and justify by reference to criteria, principles, and techniques that they have learned to apply. To put it very simply, "A rule differs from a mere regularity in being something to be followed, where non-compliance is not mere irregularity but error" (Heal 1986, p. 417).

Let us first of all consider Wittgenstein's attempt to clarify the distinction between mere regularity and normative regularity. During the Second World War, he wrote in a set of pocket notebooks devoted to his critical discussion of the philosophy of mathematics:

> There might of course be a caveman who produced *regular* sequences of marks for himself. He amused himself, e.g., by drawing on the wall of the cave: [...]
>
> —.—..—...—....—
>
> But he is not following the general expression of a rule. And we do not say that he acts in a regular way because we can form such an expression. (Wittgenstein 1937–4a, VI § 41; 1941–4b, p. 123)

Although the caveman produces regular sequences of marks (much like a "thrush always repeats the same phrase several times in its song"), we would not say that the caveman (or the thrush) is following a rule just because *we* can formulate such a rule. It takes more, namely that some "general expression of a rule" is being followed.

> Let us consider very simple rules. Let the expression of the rule be a figure, say this one:
>
> |— —|
>
> and one follows the rule by drawing a straight sequence of such figures (for example as an ornament).
>
> |— —| |— —| |— —| |— —| |— —|
>
> Under what circumstances would we say: by writing down such a figure, somebody is giving a rule? And under what circumstances: someone is following this rule when he draws this sequence? (Wittgenstein 1937–44a, VI § 42, 1941–4b, pp. 125 f.).

Under what circumstances? Conceding that "It is difficult to describe this," he presents a few thought examples:

> If one of a pair of chimpanzees once scratched the figure |— —| in the soil and thereupon the other the series |— —| |— —| etc., the first would not have given a rule nor would the other be following it, *whatever* else went on at the same time in the mind of the two of them.
>
> However, if one observed, for example, the phenomenon of a kind of instruction, of showing and imitating, of successful and unsuccessful attempts, of reward and punishment and the like; if at length the one who had been so trained put figures which he had never seen before one after another in sequence as in the first example, then we should probably say that the one chimpanzee was writing down rules which the other was following. (Wittgenstein 1937–44a, VI § 42; 1941–4b, pp. 126 f.)

The point is that "What, in a complicated surrounding, we call 'following a rule,' we should certainly not call that if it stood in isolation" (Wittgenstein 1937–44a, VI § 33; 1941–4b, p. 98). In short, " 'following a rule' is a practice" (Wittgenstein 1945–6, § 202). And "practices" are not merely identified by someone's acting in regular ways, exhibiting mere regularity in his or her conduct, but are complex activities grounded in instruction and training, in practicing and failing and learning from mistakes, in issuing and accepting positive and negative sanctions, etc. We say that someone is following a rule if it makes sense to say that he or she does this or that correctly, timely, adequately, etc.; has reached the goal, met the standard, accomplished the task. Or, on the other hand, we say that he or she has failed to follow the rule if it makes sense to say that he or she made a mistake, was late, failed, bungled up. Accordingly, following a rule is not a mental act, whether "perfectly conscious" or not. Thus, immediately after the passage quoted above, Wittgenstein addresses that very issue, asking: "But suppose that already the first time the one chimpanzee had *intended* to repeat this procedure so as to instruct the other?" And he answers firmly: "Someone can only intend something in an existing technique of acting, speaking, thinking" (Wittgenstein 1937–44a, VI §43, —translation amended; 1941–4b, p. 128).[10]

"For only through a technique can we *grasp* [*begreifen*] a regularity" (Wittgenstein 1937–44a, VI § 2; 1941–4b, p. 1).

3.4.3 The Ghost of "Tacit Knowledge" in "Practice Theory"

> When I have been taught the rule [...] and now I have been told "Go on like that": how do I know what I have to do the next time? — Well, I do it with certainty, I shall also know how to defend what I do — — that is, up to a certain point. If that does not count as a defence then there is none.'
>
> (Wittgenstein 1937–44a, *Remarks*... VI § 29; 1941–4b, MS 164, pp. 83 f.)

"Practice theory" is rooted in the mythology of "tacit knowledge." Bourdieu, for example, advances the spurious requirement that for a rule to be said to be followed, it must be not only "known and recognized" and therefore able to "be stated" but also "perfectly conscious," "constant," and "explicit" (1980a, pp. 26, 28, 91; 1980b, pp. 12, 13, 54). He even demands that for practitioners to be said to be able to follow rules, they must exhibit nothing less than "conscious obedience to consciously devised and sanctioned rules" (1980a, p. 67; 1980b, p. 39). The upshot of this requirement is, as we have seen, that Bourdieu rejects the notion of the normativity of practices (*the very notion* of "a rule that governs, directs, or orients behaviour") and instead stipulates that practices "have as their principle not a set of conscious and constant rules, but practical schemes, *opaque to their possessors*" (1980a, p. 26; 1980b, p. 12).

Giddens makes a parallel argument by positing that "practical consciousness" cannot be formulated by practitioners but rather is to be understood as "tacit knowledge that is skillfully applied in the enactment of courses of conduct, but which the actor is not able to formulate discursively" (Giddens 1979, p. 57,—cf. also pp. 6 f., 64 f.; and Giddens 1984, pp. 6, 16–23, 30). In short, "practical consciousness" is "not accessible to the discursive consciousness of actors" (Giddens 1984, p. 4). And as noted above, in Giddens the notion of "tacit" "practical consciousness" extends to "rules" that are "tacitly grasped by actors," that is, "social rules expressed first and foremost in practical consciousness" and as such "not accessible" to "discursive consciousness," in short, "rules" that actors are unable to "access" and "formulate" (1984, pp. 21 f.): "Most of the rules implicated in the production and reproduction of social practices are only tacitly grasped by actors: they know how to 'go on'" (1984, pp. 22 f.). We are, in other words, led to believe that actors generally follow "tacit rules" that they are unable to "formulate" and thus cannot cite or appeal to in justifications or sanctions.

[10] It is of some significance that Wittgenstein after the last sentence adds, in parentheses, "This 'can' is the grammatical 'can,'" meaning that the sentence "Someone can only intend something in an existing technique of acting, speaking, thinking" is not a psychological or sociological proposition but a *logical* one: a proposition about the role of the concept of "intending" in our conceptual scheme.

Schatzki also adopts a "tacit knowledge" strategy when he posits that

> Whatever abilities to go on intelligibly out of which people nonverbally proceed likewise cannot be exhaustively formulated in words. [...] The abilities to go on nonverbally that are evidenced in both actions and judgments of intelligibility and correctness cannot be adequately reproduced in linguistic formulations. [...] Knowing how to act cannot be laid out in explicit formulations. [...] It is far better to renounce the idea that rules and meanings guide or determine language use and instead allow future reflection to be guided by the idea of unformulable understandings — wherever this may lead. From this perspective, rules and meanings are really only ex post facto attempts to recoup past usage. (Schatzki 1996, pp. 51 f.)

Schatzki restates and, if possible, sharpens these propositions in an article published shortly after: "understandings of words cannot be fully presented in the form of explicit formulations." Similarly, in the case of "explicit rules," "Knowing how to use any such expression cannot be made fully explicit. But these considerations also apply to human activity at large: knowing how to proceed nonverbally likewise cannot be exhaustively formulated in words." Or even without qualification: "knowing how to act cannot be laid out in words." In sum, "knowing how to go on is a mastery of ways of speaking and acting that defies adequate representation in words, symbols, diagrams, or pictures" (Schatzki 1997, pp. 296, 299).

This entire line of argumentation trades on introducing—surreptitiously, as it were—the *absolutist* and hence metaphysical *criterion* that "rules" must be "explicit," "fully explicit," "fully presented," "adequate," " 'perfectly conscious,' and "consciously devised and sanctioned," or "exhaustively" "or adequately" "formulated" for us legitimately to say that actors are guided by them in their actions. But what does this even mean? —Consider an example. While driving home, listening attentively to the radio news, I stop for a red light at an intersection. We would ordinarily say that, by stopping at this point, I am obeying the rules of the traffic code, but according to Bourdieu, I am not, for in my stopping, while listening to the radio, I am not "perfectly conscious" of the rule. So, in order to be following a rule, on this view, I would presumably have to think of the rule, and nothing but the rule, at any point in time. But what then about the rules I have learned for how to operate the brake and wheel in order to bring the car to a full stop safely and cautiously? Can I be "perfectly conscious" of all those rules at the same time? In fact, in which sense of "perfectly conscious" can I be "perfectly conscious" of the rules of traffic lights while actually operating a car moving at, say, 50 km per hour in central Copenhagen while avoiding swarms of itinerant bicyclists, watching for jay-walking pedestrians, and, of course, other cars? Something fishy is going on in this argumentation. And what is fishy is that Bourdieu, in fact, presumes that what goes on in my mind *as I act* is constitutive of whether or not I am following a rule. Is it even intelligible to say, as does Bourdieu, that the criterion of following a rule is that the actor is "perfectly conscious" of it? If I am "perfectly conscious" of the rule but do not stop for red, am I then following the rule—merely by virtue of being "perfectly conscious" of it? Or am I violating it in spite of my being "perfectly conscious" of it? This is certainly not how our concept of acting in accordance with (or in violation of) a rule works!—Again, I stop the car, safely, at the intersection, and a passenger who has been sleeping in the back seat wakes up and asks "Why have you stopped?", and I say "There's a red light." Is my saying this not sufficient evidence that I am following the rule, even if I did not give the traffic code any thought while driving and listening to the news, or even if I, in accounting for having stopped, do not recite the relevant sections of the traffic code, word by word? Or, if I should happen to be absentminded and cross the intersection when the light has already turned yellow, and my passenger says "Uh-oh," and if I then say "Hmm, sorry!", is my accepting his inarticulate reproach not sufficient indication that I am well aware of the rule?

Similarly, take Bourdieu's requirement that rules be "explicit" to be considered operative, or Schatzki's that they be "exhaustively formulated in words" or his postulate that "Knowing how to act cannot be laid out in explicit formulations." What does *that* mean? The traffic code is surely "explicit" in as much as it is written text, but does a written text not sometimes give cause for doubt and require interpretation? Is that not why there are lawyers and judges and teachers and tutors in this world? The traffic code anyway only stipulates that drivers must stop for a red light, with the qualification that the vehicle must be brought to a stop in such a way as not to cause anxiety or alarm, and so on. But it does not stipulate, for instance, a specific rate of deceleration as a function of speed and distance. Does that make it any less "explicit"?—Again, the theoreticians are tormenting a concept from ordinary language. When we say that some expression is "explicit," we are simply saying that whatever is being expressed is sufficiently clear in the context in which it is being uttered. If a friend of mine asks me "Do you want a beer?", and I nod, then I am *perfectly explicit* even without having said a single word. The word "explicit" is not synonymous with "written," "formalized," or "codified," and to say that a rule is "explicit" merely means that it, for a given purpose in given situation for competent actors, does not give rise to doubt and call for interpretation. This is how words such as "explicit," "complete," "exhaustive," and "adequate" are ordinarily used. To say that a rule formulation, for instance, the one stating the rule of bringing the car safely to a stop when approaching an intersection, is not "explicit" etc. is unintelligible if there in actual practice is no doubt about its application among relevant parties and if actors, when prompted, justify their conduct or accept sanctions with reference to that rule. But not only are "practice theorists" tormenting ordinary language. They make some astonishing argumentative moves.

First, when, for instance, Schatzki states that "knowing how to use any such expression ["explicit rules"] cannot be made fully explicit," what is then being compared with what? Is he not comparing "knowing how" with "explicit rules"? If so, he is making statements about "knowing how" that presume that he, by some extraordinary gift, is able to give a description of what according to him "cannot be made fully explicit," which he then compares with "explicit rules"—only to conclude that the latter are not up to the task. But "What we cannot speak about we must pass over in silence" (Wittgenstein 1922, § 7).

Second, Bourdieu's "opaque" "generative schemes" and the "tacit" "rules" of Giddens and Schatzki are granted incredible and, in fact, unbelievable powers. These constructs are not only supposed to generate regularity in individual behavior but also, and this is what is so awesome, to produce "regularity" and "continuity" across individuals distributed in time and space. They never provide anything like an account of how this is supposed to happen (apart from self-defeating references to the "structures" that "structure" schemes and rules). The question then is, how do they make themselves believe in this "miracle"? Stephen Turner suggests an answer to that in the conclusion of his critique of "practice theory,"

> 'the idea of a tacit common possession, something that is itself not a text, fact or event — a "hidden collective object" shared among a certain set of persons — seems to be a plausible hypothesis. The plausibility depends on analogies to "public" things, like articulated beliefs, facts and texts. The terms for this kind of collective non-public possession, such as tacit knowledge, rely directly on these analogies. The non-public things have effects or causal powers like those of things that are themselves explicit and public. (Turner 1994, p. 102)[11]

This is a very astute observation: "The plausibility depends on analogies to 'public' things." Bourdieu's notion of "schemes" and Giddens' related notion of "practical consciousness" both subscribe to a notion of "tacit knowledge" that is somehow "shared."[12] This notion in turn relies on a picture of, especially, inscribed objects (text, formulas, tables, diagrams, drawings, photos) that derive their practical integrity and efficacy from the fact that they are "public" in the sense that they can be inspected, consulted, and referred to by the actors, the only difference being that the transcendental objects of "tacit knowledge" mythology are "opaque to their possessors," "tacit," in short: invisible and inexpressible.

A final question. Why the obsession with the notion of expressions of rules that are "fully explicit" and "exhaustive" for all times and settings? Why the insistence that for "rules" to be said to guide us in our affairs, they would have to be "articulable," "perfectly conscious," "constant," "explicit," even "fully explicit," "exhaustive," "complete," and so on? Is it because it is assumed that for a rule to guide us, it would have to eliminate all imaginable doubt, once and for all? And is it because of this metaphysical presumption that the notion of normative regularity is ruled out as unrealistic? This would seem to be the line of reasoning underlying, for instance, Bourdieu's rejection of the notion of "rule-following" for being unable to account for the distinctive "uncertainty and vagueness" that characterize practices because "practical schemes" vary "according to the logic of the situation, the almost invariably partial viewpoint which it imposes, etc." (Bourdieu, 1980a, p. 26; 1980b, p. 12; Schatzki makes a parallel move, 1996, p. 50 f.).[13] In other words, on Bourdieu's view, the application of a rule—an "explicit" rule—*cannot* take into account "the logic of the situation," the contingencies and circumstances of action. This immediately begs the question: Are these "rules" of *this* world? Indeed, is it even *thinkable* that the

[11] "Turner is surely right that if we conceive of practices as akin to tacit beliefs — hidden, inner objects, that are causally responsible for our behavior — then the very notion of a social theory of practice is ludicrous, and there are insuperable difficulties in understanding how that thing can be transmitted" (Stern 2003, p. 201).

[12] I have elsewhere developed a critique of Polanyi's notion of "tacit knowledge" (Schmidt 2012) and of the notion of "shared understanding" and similar (Schmidt 2016) and will therefore not expand on these issues here.

[13] Giddens seems to be making a converging move when he posits that "formulated rules" are a special and exceptional type of "rule" and that "most" "rules" are "social rules" that are "tacit."

expression of a rule could remove all possible doubt for all eternity? Is that notion not simply nonsensical? And does it *then* make sense to *negate* it?—An example: A courageous geographer holds a press conference at which he proclaims that he now sets out on a new expedition to explore what is north of the North Pole. A journalist protests, "But there is *nothing* there!" Or another example: A famous scholar gives a keynote talk in which he claims that the meter rod is not *precisely* 1 meter, and somebody in the audience objects that it, of course, could not be, for in nature there are no completely exact boundaries.—Are the protesters making any more sense than the mad scientists? I think not, for as Wittgenstein pointed out in a letter to Frank Ramsey, "*the negation of nonsense is nonsense*" (Wittgenstein 1927, p. 158).

If this interpretation is not wide of the mark, "practice theorists" are, so to speak, whistling in the dark to banish a terrifying ghost—instead of turning on the light.

3.4.4 The *Expression* of a Rule Is Not a *Rule*

"Following a rule" is a practice

(Wittgenstein 1945–6, *Philosophical Investigations*, § 202)

How does an "expression of a rule" work in practice?

It is trivially true that a given rule can be expressed in endless ways. One and the same rule may be articulated vocally or in writing, algebraically or in prose; it may be expressed in diagrams, charts, or schemas; it may be defined ostensively by means of gestures and examples; and so on. A rule formulation may be copied, reformulated, transcribed into another representational notation, or translated into another language—and yet be considered to be and applied as "the same." Moreover, the expression of a rule will typically play a major role in learning how to apply the rule, for instance, when teachers show pupils how to go on, give examples of how to go on, give tasks, correct mistakes, and so on, or when students use textbooks and dictionaries when learning the grammar and lexicon of a foreign language, or are examining proofs as part of learning geometry, and so forth. But expressions of rules may just as well remain an integral and continually present part of an established practice, such as the use of rulers, color charts, multiplication tables, pre-flight check lists, production schedules, routing schemes, biological nomenclatures, and so on. On the other hand, an inscription or some other semiotic artifact may have all the formal trappings of a "rule formulation"—without being applied as part of an actual practice, for a rule formulation may, for example, have become obsolete, have ceremonial status only, or may simply not be taken seriously and therefore not upheld.

It is also trivially true that the formulation of a rule is, in a sense, *finite*. It is expressed in sound waves, ink marks on a surface, and the like, and yet the rule it expresses is supposed to apply to *endless* situations. And similarly, the examples given by the teacher and the exercise tasks performed by the pupil and approved by the teacher are equally finite, and yet again, the rule the pupil is being trained to follow is supposed to apply endlessly. This occasions us to think of rules as an endless series of steps, somehow already taken in the mind, like rails in front of us, going on forever: "Whence the idea that the beginning of a series is a visible section of rails invisibly laid to infinity? Well, we might imagine rails instead of a rule. And infinitely long rails correspond to the unlimited application of a rule" (Wittgenstein 1945–6, § 218). This metaphysical picture is shattered when we realize that a *finite* series of actions, such as the teacher's examples or the pupil's homework, that are accepted as going on as instructed according the formulated rule, i.e., *in the same way*, can *also* be construed as being in accordance with an endless number of *alternative* rule formulations. This is again, in a sense, trivial but may be tricky nonetheless. A few simple cases will be helpful. First, consider the case of an ordinary signpost (⇨):

> A rule stands there like a signpost. — Does the signpost leave no doubt about the way I have to go? Does it show which direction I am to take when I have passed it, whether along the road or the footpath or cross-country? But where does it say which way I am to follow it; whether in the direction of its finger or (for example) in the opposite one? — And if there were not a single signpost, but a sequence of signposts or chalk marks on the ground — is there only one way of interpreting them? — So I can say that the signpost does after all leave room for doubt. Or rather, it sometimes leaves room for doubt, and sometimes not. (Wittgenstein 1945–6, § 85)

If the signpost, or any expression of a rule, leaves room for doubt, how can we then be said to follow a rule at all? "It may easily look as if every doubt merely *revealed* a gap in the foundations; so that secure understanding is possible only if we first doubt everything that *can* be doubted, and then remove all these doubts" (Wittgenstein 1945–6, § 87). In other words, are we to conduct our business like the man who was "always doubting before he opened his front door whether an abyss did not yawn behind it, and making sure about it before he went through the door"? Hardly, not even if the man "might on some occasion prove to be right." For we do not necessarily doubt just "because it is possible to *imagine* a doubt" (Wittgenstein 1945–6, § 84).[14] Wittgenstein concludes this line of reasoning by reminding us that the signpost is only a signpost as part of our practices: "The signpost is in order—if, under normal circumstances, it fulfils its purpose" (§ 87).

To examine more closely how an expression of a rule is made part of a practice, take the case of the daft pupil. The teacher orders him to write down series of signs according to a certain formation rule:

> Let the first of these series be that of the natural numbers in the decimal system. — How does he come to understand this system? First of all, series of numbers are written down for him, and he is required to copy them. [...] And here already there is a normal and an abnormal learner's reaction. — At first, perhaps, we guide his hand in writing out the series 0 to 9; but then the *possibility of communication* will depend on his going on to write it down by himself. — And here we may imagine, for example, that he does copy the figures by himself, but not in the right order: he writes sometimes one, sometimes another, at random. And at *that* point communication stops. — Or again, he makes "*mistakes*" in the order. — The difference between this and the first case will of course be one of frequency. — Or he makes a *systematic* mistake; for example, he

[14] "If you tried to doubt everything you would not get as far as doubting anything." In fact, "Doesn't one need grounds for doubt?" (Wittgenstein 1949–51, §§ 115, 123).

> copies every other number, or he copies the series 0, 1, 2, 3, 4, 5,... like this: 1, 0, 3, 2, 5, 4,.... Here we shall almost be tempted to say that he has understood us *wrongly*. (Wittgenstein 1945–6, § 143)

But perhaps the teacher, after some effort, manages "to wean" the pupil from the systematic mistake, "as from a bad habit":

> Suppose the pupil now writes the series 0 to 9 to our satisfaction. — And this will be the case only if he is *often* successful, not if he does it right once in a hundred attempts. Now I continue to guide him through the series and draw his attention to the recurrence of the first series in the units; and then to its recurrence in the tens. (Which means only that I use particular emphases, underline figures, write them one under another in such-and-such ways, and similar things.) — And now at some point he continues the series by himself — or he does not. [...]
>
> Now, however, let us suppose that after some efforts on the teacher's part he continues the series correctly, that is, as we do it. So now we can say that he has mastered the system. — But how far does he have to continue the series correctly for us to be able rightly to say that? Clearly, you cannot state a limit here. (Wittgenstein 1945–6, § 145)

How does the teacher determine that the pupil has understood the rule he has explained so patiently? The series can be continued endlessly but the teacher can only judge the effect of his teaching on the basis of a finite number of steps taken. Hence, one "cannot state a limit here." Wittgenstein returns to this very issue later in his *Investigations*:

> Let us return to our example ([§] 143). Now, judged by the usual criteria, the pupil has mastered the series of natural numbers. Next we teach him to write down other series of cardinal numbers and get him to the point of writing down, say, series of the form
>
> 0, n, 2n, 3n, etc.
>
> at an order of the form "+ n"; so at the order "+ 1" he writes down the series of natural numbers. — Let's suppose we have done exercises, and tested his understanding up to 1000.
>
> Then we get the pupil to continue one series (say "+ 2") beyond 1000 — and he writes 1000, 1004, 1008, 1012.
>
> We say to him, "Look what you're doing!" — He doesn't understand. We say, "You should have added two: look how you began the series!" — He answers, "Yes, isn't it right? I thought that was how I had to do it." — Or suppose he pointed to the series and said, "But I did go on in the same way."— It would now be no use to say, "But can't you see...?" — and go over the old explanations and examples for him again. In such a case, we might perhaps say: this person finds it natural, once given our explanations, to understand our order as we would understand the order "Add 2 up to 1000, 4 up to 2000, 6 up to 3000, and so on". (Wittgenstein 1945–6, §185)

In other words, the pupil is indeed daft: "This case would have similarities to that in which it comes naturally to a person to react to the gesture of pointing with the hand by looking in the direction from fingertip to wrist, rather than from wrist to fingertip" (Wittgenstein 1945–6, §185). But as we saw above, an expression of a rule—a signpost or a pointing hand—does not determine how it is to be applied.

Now, at some point in the discussion of rule-following, Wittgenstein's interlocutor asks, seemingly exasperated: "But how can a rule teach me what I have to do at *this* point? After all, whatever I do can, on some interpretation, be made compatible with the rule." Wittgenstein replies: "No, that's not what one should say. Rather, this: every interpretation hangs in the air together with what it interprets, and cannot give it any support. Interpretations by themselves do not determine meaning (Wittgenstein, 1945–6, §198), because as he points out later, "one should speak of interpretation only when one expression of a rule is substituted for another" (Wittgenstein 1945–6, §198). But the interlocutor is still not satisfied and asks, as in disbelief: "So is whatever I do compatible with the rule?" To which Wittgenstein replies with a couple of rhetorical questions: "Let me ask this: what has the expression of a rule—say a signpost—got to do with my actions? What sort of connection obtains here?" And he immediately goes on to offer the answer: "Well, this one, for example: I have been trained to react in a particular way to this sign, and now I do so react to it." But the interlocutor is not at all satisfied with Wittgenstein's reference to something as mundane as *training*, and objects: "But with this you have pointed out only a causal connection; only explained how it has come about that we now go by the signpost; not what this following-the-sign really consists in." Wittgenstein replies by reminding the interlocutor of the place of expressions of rules in our practices: "Not so; I have further indicated that a person goes by a signpost only in so far as there is an established usage, a custom" (Wittgenstein 1945–6 , § 198).

A short while later in the dialog, after Wittgenstein has tried to clarify the notion of rule-following, the interlocutor—finally, as it were—comes down to what is eating him. He now asks: "How am I able to follow a rule?" (Wittgenstein 1945–6, § 217). Replying, Wittgenstein reminds him of their very recent exchange on this very issue. As we just saw (in the paragraph above), Wittgenstein had then observed that we are *trained* to follow this or that rule: go by the signpost, extend the series 0, n, 2n, 3n, etc., and the interlocutor had objected, "But with this you have pointed out only a causal connection" (§ 198). Now, in reply to the new question "How am I able to follow a rule?", Wittgenstein says: "If this is not a question about causes" (and hence *training*), "then it is about the justification for my acting in this way in complying with the rule" (§ 217). That is, in answer to "How am I able to follow a rule?", Wittgenstein's response is the rather mundane one that we, through instruction and practicing, have learned to master the various techniques of following the various rules, and that we, when requested or challenged, justify our rule-following activities by referring—in relevant ways—to some expression of the rule in question. There is nothing to add.

But to be sure, as the hapless pupil's mastery eventually develops and matures, as the teaching situation therefore comes to an end, and as he thus becomes a practitioner, he typically will no longer be requested, on a regular basis, to explain his proceedings in relation to the expression of the rule. He is now an accomplished practitioner. At that stage, as Wittgenstein puts it in a notebook entry, "The training may of course be overlooked as mere history, if he now always calculates right. But that he *can* calculate he shows, not only to others but also to himself, in that he *calculates* correctly" (Wittgenstein 1937–44a, VI § 33; 1941–4b, pp. 97 f.). The expression of the rule (say, "Exit ⇨," "This ☛ color is called mauve," "Extend the series 0, n, 2n, 3n, etc.," or "Hold the fork in your left hand and the knife in the right") may now be used, not as the model of the rule-following technique to be learned but as the *criterion* that the rule thus expressed (and hence interpreted) has indeed been followed. If the practitioner is now asked why he is doing what he is doing, he will justify his conduct by using an expression of the rule in some shape or form, by citing the expression that was used when he learned to follow this rule or some indexical pointer to it. But if asked again how he knows what to do next and why he is taking *this* step and not *that*, he will at some point throw up his hands: "Once I have exhausted the justifications, I have reached bedrock, and my spade is turned. Then I am inclined to say: 'This is simply what I do'" (§ 217).

In another notebook entry, from 1944, this argument is developed further, taking the example of using a ruler to draw a line or otherwise tracing a line:

> Does a line compel me to trace it? — No; but if I have decided to use it as a model in *this* way, then it compels me. — No; then *I* compel myself to use it in this way. I as it were cleave to it. — But here it is surely important that I, so to speak once for all, can form the decision with the /general/ interpretation, and can hold by it, and do not at every step undertake fresh interpretation work.
>
> The line, it might be said, intimates to me how I am to go. But that is of course only a picture. And should it every time intimate something different, then I am *not* following it as a rule. And what is called "different" and "the same" can only life decide.[15]
>
> "The line intimates to me how I am to go": that is merely a paraphrase for:: — it is my *last* court of appeal for how I am to go. (Wittgenstein 1937–44a, VII § 48; 1941–4a, pp. 151 f.)

And shortly later in another entry in the same notebook:

> "The line intimates to me..." Here the emphasis is on the *impalpability* of the intimating. On this: that *nothing* stands between the rule and my action. [...]
>
> One follows the rule "mechanically". Hence one compares it with a mechanism.
>
> "Mechanical" — that means: without thinking. But *entirely* without thinking? Without *reflecting*. (Wittgenstein 1937–44a, VII § 60; 1941–4a, pp. 162, 164).

Not *mechanical*, but *without reflecting*. Or, perhaps, in other words: Not mindlessly, but also without doubting at every step, with the—fallible—confidence of practical competence. That is, if we accept what Wittgenstein reminds us of, there is no mystery here. We learn

[15] In the English and German versions of *Remarks on the Foundations of Mathematics* (Wittgenstein 1937–44a, 1937–44b), this paragraph deviates significantly from the manuscript in the *Nachlass*: "The line, it might be said, intimates to me how I am to go. But that is of course only a picture. And if I judge that it intimates this or that to me as it were irresponsibly, then I would not say that I was following it as a *rule*" (Wittgenstein 1937–44a, VII § 48; 1941–4a, p. 152). (Compare Wittgenstein,1945–6, § 222).

to follow rules (using words, making multiplications, arriving at an appointment on time) through instruction and training, and our learning consists in developing mastery of the specific techniques through which we *grasp* the specific regularities.

What tempts us to think of normative regularity as mysterious, as something that runs "deep" and remains "tacit" and "inexpressible," or, with Bourdieu, to think of the regularity of social order as something "a little miraculous," is that we, when we engage in the philosophy of social science, tend to consider rule-following in isolation from the institutions in which rule-following is learned and upheld. In the context of ordinary practical life and speech, however, when we recognize settings and activities as instances of specific practices, we typically do not bring in the history of learning and training, because we typically do not *need* to; we have learned to recognize the practices in which we already engage as effortlessly as when recognizing a face.

Conceived of in isolation, as in the case of the caveman or the chimpanzees, if there is no "general expression of the rule" and thus no instruction, training, and assessment, then there can be no explanation or justification, either. There is no "right" or "wrong." Thus, "What, in a complicated surrounding, we call 'following a rule,' we should certainly not call that if it stood in isolation" (Wittgenstein 1937–44a, VI § 33; 1941–4b, p. 98).

As Wittgenstein summarizes the argument:

> If a rule does not compel you, then you are not *following* a rule.
>
> But how am I supposed to be following it; if I can after all follow it as I will?
>
> How am I supposed to follow the signpost, if whatever I do is to be following it?
>
> But, that everything can /also/ be *interpreted* as following, does not mean that everything is following.
>
> But how then does the teacher interpret the rule for the pupil? (For he is certainly supposed to give it a particular interpretation.) — Well, how but by means of words and training?
>
> And the pupil he possesses the rule (*thus* interpreted) inwardly when he reacts to it thus and so.
>
> *This*, however, is important, namely that this reaction, which is our guarantee of understanding, presupposes, as a surrounding, particular circumstances, particular forms of life and speech. (As there is no such thing as a facial expression without a face.) (Wittgenstein 1937–44a, VII § 47; 1941–4a, pp. 149–50 [entry dated 18 March 1944])

Considered in isolation from the form of life to which expressions of rules belong and from the history of training through which their application is learned, expressions of rules—a demonstration of some dance steps, a set of instructions, a statute, a road sign, a definition, a formula, a blueprint, a recipe—are just movements, sound waves, ink marks on paper, pixels on a screen, and the like. And in isolation from that practice, the expression can be interpreted in endless ways, just as it becomes impossible to distinguish normative from natural regularity. The mystery that torment "practice theory" arises from its trying to explain normative regularity *in general*, in isolation from the *specific* practices of which expressions of rules and rule-following are constitutive.

3.5 Knowing When To Stop Digging

Our disease is one of wanting to explain.

(Wittgenstein,1937–44a, *Remarks*..., VI § 31; 1941–4b, MS 164, pp. 90–2)

The difficulty here is: to stop

(Wittgenstein,1945–8, Zettel § 314)

At some point in his *Philosophical Investigations*, Wittgenstein asks, apparently repeating a question raised by his interlocutor: "How do I recognize that this colour is red?" In reply, he suggests a somewhat rude answer: "One answer would be: 'I have learnt English'" (Wittgenstein 1945–6, § 381). —Why is this rude? To the question "Why do you turn right here?", my reply "Because this is a one-way street, and there was a sign over there" would not be considered rude, of course. For that question is asked in a particular situation in order to obtain a specific explanation of my behavior at this particular point in time at this particular location, and my answer is an explanation in terms of specific rules I learned as a child and later when taking driving lessons. This is how the concept of "rule" is applied in explanations in ordinary discourse. However, if I had said, "Because I have taken driving lessons," then it would have been very rude indeed, for my interlocutor was not asking for a biographical account but for a very specific reason for my turning *here*. That is, Wittgenstein's answer is rude because he gives a similarly general answer to the interlocutor's question to show that the question is not a question about the following of a specific rule but about rule-following *in general*. Wittgenstein is sarcastic in order to show that his interlocutor does not really know what he is asking *for*: he is asking a metaphysical question and gets a rude answer, and rightly, too.

But for a "practice theorist," Wittgenstein's explanation would be considered unsatisfactory. It would be considered rude (as intended, of course), for his explanation does not meet the "architectural requirement"[16] of the philosopher or theorist that stipulates that for an explanation to be valid, it should be a given in *general terms*, that is, in this case, in terms of some *general* principle or with reference to some universally effectual mechanism. What the theorist requires is something other than a specific explanation in terms of a specific rule (the name of a particular color, say), namely, a general explanation of behavioral regularity. How are people able to recognize the color red or follow traffic signs? How is such normative regularity even possible? Well, because people have learned to follow, say, traffic signs and are being reminded of these rules by other road users, and by the police, too. *That is the answer*. Pressing on to go deeper, beyond the explanations we give to particular questions about our conduct in particular situations, simply takes us into infinite regress. "The difficulty here is: to stop" (Wittgenstein 1945–8, § 314).

It will be remembered that when Wittgenstein's interlocutor finally asked, "How am I able to follow a rule?", Wittgenstein replied that "If this is not a question about causes,

[16] "Remember that we sometimes demand explanations for the sake not of their content, but of their form. Our requirement is an architectural one; the explanation a kind of sham corbel that supports nothing" (Wittgenstein 1945–6, § 217).

then it is about the justification for my acting in *this* way in complying with the rule" (Wittgenstein 1945–6, § 217), suggesting that if it were *not* a question about justification but about *causes*, the answer would be the rude one, "One is trained to do so" (ibid., § 206). However, Wittgenstein also gave a less rude answer to the question "How am I able to follow a rule?":

> A language-game, in which someone calculates according to a rule and places the blocks of a building according to the results of the calculation. He has learnt to operate with written signs according to rules. — One that has described the procedure of this teaching and learning, has said everything that can be said about acting correctly according to the rule. We can go no further. [...]
>
> As already said, what the (correct) following of a rule consists in cannot be described more closely than by describing the *learning* of "proceeding according to the rule". And this description is an everyday one, like that of cooking and sewing, for example. It presupposes as much as these. It distinguishes one thing from another, and so it informs a human being who is ignorant of something particular. [...]
>
> For one who gives me a description of how people are trained in following a rule and how they react correctly to the training, will himself employ the expression of a rule in the description and will presuppose that I understand it. (Wittgenstein 1937–44a, VII § 26; 1941–4a, pp. 101 f. [entry dated 6 March 1944])

Indeed, "One that has described the procedure of this teaching and learning, has said everything that can be said about acting correctly according to the rule. We can go no further."

It is in the same way with the overriding "practice-theoretical" question: How do we explain social order? This question *could* be taken as a sensible question if it was specified. It could, for instance, be a question about the evolution and development of *Homo sapiens* as a very specific form of life. This is a researchable issue addressed in ethology, primatology, paleoanthropology, archeology, etc. It could also, for example, be a question about the acquisition of linguistic skills and techniques in family life and educational institutions, about pedagogical methods, etc. It could also, for instance, be a question about how cooperative work is accomplished in an orderly manner, which would open for studies of the use of employment contracts, job descriptions, budgets, piece rates, quality assessment procedures, and the design and use of coordinative artifacts such as schedules, routing schemes, etc. (see, e.g., Schmidt 2016, pp. 329 f.). "Practice theory," however, wants to go further, and thus enters a world of nonsense.

The problem with "practice theory" is in the very question it has raised and tries to address. It set out to explain social order—not how this or that person learned to promenade without bumping into other pedestrians, or how people of this or that profession manage to get work done with given resources and on time, but social order, tout court:

> To what extent can the function of language be described? If someone is not master of a language, I may bring him to a mastery of it by training.
>
> Someone who is master of it, I may remind of the kind of training, or I may describe it; for a particular purpose; thus already using a technique of the language.

> To what extent can the function of a rule be described? Someone who is master of none, I can only train. But how can I explain the application [*das Wie*] of the rule to myself?
>
> The difficult thing here is not to dig down to the ground but rather to recognize the ground that lies before us as the ground.
>
> For the ground again and again feigns a greater depth, and when we seek to reach this, we keep on finding ourselves on the old level.
>
> Our disease is one of wanting to explain. (Wittgenstein 1937–44a, VI § 31; 1941–4b, pp. 90–2)

3.6 Collateral Damage: The Concept of "Practice"

"Practice theory" belongs to the tradition of grand social science theorizing, another term for the philosophy of social science. It began as an attempt to overcome the notion of a social order bereft of human agency that is the basic tenet of structuralism—while avoiding interactionist accounts that were seen as unable to offer explanations of social order. And in doing so, "practice theory" accepted the underlying assumption that an explanation of social order would have to meet the "architectural requirement" of grand social science theorizing: that there, hidden somewhere, must be a universal key that can (help us to) explain all and everything and that it is for the social science theoretician to construct it as a *precondition* for empirical social research to be even possible. But the notion of such a universal key is made of the same stuff as vitalism's "life principle" or "animal magnetism." It explains nothing.

In the words of Michael Lynch, "practice theory" is an attempt to construct an ontology in which "a conception of practice, or even of heterogeneous practices, is plugged into the explanatory place previously occupied by the now-discredited teleological agencies of Reason, Nature, Moral Sense, and Will." In short, it is an attempt to "overthrow 'traditional' metaphysics that replaces one prime mover with another" (Lynch 1997, p. 338). (On this issue, see also Turner 1994).

As such, "practice theory" has caused serious collateral damage. By appropriating the term "practice," which serves a critical role in everyday discourse about the relationship between actual contingent action and the general principles to which actors are committed in their action, and then using it in entirely different ways in entirely different discourses, it is a source of massive confusion. Because of its ontological aspirations, "practice theory" uses the term "practice" to designate just about any and all aspects of human life. For example, in answer to her own question, "*What is Practice?*", Ortner replies: "In principle, the answer to this question is almost unlimited: anything people do." But she then adds that "Given the centrality of domination in the ["practice theory"] model, however, the most significant forms of practice are those with intentional or unintentional political implications. Then again, almost anything people do has such implications. So the study of practice is after all the study of all forms of human action, but from a particular—political—angle" (Ortner 1984, p. 149). For Bourdieu, however, the term "practice" is used for the regularities an analyst can detect in the behavioral patterns exhibited by populations, from cosmologies and rituals to matrimonial and educational preferences, and Giddens uses the term in similar ways, while Reckwitz uses it as a shorthand way of referring to embodied routines. And finally, Nicolini, who appoints "practice" to the "basic unit of analysis" (Nicolini 2012, p. 7), declines to offer a definition (p. 9) while he rejects using the term "practice" as it is ordinarily used. Instead, he embraces an elementary category mistake by trying to conceive of "practice" as "activity" and "routine" (pp. 2 f., 219) and *at the very same time* "as tradition and community," "as accomplishment," and "as the house of the social" (Chapters 4–7). In the same vein (or fog), he posits that the "practice approach" "foregrounds" "activity" (p. 3), "body" (pp. 4, 6), "interest" (p. 6), "sense-making," and "knowing" (pp. 5, 7), which makes one wonder if there is anything left in the background.—Consequently, "practice theory" uses the very term "practice" in confusing and often also confused ways: as just another word for "regularity," "routine," "activity," "culture," "tradition," "paradigm," "embodied action," "knowing how," and so forth.

One is left thus with the question: Why do "practice theorists" want to use the very term "practice" at all? Perhaps because doing so has the advantage, for the social scientist and theorist, that the term invokes the connotations of the ordinary use of the term (say, "Has your idea actually been used in practice"), while they, at the same time, grant themselves the privilege of determining what it is that actors, unbeknown to themselves, "unconsciously" even, are *really* doing. However, as always when social scientists appropriate concepts from ordinary language and transform them into technical terms, the cost of doing so is that whatever explanations they come up with do not have *any accountable relation whatsoever* to what they purport to talk about and what the world at large believes they talk about. They are dealing in counterfeit explanations.

In sum, "practice theory" does not offer sound conceptualizations for CSCW and related practice-centered research. Rather, "practice theory" comprises a mixed bag of attempts to devise ontological (or a priori) constructs to "fill the gap" in the philosophy of social science left by now-discredited notions such as culture, tradition, structure, etc. that pretend to explain everything but, in the end, explain nothing. Like its predecessors, "practice theory" offers no conceptual means for identifying and thus comparing specific practices. The issue of criteria of sameness is completely ignored, the distinction between statistically observable regularity and normatively governed conduct is smothered, and the notion of normative regularity is drowned in the mythology of "tacit knowledge." In short, by relocating practitioners' normative commitments to rules, principles, standards, etc., their criteria of correct or incorrect conduct, and hence also their criteria of sameness, to the transcendental realm of "tacit knowledge," "practice theory" also removes itself from relevance for empirical studies of actual work practices. Instead of providing ways and means of investigating and analyzing how practitioners in different walks of life create and maintain order in their affairs, it offers pseudo-explanations. Instead of informing the necessarily strictly empirical work required in technologically oriented research, it offers "theories of practice that substitute magic and just-so stories for hard work" (Stern 2003, p. 201).

References

Anscombe, Gertrude Elizabeth Margaret (1957). *Intention*. Cambridge: Basil Blackwell. (Second ed., 1963).—Cambridge, MA, and London: Harvard University Press, 2000 (Paperback ed.).

Baltzer, Ulrich (1997). [Review of] T. R. Schatzki: *Social Practices: A Wittgensteinian Approach to Human Activity and the Social* (Cambridge: Cambridge University Press, 1996), *Zeitschrift für philosophische Forschung*, vol. 51, no. 4, October-December, pp. 660–4. <http://www.jstor.org/stable/20483904>

Bittner, Egon (1965). The concept of organization. *Social Research*. Vol. 32, no. 3, Autumn 1965, pp. 239–55.

Bourdieu, Pierre (1972). *Outline of a Theory of Practice*. Cambridge: Cambridge University Press, 1977. Transl. from *Esquisse d'une théorie de la pratique, précédé de trois études d'ethnologie kabyle*, Genève: Librarie Droz, 1972. Transl. by R. Nice.

Bourdieu, Pierre (1980a). *Le sens pratique*. Paris: Les Éditions de Minuit.

Bourdieu, Pierre (1980b). *The Logic of Practice*. Cambridge: Polity Press, 1990. Transl. from *Le sens pratique*, Paris: Les Éditions de Minuit, 1980b. Transl. by R. Nice.

Bourdieu, Pierre (1987). *In Other Words: Essays toward a Reflective Sociology*. Cambridge: Polity Press, 1990. Transl. from *Choses dites*, Paris: Éditions du Seuil, 1987. Transl. by M. Adamson.

Bourdieu, Pierre; and Loïc J. D. Wacquant (1992). *Invitation to a Reflexive Sociology*. Chicago: University of Chicago Press, 1992. Transl. from *Réponses: Pour une anthropologie réflexive*, Paris: Éditions du Seuil, 1992.—Cambridge: Polity Press, 1992.

Feldman, Martha S.; and Wanda J. Orlikowski (2011). Theorizing practice and practicing theory. *Organization Science*. Vol. 22, no. 5, September-October 2011, pp. 1240–53.

Giddens, Anthony (1979). *Central Problems in Social Theory: Action, Structure and Contradiction in Social Analysis*. Houndsmills, U.K.: Macmillan Education.

Giddens, Anthony (1984). *The Constitution of Society: Outline of the Theory of Structuration*. Cambridge: Polity Press. (Paperback ed. 1986).

Hayek, Friedrich A. (1963). Rules, perception and intelligibility. (*Proceedings of the British Academy*, London). In F. A. Hayek: *Studies in Philosophy, Politics and Economics*. London: Routledge & Kegan Paul, 1967, pp. 45–65.

Hayek, Friedrich A. (1964). The theory of complex phenomena. (M. Bunge (ed.): *The Critical Approach to Science and Philosophy: Essays in Honor of K. R. Popper*. New York: The Free Press). In F. A. Hayek: *Studies in Philosophy, Politics and Economics*. London: Routledge & Kegan Paul, 1967, pp. 22–42.

Hayek, Friedrich A. (1969). The primacy of the abstract. (A. Koestler and J. R. Smythies (eds.): *Beyond Reductionism: New Perspectives in the Life Sciences [Proceedings of] the Alpbach Symposium [1968]*. London: Hutchinson). (Lecture held at the Alpbach Symposium 7 June 1968). In F. A. Hayek: *New Studies in Philosophy, Politics, Economics and the History of Ideas*. London: Routledge & Kegan Paul, 1978, pp. 35–49.

Heal, Jane (1986). Wittgenstein, Kripke and meaning. *The Philosophical Quarterly*. Vol. 36, no. 144, July 1986, pp. 412–19.

Kuhn, Thomas S. (1962). *The Structure of Scientific Revolutions*. Chicago: University of Chicago Press. (O. Neurath; R. Carnap; and C. W. Morris (eds.): *International Encyclopedia of Unified Science*, vol. II, no. 2).—Chicago: University of Chicago Press, 1969 (2nd ed.).

Kuutti, Kari; and Liam J. Bannon (2014). The turn to practice in HCI: Towards a research agenda. In M. Jones, et al. (eds.): *CHI'14: Proceedings of the 32nd Annual ACM Conference on Human*

Factors In Computing Systems, Toronto, Canada, 26 April—1 May 2014. New York: ACM Press, pp. 3543–52.

Lizardo, Omar (2004). The cognitive origins of Bourdieu's *habitus*. *Journal for the Theory of Social Behaviour*. Vol. 34, no. 4, December 2004, pp. 375–401.

Llewellyn, Nick; and Laura Spence (2009). Practice as a members' phenomenon. *Organization Studies*. Vol. 30, no. 12, December 2009, pp. 1419–39.

Lynch, Michael (1997). Theorizing practice. *Human Studies*. Vol. 20, no. 3, July 1997, pp. 335–44.

Maton, Karl (2008). Habitus. In M. J. Grenfell (ed.): *Pierre Bourdieu: Key Concepts*. Durham: Acumen Publishing, pp. 49–65.

Mauss, Marcel (1934). Les techniques du corps. (Lecture, Société de Psychologie, 17 May 1934). *Journal de Psychologie*, vol. XXXII, no. 3–4. 1936, pp. 271–93.

McGinn, Marie (2013). *Wittgenstein's Philosophical Investigations*. London and New York: Routledge. (2nd ed., 1st ed. 1997).

Minar, Edward H. (1986). *Philosophical Investigations §§ 185–202: Wittgenstein's Treatment of Following a Rule*. PhD Dissertation. Cambridge, MA: Department of Philosophy, Harvard University. August 1986.—Garland Publishing: NewYork and London, 1990.

Minar, Edward H. (2011). The life of the sign: Rule-following, practices, and agreement. In O. Kuusuela and M. McGinn (eds.): *The Oxford Handbook of Wittgenstein*. Oxford: Oxford University Press, pp. 276–93. (Paperback ed., 2014).

Mises, Ludwig Heinrich von (1949). *Human Action: A Treatise In Economics. Volume I*. (Yale University Press: New Haven). Text ed. by B. B. Greaves. Indianapolis: Liberty Fund, 2007. <http://www.ceeol.com>

Nicolini, Davide (2012). *Practice Theory, Work, and Organization: An Introduction*. Oxford: Oxford University Press.

Ortner, Sherry B. (1984). Theory in Anthropology since the sixties. *Comparative Studies in Society and History*. Vol. 26, no. 1, January 1984, pp. 126–66.

Pitkin, Hanna Fenichel (1972). *Wittgenstein and Justice: On the Significance of Ludwig Wittgenstein for Social and Political Thought*. Berkeley, CA: University of California Press. (Paperback ed., 1993).

Polanyi, Michael (1958). *Personal Knowledge: Towards a Post-Critical Philosophy*. London: Routledge & Kegan Paul. (2nd ed. 1962).

Polanyi, Michael (1966). *The Tacit Dimension*. Garden City, New York: Doubleday.

Reckwitz, Andreas (2002). Toward a theory of social practices: A development in culturalist theorizing. *European Journal of Social Theory*. Vol. 5, no. 2, May 2002, pp. 243–63.

Ryle, Gilbert (1946). Knowing how and knowing that. (*Proceedings of the Aristotelian Society*). In G. Ryle: *Collected Papers. Volume II: Collected Essays, 1929–1968*. London: Hutchinson & Co, 1971, pp. 212–25.

Ryle, Gilbert (1968). The thinking of thoughts: What is "le Penseur" doing? (*University Lectures*, University of Saskatchewan). In G. Ryle: *Collected Papers. Volume II: Collected Essays, 1929–1968*. London: Hutchinson & Co, 1971, pp. 480–96.

Sartre, Jean-Paul (1960). *Critique de la raison dialectique. Tome I*. Paris: Gallimard.

Schatzki, Theodore R. (1996). *Social Practices: A Wittgensteinian Approach to Human Activity and the Social*. Cambridge: Cambridge University Press.

Schatzki, Theodore R. (1997). Practices and actions: A Wittgensteinian critique of Bourdieu and Giddens. *Philosophy of the Social Sciences*. Vol. 27, no. 3, September 1997, pp. 283–308.

Schatzki, Theodore R. (2001). Introduction: Practice theory. In T. R. Schatzki; K. D. Knorr-Cetina; and E. v. Savigny (eds.): *The Practice Turn in Contemporary Theory*. London and New York: Routledge, pp. 10–23.

Schatzki, Theodore R.; Karin D. Knorr-Cetina; and Eike von Savigny (eds.) (2001). *The Practice Turn in Contemporary Theory*. London and New York: Routledge.

Schmidt, Kjeld (2002). Remarks on the complexity of cooperative work. *Revue des sciences et technologies de l'information. Série Revue d'intelligence artificielle (RSTI-RAI)*. Vol. 16, no. 4–5, 2002, pp. 443–83.—[Also in K. Schmidt: *Cooperative Work and Coordinative Practices*, London: Springer, 2011 (Chapter 9)].

Schmidt, Kjeld (2011). *Cooperative Work and Coordinative Practices: Contributions to the Conceptual Foundations of Computer-Supported Cooperative Work (CSCW)*. London: Springer.

Schmidt, Kjeld (2012). The trouble with "tacit knowledge". *Computer Supported Cooperative Work (CSCW): The Journal of Collaborative Computing and Work Practices*. Vol. 21, no. 2–3, June 2012, pp. 163–225.

Schmidt, Kjeld (2016). Treacherous ground: On some conceptual pitfalls in CSCW. *Computer Supported Cooperative Work (CSCW)*. Vol. 25, no. 4–5, October 2016, pp. 325–53.—[Special issue: *Reconsidering "Awareness" in CSCW*].

Schütz, Alfred [A. Schutz] (1945). On multiple realities. (*Philosophy and Phenomenological Research*, June 1945). Text ed. by M. Natanson. In A. Schutz: *Collected Papers. Vol. I. The Problem of Social Reality*. The Hague: Martinus Nijhoff, 1962, pp. 207–59.

Schütz, Alfred [A. Schutz] (1947–51). *Reflections on the Problem of Relevance*. (Manuscript). Text ed. by R. M. Zaner and L. Embree. In A. Schütz: *Collected Papers. Vol. V: Phenomenology and the Social Sciences*. Berlin: Springer-Verlag, 2011.

Schütz, Alfred [A. Schutz] (1953). Common-sense and scientific interpretations of human action. (*Philosophy and Phenomenological Research*, September 1953). Text ed. by M. Natanson. In A. Schutz: *Collected Papers. Vol. I. The Problem of Social Reality*. The Hague: Martinus Nijhoff, 1962, pp. 3–47.

Stern, David G. (2003). The practical turn. In S. P. Turner and P. A. Roth (eds.): *The Blackwell Guide to the Philosophy of the Social Sciences*. Malden, MA, and Oxford: Blackwell Publishing, pp. 185–206.

Stern, David G. (2004). *Wittgenstein's Philosophical Investigations: An Introduction*. Cambridge: Cambridge University Press.

Turner, Stephen P. (1994). *The Social Theory of Practices: Tradition, Tacit Knowledge and Presuppositions*. Cambridge: Polity Press.

Williams, Meredith (1999). *Wittgenstein, Mind and Meaning: Toward a Social Conception of Mind*. London and New York: Routledge.

Williams, Meredith (2010). *Blind Obedience: Paradox and Learning in the Later Wittgenstein*. London and New York: Routledge.

Winch, Peter (1958). *The Idea of a Social Science and its Relation to Philosophy*. London: Routledge & Kegan Paul. (2nd ed., 1990).

Wittgenstein, Ludwig (1922). *Tractatus Logico-Philosophicus*. London: Kegan Paul, Trench & TrübnerRoutledge & Kegan Paul, London, 1961. Transl. by D. F. Pears and B. F. McGuiness. (Rev. ed., 1974).—London and New York: Routledge, 2001.

Wittgenstein, Ludwig (1927). [Letter to Frank Ramsey]. Vienna, 2 July 1927. Text ed. by B. McGuiness. In L. Wittgenstein: *Wittgenstein in Cambridge: Letters and Socuments 1911–1951*. Cambridge: Blackwell Publishers, 1995, pp. 158–9.

Wittgenstein, Ludwig (1937–44a). *Remarks on the Foundations of Mathematics*. (Manuscript, 1937–44). Transl. from *Bemerkungen über die Grundlagen der der Mathematik*. Transl. by G. E. M. Anscombe. Text ed. by G. H. von Wright; R. Rhees; and G. E. M. Anscombe. Oxford: Basil Blackwell Publishers, 1978. (Revised ed.; 1st ed. 1956).

Wittgenstein, Ludwig (1937–44b). *Bemerkungen über die Grundlagen der der Mathematik.* (Manuscript, 1937–44). Text ed. by G. H. von Wright; R. Rhees; and G. E. M. Anscombe. Frankfurt am Main: Suhrkamp, 1984. (*Werkausgabe in 8 Bänden*, vol. 6).

Wittgenstein, Ludwig (1941–44a). Band [MS 124]. (Manuscript, 6 June-3 July 1941, 5 March-19 April 1944, 3 July 1944). In L. Wittgenstein: *Wittgensteins Nachlass: The Bergen Electronic Edition.* Oxford and New York: Oxford University Press 1998.—Charlottesville, Virginia: InteLex Corporation 2003. <http://www.nlx.com/collections/124>

Wittgenstein, Ludwig (1941–44b). Taschennotizbuch [MS 164]. (Manuscript, *circa* 1941–44). In L. Wittgenstein: *Wittgensteins Nachlass: The Bergen Electronic Edition.* Oxford and New York: Oxford University Press 1998.—Charlottesville, Virginia: InteLex Corporation 2003. <http://www.nlx.com/collections/124>

Wittgenstein, Ludwig (1945–46). *Philosophical Investigations.* (Manuscript). Transl. from *Philosophische Untersuchungen.* Transl. by G. E. M. Anscombe; P. M. S. Hacker; and J. Schulte. Text ed. by P. M. S. Hacker and J. Schulte. In L. Wittgenstein: *Philosophical Investigations.* Oxford: Blackwell Publishers, 2009, pp. 1–181. (Revised 4th ed.).—[TS 227: Previously published as *Philosphical Investigations, Part 1*].

Wittgenstein, Ludwig (1945–48). *Zettel.* (Manuscript). Transl. by G. E. M. Anscombe. Text ed. by G. E. M. Anscombe and G. H. von Wright. Oxford: Basil Blackwell Publishers, 1981. (2nd ed; 1st ed. 1967).

Wittgenstein, Ludwig (1998). *Wittgensteins Nachlass: The Bergen Electronic Edition.* Oxford and New York: Oxford University Press.—Charlottesville, Virginia: InteLex Corporation, 2003. <http://www.nlx.com/collections/124>

Wulf, Volker; Markus Rohde; Volkmar Pipek; and Gunnar Stevens (2011). Engaging with practices: Design case studies as a research framework in CSCW. In P. J. Hinds, et al. (eds.): *CSCW 2011: Proceedings of the ACM 2011 Conference on Computer Supported Cooperative Work.* New York: ACM Press, pp. 505–12.

4 Making Use

Understanding, Studying, and Supporting Appropriation

GUNNAR STEVENS AND VOLKMAR PIPEK

4.1 Introduction

> In autumn 2001, I bought my first mobile phone. I want to point out that the technology did not change very much in the five years between total denial and actual use of the technology; the technology designers had little influence on the buying decision. It was rather my notion of interesting usages that evolved over the years.
>
> Pipek (2005, p. 16)

In the context of socio-informatics, the term "appropriation"—derived from the verb "to appropriate," using the definition "to set apart for or assign to a particular purpose or use" (Merriam-Webster 2011)—refers to the establishing of new social practices in the light of new technologies. So, roughly speaking, appropriation is closely related with change, although in everyday life such transformations may be slow, unnoticed, quiet, and evolutionary. The world, in other words, continues to look stable and ordered to those undertaking routine activities. Technologies, as is often said, are made "at home in the world." Moreover, in an epoch of rapid change we take innovations for granted, so that is hard to imagine how to live without, for example, electricity, washing machines, road networks, or even smartphones. Because of this power of the present, it is the role of stories and vignettes to bring once familiar situations and practices into explicit consideration.

This is true not just for the past, but also for future and otherwise alien practices. In this respect, reports of historians, ethnographers, visionaries, and design researchers face the same challenge and are what appropriation studies are all about—namely, helping readers to familiarize themselves with unknown practices and their (emerging) nature. This brief outline suggests that established orders are quite malleable, which is one of the reasons why emergence and structure are of theoretical interest, even when these issues pose no problems in everyday life.

Socio-Informatics, Volker Wulf, Volkmar Pipek, Dave Randall, Markus Rohde, Kjeld Schmidt, Gunnar Stevens (Eds). © Oxford University Press 2018. Published 2018 by Oxford University Press.

A survey of the origins of the term shows that appropriation is an ambiguous concept, used in different ways in various disciplines. The aim of this chapter is to provide an orientation to how appropriation might usefully be thought of, and why its use is becoming increasingly important. We will suggest that one important value here is to do with what it offers to the informing of design, but also to reflection about the limits of design. With regard to the latter, a common assumption is that designers are responsible for all outcomes associated with their vision. Concerning this, the concept of appropriation has a critical function in sensitizing us to the limits of design, emphasizing the openness and potentially creative use of artifacts. In addition, the concept sensitizes us to the power relation between designers and users—or, more generally, between the software industry and the consumer class (Stallman 1985). Exploring the concept of appropriation, then, in a long-term perspective plays a key role in our grounded design framework (see Chapter 1).

4.2 Get Back to Work: A Brief Survey of the Origins

The various meanings of "appropriation" are connected by a web of historical and thematic similarities. Hence, we do not seek to introduce a definition, but to give a brief overview of the scholarly traditions that contribute to the concept. With regard to the design discourse on appropriation, two main lines of development are of special interest in the history of the concept. The first line is rooted in German idealism, its elaboration by Marx, and its later adoption in activity theory. The other line of development is rooted in French post-structuralism, with de Certeau's view on the practices of the ordinary man.

In some way, the computer-supported cooperative work (CSCW) agenda represents a third branch that was influenced by both activity theory (e.g., via the Scandinavian participatory-design tradition and the German usability tradition) and post-structuralism (e.g., via Dourish and the British critical design tradition). Nevertheless, by its emphasis on appropriation *work* and appropriation *support,* CSCW provides a distinctive focus. With this stance, it allies neatly with in the concept of tailorability and that of end-user development but broadens the perspective, taking both into account: the adoption and adaptation of digital artifacts within the local context.

4.2.1 Express Yourself: Appropriation and German Idealism

> [Man] confronts the materials of nature as a force of nature. He sets in motion, his embodied nature forces, his arms and legs, head and hands in order to appropriate materials of nature in a form, which is suitable to his own life. Through his movement, he acts upon external nature and changes it, and in this way simultaneously changes his own nature. By thus acting on the external world and changing it, he at the same time changes his own nature.
>
> Marx (1973, p. 283)

The concept of appropriation originated in the late eighteenth century and initially was limited to legal questions of property and the (il-)legal possession of something. Hegel picks up on this discourse about possession to reflect on the general relationship of man with the world (cf. Keiler 1990; Braun 2004). Hegel views private property as the vehicle through which one is recognized by others as a free agent. In this way, other agents "would be able to see that a person owns something, and therefore this individual can be treated as a realized person" (Hidalgo 2013). Appropriation, in this view, can be understood as incorporating both "ownership" and expressivity (through the working of materials). Hence,

> our life is seen as self-expression also in the sense of clarifying what we are. This clarification awaits recognition by a subject, and man as a conscious being achieves his highest point when he recognizes his own life as an adequate, a true expression of what he potentially is—just as an artist or writer reaches his goal in recognizing his work as a fully adequate expression of what he wanted to say. And in one case as in the other, the "message" could not have been known before it was expressed.... The specific property of human life is to culminate in self-awareness through expression. (Taylor 1977, p. 17)

Moreover, in the moment when man recognizes his work as an expression of selfhood, man is not aliened from nature anymore but has become part of it. In this view, appropriating external conditions means to gain autonomy by recognizing the necessity of the given.

> At the same time man in acting on external nature to serve his purposes, in working, helps to transform it and himself, and to bring both sides towards the eventual reconciliation. (Taylor 1977, p. 120)

In a further step, Marx's contribution was to free the concept from its preindustrial, slightly elitist connotations. He generalizes the concept of man as an expressive being by taking everyday labor instead of artistic works as the paradigmatic case. In this view, man is constituted by labor as the realization of man in nature through appropriation. Under the capitalist mode, and relations, of production, however, people sell their labor power to others. As a result, the worker manufactures products with which he has no relation. This logic alienates man from his work. He owns the products of his work neither legally, nor cognitively, nor emotionally. Instead, the products of his labor remain completely alien to him. As a result, capitalism denies work its status as a resource for human development.

In sum, the concept of appropriation in German idealism focuses on the interplay of man and his surroundings. It is part of the expressive nature of man and implicates individual and social dimensions, as well as anthropological dimension. This, we will argue, has much to do with the concept of appropriation as learning in practice and as expansive learning, as outlined by activity theory.

4.3 Learning by Doing: Appropriation and Activity Theory

> Appropriation means very generally exploring, touching, and grasping, but also changing, repurposing, and converting, the physical and social environment. Appropriation implies the active doing of the subject, his interaction with the physical and social environment

> by making it, owning it, and, by the same token, creatively recognizing himself in it. From the appropriation perspective, human development is not adaptation to the environment. On the contrary, the environment is the place for personal development through overcoming the boundaries of limited nature. It is a mere adoption of the environment, as it prevents him from fully developing the richness of human capabilities and real humanity.
>
> Deinet (2014, translated by the authors)

In the twentieth century, the Marxian view of appropriation had a certain renaissance in activity theory, where the concept was elaborated from a psychological stance (cf. Keiler 1990). Unlike orthodox cognitive psychology, activity theory does not view the subject as an isolated entity that is detached from its environment but instead views the active engagement of the subject with its environment as being essential for individual development. In his engagement with the world, the actor appropriates the existing material and symbolic culture.

This stance also has methodological consequences. Activity theory, like other "humanistic" approaches, has an a priori objection to laboratory experiments on the grounds that they lack ecological validity. Instead, human activities should be studied in the wild, where *activity systems* are the basic unit of analysis. Moreover, research methods should be historical in order to reconstruct the socio-material genesis of the subject matter: "[to] explain a subject scientifically means to understand him through his becoming" (Holzkamp and Schurig 1973).

The core of an activity system consists of the triadic relationship of subject, object, and tools. In particular, the tool quality of things must be learned through appropriation as active, cooperative engagement in the world:

> The spoon does not meet him [the child] in the socially developed manner of its use, as embodied in the characteristics of its shape, but in its non-specific, "natural," physical properties... The mother observes this. She helps the child by engaging in what he does. In the resulting joint action the child forms the skill to use the spoon; it uses it from now on as a human subject. (Leontjew 1967, translated by the authors)

In this triadic relation, the tool has a mediation role, with both a mental quality and a material quality. The mental quality is given by the person's competency and his repertoire of routines when using the tool. In addition, activity theory emphasizes the social dimension of rules, division of labor, and community as further elements of an activity system into account (see Figure 4.1). These elements and the mediating relationships are historically formed and open to further development. In particular, activity systems do not exist in isolation; rather, they must constantly react to the external conditions in which they reside, including other related activity systems. Hereby, internal contradictions, breakdowns, and changes in the environment present driving forces. The system is continually striving for balance while encountering tension and contradiction. Appropriation relates to how such events and contradictions are handled, how changed conditions are incorporated, and as a result, which structures arise and are transformed—or might be stabilized and retrofitted under the new conditions.

Figure 4.1 Constitutive elements of an activity system: Modifications of an element or conflicts in a relationship have effects on the whole activity system and are driving forces for the further development (Source: Own diagram)

Stability is arrived at through successful internalization expressed in the formation of routinized actions, habits, attitudes, and emotions toward people, objects, and situations. Concerning the hierarchical structure of activity (Hashim and Jones 2007), internalization refers to the process where conscious actions become unconscious operations. These operations serve as a repertoire that defines the competence and tacit knowledge of a person: they are a resource that he or she can fall back on within the particular situation. The descent of formerly conscious actions could be described as the

> segmentation of appropriation... through (1) anticipation, (2) initial familiarity, (3) development of repertoire of routines and the (4) development of new forms of use. (Bødker and Christiansen 2012, p. 80)

Fluent mastery requires that new practices have to be practiced over and over again. So, fully fledged appropriation (especially concerning advanced technologies) is more of a slow, emerging process in which progress is often achieved through trial and error.

Wertsch (1998) has also argued, in a similar vein, that "the process of taking something that belongs to others" implies, for better or for worse, the reproduction of traditions, routines, and ways of judging and distinction making. In daily life, they become a second nature that is taken for granted. A prominent example is the appropriation of language:

> The word in language is half someone else's. It becomes "one's own" only when the speaker populates it with his own intention, his own accent, when he appropriates the word, adapting it to his own semantic and expressive intention. (Bakhtin 1981, p. 293)

This shared ownership of our words also pinpoints that individuals are always social beings, whose identities are expressed by the way they appropriate the objects of their environment.

Engeström (2001) develops an analysis of the process of appropriation as expansive learning and emphasizes the productive role of unfulfilled requirements, internal contradictions, and unresolved new situations. In short, conflicts are the internal and external stumbling blocks that irritate the smooth conduct of action. Because of the possible adverse consequences, such conflicts should be prevented in practice, but by the same token, they are triggers for changing activity systems and as a result present a driving force for innovation and improvement of practices and services. Appropriation as expansive learning, in this context, means a productive confrontation with such conflicts and hence new options. The process is not linear but involves a tension between physical objects, sociocultural demands, and personal motivations, often resulting in resistance. In particular, not all conflicts, situations, or new artifacts submit equally easily to appropriation; some stubbornly resist, and some remain alien (Bødker and Christiansen 2012).

Apart from the individual perspective, the process could be viewed from the activity system as a whole. Such view is more prominent in sociological work, especially with regard to the appropriation of social spaces and the concept of social space analysis. This is rooted in cultural–historical appropriation theory, which stresses the historicity of social spaces, regarding them as both the condition and the result of individual and collective human action. In addition, this view emphasizes that appropriation takes place in socio-spatial settings in which the relational interaction between individuals and spatial structures are of central importance (Spatscheck 2014). Appropriation, here, is closely related to the intervention in socio-spatial arrangements that resulted in a change of positions of the subject in the social space as well as a change of the spaces themselves. With regard to this facet, video telephony, media spaces, CCTV, and the various methods of their appropriation are good examples of intervention in socio-spatial arrangements.

In particular, the shift to the spatiality of activity systems has also lead to a renaissance of the question of ownership and private property, where the legal and political dimensions of appropriation have been rediscovered. In particular, the appropriation of spaces is a public issue that goes along with the negotiation of claims, interest, and power structures (Spatscheck 2014). These conflicts are particularly evident when homeless people in the city make public places to their own, when social structures of neighborhoods change through gentrification, or when teenagers use playgrounds, schoolyards, shopping malls, or McDonald's outlets as their second home (Deinet 2014). In such cases, appropriation is not just individual learning of how to use these environments; the everyday use and construction of social spaces become a performative demonstration of power and the enforcing of claims. Space in this sense constitutes a political area, where the participating actors in their action must capitalize their resources with regard to their social situation in pursuit of their interests (Spatscheck 2014). With regard to this, the formation of, and access to, resources presents a key aim as well as a key result of the successful appropriation.

In sum, the term "appropriation" in activity theory refers to the further development of activity systems, its elements, and the relationship among them. Regarding this, appropriation involves two levels. With respect to the individual, it refers to expansive learning and the formation of new routines, skills, and competencies (see Figure 4.2 left). As a collective process, it refers to the establishment, reproduction, or transformation of action systems where new tools, rules, routines, and division of labor find their place within the activity system. Gärling et al. (2002) also refer to this as the dual sociality of appropriation, expressing the idea that *persons change by changing their (socio-material) environment.*

4.3.1 Appropriation and de Certeau

Another strand in the history of the concept of appropriation is de Certeau's post-structural consideration of everyday practices as a place of appropriation and resistance. His interest in studying the margins of the cultural system entails taking a bottom-up view. This stance has quickly become adopted by cultural studies and critical media studies, for example.

There are striking parallels between the post-structuralist and the cultural–historical understanding of appropriation, but also considerable differences. In some way, both are heirs to the Marxian concept, but they set other priorities. The differences result in the main from different subject matter, methodology, and the role of the concept in theory building. For instance, the primary focus of activity theory is on the psycho- and socio-genesis of man. In contrast, de Certeau's primary interest was how the ordinary man gains autonomy under dominating structural conditions. As a result, he was less concerned with *successful* appropriation and more with "negative" *tactical* appropriation as resistance against alienation. Another difference is that de Certeau focuses more on everyday culture—or, more precisely, what people do with commodities of mass production. Since Adorno and Horkheimer's (2007) widely recognized essay about the cultural industry, mass production of cultural goods has been view as an instrument of power and control. In their essay, Adorno and Horkheimer paint a lamentable picture of alienated mass consumption, and de Certeau's view on appropriation corrects this in a certain respect. This topic of unequal power relations, suppression, and social discipline was a common topic in the post-structuralist era, an interest that de Certeau, for instance, shares with Foucault (Frijhoff 1999).

de Certeau's aim is to become an embedded reporter who follows the situated tactics of actors at ground level. In particular, he believes that the dominating conditions are not alone in muzzling the ordinary man, but that the common, standardized methods of the social scientist play a role as well. The scientist's role is integrative, linking things together into one single theory, and leaving out what does not fit (a critique shared by Harvey Sacks, 1963). This is an inherent effect, says de Certeau, of standardized methods. Opposed to this logic of subsumption, his aim was to give the particularities of everyday life a voice.

> Cultural history, on the contrary, works with the world as it presents and constructs itself, as a whole. It tries to account for the meaning of everything, which means that it has to start from the whole field of particularities, from the tactics of everyday life. It also means that the relationship between the regularities of history and the particularities, evasive and centrifugal, of the historical reality needs to be continuously kept in mind. (Frijhoff 1999, p. 94)

As noted, critical theory paints a lamentable picture of the culture industry. Mass consumption was thought as a one-way cultural transfer, where the content was passively consumed and received by the people. Critical theory and positivist "media effects" theories met each other at this point. Both assumed a homogeneous mass and asked, from this view, what media do to the mass instead of studying what people do with mass media

(Ruggiero 2000). With regard to the latter, de Certeau stresses that cultural goods and other symbolic systems are not passively consumed but are appropriated in such a way that a local, contextualized meaning is possible. Hence, using goods is not a one-dimensional process of assimilation of externally imposed structures of meaning, but it is an active and artful play of meaning, norms, prescriptions, and power structures (Krönert 2009). Appropriation means inconspicuous *making of consumption* branches into thousands of practices and is fabricated in them. This view is closely related to the Lévi-Strauss notion of "bricolage" as using the given and recombining them (Ahearne 1995).

> The "making" in question is a production, a poiesis... called "consumption." ... [It] is devious, it is dispersed, but it insinuates itself everywhere, silently and almost invisibly, because it does not manifest itself through its own products, but rather through its ways of using the products imposed by a dominant economic order. (de Certeau 1984, p. xiii)

In this view, appropriation resulted from unequal power relations, but it is not determined by this. Where strategic power lies with the proprietor, an enterprise, a city, or a scientific institution, tactical power is effectively the limited power of the individual to resist and remake space. Moreover, power struggles are open-ended, never-ending stories where particular power constellations, cultural forms, and artifacts never have a fixed meaning once for all.

Tactics comprise the art of relatively powerlessly making use of the situation to ensure what gains are possible. The weak use the gaps in the power structures, the blind spots in the grid of surveillance, in order to open up local conditions. This also includes steganographic tactics such as appropriating the language and culture of those in power ironically in order to disguise and hide oneself by expressing the own using the words of the other.

> For instance, the ambiguity that subverted from within the Spanish colonizers' "success" in imposing their own culture on the indigenous Indians is well known. Submissive, and even consenting to their subjection, the Indians nevertheless often made of the rituals, representations, and laws imposed on them something quite different from what their conquerors had in mind; they subverted them not by rejecting or altering them, but by using them with respect to ends and references foreign to the system they had no choice but to accept. They were other within the very colonization that outwardly assimilated them; their use of the dominant social order deflected its power, which they lacked the means to challenge; they escaped it without leaving it. The strength of their difference lay in procedures of "consumption." (de Certeau 1984, p. xiii)

The tactics of clandestine usages are hidden from producer's strategic power, and in the same way they are hidden from the standardized methods of the media scientist, as well as the positivistic innovation and adoption theories (Rogers 2010). This family of theories in question study artifacts as immutable and monolithic entities that are adopted unquestioningly. The "view from above" of use statistics says nothing about the universe of different practices, needs, rationales, constraints, and emotions. In particular, such statistics neglect the politics of use and the consequences of power struggles seen as consisting in a struggle between tactics and strategy.[1] The merit of de Certeau is that he makes us aware of the positivistic shortcomings, reinforcing the need to take the particularities of context seriously: what is of interest is the local meaning of the used artifacts; how they meld together, and for what reasons they are used seem to be of no concern. Concerning this, appropriation presents a situated, open, and open-ended process, where people are not just human factors but human actors.

Methodologically, bottom-up approaches are arguably needed, as different contexts of use are characterized by different modes of appropriation, leading to (in the context of cultural studies) a variety of everyday cultures (Hepp 1998). In particular, individual case studies are needed to do justice to the particularities of the context and the creative ways of situated use. So, instead of "How many cases have you counted?", the question in appropriation studies should be "What is the logic of this particular case and why have specific use practices emerged?".

4.4 Design in Use: Tailoring, End-User Development, and Appropriation

In the previous section, the general accounts of appropriation usually describe the phenomenon as a production of individuals and groups but are less concerned with the qualities that make a tool more or less "appropriable." This applies to material tools (e.g., a hammer) as well as immaterial tools (e.g., language expressions).

For information and communications technology, or, more concretely, software-based systems, this question deserves more attention. The semi-material nature of these tools allows one to identify, design, and implement the aspects a tool is aiming to serve, together with, but independently of, interactive aspects of its presentation at the user interface. These interactive aspects may address activities that transcend the intended purpose of software, supporting meta-activities like learning, troubleshooting, or sense-making with IT tools in relation to a use case (e.g., a help system or an interactive assistant). In addition, they may address the configuration of technologies, even to a point in which the functionality is changed or specialized to support a specific task beyond the original designers' intentions. This kind of malleability of an information system significantly impacts the space users have for appropriating a technology, and the semi-material nature of software allows much more extensive approaches to design technologies so that they serve appropriation processes of users better. We refer here to two important discourses, namely, those on end-user development (trying to align concepts from the fields of human–computer interaction, software engineering, and artificial intelligence) and tailorability (derived more from the participatory-design and CSCW communities).

[1] At this point, we like to warn against a tendency in cultural studies, too. Here, it seems trendy to subsume appropriation just under the category of power and alienation. Such a view, however, could easily lead to the glossing of context and the practices that produce it. As a result, much is said about appropriation in theory, but often relatively little about appropriation practices "in the wild."

End-user development research contributes explicitly to a design-oriented view on appropriation. In general, end-user development research is interested on how users can be empowered and supported to adapt their computerized environments to their needs:

> End-User Development can be defined as a set of methods, techniques, and tools that allow users of software systems, who are acting as non-professional software developers, at some point to create, modify or extend a software artefact. (Lieberman et al. 2006, p. 2)

Application domains for end-user development are rather diverse. In the past, the focus was on professional/work contexts, while newer studies also investigate domestic contexts. Other studies focus on how end users are making use of software ecosystems and existing infrastructures. End-user development research also builds on a long tradition to empower users making use of computers and supporting their computer literacy. This tradition includes the educational research studying computational environments as learning tools (Papert 1980), the open-source movement focusing on the users' right to customize (Stallman 1981), the research on the novice programmer and the cognitive dimension of programming (Pane and Myers 1996) and, last but not least, the participatory-design movement focusing on tailorable systems as a mean for democratization of work (Henderson and Kyng 1995). Despite their differences, all have in common the perception that the ordinary user can and should be the co-creator of the technological environment.

It is also worth mentioning that various connecting lines between end-user development and the humanistic Marxian appropriation concept exist, both in the case of Papert and in the case of the Scandinavian participatory-design tradition. Papert's constructionist view, for instance, understands learning as the progressive internalization of actions and the externalization of ideas making them tangible and shareable (Ackermann 2001). From this stance, Papert argues that the knowledge building and artifact building go hand in hand. Hence, end-user development environments should support (in his case) children to express themselves by enable them to build personal meaningful things and to conduct computational experiments to discover the (computational) world (Stevens et al. 2013). The Scandinavian end-user development tradition also shares with Marx the demand that the workplace design should not be reduced to its functional role, but it understands work also as a place for self-development and self-expression.

While having a broadly left-wing political agenda, the participatory-design movement's relationship to power seems less ideological than that of de Certeau and cultural studies, but more pragmatic—one might characterize it as a kind of social partnership between workers, trade unions, researcher, and managers (Ehn 1993). It focuses, it can be argued, quite pragmatically on how such technologies can and must be designed in support of skillful worker. From this stance, the concept of tailoring has been elaborated as a mean for workplace democratization that touches many issues like software construction, learning, organizational change, and organizational politics (Trigg and Bødker 1994).

In a narrow sense, tailoring represents an activity taking place during "use time" after the original design phase, which typically starts right after the first contact of the user with software. Tailoring shares some features, but still is different from both "use" and programming. With regard to programming, tailoring does not lead to a new system version, but modifies a given one according to local necessities (Wulf 1994). In addition, the person doing the tailoring is typically not an expert in software engineering but rather an expert in the application domain. With regard to normal use, tailoring is distinguished by three aspects. First, tailoring activities modify working tools rather than the working material. Second, tailoring activities have longer-lasting effects on the modified functions. Concerning this, Wulf and Golombek (2001) mention the creation of document templates as an example of tailoring. Third, tailoring is a kind of secondary task modifying more stable work structures, making the primary task more efficient. This functional orientation makes tailoring the environment different from, for example, constructive learning environments that are often more playfully designed. Moreover, tailoring "just for fun"—even though it is a common practice (Draxler et al. 2014)—can be dismissed as a waste of time and money. In other words, tailoring as a secondary activity comes with a cost that must be justified. In particular, tailorability initially increases software complexity, where the learning how to make use of the tailoring features needs extra time before the user might benefit from it.

This raises the question of why tailorable systems are needed and where the limits of the approach might be.

4.4.1 Contingencies, Heterogeneity, and Dynamics: Reasons To Make Software Flexible

It is an assumption underlying traditional software development methods that users do not need to tailor software artifacts because the artifacts are optimally adapted to user and the use context. Equivalently, designers—one assumes—know all about the user and the use contexts. Moreover, users form a homogeneous group, the contexts are well and formally specified, and the application domain does not change over time. In contrast, since we are in reality in a messy, unstable, and often unknown world, it can be argued that tailorable software can be used to cope with the imperfections so frequently identified. Regarding this, overlapping reasons have been outlined why usages are not perfectly anticipated at design time, and what design implications we should draw.

Contingencies of Use Situations

No matter how finely the net of user observation is knitted, no matter how users and use contexts are explored, understood, and measured—regardless of whether standardized surveys, participatory observation, or cultural probes are used—by its very nature the use context is underdetermined by data. As a result, there are always blind spots in any given context analysis, where situated use and situated needs are not anticipated. This especially holds true with the tailoristic workplace design that neglects the difference between the actual work and its formalized work description.

> Standardized representations of office work and its products, as captured in forms, diagrams, databases, or narrative text, are thus the result of articulation.... Without an

> understanding of articulation, the gap between requirements and the actual work process in the office will remain inaccessible to analysis. That is, it will be possible to describe tasks in an idealized form but not to describe the actual situation... It will always be the case that in any local situation actors "fiddle" or shift requirements in order to get their work done in the face of local contingencies. (Gerson and Star 1986, p. 258)

The underdetermined nature of the use situation is closely related to users' autonomy and their capacity to react to exceptional situations in an ad-hoc manner. By the same token, underdeterminacy limits the options for office automation, standardized workflow systems, and ergonomic design to formal task and process description, such as promoted by methods for business modeling (Scheer et al. 2005) as well as cognitive modeling (Olson and Olson 1990).

As a reaction, design for unanticipated use results in two, interwoven, interpretations: designing accountable computer systems as a resource, and designing tailorable applications (see Section 4.3.2).

Heterogeneity of Application Contexts

There are pragmatic and economic reasons why software does not perfectly fit the application context. In general, it would be desirable to develop a tailor-made software version for each client that might fit his or her particular needs. However, such individual solutions create extra costs and efforts, so that the development of a non-individualized, standard version may economically desirable. Customizable software, then, represents something of a trade-off between standardization and individualization. This also leads to an altered software adoption process: between the design and the use phase, there will be not only a learning phase, but also a phase of customization.

Depending on the scope and complexity of the application, such customization will be very different. At the one extreme, the user might just enter the mail account data to make an email client work. At the other extreme, customizing an enterprise system such as SAP and implementing it in a large organization often represents a multi-man-years large project, where the project team covers professional IT consultants, managers, and members of the involved departments. The end-user-development focus is typically in-between these extremes, but there is no clear cut-off.

Heterogeneity of Users

Users, of course, also vary considerably. They have different knowledge, cultural backgrounds, skills, and preferences. Hence, there is, in the traditional ergonomics literature, a large body of work on tailoring with regard to personalization, where tailoring is primary considered as individual effort. Also, the usability norm ISO 9241-10 includes the following personalization demand expressed by the individualization criteria:

> A dialogue is individualizable when the dialogue system allows adjustments to the task requirements, individual user preferences and user skills. (ISO 9241–10)

The norm mentions several justifications for individualization, such as linguistic and cultural differences, individual knowledge, and experience in the domain, as well as different perception, sensomotoric, and mental abilities. The norm also provides several examples like making font size, color, and key assignments adaptable, or allowing users to choose between alternative forms of representation and to enhance input options, for example, by creating their own commands.

In addition to the research on adaptable systems personalized by the user, there is a large body of research on adaptive systems that are automatically personalized for the user. The essential core is a user model that is constructed from the user input and other personalized data. The aim is to identify the user's background, preferences, and abilities in this model and adapt the system respectively. Such adaptation can relate to the user interface, the content, of the behavior of the system. One well-known example is adaptive hypermedia system:

> Adaptive hypermedia systems build a model of the individual user and apply it for adaptation to that user, for example, to adapt the content of a hypermedia page to the user's knowledge and goals, or to suggest the most relevant links to follow. (Brusilovsky 1998, p. 87)

From the perspective of appropriation, we generally have to keep a critical eye on adaptive systems for two reasons: the possible decline in user competence, and privacy concerns.

Regarding the first, the basic idea is the computer literally reads every intention, so that users make minimal effort themselves. In the long run, adaptive systems may help the user to work more efficiently. However, the danger is that personal competencies degenerate. In addition, for larger adaptive media systems, the danger is well known by now, as news feeds are tailored to the supposed interests and the mindset of the user.

The second issue arises from the fact that adaptive systems need personalized data in order to function properly. Moreover, the approach bases on the principle that the more close-meshed the observation is woven and the more data is collected, the better is the user model. From a user point of view, this poses the threat that the strategic power of the major companies increases while the tactic power of the ordinary man is weakened. Concerning such a shift in power relations, users' readiness to give personalized data away seems tactically (in de Certeau's terms) problematic.

Dynamically Evolving Contexts

The need to adapt software is also caused by the application context, and its surrounding evolves over the time (Wulf 1999). This encompasses the demands of the individual, the team, and the organization as a whole. Indeed, software requirements are a moving target was a painful learning process for software engineering (Floyd et al. 1989). In particular, feature requests often arise only in reaction to users having their first experiences of using a new system in everyday life.

With regard to the dynamics of an evolving context, Orlikowski and Hoffman (1997) have outlined three types of changes: anticipated, emergent, and opportunity-based changes. Anticipated changes are planned ahead of time and occur as intended. Emergent changes arise spontaneously out of local innovation. Opportunity-based changes are not anticipated ahead of time but are introduced purposefully and intentionally during and in response to the change process. By definition, emergent and opportunity-based changes could not have been included in a traditional requirements analysis. This reduces the chance that tailoring options exist, where users might fit the system to the new requirements. Hence, a static tailorability approach leads into the following dilemma:

> To make a part tailorable, one has to identify this part in first place and has to know how it should be tailorable [but this knowledge only evolves in the appropriation process]. (Draxler and Stevens 2006, p. 1)

A way out of the dilemma is to conceptualize tailorability not only as technical feature, but as continuing effort in an evolutionary, participatory-design process. Several related concepts have been elaborated to address this demand.

Wulf (1994), for instance, outlined an iterative-participatory process model that take tailoring activity explicitly into account. The core idea is that tailorable software allows small, anticipated changes within the use context. Larger, emergent demands are discussed in participatory workshops with the developers, so that they might be implemented in the next version. In a similar vein, Fischer and Ostwald (2002) outline SER (for *s*eeding, *e*volutionary growth, and *r*eseeding), which is an end-user-development-oriented, open-ended software development model. The central idea is that the initially deployed system continually evolves in the use context, where it alternates between periods of daily use and unplanned evolution, and periods of deliberate restructuring and enhancement.

Another concept was outlined by Draxler and Stevens (2006), with a stronger focus on mass products that are developed in an agile manner. They suggest integrating communication channels within the use context with tailoring and online help options. The aim is that users could provide feedback within the use context, for example, asking the manufacturer as well as the user community for help, and making feature requests that might be realized in the next version. While independently developed, the concept has striking similarities to commercial solutions like *GetSatisfaction* or *UsersVoice* that allow one to integrate channels within Web apps, so that customers can ask questions, submit an idea or complaint, or give praise and discuss issues within the online community.

4.4.2 Making It "Easy To Adapt": Ways of Designing Flexibility

As outlined, there are several reasons why applications do not always fit to the use context and thus may require some degree of tailorability. In particular, the terms *un*expected, *un*usual, and *un*anticipated refer to the inherent contingency and openness of practices that by their very nature cannot captured by formal models, scripts, or regulation. This is not just a complexity issue but represents a fundamental worldview problem, based on the conflation of real world practices with (formal) descriptions of those practices.

Hence, the flexibility of application context must somehow be reflected by equal flexibility in application systems. Facing the apparent contradiction of formalizing the unformalizable, we could distinguish two different but supplementing design methodologies in end-user development. The first one could be called tailorable design, focusing more on *technical flexibility*. The second one could be called technomethodological design (Button and Dourish 1998), focusing more on *interpretative flexibility*. Both, however, have in common the basic philosophy that we need understood software not such much as formalization of labor, but as tools for labor.

4.4.3 Tailorable Artifacts: Increasing the Technical Flexibility

The first design approach just mentioned primarily focuses on how software could be technically more flexible by making it more tailorable, malleable, adaptable, and customizable. This challenge has led to a series of new design approaches including component-based and service-oriented architectures, open-source software, plugin-extensible *software*, and domain-specific languages. In addition, end-user development environments have been developed in various domains, such as Web-authoring tools, mash-up editors, process and workflow editors, business intelligence report editors, and so on. One of the most well-known examples is the Excel spreadsheet (Nardi 1993). The off-the-shelf spreadsheet is of little direct value to the end user. However, the empty, application-neutral spreadsheet allows the users to create their own domain- and task-specific one or buy one from a third-party provider. Moreover, Excel demonstrates that end-user development does not have to be complicated but can create a mass product.

Another important issue relates to the question, to what extent software systems should be open and adaptable—which is also a political issue concerning the power relation between users and software companies (Stallman 1985). The one extreme is closed systems like ATMs, where users are not able to change anything. The other extreme is open systems like Emacs, where users could, in theory, change everything, increasing the power of the end users. However, open-source software is also a good example of the fact that only tech-savvy users make use of this power. This demonstrates that providing tailoring options is not sufficient for end-user empowerment. In particular, for safety, security, and complexity reasons, restricting tailoring options might be useful—and at least should be considered in end-user development as having non-technical end users in mind.

Moreover, in end-user-development research it was recognized that a gentle slope of increasing tailoring possibilities should be provided. Regarding this, in literature often three levels are distinguished: choosing between alternatives in anticipated behavior, constructing new behavior from existing pieces, and altering the artifact (i.e., reprogramming). For instance, the concept of component-based tailorability (Mørch et al. 2004) distinguishes between those three different levels:

Configuring a component. The configuration of an individual component is the easiest way to tailor a system, since this tailoring level offers the smallest complexity being limited to the so-called component slots only. Due to this restriction, the tailoring action can be supported by providing special tailoring environments. With the help of such special environments, it is much easier for the user to tailor these slots.

Changing the component composition. The changing of the composition allows for a more substantial adaptation. This level includes operations like inserting and deleting components, rewiring the components or building complex components. This level

> requires the user to understand not only the individual components but also their interactions.
>
> **Designing new components.** This level increases the opportunities for tailoring since the user is not dependent on already existing components. However, when tailoring on this level the user has to understand the underlying programming language, the component model, and the implementation details. (Stevens et al. 2006, p. 272)

Such advanced tailoring features were implemented by, for example, FreEvolve (Wulf et al. 2008) of Prospero (Dourish and Edwards 2000, p. 48). Unfortunately, such systems never moved beyond a research prototype, so that tailoring such systems has never been studied in the wild. Yet, these research prototypes serve as visionary concept studies that demonstrate the technical feasibility of, and shape an analytic lens for, studying tailoring concepts in practice.

For instance, in our study about the appropriating component-based systems such as Firefox, World of Warcraft, and Eclipse, we study how end users in everyday life make use of the three levels of configuring components, changing component composition, and designing new components (Draxler and Stevens 2011; Draxler et al. 2011). One of the insights was that most users make use only of the first two tailoring levels (configuring and changing composition). Compared to this, almost nobody, we found, created new components. In addition, the study also showed that the features used for changing compositions looked quite different from those suggested in academia. In practice, built-in plugin managers and plugin repositories were highly popular because they reduced complexity significantly for the user, but at the same time also restricted options for changing the system at this tailoring level. Nevertheless, the users' tailoring activities have led to a striking diversity of individualized installations.

Accountable Artifacts: Increasing Interpretative Flexibility

An alternative to increasing technical flexibility is to increase interpretative flexibility. Here, the user does not adapt the artifact itself but rather his way of using it (Wulf 1999). This implies that the system at hand does not prescribe a particular use practice but instead allows multiple ones.

A well-documented example of such a general-purpose tool is email. As the name indicates, the original idea behind the technology was to provide an electronic version of paper-based mail—which in itself is a general-purpose medium that could be used for many purposes, like sending informal love letters as well as formal, official documents. The same variety of usages also holds for the electronic counterpart, even allowing for the fact that legally binding notification was much more difficult to establish than when using email for informal communication. The appropriation also leads to many new practices, such as using email as an appointment book to send oneself a reminder, using it as an instant messenger, using it for spamming, and so on. In addition, various new practices to do with organizing email inboxes have emerged (Whittaker and Sidner 1996). Key email protocols like SMTP, MIME, and IMAP support this flexibility, as they do not prescribe a particular usage but focus on the interoperability of the underlying infrastructure. In contrast, more prescriptive approaches to structuring email correspondence, like the Coordinator (Winograd 1987), have had little success.

The second design approach aims to systematize such interpretive flexibility, rooting it at the theoretical level in Suchman's (1987) insight that plans for humans do not fully determine behavior but instead present a resource that could be used and adapted in specific situations. As such, computer systems should not be designed as a realization of an abstract, defined work procedure. Instead, computer systems should serve as a resource used in joint activities without a need to anticipate particular contingencies, or the order in which they might arise (Robinson 1993).

This design view adopts the much-rehearsed ethnomethodological stance to study how members structure and make accountable, through a mutually elaborative process, the situations in which they work. The seminal point for design is that these embodied methods are stable and structured—and that they are observable and analyzable by researchers as much as they are made public by members. Hence, they could be made the starting point for the design considerations.

With regard to this, system design must uncover and envision what are and will be the relevant members' methods in the application domain, what is the rationale that underpins them, and last but not least, how computational artifacts will affect them and become part of them, respectively. This view is particularly elaborated by the programmatic manifesto of *Technomethodology*:

> In contrast with the approaches to ethnomethodologically-informed design [we] consider the relationship between ethnomethodology and system design in a design context to be more than a practical matter.... System designers learn from ethnomethodology, not from ethnomethodologists or their observations.... Technomethodology attempts to align system design not so much with the details of specific working practices, as with the details of the means by which such working practices arise and are constituted. (Dourish and Button 1998, p. 412)

From this perspective, Dourish and Button (1998) analyze traditional design methodologies that abstract from the details by hiding the underlying computational mechanisms from the user. While this reduces the complexity of the user interface, it also makes these mechanisms less predictable and as a result makes it more difficult for the user to make use of them.

> The key property of human action is the way in which it is made observable and reportable in the course of its own unfolding. It is organized accountably. As someone speaks, this is how "he provides the very materials for making out what he says." Computational abstractions, being static, atomic and unexaminable, provide no such means. Abstract computational behavior is not accountable; and, for this reason, the forms of contingent, improvised (situated) action become problematized. (Dourish and Button 1998, p. 415)

While tailorable and technomethodological system design are different approaches to the problem of flexibility, they have a number of features in common. This especially holds for *Prospero*, which served as a kind of reference for technomethodological design (Dourish and Edwards 2000). On a technical level, Prospero provides *translucent* user interfaces that "open up" the internal computational mechanisms. These make the mechanisms more adaptable, but also more transparent—and thus make its working more predictable for the end users. The *translucent* interfaces provide cues to what the system is doing, why it is doing it that way, and what is likely to be done next. In short, such interfaces should make the computational action more accountable, which is a prerequisite for situated, social action and—if we understand computer systems as being actants with agency—a prerequisite for human–computer interaction altogether.

> We will be concerned here with a second approach. This is a more fundamental one, and aims to address the disparity between traditional process-driven models of interface design and the more improvisational model revealed by sociological and anthropological investigations such as Suchman's. This approach is based on a re-reading of Open Implementations' reflective self-representations as accounts that systems offer of their own activity. (Dourish and Button 1998, p. 419)

Of course, one can have reservations about such a view—to what extent, for instance, does it makes sense to speak of technical artifacts being accountable? Pragmatically, perhaps the best way of viewing the notion of "accountability" in this context is to argue that it entails the user understanding what the computer is doing, why it is doing it, and what to expect next—in short, that the application provides a reliable tool and context for doing things. Concerning this, *open implementation* might be one option, although not the only one, and maybe not the best, for improving transparency and predictability.

In sum, the merits of concepts such as radically tailorable systems and technomethodogical design are that they sensitize us to the need for system design to provide resources that help human actors to make the most of the systems that result. In addition, this thread of research shows that people do not appropriate technology in an unstructured and accidental way, but according to their interpretative and technical competencies, given the demands of the situation at hand.

4.5 Making It Work: Appropriation as Collaborative Work

The studies of technology support for cooperative work situations took appropriation work as being collaborative by nature (e.g., the negotiation of conventions to establish the nontechnological configurations of an in-work setting; see Mark et al. 1997), but initially without distinguishing it systematically from the actual configuration work ("tailoring"). The term "appropriation" in CSCW is shaped by and further develops the tailoring concept of end-user development research in recent decades. In addition to our own work in this field (e.g., Pipek and Wulf 1999; Törpel et al. 2003), important contributions to this topic have been made by Dourish (2003), Balka and Wagner (2006), and Twidale (2005). The common strand of all this work is a praxeological view, one with an affinity for ethnographic methods, a focus on tailorable workplaces, and the activities of the people making use of the situation at hand. From this stance, Dourish, for instance, defines appropriation as follows:

> Appropriation is the process by which people adopt and adapt technologies, fitting them into their working practices. It is similar to customization, but concerns the adoption patterns of technology and the transformation of practice at a deeper level. Understanding appropriation is a key problem for developing interactive systems, since it is critical to the success of technology deployment. It is also an important research issue, since appropriation lies at the intersection of workplace studies and design. (Dourish 2003, p. 465)

Tailoring is still central to this research thread. Yet, with the appropriation concept, the aforementioned authors have taken a broader perspective at the constitution-theoretical, methodological, and design-conceptual level, which has a great affinity to the outlined activity-theoretical concepts we have discussed, but with a stronger focus on the role of the digital artifact.

As mentioned, end-user development focuses on how to empower users to adapt computer systems with regard to the local context. Related to this, appropriation research asks how people might be empowered not just to tailor but to make use of the technology at hand with regard to the local context. This can also include tactical moves to "mis"-use technologies, the invention of usages, and the informal processes of learning and sense-making. In particular, if we examine in minute detail what happens during tailoring, it becomes evident that fitting a technology to the local situation is much more than just customizing it. We have characterized this "*more*" than tailoring as follows:

> Appropriation can be described as a collaborative effort of end users, who perform "appropriation activities" to make sense of the software in their work context. Besides activities to configure the software to fit into the technological, organizational and individual work context of the users ("Tailoring"), there is a larger area of technology-related communication, demonstration and negotiation activities aimed at establishing a shared understanding of how a software artefact works and what it can contribute to the shared work context. The mutual shaping of the technology and organizational contexts resemble an ongoing design process that end users perform rarely without any involvement of professional developers. (Pipek 2005, p. 3)

This "more" can be studied from two sides: from within the situation, studying how the appropriation of a new artifact appears to users, and from the outside, studying how it is embedded in the broader situation.

4.5.1 Dealing with Breakdowns: A Phenomenology of the Appropriation Situation

From within, we can ask when and how technologies become present at hand (Wulf and Golombek 2001; Stevens 2009). A phenomenological inquiry reveals that manifold small, insignificant disruptions exist that prompt reflection on the present situation, the technology at hand, and common-use practices. With Heidegger, we could call them breakdown situations; with Dewey, we can call them doubtful situations; or with Engeström, we can call them situations of expansive learning (see Figure 4.2). In such cases, the user finds him- or herself in new, unknown situations where common routines are inadequate, so that s/he must "invent" a new one in an expansive learning manner (cf. Figure 4.2).

In principle, there are various options available, constituting the dialectics of "mental" and "material" appropriation activities. We want illustrate these small steps of appropriation through the following train of thought.

> Assume that Jane wants to celebrate her birthday. She would like to send a form letter to all her friends. However, she has never done this before. This forces her to reflect on what might be a smart way to solve the problem at hand. In principle, there are a number of options, such as exploring whether Word has a form-letter function, how to use this function, how to enter the data in an appropriate form, and so on. She might also search the internet to see if a suitable Word extension or text editor that had a form-letter feature existed, and then try to install and use it. She might also be competent enough to write a Word macro (or use the situation as a trigger to learn how to do so) that is optimally adapted to her needs, or at least is good enough for her problem at hand. In this situation, it is likely that she starts with a tentative solution, which appears to her as the easiest and the most promising way. If she reached a deadlock, she might change her strategy, for example, asking someone else for advice. She further experiments until she finds a feasible way or gives up her goal.

Her tinkering leaves "mental," "social," and "material" traces. The traces are mental, in the sense that she has learned about the software and extended her skills in making use of it. The traces are social in the sense that Jane may now owe favors to the colleague she asked for help, or she may help others, for example, through a thread in a help forum dealing with how to use the form-letter function in Word. The traces are material, in the sense that she modified her Word installation or created a Word template that she can use in the future. Because of these traces, there is no need to start all over the next time she is faced in a similar situation. The traces are social in the sense that she might trigger a question-and-answer thread in a community forum, or share the resulting Word template with others. In sum, the successful mastering of a breakdown or doubtful situation is always related to the expansive growth of the individual person and the activity system as a whole.

The second seminal point is that from phenomenological point of view, it does not matter which choice is the best or most realistic from an external perspective, or that whatever option Jane realizes might be predictable. It is the internal perspective of the situation that matters. And within the actual situation, the various options are real possibilities for action, even if they are proven less than optimal afterwards. This demonstrates that learning and tailoring a tool have the same genesis: both are the results of mastering doubtful situations. It will eventually become apparent whether the appropriation is more dominated by new ways of sense-making, new ways of tool making, or both.

4.5.2 Make It Together: The Collaboration Pattern

Another focus is on the study of collaborative appropriation. This follows up on previous work on collaborative tailoring in organizations (Mackay 1990; Trigg and Bødker 1994; Wulf 1997), which has raised awareness about collaboration patterns such as the existence of sharing networks, sharing habits, and different user types with regard to customization (Wulf 1999a; Stevens et al. 2006). Mackay (1990), for instance, suggests a classification scheme where she distinguishes three user types: lead users who play with new software, first creating adaptations and then sharing with others; translators, who are less technically oriented but customize a bit and, in particular, adapt the solutions of lead users for others; and ordinary users, who use the adaptations made by the others. With regard to the incentives to share customizations, Mackay concludes:

> Users have a number of incentives to share customizations, including taking advantage of each other's work, learning new methods of accomplishing useful tasks, avoiding errors, and generally saving time. The net result is that users adopt patterns of use from each other, propagating both useful innovations and errors throughout the organization. (Mackay 1990, p. 218)

The existence of such collaboration patterns is a quite general phenomenon and is not limited to the organizational domain. In the domestic domain, for example, Grinter et al. (2005) found that the party with the biggest technical competence usually configures the home IT for others. We found a similar result with regard to the appropriation of domestic eco-feedback systems (Schwartz et al. 2014). Moreover, the collaborative patterns are strikingly similar to the adoption patterns outlined by diffusion of innovation theory.

> [Most individuals do adopt new products] not on the basis of scientific research by experts, but on the basis of the subjective evaluations of near peers who have already adopted the innovation. These peers [typically innovators and early adopters] serve as models whose behavior is imitated by others in the social system. (Rogers 2002, p. 990)

In addition, a similar pattern can be found in the case of the informal learning and sharing of tool knowledge (Wulf 1999a; Törpel et al. 2003; Twidale 2005). These similarities do not occur by accident but are deeply rooted in the fact that customizing, learning, and adopting digital artifacts are just different, intertwined ways of appropriating them.

4.5.3 Infrastructuring: Appropriation and the Emergence of Infrastructure

As outlined in Section 4.4.2, from an external view, appropriation is closely related to and expressed by the transformation of an activity system in reaction to the adoption of a new technology. In particular, in the social context of the home, the team, the organization, and the community, the adoption of new systems affects not only the individual but also the other parts of the activity system, including other tools. Local changes also trigger negotiation about the division of labor, what the work outcome should be, what are the rules for using and customizing the tools, what are the competencies, habits, and expectations of others that might have to be taken into account, and so on.

The POLITEAM study (Wulf 1997), concerning the introduction of a groupware system in a German ministry, presents an illustrative example of the coevolution of work and working tools as part of an activity system. In the POLITEAM case, Wulf (1997) observed that the adoption of the groupware also affected the division of work. For instance, before the introduction of the groupware, senior civil servants used pen and paper or Dictaphones to make drafts and corrections, which were then sent to a typing service. After the groupware was introduced, however, the civil servants used the groupware to make corrections directly in the electronic document. This new division of labor had reciprocal effects on the groupware customization. For instance, the access control rules had to be configured in such a way that civil servants also had write access. In addition, the coevolution of both technology and work required new skills from the members. For instance, civil servants had to learn how to use text editors and had to develop their typing skills.

The mutual dependencies of adoption and adaptation processes pinpoint the fact that tailoring should not be studied in isolation but should take the social embeddedness of tailoring activities into account (Pipek and Wulf 2009). However, identifying the technical and organizational ties that bind users together when using different artifacts remains problematic.

Pipek and Kahler (2006) distinguished four scenarios: a "shared-use" scenario, in which users tailor and appropriate a tool that every user uses independently and individually (individual decisions/appropriations do not influence each other directly—but maybe indirectly); a "shared-context" scenario, in which a tool is being used individually and independently, but within a shared context (e.g., an organization, a virtual team, or a workflow; here, individual decisions/appropriations may influence others, e.g., due to changed outcome qualities); a "shared-tool" scenario, where users tailor and appropriate the same tool (e.g., a shared file repository; here, the consequences of individual decisions/appropriations become tangible in a way that requires collaboration). The final scenario is the "shared-infrastructure" scenario and illustrates that if we widen the lens to consider a set of tools, devices, and technologies used by users in an (at least partially) shared context, the consequences of individual appropriations of even single-user software like a text processor become difficult to anticipate, as ties emerge from a network of conventions, workflow relations, organizational structures, and technological dependencies.

Concerning this, the broader view of appropriation helps to get a more complete picture of the interdependencies and the transformation of practices. In particular, it makes us aware of the various feedback loops and mutual influences within the activity system. Moreover, activities surrounding the computer systems in use do not exist in isolation but are linked by manifold, often implicit dependencies.

> Changes—independently of whether they are implemented by tailoring or by evolving the software—can depend on and affect changes in other applications of the IT-infrastructure and the interaction between applications. This requires coordination between tailoring and development, and cooperation between the persons responsible for tailoring and developing the different applications. And this, in turn, requires a different set of competences from users and developers. (Eriksson and Dittrich 2008, p. 31)

This interconnectedness constitutes a web of linkages that mediates between the local and global activities of appropriation and development (Wulf 1994). Most of the studies mentioned so far deal with application fields that have one single or dominant software tool. In the paper by Törpel et al. (2003), we presented a different case that sheds light on issues of scale within the evolution and appropriation of software infrastructures that involve several tools. During the observation of SIGMA, a network of 200–250 business consultants and trainers, the shared endeavor of building a groupware system for all network members was counteracted by the proliferation of various tool usages of competing products. Robertson (1998) stressed in her discussion of infrastructural decisions of SMEs (small and medium enterprises) that "shopping" for a different product is a perfectly viable alternative for end users, instead of tailoring an existing product. As a consequence, appropriation needs to be addressed as a process that involves also alternative tools that could complement the existing infrastructure. Alternative and complementing tools interact with the intended purposes users need. Both of these papers stress the creative power that users have to define their infrastructure by exchanging parts of it or assigning new meanings to it.

In order to describe these changing relations between tools and their associated sense (the purposes they are supposed to serve in a use situation), we distinguished (Törpel et al. 2003) between *proliferation*, that is, when different technologies are being appropriated for the same purpose, and *differentiation*, that is, when a technology is appropriated for many different purposes. Although a technology may be capable of serving different purposes, it is sometimes specialized for only one or a few purposes. As technological artifacts and/or associated usages change/emerge in a use context, the relations between technological artifacts and use purposes may be redefined. In this study, we also distinguished between *integration* (when one new/improved technology provides functionality for multiple existing use modes formerly realized by multiple different technologies), *standardization* (when one or more specific ways of use are objectified in one artifact), and *initiation* (when anticipated but still imaginary new use options are objectified for purposes assumed relevant to the use context). Again, none of these processes necessarily involves new technologies; they may occur through the pure repurposing of the existing infrastructure at hand.

The phenomenon of disruptions, conflicts, and breakdowns triggered by distributed innovations (and here we refer to temporal and spatial as well as epistemological distributedness) serves as the main driver for the emergence of technological systems (Hughes 1987). While activity theory is well suited for analyzing the local context of an activity system, we started to adopt Star's concept of infrastructure to get a better grip on the interconnectedness of distributed local and global activities. When investigating the phenomena of appropriation, Star's understanding of "infrastructure" is helpful because it does not refer to an infrastructure as a technical entity or a set of devices (plants, stations, switches, vehicles, etc.) and connectors (cables, pipes, streets, etc.). Instead, infrastructures are described as an ongoing affair that is equally the medium for and the outcome of cooperation practices. From this stance, Star and Ruhleder (1996, later reworked in Bowker and Star 2000) described eight salient characteristics of infrastructure (see Table 4.1). Star was not so much interested in what infrastructures *are* but what they *mean* to their users, and how they were made in everyday life.

This relational view on infrastructures portrays them as the result of a continuing, everlasting, and not necessarily intentional production of connected artifacts and meanings, a

Table 4.1 Characteristics of infrastructure and corresponding activities of infrastructuring (quoted from Pipek and Wulf 2009 and DiSalvo et al. 2012)

Characteristics of Infrastructure (Bowker and Star 2000)	**Activities of Infrastructuring (Pipek and Wulf 2009)**
Infrastructures are embedded in other social and technological structures	Activities that connect different technological and social structures Activities that change standards, routines, or traditions involved in mediating between technological and social structure
Infrastructures are transparent in invisibly supporting tasks	Activities that change the visibility of an infrastructure
Infrastructures have a spatial and temporal reach or scope	Activities that increase the longevity of an infrastructure, or that add new members, element, or application area
Infrastructures comprise taken-for-granted artifacts and organizational arrangements learned as part of membership	Activities that change, or reflect changes in, the community or communities supported
Infrastructures shape and are shaped by conventions of practices	Activities that aim at changing conventional practices or that impose existing practice on new technologies
Infrastructures are plugged into other infrastructures and tools in a standardized fashion, although they are also modified by scope and conflicting (local) conventions	Activities that change standards that mediate between infrastructures (may also include activities that aim at local specializations of standards) Activities that change the scope to which standards apply Activities that articulate or mediate conflicts
Infrastructures do not grow de novo, they wrestle with the inertia of the installed base and inherit strengths and limitations from that base	Activities that interface and align new applications with existing IT infrastructures Activities that challenge and develop existing practices
Infrastructures are invisible but become visible upon breakdown	Activities that help with articulating a breakdown Activities that enable recovery after a breakdown

process of *infrastructuring* (Bowker and Star 2000). This view on infrastructuring shares many similarities with other concepts of appropriation we have outlined, such as, for example, Engeström's newer conceptualization of activity systems. In particular, in Star's work, the role played by breakdowns is similar to that in Engeström's cycle of expanded learning and Dewey's pattern of inquiry (cf. Figure 4.2). As an interruption of the conduct of action, breakdowns are special situations that reflect on and—in reaction—transform established practices, which in turn will have an effect on the infrastructures they rely on.

The notion of infrastructure extends the scope of reflection of appropriation phenomena significantly. At one point, the discourses on tailorability and end-user development still carried a designer focus with them: most of them reflected on a single tool or technology,

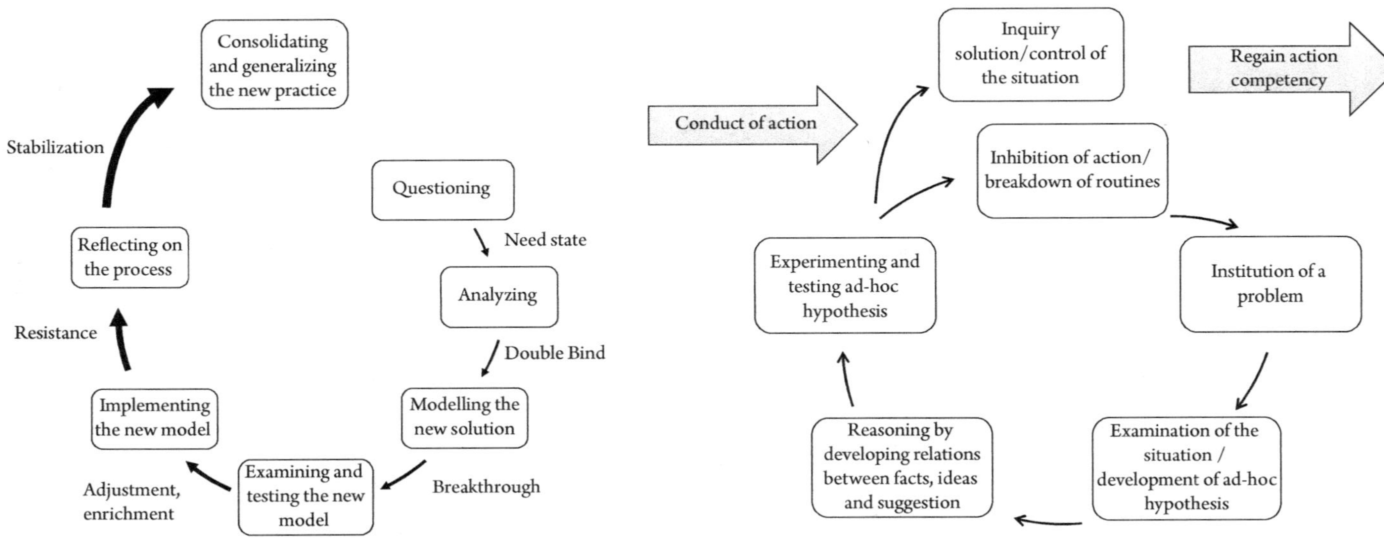

Figure 4.2 (*Left*) Engeström's cycle of expansive learning; (*right*) Dewey's pattern of inquiry

simply because the goal of deriving "implications-for-design" results in a pragmatically restricted solution space, as the activity range of a designer is defined by the tool she designs. We transcended this in our considerations about *appropriation infrastructures* (see Section 4.6.2), but the terminology that developed in the discourses around "infrastructuring" provides an arena of stakeholder activities around technology development and appropriation, one that is fresh and unprejudiced in relation to established divisions of labor or structures of professionalization (as they are associated with the contrast between design and use). Infrastructures may stabilize and reproduce through appropriation activities—for example, when users find out about an infrastructure like email and learn how to use it for their own purposes. They may also change, through appropriation, old tools by new technologies or through the development of new practices as new technologies afford them. The breakdowns described earlier may occur as elements of the infrastructure fall "out of sync" with opportunities offered by alternative tools or required by the surrounding technological context (e.g., when the demand to send large pictures and videos via email, combined with network capacities that would allow that, lead to an adaptation of the email protocols and the design of new email servers and clients), a phenomenon described as a "reverse salient" in the discourses around infrastructure.

Concerning the characteristics of infrastructures (cf. Table 4.1, left), we outlined in a previous work corresponding activities that lead to it emerging/developing (cf. Table 4.1, right). These activities have been documented in previous appropriation studies where we observed how users adopted and adapted new systems and integrated them in their local contexts, through the articulation of problems and usages as well as the sharing of tailoring artifacts (Pipek 2005; Stevens 2009). This shift of the perspective was also driven by common trends like Web 2.0, software ecosystems, agile development, and open-source communities, which also provide new opportunities for appropriation support.

4.6 Studying and Supporting Appropriation

In Section 4.4, we traced the conceptual origins of appropriation, and our actual understanding of it. While, appropriation could be roughly summarized as being all about *the work to make things work*, due to the diversity of the contexts, there will be no unified conceptual framework or even a grand theory emerging that would cover all appropriation practices and use cultures. At the same time, what level of generality might be appropriate remains an open question. In this last section, we give a brief, tentative outline about implications for studying and supporting appropriation.

4.6.1 Appropriation and Ethnographic Work

Most appropriation studies can be characterized as addressing at least one of the three following questions.

How is appropriation done in practice? This field of research is interested in the situations, people, methods, artifacts, and so on, that play a role in the appropriation of artifacts.

For instance, empirical studies show that some people make use of new technologies earlier and faster than others. Also, studies reveal that technology breakdowns, looking over the shoulder while working together, or making small talk at the water cooler, and so on, seem to be special situations that are important for the emergence and establishing of use practices. In addition, studies have identified common patterns, both temporal and spatial, which entail collaboration between different parties and which result in appropriation.

How can appropriation work be supported? How appropriation could be supported, for example, by the design of artifacts, processes, or by individual measures, is also of interest. Regarding this, it is mainly end-user development and CSCW research that has contributed to this issue (Trigg and Bødker 1994 Wulf 1999a; Stevens et al. 2006). Moreover, appropriation support in CSCW does not merely address tailoring but also is concerned with the support of articulation work and the negotiation of usages within local social networks (e.g., with peers, friends, and colleagues). A third approach, as yet not fully realized, could be characterized as the investigation of how to link appropriation with infrastructuring in a design-oriented manner.

What are the resulting practices and use cultures? A third goal of research into appropriation is to document, systematize, and classify the practices resulted from appropriation process and to understand and explain their inner logic. Understanding what practices and contexts are worth studying has to be a pragmatic matter. For instance, in design research the focus is typically on practices that have resulted from the appropriation of advanced technologies. In contrast, in the early days of CSCW, mainly the appropriation of groupware systems like email, instant messaging, shared workspace, or media spaces was a focus. Later on, the appropriation of community systems like Facebook and Wikipedia was investigated.

Due to the very nature of appropriation, there cannot be one methodology for doing appropriation studies in an appropriate manner. Nevertheless, it would seem to follow that appropriation practices, founded in the kinds of contextual, emerging use described here, require some version of "in the wild" study. However, this also means that appropriation studies could never be representative in any statistical sense. Instead, the goal of appropriation studies is to make the particular case visible, intelligible, relevant, and reportable for an external reader. In addition, design-oriented studies into appropriation will owe something to the grounded design framework (see Chapter 1).

With regard to the manifold options of conducting appropriation studies, a first approach to classifying the various types is to distinguish them with regard to the time horizons of the individual studies as they are, rather than issues that are specifically to do with the length of time needed to make sense of the appropriation issue.

It is obviously the case that, if we are to take the notion of appropriation seriously, we need to consider the time entailed in the conduct of such studies. As outlined, appropriation may take place in small steps and over variable periods of time.

With regard to the situatedness, the specific disturbances, breakdowns conflicts, and tensions, where routines get out of order, may be quickly identifiable. For instance, in one study, we analyzed, in minute detail, the user activity during a critical incident (Stevens et al. 2008). In the analysis, we could identify various strategies to cope with the situations that are described by the Dewey and Engeström logic of inquiry and expensive learning (cf. Figure 4.2). In another short-term oriented study, we installed smart meters for 2 weeks and examined the way data from this new technology was understood and used to understand better how make energy consumption is made accountable with the help of the new technology (Schwartz et al. 2013). A second reason to conduct a short-term study is capture initial, tentative glimpses about future practices. In this case, however, the actual doing is of less interest than the resulting outcome. These studies may inspire, inform, and improve design and redesign decisions relating to some kind of probe. Overall, such kinds of short-term studies serve as a means to better anticipate future appropriation. Even so, the appropriation of a new technology, the transformation of an activity system, and mastering a practice can take time. Therefore, there are grounds, wherever possible, for a more sustained commitment to understanding the appropriation of new techniques, ideas, rules, practices, and so on.

Long-term studies rely on the same bottom-up oriented methodologies as short-term studies, although they are likely to enlist a more complete approach to methodology. They form part of design-case study methodology (see Stevens et al. Chapter 1), for instance, and may implicate, for example, living lab approaches, where new technology is put in place precisely to investigate its effects over time. An example is the SMEDL living lab study based on a four-year program of research, where we studied the long-term effects that smart meters have on domestic practices and relationships (Schwartz et al. 4).

There is also a case for very long-term studies, to the extent that the studies take on a somewhat "historical" flavor. There are few such studies in the CSCW or design-research context, but they can be found elsewhere. Du Gay et al.'s (2013) study about the rise and evolution of the Sony Walkman and its impact on the media industry as well as media practices is one example of such a study.

4.6.2 Appropriation and Design

In conclusion, this chapter has been concerned with the different ways in which the concept of appropriation has been deployed, and it has asked how best to deploy this concept in pursuit of a design-related agenda. We have argued that appropriation activities are active, creative endeavors to change the technological environment to serve the intended usages of practitioners in a better way.

As a consequence, we can reflect on the functionalities a technology may provide in order to support appropriation activities. Keeping a tool interaction simple, together with providing good manuals and help systems, is vital, but the appropriation of tools is very often more a social activity than a problem of individual learning and use. Knowledge-sharing and delegation structures often develop, although in home- and other informal-use scenarios these structures are likely to be much more spontaneous and less organized than in professional environments. Appropriation support can address these social aspects of computing by supporting users as a "(virtual) community of tool/technology users," and by providing functional support for different appropriation activities that users can engage in to make use of a technology. Examples of such technological support (Pipek 2005) include:

- basic technological support: building highly flexible systems
- articulation support: providing support for technology-related articulations (real and online)
- historicity support: conceptualizing the appropriation as a process of emerging technologies and usages, for example, by documenting earlier configuration decisions and providing retrievable storage of configuration and usage descriptions
- decision support: providing voting, polling, and so on, if an agreement is required in a collaborative appropriation activity
- demonstration support: showing the usages of one user (or group group) to another user (or group); also, providing the communication channels that are required to do this
- observation support: supporting the visualization of (accumulated) information on the use of tools and functions in an organizational context
- simulation support: showing the effects of possible usage in an exemplified or actual organizational setting (this kind of support only makes sense if the necessary computational basis can be established)
- exploration support: performing simulation studies with extended support for technology configurations and test bed manipulations; may involve both individual and collaborative exploration modes
- explanation support: explaining the reasons for application behavior; this may be fully automated support or user–user/user–expert communication
- delegation support: supporting delegation patterns within configuration activities and providing remote configuration facilities
- (re-)design support: providing feedback to designers on the appropriation processes

Most of these suggestions aim to enhance the interactional capacities of a technology to allow end users to exchange and manage the use modes of a technology. They go beyond tailoring interfaces, as these use-mode changes do not necessarily require reconfigurations of the technological artifact. The user interactions that inspired this set of functionalities currently take place, for instance, in user forums of large software companies, on feedback platforms like GetSatisfaction, on expert platforms like stackoverflow.com, or by using videos to explain a technology on YouTube, but its embedment into the very technologies the interactions are about may bring additional benefit.

When we (Pipek 2005) deliberately took the professional software designer out of the equation before thinking about possible functional support for appropriation work and instead focused on interactions among users, we found that there are a number of obvious benefits of connecting the spheres of technology design with the spheres of technology usage. Designers may be able to understand the shortcomings of an existing technology when they are able to see and reflect on the appropriation activities of users. The connection may give users an understanding of the difficulties of implementing certain technological options and allow for a practice-driven prioritization of possible technology revisions.

Subsequently, we went beyond the interface level, introducing the idea of appropriation infrastructures (Stevens 2009; Stevens et al. 2010). The key idea of this approach is to embed tailoring and collaboration means within the context of use, supporting reflective, expansive learning when in a breakdown situation with the artifact present at hand. As the breakdown situation typically is not detached from the underlying infrastructure, the key idea is to provide channels in this situation to connect to other stakeholders like peers and colleagues, sysadmins, and help desk personnel, as well as developers and user communities.

The digital artifact itself can serve as a boundary object mediating between the self, the actual situation, and the social–material context. In particular, on the one hand, the software artifact provides communication channels; on the other hand, it presents the object that the communication is about. This twofold character could be used to support the articulation of the actual situation. The challenge is to make a situation readable by other stakeholders, implying that they have at least a basic understanding of the situation at hand as well as of the other stakeholders' attitudes and interests. Breakdown situations are often characterized by the absence of such understanding; a collaborative solution often requires stakeholders to inquire into the problem itself (e.g., a real or perceived breakdown, bug, or lack of knowledge) and the involvement of further stakeholders (who may be able to provide a solution or at least have knowledge that can inform the repair process; e.g., the local admin or the software developer).

When dealing with this dilemma, possible forms of support for infrastructuring activities may provide functionalities that are similar to the ones described for appropriation support, but these must be implemented as intermediary tools that work independently of the single artifact. Devices that are or become part of this infrastructure need to be prepared to interact with these tools. Pipek and Kahler (2006) distinguished between inner tailorability (the classical approaches to keep a tool modifiable at use time) and outer tailorability (approaches that improve the capabilities of a tools to work in an ensemble of tools), something that is echoed by the need for standardization in the infrastructure discourses.

With this in mind, we have outlined a modular software architecture, which is shown in Figure 4.3. The concept distinguishes spaces for personal appropriation, appropriation in self-organized groups, and appropriation in the public domain (e.g., the users of a technology); each of these spaces aims to provide tools to create as well as to explore adaptations and ideations. The infrastructure should also be context aware, meaning that the spaces for reflection should be directly accessible from the practice.

The architecture is split into a shared, or backend, part of the infrastructure, and a local, or client, part that integrates the infrastructure into the context of an application. The right side of the figure represents other agents of the product community (considered experts with various levels of technological expertise, from simple users to professional developers) who are connected to the appropriation infrastructure. Functional modules of this architecture may span backend as well as client implementations. We consider four modules to be crucial:

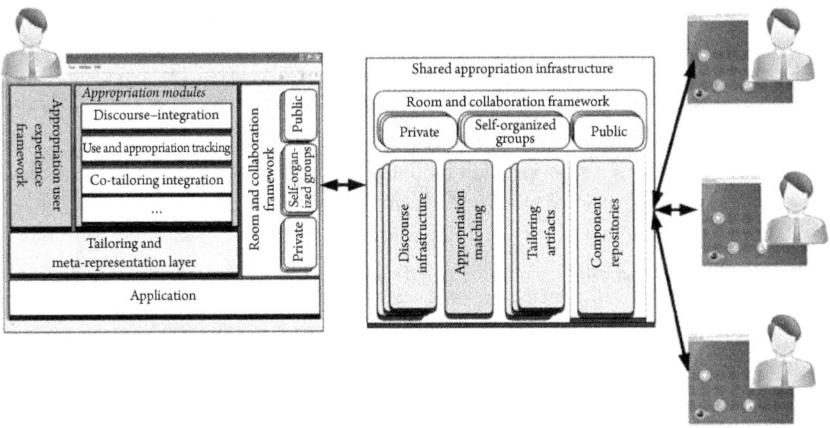

Figure 4.3 Architecture of a next generation of appropriation infrastructure (taken from Stevens 2009, p. 183)

- *The appropriation user experience framework*: This framework is a module that is responsible for weaving the shared infrastructure into the skin of the technology, guaranteeing a consistent user experience, regardless of the modular composition. The visual presentation and the responsible computational mechanisms, as well as the corresponding discussions, are supposed to refer to each other to simplify the transition between usage, usage discourse, and artifact modification. The framework should provide an extension point that allows one to plug in additional and domain-specific connection strategies.
- *The discourse infrastructure module*: The function of this module is to foster the social process of sense-making and negotiation around the used technology. It may implement many of the support mechanisms described in Section 4.5.2. The module consists of two parts: the shared part is responsible for storing and managing the actors' discourses, while the local part is responsible for integrating the discourses into the application in terms of adequate location and visualization at the interface.
- *The cooperative tailoring module*: This module is responsible for dealing with the technological aspects of a cooperative solution. The main role of its shared part is to offer management repositories that store and manage pre-made components as well as tailoring artifacts. The local part embeds the shared repository into the application context and should support a cooperative tailoring model.
- *The space and collaboration framework*: This module is responsible for providing user management and access control functionalities. An addition, it maps the logical space concept to the physical layer of distributed computing. In particular, the reference configuration file should offer the different types of spaces previously mentioned.

Based on the data this infrastructure produces and manages, additional services become possible. User recommendations may be generated automatically, based on the analysis of individual and collective histories of use. The histories need to be tracked and collected locally and may be matched with similar histories in the shared part of the appropriation infrastructure.

Besides these different appropriation modules, the architecture contains a set of common modules to manage and configure the technologies (e.g., a component management and configuration framework). A modular conceptualization of an appropriation infrastructure, and, in particular, the architectural separation of the appropriation support modules from the running instances of the applications under consideration, help to increase the extensibility and evolvability of the framework beyond the scope of a single application.

4.7 Concluding Remarks

As we have shown in the previous sections, appropriation has a long history. In this history, its meaning has often entailed some slippage, and various schools of thought have stressed different elements. Even so, a number of family resemblances remain. The various textures of the concept revolved about themes like the productive power of man, the relation between man and nature, as well as between man and society, and the reproduction, transformation, and growth of culture, practices, and mankind following Goethe's dictum: "What you have inherited from your fathers, acquire it in order to possess it."

The renewed interest in the concept also resulted from the lacunae in the positivistic mainstream of the traditional discourses concerned with technology development (information systems and software engineering). In simple terms, positivistic ideology perceives any deviation in practice from the theoretic model as random, and that the purpose of scientific endeavor is to build more accurate models that minimize such "errors." In particular, a technological determinism strand treats windows of opportunities, particularities of context, and practices and activities of the human subject as irrelevant to the design and development of new artifacts. For this stance, appropriation phenomena still do not exist. However, in the 1980s and 1990s, various ethnographic studies revealed that technologies such as the Sony Walkman, the Lotus Notes groupware system, the Worm Community System, and so on. are, in practice, used in manifold ways. In itself, this point would scarcely be worth mentioning, were it not for the fact that for the various kinds of models typically deployed in the service of design, as with the social sciences, this comes as something of a surprise. The phenomenon of *unanticipated use* was a *scandal* as well as *surprising fact.*

In reaction, the observed manifold forms of usages are understood to be the result of an open-ended appropriation process. Depending on the perspective adopted, the assessment of this process, however, has been different: more left-wing researchers, for instance, interpreted the appropriation of, for instance, space as a tactic of the ordinary man expressing resistance to the prevailing order, while others interpret it as a kind of unfaithful, deviant technology use that can lead to reduced productivity. Despite the differences, both interpretations focus on *unanticipated use* as subject matter, which has to be explained. As a matter of course, *anticipated use* is presumed to be the dominant form.

In comparison, we firmly believe that the concept of appropriation should not start from *unanticipated use* as theoretical point of departure; instead, we regard *orderly use* itself as in need of explanation. In other words, appropriation is constituted in the interplay of technology development and situated appropriation *work*, where the outcomes have to be understood as *practical inquiry* or as *infrastructuring*. In contrast to technological determinism *orderly use* is not seen as being caused by external factors but is a product of creative actions dealing with the demands and opportunities of the situation at hand.

This view has an impact on the role of abstractions, concepts, and theoretic models, too. As has been said elsewhere in this book, the positivistic stance has a tendency to postulate simple cause–effect models and to interpret regularities in technology use as simple causalities without further analysis. This, in turn, produces conceptual apparatuses that gloss over the transformative and emergent quality of appropriation process. At the same time, no generalization is an absurd alternative, since we see, over and over again, that in given settings, work is done in typical ways. The single case, then, is never wholly innocent of preexisting knowledge, concepts, or categories. What is at stake is what kind of use one might make of them. It is the view of the author that, following Herbert Blumer, we should see such examples from previous work as *illuminating*. Existing knowledge, research results, theories, categories, and so on, can sensitize researchers to what cases and phenomena are already documented, and within which academic discourses new findings can be positioned. A vital component of this is the business of making the relevance of newly acquired data evident to the reader—for example, by drawing analogies, making a contrast, and so on. There remains a considerable space for empirical appropriation studies, specifically with a design-oriented impetus. They need to be open in their focus and curious in their manner of exploring practices and innovative IT designs. Looking at the phenomenon of appropriation work is an obvious strategy in the framework of grounded design (see Chapter 1).

There is not any deterministic relationship between the design of IT artifacts and their appropriation, and this is precisely what necessitates a specific focus on appropriation. It is likely as argued here, that certain designs, that is, those with better "appropriability," have a higher likelihood of impacting practice positively. The focus on "design," in and of itself, presumes a certain relationship between the functionalities of the artifact and the kinds of use to which it will be put. To assert no such relationship would, of course, be a bizarre argument, but to assert that any given design does not wholly close down the various possibilities of use, and, more strongly, that the objective of designing in such a way that maintaining or opening up this space for flexibility is a desirable objective is a different position.

Last, but not least, supporting the creative, purposeful activities that contribute to the successful establishment of usages, the question is of how to put improved "appropriability" into the design of technologies. Much of what has been discussed in this chapter concerns the possible avenues that facilitate the tailoring of, at minimum, interfaces and, more ambitiously, functionality and infrastructure development. Tied to this, but with arguably even greater ambition, is the prospect that "appropriation support" functionalities will provide a fruitful research arena. With the concept of approbation infrastructures, we have touched this topic, but it needs to be further elaborated, especially with regard to the new technological infrastructures emerging around "ubiquitous computing" and the "internet of things." In initial approaches to develop "sociable technologies," Ludwig et al. (2014, 2017) address the complicated relations that make the analysis of and the design for appropriation activities in the "Internet of things" era even more difficult. The same, complex issues occur when we address the area of 3D printing and the "hacking" and "making" cultures that have grown up around it. Regarding this, the materiality of appropriation practices becomes a renaissance—thus completing the circle to the Hegel/Marxian beginning of the concept.

References

Ackermann, E. 2001. "Piaget's constructivism, Papert's constructionism: What's the difference." *Future of Learning Group Publication* 5 (3): 438.

Adorno, T., and Horkheimer, M. 2007. "The culture industry: Enlightenment as mass deception." In S. Redmond and S. Holmes, eds., *Stardom and Celebrity: A Reader*. Los Angelos: Sage, 34–43.

Ahearne, J. 1995. *Michel de Certeau: Interpretation and Its Other*. Redwood City: Stanford University Press.

Bakhtin, M. M. 1981. *The Dialogic Imagination: Four Essays*. Austin: University of Texas Press.

Balka, E., and Wagner, I. 2006. "Making things work: Dimensions of configurability as appropriation work." In *CSCW'06*. New York: ACM, 229–38.

Bødker, S., and Christiansen, E. 2012. "Poetry in motion: Appropriation of the world of apps." In *ECCE'12*. New York: ACM, 78–84.

Braun, K.-H. 2004. "Raumentwicklung als Aneignungsprozess." In U. Deinet and C. Reutlinger, eds., *"Aneignung" als Bildungskonzept der Sozialpädagogik*. Wiesbaden: VS Verlag für Sozialwissenschaften, 19–48.

Brusilovsky, P. 1998. "Methods and techniques of adaptive hypermedia." In P. Brusilovsky, A. Kobsa, and J. Vassileva, eds., *Adaptive Hypertext and Hypermedia*. Dordrecht: Kluwer, 1–43.

Button, G., and Dourish, P. 1996. "Technomethodology: Paradoxes and possibilities." In *CHI'96*. New York: ACM, 19–26.

de Certeau, M. 1984. *The Practice of Everyday Life*, trans. S. Rendall. Oakland: University of California Press.

Deinet, U. 2014. "Raumaneignung Jugendlicher Zwischen Schule, McDonald's Und Der Shopping Mall." In U. Deinet and C. Reutlinger, eds., *Tätigkeit-Aneignung-Bildung: Positionierungen Zwischen Virtualität Und Gegenständlichkeit*. Sozialraumforschung und Sozialraumarbeit, Vol. 15. Wiesbaden : Springer VS, 215–32.

DiSalvo, C., Clement, A., and Pipek, V. 2012. "Participatory design for, with, and by communities." In J. Simonsen and T. Robertson, eds., *International Handbook of Participatory Design*. Oxford: Routledge, 182–209.

Dourish, P. 2003. "The appropriation of interactive technologies: Some lessons from placeless documents." *Computer Supported Cooperative Work* 12 (4): 465–90.

Dourish, P., and Button, G. 1998. "On 'technomethodology': Foundational relationships between ethnomethodology and system design." *Human–Computer Interaction* 13 (4): 395–432.

Dourish, P., and Edwards, W. K. 2000. "A tale of two toolkits: Relating infrastructure and use in flexible CSCW toolkits." *Computer Supported Cooperative Work* 9 (1): 33–51.

Draxler, S., Jung, A., Boden, A., and Stevens, G. 2011. "Workplace warriors: Identifying team practices of appropriation in software ecosystems." In *CHASE'11*. New York: ACM, 57–60.

Draxler, S., and Stevens, G. 2006. *Getting Out Of A Tailorability Dilemma*. Available at https://s3.amazonaws.com/academia.edu.documents/2682924/Draxler_and_Stevens_-_2006_-_Getting_Out_of_a_Tailorability_Dilemma.pdf?AWSAccessKeyId=AKIAIWOWYYGZ2Y53UL3A&Expires=1502838999&Signature=K0%2FCULHp5yAYE2WMCuoj94K9pCI%3D&response-content-disposition=inline%3B%20filename%3DGetting_out_of_a_tailorability_dilemma.pdf (accessed August 15, 2017).

Draxler, S., and Stevens, G. 2011. "Supporting the collaborative appropriation of an open software ecosystem." *Computer Supported Cooperative Work* 20 (4–5): 403–48.

Draxler, S., Stevens, G., and Boden, A. 2014. "Keeping the development environment up to date: a study of the situated practices of appropriating the Eclipse IDE." *IEEE Transactions on Software Engineering* 40 (11): 1061–74.

Du Gay, P., Hall, S., Janes, L., Madsen, A. K., Mackay, H., and Negus, K. 2013. *Doing Cultural Studies: The Story of the Sony Walkman*. London: Sage.

Ehn, P. 1993. "Scandinavian design: On participation and skill." In D. Schuler and A. Namioka, eds., *Participatory Design: Principles and Practices*. Boca Raton: CRC Press, 41–77.

Engeström, Y. 2001. "Expansive learning at work: Toward an activity theoretical reconceptualization." *Journal of Education and Work* 14 (1): 133–56.

Eriksson, J., and Dittrich, Y. 2008. "Achieving sustainable tailorable software systems by collaboration between end-users and developers." In S. Clarke, ed., *Evolutionary Concepts in End User Productivity and Performance: Applications for Organizational Progress: Applications for Organizational Progress*. Hershey, PA: IGI Global, 19–34.

Fischer, G., and Ostwald, J. 2002. *Seeding, Evolutionary Growth, and Reseeding: Enriching Participatory Design with Informed Participation*. Available at http://l3d.cs.colorado.edu/~Gerhard/papers/pdc2002-ser.pdf (accessed November 2017).

Floyd, C., Reisin, F.-M, and Schmidt, G. 1989. "STEPS to software development with users." In *ESEC'89* Berlin/Heidelberg: Springer, 48–64.

Frijhoff, W. 1999. "Foucault reformed by Certeau: Historical strategies of discipline and everyday tactics of appropriation." In J. Neubauer, ed., *Cultural History after Foucault*. Piscataway: Transaction Publishers, 83–100.

Gärling, T., Biel, A., and Gustafsson, M. 2002. "The new environmental psychology: The human interdependence paradigm." In R. B. Bechtel and A. Churchman, eds., *Handbook of Environmental Psychology*. New York: John Wiley & Sons, 85–94.

Gerson, E. M., and Star, S. L. 1986. "Analyzing due process in the workplace." *ACM Transactions on Information Systems* 4 (3): 257–70.

Grinter R. E., Edwards, W. K, Newman, M. W., and Ducheneaut, N. 2005. "The work to make a home network work." In *ECSCW'05*. Dordrecht: Springer, 469–88.

Hashim, N. H., and Jones, M. L. 2007. *Activity Theory: A Framework for Qualitative Analysis*. Available at http://ro.uow.edu.au/cgi/viewcontent.cgi?article=1434&context=commpapers (accessed August 15, 2017).

Henderson, A., and Kyng, M. 1985. "There's no place like home: Continuing design in use." In R. M. Baecker, *Readings in Human–Computer Interaction: Toward the Year 2000* (2nd edition). San Francisco: Morgan Kaufmann Publishers, 793–803.

Hepp, A. 1998. "Fernsehaneignung Und Alltagsgespräche." In *Fernsehaneignung Und Alltagsgespräche*. Wiesbaden: VS Verlag für Sozialwissenschaften, 203–10.

Hidalgo, D. 2013. "Ownership and private property from the perspectives of Hegel and Marx." *The Agora: Political Science Undergraduate Journal* 3 (2): 139.

Holzkamp, K. and Schurig, V. 1973. "Zur Einführung." In A. N. Leontjew and K. Holzkamp, eds., *Probleme der Entwicklung des Psychischen*. Frankfurt am Main: Athenäum Fischer Taschenbuch, S. XI–LII. Hughes, T. P. 1987. "The evolution of large technological systems." In W. E. Bijker, T. P. Hughes, and T. J. Pinch, eds., *The Social Construction of Technological Systems: New Directions in the Sociology and History of Technology*. Cambridge, MA: MIT Press, 51–82.

Keiler, P. 1990. "Aneignung." In H. J. Sandkühler, ed., *Europäische Enzyklopädie zu Philosophie und Wissenschaften*, Hamburg: Meiner, 118–27.

Krönert, V. 2009. *Michel de Certeau: Alltagsleben, Aneignung Und Widerstand*. Wiesbaden: VS Verlag für Sozialwissenschaften.

Leontjew, A. N. 1967. *Probleme Der Entwicklung Des Psychischen*. Berlin: Volk und Wissen.

Lieberman, H., Paternò, F., Klann, M., and Wulf, V. 2006. "End-user development: An emerging paradigm." In H. Lieberman, F. Paternò, and V. Wulf, eds., *End User Development*. Dordrecht: Springer, 1–8.

Ludwig, T., Stickel, O., Boden, A., and Pipek, V. 2014. "Towards sociable technologies: An empirical study on designing appropriation infrastructures for 3d printing." In *DIS'14*. New York: ACM, 835–44.

Ludwig, T., Stickel, O., Boden, A., and Pipek, V. 2017. "3D printers as sociable technologies: Taking appropriation infrastructures to the Internet of Things." *ACM Transactions on Computer-Human Interaction*, 24 (2): 17.

Mackay, W. E. 1990. "Patterns of sharing customizable software." In *CSCW'90*. New York: ACM, 209–21.

Mark, G., Fuchs, L., and Sohlenkamp, M. 1997. "Supporting groupware conventions through contextual awareness." In *Proceedings of The Fifth European Conference on Computer Supported Cooperative Work*. Dordrecht: Springer, 253–68.

Marx, K. 1973. *Grundrisse*. London: Penguin Books.

Merriam-Webster. 2017. "appropriate." *Merriam-Webster.com*. Available at http://www.merriam-webster.com (accessed August 15, 2017).

Mørch, A. I., Stevens, G., Won, M., Klann, M., Dittrich, Y., and Wulf, V. 2004. "Component-based technologies for end-user development." *Communications of the ACM* 47 (9): 59–62.

Nardi, B. A. 1993. *A Small Matter of Programming: Perspectives on End User Computing*. Cambridge, MA: MIT Press.

Olson, J. R., and Olson. G. M. 1990. "The growth of cognitive modeling in human–computer interaction since GOMS." *Human–Computer Interaction* 5 (2–3): 221–65.

Orlikowski, W., and Hoffman, D. 1997. "An improvisational model for change managment: The case of groupware technologies." In T. W. Malone, R. Laubacher, and M. S. Scott Morton, eds., *Inventing the Organizations of the 21st Century*. Cambridge, MA: MIT Press, 265–82.

Pane, J., and Myers, B. 1996. *Usability Issues in the Design of Novice Programming Systems*. Available at http://repository.cmu.edu/cgi/viewcontent.cgi?article=1818&context=isr (accessed August 15, 2017).

Papert, S. 1980. *Mindstorms: Children, Computers, and Powerful Ideas*. Basic Books, Inc.

Pipek, V. 2005. *From Tailoring to Appropriation Support: Negotiating Groupware Usage*. Oulu: Oulun Yliopisto.

Pipek, V., and Wulf, V. 1999. "A groupware's life." In *ECSCW'99*. Dordrecht, Springer, 199–218.

Robertson, T. 1998. "Shoppers and tailors: Participative practices in small Australian design companies." *Computer Supported Cooperative Work* 7 (3): 205–21.

Robinson, M. 1993. "Design for unanticipated use....." In *ECSCW'93*. Dordrecht: Springer, 187–202.

Rogers, E. M. 2002. "Diffusion of preventive innovations." *Addictive Behaviors* 27 (6): 989–93.

Rogers, E. M. 2010. *Diffusion of Innovations*. New York: Simon and Schuster.

Ruggiero, T. E. 2000. "Uses and gratifications theory in the 21st century." *Mass Communication and Society* 3 (1): 3–37.

Sacks, H. 1963. "Sociological description." *Berkeley Journal of Sociology* 8 (1): 1–16.

Scheer, A.-W., Thomas, O., and Adam, O. 2005. "Process modeling using event-driven process chains." In M. Dumas, W. M. van der Aalst, and A. H. ter Hofstede, eds., *Process-Aware Information Systems*. Hobroken, NJ: John Wiley & Sons, 119–46.

Schwartz, T., Stevens, G., Ramirez, L., and Wulf, V. 2013. "Uncovering practices of making energy consumption accountable: A phenomenological inquiry." *ACM Transactions on Computer–Human Interaction* 20 (2): 12.

Schwartz, T., Stevens, G., Jakobi, T., Denef, S., Ramirez, L., Wulf, V., and Randall, D. 2014. "What people do with consumption feedback: A long-term living lab study of a home energy management system." *Interacting with Computers* 27 (6): 551–76.

Spatscheck, C. 2014. "Aneignungsprozesse Gestalten Und Begleiten." In U. Deinet and C. Reutlinger, eds., *Tätigkeit-Aneignung-Bildung: Positionierungen Zwischen Virtualität Und Gegenständlichkeit*, Sozialraumforschung und Sozialraumarbeit, Vol. 15. Wiesbaden: Springer VS, 113–24.

Stallman, R. M. 1981. *EMACS: The Extensible, Customizable Self-Documenting Display Editor*. Available at https://www.gnu.org/software/emacs/emacs-paper.html (accessed August 15, 2017).

Stallman, R. M. 1985. *The GNU Manifesto*. Available at http://www.gnu.org/gnu/manifesto.html (accessed August 15, 2017).

Star, S. L., and Ruhleder, K. 1996. "Steps toward an ecology of infrastructure: Design and access for large information spaces." *Information Systems Research* 7 (1): 111–34.

Stevens, G. 2009. *Understanding and Designing Appropriation Infrastructures*. Available at http://dokumentix.ub.uni-siegen.de/opus/volltexte/2010/433/ (accessed August 15, 2017).

Stevens, G., Boden, A., and von Rekowski, T. 2013. "Objects-to-think-with-together." In Y. Dittrich, M. Burnett, A. Mørch, and D. Redmiles, eds., *4th International Symposium on End User Development*. Berlin: Springer, 223–8.

Stevens, G., Quaisser, G., and Klann, M. 2006. "Breaking it up: An industrial case study of component-based tailorable software design." In H. Lieberman, F. Paternò, and V. Wulf, eds., *End User Development*. Dordrecht: Springer, 269–94.

Stevens, G., Draxler, S., and Wienke, I. 2008. "Zum Handeln in Krisensituationen: Ein Beitrag Zur Strukturationsdebatte." In M. Bichler, ed., *Multikonferenz Wirtschaftsinformatik 2008*. Berlin: GITO mbH Verlag, 281–2.

Suchman, L. A. 1987. *Plans and Situated Actions: The Problem of Human–Machine Communication*. Cambridge: Cambridge University Press.

Taylor, C. 1977. *Hegel*. Cambridge: Cambridge University Press.

Törpel, B., Pipek, V., and Rittenbruch, M. 2003. "Creating heterogeneity: Evolving use of groupware in a network of freelancers." *Computer Supported Cooperative Work* 12 (4): 381–409.

Trigg, R. H., and Bødker, S. 1994. "From Implementation to design: Tailoring and the emergence of systematization in CSCW." In *CSCW'94*. New York: ACM., 45–54.

Twidale, M. B. 2005. "Over the shoulder learning: Supporting brief informal learning." *Computer Supported Cooperative Work* 14 (6): 505–47.

Wertsch, J. V. 1998. *Mind as Action*. Oxford: Oxford University Press.

Whittaker, S., and Sidner, C. 1996. "Email overload: Exploring personal information management of email." In *CHI'13*. New York: ACM, 276–83.

Winograd, T. 1987. "A language/action perspective on the design of cooperative work." *Human–Computer Interaction* 3 (1): 3–30.

Wulf, V. 1994. "Anpaßbarbarkeit Im Prozeß Evolutionärer Systementwicklung." *GMD-Spiegel* 24 (3) 41–6.

Wulf, V. 1997. "Organisatorischer Wandel Bei Einführung von Groupware." In H. Krallmann, ed., *Wirtschaftsinformatik'97*. Heidelberg: Physica, 167–81.

Wulf, V. 1999. Evolving cooperation when introducing groupware: A self-organization perspective. *Cybernetics and Human Knowing* 6 (2): 55–75.

Wulf, V., and Golombek, B. 2001. "Direct activation: A concept to encourage tailoring activities." *Behaviour and Information Technology* 20 (4): 249–63.

Wulf, V., Pipek, V., and Won, M. 2008. "Component-based tailorability: Enabling highly flexible software applications." *International Journal of Human-Computer Studies* 66 (1): 1–22.

5 A Bridge Too Far?

Critical Remarks on the Concept of "Infrastructure" in Computer-Supported Cooperative Work and Information Systems

CHARLOTTE P. LEE AND KJELD SCHMIDT

But I think we might be going a bridge too far.
Lieutenant General Frederick Browning[1]

In the course of the last century or two, large-scale technical structures such as water and sewer systems, railways, electrical telegraph systems, administrative archives, electrical power distribution, telephony, satellite navigation, and now, of course, the Internet and the services facilitated by it—email, the World Wide Web (WWW), search engines, online repositories, etc. and, not least, organizational and interorganizational coordination technologies such as enterprise resource planning (ERP) systems, supply-chain management systems, and medical record systems have been constructed and have become critical features of our civilization (e.g., Delgado 1979; Perrow 1984; Bijker et al. 1987; Mayntz and Hughes 1988; Yates 1989; La Porte 1991; Bud-Frierman 1994; Rochlin 1997; Abbate 1999; Gillies and Cailliau 2000; Yates 2005; Levinson 2006; Car et al. 2008a, 2008b;

[1] "On the narrow corridor that would carry the armored drive, there were five major bridges to take. They had to be seized intact by airborne assault. It was the fifth, the crucial bridge over the Lower Rhine at a place called Arnhem, sixty-four miles behind the German lines, that worried Lieutenant General Frederick Browning, Deputy Commander, First Allied Airborne Army. Pointing to the Arnhem bridge on the map he asked, 'How long will it take the armor to reach us?' Field Marshal Montgomery replied briskly, 'Two days.' Still looking at the map, Browning said, 'We can hold it for four.' Then he added, 'But, sir, I think we might be going a bridge too far'" (The final conference at Montgomery's Headquarters on Operation Market-Garden, 10 September 1944, as recalled by Major General Roy E. Urquhart, quoted in Ryan 1974, pp. 9, 89).

Socio-Informatics, Volker Wulf, Volkmar Pipek, Dave Randall, Markus Rohde, Kjeld Schmidt, Gunnar Stevens (Eds). © Oxford University Press 2018. Published 2018 by Oxford University Press.

Pollock and Williams 2009; Stead and Lin 2009). The study of computing infrastructures, in particular, has grown significantly due to the rapid proliferation and ubiquity of large-scale IT-based installations. At the same time, recognition has also grown of the usefulness of such studies as a means for understanding computing infrastructures as material complements of practical action. Subsequently, the concept of "infrastructure" has gained increasing importance in Computer-Supported Cooperative Work (CSCW) as well as in neighboring areas such as Information Systems (IS) research and Science and Technology Studies (STS). However, as scholarly study of infrastructures (especially of those that depend on computing technologies) has unfolded, the very concept of "infrastructure" has been applied in different discourses, for different purposes, in myriad different senses. The concept of "infrastructure" has become increasingly muddled over time. Disparities in use of the concept have become an immense source of confusion (Schmidt and Bansler 2016). The unquestioned and seemingly unnoticed use of the term "infrastructure" in myriad ways is hobbling the development of the area.

While we do not attempt a comprehensive review of this vast literature, we do trace some influential lines of thought and how these come together and also diverge. This work presents a critical investigation of the vicissitudes of the concept of "infrastructure" over the last 35 years. The aim of this work is to foster greater clarity to help further develop this line of computing research and the practices it both studies and supports.[2] The broadening scope of the concept of *infrastructure* has brought more researchers and a greater variety of orientations and methods to the table to the great benefit of the research area. While it is neither necessary nor desirable to have a singular approach or focus for the study of infrastructures, the rapid growth of the area has led to a substantial amount of confusion. The broadening scope of the concept has also been useful for positioning sociotechnical research as important, if not crucial, for continuing advances in the successful development, maintenance, and use of technological infrastructures. Having successfully reframed the discussion around infrastructure as a sociotechnical one, greater precision is now required for distinguishing the elements that interact within and without infrastructure. Imagine if you will a surgeon who does not have the vocabulary or grammar to distinguish between heart and lungs. This would not make surgery impossible, but it would make it far more difficult. More precision is needed in defining our terms, objects of study, and the interactions between myriad nested and overlapping practices, technical components, and sub-components. Ultimately, we need increasingly sophisticated conceptual tools for understanding, talking about, and working on the problem spaces in which we are intervening.

A place to begin this discussion is to observe that the very word "infrastructure" has a surprisingly short history and that the term, nonetheless, is used quite flexibly in everyday discourse. It seems to have originated in in the late nineteenth century in French

[2] This study was conceived during Lee's stay at Copenhagen Business School as a visiting scholar (Fall 2015). Lee's research has been supported by US National Science Foundation (NSF) grants: IIS-0954088, ACI-1302272, and OCI-1220269. Schmidt's research has been supported by the Velux Foundation under the "Computational Artifacts" project (VELUX33295).—We want to express our gratitude to Professor Jørgen Bansler, University of Copenhagen, for very helpful critical comments and suggestions, and to Dr Drew H. Paine, Lawrence Berkeley National Lab (formerly University of Washington), for helpful feedback and copyediting.

railroad engineering as a way to refer to the ballast, subgrade, and subsoil supporting the tracks, as opposed to the "superstructure" in the form of tracks, station buildings, and rolling stock.[3] However, its use soon extended to refer to material structures underpinning other structures such as buildings and roads. In English, its wider use seems to have begun during the Cold War with the establishment of NATO's Infrastructure Committee tasked with the establishment of "static buildings and permanent installations required to support military forces" such as headquarters, pipelines, airfields, signal communications, information systems, air defense systems, storage depots, port facilities, and maintenance bases (NATO 2001). From that usage, the term was extended to refer to the system of public works of a country, state, region, or city (water and sewage, electrical power, railroads, etc.) and then in the 1970s, by analogy, to sociotechnical systems or entire industries sustaining the economic life of a country, such as postal services, shipping and container transportation, trucking, aviation, banking, etc. Thus, when one today mentions a country's "railroad infrastructure," one may be referring to the railroad system *as a service* running the entire system of resources in the form of technical structures (tracks, signal systems, stations, etc.), the ongoing operation of trains, signals, and switches, as well as the administration of its operation, such as the provision of schedules, ticketing services, maintenance, etc. Still, while used flexibly, in ordinary discourse the concept of "infrastructure" refers to a technical facility that provides a service to the wider world: by supporting tracks, by affording the movement of trains, by supporting the transportation of goods and people, and so on. The point of its use is that it refers to a system that under some description supports another: an infrastructure in its relation to a superstructure.

5.1 "Infrastructural Resources"

In the general computing-related discourse, the term "infrastructure" was originally introduced and used, as a key analytic concept, in the research area *social studies of computing* by Rob Kling, Walt Scacchi, and Tom Jewett (Kling and Scacchi 1982; Kling 1987; Jewett and Kling 1991). The research problem Kling et al. were addressing was not one of technology development and systems design, nor one of general public policy, but one of sociology of technology: "What influences the adoption of new computer-based technologies? How are particular computer-based technologies ordinarily used? What are the social consequences of using computer-based technologies?" (Kling 1987, pp. 307 f.). They were exploring ways of understanding computing as social action, and for that purpose, they needed to see computing technology and computer systems not as something that (somehow) arrives out of the blue but rather as something that is inherently "social," in its inception as well as in use. Thus, in a programmatic paper, Rob Kling and Walt Scacchi (1982) subjected conventional conception of computing to an incisive critique:

[3] *"Le passage des trains, dont la masse est souvent très lourde et animée de grandes vitesses, communique en effet à la voie et à l'infrastructure des vibrations qui causent des ébranlements dangereux pour les ouvrages mal fondés,"* in contrast to *"la superstructure, c'est-à-dire [...] la voie et des stations et de la fourniture du matériel roulant"* (Bricka 1894, pp. 3, 126). (For an overview of the etymology, see Lewis 2008).

> Most scholarly and professional examinations of the social and economic repercussions of new computing developments are based on a highly simplified conception of computing and social life. This conception focuses on certain explicit economic, physical, or information processing features of a technology. For the sake of simplicity, the social context in which the technology is developed and used, and the history of participating organizations, are ignored. [...] This conception informs many analyses of computing and related activities: of the payoffs of new computing developments, of the costs to be borne by developers and the broader public, of the extent to which different management strategies will yield more reliable and broadly workable computer-based systems. (Kling and Scacchi 1982, p. 2)

Against this conception, dubbed the "discrete-elements model of computing," they sketched an alternative "web model" approach. Where the "discrete-elements model of computing" conceives of a computing resource as "a particular piece of equipment, application, or technique," the "web model" conceives of a computing resource as "an ensemble of equipment, applications, and techniques." Both approaches conceive of these computing resources—a "particular piece" or "an ensemble"—as the unit of analysis, its "focal computing resource."

As the decisive move in this attack, the concept of "infrastructure" was invoked, and due to the central role it was assigned, the term was given a formal definition:

> *Infrastructure* refers to those resources which help support the provision of a given service or product. The infrastructure for providing computer-based services includes resources such as skilled staff and good operations procedures, as well as physical systems such as reliable "clean" electrical energy and low-noise communication lines. (Kling and Scacchi 1982, p. 7, n. 2, and pp. 18 f.)[4]

According to Kling and Scacchi, for both approaches—the "discrete-elements models" and the "web models"—the "infrastructure for supporting the focal computing resource and the organizational procedures by which it [the resource] is organized and sustained are critical elements." Similarly, each approach presumes that the "computer-based service is provided through a set of structured computing resources and organized infrastructure." So far, they are on parallel tracks. However, the former approach presumes that deploying, managing, and establishing procedures for these "infrastructural resources" ("structured computing resources" as well as "organized infrastructure[s]") is "separable from deployment of the focal computer-based technology." Hence, on this view, "Infrastructure, either technical or administrative, is a neutral resource." In contrast, on the "web model" view, the "computer-based systems" are conceived of as "a form of social organization." Hence, "Like any organization or institution, it [the organized infrastructure] is not necessarily neutral" (Kling and Scacchi 1982, pp. 7 f.; Kling 1987, pp. 311 f.).

[4] This definition was upheld and even sharpened later: "*Infrastructure* is a useful concept in analyses of computing support — it denotes all the resources and practices required to help people adequately carry out their work" (Kling and Scacchi 1982; Kling 1987). Infrastructure for computing refers to a variety of organizational arrangements for supporting computing, including recharge systems and purchasing procedures, as well as the human resources [...]" (Jewett and Kling 1991, pp. 247 f.).

Hence the motivation for introducing the notion of "infrastructure": "We find the term infrastructure useful to denote these supporting resources for computing development. They are often taken for granted, and priority is placed on the leverage to be gained by new computing developments" (Kling and Scacchi 1982, p. 20). Kling and his colleagues introduced the concept of "infrastructure" so as to be able to treat the organizational and practical aspects of computing on the same level as computing equipment and thus to bring to attention the invisible work and the hidden costs required of establishing the organizational framework for computing as well as the often undisclosed conflicts of interest at play in such large-scale organizational interventions.

However, the way the term "infrastructure" is used here is a source of potential confusion. The authors explicitly distinguished between "the focal" computing facility on the one hand and, on the other, the supplementary technical resources, organizational arrangements, and human skills required for it to operate. This distinction is clear enough, in that it reflects the purpose of bringing to the fore the organizational and practical embeddedness of computing. So far, the authors are in accord with the ordinary use of the term "infrastructure." For as already mentioned, when one talks about a country's railroad infrastructure, one will be referring to the service provided by the technical structures or installations and equipment of the railroad system in operation. And one may also, in describing the railroad services, refer to the technical installations (tracks, etc.) as the infrastructure of a country's railroad service, that is, the infrastructure of an infrastructure. So far, so good. But would one refer to, say, the administration of operations, etc., of a railroad system as the *infrastructure* of the system of tracks, etc.? Hardly. That would be utterly perplexing. Much of the trouble with the notion of "infrastructure" in CSCW and IS probably stems from this terminological choice.

In so far as the "focal" entity of the given study is clearly identified, the ambiguity can be handled (with care), just as we, in daily language, can refer to the railroad system, the sewer system, the power systems, and so on as "infrastructures" in both senses: as technical installations and as organized technical services. However, the ambiguity becomes unwieldy as soon as the "focal" entity, and by implication the "infrastructure" defined as its organized context, becomes heterogeneous and distributed. The focus then becomes blurred. Kling and Scacchi, for example, already open this can of worms when they go on to say that a crucial characteristic of the "web models" approach is the assumption that "Each computer-based service is provided through a set of structured computing resources and organized infrastructure[s]" (Kling and Scacchi 1982, p. 8). This raises a question: How does one identify what is "focal" and what is not? In the case of, say, the railroad system, there are, so to speak, only two levels: the organized transportation service and the technical structure it depends on (if we may be allowed to disregard the fact that maintenance services also use the rail tracks and so on). But in the case of a "computer-based service" "provided through a set of structured computing resources and organized infrastructure[s]," it is difficult and potentially impossible to determine what's what. What would here be the criterion for determining the "focal" entity?

Kling et al. did not address that question, for at the time the question had hardly been raised as a real-life question yet. Distributed computing was still in its infancy: The essential email protocol SMTP was not specified until August 1982, that is, in the same year as

Kling et al.'s study (Postel 1982; Hardy 1996), and TCP/IP was only made the underlying protocol of ARPANET in January 1983 and did not become practical reality until the end of the 1980s (Quarterman 1990; Abbate 1999; Gillies and Cailliau 2000). That is, in 1982 and even in 1987, it made perfect sense not to consider "the focal computing resource" a problematic notion.

5.2 "Information Infrastructures" 1.0

The widespread use of the term "infrastructure" in computing can be dated quite precisely to around 1990, when it appeared in the form of the term "information infrastructure." Until then, in the decades up to 1990, the term "infrastructure" was hardly used in the computing literature; instead the term "network" (or "computing network") reigned supreme, for the simple reason that it precisely describes an essential topological feature of the facilities: their being distributed and yet interconnected. But by the late 1980s, the Internet protocol TCP/IP had become the standard communication protocols in ordinary computer operating systems. Given this vast and potentially global computing and communication platform, the interest of technologists and government officials turned to the question of how to exploit this new resource: What *services* could or should be built on top of it? Provided, organized, maintained by whom? In the ensuing discussion, such services were dubbed "infrastructures" and, with increasing frequency, "information infrastructures" (e.g., Cerf 1987; FCCSET 1987a, 1987b; Kahin 1990b, 1992; McGarty 1992; Kahin 1997).[5]

The notion of "infrastructure" introduced by Kling and Scacchi a decade earlier, in 1982, had no apparent influence on this movement. Indeed, by 1992, the paper by Kling and Scacchi (1982) does not seem to have received any citations (other than in Kling's own later papers: Kling 1987; Jewett and Kling 1991). In fact, the issue addressed around 1990 by the technologists, administrators, and government officials was not the sociological issue of how the social organization of computing might be subjected to a critical analysis that did not, from the very beginning, presume computing to be a "neutral" entity. The issue was now rather that of exploring and planning how to exploit the Internet.

Around 1990, two broad and interrelated initiatives gained momentum.

On the one hand, the US National Science Foundation (NSF) began to explore ways in which the Internet could provide the technical platform for scientific research. In a very influential white paper, William Wulf, then Assistant Director of NSF's Directorate for Computer and Information Science and Engineering, outlined the idea of a "national collaboratory," defined as

[5] The term "information infra-structure" was originally coined by the US Domestic Council Committee on the Right of Privacy in 1976 in a report on National Information Policy (US DCCRP 1976; cf. also Bearman 1986; Kahin 1997, p. 164). But the (scholarly) use of the term "information infrastructure" increased explosively around 1990, from about 900 articles in 1980–9, to 16,300 in 1990–9, that is, by a factor of 18. In the next decade, 2000–9, the total reached 29,300 (calculated on the basis of http://scholar.google.com).

> a "center without walls", in which the nation's researchers can perform their research without regard to geographical location — interacting with colleagues, accessing instrumentation, sharing data and computational resources, [and] accessing information in digital libraries. (Wulf 1989, p. 1)

In the context of this chapter it is important to note that the "national collaboratory" was envisioned as more than "a mere interconnection of computers; it was envisioned as offering a complete infrastructure of software, hardware, and networked resources" (Cerf et al. 1993, p. vii). The notion of a "national collaboratory" was further explored in March 1989 at a two-day workshop organized by Joshua Lederberg and Keith Uncapher and supported by NSF (reported in Lederberg and Uncapher 1989). In the words of a later report, "The workshop enthusiastically endorsed the concept and in general terms identified the technologies and services that would have to exist or be developed to provide the necessary infrastructure" (Cerf et al. 1993, p. vii).

Four years later, the Committee on a National Collaboratory under NSF's Computer Science and Telecommunications Board undertook a "year-long effort to study the needs of scientists for computing and information technology to facilitate collaboration, and to relate those needs to the development and use of collaboratories" (Cerf et al. 1993, p. vii). In the course of this work, the idea of one "national collaboratory" was abandoned:

> As the study progressed, the idea of developing a single national collaboratory was replaced by the idea of developing multiple scientific collaboratories. These collaboratories would share network and computing resources, software, and infrastructure but would have unique features dictated by the needs of particular scientific disciplines. Recognition of those varying needs drove the shift in focus from a single national collaboratory to many scientific collaboratories. (Cerf et al. 1993, p. viii)

Thus, instead of a monolithic collaboratory, the committee recommended that the NSF establish a "collaboratory testbed program" with multiple "collaboratories":

> Because scientific disciplines vary in numerous ways, it should not be assumed that one mode of collaboration or one set of collaboration tools can fit all needs. Therefore, the committee recommends that the proposed research program establish several collaboratory testbeds, which should be tailored to the needs of particular groups of scientists in their respective fields. (Cerf et al 1993, p. 3)

Ten years later and based on a decade of practical experience of a host of studies, this program morphed into the "cyberinfrastructures" research program. (We will address this later in this chapter).

On the other hand, also around 1990, US and other national policy makers began exploring ways to obtain benefits for society at large from adding services on top of the Internet. Such visions were presented in a *Bluebook* entitled *Grand Challenges: High-Performance Computing and Communications*, published by the White House Office of Science and Technology Policy (OSTP) in 1991:

> In addition to serving the needs of the scientific and research communities, the NREN [National Research and Education Network] will provide valuable experience necessary for the successful development of a broader, privately-operated national information infrastructure. Such an infrastructure would allow consumers, businesses, and schools and government at all levels to share quality information and entertainment when and where they want it at a reasonable cost. (OSTP 1991, p. 17)

Based on these ideas, and primarily at the initiative of Senator Al Gore, the US Congress on 9 December passed the *High Performance Computing Act of 1991*, which foresaw the development of "an information infrastructure of data bases, services, access mechanisms, and research facilities available for use through the Network [i.e., the Internet]" (US Congress 1991, § 3.1.C).

This initiative received further momentum during the Clinton administration (1992–2001). As one of its first measures in this context, it created, in 1993, the Information Infrastructure Task Force (IITF) consisting of high-level representatives of the federal agencies that played a role in advancing the development and application of information technologies. Tasked to articulate and implement the administration's vision for the "National Information Infrastructure" (NII), it quickly published an *Agenda for Action* outlining the administration's vision of NII (IITF 1993). Here, the notion of "information infrastructure" was discussed in some detail:

> The phrase "information infrastructure" has an expansive meaning. The NII includes more than just the physical facilities used to transmit, store, process, and display voice, data, and images. [...] [B]eyond the physical components of the infrastructure, the value of the National Information Infrastructure to users and the nation will depend in large part on the quality of its other elements:
>
> - The information itself, which may be in the form of video programming, scientific or business databases, images, sound recordings, library archives, and other media. Vast quantities of that information exist today in government agencies and even more valuable information is produced every day in our laboratories, studios, publishing houses, and elsewhere.
> - Applications and software that allow users to access, manipulate, organize, and digest the proliferating mass of information that the NII's facilities will put at their fingertips.
> - The network standards and transmission codes that facilitate interconnection and interoperation between networks, and ensure the privacy of persons and the security of the information carried, as well as the security and reliability of the network.
> - The people largely in the private sector who create the information, develop applications and services, construct the facilities, and train others to tap its potential. Many of these people will be vendors, operators, and service providers working for private industry. (IITF 1993, pp. 7 f.)

That is, the NII was conceived of as a set of *services* providing content ("the information itself...") by means of the facilities of the Internet and concomitant software and protocols.

Note that the "information infrastructure" might as well have been conceived of and termed "information superstructure," in as much as what was talked about were service facilities to be erected upon the infrastructure in the form of the Internet. From the point of view of computer-network engineering, this would have made perfect sense. But the add-on facilities expected to be developed were probably called "information infrastructures" because they were seen as service-providing utilities on par with water and power supplies, and in order to distinguish them from those of the computing network (the Internet proper). Anyway, a distinction was introduced between the underlying structure of the Internet and the facilities that, running on this distributed platform, would provide "information content," the "information infrastructure."[6]

However, there is an inherent ambiguity with the term "information infrastructure." What exactly is it meant to denote: form or content? Let us take the case of an ordinary city library. This can most certainly be referred to as part of the city's "information infrastructure" in that it, by giving free access to books, newspapers, magazines, etc., provides an "information" service to the citizens of that city. In this case, what is the "information infrastructure"? Is it the collection, etc., or is it the classification scheme for managing the collection? Does the infrastructure change whenever new books are acquired or old books discarded? In the context of public policy discourse, in which the term "information infrastructure" emerged, the distinction between form and content is of little or no concern. In that kind of context, a country's railroad infrastructure is considered *as a whole*: tracks, rolling stock, station buildings, personnel, ticket sales, administrative procedures, all of it: the entire rail transportation industry. Similarly with a library: From the point of view of the "information infrastructure" discourse, a library is seen as a unitary service facility: books, shelves, buildings, archives, staff, acquisition budgets, and lending procedures, all of it. In other words, from the point of view of public policy discourse, the "information infrastructure" is *both* form and content.—But from the point of view of designing and managing it, a notion of "information infrastructure" that conflates form and content makes little or no sense. Different design issues are at play: there is an issue of the design of a reasonably comprehensive and yet manageable classification scheme, and there is the different "design" issue of selecting which books etc. to acquire. Of course, while distinctly different, these design issues cannot be completely separated. Acquisition policies are, for instance, constrained by the storage capacity of the library: meters of shelf-space or terabytes of server capacity. Similarly, the classification scheme (catalog, index, shelf labels, etc.) has to match the variety of documents acquired. Still, while the issues cannot be *completely* separated, they are anyway distinctly different.—This ambiguity is inherent in the public policy discourse on "infrastructures."

5.3 "Infrastructural Inversion"

In the early 1990s, networked computing became practical reality. By the end of the 1980s, TCP/IP had become standard in practically all operating systems. Hence, the issue of building services on top of the Internet was no longer merely a vision in public

[6] Brian Kahin (Harvard) and McGarty (MIT) both made attempts to distinguish explicitly between "network," "architecture," and "infrastructure" (Kahin 1990a; McGarty 1991, 1992).

policy debates but was beginning to take shape, as exemplified by the experimental work initiated by the NSF in 1990 on the "national collaboratory" and of course the WWW (launched at CERN in December 1990).[7]

A pioneering study of one of the first efforts to build a "collaboratory" was undertaken by Leigh Star and Karen Ruhleder from 1991 to 1994 and was reported in a CSCW conference paper (1994) that was shortly after reworked into a journal article (1996). This study has been hugely influential, which can be seen from the fact that the two articles together have received more than 1,700 citations.[8] It has also, by virtue of the eminent role is has played in the subsequent infrastructure literature, contributed significantly to the confusion that is now obvious. We will therefore deal with it in some depth.

The study investigated the building of a communication and publishing system, the Worm Community System (WCS), which was meant to support the cooperative effort of the global community of biologists engaged in sequencing the gene structure and studying other characteristics of the nematode (roundworm) *Caenorhabditis elegans*: "The vision was of a kind of supra-laboratory stretched over the entire scientific community. The needs for both standards and customizable components were equally strong. The system development process also became an effort to bring together communities of practice with very different approaches to computing infrastructure" (Star and Ruhleder 1996, p. 112).

However, the WCS project ended in "ultimate failure" (Star and Ruhleder 1996, p. 112), not because the *C. elegans* community had no need for collaboration technology to support its widely distributed cooperative effort, but basically because the WCS lost out to competing computing services and technologies: "the WCS fits well the cognitive map of the scientist with respect to information: links between disparate pieces, graphical representations, layers of detail, etc. Yet relatively few worm biologists have 'signed on' to WCS, even as the community itself is growing rapidly" (ibid., p. 131). And the cause of the failure, according to Star and Ruhleder, was that the WCS in its design was a "closed system." It could run only a very constrained selection of work stations and operating systems: "The World-Wide Web, on the other hand, can be accessed from a broad variety of terminals and connections, and Internet computer support is readily available at most academic institutions and through relatively inexpensive commercial services" (ibid.).[9]

[7] Before the end of the 1990s, the term "the Internet" had also, by and large, replaced earlier terms such as "the information superhighway" (Kahin 1997, pp. 184 f.). Likewise, in public policy discourse and in ordinary language in general, the term "information infrastructure" has been replaced by the term "Internet" as a general reference to the Internet (as defined by the Internet protocol suite (TCP/IP, etc.) and the underlying physical structure of cables and routers) *as well as* everything that has been put on top of it: email, the WWW, the WWW indexing services (Google, Yahoo), the databases to which one can get access via these services such as Wikipedia, and the various "social media."

[8] The 1996 article has received 1,480 citations (according to http://scholar.google.com, accessed December 2016).

[9] The second author of this chapter was involved in a similar—and similarly failed—attempt to build a dedicated communication and publishing system for European mathematicians (Schmidt and McAlpine 1988).

As an "analytic framework" to understand that experience and its failure,[10] Star and Ruhleder invoked the notion of "infrastructure" as ostensibly used by Kling and his colleagues (they cite Kling and Scacchi 1982; Jewett and Kling 1991). But where Kling et al. had inverted the usual relationship between infrastructure and superstructure by shifting focus from the computing system to its practical organizational embeddedness and dubbed it "infrastructure" while still maintaining the computing system as the "focal" entity, Star and Ruhleder went much further. Their concern was stated quite explicitly:

> Most of us, in speaking loosely of infrastructure, mean those tools which are fairly transparent for most people we know about, wide in both temporal and spatial scope, embedded in familiar structures — like power grids, water, the Internet, airlines. That loose talk is perfectly adequate for most everyday usage, but is dangerous when applied to the design of powerful infrastructural tools on a wide scale, such as is now happening with "national information infrastructures". Most importantly, such talk may obscure the ambiguous nature of tools and technologies for different groups, leading to de facto standardization of a single, powerful group's agenda. (Star and Ruhleder 1996, pp. 113 f.)

The point seems to be that since "information infrastructures," as envisioned in the discussions about "collaboratories" and the NII of the early 1990s, would not merely provide elementary data communication conduits such as basic computing networks but also "information" *content*, research would need to address the classification schemes and standards that, inexorably, are incorporated in networked computing facilities as soon as such facilities, as "information infrastructures," provide content. Hence, "infrastructures" could no longer be conceived of narrowly as large-scale technical installations. It was, rather, necessary to shift focus to take into account issues as potentially problematic, politically and socially, as classification schemes and standards. A narrow focus would be "dangerous" because it would "obscure" conflicts of interest and thus marginalize or suppress the concerns of less "powerful" stakeholders. To shift focus, Star and Ruhleder argued for a reconceptualization of the very concept of "infrastructure." What they proposed was, citing what Geof Bowker shortly before had dubbed an "infrastructural inversion" (Bowker 1994, p. 235), "a figure-ground gestalt shift."

They begin their argumentation by raising a deliberately astonishing question: "When is an Infrastructure?", citing Yrjö Engeström for the question "When is a tool?" (1990, p. 175). Having argued that "A tool is not just a thing with pre-given attributes frozen in time—but a thing becomes a tool in practice, for someone, when [!] connected to some particular activity," they went on to state that "By analogy, infrastructure is something that emerges for people in practice, connected to activities and structures" (Star and Ruhleder 1996, p. 112):

[10] It is, of course, beyond the scope of this chapter to discuss the analysis of the case, but it should anyway be mentioned that Star and Ruhleder actually do not employ this "analytic framework" in their analysis of the case; they instead apply a communication model developed by the cyberneticist anthropologist Gregory Bateson.

When, then, is an infrastructure? Common metaphors present infrastructure as a substrate: something upon which something else "runs" or "operates," such as a system of railroad tracks upon which rail cars run. This image presents an infrastructure as something that is built and maintained, and which then sinks into an invisible background. It is something that is just there, ready-to-hand, completely transparent.

But such a metaphor is neither useful nor accurate in understanding the relationship between work, practice and technology. It is the image of "sinking into the background" that concerns us. Furthermore, we know that such a definition will not capture the ambiguities of usage referred to [when it is observed that] without a Braille terminal, the Internet does not work to support a blind person's communication. And for the plumber, the waterworks system in a household connected to the city water system is target object, not background support. Rather, following Jewett and Kling (1991), we hold that infrastructure is a fundamentally relational concept.[11] It [?] becomes infrastructure in relation to organized practices. Within a given cultural context, the cook considers the water system a piece of working infrastructure integral to making dinner; for the city planner, it becomes a variable in a complex equation. Thus we ask, *when*—not *what*—is an infrastructure.

Analytically, infrastructure appears only as a relational property, not as a thing stripped of use. Bowker (1994) calls this "infrastructural inversion," a methodological term, referring to a powerful figure-ground gestalt shift in studies of the development of large scale technological infrastructure [...]

An infrastructure occurs when the tension between local and global is resolved. That is, an infrastructure occurs when local practices are afforded by a larger-scale technology, which can then be used in a natural, ready-to-hand fashion. (Star and Ruhleder 1996, pp. 112–14)

Thus "inverted," "infrastructure emerges with the following dimensions":

[1] *Embeddedness.* Infrastructure is "sunk" into, inside of, other structures, social arrangements and technologies;

[2] *Transparency.* Infrastructure is transparent to use, in the sense that it does not have to be reinvented each time or assembled for each task, but invisibly supports those tasks;

[3] *Reach or scope.* This may be either spatial or temporal — infrastructure has reach beyond a single event or one-site practice;

[4] *Learned as part of membership.* The taken-for-grantedness of artifacts and organizational arrangements is a *sine qua non* of membership in a community of practice [...];

[11] At this place in the first version of their article, Star and Ruhleder (1994, p. 253) boldly stated "that infrastructure is [!] fundamentally and always a *relation*, never a thing." But it is incomprehensible to say that "an infrastructure *is* a *relation*, not a thing." On one hand, when we refer to something as an "infrastructure," we are referring to something *in* its relation to something else. On the other hand, it is surely the *concept* of "infrastructure," not the railroad system or the water system, that is "relational" in that it (logico-grammatically) presumes some "superstructure."

> [5] *Links with conventions of practice.* Infrastructure both shapes and is shaped by the conventions of a community of practice [...];
>
> [6] *Embodiment of standards.* Modified by scope and often by conflicting conventions, infrastructure takes on transparency by plugging into other infrastructures and tools in a standardized fashion;
>
> [7] *Built on an installed base.* Infrastructure does not grow *de novo*: it wrestles with the "inertia of the installed base" and inherits strengths and limitations from that base [...];
>
> [8] *Becomes visible upon breakdown.* The normally invisible quality of working infrastructure becomes visible when it breaks [...]. (Star and Ruhleder 1996, p. 113)

On this conception, the word "infrastructure" is not used for large-scale technical installations, nor is it—as in public policy discourse—used for such installations *in their capacity of providing* a support service, but is rather used for the *integration* of resources in "local practices."

The argument is muddled, however, and needs unpacking. Several distinctly different lines of reasoning are entwined: (1) the concept of "infrastructure" is a "*relational*" concept; (2) "infrastructure" "*emerges*" as the result of a "gestalt shift"; (3) technical resources "become," "occur," or "emerge" as "infrastructure" and can only be considered as such when enacted as part of "organized practices"; and (4) different practices, different conceptions of infrastructure. What makes the argument muddled is, primarily, that these propositions are implicitly taken to be identical, which they obviously are not. Let us consider them in turn.

First, Star and Ruhleder argue that "infrastructure appears only as a relational property, not as a thing stripped of use." The concept of "infrastructure" should not simply be understood as a notion of large-scale technical artifacts but as a "fundamentally relational concept": "It becomes infrastructure in relation to *organized practices*," that is, in as much as "it" from the point of view of some (identifiable) "organized practices" "sinks into an invisible background." In other words, something—*anything*, really—is an "infrastructure" if it is in such a relation to something else that it serves the function of a resource that is routinely and unproblematically taken for granted: "It is something that is just there, ready-to-hand, completely transparent."

Now, it is (logico-grammatically) indisputable that something cannot be said to be an "infrastructure" without its being an infrastructure *of* something else, just as something cannot be said to be "supportive" without being supportive of something else or "a means" without being a means for some end. One could thus also say that "infrastructure" is a transitive noun. To that extent, the notion of a "relational concept" is clear enough, although it is a rather overwrought way of expressing the obvious.

Second, there is a sense in which one can say that, when applying a figure-ground gestalt shift, one makes what was the ground "emerge" as focus. Thus, one may say that when one shifts attention from the computing system to the organized practices supporting it, as did Kling et al., one thereby makes these otherwise taken-for-granted phenomena "emerge." Thus, one may say with Star and Ruhleder that "infrastructure emerges', as a result of inversion" (1996, p. 113). But infrastructures "emerge" only in that they become objects of attention and, in that particular sense, "visible." In other words, the gestalt shift is an analytic move. It is not the ground that shifts; it is *the analyst's attention*. Nor is it the infrastructure that "emerges" or resources that "become" infrastructure; it is the analyst who reconceives his or her object of attention. There is surely a temporal dimension to the analyst's shift of attention but not to something's being infrastructure. Does the moon "emerge" from the sky when an astronomer trains her telescope on it? The talk about the ground emerging as a focus is ultimately an elaborate way to call for the study of the mundane or ordinary—a call that is absolutely key for CSCW—but at the same time not itself revolutionary for CSCW or for the study of practice (and by extension what practitioners themselves are focusing on) within CSCW. That said, the call has played an important and useful political role for justifying this kind of research.

Third, Star and Ruhleder state that "It [?] becomes [!] infrastructure in relation to organized practices." If "it" here refers to some technical installation, which in context seems the most likely interpretation, the proposition may mean different things: the installation is only ("it becomes") an infrastructure to the extent that it is incorporated into organized practices; *or* the technical installation is only ("it becomes") an infrastructure *when* actually used as such by organized practices. It is tautology to say that a technical installation is only an infrastructure to the extent that it is incorporated into organized practices. If human civilization ceased to exist, mechanical or electronic structures would not be infrastructures, just as tools would not be tools but just material objects. It may be appropriate to remind us that a technical installation is only an infrastructure to the extent that it has been incorporated into organized practices, but it is a source of confusion to talk about tools and infrastructures as having a temporal dimension. But while it is tautology to say that a chair is only a chair for a life form for which sitting in chairs is a routine occurrence, it is nonsense to say, following Engeström, that the chair is only a chair *when* occupied and thus ceases to be a chair *when* it is not being used, for instance, while its owners are absent or asleep in their beds. In the same way, a hammer does not cease to be a hammer *when* lying on the workbench or in the tool box or *when* it is being manufactured or is on display in the hardware store. A hammer, of course, ceases to be a hammer when melted as scrap in a steel plant, but apart from that, "tool-ness" does not have a temporal dimension. Being a tool is not a process or an activity; it does not have duration. The question "When is an Infrastructure?", while it may serve to direct attention to the need to study instances of actual practice, is, ultimately, unintelligible.

Fourth, consider again the proposition, "It becomes infrastructure in relation to *organized practices*." There is a third possible interpretation, namely, that the given installation is only an infrastructure for the particular organized practices by which it is a taken-for-granted resource, in contrast to organized practices that, for instance, build or maintain it. It makes obvious sense to say that a technical installation is only an infrastructure "in relation to organized practices." Notice, however, that the notion of a "relational" concept here is used differently than in the sense discussed above (the infrastructure/superstructure relation), namely, in the sense that the identity and extension of the infrastructure is determined by ("in relation to") certain organized practices that thereby stand as the "focal" entity, the unit of analysis (the role played by the "focal" computing system in Kling et al.).—But it is another source of confusion to reinterpret "in relation to" as "*relative to*." To take the water system example: "Within a given cultural context, the cook considers the water system a piece of working infrastructure integral to making dinner; for the city planner, it becomes a variable in a complex equation" (Star and Ruhleder 1996, p. 113). Here, the water system is considered an infrastructure for the cook ("within a given cultural context"), whereas for the city planner, it is a parameter in the overall planning task (and presumably for the plumber an artifact to maintain or reconfigure). On that view, we cannot talk about the water system as an infrastructure spanning these *different* practices. But that is, of course, a completely arbitrary conceptual imposition. The simple fact that citizens of all stripes—consumers, planners, technicians, etc., are able to engage in sensible debates about the water system or the power system is simply ignored. While the cook considers the water system "a piece of working infrastructure," the city planner in her work surely conceives of the contemplated extensions to the water system as extensions to the *same* water supply infrastructure (next to the power and transportation infrastructures), just as the plumber, in implementing some of the local extensions, considers those pipes and fittings as elements in the *same* infrastructure. The water system is simply ordinarily conceived of as *one* infrastructure, by virtue of the fact that it is a (large) system of hierarchically configured components that are mechanically connected and designed to work in a reasonably dependable causal manner (ensuring the flow of water). That is, the system has functional unity. It is thus the same system they are dealing with; they are just doing different things with it. Their practices are quite different but nonetheless interlinked by the functionally unitary system. However, by imposing a radically "relational" (or rather *relativistic*) notion of "infrastructure," Star and Ruhleder officially rule out any talk of the water system as an infrastructure for practitioners other than water consumers.

Let us summarize. To a large extent, the muddled argument offered by Star and Ruhleder is surely simply an indication that this was the very first attempt to formulate a research program for investigating computer-based information infrastructures spanning distinctly different work practices. The "infrastructural inversion" was proposed as a way of foregrounding or focusing on the practices and conflicts of interest that might otherwise have remained unrecognized or, as they preferred to express it, "invisible." But it does so at a high cost. The program outlined by Star and Ruhleder—predicated on the notion that "infrastructure" is a "relational" or relativistic or even a temporal concept—only seems to work because it makes a virtue of the ambiguity afforded by entwined lines of argument. The result is ambiguity in almost all sentences in which the word "infrastructure" occurs in the very text by Star and Ruhleder (1996). If it is accepted that "infrastructure appears only as a relational property, not as a thing stripped of use" (p. 112), or that "Information infrastructure is not a substrate which carries information on it, or in it, in a kind of mind-body dichotomy" (p. 118), what then is meant by "infrastructure" in expressions such as: "a large-scale information infrastructure" (pp. 112, 131), "very large scale systems such as the US National Information Infrastructure" (p. 117), "large-scale information and communication infrastructures" (p. 129), or "computing infrastructures, including gophers, FTP sites, etc." (p. 131)?—Having deprived themselves and the rest of us of using "infrastructure" in the ordinary sense, they obviously cannot cope without using it in exactly that way. The same semantic oscillation can be observed in Bowker and Star's *Sorting Things Out* (1999). For example: "[Infrastructural] inversion is a struggle against the tendency of infrastructure to disappear (except when breaking down)" (p. 34). In which sense of "infrastructure" can it said to be able to "disappear" and "break down"? Using the term in both senses—in the ordinary as well as in the "inverted" sense—is a source of the ambiguity that hobbles infrastructure studies. If we, following Star and Ruhleder as well as Star and Bowker, use "infrastructure" to denote some technical installation *in its being* "transparent," taken-for-granted, "disappeared," or "invisible," then we are at a loss for words to describe that which "emerges" when "breakdown" occurs, namely, that installation as an infrastructure in the ordinary sense.

Worse, however, as a result of the "inversion," the term "infrastructure" can be used to mean just about anything. This licenses not just semantic drift but a conceptual landslide. For example, according to Star and Bowker "information infrastructures" "provide the tools—words, categories, information processing procedures—with which we can generate and manipulate knowledge" (Star and Bowker 1995, p. 41). Words, categories, and procedures as "infrastructures"? This is to stretch the notion of "infrastructure" to the breaking point. This conceptual slide becomes even more obvious in the extensive discussion devoted to "infrastructural inversion" in Bowker and Star's *Sorting Things Out* (1999, p. 33). Presented as an example of "Scientific inversions of infrastructure," Bowker and Star mention the collection *The Right Tools for the Job: At Work in Twentieth-Century Life Sciences* (edited by Clarke and Fujimura 1992):

> The purpose of this volume was to tell the history of biology in a new way – from the point of view of the materials that constrain and enable biological researchers. Rats, petri dishes, taxidermy, planaria, drosophila and test tubes take center stage in this narrative. The standardization of genetic research on a few specially-bred organisms (notably drosophila) has constrained the pacing of research, and the ways the questions may be framed, and has given biological supply houses an important, invisible role in research horizons. While elephants or whales might answer different kinds of biological questions, they are obviously unwieldy lab animals. While pregnant cow's urine played a critical role in the discovery and isolation of reproductive hormones, no historian of biology had thought it important to describe the task of obtaining gallons of it on a regular basis. Adele Clarke (1998) puckishly relates her discovery, in the memoirs of a biologist, of the technique required to do so: tickle the cow's labia in order to make her urinate. A starkly different view of the tasks of laboratory biology emerges from this image. It must be added to the processes of stabling, feeding, impregnating, and caring for the cows involved. The supply chain, techniques and animal handling methods had to be invented along with biology's conceptual frame; they are not accidental, but constitutive.
>
> Our infrastructural inversion with respect to information technologies and their attendant classification systems follows this line of analysis. (Bowker and Star 1999, p. 36)

In the quoted passage, are "rats, petri dishes, taxidermy, planaria, drosophila and test tubes" the (inverted) "infrastructure"? Does "infrastructure" then simply mean the infinite assortment of *stuff* upon which a practice, any practice, relies? If so, "infrastructural inversion" then simply means focusing on the (mundane) practicalities of a given practice—methods, techniques, materials, tricks of the trade—from the point of view of the history of their development and integration. Such a focus is, of course, most useful for the purposes of studying the mundane practicalities of cooperative work, but do we have to call what we thus focus on "*infrastructure*" and thereby lose the ability to talk clearly and systematically about—exactly!—large-scale technical installations? More than that, do we, in order to be able to focus on the practicalities of work in a world of large-scale technical installations, have to abandon what is *specific* to large-scale technical installations, as the semantic conflation implied by the inversion would suggest? We suggest that the very methodological move of "infrastructural inversion" tends to spin out of control.

The "infrastructural inversion" is a source of considerable confusion and presses researchers into contortions where anything (not just petri dishes and bovine urine but also words and categories) that is used as a resource in some sense in an organized practice can be seen as an *infrastructure* for just that practice. But at the same time, and as a result of the advocated "inversion," Star and Ruhleder are themselves unable to apply that language to their case. The "decentralized technologies" they address in their study and that motivate their conceptual analysis are characterized by spanning multiple and often very different practices. The setting they studied was, in their own words, characterized by "communities of practice with very different approaches to computing infrastructure," "very different practices, technologies and skills," etc. Given that, and given the "relational" conception they advocate (something is only an "infrastructure" "in relation to" particular "organized practices"), there is no reason at all for them to even try to use the notion of "infrastructure" in analyzing the case. For *which* practice is what they characterize as an "infrastructure" in fact an infrastructure (in the inversed sense)? What is the focal entity by means of which the scope of the infrastructure is defined? In short, Star and Ruhleder's proposed interpretation of the concept of "infrastructure" cannot be applied to the kind of problem it was originally designed to handle.

Now, a less radical relational notion of "infrastructure" may be possible. Different practices typically rely on different infrastructures. The chef, in his work, relies on, inter alia, the water system that yields clean running water, but also electrical power for cooling and heating food items; deliveries and removal of refuse; and so on, just as the city planner in her planning work relies on resources such as drawing archives, and the plumber in his maintenance work relies on the resources such as tools and materials at hand in his van. — Leigh Star may have been suggesting just that a few years later when she argued that the ordinary understanding of infrastructure gets complicated "when one begins to investigate large-scale technical systems in the making, or to examine the situations of those who are not served by a particular infrastructure":

> For a railroad engineer, the rails are not infrastructure but topic. [...] One person's infrastructure is another's topic, or difficulty. [...] So, within a given cultural context, the cook considers the water system as working infrastructure integral to making dinner. For the city planner or the plumber, it [!] is a variable in a complex planning process or a target for repair. (Star 1999, p. 380)

That is, one group's support structure is another group's everyday work of design, maintenance, and upgrade (Ribes and Finholt 2007). This much is clear. This pragmatist definition of "infrastructure" is sufficient to forestall endless discussions of "what is really infrastructure" and instead directs the research to examine the intersection of multiple organized practices: what is supporting the work of somebody, and who is sustaining those relationships (Ribes and Lee 2010)? But notice the role the innocuous pronoun "it" plays in the passage by Star quoted above: "it" ("the water system") is now referred to as a self-evident entity with well-defined boundaries. The role played by the ordinary notion of "infrastructure" has now been taken over by the concept of "system." Of course, in the case of a water system, identifying and delimiting the focal entity poses no problem; but what is the "system" when we are trying to investigate "decentralized technologies" used in multiple organized practices across wide geographical distance? —We have been taken on a very long detour, only to arrive back where we started. What is the criterion for determining the focal entity?

Finally, a question is pleading to be raised: Why this insistence on taking the ordinary term "infrastructure" through these inversion somersaults? One answer is that Star and Ruhleder—as well as the rest of us—are struggling to understand and articulate a relation between our practices and our technical artifacts that is particularly acute when it comes to large-scale distributed systems based on computing technology. For while computational artifacts, such as spreadsheets and word processors, can be compared to and largely understood as machines, on par with power looms and automatic gear shifts, and while complex computational artifacts such as airline reservation systems and accounting systems can be compared to and understood as machine systems, on par with newspaper printing presses, it is difficult to do so for the kinds of machinery that are explored here. The complex computational artifacts that are being addressed here span local practices, typically with diverging standards and policies of data curation, and different preferences for data sharing, but they also, and most importantly, incorporate, in computational form, standardized coordinative protocols such as data representation metrics, notations, classification schemes, etc. Hence the insistence that "information infrastructures" are not just computers connected with cables and routers but somehow also encompass standards and policies and practices of their maintenance. This concern is then further strengthened by the fact that these complex computational artifacts often evolve over time in an open-ended process. The ordinary use of the term "infrastructure," especially as used in public policy discourse, seems to meet these concerns quite well, as it can be used to express a complex of "the technical" and "the social" (as in "the city's transportation infrastructure"). The problem with this, in the context of the development of computing technologies for these kinds of application, is that it, by conflating technical artifacts and the practices in which they are used, forestalls the necessary clarity with respect to *what* is to be designed for *which* practices. It can be (and has been) useful to use terms like "man–machine system," "human–computer interaction," "sociotechnical system," "socio-materiality," and so on, so long as and *only* so long as we are still able to distinguish and articulate the artifact to be designed from the setting in which it is used. And for that purpose, we need to be able to distinguish, as clearly as possible, the *computational representation* of objects, procedures, protocols, notations, classifications, etc., from the objects, procedures, protocols, notations, classifications, etc., of the *practices* in which the computational representations are applied. If we use the same word, say, "infrastructure," for both aspects, we will have great difficulties making progress (for a more elaborate discussion, see Schmidt and Bansler 2016).

Subsequent efforts to apply and further develop the concept of "infrastructure" have provided ample demonstration of these difficulties, as the ambiguities and contradictions that have beset the "infrastructure" discourse from the very beginning continue to hamper us at every other turn.

5.4 "Information Infrastructures" 2.0

Over the last two decades an ambitious attempt to develop a systematic and comprehensive approach to "information infrastructures" has been undertaken by a network of (primarily Norwegian) researchers comprising Ole Hanseth, Eric Monteiro, Gunnar Ellingsen, and many others (e.g., Hanseth et al. 1996; Hanseth and Monteiro 1998; Hanseth and Lundberg 2001; Rolland and Monteiro 2002; Ellingsen and Monteiro 2003; Hanseth and Lyytinen 2004; Ellingsen and Røed 2010; Hanseth and Lyytinen 2010; Monteiro et al. 2013).

In all this, Hanseth et al. draw upon and try to unite the "infrastructure" movements we have discussed: on the one hand, the public policy discourse on "information infrastructures" (e.g., McGarty 1992; Smarr and Catlett 1992) and the related information systems literature on organizational "information infrastructures" (e.g., Weill and Broadbent 1998), and on the other, the "inversion" tradition initiated and represented by Kling et al. and Star et al. In doing so, they try to develop a unified conceptualization informed by the "actor network theory" of Michel Callon and Bruno Latour.

All in all, this tradition has resulted in a very rich body of literature that bridges from ethnographic studies to conceptual work and tries to address a very diverse spectrum of "infrastructures," from the Internet at large, to domain-specific "infrastructures," to "infrastructures" servicing particular local practices, and the research questions driving the research reach from the policy and management issues of identifying opportunities and anticipating impact to issues of designing and implementing large-scale technical facilities under conditions of practical contingencies. In the course of its development, this tradition has produced a range of in-depth studies of the role of large-scale computational infrastructures in complex cooperative work settings, such as studies of corporate Electronic Data Interchange (EDI) implementations (Hanseth and Monteiro 1997; Hanseth and Braa 2001); ERP systems (Hanseth and Braa 2001; Hanseth et al. 2001); electronic patient record (EPR) systems, and similar IT-based healthcare systems in a wide spectrum of clinical practices (Hanseth and Lundberg 2001; Ellingsen and Monteiro, 2003, 2006; Ellingsen and Røed 2010; Aanestad and Jensen 2011; Larsen and Ellingsen 2012; Silsand and Ellingsen 2014); surveyor support in a maritime classification company (Rolland and Monteiro 2002; Monteiro and Rolland 2012); IT support for environmental monitoring in subsea oil and gas production (Parmiggiani et al. 2015), and so on.

The overarching conceptualization of "information infrastructures" is that they are characterized by developing in a way entirely different from other technical systems, in that they are characterized by being "enabling, shared, open, socio-technical, heterogeneous, and [an] installed base" (Hanseth and Monteiro 1998, p. 10), or a "*shared, evolving, heterogeneous installed base of IT capabilities among a set of user communities*" (Hanseth and Lyytinen 2004, pp. 207, 208, 213). That is, an "information infrastructure" cuts across local practices; it is not strictly speaking *designed*, or only designed embryonically, but is rather an evolving "installed base" encompassing a vast number of technical components of different kinds. In exploring these issues, this tradition highlights the tension between standardization and flexibility; the tension between the global and the local; and the tension between the inertia of the installed base and the dynamically changing technologies and practices that depend on that installed base.

This impressive portfolio of studies contributes much needed studies of economically vital collaboration technologies in actual use and provides a critical corrective to the mainstream program in CSCW that focuses on supporting small-group interaction (Monteiro et al. 2013).

There is, however, a deep ambiguity in its use of the term "infrastructure." In accordance with their original and overriding commitment to public policy and managerial discourses concerning "information infrastructures," Hanseth et al. use the term "information infrastructures" in more or less the same way as it was used when the very notion was launched in the US (with a big bang) around 1990. In fact, in their widely cited paper entitled "Developing Information Infrastructure" (Hanseth et al. 1996), as well as in their unpublished but also widely cited book manuscript (1998, pp. 45–9), Hanseth et al. followed McGarty's characterization of the concept of "infrastructure" (McGarty 1992), remarking that he "gives a rather extensive and precise definition of [information infrastructures] with the following keywords: shareable, common, enabling, physical embodiment of an architecture, enduring, scale, and economically sustainable" (Hanseth et al. 1996, p. 409; Hanseth and Monteiro 1998, pp. 45–9), just as they joined Smarr and Catlett (1992) in conceiving of "information infrastructures" as "computer networks *with associated services*" (Hanseth et al. 1996, p. 409; Hanseth and Monteiro 1998, p. 43 [emphasis added]). That is, they used the term "information infrastructures" as it was used in public policy discourse: a large-scale technical facility conceived of, from the point of view of society at large, as an information-provisioning *service*.

In accordance with this perspective, they "do not see an infrastructure as some kind of purified technology, but rather in a perspective where the technology cannot be separated from social and other non-technological elements, i.e. as an actor-network" (Hanseth and Lundberg 2001, p. 349). In other words, on this view "information infrastructures" "are not pure technical artifacts, but complex heterogeneous actor-networks" (Hanseth and Braa 2001, p. 263). In the context of public policy discourse and, related to this, in the context of management studies and social studies of technology, this is sufficiently clear. In fact, this use of the term "infrastructure" is in accordance with the ways it is ordinarily used. Ambiguity, however, wells up nonetheless, and does so in three ways.

First, there is a perennial problem with the criterion of inclusion. Hanseth and Lyytinen, for instance, echo the notion of "information infrastructures" as defined by Hanseth and Monteiro (1996) and reiterated by Hanseth and Lyytinen (2004), but then also distort it, when they state that

> we will define an [Information Infrastructure] as *a shared, open* (and unbounded), *heterogeneous* and *evolving* socio-technical system (which we call *installed base*) consisting of a set of IT capabilities[12] and their user [!?], operations and design communities (Hanseth and Lyytinen 2010, p. 4)

Here the concept of "information infrastructure" begins to stumble. In so far as an "information infrastructure" is conceived of as a shared, open, heterogeneous, and evolving sociotechnical system consisting of a set of IT capabilities *and* their operations and design communities, we are still within the framework of the public policy discourse or the organizational IT management discourse. We are supposedly still talking about an "infrastructure" as a *support* structure. But when the authors include "user communities" as part of the "infrastructure," is the "infrastructure" now supporting itself, levitating as if by magic, or is it doing self-service, perhaps? The concept is no longer taken as "relational," as a concept that *presumes* a superstructure for which it provides support, but is rather taken as a concept of *a thing in itself*, as synonymous with, say, "a sociotechnical system." —The tendency to use "infrastructure" as synonymous with "sociotechnical system" is also visible in Hanseth and Lundberg article on "work oriented infrastructures" in a radiology clinic (2001):

> We also include in the infrastructure the institutionalized communication forms used: the request/response communication, the daily meetings, and the ad-hoc conversations. This infrastructure is supported by a more general one consisting of transporters, trolleys, shelves, tables, personal callers, phones and fax machines, secretaries, other support staff (medical assistants), PACS, RIS and their computer and network infrastructure [...], etc. (Hanseth and Lundberg 2001, p. 355)[13]

Including "ad-hoc conversations" is no slip of the pen. It is a deliberate move:

> Seeing orders, reports, images, meetings and ad-hoc conversation as infrastructure is in conflict with a narrow, and rather conventional, understanding of infrastructure as just material structures like roads, cables (for telephone or electric power transmission), water pipes, etc. But we want to look at the orders and reports as well as the immaterial phenomena such as meetings and conversations as infrastructure because
>
> - they constitute together the foundation upon which the collaboration and division of labour between radiologists and clinicians rest
> - the different elements are linked together in the sense that each of them is based upon the existence of the others, and the role of each is defined in terms of how this role fits together with and links with the other elements' roles. (Hanseth and Lundberg 2001, p. 355)

[12] "We denote an IT capability as the possibility and/or right of the user or a user community to perform a set of actions on a computational object or process. [...] IT capabilities are viewed here *solely as engineered artifacts*" (Hanseth and Lyytinen 2010, p. 2).

[13] PACS: Picture Archiving and Communication System; RIS: Radiology Information System.

Yes, there is no reason to restrict the use of the term "infrastructure" to "material structures." In fact, as argued, in ordinary language, we do not impose such a restriction. It is certainly legitimate to use the term "infrastructure" to denote not only a material structure but also the support offered to another system by an organized effort *by means of* that structure, that is, to talk about a sociotechnical system *as a service*. This is how the term is ordinarily used in public policy discourse, and the rational point of saying that the concept of "infrastructure" is "relational." And it is, of course, an open issue whether it is helpful to talk about the sociotechnical setting of a particular cooperative work practice as an "infrastructure," rather than simply a "material setting" or, say, an "ordering system." But without clarity about the point of using the very term "infrastructure" and about the criteria of what is included and what is not, the use of the concept "information infrastructure" is dodgy and easily ends in a vicious circle. So, are cables, routers, and the electronic circuits of running software "infrastructures" *in the same sense* as digital images or stacks of paper with orders? And are these material structures "infrastructures" *in the same sense* as, for instance, "immaterial phenomena" such as meetings or conversations? Are they simply "infrastructures" because they *in some sense can be said to be* involved in the cooperative effort in question? Would that not be to substitute metaphor for concept? Imagery and orders, for instance, may certainly be said to be part of the infrastructure of radiology work but they can hardly be said to evolve in the same sense as, say, an EPR system. What is gained by transforming the concept of "infrastructure" into an abstract category on par with, for instance, "resource" or "useful stuff," and conceiving of "the motley of artifacts and materials of our lives as instances of such an all-encompassing category" (Schmidt and Bansler 2016)?

Second, in order to avoid the impending ontological avalanche, clear criteria of inclusion and exclusion are necessary. Describing some facility as an "infrastructure" is an analytic operation: We highlight the *specific* relation of dependence/support, and in so doing, we include under "infrastructure" that which is considered to be *specific* to the relation from the point of view of what is supported (a superstructure of applications or society at large or a particular cooperative work arrangement). The concept of "infrastructure" should be used with great care. Thus, in the case of the cooperative work arrangement of a radiology clinic, it might be relevant to include orders, reports, images, etc. as "infrastructure," in so far as these types of artifact are essential to the specific practices of the radiological clinic. But are these ad-hoc conversations *specific* to these practices? Can something as transitory as ad-hoc conversations be said to be part of an "infra*structure*," in any sense of the word? Does it make sense to include under "infrastructure" phenomena that occur contingently and sporadically? It is, we submit, an analytic problem of the first order to determine what is included as essential to this particular setting, and what is not.

And third, these ambiguities and terminological slides are perhaps rooted in the very concept of "infrastructure" as appropriated by Hanseth et al. from the public policy discourse of the early 1990s, from which Hanseth et al., as mentioned, derived their conception of "information infrastructure" as a "shared, evolving, heterogeneous installed base of IT capabilities." The exemplars discussed in the texts founding this tradition are the Internet (in which Hanseth et al. include email and the WWW) as well as EDI, healthcare systems, etc. (Hanseth et al. 1996; Hanseth and Monteiro 1998; Hanseth and Lyytinen 2004, 2010). Let us consider the Internet. In which sense can it be said to be "evolving" and "heterogeneous"? This is not at all evident. What are the criteria of sameness (and hence also change) presumed when talking about evolution and heterogeneity? In the context of a technical discourse (as opposed to public policy discourse), the criterion of inclusion would be the suite of Internet protocols (TCP/IP, etc.), so that machines (hosts, routers, laptops, mobile devices, printers, CNC machines...) running TCP/IP and thus having an IP-number are included. That, we submit, would make the Internet very well defined and not heterogeneous at all. The same would apply to email or the WWW. Defined by protocols such as POP, IMAP, and SMTP, and HTTP and HTML, respectively, these are well-defined infrastructures. Of course, protocols may change, and new protocols may be added, but this is hardly qualitatively different from updating any other multi-user system.

According to Hanseth et al., information infrastructures are "heterogeneous" in that they "are more than 'pure' technology, they are rather *socio-technical networks*." Thus, "Infrastructures are heterogeneous concerning the qualities of their constituencies. They encompass technological components, humans, organizations, and institutions" (Hanseth and Monteiro 1998, p. 43). Or in similar words, "information infrastructures are at any moment of time *heterogeneous*: they contain components of multiple sorts—diverse technological components as well as multiple non-technological elements (individual, social, organizational, institutional etc.) that are necessary to sustain and operate the infrastructure" (Hanseth and Lyytinen 2004, p. 215). The reason for this conception is the (unsurprising) observation that "An information system does not work [...] if not the users are using it properly" (Hanseth and Monteiro 1998, p. 43). That is, the heterogeneity Hanseth et al. find in their studies is a manifestation of their methodological stance according to which they reject distinguishing between "the technical" and "the social."[14] The heterogeneity is an artifact of their insistence on extending the notion of "infrastructure" to include "components of multiple sorts." One result of this stance is that ambiguity is unrestrained. When they, for example, say that "components are connected in complex ways and they change constantly" and that "clean interfaces between layers of the architecture are critical," or when they talk about "protocol stacks" and "variations of heterogeneity as a result of the architectural layering" (Hanseth and Lyytinen 2004, p. 215)—the scope of these observations is quite blurred. In the context of technical design, the ensuing ambiguity seems quite unwieldy.

In sum, then, the conceptual difficulties that emerge in this tradition seem to stem from trying to make the same conceptual apparatus bridge from a public policy discourse to a management discourse to a technical design discourse.

5.5 "Cyberinfrastructures"

By the turn of the century, the movement to build "information infrastructures" to support scientific research work had gained momentum. What had been but a vision when

[14] "Actor network theory views society as a completely interwoven socio-technical web. It consists of a highly heterogeneous network of actors, institutional arrangements, textual descriptions, work practices and technical artefacts" (Hanseth and Monteiro 1997, p. 185).

the plans for NSF's "collaboratory testbed program" were drafted and debated in the early 1990s (e.g., Cerf et al. 1993) was now solid experience from a large number of testbeds and evaluation studies (for a very useful overview, see Finholt 2003). To take stock of what had been achieved and what the prospects were, NSF published, in the course of 2003–5, about thirty workshop reports and similar studies on the experiences with building and using cyberinfrastructures in various scientific disciplines: Atmospheric Sciences, Biological Sciences, Chemistry, Earth Sciences, Engineering Design, Engineering Research, Environmental Research, Geoscience, Humanities, Materials Research, Mathematical Sciences, Ocean Sciences, Physical Sciences, Polar Science, and Social Sciences.[15]

As part of this, quite impressive, assessment exercise, the term "collaboratory" was superseded by the term "cyberinfrastructure" and was thereby brought into line, terminologically at least, with the broader movement engaged in building "information infrastructures." The term "cyberinfrastructure" was coined in the early 2000s by a "Blue Ribbon" panel formed by the NSF on the future of scientific computing in a publication colloquially referred to as the "Atkins report" (Atkins et al. 2003). With the added push of funding from the NSF specifically for research related to "cyberinfrastructure," the term grew in prominence and subsequently joined the developing "infrastructure" lexicon.[16]

The main push for "cyberinfrastructure" research at that time, and still today, although to a lesser degree, was for the development and use of high-performance computing (fast internetworked) and complementary applications and services for scientific work. At this time, however, the notion of "infrastructure" was closer to the original notion of a technical infrastructure in that it is actually a material substrate:

> The charge to the Panel is premised on the concept of an advance infrastructure layer on which innovative science and engineering research and education environments can be built. [...] The newer term *cyberinfrastructure* refers to infrastructure based upon distributed computer, information and communication technology. If *infrastructure* is required for an industrial economy, then we could say that *cyberinfrastructure* is required for a knowledge economy. (Atkins et al. 2003, p. 5)

The Atkins report did mention in passing the importance of investigating sociological aspects of cyberinfrastructure for success: "Much of the effort under way to use cyberinfrastructure for collaborative research is not giving adequate attention to sociological and culture barriers to technology adaption that may cause, failure, even after large investments" (Atkins et al. 2003, p. 12). Nevertheless, social aspects were not explicitly called out as part of the cyberinfrastructure:

> The base technologies underlying cyberinfrastructure are the integrated electro-optical components of computation, storage, and communication that continue to advance in raw capacity at exponential rates. Above the cyberinfrastructure layer are software

[15] For an index, see http://www.nsf.gov/cise/aci/reports.jsp.

[16] It should be noted that there is a compatible and overlapping research program both in Europe and in the United States around the concepts of e-Research and e-Science (Jirotka et al. 2013), but as our focus here is on notions of "infrastructure" per se, we do not address that literature here.

> programs, services, instruments, data, information, knowledge, and social practices applicable to specific projects, disciplines, and communities of practice. Between these two layers is the *cyberinfrastructure* layer of enabling hardware, algorithms, software, communications, institutions, and personnel. This layer should provide an effective and efficient platform for the empowerment of specific communities of researchers to innovate and eventually revolutionize what they do, how they do it, and who participates. (Atkins et al. 2003, p. 5)

But a few years later, the notion of "cyberinfrastructure" underwent the same semantic slide we have already seen. In 2006 and 2007, the NSF sponsored two workshops bringing together prominent researchers interested in cyberinfrastructure (Edwards et al. 2007; Cummings et al. 2008). The direct impact of these workshops and resulting reports is open to debate; however, they are indicative of an almost simultaneous push forward in both the "information infrastructure" and "infrastructural inversion" approaches to cyberinfrastructure research.

In its understanding of the idea of "cyberinfrastructure," the report *Understanding Infrastructure: Dynamics, Tensions, and Design*, written by Paul Edwards, Steven Jackson, Geof Bowker, and Cory Knobel (2007), draws explicitly on the work of Star and Ruhleder and defines "cyberinfrastructures" as

> the set of organizational practices, technical infrastructure and social norms that collectively provide for the smooth operation of scientific work at a distance. All three are objects of design and engineering; a cyberinfrastructure will fail if any one is ignored. (Edwards et al. 2007, p. 6)

On this view, then, "cyberinfrastructures" are a "set of organizational practices, technical infrastructure and social norms." Again, this is not quite intelligible. As we have seen, one can certainly, in the context of public policy discourse, talk of the "transportation infrastructure" of a country, in reference to the technical infrastructure and the organization of its operation, since the scope of the entity is defined by the given social unit for which this entity is a resource ("country"). But in the case of "cyberinfrastructures," how is "scientific work" distinct from "the set of organizational practices, technical infrastructure and social norms"? That is, there does not seem to be a social unit—"scientific work"—of which it makes sense to say that it relies on a "set of organizational practices, technical infrastructure and social norms."[17] Here the "infrastructural inversion" seems to have lost sense of what is what. Nevertheless, the Edwards et al. report pushes slightly past earlier framing of infrastructure as "relational" and as existing "in relation to organized practices" by bringing back in the notion of "systems":

> The growth, consolidation, and splintering phases of the historical model mark a key transition from homogeneous, centrally controlled, often geographically local systems

[17] Edwards et al. mainly discuss the notion of "social norms" in terms of the different norms of different scientific domains with respect to data sharing, but there is no explicit discussion about norms as part of what defines "cyberinfrastructures."

> to heterogeneous, widely distributed networks in which central control may be partially or wholly replaced by coordination.
>
> In general, and specifically in the meaning of the cyberinfrastructure framework, *infrastructures are not systems*. Instead, they are networks or webs that enable locally controlled and maintained systems to interoperate more or less seamlessly. [...] Thus we define a spectrum running from systems (centrally organized and controlled) to networks (linked systems, with control partially or wholly distributed among the nodes) to webs (networks of networks based primarily on coordination rather than control). (Edwards et al. 2007, pp. 11 f.)

That is, "infrastructures" are not "systems," for they are constituted by "coordination," as opposed to "central control," but they are still conceived of as heterogeneous "networks of systems," each having different control structures and stakeholders. Here, then, we see a shift whereby the notion of "coordination," a hierarchy of coordination really, becomes central to the idea of "cyberinfrastructure" and where "infrastructures" are conceptually, although not geographically or politically, bounded by the notion of "systems." That is, in spite of the nod to Star and Ruhleder, the problem of identifying the focal entity that first Kling and then Star and Ruhleder tried to address (in different ways) is bypassed by Edwards et al. as they, ultimately, anchor the notion of "cyberinfrastructure" in "systems." On one hand, "cyberinfrastructures" are conceived of as "organizational practices, technical infrastructure and social norms" and, on the other, as "heterogeneous, widely distributed networks in which central control may be partially or wholly replaced by coordination." In short, it was obviously as difficult for this report to pin down what was meant by "cyberinfrastructure" as it was for the Atkins report.

Whereas the report by Paul Edwards et al. (2007), built upon the "infrastructural inversion" approach, another NSF workshop, held soon afterwards with a different set of prominent researchers, namely, Jonathon Cummings, Tom Finholt, Ian Foster, Carl Kesselman, and Katherine Lawrence, resulted in a report that represents another approach to studying "cyberinfrastructure": *Beyond Being There: A Blueprint for Advancing the Design, Development, and Evaluation of Virtual Organizations* (Cummings et al. 2008). Researchers in this vein, like others before them, faced confusion about the conceptual separation between the notions of "virtual organizations" and "cyberinfrastructures." The report opens by stating:

> A virtual organization (VO) is a group of individuals whose members and resources may be dispersed geographically and institutionally, yet who function as a coherent unit through the use of cyberinfrastructure (CI). A VO is typically enabled by, and provides shared and often real-time access to, centralized or distributed resources, such as community-specific tools, applications, data, and sensors, and experimental operations. (Cummings et al. 2008, p. v)

The notion of "cyberinfrastructure" as that which enables "virtual organizations" to remain coherent is iterated several times, but at the same time the notion of "cyberinfrastructure" itself remains rather hazy. In fact, despite the stated decisive role ascribed to cyberinfrastructures, the report does not define what is meant by "cyberinfrastructure." However, the report does go on to state that

> [virtual organizations] may be known as or composed of systems known as collaboratories, e-Science or e-Research, distributed workgroups or virtual teams, virtual environments, and online communities. (Cummings et al. 2008, p. v)

The definitions are rather circular since some of the terms that "virtual organizations" are supposed to be "known as," such as "collaboratories" or "e-Science," also happen to be used as *synonyms for cyberinfrastructures themselves*. In a way, like the term "infrastructure" began to refer not only to the substrate but the superstructure (services included), "cyberinfrastructure" began to be considered as not only that which supports "virtual organizations" but in fact to *be* "virtual organizations."[18]

While both of these workshops and subsequent reports had different but overlapping antecedents, that is, US information sciences and US organization science, respectively, they also had shared interests in contextualizing the "big iron" of high-speed computing in terms of socially situated use and actual work practices. This progression toward prioritizing social aspects was in part due to experiences in computing that demonstrated that attending to organizational issues was critical to the success of the cyberinfrastructure mission in supporting science (Finholt 2003; Finholt and Birnholtz 2006; Foster and Kesselman 2006). Sociotechnical researchers, building in part on earlier work on collaboratories (Finholt and Olson 1997; Finholt 2002) and also on the work of Star and Ruhleder (1996) and Star (2002), were quick to heed the call to explore the concerns and social structures related to cyberinfrastructure (e.g., Karasti et al. 2006; Lawrence 2006; Lee et al. 2006; Ribes 2006).

Taking a Latourian turn, researchers "followed the network" and found that, in order to understand cyberinfrastructures, the larger ecosystem of organizational formations and concomitant systems also needed to be studied (e.g., Pollock et al. 2007; Bietz et al. 2010; Monteiro et al. 2013; Ribes 2014; Cohn 2016).

However, despite the reasonableness of expanding the scope of cyberinfrastructure investigations to include the organizations that cyberinfrastructures both support and rely upon, the concept of "cyberinfrastructure," and by extension the concept of "infrastructure," became extremely convoluted. By this time, "infrastructure" was conceived of as including, in addition to the technical substrate, services that overlay the technical substrate, skilled staff, organized practices, social norms, virtual organizations, and—in the vein of infrastructural inversion—anything that routinely and unproblematically supports any organized practices.

5.6 "Infrastructuring"

The latest turn in the life of the concept of "infrastructure" in CSCW and nearby areas occurred as researchers in the mid-2000s undertook another "infrastructural inversion." It will be remembered that Star and Ruhleder, in deconstructing the concept of

[18] In fact, one of the authors of this chapter contributed to this controversial expansion (Bietz and Lee 2009; Bietz et al. 2012).

"infrastructure," or rather re-constructing it as a "relational" one, went so far as to make the term "infrastructure" a process term ("When is infrastructure?" Star and Ruhleder 1996). This radical inversion then inspired researchers to construct the neologism "infrastructuring":

> Bringing the long-term perspective and infrastructure work to the forefront of priorities creates a need for change in approaches to information systems design and technology development, particularly large-scale collaboration infrastructures. [...] Theoretical challenges suggest moves from technologies as high-tech devices towards more inclusive conceptualizations of thickly interwoven socio-technical infrastructures encompassing mundane technologies and practices and information systems design from one-time technology development towards ongoing processes of infrastructuring. Together these openings challenge us to explore *designing for infrastructuring*, i.e. how to design for the blurring of borders between use and design, for ongoing changes, ease of maintenance, and tailoring of flexible and adaptable systems. (Karasti and Baker 2004, p. [8])

Similarly, also with a view to "blurring the borders between use and design," Pipek and Wulf use the notion of "infrastructuring" to "subsume *all* activities that contribute to a successful establishment of usages under the term "infrastructuring" to avoid confusion with classic notions of design as design-before-use performed by professional designers" (Pipek and Wulf 2009, p. 450). They later further specify that they "use the term infrastructuring to distinguish ourselves from notions of design that only refer to professional, or to put it better, professionalized design activities":

> It is the degree of professionalization with regard to (technical) competencies that leads to the distinction between users and designers. Based on this distinction, traditional design methodologies in IS prioritize the designers' perspective in a way that obstructs the perception of the users' contributions to the improvement of infrastructures. However, the users' perspective on developing IT infrastructure is actually broader. It includes the transition from old to new routines and usage patterns, and it is more diverse. While product-related choices in the application domain may seem straightforward to the designer, any organizational unit and any individual actor confronted with new systems has to find ways to integrate them into existing work practices. (Pipek and Wulf 2009, p. 457)

That is, "infrastructuring" is proposed as a short-hand way of referring to the social, organizational, educational, and technical processes (design and redesign, implementation and introduction, adaptation and adoption, combination and recombination) through which complexes of technical artifacts become integrated into practices as taken-for-granted technical resources. It is meant as a placeholder for a host of interdependent and intersecting issues that only with difficulty can be investigated separately, if at all. And sure enough, the move to rally around "infrastructuring," rather than "infrastructure," seems to have provided new space for researchers to investigate the processes and practices involved in the evolution of infrastructures.

Such conceptual moves are often useful in scientific work, but they have a price. The introduction of a particular technical term for such loose heuristic use may lead the innocent or credulous to believe that a coherent research program or even *a theory* has been established when in fact nothing of the sort has happened. It may thus forfeit the very purpose of introducing it. Whether this will happen to the notion of "infrastructuring" is to be seen, but the risk is obvious.

Anyway, the conceptual problems we have discussed concerning the different uses of the concept of "infrastructure" are already visible in these programmatic articles. It is, for example, striking that the "infrastructural inversion" approach that has been invoked to justify using the term "infrastructure" as a verb (or rather, a verb in its gerund form: "infrastructuring") is immediately abandoned again and forgotten when, for example, Karasti and Baker refer to "large-scale collaboration infrastructures" in one of the ordinary senses of "infrastructure" (technical resource or sociotechnical service) or when Pipek and Wulf use terms such as "e-infrastructure," "IT infrastructure," etc. in the ordinary sense of technical installations. Again, the issue of how to identify and delimit the focal entity that occupied Kling et al. as well as Star and Ruhleder has been abandoned. This is especially obvious when Pipek and Wulf propose to "subsume *all* activities that contribute to a successful establishment of usages under the term 'infrastructuring.' " It is thus not clear if the technical resources that Pipek and Wulf have in mind when they investigate "infrastructuring" are of the same kind as or are comparable to the "large-scale collaboration infrastructures" Karasti and Baker are referring to. It is not even clear if they use the term "infrastructure" to refer to a large-scale technical resource, as opposed to the array of artifacts and resources available in a particular work setting:

> In our framework, the work infrastructure of a worker or organization is *the entirety of devices, tools, technologies, standards, conventions, and protocols on which the individual worker or the collective rely* to carry out the tasks and achieve the goals assigned to them. These elements are interconnected mainly in two ways: either in a technological sense that the functioning and utility of elements depends on other elements, or through use-based ties motivated by a shared interest of users or shared organizational aspect (work task, department, etc.). Dependencies may be transitive [...]. While our general definition does not exclude non-IT devices, we consider IT devices and technologies to play a crucial role in the ensemble of tools and technologies. (Pipek and Wulf 2009, p. 455 [emphasis added])

There may be much to be gained by such an inclusive approach: "the entirety of devices, tools, technologies, standards, conventions, and protocols on which the individual worker or the collective rely to carry out the tasks and achieve the goals assigned to them." But then the very term "infrastructure" gets in the way. What unites all these entities is merely the fact that they somehow, in some fashion, belong to the ensemble of artifacts and techniques upon which practitioners can be said depend in their work. This approach then faces the same methodological problems faced by the "information infrastructure" approach as discussed above.

5.7 Using the Concept of "Infrastructure": Proceed with Caution!

We have traced a multitude of paths that meander and sometimes cross. The notion of "infrastructure" has shifted, expanded, and developed in manifold ways over time. In many ways, the CSCW and IS communities have been circling around the concept of "infrastructure" without defining or otherwise determining its point or its boundaries. What is striking in the use of the term "infrastructure" in CSCW and vicinity is not only that the term is used quite variably. What is perhaps more striking is that the various authors do not seem to realize this. Star et al. refer to Kling et al., and Hanseth et al. refer to Kling et al. and Star et al., and subsequent authors refer to this disparate body of literature in varying combinations. But what is most striking is that the term "infrastructure" is being used for distinctly different purposes and to denote distinctly different phenomena.

Let us summarize. We can distinguish at least four different discourses and related meanings of the term "infrastructure" in this literature:

- "infrastructure" as something that somehow provides essential support for something else; "infrastructure" here is broad, encompassing, and extremely ambiguous with very little or no distinction between what is or is not included or excluded in "infrastructure";
- "infrastructure" as an assemblage of artifacts (and perhaps even activities and "users") in operation as providing support and/or service to some social system (nation, city, industry, firm, research community, organized practice); "infrastructure" here is also very broad and ambiguous—including any material artifact that supports a practice or organization;
- "infrastructure" as technical structure or installation or material substrate ("networked computing") conceived of in terms of its structure *and* the services it provides to some social system: infrastructure and superstructure;
- "infrastructure" as technical structure or installation or material substrate ("networked computing") conceived of in terms of its structure: the material interdependencies of its components and processes; in the case of computing technologies, these processes include regular electronic or optical pulses, protocols, messages, etc.

As we have tried to demonstrate, this range of meanings is a bridge too far. If by "infrastructure" we may mean a technical installation, or an assemblage of stuff, or even an assemblage of both artifacts *and* their users, then we would not know what we are talking about, nor would anybody else.

We therefore recommend that the semantic landslide triggered by the "infrastructural inversion" be halted. One can talk about "infrastructure" in *the narrow sense* of a technical structure or installation ("networked computing")—computing infrastructures as running code (running over networked computing devices), and the representations of running code in the form of programs, protocols, and interfaces. One may then talk about the Internet as defined by the suite of protocols as a specific infrastructure, just as one may focus on other infrastructures defined by other protocols, such as HTTP, IMAP, and SMTP, or the proprietary protocols and interfaces at higher "levels," such as organizational information systems or "social media."

One can also talk about "infrastructure" in *a broader sense* of a technical structure *in operation*, that is, *as providing some service*, giving support, etc. "Infrastructure" in this broader sense thus basically means the same as "socio-technical system," in that any talk about a technical structure *in operation* presumes the competent organized practices of its operation and maintenance.—But it is here crucial that we remember that when we talk about "infrastructure," we are engaged in an operation of abstraction in which we highlight the relation between the technical structure and its superstructure. While it is critically important to investigate the organized practices that operate and maintain a technical infrastructure and its technical components, it is a source of massive confusion to *categorize* as part of the infrastructure, *on par with technical components*, the activities, interactions, skills, people, etc. required for the infrastructure to operate. After all, when we refer to a hammer as a useful tool, we do not categorize the arm holding it or the man wielding it as part of the hammer; however, when designing or selecting a hammer, we may very well consider the strength or preferences of the prospective hammerer. This designation of what is and is not part of the hammer is a matter of conceptual clarity and not a matter of saying that the hammerer or the method and qualities of hammering do not matter.

However, one may also, in the context of studying a particular work practice, address the ways in which the various computational infrastructures are adopted and incorporated in that practice. In the context of such practice-centered studies, one may talk about *heterogeneous* complexes of technical infrastructures (e.g., the Internet suite of protocols; HTTP, IMAP, and SMTP; SQL-based organizational databases connected via CGI; ERP systems such as SAP R3; etc.) as configured in the particular application context, and how they are integrated with the whole range of assorted artifacts, materials, and processes pertinent to that practice. It is here crucial, however, that the focal entity, *the practice*, is clearly identified, for without that, any attempt at comparative analysis and reasoned generalization will be critically hampered.

5.8 Implications and Conclusions

Although used in manifold, often contradictory ways, the notion of "infrastructure" has served a useful purpose in that it serves to frame and focus the issue of understanding computational artifacts in the larger practical context of their use. Notions such as "infrastructuring" and "infrastructure-as-virtual-organization" are used to enable and encourage the growing ranks of researchers in "infrastructure" studies to explore how people actually use or develop computing technologies in a larger context.

The importance of this becomes evident when one considers that the historic biases of the IS and CSCW fields toward research projects that lend themselves to post hoc evaluation of entire readily deployable prototypes has driven early research in those areas toward efforts to develop novel, effectively discrete artifacts that support a constrained set of practices. In fact, large-scale computing systems, especially those that transcend local practices and connect otherwise disconnected practices, have tended to be marginalized in CSCW (Monteiro et al. 2013). Studies of infrastructure present a necessary challenge to CSCW because such studies are preoccupied with infrastructures that are created to regulate, connect, and intersect with local practices. Now, thanks to the contributions from infrastructure studies, this has more recently given way to research focusing not only on the use of existing technical infrastructures but also on how infrastructures are developed in relation to specific work practices, and how infrastructures are sustained over time, including through leveraging other, related infrastructures.

The gamut of traditional and infrastructure approaches necessarily deal with notions of embeddedness—as both a product and a resource (Bietz et al. 2010)—and consider stakeholders (Lee et al. 2010) and sources of innovation in infrastructure to be manifold and more diverse than traditional notions of information technology design would accommodate (Pipek and Wulf 2009). In order to take more seriously the situatedness of infrastructure development in particular work contexts—and to begin to reconcile global notions of infrastructure with CSCW studies of locally grounded work practices—research in Europe has coined concepts such as "work-oriented infrastructures" to highlight how infrastructures are "developed to support specific work tasks" (Hanseth and Lundberg 2001) and "work infrastructures" to highlight "how the technologies undergoing design, and the design process itself, are embedded in an existing work environment" (Pipek and Wulf 2009). This latter work lay the ground work for more recent work on "appropriation infrastructure," which is yet another trope to show how grassroots "usages" become embedded in larger infrastructures.

Investigating notions of the sustainability of infrastructure has resulted in a variety of overlapping notions such as the practices of "aligning" and "leveraging" actors across groups, organizations, and infrastructures (Bietz et al. 2010; Bietz et al. 2012; Vertesi 2014), designing for graceful obsolescence (Cohn 2013), resolving differing temporalities or rhythms of stakeholders (Steinhardt and Jackson 2014), and investigating the work and technologies that sustain the availability of core resources and services over time (Ribes 2006). This latter work in the US represents a mélange of practice-centered work and more STS-style conceptual explorations or some combination of those.

All in all, what studies of infrastructure have indeed accomplished, and that very successfully, is to create a space in which researchers can take seriously the practices and wider technical and organizational milieu in which computational artifacts are created and used.

In sum, what emerges from our critical investigation of the vicissitudes of the concept of "infrastructure" over the last 35 years is that the various attempts to develop the concept of "infrastructure" apply a perspective that is complementary to important strands of CSCW research. The ("indigenous") research program of CSCW explores collaboration technologies from the point of view of local work practices (Schmidt and Bannon 2013) and conceives of technologies as necessary but contingent complements of such practices, "practice" here being constituted by the norms, rules, and conventions to which practitioners are observably committed. The study of locally situated practices can actually span a fair number of concerns because practices are not discrete entities; there are families of practices, with variations and overlapping characteristics. Even so, while CSCW derives its strength from its focus on actual, locally situated practices—the focus on the local is also CSCW's weakness.

Branches of infrastructure research offer a necessary corrective to the focused emphasis in CSCW on the local. Infrastructures, after all, can impose regulatory regimes on local practices (administrative workflow systems, production planning and control systems, healthcare information systems, cyberinfrastructures, etc.). At the same time, infrastructures not only provide constraints to local practice but also provide resources for the creation of new practices and artifacts and for the creation of new infrastructures themselves. If we see infrastructures as providing regulatory and other constraints as well as resources for local practice, the question of how to approach the relationship between local practice and infrastructure becomes pressing. The investigation of infrastructure and local practice can be approached and scoped in a number of ways, such as:

- by focusing on a particular social setting, researching practices (in the Star and Ruhleder sense) or a family of practices (e.g., the work of nurses at Clinic X, or the clinical work of nurses and doctors at Clinic X at *this* address); in this case, we work from the family of practices outward and across to multiple applications or systems;
- by focusing on a particular class of social settings and researching practices or of a family of practices (e.g., the clinical work in oncology, or clinical work in general); in this case, we work again from the family of practices outward and across to multiple applications or systems; in this example, we scale up to look at multiple local settings;
- by focusing on a particular technical structure and researching the practices they enable and support, including those practices that may be otherwise unrelated; the unit of analysis is here the web of practices that intersect a technical system or kinds of component of a technical system such as data structure, data collection, protocol, portal (web interface), application, or instrument;
- by focusing on a particular class of technical structures; this applies the same approach as for focusing on a particular technical structure but, in this case, we scope a particular technical structure across multiple settings to explore differences and commonalities between technical structures and the webs of practices they enable and support;
- by focusing on coordination among infrastructure-spanning practices and technical structures, researching management and coordination practices across heterogeneous, distributed "systems of systems"—these heterogeneous systems of systems frequently lack central control, and research thus tends to focus on system, and perhaps infrastructure-spanning practices, artifacts, and coordination; in this type of work, artifacts and practices may have characteristics of being local *and* global simultaneously or serially and of being pertinent and useful in multiple workflows and in practical time frames or temporalities.

This list is not intended to be a checklist or a directive, but rather as means to make sense of the landscape of how studies of infrastructure are attempting to transcend local concerns with concerns that have to do with the conceptual, geographic, and temporal reach of technical structures that have been described as "infrastructure." Indeed, studies often combine elements of the above, and we do not call for mutual exclusivity, only awareness.

While the importance of the relationship between the local and the global have already been pointed to in previous research (Ribes and Finholt 2007) and suggested in the notion of "embeddedness" (Star and Ruhleder 1996; Bowker and Star 1999), we here call for further exploration and a great deal more articulation of the specific artifacts that are embedded, and, furthermore, of the actual practices that are undertaken in order to embed these artifacts and keep them embedded. In this way, infrastructure studies can offer a useful corrective for CSCW so that local work practices are studied but also transcended. The point is, of course, not to abandon or ignore work practice but rather to not only *situate* work practices within a larger context but also to actually understand the *dialogic and emergent relationship between* work practices and the practices and artifacts that are part of a larger sociotechnical milieu—however that milieu is scoped.

The slipperiness of "infrastructure" concepts has been understandable in what was a rapidly developing area, but now, some decades in, clarifications are necessary for the further articulation of differences within studies of infrastructures so that we might ensure that we are comparing like with like or at least being purposeful and circumspect when we are comparing phenomena that are not the same. Further conceptual clarity will not only allow the definition of subareas and spin-offs as demanded by research and design but might also enable the discovery of nuances in how practices play out within and across the context of larger sociotechnical frames. We are not arguing for a singular approach to the study of infrastructures—far from it. What we are calling for is for infrastructure scholars to (a) clearly define what is meant by "infrastructure" for each study; (b) clearly explicate the focal entity and hence the criteria of inclusion; (c) delineate the scope and limits of the set of phenomena (including infrastructure) actually being studied; and (d) explicitly articulate the relationship of the myriad artifacts, techniques, and practices under study to the infrastructure as defined. Whether those artifacts and practices are conceived of within, across, or outside of the infrastructure in question is of significant consequence for future studies. Greater empirical, conceptual, and analytical precision is necessary for the continuing advancement of computer-supported cooperative work itself as well as for the study and support of massively proliferating technical infrastructures.

References

Aanestad, Margunn; and Tina Blegind Jensen (2011). Building nation-wide information infrastructures in healthcare through modular implementation strategies. *Journal of Strategic Information Systems*. Vol. 20, no. 2, June 2011, pp. 161–76.

Abbate, Janet Ellen (1999). *Inventing the Internet*. Cambridge, MA, and London: The MIT Press. (Paperback ed., 2000).

Atkins, Daniel E., et al. (2003). *Revolutionizing Science and Engineering Through Cyberinfrastructure: Report of the National Science Foundation Blue-Ribbon Advisory Panel on Cyberinfrastructure.* Washington, DC: National Science Foundation, January 2003. <http://www.nsf.gov/cise/sci/reports/atkins.pdf>

Bearman, Toni Carbo (1986). National Information Policy: An insider's view. *Library Trends,* Summer 1986, pp. 105–18.

Bietz, Matthew J.; and Charlotte P. Lee (2009). Collaboration in metagenomics: Sequence databases and the organization of scientific work. In I. Wagner, et al. (eds.): *ECSCW 2009: Proceedings of the 11th European Conference on Computer-Supported Cooperative Work, 7–11 September 2009, Vienna, Austria.* London: Springer, pp. 243–62.

Bietz, Matthew J.; Eric P. S. Baumer; and Charlotte P. Lee (2010). Synergizing in cyberinfrastructure development. *Computer Supported Cooperative Work (CSCW).* Vol. 19, no. 3–4, August 2010, pp. 245–81.

Bietz, Matthew J.; Toni Ferro; and Charlotte P. Lee (2012). Sustaining the development of cyberinfrastructure: An organization adapting to change. In S. E. Poltrock, et al. (eds.): *CSCW 2012: Proceedings of the ACM 2012 Conference on Computer Supported Cooperative Work.* New York: ACM Press, pp. 901–10.

Bijker, Wiebe E.; Thomas P. Hughes; and Trevor J. Pinch (eds.) (1987). *The Social Construction of Technological Systems: New Directions in the Sociology and History of Technology.* Cambridge, MA, and London: The MIT Press. (Paperback ed., 1989).

Bowker, Geoffrey C. (1994). Information mythology: The world of/as information. In L. Bud-Frierman (ed.): *Information Acumen: The Understanding and Use of Knowledge in Modern Business.* London and New York: Routledge, pp. 231–47.

Bowker, Geoffrey C.; and Susan Leigh Star (1999). *Sorting Things Out: Classification and Its Consequences.* Cambridge, MA: MIT Press.

Bricka, Charles (1894). *Cours de chemins de fer: professé à l'École Nationale des Ponts et Chaussées.* Paris: Gauthier-Villars et Fils.

Bud-Frierman, Lisa (ed.) (1994). *Information Acumen: The Understanding and Use of Knowledge in Modern Business.* London and New York: Routledge.

Car, Josip, et al. (2008a). *The Impact of eHealth on the Quality and Safety of Healthcare: A Systemic Overview & Synthesis of the Literature: Report for the NHS Connecting for Health Evaluation Programme.* University of Edinburgh, March 2008.

Car, Josip, et al. (2008b). *The Impact of eHealth on the Quality and Safety of Healthcare: A Systemic Overview & Synthesis of the Literature: Report for the NHS Connecting for Health Evaluation Programme: Extended Executive Summary.* University of Edinburgh, March 2008.

Cerf, Vinton (1987). Information infrastructure. *IEEE Network.* Vol. 1, no. 3, July 1987, pp. 52–3.

Cerf, Vinton G., et al. (1993). *National Collaboratories: Applying Information Technology for Scientific Research.* Washington, DC: The National Academies Press.—Committee on a National Collaboratory: Establishing the User-Developer Partnership; Computer Science and Telecommunications Board (CSTB); Commission on Physical Sciences, Mathematics, and Applications; National Research Council. <http://www.nap.edu/catalog/2109/national-collaboratories-applying-information-technology-for-scientific-research>

Clarke, Adele E. (1998). *Disciplining Reproduction: Modernity, American Life Sciences, and the Problems of Sex.* Berkeley, CA, etc.: Univ of California Press.

Clarke, Adele E.; and Joan H. Fujimura (1992). *The Right Tools for the Job: At Work in Twentieth-Century Life Sciences.* Princeton, New Jersey: Princeton University Press.

Cohn, Marisa Leavitt (2013). *Lifetimes and Legacies: Temporalities of Sociotechnical Change in a Long-Lived System.* PhD diss. Irvine, CA: Information and Computer Science, University of California, Irvine.

Cohn, Marisa Leavitt (2016). Convivial decay: Entangled lifetimes in a geriatric infrastructure. In D. Gergle, et al. (eds.): *CSCW 2016: Proceedings of the 19th ACM 2014 Conference on Computer Supported Cooperative Work and Social Computing, San Franscisco, 27 February—2 March 2016.* New York: ACM Press, pp. 1511–23.

Cummings, Jonathon; Thomas A. Finholt; Ian Foster; Carl Kesselman; and Katherine A. Lawrence (2008). *Beyond Being There: A Blueprint for Advancing the Design, Development, and Evaluation of Virtual Organizations.* Washington, DC: National Science Foundation, May 2008.—Final Report on Workshops on Building Effective Virtual Organizations. <http://citeseerx.ist.psu.edu/viewdoc/download?doi=10.1.1.205.6126&rep=rep1&type=pdf>

Delgado, Alan (1979). *The Enormous File: A Social History of the Office.* London: John Murray.—Chicago: ARTFL Encyclopédie Projet, University of Chicago, 2008.

Edwards, Paul N.; Steven J. Jackson; Geoffrey C. Bowker; and Cory P. Knobel (2007). *Understanding Infrastructure: Dynamics, Tensions, and Design: Report of the workshop, "History and Theory of Infrastructure: Lessons for New Scientific Cyberinfrastructures".* Washington, DC: National Science Foundation, January 2007. <https://deepblue.lib.umich.edu/bitstream/handle/2027.42/49353/UnderstandingInfrastructure2007.pdf?sequence=3&isAllowed=y>

Ellingsen, Gunnar; and Eric Monteiro (2003). A patchwork planet: Integration and cooperation in hospitals. *Computer Supported Cooperative Work (CSCW).* Vol. 12, no. 1, February 2003, pp. 71–95.

Ellingsen, Gunnar; and Eric Monteiro (2006). Seamless integration: Standardisation across multiple local settings. *Computer Supported Cooperative Work (CSCW).* Vol. 15, no. 5–6, December 2006, pp. 443–66.

Ellingsen, Gunnar; and Kristoffer Røed (2010). The role of integration in health-based information infrastructures. *Computer Supported Cooperative Work (CSCW): The Journal of Collaborative Computing.* Vol. 19, no. 6, December 2010, pp. 557–84.

Engeström, Yrjö (1990). *Learning, Working and Imagining: Twelve Studies in Activity Theory.* Helsinki: Orienta-Konsultit Oy.

FCCSET (1987a). *A Report to the Office of Science and Technology Policy on Computer Networks to Support Research in the United States: A Study of Critical Problems and Future Options. Volume I: Recommendations* Washington, DC: Subcommittee on Computer Networking, Infrastructure, and Digital Communications; Committee on Computer Research and Applications; Federal Coordinating Council on Science, Engineering, and Technology (FCCSET), November 1987. Edited by G. Bell.—Document prepared by the Computing and Communication Division, Los Alamos National Laboratory, Los Alamos, New Mexico.

FCCSET (1987b). *A Research and Development Strategy for High Performance Computing.* Washington, DC: Executive Office of the President, Office of Science and Technology Policy, 20 November 1987.

Finholt, Thomas A. (2002). Collaboratories. *Annual Review of Information Science and Technology.* Vol. 36, no. 1, January 2002, pp. 73–107.

Finholt, Thomas A. (2003). Collaboratories as a new form of scientific organization. *Economics of Innovation and New Technology.* Vol. 12, no. 1, January 2003, pp. 5–25.

Finholt, Thomas A.; and Jeremy P. Birnholtz (2006). If we build it, will they come? The cultural challenges of cyberinfrastructure development. In W. S. Bainbridge and M. C. Roco (eds.): *Managing Nano-Bio-Info-Cogno Innovations: Converging Technologies in Society.* Dordrecht: Springer, pp. 89–101.

Finholt, Thomas A.; and Gary M. Olson (1997). From laboratories to collaboratories: A new organizational form for scientific collaboration. *Psychological Science.* Vol. 8, no. 1, January 1997, pp. 28–36.

Foster, Ian; and Carl Kesselman (2006). Scaling system-level science: Scientific exploration and IT implications. *Computer*. Vol. 39, no. 11, November 2006, pp. 31–9.

Gillies, James; and Robert Cailliau (2000). *How the Web was Born: The Story of the World Wide Web*. Oxford: Oxford University Press.

Hanseth, Ole; and Eric Monteiro (1997). Inscribing behaviour in information infrastructure standards. *Accounting, Management and Information Technologies*. Vol. 7, no. 4, October-December 1997, pp. 183–211.

Hanseth, Ole; and Eric Monteiro (1998). Understanding Information Infrastructure. [Unpublished book manuscript]. 27 August 1998. <http://heim.ifi.uio.no/oleha/Publications/bok.pdf>

Hanseth, Ole; Erik Monteiro; and Morten Hatling (1996). Developing information infrastructure: The tension between standardization and flexibility. *Science, Technology, & Human Values*. Vol. 21, no. 4, October 1996, pp. 407–26.

Hanseth, Ole; and Kristin Braa (eds.) (2001). IT Infrastructures. [Special theme of] *Computer Supported Cooperative Work (CSCW)*, vol. 10, no. 3–4. September 2001, pp. 261–396.

Hanseth, Ole; Claudio U. Ciborra; and Kristin Braa (2001). The control devolution: ERP and the side effects of globalization. *The Data Base for Advances in Information Systems*. Vol. 32, no. 4, 2001, pp. 34–46.

Hanseth, Ole; and Nina Lundberg (2001). Designing work oriented infrastructures. *Computer Supported Cooperative Work (CSCW): The Journal of Collaborative Computing*. Vol. 10, no. 3–4, September 2001, pp. 347–72.

Hanseth, Ole; and Kalle Lyytinen (2004). Theorizing about the design of Information Infrastructures: Design kernel theories and principles. *Sprouts: Working papers on information environments, systems and organizations*. Vol. 4, no. 4:12, pp. 207–41.

Hanseth, Ole; and Kalle Lyytinen (2010). Design theory for dynamic complexity in information infrastructures: the case of building internet. *Journal of Information Technology*. Vol. 25, no. 1, March 2010, pp. 1–19.

Hardy, Ian R. (1996). *The Evolution of ARPANET email*. History thesis paper. Berkeley, CA:University of California at Berkeley. 13 May 1996. <http://www.ifla.org.sg/documents/internet/hari1.txt>

IITF (1993). *The National Information Infrastructure: Agenda for Action*. Washington, DC: Information Infrastructure Task Force (IITF), Department of Commerce, 15 September 1993. Edited by R. H. Brown.

Jewett, Tom; and Rob Kling (1991). The dynamics of computerization in a social science research team: A case study of infrastructure, strategies, and skills. *Social Science Computer Review*. Vol. 9, 1991, pp. 246–75.

Jirotka, Marina; Charlotte P. Lee; and Gary M. Olson (2013). Supporting Scientific Collaboration: Methods, tools and concepts. *Computer Supported Cooperative Work (CSCW)*. Vol. 22, no. 4–6, August-December 2013, pp. 667–715.

Kahin, Brian (1990a). *The NREN as a Quasi-Public Network: Access, Use, and Pricing*. John F. Kennedy School of Government, Harvard University, February 1990.—90–01.

Kahin, Brian (1990b). RFC 1191: Commercialization of the Internet: Summary Report. *Request for Comments*, no. 1191. Network Working Working Group. November 1990.—[Memo based on a workshop held by the Science, Technology and Public Policy Program of the John F. Kennedy School of Government, Harvard University, 1–3 March 1990.] <https://www.ietf.org/rfc/rfc1192.txt>

Kahin, Brian (ed.) (1992). *Building Information Infrastructure*. New York: McGraw-Hill.

Kahin, Brian (1997). The U.S. National Information Infrastructure Initiative: The market, the net, and the virtual project. In B. Kahin and E. J. Wilson (eds.): *National Information Infrastructure Initiatives: Vision and Policy Design*. Cambridge, MA: MIT Press, pp. 150–89.

Karasti, Helena; and Karen S. Baker (2004). Infrastructuring for the long-term: Ecological information management. In: *HICSS 2004: Proceedings of the 37th Annual Hawaii International Conference on System Sciences, 5–8 January 2004*. Los Alamitos, CA, etc.: IEEE Computer Society Press. <http://ieeexplore.ieee.org/stamp/stamp.jsp?tp=&arnumber=1265077&isnumber=28293>

Karasti, Helena; Karen S. Baker; and Eija Halkola (2006). Enriching the notion of data curation in e-science: data managing and information infrastructuring in the long term ecological research (LTER) network. *Computer Supported Cooperative Work (CSCW)*. Vol. 15, no. 4, August 2006, pp. 321–58.

Kling, Rob (1987). Defining the boundaries of computing across complex organizations. In R. J. Boland, Jr and R. Hirschheim (eds.): *Critical Issues in Information Systems Research*. New York: Wiley and Sons, pp. 307–62.

Kling, Rob; and Walt Scacchi (1982). The web of computing: Computing technology as social organization. *Advances in Computers*. Vol. 21, pp. 1–90.

La Porte, Todd R. (ed.) (1991). *Social Responses to Large Technical Systems: Control or Anticipation*. Dordrecht, Boston, and London: Kluwer Academic Publishers.

Larsen, Eli; and Gunnar Ellingsen (2012). Establishing a core health record; A case study from Norwegian healthcare. In J. Dugdale, et al. (eds.): *COOP 2012: From Research to Practice in the Design of Cooperative Systems: Results and Open Challenges. Proceedings of the 10th International Conference on the Design of Cooperative Systems, 30 May—1 June 2012 [Marseille, France]*. London: Springer, pp. 1–15.

Lawrence, Katherine A. (2006). Walking the tightrope: The balancing acts of a large e-research project. *Computer Supported Cooperative Work (CSCW)*. Vol. 15, no. 4, August 2006, pp. 385–411.

Lederberg, Joshua; and Keith Uncapher (1989). *Towards a National Collaboratory: Report of an Invitational Workshop at the Rockefeller University, March 17–18, 1989*. Unpublished report. Washington DC: Directorate for Computer and Information Science and Engineering, National Science Foundation.

Lee, Charlotte P.; Matthew J. Bietz; and Alex Thayer (2010). Research-driven stakeholders in cyberinfrastructure use and development. In W. W. Smari and W. K. McQuay (eds.): *CTS 2010: International Symposium on Collaborative Technologies and Systems (CTS), 17–21 May 2010*. Washington, DC: IEEE Press, pp. 163–72.

Lee, Charlotte P.; Paul Dourish; and Gloria Mark (2006). The human infrastructure of cyberinfrastructure. In P. J. Hinds and D. Martin (eds.): *Proceedings of CSCW'06: The 20th Anniversary Conference on Computer Supported Cooperative Work, Banff, Alberta, Canada, 4–8 November 2006*. New York: ACM Press, pp. 299–308.

Levinson, Marc (2006). *The Box: How the Shipping Container Made the World Smaller and the World Economy Bigger*. Princeton and Oxford: Princeton University Press.

Lewis, Stephen (2008). The etymology of infrastructure and the infrastructure of the Internet. *Hak Pak Sak*. 22 September 2008. <https://hakpaksak.wordpress.com/2008/09/22/the-etymology-of-infrastructure-and-the-infrastructure-of-the-internet/>

Mayntz, Renate; and Thomas P. Hughes (eds.) (1988). *The Development of Large Technical Systems*. Frankfurt am Main, Germany, and Boulder, Colorado: Campus Verlag and Westview Press.

McGarty, Terrence P. (1991). Communications Networks: A Morphological and Taxonomical Analysis. In: *Private Networks and Public Objectives Conference, Columbia University*. Cambridge, MA <http://citeseerx.ist.psu.edu/viewdoc/download?doi=10.1.1.558.7054&rep=rep1&type=pdf>

McGarty, Terrence P. (1992). Alternative networking architectures: Pricing, policy, and competition. In B. Kahin (ed.): *Building Information Infrastructure*. New York: McGraw-Hill, pp. 218–70.—[Originally presented at John F. Kennedy School of Government, Harvard University, 30 November 1990].

Monteiro, Eric; and Knut H. Rolland (2012). Trans-situated use of integrated information systems. *European Journal of Information Systems*. Vol. 21, no. 6, November 2012, pp. 608–20.

Monteiro, Eric; Neil Pollock; Ole Hanseth; and Robin Williams (2013). From artefacts to infrastructures. *Computer Supported Cooperative Work (CSCW)*. Vol. 22, no. 4–6, August-December 2013, pp. 575–607.

NATO (2001). *50 Years of Infrastructure: NATO Security Investment Programme: Sharing Roles, Risks, Responsibilities, Costs and Benefits*. NATO Infrastructure Committee. Edited by J. Astbury. <http://www.nato.int/structur/intrastruc/50-years.pdf>

OSTP (1991). *Grand Challenges: High Performance Computing and Communications, The FY 1992 U.S. Research and Development Program. To Supplement the President's Fiscal Year 1992 Budget*. Washington, DC: Committee on Physical, Mathematical, and Engineering Sciences, Federal Coordinating Council for Science, Engineering, and Technology, Office of Science and Technology Policy.—Washington DC: National Science Foundation, 1991.—[A.k.a. *FY 1992 Blue Book*].

Parmiggiani, Elena; Eric Monteiro; and Vidar Hepsø (2015). The digital coral: Infrastructuring environmental monitoring. *Computer Supported Cooperative Work (CSCW)*. Vol. 24, no. 5, October 2015, pp. 423–60.

Perrow, Charles (1984). *Normal Accidents: Living with High-Risk Technologies*. New York: Basic Books.

Pipek, Volkmar; and Volker Wulf (2009). Infrastructuring: Toward an integrated perspective on the design and use of information technology. *Journal of the Association for Information Systems*. Vol. 10, no. 5, May 2009, pp. 447–73.

Pollock, Neil; and Robin Williams (2009). *Software and Organizations: The Biography of the Enterprise-Wide System or how SAP Conquered the World*. London and New York: Routledge.

Pollock, Neil; Robin Williams; and Luciana D'Adderio (2007). Global software and its provenance: Generification work in the production of organizational software packages. *Social Studies of Science*. Vol. 37, no. 2, April 2007, pp. 254–80.

Postel, Jonathan Bruce (1982). *RFC 821: Simple Mail Transfer Protocol. Request for Comments*, no. 821. Network Working Group. August 1982. <http://www.armware.dk/RFC/rfc/rfc821.html>

Quarterman, John S. (1990). *The Matrix: Computer Networks and Conferencing Systems Worldwide*. Bedford, MA: Digital Press.

Ribes, David (2006). *Universal Informatics: Building Cyberinfrastructure, Interoperating the Geosciences*. Ph.D. diss. San Diego, CA:University of California, San Diego. <http://escholarship.org/uc/item/2gf7b45n>

Ribes, David (2014). The kernel of a research infrastructure. In S. Fussell, et al. (eds.): *CSCW 2014: Proceedings of the 17th ACM 2014 Conference on Computer Supported Cooperative Work and Social Computing, Baltimore, Maryland, 15–19 February 2014*. New York: ACM Press, pp. 574–87.

Ribes, David; and Thomas A. Finholt (2007). Tensions across the scales: Planning infrastructure for the long term. In T. Gross, et al. (eds.): *GROUP 2007: International Conference on Supporting Group Work, 4–7 November 2007, Sanibel Island, Florida, USA*. New York: ACM Press, pp. 229–38.

Ribes, David; and Charlotte P. Lee (2010). Sociotechnical studies of cyberinfrastructure and e-research: Current themes and future trajectories. *Computer Supported Cooperative Work (CSCW)*. Vol. 19, no. 3–4, August 2010, pp. 231–44.

Rochlin, Gene I. (1997). *Trapped in the Net: The Unanticipated Consequences of Computerization*. Princeton, New Jersey: Princeton University Press.

Rolland, Knut H.; and Eric Monteiro (2002). Balancing the local and the global in infrastructural information systems. *The Information Society*. Vol. 18, no. 2, 2002, pp. 87–100.

Ryan, Cornelius (1974). *A Bridge Too Far*. New York: Simon & Schuster.

Schmidt, Kjeld; and Liam J. Bannon (2013). Constructing CSCW: The first quarter century. *Computer Supported Cooperative Work (CSCW)*. Vol. 22, no. 4–6, August-December 2013, pp. 345–72.

Schmidt, Kjeld; and Jørgen Bansler (2016). Computational artifacts: Interactive and collaborative computing as an integral feature of work practice. In A. D. Angeli, et al. (eds.): *COOP 2014: 12th International Conference on the Design of Cooperative Systems, 23–27 May 2016, Trento, Italy*. London: Springer, pp. 21–38.

Schmidt, Kjeld; and Gordon McAlpine (1988). *Euromath: Requirements Analysis Report*. Lyngby, Denmark: Dansk Datamatik Center, October 1988.

Silsand, Line; and Gunnar Ellingsen (2014). Generification by translation: designing generic systems in context of the local. *Journal of the Association for Information Systems*. Vol. 15, no. 4, April 2014, p. 177.

Smarr, Larry L.; and Charlie E. Catlett (1992). Life after Internet: Making room for new applications. In B. Kahin (ed.): *Building Information Infrastructure*. New York: McGraw-Hill, pp. 144–73.

Star, Susan Leigh (1999). The ethnography of infrastructure. *American Behavioral Scientist*. Vol. 43, no. 3, November 1999, pp. 377–91.

Star, Susan Leigh (2002). Infrastructure and ethnographic practice: Working on the fringes. *Scandinavian Journal of Information Systems*. Vol. 14, no. 2, 2002, pp. 107–22.

Star, Susan Leigh; and Geoffrey C Bowker (1995). Work and infrastructure. *Communications of the ACM*. Vol. 38, no. 9, September 1995, p. 41.

Star, Susan Leigh; and Karen Ruhleder (1994). Steps towards an ecology of infrastructure: Complex problems in design and access for large-scale collaborative systems In J. B. Smith; F. D. Smith; and T. W. Malone (eds.): *CSCW'94: Proceedings of the Conference on Computer-Supported Cooperative Work, 24–26 October 1994, Chapel Hill, North Carolina*. New York: ACM Press, pp. 253–64.

Star, Susan Leigh; and Karen Ruhleder (1996). Steps towards an ecology of infrastructure: Complex problems in design and access for large-scale collaborative systems. *Information Systems Research*. Vol. 7, no. 1, March 1996, pp. 111–34.

Stead, William W.; and Herbert S. Lin (eds.) (2009). *Computational Technology for Effective Health Care: Immediate Steps and Strategic Directions*. Washington, DC: National Academies Press.

Steinhardt, Stephanie B.; and Steven J. Jackson (2014). Reconciling rhythms: plans and temporal alignment in collaborative scientific work. In S. Fussell, et al. (eds.): *CSCW 2014: Proceedings of the 17th ACM 2014 Conference on Computer Supported Cooperative Work and Social Computing, Baltimore, Maryland, 15–19 February 2014*. New York: ACM Press, pp. 134–45.

US Congress (1991). *High Performance Computing Act of 1991*. Washington, DC: 102nd United States Congress, 9 December 1991.—Pub.L. 102–94.

US DCCRP (1976). *National Information Policy: Report to the President of the United States Submitted by the Staff of the Domestic Council Committee on the Right of Privacy; Honorable Nelson A. Rockefeller, Chairman*. Washington DC: National Commission on Libraries and Information Science.

Vertesi, Janet (2014). Seamful spaces: Heterogeneous infrastructures in interaction. *Science, Technology & Human Values*. Vol. 39, no. 2, March 2014, pp. 264–84.

Weill, Peter; and Marianne Broadbent (1998). *Leveraging the New Infrastructure: How Market Leaders Capitalize on Information Technology*. Cambridge, MA: Harvard Business School Press.

Wulf, William Allan (1989). The national collaboratory—A white paper. 20 December 1988—[Printed as Appendix A to: Joshua Lederberg and Keith Uncapher (1989). *Towards a National Collaboratory: Report of an Invitational Workshop at the Rockefeller University, March 17–18,*

1989. Directorate for Computer and Information Science and Engineering, National Science Foundation.].

Yates, JoAnne (1989). *Control through Communication: The Rise of System in American Management*. Baltimore and London: Johns Hopkins University Press.

Yates, JoAnne (2005). *Structuring the Information Age: Life Insurance and Technology in the Twentieth Century*. Baltimore and London: Johns Hopkins University Press.

Part II

Methodological Positionings

6 Investigation and Design

DAVE RANDALL

6.1 Introduction

The problem of how best to relate design activities to the world in which its results are embedded is a long-standing one. Designed products of whatever kind by definition constitute a potential intervention in the world. Nevertheless, and of course, we do not and cannot know in advance what that intervention will look like in any detail, since that will be the product of the feasibility of both technological and organizational changes and of the deliberations about such matters, which go on both in and between organizations. This has not precluded a variety of attempts to characterize potential futures. They typically involve a strategy for describing what the world looks like now and understanding whether and how the deployment of new technology might bring about the changes intended. A range of epistemological commitments can be discerned in respect of this difficult and complex agenda. They include, for brief mention, an "engineering" paradigm associated with structured design; the analysis of goals and means hierarchies (associated with some versions of cognitive science) for the purposes of interrogating "usability," and a more sociological/anthropological (and humanistic psychological) perspective allied to concern for the "situated." Some paradigms, if not all, recognize that design inevitably involves choices. That these choices may be ethical or political in nature is not always equally recognized. This has led to what we might term a "critical" response and is evident in such perspectives as participatory design (see Chapter 7), value-sensitive design, "critical design ethnography" (see, e.g., Barab et al. 2004), and reflective design (Sengers et al. 2005), to name but a few. Understanding what motivates all these broad stances and their relative merits at both a theoretical and a methodological level would require a much more extensive treatment than is possible here, and I do not attempt to do so. My interest is more specific. It lies precisely in the "turn to the social" and what it might mean as the "ethnographic" stance is deployed in a wider range of contexts and, not to put too fine a point on it, in circumstances that could scarcely have been envisaged at the outset. That is, it has to do with the degree to which interdisciplinarity in relation to design entails a need

Socio-Informatics, Volker Wulf, Volkmar Pipek, Dave Randall, Markus Rohde, Kjeld Schmidt, Gunnar Stevens (Eds). Published 2018 by Oxford University Press.

for new methodologies, concepts, theories, and so on, or, conversely, whether it makes more sense for the various disciplines that have concerned themselves with human behavior more generally—psychology, sociology, anthropology, social psychology, and so on—to colonize such terrain (see, e.g., Forsythe 1999; Dourish 2006) The main thrust of the argument in this chapter is as follows.

First, I aim to examine the relationship between disciplinary interests and "interdisciplinarity" in the design context. I argue that investigation of present circumstance, or context, does not require the *conceptual* work of disciplines—anthropology, sociology, or what have you—that is sometimes argued for. If, as I suggest, the problematic is a genuinely interdisciplinary one, then a careful consideration of what that might mean is necessary. As Harper et al. intimate

> This [would] apply equally well to the methodological concerns of any discipline (and reflects the fact that many cross disciplinary exchanges are dialogues of the not-listening-very-carefully type). These concerns would include what kind of data is viewed as relevant, what kind of concepts best organize that data, what kinds of theory can be developed from it, and so on, these developments take place "to date with surprisingly limited trading of ideas across disciplinary boundaries" (Crowley and Zentall 2013, p. 1). Why is this? What limits do the disciplines set for themselves such that this trade is so difficult to establish and maintain? Why is it that where such attempts are made, they are routinely challenged, or worse, ignored by those entrenched within particular frameworks? What is the history of the concepts that the disciplines hold so dear and why do they persist? (Harper et al. 2016, p. 6)

Rather, what is required, as various commentators have suggested, is a turn toward "practice-based" computing. That is, first, where Reckwitz (2002b) suggests that the concept of practice allows for sociology to resolve many of its epistemological problems, I suggest that "practice-based computing" does some similar work in design-related contexts. Second, a feature of the current obsession with disciplinary tropes is the view that "ethnography" is a method, a notion that a proper reading of original texts would quickly dispel. The consequence has been a certain methodological "fetishism" (see, e.g., Burman 1997),[1] which, I suggest, unnecessarily problematizes investigative effort. The "turn to the social," as it has been called, does not, I will argue, require us to have a "purist" approach to our studies, for the simple reason that the problem space associated with interdisciplinary work is (or, at least, can be) very different from that defining anthropology or sociology. It follows that, considered appropriately as relevant to the problem of design, what is termed "ethnography" encompasses a number of so-called methods. It also follows that the range of possible concepts that might be deployed in order to relevantly explain one's observations might also be different. All, however, can be subsumed under an analytic commitment to the examination of practice. An evidently related theme has to do with the theoretical and conceptual choices made in order to turn these

[1] The term was originally applied to the notion that all features of social life can and should be subjected to quantitative analysis. Here, I am arguing that the same tendencies are to be seen in some versions of qualitative analysis. The notion of "coding" as a sine qua non in grounded theoretical work is a prime example.

observations into design-relevant material. I will attempt to characterize the different methodological choices under the umbrella of the "turn to the social" that have been made in recent years and say something about what motivates them.

Third, therefore, and associated with this eclectic view of investigation, we need to adopt an equally eclectic view of "design" and show how these moves can be associated with varying conceptions of what the design problem might be. Thus, the possible ways in which investigative work may relate to design might include the following: understanding, delineating, characterizing, or scoping the design space; understanding how objects and operations relate to the categories inherent in specific practices; comparing settings with a view to establishing similarities and differences; evaluating the roles that specific artifacts play in work practices and their evolution; and comparing them across domains. The point is that this is an entirely nontrivial, although rather underexamined, issue. While it may be true that academic research projects and even many commercial undertakings may involve a specified design outcome, this is not universally true. Moreover, it would seem reasonable to argue that the more complex the setting under investigation, the more open the design possibilities are.

6.2 The "Turn to the Social"

The "turn to the social," marked initially by work such as that of Suchman and Wynn (1984), Suchman (1987), Hughes et al. (1992), and Heath and Luff (1991), is often associated (for no good reason) with an ethnographic preference. As has been pointed out before (see Randall et al. 2007), properly considered, the term "ethnography" originates in a peculiarly sociological/anthropological version of "fieldwork" but became popular in an interdisciplinary context (such as computer-supported cooperative work [CSCW]) from the late 1980s onward as a means to examine work in a detailed and contextual fashion.[2] Relatively little has been said about whether the different purposes associated with interdisciplinary work have consequences for the character of ethnographic work, and that will be the theme of this chapter. The "turn" mentioned above was predicated on a critique, one that ranged from artificial intelligence to photocopier repair and that owes its presence in CSCW, of course, to Lucy Suchman. The gist of Suchman's (1987) argument was that the "planful" conception inherent in most design methodologies was not sufficient to explain either human conduct, in whatever context, or the actual use to which such technologies might be put. There was an analytic contrast, that is, to be made between "plans" and, as we all now know, "situated action." The remedy for the neglect of context was the careful, detailed examination of human conduct through a "situated" analytic lens. Over 20 years and more, this view came to enact a powerful vision of how studies might be conducted such that they in some way support the work of design. In sum, Suchman and others might be read as suggesting a radical reinvention of the

[2] As Bannon et al. point out in a recent paper (Bannon et al. 2011), there is a long European tradition of fieldwork under a variety of perspectival auspices that has remained, in some part, subterranean in CSCW and human–computer interaction (HCI) communities.

description–analysis–prescription procedures that, at a very general level, can be said to characterize the design process.

Some version of "ethnography" was seen as a potential remedy. Nevertheless, and as the distinction between "ethnography" and other forms of fieldwork implies (see Randall et al. 2007), ethnography is not, and never was, a specific *method* in the sociological canon (or elsewhere). What actually distinguishes it is a distinctive *analytic* stance. Hence, as Clifford Geertz (probably the most famous anthropologist of the last 50 years), says: "And it is in understanding what ethnography is, or more exactly what doing ethnography is, that a start can be made toward grasping what anthropological analysis amounts to as a form of knowledge. This, it must immediately be said, is not a matter of methods" (Geertz 1973, p. 214). In a similar vein, James Clifford and George Marcus (equally celebrated anthropologists) have argued that ethnography is a necessarily partial and incomplete project. Thus, "ethnographic truths are thus inherently partial—committed and incomplete. This point is now widely asserted—and resisted at strategic points by those who fear the collapse of clear standards of verification" (Clifford and Marcus 1986, p. 2). Again, I do not have the space to examine a subtle argument in detail. Suffice it to say that it implies at the very least that ethnography is inevitably conducted from a viewpoint, that the "cultures" we purport to examine do not have the homogenous existence our writing suggests, and that our descriptions of settings are rhetorically constructed. Now, we do not have to accept a radically subjectivist vision of ethnographic practice in order to see the consequences of such a position for design-related work. At a minimum, it means that (1) our findings will always be a function of our analytic purpose (which will include decisions about the problem space we choose to inhabit), (2) our writing will reflect our identification of what are—for us—the relevant problems within that space, and (3) relevance should be made evident to the audience for our work in what we write, and that audience is, in some part, designers. It also follows that decisions about appropriate methods (including such matters as degree of "immersion" in the setting, what observer "role" to adopt [see Gold 1958; Spradley 1980; Adler and Adler 1987], etc.) are a function of decisions about the problem space in question and how it is determined (and, just as importantly, how such decisions might be transformed over time and/or in consultation with our "audience"). It is likely, then, that our conception of the "problem space" will be an emergent one. This does not necessarily mean that it will emerge directly from ethnographic findings. It may well mean, and arguably should mean, that it will emerge from the constellation of interests and practices that we can think of as being to do with "design."

This point is often ignored or at least misunderstood. It is part of our argument that "method" has become something of a fetish, such that it is argued that only professional anthropologists/sociologists have the requisite skills to conduct observational work, acquired after a substantial and rigorous period of training. Just as importantly, of course, only those disciplinary experts will have the skills to develop appropriate conceptual and/or theoretical formulations. This could be why the "methods" section in conference papers has become obligatory in a way that is directly analogous to Dourish's (2006) observations about "implications for design." Put another way, I will assert that, while there are good grounds for carefully interrogating method when statistical or similar devices are deployed in order to validate findings, such interrogations are less appropriate when applied to qualitative findings. This is an extremely important, if somewhat controversial, point. Having said that, it is not new. Glaser and Strauss, and I use their work merely for the purposes of exemplifying, were arguing in 1968 that "these critics, in their zeal for careful verification and for a degree of accuracy they never achieve, have forgotten both the generation of theory and the need for carefully appraising the *different standards of plausibility* necessary for sociology's *diverse* tasks" (Glaser and Strauss 1967, p. 223 [our emphasis]). They go on to say, "The theory that emerges from the researcher's collection and analysis is in one sense equivalent to what he knows systematically about his own data" (Glaser and Strauss 1967, 225). Now, this is not an excuse for lying or laziness. It is specifically an argument for careful comparison of selected data. Their enterprise can be loosely characterized as an effort to answer the charge, which comes from critics in the "quantitative" camp of sociologists, that case study methods provided no means for generalization. By definition, then, such work is conceptual and/or theoretical. It does not entail a commitment to specific forms of coding procedure or any sequential order. Thus, as Corbin and Strauss observe, "as any experienced researcher will tell you if pressed to think about the matter, research really is a rather 'messy affair'" (Corbin and Strauss 1990, p. 32). Indeed, if it did require such a commitment to methodical procedures then Glaser and Strauss (who originally formulated the approach) were not in fact doing grounded theory—despite their evident belief that they had invented the term.[3] Now, in making this point, we recognize that a very significant body of work has developed around this original formulation (e.g., Charmaz 2006; Bryant and Charmaz 2007), and much remains contested. Regardless, our point is that the importance of such matters as coding in grounded theory, according to its originators, is not to reveal the details of a method but to aid the researcher think systematically about their *analysis*.

Method follows purpose. Many, if not all, of the significant debates in the CSCW and human–computer interaction (HCI) arenas over the last few years have actually been debates about purpose (see Dourish 2006; Crabtree et al. 2009). What is puzzling, we suggest, is that such debates take place in a design vacuum. That is, and despite the recent rise of "design research" as a distinctive project (see, e.g., Hevner and Chatterjee 2010; Rohde et al. 2017), there has been little serious examination of how ethnographic analysis might relate to different kinds of design agenda. Large-scale cooperative-systems design, after all, is likely to be quite different from consumer-product design. Design, it will be argued here, has been singularly underspecified.

Ethnography remains a contested site. It has been used for a variety of theoretical and analytic purposes, including structural–functionalist, Marxist, feminist, ethnomethodological, interpretivist, and so on. In the specific context of CSCW and HCI, it has been used in association with participatory design, activity theory, distributed cognition, actor network theory, ethnomethodology, and so on. In design-related communities like CSCW and HCI, the ethnographic project has tended toward (although not exclusively) a certain kind of analytic focus. Roughly speaking, this entails a commitment to the point

[3] I might note here that substantive work by Glaser and Strauss, such as *Time for Dying* (1967), contains no examination of coding procedures at all.

of view of the actor; some kind of preference for study of the way actors order their activities; an interest in the skills, competencies, and "artfulness" that actors bring to their efforts; and an interest in the use of artifacts. It presupposes no particular data collection techniques (we should remind ourselves that the classic anthropologists had no recourse to the recording methods we possess today and seldom bothered themselves with anything resembling, for instance, a transcript), no rules concerning time taken, and no uncontested position concerning truth and objectivity. It can also, and sometimes does, have a relationship to political or moral positioning (see, e.g., Marcus 1995; Dourish 2006), such that ethnographers can be seen as "circumstantial activists." It is, however, no part of this chapter to adjudicate these competing views of what the appropriate theoretical auspices of ethnography might be. It is rather to examine how it is that new circumstances have led to new methodological and conceptual choices and to further examine how this ramifies in relation to design activities. If we accept that method follows purpose, as I have been at pains to suggest, the task is to examine the burgeoning eclecticism of method and approach under the wide umbrella of "ethnography," in order to understand better what purposes are in play. Below, then, I examine some of the dimensions along which these purposes might vary. The first of these is the move to new domains of enquiry.

6.2.1 The Domain

We might anticipate that an interdisciplinary field like CSCW and its cognates would have seen a massive expansion in the number and range of studies conducted. And, in a sense, we have. If Hughes et al. (1994) are to be believed, the early studies were largely concerned with "control rooms" (see Heath and Luff 1991; Hughes et al. 1992). While this was probably never true—white-collar office work was already a topic of enquiry, as was manufacturing—it certainly characterized a body of work that focused on small, self-contained, face-to-face working environments. The reasons for this were obvious—time, money, and effort are limited resources, and such investigations are self-evidently more "manageable" than long-term studies of complex environments. They also (arguably) favored attention to cooperation over coordination. Nevertheless, the evolution of new technologies such as large databases, the Internet, mobile devices, social networking, and so on, had a number of consequences for ethnographic work. While I have been and remain skeptical about the claims of "virtual" ethnography, some evident methodological shifts are attendant on these technological and social changes. These are that the "site" of any given ethnography is arguably less self-evident than previously supposed, that the specific methods employed by ethnographers might need adjustment, and that we might need to rethink our orientation to "work," as the distinction between work and nonwork (arguably) becomes more permeable. Again, this has not been without controversy. Schmidt (2011) argues, for instance, that the move to studies of social networking, cell phone use, technology in the home, and so on, are less well founded than they might be, often being based on some casual acceptance of a number of sociological tropes that are, in fact, contested. Regardless, the fact is that where CSCW quickly moved "out of the control room," it now seems to have radically expanded its remit. One of the simplest comparisons we might make is between the domains being investigated in the early years of CSCW under ethnographic auspices, and those under investigation today. Many studies have moved "out of the work site" altogether. There are arguably just as many, if not more, studies of settings that do not involve paid work as there are studies of settings that do. For example, an increasing number of ethnographic studies have concentrated on domestic and leisure activities (see, e.g., Harper 2003; Crabtree and Rodden 2004a; Neustaedter et al. 2010; Ogonowski et al. 2013), mobilities of one kind or another (see, e.g., Palen and Saltzman 2002; Meurer et al. 2014), and gaming (see, e.g., Brown and Bell 2004; Crabtree et al. 2004b; Randall 2011). Just as strikingly, the rise of the Internet has produced a remarkable expansion in studies of "online" behaviors of one kind or another.

Now, in and of itself, this eclecticism does not matter a great deal. Ethnographers will go where they wish (or where they are allowed to go and/or are funded to do so). However, it does raise the issue of what a foundational concept for practice-based computing might look like. This is not because I strongly favor research into domestic environments, game playing, the "mobile" life of teenagers, and so on, but because I favor an indeterminate view of the relationship between technology and social life. To the degree that Web and mobile technologies are blurring boundaries, this raises problems both for the relevance of the domain and for the scope of the technology. If this blurring is taking place and if it is also true that digital technology is mediating more and more aspects of our lives, then certain questions are raised, questions that certainly impinge on the analytic auspices of ethnographic enquiry and its relationship to design. In turn, and as a result, another source of variation lies in new strategies that we consider to be ethnographic.

6.2.2 Ethnographic Strategies

The sheer range of strategies associated with the ethnographic program is striking. Briefly, ethnomethodology, conversation analysis, cultural and "technological" probes, interaction analysis, interaction design, pattern languages, "living labs," and contextual inquiry, as well as an array of theoretical and conceptual frameworks (some of which are mentioned above), have all laid claim to some version of ethnographic practice. In addition, the particularities of the online world have led to specific claims about "digital," "trace," or "virtual" ethnography. All, despite these manifest variations, share the common feature that they are, in some sense, "user centered." That is, some marriage between user practices, user needs, or user "wants" and a design intervention is the desired outcome.

Early work, and one can take as an exemplar of this position the work that has emanated over a 20-year period from the so-called Lancaster school in the UK, was largely concerned with examining what the relationship between ethnography and design might look like, rather than attempting to produce any specific design recommendations. This work (Hughes et al. 1992) outlined the way in which such ethnographies had to be attentive, in some way, to designers' concerns:

> Directed toward system use and system design, this implies placing an emphasis on studying the functionalities of a technological system as they evolve from their incorporation into the socially organised work activities of those who use them; rather

> than, as in many cases, functionalities as the system's designers might imagine them to be. (Hughes et al. 1992, p. 124)

Nevertheless, these studies posited no strong relationship:

> The emphasis here is on "potential" since there are important questions about how such studies might be incorporated into the design process. This is not a complaint but a recognition of the fact that the alliance between ethnography and systems design is, as yet, but the nomination of an agenda rather than signifying any body of achievement. (Hughes et al. 1992, p. 124)

They insisted on a particular character for this work, the "rich, highly detailed, highly textured, but nevertheless partial and selective descriptions associated with ethnography" (Hughes et al. 1992, p. 134) but, it was admitted, such studies "would seem to contribute little to resolving the designer's problem where the objective is to determine what should be designed and how" (Hughes et al. 1992, p. 134).

Recommendations in these early and somewhat naive years centered on the search for an ongoing engagement with the concerns of designers, with ethnographers using

> a dialogic process in which, initially, the fieldworker was interrogated by the rest of the research team. As indicated, this took the form of questions such as "what happens if...?", "how is this done...?", "what would be the consequences of doing X?", and so on. (Hughes et al. 1992, p. 135)

At the same time, designers were engaged in trying to formulate questions that the ethnographer might answer (see Hughes et al. 1992). Again, however, the thrust of these early papers lay in the difficulties of producing answers:

> From our point of view as sociologists these questions gave more directed attention as to how the ethnographic analysis of the work should be examined and analysed... For us, such questions were not easily answerable by reference to work which is as subtle and complex as our ethnographic analysis had shown controlling to be. Our methodological point of view of treating the system as a "motile configuration" of working practices, activities and technology, made it difficult for us to draw the distinctions necessary to provide answers to such questions. (Hughes et al. 1992, p. 135)

How, then, and in the light of a great deal of water passing under the bridge since the time of the early Lancaster work, are we to understand how the "motile configuration of working practices, activities and technology" can best be understood. As already intimated, the concept of practice offers illumination.

Unfortunately, and as so often with disciplinary renderings, much effort is wasted in trying to provide definitions at some level of generality. Examples of a more or less "sociological" treatment of the concept of practice can be found in the work by Reckwitz (2002a, b), who is mainly concerned with the "bodily and mental" construction of routine; Bourdieu (1977), for whom practice is structured by "fields" and "doxa"; Giddens (1984), who is primarily interested in the way in which both constrain and afford our practices; Geertz (1973), for whom practices are symbolically constructed; Knorr-Cetina et al. (2005), who are concerned with constructing typologies of practice (e.g., integrative vs. dispersed); and Nicolini (2012), who provides a synthesis for those interested in organizational studies (see Chapter 1 in this book for a critique). As Miettinen et al. (2009) point out, such theories are in the main deployed in the ongoing attempt to deal with the structure/agency debate. Certainly, Orlikowski's (2000) well-known approach does nothing to dispel that view.

The question for design-oriented studies is whether such theoretical abstractions, which, as has been pointed out, are essentially concerned with sociological matters, have any important consequences for design. It would be my contention that they do not. I am not the first to point out that sociology's perennial interest in the problem of "order" seldom, if ever, translates into a concern for how order is practically managed. Now, there may be many themes that could arguably be addressed in pursuit of such an interest, some of which are rehearsed by Randall et al. (2007). In an effort to characterize, rather than define, the idea that our analytic interest in practice should be design related, they refer to issues such as the ways in which practice is ecologically determined, is sequentially organized, takes place in a working division of labor, is socially organized through awareness (or "heed"), is typically constrained by various material factors, is coordinated, is skillful and/or knowledge based (see, e.g., Westrup 2002), and can be said to be constructed in rule-based routines but (sometimes) beset by "troubles." Practices also take place in a normative context, such that considerations of how "things ought to be done" sometimes affect them. Such latter considerations range from assumptions about routine right though to political and moral judgments. Regardless, and to return to our point, such analytic foci are not intended to illustrate *that* practices relate in some way to work and the use of technology, but to reveal *how* such practices are constituted in relation to work.

Having said all this, whether any significant move has been made since then to bridge the gap between investigation and design at anything other than a descriptive level remains something of a moot point. At least three ways of filling in this gap have been suggested. One is the active involvement of users in the design process. The second is to provide a theoretical grounding for the design process. The third—which is not separate from the first two—is to treat design explicitly as a political process.

6.3 Design Research

6.3.1 Involving Users

One evident feature of these studies is that they made relatively little use of users themselves, except as an object of study. A way of thinking about this is to see the relationship between ethnography and design as entailing a problematic balance between "what happens now" and what changes new technology will bring. This can be seen as a problem of time in more than one sense. Ethnographic studies can both take a great deal of time (although there is no special reason why they should) and may, paradoxically, be positioned at a point in the design life cycle such that they provide us with little or no information about the impact of interventions (although, again, there is no reason why this should necessarily be true). That is, the vision of "concurrent" ethnography offered by Hughes et al. does not seem, for the most part, to reflect take-up in the "real world." Later work (see Crabtree 1998; Voss et al. 2008) focused on a more active involvement on the part of users and stressed the way in which ethnography could be used in conjunction with some form of participatory design or, in a more elaborate form, could form the basis for "co-construction" (see, e.g., Kensing et al. 1998). Participatory design has sought to involve users in the co-design and development of computer systems for many years. This was seen to have a number of benefits, not least the democratization of processes, the improvement of organizational knowledge and, ultimately, systems that "fit" working life better. Latterly, participatory design has moved beyond the work area and became a relevant topic for the domestic context as well. Research around participatory design has explored various methods and tools that focus on the involvement of users in (re-)design processes (see, e.g., Greenbaum and Kyng 1991; Bødker et al. 2004; see also Chapter 7). Bødker et al. (2001), for instance, argue for a mutual and iterative learning process between designers and users. Participation here is seen as ongoing and continuous, such that some shared understanding of problems and needs can be derived. Nevertheless, whatever co-construction seems to offer as an adjunct to descriptive work, there remain a number of issues that have to do with organizational complexity and the heterogeneous and sometimes mutually accomplished nature of tasks, not to mention the balancing of stakeholders' rights and responsibilities. Other interventions can be mentioned here, notably cultural and technology probes. Gaver (1999), for instance, introduced the concept of cultural probes, stimuli that encourage and allow participants to reflect creatively. This concept was adopted in several ways, for example, with technology probes that inspired design for and with families (Hutchinson et al. 2003). Crabtree and Rodden (2004a) also experimented with different techniques to explore the home and highlighted the importance of self-documentation methods compared to full-time standard recording. Lindquist et al. (2007) described the use of several self-documentation and design methods of a cross-generational long-term project and reflected on their aptitude for domestic settings. These initiatives share a common feature, which is a concern for how to develop an understanding of the possible shape and role of new technology, in addition to the picture of current practice that traditional, and largely observational, ethnographic approaches might afford.

This shift arguably brings with it different choices and new problems concerning suitable users, time of user involvement, choice of adequate methods for the specific purpose envisaged, and so on (Randall et al. 2007). This has involved, inter alia, the deployment of ethnographically oriented investigations in order to understand the domestic context (e.g., O'Brien et al. 1999), methods for exploring new design ideas with users (e.g., Bernhaupt et al. 2008), and approaches to understanding how users appropriate new technology and its impact on users' habits. One such approach is usually referred to as the "living lab." "Living labs" have been offered as a solution to some of the difficulties rehearsed above. The term "living lab," apparently first used by William Mitchell at the MIT media lab, reflected a concern for real-world contexts married to the provision of a means to introduce new technology. They provide a research infrastructure for *long-term* user involvement in participatory-design processes and a test bed for evaluation procedures. Whether or not they actually do so seems to depend on the "living lab" in question. There are a variety of possibilities inherent in the concept. However, all directions have a common understanding of a living lab as an open and innovative research framework, with a strong focus on user centric research methods, that is, methods that can be applied in multiple real life environments for "sensing, prototyping, validating and refining complex solutions" (Eriksonn et al. 2006). Users take on an active role in the co-creation of the design process by providing ideas and experiences from real-use contexts and stimulate research due to long-term involvement. These properties, one can argue, distinguish the living lab method from other research methods (see Chapter 10).

6.3.2 Theorizing Design Research

Paradoxically, progress toward a different and more flexible standard in respect of the validity (or at least, plausibility) of our investigative endeavors has been accompanied by attempts to provide a new rigor in design. This move is often referred to as "design research" and is associated with work by, for instance, Hevner and Chatterjee (2010) and Edelmann et al. (2007). Hevner and Chatterjee characterize the agenda as follows:

> Design science research is a research paradigm in which a designer answers questions relevant to human problems via the creation of innovative artifacts, thereby contributing new knowledge to the body of scientific evidence. The designed artifacts are both useful and fundamental in understanding that problem. (Hevner and Chatterjee, 2010, p. 5)

Proponents of the "design-science" paradigm are insistent that their problematic is distinct from natural science:

> Behavioral science, which draws its origins from natural science paradigm, seeks to find the truth. It starts with a hypothesis, then researchers collect data, and either prove or disprove the hypothesis. Eventually a theory develops. Design science on the other hand is fundamentally a problem-solving paradigm whose end goal is to produce an artifact which must be built and then evaluated. (Hevner and Chatterjee, 2010, p. 5)

In addition, they insist, with the same somewhat cavalier (not to say mistaken) assumptions, that their problematic is distinct from more qualitative approaches:

> First, complex design problems can no longer be solved without prior or parallel research. It should be noted that design research cannot be equated with consumer research or variations of it that take the form of ethnomethodology, i.e. an empirical science that examines the behaviour of consumers in their everyday environments and thus refrains from carrying out laboratory research. (Edelmann et al. 2007, p. 3)

Now, we need not engage with the (absurd) view that behavioral science typically draws from natural science assumptions, nor with the view that ethnomethodology is a form of consumer research; instead, we can focus on the idea that design research is a "problem-solving" paradigm. The agenda is obviously to move the concept of "design" away from a naive position toward something that is theoretically informed. March and Storey (2008) put it this way:

> Thus, a design science research contribution requires (1) identification and clear description of a relevant organizational IT problem, (2) demonstration that no adequate solutions exist in the extant IT knowledge-base, (3) development and presentation of a novel IT artifact (constructs, models, methods or instantiations) that addresses the problem, (4) rigorous evaluation of the IT artifact enabling the assessment of its utility, (5) articulation of the value added to the IT knowledge-base and to practice, and (6) explanation of the implications for IT management and practice. (March and Storey 2008, p. 726)

Of course, the ethnographic position would be that evolving "clear" descriptions of problems is precisely where qualitative work has a role to play. All of the complexities I have been at pains to explicate above require investigative procedures that are only contingently applied. Perhaps this is why they are typically underspecified at the analytic level, in much the same way that "design" has been underspecified in the ethnographic agenda. If so, then there is an obvious need for some sort of integrative perspective, one that both recognizes the eclecticism of method entailed in design-related investigation and takes design seriously.

What is clear is that design-relevant ethnography needs active engagement from all parties. The actual balance of contribution from ethnographer, ethnographic record, user, and designer is likely to be worked out in-situ, but the principle that all need to be involved in some degree is foundational to the practice-oriented project. More fully worked-out versions of this might entail something like a "design case study" methodology that links ethnographical work with the co-construction of innovative IT artifacts and the iteration of given practices (Pipek and Wulf 2009; Rohde et al. 2009, 2017). A design case study covers typically three research activities: (1) it empirically analyzes the given practices in a specific field of application, (2) it co-constructs an innovative ICT artifact related to the findings of the first phase, and (3) it investigates the appropriation of the technical artifact over a longer period of time (Wulf et al. 2011, 2015). While there is a certain logical sequentiality, the three research activities can, at least in parts, be conducted in an iterative manner. Such approaches are marked by an analytic flexibility, such that procedures are judged in relation to domain and technology relevance rather than intellectual purity. Put simply, approaches of this kind can incorporate both careful and detailed empirical analysis and perform a critical, questioning role as well.

6.3.3 The Politics of Design

A further issue, as has been indicated by a number of authors from both the participatory-design and the "postmodern" ethnographic traditions, is one that implicates a political or moral universe. There is no question that engaging in something like the "processual character of interaction," a way of describing "practice," is not going to provide us with answers to questions of that kind, and they may well be questions worth asking. Nevertheless, a plausible rendering of "lived experience" can at least incorporate the way in which people typically and visibly orient to politics, morality, emotional life, sentiment, and so on. What we do with that subsequently largely depends on our own commitments. Ethnomethodologists, who take a resolutely "indifferent" line to such matters, are not, and never were, in the business of providing a vehicle for solving moral, political, or social problems (whether other stances are more successful is a matter for one's own enthusiasms), and, arguably, "postmodern" stances are not appropriate either for providing the kind of detailed, sometimes processual data that ethnomethodologists wish to provide or for the kind of analytic work that ethnomethodologists wish to do. For the purposes of this chapter, I do not wish to take any sides in respect of what commitments people wish to make but will be content with a couple of observations. First, the issue of what is a necessary or sufficient stance in relation to all the different design problems and policies one might encounter, including the different ways in which the protagonists construe their tasks, is not one that is solved by casting the debate in terms of the "replacement" of one stance by another. Second, this implicates the vexed question of "what the designer does or does not know." Crabtree et al. (2009) are insistent that

> we do not dispute the need for critical reflection in design or any other technical practice as that notion is ordinarily understood... but then we would argue that designers and users are already possessed of that faculty. As Garfinkel... argued long ago, members—be they "designers" or "users"—are not in real life the cultural dopes represented in theoretical models of society and the value schemes they represent and reflect. We would also argue, as any member of the HCI community will recognize, that social responsibility has long been a core concern of designers and is a recurrent theme at CHI. (Crabtree et al. 2009, p. 884)

Dourish (2006), apparently in contrast, suggests

> I will argue two primary points. First, that the focus on implications for design is misplaced, misconstruing the nature of the ethnographic enterprise; and second that, ironically, in so doing, it misses where ethnographic inquiry can provide major insight and benefit for HCI researchers.
>
> Sometimes, after all, the most effective outcome of a study might be to recommend what should not be built rather that to recommend what should. More to the point, an analysis of the cultural and social organization of some particular setting or occasion is often best articulated independently of specific systems, technologies, or design briefs. (Dourish 2006, p. 542)

Of course, our point is that the contrast does not take a logical form (A not B), but becomes apparent when one analytic choice among many possible choices is made. I do not want to engage in a discussion about whether "misrepresentation" is what is going on or what is "best" might turn out to be, but it is clear that in this view, design can somehow be remedied by an ethnographic engagement independent of specific design decisions or evaluations. And so it might. The ethnomethodological critique (for that is what it is) of the notion that people are "cultural dopes" or "puppets" is not, however, particularly relevant here. Garfinkel's argument traded on a specific, and entirely justified, criticism of a sociological approach that sees people merely as subject to various social influences or causes. In contrast, he wanted to point to the ways in which members are demonstrably interactionally competent, and indeed they are. The concept of "member" means precisely that a set of skills and competences are displayed in the production of the setting in question. It does not problematize the idea that knowledge, expertise, and even political awareness may be socially distributed or distributed in such a way that it draws the disapproving look of the cultural anthropologist. In sum, my aim in exploring these issues is to try to show that "being useful" does not entail "critical" as against "service" positions but can easily entail both. Moreover, this has been evident for some time (see Randall et al. 1993). Where we entirely agree with Crabtree et al. is that "replacing" careful empirical work with cultural generalizations is not desirable. The degree to which this is actually taking place, however, is an open question.

Intervention

The careful analysis of "situated" activity is a modest endeavor and is a useful place to start at in relation to design work. It is not the only place to start, or necessarily the best, nor is it obvious that that it will answer all the many and complex questions we choose to ask when we talk about "design." Of course, a singular difficulty in any such discussion would be the difficulty (impossibility) of demonstrating the superiority of any approach to ethnography on empirical grounds. The reasons for this are obvious. We would need an agreement over what a "good" design outcome was, and an agreement about the connections between the various steps that led to it and how to prove it (i.e., that designers were, in fact, paying any attention to ethnographic results and that this could be demonstrated). We have none of those things. Hughes et al. (1992) suggested that

> we describe the dialogues involved in rendering these observations "informative" for systems design, and the mutual translations implied in attempting to reconcile sociological with software engineering questions about supporting the work. We conclude by specifying some features of cooperative work which an engineering approach is in danger of overlooking. (Hughes et al. 1992, p. 123)

That there is a continuing need to engage in these dialogs and to critically engage with overmechanical conceptions of design seems to be, even so, something that all parties in practice-based research should orient toward.

Three features of late capitalism arguably demand this complex engagement with ethnographic data. The first is the fact of organizational and cross-organizational complexity, allied to the ongoing evolution of professional roles. The second is the design dynamic, such that instead of there being a simplistic narrative around "requirements," researchers need to recognize different forms of engagement at different times. There has to be a recognition of the various ways in which organizational (and other) stakeholders will intervene in the design process. This process must also involve, in some sense, the "user"; but again, the same features of late capitalism mean that the complexities of stakeholder positions need to be recognized. "Co-construction" will not be a simple business. Third, we need to recognize that, whatever design process we engage in, the process of appropriation may, to a degree, be independent of it (see Chapter 4). We cannot, in other words, assume that we will know in advance who will appropriate new technology, nor can we determine how they will do so. This means that ethnographic engagement must be based in some kind of action research and must be dynamic and reflexive.

Out of this work and countless other examples like it, we can glean—leaving aside the posturing of protagonists—certain principles that can be seen as central to the practice-oriented project and as clear gains for design work. These are as follows:

1. Detailed, careful ethnographic work is probably valuable in most and may be necessary in some design-relevant cases.
2. There can be no *deterministic* relationship between ethnographic "thoroughness," orientation to detail, sequential analysis, or what have you, and "design." The reason is, quite simply, that design requirements will vary according to the kind of design in question.
3. In some sense, critique is fundamental to the practice-based design project, but we do not always agree on what kind of critique is most useful. As suggested above, the lineaments of dispute here have to do with the degree to which such critique should take a form appropriate to the field of practice-based design or should revert to disciplinary interest on the grounds that disciplinary specialists know best.
4. We must not forget that the main contribution of CSCW and HCI to design has been their insistence on the dialogic processes between user, designer, and ethnographer. Having said that, the character of these processes will depend on a number of specific domain-related issues, including whether the domain in question is well understood, the degree to which it is "bounded," the complexity of the stakeholder structure, and so on.

All of these questions remain largely unresolved.

6.4 Conclusion

The purpose of this chapter has been to argue for a nondeterminist relationship between investigation and design and, closely allied to this, a nonfetishistic view of what ethnography (as one investigative technique) entails (specifically in relation to method). CSCW has, without question, been a vehicle for enormous gains in our understanding of, and contribution to, thinking about design. This process has not stopped. The development of digital technology, the increasing complexity of organizational life, and the sheer degree of connectivity available for social purposes has meant that ethnographic engagement of some form has become a "preferred bidder," competing with old and simplistic measures of "task," technology, and allocation of function.

Of course, system designers, and those plying similar trades, continue to do their work regardless of the critiques offered from whatever source. As such, they are much like the scientist who continues to do science, oblivious and indifferent to the critiques offered by the "studies of science and technology" movement. As suggested in this chapter, there are a number of arguments concerning the relationship between ethnography and design, and the putative preference for one form over another, and we should take these very seriously. As with so many aspects of intellectual life, the debate can be cast as one about the relative merits of rigor and imagination.

Another element that has been extensively debated by the various protagonists is the "relationship to design." We saw how at least two different conceptions of "use" are in play: one that sees a tight coupling between data and design, and one that advocates a step back from that presumption (but nowhere suggests one cannot usefully couple these two things) in order to reflect more critically on the process and thereby serve another purpose. This is the point, of course, because the argument is precisely an argument about purpose. Dourish (2006), it can be argued, is suggesting that the links between ethnography and design need not be represented in such a way as to *speciously* couple ethnography and design, rather than suggesting no coupling at all. One obvious feature of ethnographic practice, as opposed to the way it is represented in published work, in reports, or what have you, is that any given ethnography can serve many purposes. One issue is evidently, as stated in "Intervention," above, that no *deterministic* relationship between ethnography of whatever kind and design has ever been established in the workplace or elsewhere. How strong a relationship, however, is going to depend on the quality of the ethnographic work done (under whatever auspices), the work of establishing relevance through dialogic engagement with users and designers, and through the recognition that different domains pose different kinds of problems. This latter issue is, I believe, extremely important and does not directly arrive out of any perspectival stance. The commitments outlined in this chapter do not on their own produce for us relevant settings or relevant choices about how to deal with aspects of those settings, because they must somehow be related to the design questions that someone, somewhere, has at some point in time (and there is no particular reason to suppose that design questions are only asked by "designers" except in the narrow, and tautological, sense). These questions could well be the product of a critical imagination and may well be important, but they are simply not the same questions that ethnomethodologists, or others primarily interested in descriptive work, would ask. This does not make them irrelevant. Once we have made choices about the kinds of questions we are interested in and where we might find answers to them, of course, we can approach them in ways recommended by various perspectival interests. In design terms, in other words, what to look at it is just as important as how to look at it.

If, as I suggest, the various controversies around the ethnographic project remain largely unresolved, then it behooves me to make some modest suggestions about future avenues in the field of practice-based design:

1. CSCW and HCI, as design-relevant communities (along with many other semidiscrete enterprises), need to learn to avoid endless neologism and instead build

toward some modest general concepts founded in empirical studies. Such generalizations may well emanate from the way in which we conceptualize practices.

2. We, as members of these communities, need to break free of the rather casual insistence that ethnography should "feed" design in any kind of deterministic way but, at the same time, should not reverse into sociological and anthropological critique for its own sake. The CSCW/HCI "voice" can and must remain distinctive. It does so, I suggest, through the resolute insistence on enquiry into practice.
3. We also need to take into consideration that there is a range of factors that extends beyond the immediate descriptive/analytic focus; while this is rather too readily glossed as the "wider organization," there is no question that practices do take place in a normative context.
4. The most important, and unresolved, question has to do with the status of the corpus. If we assume that existing contributions to the business of description are largely unproblematic, then debates about analytic focus and the nature of intervention/prescription take precedence. These, I argue, have to do with the conceptual foundations of the ethnographic project and what the status of generalization might be in relation to the corpus of work that has developed. We have not even begun to deal with this problem.
5. Embedded in the claims made by both Schmidt (2011) and by Crabtree et al. (2009) is the idea that the fundamental purpose of ethnographic work in relation to design is to be useful in some way. It should, in some sense, contribute directly to the design process. In contrast, Dourish (2006), for instance, has been read as suggesting a drawing back from this coupling between ethnography and "design" largely in keeping with the critical claims we associate with sociology and anthropology. Now, one of the critical issues that needs to be carefully unpacked concerns the relationships between an ethnography (the "hanging around"; the grasping for "understanding," "interpretation," or explanation, depending on where one stands), the record that is produced of that activity (in respect of "data," argument, published papers, etc.), and the purposes attached to both of these things. After all, the debate we are trying to make sense of depends on what we think is going on when someone does an ethnography for whatever purpose. The thrust of Dourish's argument, at least as I see it, is twofold: the reporting of ethnographic results is impoverished if those results are to be considered *only* in terms of "implications for design," and it is a mistake to conceive of the ethnographic function as consisting in servicing a "design brief." To do so, in his view, which he shares with Bell (see, e.g., Bell and Dourish 2007), is to concede too much to the mechanical, "engineering" version of design I mention in "Intervention." These would seem to be entirely sensible judgments. However, there is an important issue to be resolved before we can judge their significance. This has to do with whether such claims for tight coupling are routinely made or realized. In fact, existing practice, I would suggest, rarely fits this model at all, except at a rhetorical level. Much of the early Lancaster work can be read as a caution against such a view, and, indeed, the proposal that ethnographies should, at least in the first instance, be "innocent" and that ethnographies can both

service design and furnish a critique at the same time has been around for a long time now (see Hughes et al. 1992; Randall et al. 1993).

6. In any event, I might argue that in this body of work, an invitation is being issued to designers to look at things anew (a critical role) instead of the serving up of data in some putative "service" role. Again, there is little to disagree with about the idea that some kind of critique might be embedded in our descriptions. We might not always agree, however, about *what kind of* critique is most valuable or, for that matter, *why*. Some clarification is perhaps needed here. The retreat from realism that we see in the "postmodern" literature on ethnography (see, e.g., Clifford and Marcus 1986; Clifford 1988) and, more specifically, in the context of "design" (Dourish 2006; Bell and Dourish 2007) has been accompanied by a variety of arguments concerning the relationship of different forms of ethnography to design, some of which make more sense than others and all of which tend to be conflated. My aim in exploring these issues is to try to show that "being useful" does not entail viewing the "critical" as against a "service" role as mutually exclusive.
7. Last, it is by no means clear that a strong and necessary relationship between ethnography of whatever kind and design has ever been established in the workplace, and certainly not that such a relationship will exist in public and private spaces not associated with paid work. It is, further, by no means clear that the processes of design will remain the same across the various different domains that are increasingly subject to the gaze of "ubiquitous computing," the "Internet of things" "big data," Internet-mediated social behaviors, and so on. We are only at the beginning of our investigations of the phenomena that attach to them. We do not know what kinds of analytic commitment—notably, the close attention to the sequential ordering of work activities—that have characterized much of our work hitherto will remain relevant because we do not yet fully understand what kinds of design problem may evolve. In addition, the problem of design cannot be considered in the absence of a consideration of designers. What is striking about arguments about "design" is that they take place in a biographical and characterological vacuum. We have no real evidence concerning the ability of designers, whoever they might be, to engage "reflexively" in their work, and it seems reasonable to suggest that this might depend in part on the kind of work they are doing and the cultural milieu they inhabit. One thing is certain—that the problems become more, rather than less, complex.

References

Adler, P. A., and Adler. P. 1987. *Membership Roles in Field Research*. London: Sage.

Bannon, L., Schmidt, K., and Wagner, I. 2011. "Lest we forget: The European field study tradition and the issue of conditions of work in CSCW research." In *ECSCW'11*. Dordrecht: Springer, 213–32.

Barab, S. A., Thomas, M. K., Dodge, T., Squire, K., and Newell, M.. 2004. "Critical design ethnography: Designing for change." *Anthropology and Education Quarterly* 35 (2): 254–68.

Bell, G., and Dourish, P. 2007. "Back to the shed: Gendered visions of technology and domesticity." *Personal and Ubiquitous Computing* 11 (5): 373–81.

Bernhaupt, R., Obrist, M., Weiss, A., Beck, E., and Tscheligi, M. 2008. "Trends in the living room and beyond." *CIE* 6 (1): 5.

Bourdieu, P. 1977. *Outline of a Theory of Practice*. Vol. 16. Cambridge: Cambridge University Press.

Bødker, S. and Christiansen, E. 2004. "Designing for ephemerality and prototypicality." In *DIS'04*. New York: ACM, 255–60.

Bødker, S., Krogh, P. G., and Petersen, M. G. 2001. "The interactive design collaboratorium." In *INTERACT'01*. Amsterdam: IOS Press, 51–8.

Brown, B., and Bell, M. 2004. "CSCW at play: 'There' as a collaborative virtual environment." In *CSCW'04*. New York: ACM, 350–9.

Bryant, A., and Charmaz, K. (eds.). 2007. *The Sage Handbook of Grounded Theory*. London: Sage.

Burman, E. 1997. "Minding the gap: Positivism, psychology, and the politics of qualitative methods." *Journal of Social Issues* 53 (4): 785–801.

Charmaz, K. 2006. *Constructing Grounded Theory: A Practical Guide Through Qualitative Analysis*. London: Sage.

Clifford, J. 1988. *The Predicament of Culture: Twentieth Century Ethnography, Literature and Art*. Cambridge, MA, Harvard University Press.

Clifford, J., and Marcus, G. (eds.). 1986. *Writing Culture: The Poetics and Politics of Ethnography*. Berkeley: University of California Press.

Corbin, J., and Strauss, A. 1990. *Basics of Qualitative Research*. London: Sage.

Crabtree, A. 1998. "Ethnography in participatory design." In *PDC'98*. Seattle: Computer Professionals for Social Responsibility, 98–105.

Crabtree, A., Benford, S., Greenhalgh, C., Flintham, M., Anastasi, R., Drozd, A., Adams, M., Tandavanitj, N., and Steed, A. 2004. "Orchestrating a mixed reality game 'on the ground.'" In *CHI'04*. New York: ACM, 391–8.

Crabtree, A., Button, G., and Rodden, T. 2009. "Ethnography considered harmful." In *CHI'09*. New York: ACM, 879–88.

Crabtree, A., and Rodden, T. 2004. "Domestic routines and design for the home." *Computer Supported Cooperative Work* 13 (2): 191–220.

Crowley, P. H., and Zentall, T. R. (eds.). 2013. *Comparative Decision Making*. Oxford: Oxford University Press.

Dourish, P. 2006. "Implications for design." In *CHI'06*. New York: ACM, 541–50.

Edelmann, K. T., Erlhoff, M., Schneider, B., Michel, R., Jonas, W., and Grand, S. 2007. *Design Research Now: Essays and Selected Projects*. Basel: Birkhäuser Basel.

Eriksson, M., Niitamo, Kulkki, S., and Hribernik. 2006. "Living labs as a multi-contextual R&D methodology." In *ICE"06*. Piscataway: IEEE Press, 1–8.

Forsythe, D. E. 1999. "'It's just a matter of common sense': Ethnography as invisible work." *Computer Supported Cooperative Work* 8 (1–2): 127–45.

Gaver, B., Dunne, T., and Pacenti, E. 1999. "Design: Cultural probes." *Interactions* 6 (1): 21–9.

Geertz, C. 1973. *The Interpretation of Cultures: Selected Essays*. New York: Basic Books.

Giddens, A. 1984. *The Constitution of Society: Outline of the Theory of Structuration*. Oakland: University of California Press.

Glaser, B., and Strauss, A. 1967. Time for Dying. Chicago: Aldine.

Gold, R. L. 1958. "Roles in sociological field observations." *Social Forces* 36 (3): 217–23.

Greenbaum, J., and Kyng, M. 1991. *Design at Work: Cooperative Design of Computer Systems*. Boca Raton: CRC Press.

Harper, R. (ed.). 2003. *Inside the Smart Home*. London: Springer-Verlag London.

Harper, R., Randall, D., and Sharrock, W. 2106. *Choice*. Cambridge: Polity Press.

Heath, C., and Luff, P. 1991. "Collaborative activity and technological design: Task coordination in London Underground control rooms." In *ECSCW'91*. Amsterdam: Kluwer Academic Publishers, 65–80.

Hevner, A., and Chatterjee, S. 2010. *Design Research in Information Systems: Theory and Practice*. Berlin: Springer.

Hughes, J., King, V., Rodden, T., and Andersen, H. 1994. "Moving out from the control room: Ethnography in system design." In *CSCW'94*. New York: ACM, 429–39.

Hughes, J., Randall, D., and Shapiro, D. 1992. "From ethnographic record to system design." *Computer Supported Cooperative Work* 1 (3): 123–41.

Hutchinson, H., Mackay, W., Westerlund, B., Bederson, B. B., Druin, A., Plaisant, C., Beaudouin-Lafon, M., Conversy, S., Evans, H., Hansen, H., and Roussel, N. 2003. "Technology probes: Inspiring design for and with families." In *CHI"03*. New York: ACM, 17–24.

Kensing, F., Simonsen, J., and Bodker, K. 1998. "MUST: A method for participatory design." *Human–Computer Interaction* 13 (2): 167–98.

Knorr-Cetina, K., Schatzki, T. R., and Savigny, E. von (eds.) 2005. *The Practice Turn in Contemporary Theory*. Abingdon-on-Thames: Routledge.

Lindquist, S., Westerlund, B., Sundblad, Y., Tobiasson, H., Beaudouin-Lafon, M., and Mackay, W. 2007. "Co-designing communication technology with and for families: Methods, experience, results and impact." In N. Streitz, A. Kameas, and I. Mavrommati, eds., *The Disappearing Computer*. Berlin/Heidelberg: Springer-Verlag Berlin Heidelberg, 99–119.

March, S. T., and Storey, V. C. 2008. "Design science in the information systems discipline: An introduction to the special issue on design science research." *MIS Quarterly* 32 (4): 725–30.

Marcus, G. 1995. "Ethnography in/of the world system: The emergence of multi-sited ethnography." *Annual Review of Anthropology* 24 (1): 95–117.

Meurer, J., Stein, M., Randall, D., Rohde, M., and Wulf, V. 2014. "Social dependency and mobile autonomy: Supporting older adults' mobility with ridesharing ICT." In *CHI'14*. New York: ACM, 1923–32.

Miettinen, R., Samra-Fredericks, D., and Yanow, D. 2009. "Re-turn to practice: An introductory essay." *Organization Studies* 30 (12): 1309–27.

Neustaedter, C., Judge, T. K., Harrison, S., Sellen, A., Cao, X., Kirk, D., and Kaye, J. 2010. "Connecting families: New technologies, family communication, and the impact on domestic space." *GROUP'10*. New York: ACM, 363–6.

Nicolini, D. 2012. *Practice Theory, Work, and Organization: An Introduction*. Oxford: Oxford University Press.

O'Brien, J., Rodden, T., Rouncefield, M., and Hughes, J. 1999. "At home with the technology: An ethnographic study of a set-top-box trial." *ToCHI* 6 (3): 282–308.

Ogonowski, C., Ley, B., Hess, J., Wan, L., and Wulf, V. 2013. "Designing for the living room: Long-term user involvement in a living lab." In *CHI'13*. New York: ACM, 1539–48.

Orlikowski, W .J. 2000. "Using technology and constituting structures: A practice lens for studying technology in organizations." *Organization Science* 11 (4): 404–28.

Palen, L., and Saltzman, M. 2002. "Voice-mail diary studies for naturalistic data capture under mobile conditions." In *CSCW'02*. New York: ACM, 87–95.

Pipek, V., and Wulf, V. 2009. "Infrastructuring: Towards an integrated perspective on the design and use of information technology." *Journal of the Association of Information System* 10 (5): 306–32.

Randall, D. 2011. "All in the game: Families, peer groups and game playing in the home." In R. Harper, ed., *The Connected Home*. Dordrecht: Springer, 111–31.

Randall, D., Harper, R., and Rouncefield, M. 2007. *Fieldwork for Design: Theory and Practice.* Dordrecht: Springer.

Randall, D., Hughes, H., and Shapiro, D. 1993. "Systems development: The fourth dimension: Perspectives on the social organisation of work." In P. Quintas, ed., *The Social Dimensions of Software Engineering.* New York: Ellis Horwood, 197–214.

Reckwitz, A. 2002a. "The status of the 'material' in theories of culture: From 'social structure' to 'artefacts.'" *Journal for the Theory of Social Behaviour* 32 (2): 195–217.

Reckwitz, A. 2002b. "Toward a theory of social practices: A development in culturalist theorizing." *European Journal of Social Theory* 5 (2): 243–63.

Rohde, M., Brödner, P., Stevens, G., and Wulf, V. 2017. "Grounded design: A praxeological IS research perspective." *Journal of Information Technology* 32 (2): 163–79.

Rohde, M., Stevens, G., Brödner, P., and Wulf, V. 2009. "Towards a paradigmatic shift in IS: Designing for social practice." In *DESRIST'09*. New York: ACM, 15.

Schmidt, K. 2011. The concept of "work" in CSCW. *Computer Supported Cooperative Work* 20(4–5): 341–401.

Sengers, P., Boehner, K., David, S., and Kaye, J. J. 2005. "Reflective design." In *CC'05*. New York: ACM, 49–58.

Spradley, J. P. 1980. *Participant Observation.* New York: Wadsworth Thomson Learning.

Suchman, L. 1987. *Plans and Situated Actions: The Problem of Human-Machine Communication.* New York: Cambridge University Press.

Suchman, L., and Wynn, E. 1984. "Procedures and people in the office." *Information Technology and People* 2 (2): 133–1.

Voss, A., Hartswood, M., Procter, R., Rouncefield, M., Slack, R., and Buscher, M. 2008. *Configuring User-Designer Relations: Interdisciplinary Perspectives.* Dordrecht: Springer.

Westrup, C. 2002. "On retrieving skilled practices: The contribution of ethnography to software development." In Y. Dittrich, C. Floyd, and R. Klischewski, eds., *Social Thinking, Software Practice.* Cambridge, MA: MIT Press, 95–110.

Wulf, V., Müller, C., Pipek, V., Randall, D., Rohde, M., and Stevens, G. 2015. "Practice-based computing: Empirical grounded conceptualizations derived from design case studies." In V. Wulf, K. Schmidt, and D. Randall, eds., *Designing Socially Embedded Technologies in the Real-World.* London: Springer-Verlag London, 111–50.

Wulf, V., Rohde, M., Pipek, V., and Stevens, G. 2011. "Engaging with practices: Design case studies as a research framework in CSCW." In *CSCW'11*. New York: ACM, 505–12.

7 Critical Reflections on Participation in Design

INA WAGNER

7.1 Introduction

If "practice" is to be a catchall term for the investigation of the way users and others interact with each other and with technology, it must also engage with the practices of designers and, more specifically, with the joint enterprises of designers and users. This, of course, has been the continuing theme of participatory design. Participatory design as a practice has been around for more than 40 years. It has its biannual conference—the PDC—and in 2012 the community that has been keeping participatory design alive published the *International Handbook of Participatory Design* (Simonsen and Robertson 2012). This was considered a major step, since publications in the field were widely dispersed and sometimes difficult to find and retrieve. The handbook offers an overview of the history of participatory design, describes methods and techniques, and provides some directions for meeting "future challenges."

However, despite a strong tradition, an impressive list of inspired and inspiring projects, and major methodological contributions to design practice, participatory design remains somewhat marginal. Many of the creative participatory techniques that the participatory-design community has developed have spread out, inspiring the field of human–computer interaction. Some of these techniques have also been taken up by the IT industry. Demonstrating how to engage users in the design of IT artifacts is often thought of as the main contribution of the participatory-design community to the field of computing. However, the ambition of participatory designers reaches beyond mere user involvement. Participatory design has a strong moral and political commitment, and it aims at including users in *all* design decisions from the start of a project:

> Perhaps the core principle of participatory design is that people have a basic right to make decisions about how they do their work and indeed any other activities where they might use technology. This is also the most contested aspect of participatory design, its most directly stated ethical commitment and its main point of difference

Socio-Informatics, Volker Wulf, Volkmar Pipek, Dave Randall, Markus Rohde, Kjeld Schmidt, Gunnar Stevens (Eds). © Oxford University Press 2018. Published 2018 by Oxford University Press.

> to more mainstream user- or human-centred design approaches. (Robertson and Wagner 2012, p. 65)

It is this normative dimension that makes participatory design different from user-centered design and other efforts at engaging users in design. However, as a recent controversy about a statement by Morten Kyng (2010a) shows, this political commitment is contested, even among participatory designers. Kyng maintains that

> we have to demonstrate that [participatory design] can deliver [information and communications technology (ICT)] designs that appeal both to users and to those who pay. To do so we need to deconstruct the current discussions on "politics" and find new practical ways to cater for the [participatory design] aspects of ICT design, including user interests. If we continue with the current focus on politics and techniques only, we run the risk of ending up in a situation where a diminishing group of [participatory design] researchers do politically correct research projects while the next practices of ICT design are being shaped by others whose main interest in users are as providers of useful input to traditionally, management controlled processes. (Kyng 2010a, p. 50)[1]

This statement reflects the experience that in many real-world contexts, designers may find themselves confronted with multiple stakeholders striving for different design results, and they may not be successful in resolving the conflicts between those different claims and interests. As Kyng stresses in his reply to the comments by Ellen Balka, Helena Karasti, and Dan Shapiro, "A lot of the solutions to how to do [participatory design] when [participatory design] was with workers at workplaces with trade unions safeguarding user interests do no longer work" (Kyng 2010b, p. 97). Hence, participation of users in all design decisions may be rather difficult to practice, for a variety of reasons.

Why is this so? One limitation that has been only marginally addressed within the participatory-design community has to do with the complexity of a setting and project. For example, in their study of an electronic patient records project within a large hospital trust, Martin et al. (2009) describe the difficulties of handling everyday practicalities of very large projects in complex contexts. In many instances, the exigencies of keeping the project on track resulted in participatory concerns being at times marginalized. Another limitation to participation is to do with issues of power. Although power relations represent a critical issue in the minds of participatory designers, in-depth analyses of how power relations come to bear on design decisions and how they shape the design result are rare. Bratteteig and Wagner (2016) provide an analysis of power and decision-making in a series of participatory-design projects, arguing that

> power is an explanatory concept: it helps see why some things are done in a certain way and not otherwise. In parts this "why" points at particular people, their skills (which we may think of in terms of power/knowledge), or their authority; in parts at structural constraints and opportunities; in parts at the "logics" of a practice. The notion of power

[1] "ICT" stands for "information and communications technology."

> suggests that the design result inter alias depends on a specific constellation of actors and resources. (Bratteteig and Wagner 2016, p. 470)

However, there is a long way from understanding power in an organization or community to being able to deal with it in a productive way: how many participatory designers are embedded in an organization where they have a voice?

Another important constraint that participatory designers face is that a project often ends before designers can even start supporting users in integrating what has been designed into their everyday practice. This also means not being able to observe, understand, and heed the evolving new practices around a system or application. A weakness of participatory design is that there are only a few evaluation studies that "demonstrate" that the successful outcomes of a project are in fact due to the practices of participation or user involvement in a particular project and context. Bossen et al. (2010) have addressed this issue through the term "user gains." They contend that such gains are rarely assessed in participatory-design projects, for a variety of reasons:

> How people appropriate the opportunities offered in individual design projects, and how these materialize in ways of working and living remain relatively unexplored. Most [participatory design] projects evaluate the process and outcome during the process and at the end. Studies of subsequent effects on working conditions or organizational changes in connection with [participatory design] projects are rare, which is partly related to the fact that many projects remain research and exploratory projects. (Bossen et al. 2010, p. 142)

Hence, it is necessary to make observing the "appropriation work" of users part of a research strategy in participatory design. This is what Wulf et al. (2015) argue, referring to a series of such empirical studies, which show the nitty-gritty details of activities that may make an IT artifact work, "from simple sense-making efforts to detailed configuration efforts to make a new technology fit an existing practice" (Wulf et al. 2015, p. 115). We could say that for a participatory-design project to be successful, it has to result in an IT artifact that can be (and in fact *is*) appropriated in real use. Bratteteig and Wagner (2016) propose that one should think of a participatory-design result as one that increases the "power to" (or agency) of future users: for example, it provides them with the knowledge and tools to enhance their (work) practices, allows them continue living in their homes although needing daily care, or increases "workplace democracy" by giving them a "voice" in matters of concern they did not have before (e.g., Bjerknes and Bratteteig 1995).

A salient question here is whether such a design result would have been possible without the participation of users in all stages of a design process. While a general answer to this question is not possible, the drive to be as inclusive of users as possible in the context of a particular project is central to participatory design.

These and other critical issues raise the question of whether participatory design is clearly distinct from and goes beyond user-centered design. Kyng's answer is that the program itself should be "modernized" so as to be able to "deliver ICT designs that appeal both to users and to those who pay" (Kyng 2010a, p. 50). He emphasizes that "the [participatory design] research community do not have to agree—especially not on politics and priorities" (Kyng 2010b, p. 93), pointing at a multifaceted future for participatory design. But how can we imagine such a future? What are the challenges ahead?

Among the critical but sympathizing voices is Dan Shapiro, who reasons in favor of a more "proactive" participatory design:

> Participatory design as a community of practitioners should seriously consider claiming an engagement in the development of large scale systems, and more particularly an engagement with the procurement and development of systems in the public sector, and should devise a collective strategy for doing so. (Shapiro 2005, p. 32)

Participatory design is excellent for understanding the widespread "procurement failures" of large-scale commercial and public software that, Shapiro contends, result "from a failure properly to understand the nature of users' activities and what they need" (Shapiro 2005, p. 30). Hence, there is an important role for participatory designers. However, he adds, participatory design so far has had little success in contributing to the design of most of the systems we are using today.

Another set of critical (and, at the same time, sympathetic) arguments refers to the role and possible contributions of participatory design with respect to the numerous social changes we are currently experiencing. Many things have changed since the time of the first successful participatory-design projects, which took place in industry, in collaboration with trade union representatives. One big change is in technology: there is less and less demand for tailored systems for work, while all sorts of "new media" (e.g., ubiquitous and pervasive technologies) and "social media" (including "technologies for communities") are gaining prominence. The fact that application development today is evolutionary, with users being able to choose between myriads of applications and off-the-shelf technologies, has to be accounted for. This raises the question as to whether participatory design is primarily concerned with the design of an IT artifact (which may be bought or easily assembled) or whether it is primarily concerned with other "design issues, such as those associated with, for example, providing elderly people with hands-on experience with mobile devices (Müller et al. 2015), or helping immigrant women market their products (Björgvinsson et al. 2010). At the same time, new forms of participation, such as, for example "living labs" (see Chapter 10) are emerging, and there is also a more widespread interest on the part of participatory designers in engaging in democratizing efforts beyond technology design (e.g., Ogonowski et al. 2013).

Linked with this are changes in the nature of the potential participants or "constituencies" of participatory-design projects: we see more and more projects with particularly vulnerable participant groups (e.g., very old and frail people; people with dementia or other mild forms of cognitive impairment; immigrant youth; and children), projects that involve whole communities, and projects in "distant" social and cultural contexts (e.g., in developing countries). There are also participatory-design projects for which it is not so clear who the future users will actually be. This is the case, for example, for projects concerning citizens' interactions with their municipality, as there can be many different types of citizens to account for and their engagement may be temporary. In these contexts, as Bødker and Zander (2015) maintain, "long-term issues of sustainability and political strategy must be addressed" (Bødker and Zander 2015, p. 55).

This chapter looks from the past to the possible future of participatory design in several steps:

- it looks back at the political roots of participatory design and what has changed since
- it unpacks the notion of participation by asking "Participation in what?" and "With which result?"
- it suggests ways to address power relations in participatory design and discusses why this might need to be done
- it discusses some of the critical issues participatory design faces today and how participatory designers address those

While some of the issues raised in this chapter are addressed systematically in the participatory-design literature, others are not. Hence, in some cases I will provide a view that is grounded in literature on participation and democracy from other fields of participatory engagement. The chapter ends by formulating thoughts on the future of participatory design.

7.2 Participatory Design: The Political Roots

Looking at the roots that have inspired "participatory action about technologies," Kensing and Greenbaum (2012) point at the political economy and worker's movements of the 1960s and 1970s, at democracy and its extension to the workplace, and at feminism, "the grass-roots movement of women asking questions and initiating change through direct actions" (Kensing and Greenbaum 2012, p. 31). Much has been written about how the workers' movement and the struggle for industrial democracy were the driving forces of the seminal projects on the "new technology and work environment" of the 1970s and 1980s, with most of the projects taking place in Scandinavia and Germany. Of major influence in Scandinavian countries was the work of Thorsrud and Emery, who made a strong case for extending plant-level negotiations and argued that some real managerial power must be transferred to employees. They also observed that this is only possible if "a large portion of the employees are both willing and able to participate" (Thorsrud and Emery 1970, p. 188).

Participatory design was formed as part of the industrial democracy movement. In the "Iron and Metal Project" (Nygaard and Bergo 1975) and the UTOPIA project (Ehn 1989), researchers sought collaboration with trade unions, which had been highly critical of how employers introduced and used IT systems. In the words of Kristen Nygaard himself, in his retrospective "Opening Speech" at IRIS, August 10, 1996:

> From 1967 on I became a member of a Trade Union discussion group on information technology. It is interesting to note that a large fraction of the young trade unionists in

> the group since became top leaders of the Norwegian trade unions. The group members came from a wide range of sectors in the society: Job shops, chemical plants, transportation, white collar work, hotels and restaurants, the public sector. I was the only researcher in the group and had for that reason special functions in our work. But the other members had their own areas of competence, equally important for the task. We first discussed possible consequences of the imminent introduction of information technology in various sectors, then how we should build up our own competence. We never considered building that competence by teaching to union members the curriculum used by programmers, engineers or managers. Knowledge is organised for a purpose and reflects the world view of the authors in terms of corporate values, power structures, objectives to be achieved etc. Uncritical acceptance of such material would make us brainwash ourselves. What we needed was a re-examination of information technology based upon the world view of the union members, emphasising solidarity, industrial democracy, safe employment, safe working conditions, decent wages, etc. (Nygaard, 1996, p. 11)

That is, the emphasis of participation was internally related to the emancipatory aim of the industrial democracy movement. The point of participation was not just "giving workers a voice" but (researchers assisting in) providing workers with the knowledge and the tools that would enable them to organize for the purposes of becoming masters of their working lives. The very first sentence of Pelle Ehn's influential *Work-Oriented Design of Computer Artifacts* (1989) places industrial democracy at the center of participatory design:

> This thesis is an inquiry into the human activity of designing computer artifacts that are useful to people in their daily activity at work. The emphasis is on opportunities and constraints for industrial democracy and quality of work. (Ehn 1989, p. 3)

The Collective Resource Approach (CRA) to design explicitly aimed at "democracy and skill" (Ehn and Kyng 1987, p. 56) for the workers. The ambition was

> [to encourage] workers and their unions to take the initiative from management rather than reacting to management's proposals and demands. In order to do so, workers and local unions must learn about the design and use of new technologies, their likely impacts on jobs and working conditions, as well as possible alternatives. (Kraft and Bansler 1994, p. 75)

Among the major results of these early projects was a general data agreement for the national Labour Union, and later legislation that regulated employees' influence and participation in changes in the workplace and its IT solutions (Mathiassen et al. 1983). But there was also the idea of providing "interactive computer-support for workers," as Ehn and Kyng wrote in a paper in which they presented the "tool perspective" to systems design. In the UTOPIA project, the researchers collaborated with the graphical workers' union to make a tool that would strengthen the workers' position—and job security—at a particular newspaper. To do this, the designers built mock-ups that the graphical workers could use to simulate page makeup, so that the designers could observe them and thus get a better understanding of the technical issues involved. This required participatory designers to get directly involved in the politics of the workplace.

Among the early participatory-design projects were also those that were not primarily political, in the sense of furthering industrial democracy in a whole industry or for a particular group of skilled workers. One example of such is the Florence project. In this project, participatory designers collaborated with the nurses in two hospital wards to develop an application that would support them in their daily work, largely following the nurses' views and suggestions. As Bjerknes and Bratteteig (1988) wrote:

> Our system would probably not be useful in any other place. However, the idea of distribution of information about coordination of work could easily be transferred to other wards. But the layout of the Work Paper (and some of the information) would have to be redesigned and tailored to the actual ward. One part of the explanation for this is that the idea for the Work Paper System came originally from the nurses in the cardiology ward. (Bjerknes and Bratteteig 1988, p. 260)

The focus of the Florence project was on the daily work of nurses, facilitating their individual tasks and supporting the distribution of information and coordination of work among the nurses. The idea was also that experiences with the participatory process would enable nurses to better define the requirements for any future system they would need.

Comparing and contrasting these early participatory-design projects shows that two elements were there from the beginning: a wider political interest in empowering workers, and a commitment to supporting them in their everyday work. For both the Iron and Metal Project and the UTOPIA project, the aim was the maintenance and development of the collective competencies of the workers, with software construction as a means to this end (rather than being an end in itself). In the Florence project, the participating nurses rejected the original project vision that an IT system should strengthen the nurses' position vis-à-vis that of other professional groups (e.g., medical doctors). Instead, the nurses emphasized that there was a need for collaboration with everyone in the ward, including the medical doctors. Hence, the aim of the Florence project switched to focusing on developing a different IT solution, one that would be practically useful in a particular context.

One of the key concepts of participatory design from its very beginnings was "mutual learning" (Bjerknes and Bratteteig 1995). Reflecting on the learning that took place in the Florence project, Bratteteig (1997) described it as being a two-way process:

> Mutual learning means that users and designer learn from each other during the design process, and both qualify themselves with respect to the systems development process they are involved in. Systems design includes to understand and to create: the way we understand a phenomenon influences the way we give form to it, and vice versa. The understanding part of design is "fed" by learning processes during design and before the actual design takes place. Mutual learning is important when different categories of people participate in the design process, typically users and informaticians. The mutual

> learning typically deals with knowledge about the application area and the work that the future computer system is supposed to support, as well as technology and possible applications of new technology. (Bratteteig 1997, p. 1)

We can say that "mutual learning," as a guiding principle, was and is still at the heart of participatory-design methods and techniques. It expresses respect for "people's expertise and their rights to represent their own activities to others, rather than having others do this for or to them" (Robertson and Wagner 2012, p. 65). Also Ehn and Kyng (1985) referred to it in describing the "tool perspective":

> According to our experience it seems fruitful from the beginning of a development project to bring together a group of people with the necessary profession-oriented, technical, and organizational skills. This makes a process of mutual learning possible in which for instance graphical workers learn about the technical possibilities of computers, bit-mapped displays, lasers, etc., and the computer specialists learn about the work of the profession in question. (Ehn and Kyng 1985, p. 14)

This is maybe the strongest link between participatory design as a movement and a larger discourse on democracy and participation, which is connected with the notion of "civil society," which dates back to the 1980s, when it was a key concept in anti-dictatorial critiques in Latin America and Eastern Europe (Kocka 2000). Like participatory design, the notion of "civil society" has a strong process dimension, building on discourse—the existence of a diversity of perspectives, the existence of conflict, and the need for negotiation. It also has a strong moral basis, with connotations of values such as autonomy, democratic self-realization, self-organization, and solidarity. The philosopher Martha Nussbaum (2003) links participation to social justice. She has argued that merely giving participants the right to participate in a project is not sufficient; it is also necessary to *enable* citizens to think, imagine, voice their opinion and interests, and negotiate issues that are of concern for them. Carol Pateman (1970, p. 43) adds "the human results that accrue from the participatory process" to the notion of participation:

> One might characterize the participatory model as one where maximum input (participation) is required and where output includes not just policies (decisions) but also the development of the social and political capacities of each individual, so that there is "feedback" from output to input. (Pateman 1970, p. 44)

While it is debatable how much the participatory-design movement was shaped by this wider societal discourse on participation and learning, it seems to strongly influence what participatory designers think about participatory design today and the kind of activities they engage in. While for some projects the design of a useful IT solution in support of users' practices is (still) in the foreground, others focus on larger societal issues with the aim of engaging citizens in developing solutions that may or may not make use of modern technology. Hence, we observe a kind of "rapprochement" between participatory design and participatory projects in areas of life, such as the environment, community and urban development, and healthcare.

7.3 Participation in What? Unpacking the Concept

When looking at how participatory design is practiced in different contexts and projects, we see that participation can mean different things and that there are even contradictory assumptions about what it means to participate: "An infinitely malleable concept, 'participation' can be used to evoke—and to signify—almost anything that involves people" (Cornwall 2008, p. 269).

A key principle of participatory design is that people have a basic right to make decisions about how they do their work and, indeed, how they perform any other activities where they might be supported by an IT artifact. This places participation in decision-making at the core of participatory design. Foundational to participatory design is also the belief "that the people who do a particular activity (including work) know most about how it gets done. So involving them in the design of the technologies they will use means that the outcomes are more likely to be successful" (Robertson and Wagner 2012, p. 65). This is one of the key assumptions of participatory design: the participation of users in the design will result in better outcomes.

Bratteteig and Wagner (2016) proposed a scheme for assessing the depth of participation, using a set of distinctions (see Figure 7.1). They sought to clarify what determines the possibility of users participating and what it is exactly that users (and other stakeholders) participate in.

The power to create choices is essential to participatory design: the opening up of alternative choices, and hence, alternative designs, is fundamental to achieving a "good" design. Users can, however, have many different roles in this process, from defining the problems the choices are an answer to, to merely delivering ideas. Creating choices requires "knowing a practice." Pelle Ehn (1988) made use of Wittgenstein's notion of "language-games" to describe this process:

> It is hard to see how we as designers of computer artifacts for page make-up could manage to come up with useful designs without understanding how the knife is used or what counts as good layout. For this purpose we had to have access to more than what can be stated as explicit propositional knowledge. This we could only achieve by at least to some extent participate in the language-games of use of the artifacts. Hence, participation is not just a question of users participating in the language-game

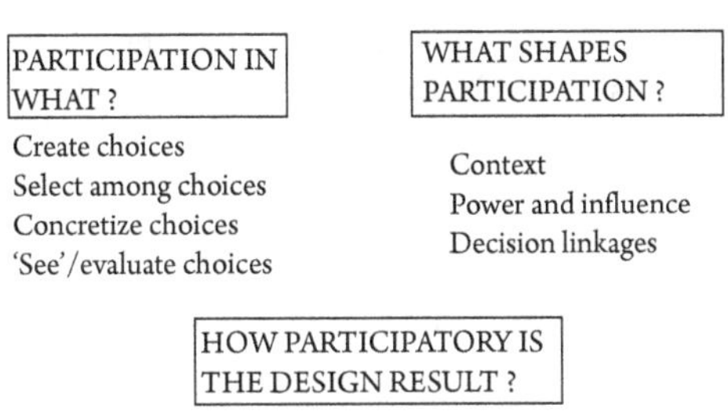

Figure 7.1 Dimensions of participation (Bratteteig and Wagner 2016)

> of design, but perhaps more fundamentally designers participating in use. (Ehn 1988, pp. 148 f.)

In participatory design, some of the choices emerge from ethnographic accounts of (work) practices and the ways that the different participants "read" them. Other choices open up while participants together engage in imagining possible futures. Participatory-design projects use techniques that help participants widen their choices rather than close the problem/solution space too early, thus handling openness and multiplicity. Müller et al. (2012) describe how, through working with residents of a care home in the form of "Internet days," this approach helped to sensitize the designers to the life circumstances of elderly people, drawing "attention to interests and (past) moments in the residents' lives which otherwise would have been neglected" (Müller et al. 2012, p. 2675). Similar to what occurred in some of the classic participatory-design projects, such as the UTOPIA project or the Florence project, the "Internet days" allowed users to, in principle, understand the technical possibilities that might be available:

> The ongoing exchange between residents, staff and students/researchers generated mutual knowledge in an ongoing dialogue of offering, asking, exploring and listening—"what can the students and the technology offer for me" and "what could be of interest for her/him." These evolving methodological and analytic choices led us to three important empirical categories, which were helpful to understand the very specific life circumstances of residents in a German care home, residents who have experienced a number of transitions in their lives. These categories are "sociality", "trust", and "memory." (Müller et al. 2012, p. 2645)

These categories informed the choices that users and designers came up with in this project.

When IT artifacts are designed, many choices are technical. While these depend on the knowledge and the resources designers bring into a project, participatory design is about making it possible for designers and users to come up with technical solutions by having them communicate through mock-ups and prototypes. In one project that was conducted with residents of a care facility, observing how participants handled different devices led to some "fairly evident" choices:

> Thus, whilst some people were eager to experiment with the controllers, mouse and keyboard themselves, others were not. It was evident to us, for instance, that we needed to experiment with input devices which must be very easy to handle for the elderly, and which connect directly to basic functionalities and information like weather information, news from the city and recent photos from organized activities. (Müller et al. 2012, p. 2645)

The next issue for a participatory-design project is how to arrange for decision-making: who decides which of the different options to pursue, and how is this decision arrived at? This selection process can be more or less participatory. In the Florence project, the decision about which of the choices to implement happened in a negotiation meeting, where both the designers and the nurses brought a list of their respective priorities. The nurses' priorities ended up being selected, although they were difficult to implement technically. At the other end is Sisom, a participatory-design project about designing a mobile application for children with cancer, where the application would help them document their symptoms before seeing a medical doctor. The Sisom project was participatory, following Alison Druin's method for participatory design with children (Druin 2002). Although in this case, the children who participated had a "voice," they did not participate in the design decisions that the project team took in their absence. Their role was to provide ideas for the user interface, and a language for talking about symptoms. The decision to limit their participation was justified by the need to follow the project vision (and also by the fact that they were children, although whether the latter reason was actually valid could be contested):

> In our work we had to make sure to meet the goals of *Sisom* and a set of pre-defined criteria. Especially, we had to ensure to design software that could help children to report their symptoms and problem experiences, without being too time-consuming and challenging. Not all of the children's ideas were therefore, feasible. (Ruland et al. 2006, p. 634)

Moreover, as the hospital's medical staff had advised against including actual cancer patients in the project, seeing them as being too weak and vulnerable to participate in the workshops, healthy school children were asked to participate instead. Ensuring that all the relevant perspectives are included in a project, also known as the "representativity problem," is a well-known issue in participatory design:

> The ethical issue that arises here is not only how to make limitations to participation transparent but how to make the decision on where the limitation comes in and why: is the limitation due to legal constraints or costs; is it due to medical concerns; or is it just simpler working with healthy children? (Robertson and Wagner 2012, p. 73)

Limiting the participation of very old people could be justified with similar arguments. However, the "Neighborhood Project" (Müller et al. 2015) is an example of a project were key design decisions were taken together with the participating elderly tenants, who voiced their preferences concerning the options of asking for and offering help, what to make visible to whom, and the kind of common activities it would be fun to organize. Their "categories of trust and privacy" were directly translated into a user interface that allowed them to choose the "buildings" (i.e., the people living in these buildings) to which some of their interactions would be visible.

There are different types of design decisions. Some decisions may involve user participation, while others may have already been framed from the start by, for example, a strong vision; institutional constraints; the composition of the project team, who from the beginning may emphasize certain properties of the design solution; the research interests that the designers bring into a project; underlying (constituent) technologies and infrastructures; and so on. The point at which design decisions are taken is where one can see how much users' contributions, choices, and observations are taken into account.

Another question in participatory design is how and to what extent users can possibly collaborate in the design of the artifact itself. In the context of an IT project, the concretizing of choices in an evolving set of prototype realizations is mainly in the hands of the designers. Whether or not users will be able to participate in this process will depend on the technical ambition and complexity of the project. However, while users may not be able to engage in the technical development itself, participatory design encourages forms of expression and concretization that are easier to master, such as building mock-ups and enacting scenarios of use. Recent examples of such mock-ups include those built by young people with diabetes (Glasemann and Kanstrup 2008), and those built by families to address issues of electricity consumption in private households (Kanstrup and Christiansen 2006). One of the important points here is that prototyping, a solution made material, *is* decision-making, as it eliminates choices and influences the allocation of resources. Making some choices material can mean that they are hard or costly to "undo," because of a lack of resources or project time, or because other, interlinked choices have already been made.

Typical of the practice of participatory design is the involvement of users in the "seeing and evaluating part" of design moves, when choices are tested in use and eventually questioned. This test situation should be as real as possible. This may be difficult to arrange, for example, in an emergency situation, where the risks of doing something wrong or being too slow is high. In these kinds of situations, such as a car accident (Büscher et al. 2008), a fire or a power outage (Ley et al. 2012), researchers may introduce a prototype in a training session that prepares actors for a real emergency event. The main point is that users should have the ability to "see" and evaluate a design idea in as real a situation as possible, as their experience can help improve the design by indicating where redesign is needed. For example, the collaborative urban planning project IPCity (e.g., Wagner 2012) was a participatory-design project where the participants—urban specialists, representatives of different interest groups, and normal citizens—substantially contributed through "seeing/evaluating" the prototypes:

> They tried hard to perform well allowing designers to learn how to improve the interaction design; they selected (and ignored) content to work with; they were active in the handling of some of the shortcomings of the representations of the site; they met the instability of the prototype, in particular the tracking mechanism. Not only this: they also challenged a premise that was close to the heart of the urban specialists: the need for precision in representing objects in an urban environment at the right scale. Most of the workshop participants, in particular the "normal" citizens, did not see the need for precision at the stage of vision building. Their "seeing" clashed with the "seeing" of professional architects. The choice of the non-expert users strengthened the designers' decision not to prioritize "precision" (Bratteteig and Wagner 2016, p. 453).

Finally, Bratteteig and Wagner (2016) argue that, although users may not participate fully in all design decisions, a participatory-design project can nevertheless produce results that are satisfactory to participants. Nygaard and Bergo (1975) have also emphasized this:

> It is essential both for the NCC1 and the MWU that the project gives results. But how are we to decide what is to be regarded as a result? We feel that the right thing to do is to initiate a self-accelerating activity within the MWU.... Measured by this standard, research reports are only useful to the extent they are releasing central and local action within the MWU. (Nygaard and Bergo 1975, p. 7).

The ambition of the early participatory-design projects was to increase "workplace democracy by giving the members of an organization the right to participate in decisions that are likely to affect their work" (Bjerknes and Bratteteig 1995, p. 74). Workplace democracy can be supported by different means. While in participatory design one of the main points of attention is the design of IT-based artifacts, important types of outcomes are new knowledge and skills, new or improved work practices, and new collaborations and networks. As many participatory-design projects today have moved from workplaces to supporting communities and different "publics," emphasizing a wider range of possible outcomes is important. One of the problems the participatory-design community is facing is that studies of how users appropriate these potential outcomes of a participatory-design project are rare. Hence, there is a lack of evidence whether the "central and local action" Nygaard and Bergo (1975) were looking for actually happens once a project has ended.

Looking back at the selection of participatory-design projects that are discussed in this chapter, we can say that their outcomes are of different kinds. The UTOPIA project was primarily aimed at developing a tool that would strengthen the position of the graphical workers vis-à-vis the owner of the newspaper. The Florence project resulted in a system that supported nurses in doing their work. Even when the working prototype had to be abandoned after a year because the machine it used broke down, it was later used to formulate a requirement specification when the hospital invested in a new IT system for nurses. The Sisom system, which is still in use in the hospital, gives ill children a voice in consultations with medical doctors, using a language that is close to their own. Moreover, the children have their opinion recorded and documented in the hospital system. Although IPCity had a strong participatory result—giving citizens the possibility to co-construct ideas for an urban site—this level of participation turned out to be impossible to maintain in the future. This was partly to do with the complexity of the prototype, and partly with the immense preparatory effort needed to make such participatory planning events happen in the context of real urban projects. The "Neighbourhood Project," as well, struggled to maintain levels of participation beyond the end of the project, pointing to the fact that

> in order to let the tenants and other stakeholders be able to use the developed infrastructure after project end, a perspective on sustainability of both the current technology appropriation process and the maintenance of the technology as well as the development of further service design has to be taken. (Müller et al. 2015, p. 2303)

Hence, even if the design result is participatory in the sense of increasing users' "agency" (or "power to"), there are issues of long-term sustainability that participatory designers face.

7.4 Thinking about Power Issues in Participatory Design

There are different viewpoints on the ways in which power issues should be dealt with in participatory design. Hartswood et al. (2002), who prefer the term "co-realisation," have a clear position:

> Co-realisation's approach is not to intervene in the politics of design as participatory design has tended to do with a predefined programme. Rather, co-realisation takes the view that politics is a members' matter to be worked through in context. (Hartswood et al. 2002, p. 14)

While it is not clear what kind of "predefined programme" Hartswood et al. refer to, they point at the need for participatory designers to understand the context of use, or "the politics of the place." From this perspective, politics "is a member's matter." An example is that of Blomberg et al. (1996), who describe the politics of making litigation work in a law firm invisible and how they came to appreciate the work of coding enormous amounts of documents. In this sense, understanding power relations in a participatory-design project's setting—be it a law firm, a residential home for elderly people, or a hospital ward—is critical to developing a successful design result predicated on participation.

Power relations are also part of the dynamics of a participatory-design team, in which stakeholders with different interests and different types of competence and knowledge collaborate. Understanding these dynamics is critical for having a realistic view of the possibilities and limitations of participation. Power issues in participatory design can be addressed on several levels, by determining, for example, who is invited to participate, how and by whom "representations" of practices and situations of use are constructed, how and by whom the design space is developed, how solutions will be selected and implemented, and who will benefit from the design.

Power issues can be looked at from a diversity of theoretical angles. In a discussion of the claim that "power" is a relational concept, Hannah Pitkin (1973) introduced the distinction between "power to" and "power over," stressing that these two uses of the word "power" express rather different phenomena. "Power over" another person ("by his getting the other to do something, but also by his doing something to the other") is a relational concept. "Power to" denotes "capacity, potential, ability, or wherewithal" (Pitkin 1973, p. 276):

> One man may have power over another or others, and that sort of power is indeed relational, though it is not a relationship. But he may have the power to do or accomplish something all by himself, and that power is not relational at all; it may involve other people if what he has power to do is a social or political action, but it need not (Pitkin 1973, p. 277)

The distinction Pitkin proposes is based on different ways of using the word "power." This does not mean that both types of power cannot occur in the same situation. For example, increasing users' "power to" may also increase their "power over." One could argue, for example, that UTOPIA primarily aimed at developing a tool that would be instrumental in increasing the graphical workers' "power over" the owner of the newspaper, or at least reduce the owner's "power over" the graphical workers. In contrast, while the Florence project started out aiming to increase the nurses' "power over," for example, doctors, it turned out that the nurses preferred to have a tool that would allow them to have more "power to" carry out certain tasks. Similarly, the IPCity project developed a tool that primarily increased citizens' "power to" engage in collaborative urban planning. But, in this case, such "power to" can also turn into "power over," when the citizens' ability to build and express their own vision for a project provides them with a strong sustainable commitment to involvement in decision-making.

The modern discourse on power is dominated by the work of Michel Foucault. In "The subject and power," he suggests asking "By what means is it [power] exercised?" and "What happens when individuals exert (as they say) power over others?" (Foucault 1982, p. 786). This leads him to distinguish between power relations (what Pitkin calls "power over") and power that is "exerted over things and gives the ability to modify, use, consume, or destroy them" (Foucault 1982, p. 786). Hence, for Foucault, power is also a "capacity." Power not only results in marginalization, exclusion, nondecision, and nonaction; it also supports and structures people's fields of options, decisions, and practices. In particular, Foucault's notion of "power/knowledge" has been taken up widely to denote the privileges connected with knowledge. Using Foucault's work *Discipline and Punish* as an example, Hall (2001) explicates:

> To study punishment, you must study how the combination of discourse and power—power/knowledge—has produced a certain conception of crime and the criminal, has had certain real effects both for the criminal and for the punisher, and how these have been set into practice in certain historically specific prison regimes. (Hall 2001, p. 76)

The term "power/knowledge" implies the ability to define issues, thus "normalizing" them so that they can be recognized and resolved and translating them into a language that makes them amenable to particular interventions (albeit at the expense of others). In the early days of participatory design, one important aim was counteracting the "power/knowledge" of designers and their highly specialized technical language, instead enabling designers and users to discuss possible technical solutions by having them communicate through mock-ups and prototypes instead of a specific formal language.

Even so, in a participatory-design project, different types of expert knowledge come into play, and it may be important to look at how accessible these are, how dominant they are, how open to criticism they are, and how much they become shared. In the case of the IPCity project, different types of power/knowledge shaped the design process, such as the importance of urban expertise for understanding "how to represent an urban situation," the artists' skills to visualize and edit what participants would see, and technical expertise (and the design decisions that were shaped by technical competences and research interests), which was difficult to challenge but also vulnerable to criticism (due to the instability of the prototypes that were evaluated in the context of urban projects). Foucault was immensely critical about particular ways of conceptualizing, categorizing, and measuring. His work on psychiatric institutions and how they classify people in order to subject them to particular regimes is well known, as well as his work on how sexuality is defined and experienced. The dominant discourses on aging or living with dementia are other examples where power/knowledge comes into play; Müller et al. (2012) and Wan et al. (2014) address these critically, using fieldwork to identify, understand, and account for the enormous diversity and complexity of real-life situations of people with dementia and the people that take care of them.

"Power to" and "power over" are categories that are useful when thinking about the design result. From a process perspective, however, design decisions in a participatory-design project are the result of a complex interplay of regulatory mechanisms, which include influence, trust, and loyalty (Bratteteig and Wagner 2014). In addition, Pitkin stresses that power and influence differ in important ways, although situations may involve both. In contrast to power, influence is based on reputation and persuasiveness; it is realized through giving explanations and trying to convince. To exert influence means to get others agree with one's claims, opinions, or intentions:

> While power represents an intervention in the action space of others, influence has to begin with one's interaction partners' own dispositions to act: how they develop opinions and take decisions and not—as in the case of power—with pushing through what already has been decided. (Zündorf 1986, p. 38)

Influence as a regulating mechanism is common in design decisions requiring highly specialized, mostly technical expertise; so is trust. Building trust is a key issue in participatory-design projects involving particularly vulnerable users. For example, Wan et al. (2014) point at the time it takes to get access to people with dementia, since "many dementia-affected families feel reluctant to discuss this sensitive topic with unfamiliar people. It required, as is always the case in such sensitive settings, the development of trust in our motives and our ability to behave responsibly over time" (Wan et al. 2014, p. 3989). Involving people with dementia and their families in testing and evaluating prototypes requires helping them build "trust in the system." Trust is a basic requirement for design decisions to happen in a participatory way in such situations, and it can only be built through designers listening to the voices of dementia-affected people and their families and acknowledging them.

Participation in design is also shaped and constrained by institutionalized aspects of power; however these may not be amenable to negotiation and can limit what can be achieved in a participatory-design project. The aims of a project, such as developing a product that fits an existing IT infrastructure, meets deadlines, meets budget restrictions, or conforms to the "rules" the world outside the project impose, may limit the possibilities for widening the design space and maintaining it in an open fashion. When performing a participatory-design project within an organization that is supposed to use the design, structural aspects may have a decisive impact on what can be achieved. For example, in the Neighbourhood Project, the interests of the cooperating housing company had to be kept in mind, and some design decisions were taken to "keep the consortium stable" (Müller et al. 2015, p. 2302).

In the context of citizen participation, Gaventa (2005) has introduced the notion of "participatory spaces," reflecting on how to influence the power relations that determine the boundaries of such spaces, what is possible within them, and who may enter such spaces, which also determines which identities, discourses, and interests will be present in such a space. He distinguishes between *closed spaces*—which refers to decision-making made behind closed doors—arguing that many civil society efforts focus on opening up such spaces through greater public involvement, transparency, or accountability; *invited spaces*—new spaces "into which people (as users, citizens, or beneficiaries) are invited to participate by various kinds of authorities, be they government, supranational agencies or non-governmental organizations" (Gaventa 2005, p. 12); and *claimed/created or "third" spaces*—where social actors create spaces for themselves.

Addressing power relations in participatory design is about how to claim and/or create spaces for participation. It is also about achieving a wider diversity and fluidity of spaces of engagement in a project. Gärtner and Wagner (1996) have used the notion of a "social arena" (Strauss et al. 1985; Clarke 1991) in their analysis of participation in industrial projects, specifically identifying the following three arenas: the political and policy-making context (Arena A); the institutional/organizational context for action (Arena B); and the context of design—support of work practice, public spaces for community involvement, and so on (Arena C; see also Balka et al. 2008). Arena C is where participatory-design projects are most successful in claiming/creating participatory spaces, at least temporarily, although one problem is that participatory designers rarely have the opportunity to continue their engagement in a work organization in order to help embed the design in everyday work practices. It can be challenging to move a participatory-design project up into Arenas B and A, which are very often "closed" spaces, even though it may be necessary to do this in order to resolve some of the problems encountered in Arena C. One example of a domain where such a move might be required is healthcare, where the drive toward "new public management," often requiring a strong focus on standardization and cost containment, may have a profound impact on the design space (see, e.g., Reidl et al. 2008).

Revisiting research within a pediatric emergency department, Bjørn and Boulus-Rødje (2015) make the case that researchers in computer-supported cooperative work should enter "a large manoeuvrable space for political interventions" (Bjørn and Boulus-Rødje 2015, p. 344), arguing, "The researcher's task was not simply to reproduce the user perspective, but instead to provide perspectives that were outside the nurses' and the application specialists' conceptual understandings and domains" (Bjørn and Boulus-Rødje 2015, p. 341). They describe how their design project became a "political object" and how it became difficult, maybe even impossible, to detach analytical sensibility from the political issues' (Bjørn and Boulus-Rødje 2015, p. 343).

One of the reasons why many participatory-design projects remain "small" and exploratory in nature is that a project with multiple stakeholders, issues that are highly complex to understand and negotiate, and complex organizational structures or institutional assets may be difficult to handle. One problem in the participatory-design community is that since the days when researchers collaborated with trade unions to empower workers, the field has lacked a clear political strategy that goes beyond single projects.

On the other hand, participatory design is moving in new directions that, ultimately, may change how we think about the relation of participation with design. These are discussed in Section 7.5.

7.5 New Directions for and Forms of Participation

Within the last 10 years, new types of participatory-design projects have been undertaken that broaden the scope of participatory design in a variety of ways. Much of this has been inspired from experiments with participation in other domains, dealing with broader societal issues. Many participatory-design projects today seek to collaborate with people who are marginalized or have special needs, giving voice to them. Moreover, participatory design has moved from workplaces to communities or different kinds of "publics." Moves such as designing for configurability, end-user development, and the design of IT infrastructures made possible by new technologies, all of which are broadly covered in this book, also have implications for participatory design.

7.5.1 A New "Clientele" for Participatory Designers?

A strong momentum originates in the engagement of some participatory designers (not necessarily of IT solutions but of products or services of all sorts) who work with neglected or particularly vulnerable groups in different parts of the world and in different cultures, including poor countries.

There is a tradition of engaging children in participatory design, and many applications supporting learning or "just having fun" have been developed with children as active participants (for a discussion of early work, see Druin 2002). Many museum projects today have children as a main user group in mind. Core assumptions here are that children are not just "young adults," that they "have their own likes, dislikes, curiosities, and needs" (Druin 2002, p. 1), that they may be particularly open to playful and unusual interfaces, and that, in many cases, they may know better than parents and teachers what they really need. Some of participatory-design projects that involve children address problems beyond play and learning, for example, Sisom, for which the user group was meant to be children with cancer.

Another example is a product-design project involving children with prosthetic legs in Cambodia (Hussain 2010). Referring to participatory design and the notion of "empowerment," Hussain describes how she had to go into the villages to be able to engage with the children and invent techniques that enable and encourage them to express their experiences and needs; one of the young participants in her study, "Vannak,"

> wrote that he would like to have a prosthetic leg that: Has a big enough foot; Has the appearance of a living leg; The liner soft and thicker than now; The outside socket is not too tight; From the ankle down please make it like a natural foot. (Hussain 2010, p. 113)

These children obviously fall into a residual category, in several ways: they live in small villages in a poor country, they are victims of war, and they do not present a big market segment. In the words of Star and Bowker (2007), they fall between the cracks and are "unspeakable"—there is no language in product design that would make it possible to describe their experiences and needs. What the project achieved was to make the children's lived experience "speakable" and visible.

The list of "particularly vulnerable user groups" may be extended to include old and frail people, youth with mental problems, people with dementia, asylum seekers, poor immigrants, and so forth. Wulf et al. (2013), who studied political activists in a Palestinian village, provide an example of making the situation of these people visible to a wider research community, with a focus on "how internet and social media applications were appropriated in this struggle" (Wulf et al. 2013, p. 1979). Although this was an ethnographic study and not a participatory-design project, it points to some of the challenges of working in such a context, which have been addressed by ethnographers (and much less in the participatory-design literature). Burman et al. (2001), reflecting on a study of girls and violence, write: "There is no such thing as a 'neutral' account of violence" (Burman et al. 2001, p. 14). There is also no neutral study of people in a highly politicized, conflictual context, and it may be difficult for researchers to arrive at an adequate understanding of what they observe. There is an obvious issue of representation and interpretation: whose voices are being heard? Are other, potentially relevant, voices being excluded? Reaching conclusions in such a case is a particularly "political, contested and unstable activity" (Maynard and Purvis, 1994, p. 7).

Reflecting on a project to develop an indigenous knowledge management system in a community in Namibia, Winschiers-Theophilus et al. (2010) point at similar challenges. More specifically, they observe:

> Major gaps existed between the international team of design researchers and the local participants based on "contrasting sense of self, individuality and community, orality versus print-based literacy, and technological skills versus local situational knowledge." (Winschiers-Theophilus et al. 2010, p. 2)

Community participation is a strong value and a well-established practice in South-African rural communities. As this was a participatory-design project, the challenges included not only how to introduce thinking about design issues into this tradition but also how to find the appropriate ways of representing villagers' knowledge. Difficulties ranged from villagers not knowing how to use maps, to the fact that they "did not prioritize effectiveness and user satisfaction in the way we typically evaluate 'usability'" (Winschiers-Theophilus et al. 2010, p. 9).

Practicing participatory design may be difficult unless participants acquire sufficient literacy in ICT literacy. Hence, including non-technical users outside of work settings (i.e., in their homes or in public spaces) poses particular challenges. The studies by Käfer et al. (2014) and Müller et al. (2012) provide good examples of the kind of learning situations participatory designers arrange for to help elderly people to familiarize themselves with modern technologies, which not only may give them an immediate advantage in everyday life but also can enable them to, at a later stage, participate in creating choices and testing evolving prototypes. Engaging elderly people in imagining future design may require some creativity, Joshi and Bratteteig (2015) argue:

> As a way of increasing the old residents' understanding of technology design we arranged "testing of materials." An example is the co-construction of the radio buttons: we brought buttons with very different properties: form, size, material, color etc. and had them look and feel their way to a decision about the best solution. The pedagogy principle of "show, not tell" was also useful for understanding the interaction mechanisms as well as the possibilities for design options. (Joshi and Bratteteig 2015, p. 24)

Looking at these "special kinds" of users—from children, to old and frail people, to villagers in Namibia—a number of interesting questions arise. One of these questions is whether giving voice to marginalized people, or people who inhabit "residual categories," should be considered a moral obligation of participatory designers. To some extent, it always is, as participatory design is explicitly committed to having different voices being heard, understood, and heeded to be truly participatory. So, there is always the obligation to look out for those that may have been forgotten or excluded or could not be "found" in a project. As Chambers (1999), a pioneer of a participatory approach to working in rural communities, has argued, "Those who are younger or very old, female, of low status groups and/or poor, deprived, disabled and weak will tend to be left out unless care is taken to find them and bring them in" (Chambers, p. 183).

Another question is how to account for the limited possibilities of some user groups to participate. One principle that participatory-design projects take rather seriously is that of "mutual learning," that is, inventing new techniques of involving people who come from other cultures, have limited physical abilities and strength, or problems to remember. However, ethical problems may arise that may be difficult to resolve. As was the case in a project with people with dementia, where it became difficult to find participants for evaluating the prototype,

> it was significantly harder to find participants for the field evaluation than for the pre-study. The reasons are manifold. Along with the project progress, the problems of the affected persons had also progressed. They were now either not able to walk, or the caregivers were too afraid to let them walk freely. The institutions were also very cautious in relation to testing, because of the possible philosophical or legal ramifications associated with technology failure. (Wan et al. 2016, p. 6)

Another example comes from a project to design a special toileting facility for people with physical disabilities. During the testing, a user broke into tears,

> possibly as a reaction to having failed in a task he had been asked to perform. The task required a capacity in the participant, namely raising his voice, which had been affected as a result of his recent stroke. A successful rehabilitation made the man physically appear a healthy volunteer to the research team. What the team could not foresee was how the man's failure to activate an alarm with his voice would mean a sad reminder of the loss of health and control in his life. (Rauhala 2011, p. 56)

These examples suggest that notions about what it means to participate have to be critically examined and that new ones should be found that can be used to identify the agenda of particularly vulnerable, weak, or inexperienced users and enable them to voice their own concerns or questions and imagine possible futures. An observation that many participatory designers working with very old people share is the power that societal prejudices that define elderly people as being afraid of new technology and unable to integrate them into their lives can have. The same holds for children, as the example of the Sisom project shows. For the case of "participatory research," Thomas and O'Kane (1998) demonstrate how it is possible to be open to children's agenda, have them voice their own concerns or questions, use participatory research techniques to give them control over the process, and also have them participate in the interpretation and analysis of research data.

Another observation that stands out is that the sheer diversity of users' life situations, capabilities, and ideas of what constitutes a "good life" may mean that there is possibly not one "participatory design result." Wan et al. (2016) make this clear in their study of people with dementia, their families, and the caretaking institutions (which can subscribe to rather different caretaking philosophies): in such a context, "it is often not possible to find 'clear-cut' solutions" (Wan et al. 2016, p. 30). Thus, taking account of the specificity of each care situation may lead to participatory designers having to develop highly individualized solutions. Joshi and Bratteteig (2015) in a participatory-design project with very old people, remark that "ageing meets us in very different ways; hence the diversity is not easily represented through a few participants," concluding that "we take the participants to represent themselves rather than pre-defined groups of people" (Wan et al. 2016, p. 23). This is an interesting turn of perspective from wider issues of participation and democracy to the idea of using IT to support individual people in their activities.

7.5.2 Extending Participation to Communities

While participatory-design projects traditionally focus on an IT artifact as an important part of their outcome, community projects no longer necessarily do. While IT artifacts may play a certain role, community projects move the project focus away from the design of IT artifacts toward a wider array or mix of interventions and more toward community development, with a focus on environmental or urban planning issues, migration, and so forth. Hence, the main aim of such projects may be formulated to extend the range of participants and widen people's options. In their introduction to *Communities and Technologies*, which is an edited collection of research articles, Huysman et al. (2003) write that

> communities are social entities whose actors share common needs, interests, or practices: they constitute the basic units of social experience.... within a global knowledge-based society, communities play a pivotal role. Problems such as new forms of political participation and civic engagement, the maintenance of cultural identities, or the integration of minorities need to be tackled on the community level. (Huysman et al. 2003 , p. xi)

While this definition resonates with the notion of "communities of practice" (Lave and Wenger 1991), communities can, of course, also be legal entities with their own political bodies. Di Salvo et al. (2012) stress that there are many kinds of communities: while some of them—for example, neighborhood, town, or regional communities—are based on geographical proximity, others are organized around particular concerns. The authors then provide a series of examples of participatory-design projects with different types of communities, reflecting on the changing role of participatory designers in such projects.

There is an enormous amount of literature dealing with issues of participation with respect to communities. In the context of participatory design, it is interesting to see how participatory designers engage with the concept of community. Some of the challenges these new types of participatory-design projects bring with them are well described by Brereton and Buur (2008) in discussing their work in an urban community in Australia. The questions they address help understand how the conditions for participatory design change when there is no longer a single organization that might represent a community that is heterogeneous and distributed. Relationships in a community are complex, and so this may require the development of new tools and techniques for these types of engagement. The authors' solution in this project was to install an electronic noticeboard in a local convenience store. One of their key observations refers to the experience of having to open up to interests that participatory designers may not be used to addressing:

> If the project is to grow, the next step potentially involves working out issues such as business models, public/private ownership, open sourcing and location of other noticeboards. Achieving balance between business and other community interests must be negotiated. Business is part of the community fabric. However, at each step the ability of the general public to participate in the design and to secure rights to use is also at stake. The attempt to appropriate public space for community use is less a matter of known design process and more a matter of strategic engagement with local business leaders and political leaders who have aligned interests and who can benefit from and support the project. (Brereton and Buur 2008, p. 105)

Working in a community extends the spectrum of political fields that participatory designers may have to enter. This may give rise to complicated situations that the designers may not be well equipped to handle. Björgvinsson et al. (2010) describe how, in a project in the Malmö living lab with a group of Arab immigrant youth, controversies arose about the choice of partners, which included a company engaged in building transportation infrastructure in East Jerusalem. Working with "marginalized social movements" in the Malmö living lab, Björgvinsson et al. (2012) have formulated political engagement in and with communities programmatically as "agonistic participatory design," which is about aligning "participants around a shared, though problematic or even controversial object of design" (Björgvinsson et al. 2012, p. 109). "Agonism," a concept that goes back to Chantal Mouffe, expresses forms of debate and confrontation that allow for "constructive controversies between 'adversaries'.... These activities are full of passion, imagination and engagement" (Björgvinsson et al. 2012, p. 109).

What these two examples highlight is that when engaging with a community, the identification of stakeholders and their perspectives, and developing adequate political strategies to deal with them, may constitute *the* most time-consuming and difficult task of the participatory designer. While "whose side to take" may turn out the paramount question in some projects, in others "what can we possibly contribute" may become a critical issue. For example, Yerousis et al. (2015), reflecting on bringing computer clubs to a Palestinian refugee camp, mention that "the Jalazone clubhouse sessions had to be frequently cancelled as violent clashes erupted between in-camp youngsters who threw stones and burnt tires, and the IDF who responded with the firing of tear gas, rubber-coated bullets" (Yerousis et al. 2015, p. 3757). For me, this is not only a question of "whatever one's stance on Arab–Israeli conflict" (Yerousis et al. 2015, p. 3757) but a question of what I, as a researcher and a participatory designer, can possibly contribute.

When working in a community, participatory designers may have to question their practices and competences in a rather radical way. Who the legitimate participants are in a particular project may be far from obvious; the goals the project aspires to reach may be highly controversial. Community projects move in two directions. One is to foster the public deliberation of issues or, as Ehn (2008) phrases it, "designers participating in public controversial things outside the boundaries of the safe design project" (Ehn 2008, p. 92). He refers to Dewey's notion of "public" as being constituted by people who can be brought together for a particular purpose. "Controversial things" may involve a multiplicity of publics, and each of them is characterized by heterogeneity and conflict. Addressing one or more publics, and possibly bringing technology to these publics in support of whatever moves them, takes participatory design close to the notion of civil society. Cornwall (2008) forwards a nuanced notion of community participation, arguing that "the intentionality of those who initiate community participation or use participatory methodologies to facilitate community development is only part of the story" (Cornwall 2008, p. 274). She continues:

> The very public nature of some forms of consultation can serve as a space for the airing of grievances that may become more difficult for those in power within and beyond the community to ignore... Equally, the most transformational intentions can meet a dead end when 'intended beneficiaries' choose not to take part, or where powerful interest groups or gatekeepers within the community turn well-meaning efforts on the part of community development workers to their own ends. (Cornwall 2008, p. 274)

Another direction that participatory designers engaging with communities are taking is toward new forms of designing products and services for which special skills and/or special needs may exist in a particular community. Björgvinsson et al. (2010) refer to a wider discourse on "democratizing innovation," which has been inspired by a rather controversial debate on what recognizing users as potentially creative producers actually may mean. A source of inspiration is the work of the Italian designer Ezo Manzini and the group around him:

> Spreading design practices where new ideas emerge from a variety of actors directly involved in the problem to be addressed: end-users, grass-roots designers, technicians and entrepreneurs, local institutions and civil society organisations. In this perspective, design is no longer just a tool for the development of functional innovative consumer products, but is increasingly seen as a process for radical change—developing

> services, systems and environments supporting more sustainable lifestyles and consumption habits. (Bannon and Ehn 2012, p. 55)

In this case, technologies are used to support social innovation. The notion of design is extended, covering "services, systems and environments," and the users are all kinds of practitioners and institutions that may contribute to and ultimately benefit from their design. The role of designers is expanded, as Mazé (2014) observes:

> Many approaches to designing for social innovation are concerned with the community-based or -led approaches to the provision of social services and resources, such as habitation, education, care, mobility and food... In these and related approaches, "the social" has become the object of design..., with profound effects on how design is understood and practiced. (Mazé 2014, p. 2)

7.5.3 Toward "Infrastructuring"

In the 1990s, within the participatory-design community, there was a marked interest in what was called at that time the "tailorability" of systems. Researchers started looking at people who worked as "user-designers" by customizing software to the needs of users in companies, as well as at end-user programming and development (see Chapter 4). Trigg and Bødker (2004), in their study of "tailoring" ("tinkering," "translating," or "gardening," as it was called by others) at the workplace, identified a wide variety of tailoring skills, from building/modifying buttons, to writing macros, and programming on the PC, all of which involved manipulating otherwise "invisible" codes. Much of the tailoring work they observed had to do with defining, sharing, and distributing "standards" (forms, macros) within the organization.

The interest in tailoring has continued, with an emphasis on making it possible for users to appropriate devices in use, by customizing and extending them according to their varying skills and needs. It has, for example, led to the notion of participatory programming, which Letondal and Mackay (2004) view "as a logical extension of participatory design, in which users participate in the creation of software tools they can ultimately tailor and program themselves" (Letondal and Mackay 2004, p. 31). Rodden et al. (2004) discuss configurability as users making sense of technology and see this as being dependent on users "making the technology relevant to the practical circumstances of *their* everyday lives" (Rodden et al. 2004, p. 75). Based on examples from healthcare and architecture, Balka and Wagner (2006) discuss different dimensions of configurability, like "placement and assembly, appropriation in use, integrating the system, and so forth," arguing that configuring the social context may be "much more critical to the functioning of the technology than configuring the system itself" (Balka and Wagner 2006, p. 237); Newman et al. (2002) argue "that systems should inherently support the ability of users to assemble available resources to handle their tasks" (Newman et al., p. 148); Pipek (2005) discusses strategies for designing tools that can be appropriated in use; and Stevens et al. (2010) use the notion of "appropriation infrastructure," emphasizing "that the social construction of IT artifacts should be tightly integrated in the material construction of

IT artifacts in bridging design and use discourses" (Stevens et al., p. 58) while Lieberman et al. (2006) refer to "end-user-development" as "empowering end-users to develop and adapt systems themselves" (Lieberman et al. 2016, p. 1).

These different terms and perspectives reflect the changing nature of technologies. They point to the fact that there is a strong link between the ways IT artifacts are constructed and the possibilities for facilitating appropriation in use. The notion of "infrastructuring" takes this debate a step further, connecting it with participatory design. It places an emphasis on collaboratively building resources that can be aligned, making them usable in and across different contexts for varying purposes. As Lee and Schmidt show in Chapter 5, there is an "inherent ambiguity" in the ways the term "information infrastructure" is used. They add: "But what is most striking is that the term 'infrastructure' is being used for distinctly different purposes and to denote distinctly different phenomena" (p. 206). For example, Ciborra and Hanseth (1998) discuss knowledge in an organization as infrastructure, Hanseth and Lundberg (2001) refer to large-scale "computer networks with associated services" (Hanseth and Lundberg 2001, p. 409), and Pipek and Wulf (2009) use the term "IT based work infrastructures," as "the entirety of devices, tools, technologies, standards, conventions, and protocols on which the individual worker or the collective rely to carry out the tasks and achieve the goals assigned to them" (p. 455).

The recent terminological shift from "infrastructure" to "infrastructuring" adds to this confusion. First of all, it refers to an activity. Pipek and Wulf (2009) define it as the design activity of improving work infrastructures. They also use it for describing "methodological and tool support for all stakeholders' activities that contribute to the successful establishment of an information system usage" (p. 447), emphasizing the perspective of users. "Infrastructuring" is about activities that help establish the usage of an information system. Another source of ambiguity is that, although the term "information infrastructure" was largely introduced to address exactly large-scale computer-based systems spanning multiple local practices (see Chapter 5), it is also used for describing local phenomena, as in Karasti and Baker (2008), who study "community members growing their own information infrastructure for community purposes" (Karasti and Baker 2008, p. 212), arguing that

> traditional perspectives on use, design, and participation make it difficult to capture, value and potentially support activities that community codesigners perform in order to make use of information systems including experience-based meta-level learning about design, managing the continuity of data and information infrastructure, and developing "home-grown" methods that account for and appreciate communities for what they are—heterogeneous yet sustainable environments where members engage with common interests and learning. (Karasti and Baker 2008, p. 220)

In this paper, they use the term "infrastructure work" for describing the activities of the community codesigners they observed. From this perspective, "infrastructuring" is about designers and users appropriating technologies in support of local practices, such as providing local data for specific community interests (Karasti and Baker 2008) or engaging in “democratic innovation” (Björgvinsson et al. 2010). It is about creating the resources for the configuring and reconfiguring of socio-material environments in which new practices may emerge. These resources may be used in many different contexts, including places that would not have been considered before as hosts of technologies, such as a bus, a local convenience store, or a shelter for homeless people.

What is participatory design in this context? Is it about preparing for such environments (or infrastructures) to be configured and appropriated? Is it about supporting the emergence of something new in these environments? Or is it about heeding what has been learned and making it available to others? Pelle Ehn (2008), who has championed the term “infrastructuring” in the participatory-design community, defines it as “binding design-games of designers and future designers/users together” (Ehn 2008, p. 92), what he also calls “meta design.” This emphasizes the aspect of making infrastructures appropriable in use. He also evokes the old idea of participatory design supporting industrial democracy, reformulating it as “a focus on infrastructuring in support for communication and community building free of coercion at use time” (p. 99). Inspired by (among other activities) the Atelier project (Binder et al. 2010), he proposes to take inspiration from a variety of notions when thinking about how to design infrastructures; such notions include “thick” infrastructures (which take account of “the mutual constitution of the social and the technical and the heterogeneity of potential design-games” [Ehn 2008, p. 99]), design patterns, ontologies, ecologies (of devices), the DIY approach, the “creative commons,” and other public infrastructures.

Hence, is participatory design about building infrastructures or is it more about supporting users in making use of existing infrastructures for specific purposes? Infrastructures are already out there, one might argue. A fascinating recent example is how new political movements, such as DiEM25 (the European left-wing platform launched by Yanis Varoufakis) or, before that, the populist social movement M5S (for Movimiento 5 Stelle) in Italy, with Beppe Grillo as its main proponent, use the Internet as their main information infrastructure. Members of M5S do not meet face to face but interact through blogs and Skype meetings. All written material is made public, and meetings are streamed for interested people following online in real time. M5S fully benefits from ongoing “infrastructuring.” Does it need a participatory designer? What would her or his task be in an environment where people are perfectly capable of taking care of their own agenda?

Another open question concerns the idea of “design in use,” which implies that users become designers when appropriating IT artifacts. There are vastly different opinions within the participatory-design community as to whether users do, in fact, become designers. It all depends on what is meant by design. As numerous examples from the Florence project (Bjerknes and Bratteteig 1988) to, for example, the *maXi* project, which supports everyday living with diabetes (Kanstrup 2012), demonstrate, users can indeed contribute to design with sketches, mock-ups, scenarios, and other forms of creating design ideas. But what when an IT artifact has been handed over? When looking at the work needed for appropriating an IT artifact, we need to distinguish between the work that goes into developing the organizational context in which the artifact will be embedded and the new practices that make it usable and useful, and adapting the IT artifact itself to evolving uses in changing contexts. The latter will most likely require more specialized designer skills, including programming. When we want to avoid using the term "design" in a rather general way, it is useful to keep this distinction in mind and also be clear about what we mean by users "designing-in-use."

What the notion of "infrastructuring" may also point to is the need to move from the local to concerns that may be in common to a diversity of stakeholders and communities. What exactly is the role of participatory design in such a move?

7.5.4 And What about Work?

And what about work? Has it disappeared altogether from the attention of participatory designers? In "The diversity of participatory design research practice at PDC 2002–2012," Halskov and Hansen (2015) do not even mention work as a key area of participatory design. However, in some places experienced participatory designers continue their good work, for example, supporting collaboration in crisis management or work in healthcare institutions. The latter field is particularly suitable for participatory design, as in it there is a need for tailored solutions for highly complex practices, where considerable technical challenges have to be met. If participatory designers went back to industry, they would meet similar circumstances. Schmidt (2011b) makes an argument for coordination technologies in general:

> More importantly, it is—on principle—technically and economically feasible for these coordination technologies to be designed in such a way that ordinary workers, of whatever profession, can devise, adopt, modify, and control the rules according to which their work is coordinated by machine systems. These potentials have only been realized sporadically, however. (Schmidt 2011b, p. 394)

Hence, there is a wide field for participatory design, which would require substantial engagement and make a difference to workers. These projects would benefit from the possibility of a "long-term engagement," with designers becoming "more committed to the moral order of the workplace" (Hartswood et al. 2002, p. 25).

Another challenge is the distributed nature of much service and production work today, with, for example, call centers in India taking care of customer complaints in the whole world, and global production networks in place in key industries like the production of cars, chips, or large-scale buildings and infrastructures. The fact is that there is little reflection in the participatory-design community on how to design for work under these circumstances, with some exceptions. For example, in the context of the HISP project, a community-based approach rather than one focused on the workplace is recommended, since "the typical arena for movements for social change in developing countries is the political 'grassroots', rather than the workplace" (Titlestad et al. 2019, p. 31). Not surprisingly, researchers stress cultural differences and the difficulties of establishing collaboration spaces between globally distributed engineering teams (see, e.g., Jensen and Bjørn 2011). While there are traditions of participation in some cultures, it may be almost impossible to achieve participation in others. And, if as in the case of sub-Saharan Africa, there is a strong culture of participation, it may be one that is different from Western notions of participation (Winschiers-Theophilus et al. 2010). Arriving at a shared decision may take a long time and involve rituals and forms of reasoning that "draw upon local epistemologies" (Winschiers-Theophilus et al., p. 2).

Moreover, in global production networks, participatory designers may have to account for the completely different political conditions under which work is organized. For example, think of China, where workers have just begun organizing themselves, fighting for better wages and working conditions, making their concerns public by using mobile phones and the Internet, and using effective political strategies:

> By turning the Taylorist system around, that is, by using the carefully designed just-in-time workflow so as to identify strategic weak spots, and then paralyzing these by walking out—[the workers] thereby [show] the essential value of their work. (Schmidt 2011a, p. 5)

What participatory design would need in these culturally distant and/or globalized contexts is a political strategy for being able to ensure "participatory results," for example, IT-based solutions that help practitioners to play a more active and informed role in the planning and coordination of their work.

7.6 Thoughts for the Future of Participatory Design: Open Issues

This concluding section addresses four open and controversial issues:

- How much participation, and in what, makes a project participatory?
- Is participatory design in need of a vision or other, more general strategies in order to become effective?
- What is the "design part" of participatory design?
- How can the outcomes of participatory design be made sustainable in the long term?

How much participation, and in what, makes a project participatory? Participatory designers are committed to sharing power with users, but viewpoints on how this should be done, and to what extent, vary considerably (Halskov and Hansen 2015). In Bratteteig and Wagner (2016), we have taken a strong stance, arguing that it is important to be clear about what users actually participate in when collaborating in a participatory-design project. This is a question that can only be answered empirically, by looking more closely into decision-making in participatory-design projects. Users do not need to participate in all design moves to contribute to a design result that increases their "power to." However, we also maintain that such a design result would not have been possible without users' contributions. Hence, moving the focus from the process "as such" to its outcome does not make the commitment to share power with users obsolete. Key to participatory design is not merely having users "deliver ideas" but giving them a voice in defining the problems the choices are an answer to. However, the weak point in this argument is surely the following: how we can possibly know that a design result increases the "power to" of users unless we observe "real use"?

Is participatory design in need of a vision or other, more general strategies in order to be successful? Morten Kyng proposes to "modernize" participatory design, making a plea for being more practical (rather than political in a principled way) by taking account of the diversity of stakeholders, including "those who pay" in a project. It is important to stress that his idea is for participatory design "to contribute to the 'next practices' of ICT design" (Kyng 2010a, p. 50). Hence, he is thinking of participatory design as striving for design solutions in which ICT has a part!

In contrast, in the following comment, Dan Shapiro questions how "bendable" and "adaptable" participatory design can be without losing its integrity, reflecting on what might happen if participatory designers give up on "politics" and go mainstream:

> The most painful question is whether the incorporation of [participatory design] into the mainstream of academic and commercial practice has gone so far as actually to make its relationship to users quite exploitative and nakedly instrumental, and to make our repeated claims about the centrality of continuously involving users quite rhetorical and hypocritical. This dismaying revelation is actually quite credible, and should cause many of us to reflect critically on what we do. (Shapiro 2010, p. 73)

One way of contributing to this debate is to go back to the question of the outcome of a participatory-design project: does it, when the project ends, result in the kind of "central and local action" Nygaard and Bergo (1975) were looking for? Traditionally, participatory design puts the needs and concerns of users into the center. Kristen Nygaard emphasized the importance of designers respecting users' decisions, even if they disagree with them. There is a potential conflict between a "vision" that is driven by imagination and political commitment, and what participants think they need, which can range from "big" ideas of how to change and enrich practices, to more modest design results. A participatory solution to this potential conflict is to make it a subject of collaboration: having users contribute to shaping the "vision." This may involve "manifold forceful but tolerant disputes among passionately engaged publics" (Björgvinsson et al. 2012, p. 128).

Still, the following question remains: is participatory design more than just a commitment to involving users, and a set of techniques for possibly achieving this? Is there a strong moral and political commitment in participatory design, and in which ways does it differ from the old commitment to industrial democracy? In Ernst Bloch's *The Principle of Hope* (1995), the author made an important distinction between abstract utopias that are unembedded in reality, and concrete utopias that are grounded in the possible. To Bloch, a concrete utopia is a horizon, a place beyond reach but within view. Can we be practical, developing design results that increase users' "power to" without referring to such concrete utopias, possibly turning them into a political program and strategy?

There are several avenues one might consider taking. One is to think about alternatives to the vision that the mainstream of funding agencies and engineers may promote; to challenge, appropriate, and redefine them, as in the example of projects where deeply engaging with very old people requires deconstructing the dominant images of aging, and the discourses that maintain such images. Another avenue would build on a discourse on ethical (and political) issues of design and use, addressing not only questions of solidarity, equality, autonomy, the need for privacy, and the need to respect people's right to maintain boundaries, but also issues such as workers' abilities to control workloads and maintain and develop skills and competencies, or the tensions between global and local concerns. Participatory designers are good at making concepts such as these "concrete," connecting them to users' practices and experiences, so as to understand what they may mean in different contexts. I personally consider addressing key societal issues an important part of participatory design.

As many participatory-design projects today have moved from workplaces to supporting communities and different "publics," they have to deal with a multiplicity of issues for which "design" is not necessarily an answer. Hence, *what is the "design part" of participatory design* today? This begs the question, "Design of what?" Technology development (which is enormously complex) or the design of specific IT systems "per se" was never an explicit aim of participatory design. Still, in many participatory-design projects, the decision that IT artifacts of some kind would be part of the design result was always there, without necessarily being explicitly questioned. There are technologically ambitious participatory-design projects. However, by looking at some of the newer projects, we can see that the issue of IT support has moved to the background. The "design" part in these projects may range from the graphical design of posters and leaflets to experimenting with social media and configuring off-the-shelf devices and applications. This also reflects the fact that, in many cases, there is no longer the need to develop IT artifacts from scratch. Hence, is participatory design still a "distinctive brand" that is different both from user-centered design and from participatory projects of varying nature in a wide range of domains?

This brings me to my final point, which is to do with *how can the outcomes of participatory design be made sustainable in the long term*? This point has two sides: how can participatory designers actively shape the conditions in which a design result can actually be put to use, in order to learn from how users appropriate it, and how can they help users (and the organizations or communities they are embedded in) sustain the practices that have been developed? This problem calls for a political strategy, obliging participatory designers to engage with research policies (on a national and international level); funding agencies, with their reimbursement schemes; the business perspectives of project partners; and so forth.

Issues of sustainability have been addressed by many participatory designers (e.g., Gärtner and Wagner 1996; Kensing and Blomberg 1998). While the early discussion focused on how to sustain the outcomes of a participatory-design project within an organization, projects with communities face different problems. For example, Merkel et al. (2004) maintain that working on strategies for long-term sustainability in community groups is key to their engagement. After collaborating with the officials of a municipality, as well as its citizens, Bødker and Zander (2015) observed that "it is essential that there is some organization that can accumulate and hold on to the experiences of the participants and activate them in later design" (Bødker and Zander 2015, p. 56). They also point to the problem of motivating citizens to engage in a participatory-design project with a long-term perspective, asking:

> What makes early movers or citizens who are engaged through an established NGO interested in participation with long-term perspectives in mind, as some kind of representatives of future citizens? And how do their insights get accumulated for future projects? (Bødker and Zander 2015, p. 56)

Design result sustainability continues to be an unresolved or difficult-to-resolve issue in participatory-design projects. It is a complex issue with many technical organizational, political, and financial aspects.

7.7 Concluding Remarks

In my view, participatory design *is* a political program that engages users in the design of IT-based solutions for practical problems, with the intent of increasing users' "power to." Pitkin roots the notion of power in organization or, as she phrases it, following Hannah Arendt, public life:

> What distinguishes public life, then, is not that it has important substantive consequences for many people; for that could be true of large-scale private power, or economic activity, or childrearing practices. What distinguishes politics, as Arendt and Aristotle said, is action—the possibility of a shared, collective, deliberate, active intervention in our fate, in what would otherwise be the by-product of private decisions. Only in public life can we jointly, as a community, exercise the human capacity "to think what we are doing," and take charge of the history in which we are all constantly engaged by drift and inadvertence. (Pitkin 1981, p. 344)

Industrial democracy was a program rooted in public life and made participatory design relevant beyond single projects.

Today, participatory design seems to be moving in several different directions. Morten Kyng represents one of these directions. While adhering to developing ICT-based solutions, also with the goal of preventing "the next practices are being shaped by others" (Morten Kyng 2010, p. 50), he emphasizes the need to be practical. At the same time, ICT design fades out of the focus of participatory design and has to some extent been replaced by the idea of "infrastructuring," a new way of expressing older concerns with supporting appropriation in use. However, the technical challenges of achieving this are mostly addressed by other research communities, for example, those interested in end-user development (e.g., Lieberman et al. 2006), with some exceptions (see, e.g., Fischer and Herrmann 2015). Although many researchers today do engage with marginalized vulnerable groups and with communities, following "commitments to human rights and civil society" (Robertson and Wagner 2012, p. 66), they do so without a political program that is built and shared with others as part of "public life" (Pitkin 1981).

References

Balka, E., and Wagner, I. 2006. "Making things work: Dimensions of configurability as appropriation work." In *CSCW'06*. New York: ACM, 229–38.

Balka, E., Bjørn, P., and Wagner, I. 2008. "Steps toward a typology for health informatics." In *CSCW'08*. New York: ACM, 515–24.

Bannon, L., and Ehn, P. 2012. "Design matters in participatory design." In J. Simonsen and T. Robertson, eds., *Routledge International Handbook of Participatory Design*. London/New York: Routledge, 37–63.

Binder, T., Ehn, P., Jacucci, G., De Michelis, G., Linde, P., and Wagner, I. 2011. *Design Things*. Cambridge, MA: MIT Press.

Bjerknes, G., and Bratteteig, T. 1988. "Computers: Utensils or epaulets? The application perspective revisited." *AI and Society* 2 (3): 258–66.

Bjerknes, G., and Bratteteig, T. 1995. "User participation and democracy: A discussion of Scandinavian research on system development." *Scandinavian Journal of Information Systems* 7 (1): 73–98.

Björgvinsson, E., Ehn, P., and Hillgren, P. A. 2010. "Participatory design and democratizing innovation." In *PDC'10*. New York: ACM, 41–50.

Björgvinsson, E., Ehn, P., and Hillgren, P.-A. 2012. "Agonistic participatory design: Working with marginalised social movements." *CoDesign* 8 (2): 127–44.

Bjørn, P. and Boulus-Rødje, N. 2015. "The multiple intersecting sites of design in CSCW research." *Computer Supported Cooperative Work* 24 (4): 319–51.

Bloch, E. 1995. *The Principle of Hope*. Cambridge, MA: MIT Press.

Blomberg, J., Suchman, L., and Trigg, R. 1996. "Reflections on a work-oriented design project." *Human-Computer Interaction* 11 (3): 237–66.

Bødker, S., and Zander, P.-O. 2015. "Participation in design between public sector and local communities." In *C&T'15*. New York: ACM, 49–58.

Bossen, C., Dindler, C., and Iversen, O. S. 2010. "User gains and PD aims: Assessment from a participatory design project." In *PDC'10*. New York: ACM, 141–50.

Brattetieg, T. 1987. *Mutual Learning: Enabling Cooperation on Systems Design*. Available at http://s3.amazonaws.com/academia.edu.documents/6330326/TBMutual_Learning.pdf?AWSAccessKeyId=AKIAIWOWYYGZ2Y53UL3A&Expires=1510873923&Signature=X9fTAWCwt%2FMjymZflRUmp9P7byY%3D&response-content-disposition=inline%3B%20filename%3DMutual_learning._Enabling_cooperation_in.pdf (accessed November 16, 2017).

Bratteteig, T., and Wagner, I. 2012. "Disentangling power and decision-making in participatory design." In *PDC'12* . New York: ACM, 41–50.

Bratteteig, T., and Wagner, I. 2014. *Disentangling Participation: Power and Decision-Making in Participatory Design*. Cham: Springer International.

Bratteteig, T., and Wagner, I. 2016. "Unpacking the notion of participation in participatory design." *Computer Supported Cooperative Work* 25 (6): 425–75.

Brereton, M., and Buur, J. 2008. "New challenges for design participation in the era of ubiquitous computing." *Co-Design* 4 (2), 101–13.

Burman, M. J., Batchelor, S. A., and Brown, J. A. 2001. "Researching girls and violence: Facing the dilemmas of fieldwork." *British Journal of Criminology* 41 (3): 443–59.

Büscher, M., Kristensen, M., and Mogensen, P. H. 2008. "Making the future palpable: Notes from a major incidents future laboratory." *International Journal of Emergency Management* 5 (1–2): 145–63.

Chambers, R. 1999. *Whose Reality Counts? Putting the First Last*. London: Intermediate Technology Publications.

Ciborra, C. U., and Hanseth, O. 1998. "Towards a contingency view of infrastructure and knowledge: An exploratory study." In *ICIC'98*. Atlanta: AIS, 263–72.

Clarke, A. 1991. "Social worlds/arena theory as organizational theory." In D. R. Maines, ed., *Social Organization and Social Processes: Essays in Honor of Anselm Strauss*. Edison, NJ: Aldine Transaction.

Cornwall, A., 2008. "Unpacking 'participation': Models, meanings and practices." *Community Development Journal* 43 (3) 269–83.

Di Salvo, C., Clement, A. and Pipek, V. 2012. "Participatory design for, with and by communities." In J. Simonsen, and T. Robertson, eds., *International Handbook of Participatory Design*. London/New York: Routledge, 182–209.

Druin, A. 2002. "The role of children in the design of new technology." *Behaviour and Information Technology* 2 (1), 1–25.

Ehn, P. 1988. "Playing the language-games of design and use-on skill and participation." *ACM Sigois Bulletin* 9 (2–3) 142–57.

Ehn, P. 1989. *Work-Oriented Design of Computer Artifacts*. Hillsdale, NJ: Lawrence Erlbaum Associates.

Ehn, P. 2008. "Participation in design things." In *PDC'08*. New York: ACM, 92–101.

Ehn, P., and Kyng, M. 1985. *A Tool Perspective on Design of Interactive Computer Support for Skilled Workers*. DAIMI Report Series PB-190. Århus: Århus University: Department of Computer Science.

Ehn, P., and Kyng, M. 1987. "The collective resource approach to systems design." In G. Bjerknes, P. Ehn, and M. Kyng, eds., *Computers and Democracy: A Scandinavian Challenge*. Aldershot: Avebury, 17–57.

Fischer, G., and Herrmann, T. 2014. "Meta-design: Transforming and enriching the design and use of socio-technical systems." In V. Wulf, K. Schmidt, and D. Randall, eds., *Designing Socially Embedded Technologies in the Real-World*. London: Springer-Verlag London, 79–109.

Foucault, M. 1982. "The subject and power." *Critical Inquiry* 8 (4): 777–95.

Gärtner, J., and Wagner, I. 1996. "Mapping actors and agendas: Political frameworks of systems design and participation." *Human-Computer Interaction* 11 (3): 187–214.

Gaventa, J. 2005. Reflections on the Uses of the "Power Cube" Approach for Analyzing the Spaces, Places and Dynamics of Civil Society Participation and Engagement. Available at http://www.powercube.net/wp-content/uploads/2009/11/reflections_on_uses_powercube.pdf (accessed October 13, 2017).

Glasemann, M., and Kanstrup, A. M. 2008. "Evoking creativity: Young diabetics design their own mobile diabetes supporter." In *Danish HCI Research Symposium* 2008. Aalborg: Aalborg University, 37–41.

Hall, S. 2001. "Foucault: Power, knowledge and discourse." In M. Wetherell, S. Taylor, S. Yates, eds., *Discourse Theory and Practice: A Reader*. London: Sage, 72–81.

Halskov, K., and Hansen, N. B. 2015. "The diversity of participatory design research practice at PDC 2002–2012." *International Journal of Human-Computer Studies* 74, 81–92.

Hanseth, O., and Lundberg, N. 2001. "Designing work oriented infrastructures." *Computer Supported Cooperative Work* 10 (3–4): 347–72.

Hartswood, M., Procter, R., Slack, R., Voß, A., Büscher, M., Rouncefield, M., and Rouchy, P. 2002. "Co-realisation." *Scandinavian Journal of Information Systems* 14 (2): 9–30.

Hussain, S. 2010. "Empowering marginalised children in developing countries through participatory design processes." *CoDesign* 6 (2): 99–117.

Huysman, M. H., Wenger, E., and Wulf, V. (eds.). 2003. *Communities and Technologies.* Berlin/ Heidelberg: Springer Science+Business Media.

Jensen, R., and Bjorn, P. 2011. "Divergence and convergence in global software development." In *COOP'11.* Dordrecht: Springer, 123–36.

Joshi, S. G., and Bratteteig, T. "Assembling fragments into continuous design: On participatory design with old people." In H. Oinas-Kukkonen, N. Iivari, K. Kuutti, A. Öörni, and M. Rajanen, eds., *Nordic Contributions in IS Research.* Cham, Springer International, 13–29.

Käfer, J., Stein, M., and Meurer, J. 2014. "Hands-on-Activities als Werkzeug im participatory design mit Senioren." In *Mensch und Computer 2014.* Berlin: De Gruyter, 335–8.

Kanstrup A. M. 2012. "A small matter of design: An analysis of end users as designers." In *PDC'12.* New York: ACM, 109–18.

Kanstrup, A. M., and Christiansen, E. 2006. "Selecting and evoking innovators: Combining democracy and creativity." In *NordiCHI'06.* New York: ACM, 321–30.

Karasti, H. and Baker, K. 2008. "Community design: Growing one's own information infrastructure." In *PDC'08.* New York: ACM, 217–20.

Kensing, F., and Blomberg, J. 1998. "Participatory design: Issues and concerns." *Computer Supported Cooperative Work* 7 (3–4): 167–85.

Kensing, F., and Greenbaum, J. 2012. "Heritage. Have a say." In J. Simonsen and T. Robertson, eds., *International Handbook of Participatory Design.* London/New York: Routledge, 21–36.

Kocka, J. 2000. "Zivilgesellschaft als Problem und Versprechen." In M. Hildermeier, J. Kocka, and C. Conrad, eds., *Europäische Zivilgesellschaft in Ost und West: Begriff, Geschichte, Chancen.* Frankfurt: Campus Verlag, 13–39.

Kraft, P., and Bansler, J. P. 1994. "The collective resource approach: The Scandinavian experience." *Scandinavian Journal of Information Systems* 6 (1): 71–84.

Kyng, M. 2010a. "Bridging the gap between politics and techniques: On the next practices of participatory design." *Scandinavian Journal of Information Systems* 22 (1): 49–68.

Kyng, M. 2010b. "On the multifaceted future of participatory design." *Scandinavian Journal of Information Systems* 22 (1): 93–102.

Lave, J., and Wenger, E. 1991. *Situated Learning: Legitimate Peripheral Participation.* Cambridge: Cambridge University Press.

Letondal, C., and Mackay, W. E. 2004. "Participatory programming and the scope of mutual responsibility: Balancing scientific, design and software commitment." In *PDC'04.* New York: ACM, 31–41.

Ley, B., Pipek, V., Reuter, C., and Wiedenhoefer, T. 2012. "Supporting improvisation work in inter-organizational crisis management." In *CHI'12.* New York: ACM, 1529–38.

Lieberman, H., Paternò, F., Klann, M., and Wulf, V. 2006. "End-user development: An emerging paradigm." In H. Lieberman, F. Paternò, and V. Wulf, eds., *End User Development.* Dordrecht: Springer, 1–8.

Martin, D., Mariani, J., and Rouncefield, M. 2009. "Practicalities of participation: Stakeholder involvement in an electronic patient records project." In M. Büscher, R. Slack, M. Rouncefield, R. Procter, M. Hartswood, and A. Voss, eds., *Configuring User-Designer Relations.* London: Springer-Verlag London, 133–55.

Mathiassen, L., Rolskov, B., and Vedel, E. 1983. "Regulating the use of EDP by law and agreements." In U. Briefs, C. Ciborra, and L. Schneider, eds., *Systems Design For, With, and By the Users.* Amsterdam: North-Holland, 251–64.

Maynard, M., and Purvis, J. (eds.). 1994. *Researching Women's Lives from a Feminist Perspective.* London: Taylor & Francis.

Mazé, R. 2014. "Our common future? Political questions for designing social innovation." Available at http://s3.amazonaws.com/academia.edu.documents/36128856/20140317_drs.pdf?AWS

AccessKeyId=AKIAIWOWYYGZ2Y53UL3A&Expires=1507904423&Signature=w57IPV0O%2BjnOnv%2FASFmRvKz80HY%3D&response-content-disposition=inline%3B%20filename%3DOur_Common_Future_Political_Questions_fo.pdf (accessed October 13, 2017).

Merkel, C. B., Xiao, L., Farooq, U., Ganoe, C. H., Lee, R., Carroll, J. M., and Rosson, M. B. 2004. "Participatory design in community computing contexts: Tales from the field." In *PDC'04*. New York: ACM, 1–10.

Müller, C., Hornung, D., Hamm, T., and Wulf, V. 2015. "Practice-based design of a neighborhood portal: Focusing on elderly tenants in a city quarter living lab." In *CHI'15*. New York: ACM, 2295–304.

Müller, C., Neufeldt, C., Randall, D., and Wulf, V. 2012. "ICT-development in residential care settings: Sensitizing design to the life circumstances of the residents of a care home." In *CHI'12*. New York: ACM, 2639–48.

Nussbaum, M. 2003. "Capabilities as fundamental entitlements: Sen and social justice." *Feminist Economics* 9 (2–3): 33–59.

Newman, M. W., Sedivy, J. Z., Neuwirth, C. M., Edwards, W. K., Hong, J. I., Izadi, S., Marcelo, K., and Smith, T. F. 2002. "Designing for serendipity: Supporting end-user configuration of ubiquitous computing." In *DIS'02*. New York: ACM, 147–56.

Nygaard, K. 1996. "'Those were the days'? Or 'Heroic times are here again'?" *Scandinavian Journal of Information Systems* 8 (2): 6.

Nygaard, K., and Bergo, O. T. 1975. "The trade unions: New users of research." *Personnel Review* 4 (2): 5–10.

Ogonowski, C., Ley, B., Hess, J., Wan, L., and Wulf, V. 2013. "Designing for the living room: Long-term user involvement in a living lab." In *CHI'13*. New York: ACM, 1539–48.

Pateman, C. 1970. *Participation and Democratic Theory*. Cambridge: Cambridge University Press.

Pipek, V., and Wulf, V. 2009. "Infrastructuring: Toward an integrated perspective on the design and use of information technology." *Journal of the Association for Information Systems* 10 (5) 447–73.

Pipek, V. 2005. *From Tailoring to Appropriation Support: Negotiating Groupware Usage*. Oulu: University of Oulu.

Pitkin, H. F. 1973. *Wittgenstein and Justice*. Berkeley/Los Angeles: University of California Press.

Pitkin, H. F. 1981. "Justice: On relating private and public." *Political Theory* 9 (3): 327–52.

Rauhala, M. 2011. "When ethical guidance is missing and do-it-yourself is required: The shaping of ethical peer review in the FRR project." In J. F. M. Molenbroek, J. Mantas, and R. de Bruin, eds., *A Friendly Rest Room: Developing Toilets of the Future for Disabled and Elderly People*. Assistive Technology Research Series. Vol. 27. Amsterdam: IOS Press, 49–59.

Reidl, C., Tolar, M., and Wagner, I. 2008. "Impediments to change: The case of implementing an electronic patient record in three oncology clinics." *PDC'08*, New York: ACM, 21–30.

Robertson, T., and Wagner, I. 2012. "Ethics: Engagement, representation and politics-in-action." In J. Simonsen and T. Robertson, eds., *International Handbook of Participatory Design*. London/New York: Routledge, 64–85.

Rodden, T., Crabtree, A. Hemmings, T., Koleva, B., Humble, J., Åkesson, K. P., and Hansson, P. 2004. "Between the dazzle of a new building and its eventual corpse: Assembling the ubiquitous home." *DIS'04*. New York: ACM, 71–80.

Ruland, C. M., Slaughter, L., Starren, J., and Vatne, T. M. 2006. "Children as design partners in the development of a support system for children with cancer." In *NI'06*. Amsterdam: IOS Press, 80–5.

Schmidt, K. 2011a. "Reflections on the visibility and invisibility of work." In G. C. Bowker, S. Timmermans, A. E. Clarke, and E. Balka, eds., *Boundary Objects and Beyond: Working with Leigh Star*. Cambridge, MA: MIT Press, 345–50.

Schmidt, K. 2011b. "The concept of 'work' in CSCW." *Computer-Supported Cooperative Work* 20 (4–5): 341–401.

Shapiro, D. 2005. "Participatory design: The will to succeed," In *CC'05*. New York: ACM, 29–38.

Shapiro, D. 2010. "A modernised participatory design? A response to Kyng." *Scandinavian Journal of Information Systems* 22 (1), 69–76.

Simonsen, J., and Robertson, T. (eds.). *International Handbook of Participatory Design*. London/New York: Routledge.

Star, S. L., and Bowker, G. 2007. "Enacting silence: Residual categories as a challenge for ethics, information systems, and communication," *Ethics and Information Technology* 9 (4): 273–80.

Stevens, G., Pipek, V., and Wulf, V. 2010. "Appropriation infrastructure: Mediating appropriation and production work." *Journal of Organizational and End User Computing* 22 (2): 58–81.

Strauss, A., Fagerhaugh, S., Suczek, B., and Wiener, C. 1985. *Social Organization of Medical Work*. Chicago/London: University of Chicago Press.

Thomas, N., and O'Kane, C. 1998. "The ethics of participatory research with children." *Children and Society* 12 (5): 336–48.

Thorsrud, E., and Emery, F. E. 1970. *Mot en ny bedriftsorganisasjon: Eksperimenter i industrielt demokrati. 2.utg*. Oslo: Tanum.

Titlestad, O., Staring, N., and Braa, J. 2009. "Distributed development to enable user participation multilevel design in the HISP network." *Scandinavian Journal of Information Systems* 21 (1): 27–50.

Trigg, R., and Bødker, S. 2004. "From implementation to design: Tailoring and the emergence of systematization." In *CSCW'94*. New York: ACM, 45–54.

Wagner, I. 2012. "Building urban narratives: Collaborative site-seeing and envisioning in the *MR Tent*." *Computer Supported Cooperative Work* 41 (1): 1–42.

Wan, L., Müller, C., Wulf, V., and Randall, D. 2014. "Addressing the subtleties in dementia care: Pre-study & evaluation of a GPS monitoring system." In *CHI'14*. New York: ACM, 3987–96.

Wan, L., Müller, C., Wulf, V., and Randall, D. 2016. "Design of a GPS monitoring system for dementia care and its challenges in academia-industry project." *ACM Transactions on Computer-Human Interaction* 23 (5): 31.

Winschiers-Theophilus, H., Chivuno-Kuria, S., Kapuire, G., Bidwell, N., and Blake, E. 2010. "Being participated: A community approach." In *PDC'10*. New York: ACM, 1–10.

Wulf, V., Müller, C., Pipek, V., Randall, D., Rohde, M., and Stevens, G. "Practice-based computing: Empirical grounded conceptualizations derived from design case studies. In V. Wulf, K. Schmidt, and D. Randall, eds., *Designing Socially Embedded Technologies in the Real-World*. London: Springer-Verlag London, 111–50.

Wynne, B. 2002. "Risk and environment as legitimatory discourses of technology: Reflexivity inside out?" *Current Sociology* 50 (3): 459–77.

Yerousis, G., Aal, K., von Rekowski, T., Randall, D. W., Rohde, M., and Wulf, V. 2015. "Computer-enabled project spaces: Connecting with Palestinian refugees across camp boundaries." In *CHI'15*. New York: ACM, 3749–58.

Zündorf, L. 1986. "Macht, Einfluß, Vertrauen und Verständigung. Zum Problem der Handlungskoordinierung in Arbeitsorganisationen." In R. Seltz, U. Mill, and E. Hildebrandt, eds., *Organisation als soziales System*. Berlin: Sigma Verlag, 33–56.

8 Integrated Organization and Technology Development

A Critical Evaluation

MARKUS ROHDE AND VOLKER WULF

8.1 Introduction

The domain of work has developed a myriad of social practices that are often shaped by information and communications technology (ICT) infrastructures. The introduction of additional IT artifacts, of course, affects these practices and the related patterns of communication. While management and IT specialists plan for certain effects of a system's introduction, unintended use of the system can play a central role (Orlikowski 1996; Pipek and Wulf 1999, 2003). Therefore, the (unanticipated) appropriation of IT artifacts by their users is an important phenomenon (see Pipek 2005; Stevens 2009; also see Chapter 4). Given the existence of IT-related organizational change and adjustments related to the appropriation of software, the development of IT in organizations faces an iterative challenge:

- the existence of IT artifacts allows for new work practices
- these practices raise new requirements for technological support

This phenomenon causes a significant degree of difficulty in software engineering projects (see Rönkkö et al. 2005).

With regard to the design of IT infrastructures in support of cooperative work, a dialog between designers and users is required. The "participatory-design" community (e.g., Greenbaum and Kyng 1991; Ehn 1993; Kensing and Blomberg 1998; also see Chapter 7) has developed over time, using a variety of different techniques for user participation in (iterative) design processes. However, the participatory-design community, we feel, tends to underestimate the relevance of unanticipated use and design-relevant outcomes of IT appropriation over longer periods of time.

Socio-Informatics, Volker Wulf, Volkmar Pipek, Dave Randall, Markus Rohde, Kjeld Schmidt, Gunnar Stevens (Eds). © Oxford University Press 2018. Published 2018 by Oxford University Press.

To cope with the intertwined complexity of individual, social, and technological change, we have developed, over time, a practice-based research perspective. As a first step, we propose a process-oriented framework for the design and introduction of IT artifacts into organizational practice: integrated organization and technology development (OTD), which tackles organizational-practice problems for which one solution could be the appropriation of properly designed IT artifacts. The OTD framework proposes that the design of new IT functionality, and the tailoring of existing ones, should be conducted in association with attention to activities of organizational and personal development (Wulf and Rohde 1995).

In parallel with our work, related approaches to analyzing, reflecting, and developing work practices have emerged. Focusing on the development of work systems, Kuutti proposed an approach called formative experiment or developmental work research methodology, which is based on action research methods (Kuutti 1991, 540 ff.). This approach includes four methodological phases: analysis, the formation of instruments, the application of these instruments, and the evaluation of effects. A different school of thinking prefers ethnographic approaches for technology development (see Blomberg et al. 1992). Ethnographic methods concentrate for the most part on observation, interviews, and video analyses. In this context, the relevance of participation (of some kind) is considered to be a crucial characteristic of the ethnographic approach (Blomberg et al. 1992, 139 f.).

With its emphasis on the integrative aspects of technological and social systems, science and technology studies can be seen as a disciplinary area that had theoretical interests in what we can gloss here as the "sociotechnical" and that preceded later approaches such as the Scandinavian participatory-design method MUST (Kensing et al. 1996; Kensing and Blomberg 1998; Kensing et al. 1998; Bødker et al. 2005) or the OTD framework presented here. More recently, Fischer and Ostwald, in the early 2000s, introduced their participatory-design method and process model SER (for seeding–evolutionary growth–reseeding), which is based on a concept of "informed participation" (Fischer and Ostwald 2002), following the meta-design approach (Fischer 2003). In the information systems community, Peter Checkland's soft systems methodology did similar work (see, e.g., Checkland 1989). It should perhaps be pointed out that only later did Checkland focus more explicitly on IT (see Checkland and Holwell 1997). In this context, the OTD framework offers one possible mindset for orientation toward groupware development projects.

In the following, we present the OTD framework and describe its application in a series of research projects.

8.2 The Framework of Integrated OTD

First described in the middle of the 1990s, OTD was applied as a framework for research projects developing and introducing groupware into organizations. Our thinking in the early 1990s was influenced by different intellectual traditions and normative positions emerging from the German discourse on computers and society.

Traditional computer science approaches seemed not to take the social embeddedness of ICT sufficiently into account, and this meant that normative concerns were not seen to be relevant and hence were seldom dealt with. Criticizing the mainstream in software engineering, Floyd et al. (1989) proposed STEPS—an evolutionary and participative process framework to build software for and with users. Their work was grounded in the kind of analysis associated with the Scandinavian school of participatory design (Floyd et al. 1989). Coy (1989), similarly, had asked for an extension of the theoretical foundation of computer science beyond purely formal conceptions.

Work-psychology research in the tradition of Leontjew's (1974) activity theory argued, at roughly the same time, that the human quality of (computer-supported) work was, importantly, determined by organizational factors, such as the overall task of an organization, and the division of labor among its workers (Hacker 1986). Discourses in management science indicated major problems with Tayloristic principles of organizational design, as they were not able to deal with the increasing differentiation and dynamics of market needs (Brödner 1985; Womack et al. 1990; Hammer and Champy 1993). Overcoming Taylorism seemed desirable as well from a normative perspective, which was grounded in work-psychology findings about work satisfaction, motivation, and so on (Brödner 1986; Hacker 1986). At the same time it became obvious that post-Tayloristic concepts of work would require different approaches for IT support (Brödner 1986; Schmidt and Bannon 1992; Wulf 1992). OTD seemed to be related to these in very significant ways. Thus, to overcome this gap in the state of the art, we suggested the process framework of OTD, to facilitate change in organizational structures and cultures with their supporting IT infrastructure.

OTD is defined as "the process of change of an organization in which an organization and technology are designed and developed in a task- and needs-oriented fashion by the members affected through integrated means: the organization members affected consider the existing problems, search and evaluate the problems' causes, and negotiate a process of problem solving. OTD only takes place if the members affected are willing and able to define contents and course of the OTD-process, and are immediately taking part" (Hartmann 1994, p. 311, translation by the authors).

The OTD process is characterized by the development of the workplace, the development of the organizational and technical systems in the workplace, the management of (existing) conflicts by discursive and negotiative means, and the immediate participation of the organizational members affected, all of which take place in parallel (see Hartmann and Rohde 1993). OTD is based on the assumption that there exist several ways of designing organizational structures and processes, rather than "one best way." So, the division of labor, the distribution of tasks among different organizational subunits, the specific design of workflows, individual degrees of freedom, the role and conditions of ICT use in the work process, and the design of technical support are negotiated in a participatory manner.

Three elements are central to this framework:

1. *The integration of individual, organizational, and technological change*: The process is intentionally set up in reaction to a problem perceived in daily work practice. After

the process is set up, the situation is analyzed with regard to organizational, professional/role, and technological dimensions. Based on such integrated analysis, alternatives for interventions are suggested and discussed. Based on the outcome of these discussions, interventions with regard to technology, the formal and informal aspects of an organization, and the qualification of its members are suggested, planned, and finally implemented.

2. *The change process is expected to happen in a participatory manner*: A problem perceived by practitioners is the starting point of the change process. From the initiation of the process, it is driven by practitioners' needs and their direct involvement in the analysis, planning, and implementation of interventions. Change agents (possibly external), such as researchers, can also get involved in support of the change process. When participants lack expertise in the change management process, a typical problem in highly Tayloristic organizations, it is expected that specific training (qualification for participation) will compensate for this.
3. *The process framework is conceptualized in an iterative and evolutionary way:* Due to the fact that the organizations' environments are constantly changing, and because an integrated development of practices requires an equally dynamic exploration of ideas, three levels of evolutionary cycles are envisioned:
    - cycles involving individual process steps, for example, prototyping technical artifacts
    - cycles involving iterations within the integrated change process, for example, reiterating the planning phase when certain interventions do not work as planned
    - cycles involving different instances of the change process, for example, where, after a change is implemented, it turns out that a new problem occurs that necessitates the redevelopment of appropriate practices

The OTD framework distinguishes between the primary task of an organization (i.e., the establishment of an appropriate work system in the organizational practice, to fulfill the organization's aims) and the secondary task (to develop, adapt, and—if necessary—reorganize the "work system," which consists of organizational structures, cultures, practices, technical systems and tools, and human resources and competencies).

Both tasks are understood as analysis–development–evaluation–adaptation/reorganization cycles. Within the primary task, the existing work system is evaluated and designated as in need of adaptation or reorganization if problems occur. The development (and the adaptation/reorganization) of the work system is another cycle in itself: the definition of a problem within the work system of an organization leads to the establishment of a reorganization process that consists of an initial analysis, the creation of options, the planning of interventions, the realization of these interventions (for organizational development, tailoring and redesign of technical systems, and measures for qualification), and then the analysis of the new system. Being a participatory process, this second task cycle should be accompanied by appropriate measures for qualification for the participation of organization members.

After a new modified work system has been developed, this system is again implemented and evaluated in terms of new organizational practice. Within this organizational practice, the work system is administrated, appropriated, and adapted on the different organizational, technical, and qualifying levels, according to the requirements of the organization's primary task.

Although the early OTD concept focused on the development of the "work system" (e.g., human work design, workplace studies) as the central task, when Rohde (2007) analyzed five longitudinal case studies—applying the framework to different organizational settings over one decade—he found that groupware support was not necessarily limited to work systems but might also focus on (collaborative) learning systems and community building. Furthermore, Rohde (2007) came up with some reformulations of OTD, especially with regard to some of the theoretical limitations of the original model. The empirical insights showed that some relevant sociocultural processes had not been considered in the original OTD framework. This was elaborated especially with regard to the design and introduction of groupware applications for informal and virtual (respectively hybrid) organizations, (social) networks, and communities. Therefore, Rohde (2007) added socioconstructivist and sociocultural theories to OTD, in order to analyze their implications for social identification (Tajfel 1982; Tajfel and Turner 1986), trust building, social capital (Bourdieu 1986; Cohen and Prusak 2001; Huysman and Wulf 2004), and community learning (Lave and Wenger 1991) within OTD projects.

The reconstituted OTD framework provides a combination of theoretical concepts for the orientation of research projects regarding the introduction and adaptation of groupware systems into organizational practices by mainly applying the following ethnographic, qualitative, and participatory methods:

- qualitative interviews
- participant observation
- scenario-based methods
- different kinds of workshops on data collection, process, and requirements analysis
- participatory design of technical prototypes
- training measures for qualification of project participants, organization members, and technology users

Rather than being a well-defined plan for ICT design projects, the framework describes an ideal, typical OTD process, intended to help researchers and participants for orientation in their respective projects.

In the first step of the change process, the actual state has to be analyzed with respect to organizational structure, technology, and qualification. Depending on the organizational subunit's problems and goals, different methods are used for such an analysis. This analysis can consist merely of a group discussion of the organization's members, to develop a common understanding of the problem. Such a discussion can be prepared by change agents using open interviews or different (work-)psychology instruments for task and work analysis.

Having clarified the situation with regard to organizational problems, it seems important to generate alternative approaches regarding solutions. These alternatives may include different combinations of organization, technology, or qualification development. Thus, the members of the organization can discuss and find a general consensus regarding an appropriate solution. These options can be created by the members of the organization themselves, or by change agents. The agents' job is to propose alternatives that are agreeable to all parties involved. Thus, it may be helpful to present work situations with the help of textual or graphical scenarios or organizational or technological prototypes to facilitate mutual understanding.

Based on this discussion, the members of the organizational unit have to decide on interventions in organizational, technological, and personal dimensions in order to realize the development options chosen. A certain approach for these interventions has been proposed by Fuchs and Hartmann (1993) and Hartmann et al. (1994). They describe software development as an iterative problem-solving process characterized by the participation of end users. The scientific knowledge of external change agents, the needs and demands of users, and the interests of system designers have to be integrated within this process (see Fuchs and Hartmann 1993, p. 361). Therefore, they developed a scheme for problem-solving, integrating problem analysis, defining goals, choosing adequate problem-solving operators, and evaluating the results. This problem-solving scheme is combined with corresponding phases of software development, and a qualification program for user participation (Fuchs and Hartmann 1993, p. 365). This approach is based on both inductive and deductive derivations of goals and problem-solving operators. Thus, the authors' main interest in developing user qualification is directed toward the development of analytical, synthetical, and dialectical skills for problem-solving and conflict management. These are developed in and through methods such as group discussion, group training, communication training methods, and theme-centered interaction.

In relation to the design and introduction of groupware, the original OTD framework does not differ explicitly between the development of new IT systems "from scratch" and the redesign of existing groupware systems. Empirical evidence, however, has shown the relevance of processes of redesign, tailoring, and adaptation of existing systems. Therefore, groupware design and introduction projects, it was felt, should include extremely generic and flexible groupware systems that would allow for appropriation practices, participatory tailoring, and adaptation (see Chapter 2).

When we then evaluated the integrated OTD framework, we found that the framework required some conceptual refinement. We initially understood changes in work practices to be the result of planned interventions at the time of their (evolutionary) implementation. However, empirical studies published in the late 1990s, showed that organizational change following the introduction of groupware can also happen in an opportunistic manner, a long time after its implementation (Orlikowski 1996; Pipek and Wulf 1999).

Similarly, learning was originally conceptualized as happening in a planned manner during the change process. However, while formal learning, in the sense of qualifying, is important for enabling change, the informal mode of learning is also important, both for making sense of an IT artifact and for developing work practices (e.g., Lave and Wenger 1991; Wulf 2000; Twidale 2005).

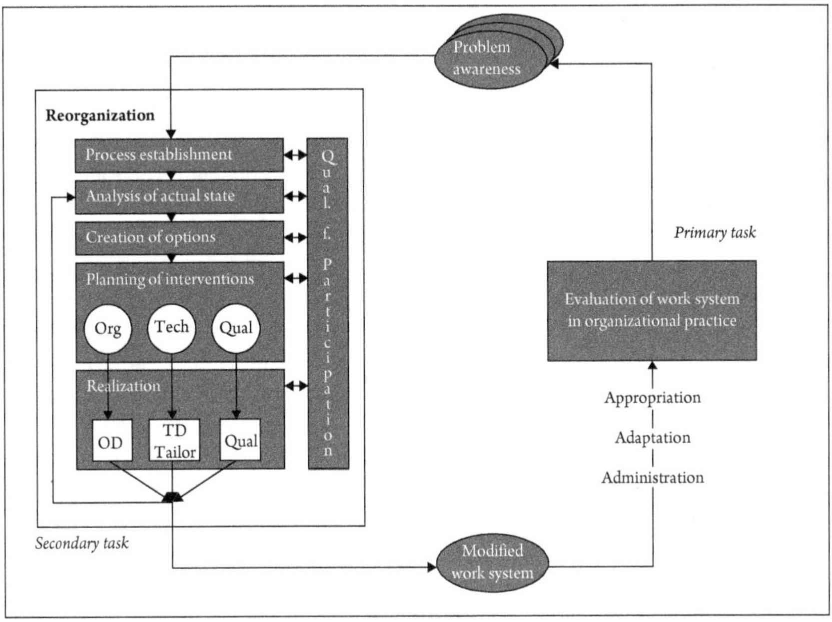

Figure 8.1 Orientation framework: "Integrated Organization and Technology Development"

To cope with these insights, the integrated change process has to be understood as, in principle, ongoing.

The interventions depicted on the left side of the process framework shown in Figure 8.1 may contribute to informal learning and emergent changes in work practice. When discussing extensions of the STEPS process model, we suggested that the IT artifacts should be tailorable by the users (Wulf 1994; Wulf et al. 2008). To overcome the conceptual shortcomings, the right side of the framework shown in Figure 8.1 should be further elaborated. It should be understood as a complex, self-organized, and partially discontinuous long-term alignment between organizational and technological learning and change. Understanding and supporting these activities requires further research. A new development cycle starts in the case where a formal change process is set up again.

8.3 Applying the Framework in Practice

While the OTD framework has influenced our thinking ever since, in only few of our projects was there the mandate to tackle organizational change related to the introduction of IT explicitly. Here we want to focus on experiences gained in two projects: OrgTech (Iacucci et al. 1998; Stiemerling et al. 1998; Wulf et al. 1999) and the Iran Non-Governmental Organization Community System (NGO-CS) project (Rohde 2004).

8.3.1 OrgTech: Supporting Maintenance Work in a Steel Mill

OrgTech: The Case

Being responsible for the maintenance of a steel mill, a group of middle managers agreed to work with a consortium of two research institutions (Fraunhofer Institute for Graphical Data Processing (FhG-IGD) and our group, at that time at the University of Bonn) as well as a business consultancy that specialized in facilitating organizational development processes following a post-Tayloristic paradigm. The projected aimed at exploring the opportunities of "innovative" (at that time) IT applications such as video conferencing, application sharing, and 3D computer-aided design (CAD), in order to overcome the rather formal division of labor in the steel mill's maintenance department. Additionally, the managers wanted to investigate how to better integrate external engineering firms into their internal maintenance engineering, work planning, and manufacturing processes. While the external engineers worked mainly with their internal engineering correspondents, both of these sets of actors had little contact with the work planning and manufacturing units. The maintenance of the steel mill additionally suffered from conflicts between the centrally responsible unit and local acting plant operators, who carried out modifications at their plants without central involvement.

The project was funded by the EU and the State of North Rhine–Westphalia, within a funding scheme for structural adjustment. The project was established, on the steel mill's side, by the heads of the maintenance department and the head of the construction department. Both of them were in charge of central organizational units that were in competition with the different plant operators. They also asked two external engineering offices to participate in the project—these offices supplied services to the maintenance engineering department. At least one of them viewed the steel mill's managers' invitation with some reservations and some suspicion.

The link to the steel mill's middle managers was built by a department head from one of our partners from FhG-IGD—a research institute with a high technical reputation. He had known these managers for some time. The middle managers, both with a PhD in mechanical engineering, seemed to be driven by a certain curiosity to explore what type of insights a research-based project team could achieve in their field of operation, and which type of change processes would emerge. However, later on in the project, we learned that the manager responsible for the maintenance department had hired, in parallel, a professional consultancy firm to reorganize his manufacturing unit.

We started the project with a kickoff workshop in which we asked the participants from the different organizations to point out problems related to technological, organizational, and qualification issues. Based on the results of the workshop, we conducted an extensive interview study in different organizational units of the steel mill and in the two engineering offices (Wulf et al. 1999; Nett et al. 2000). Based on these results, a workshop was conducted at FhG-IGD to present ten different IT applications that offered some potential for overcoming identified problems. In a second workshop, the results of the pre-study were presented to members of the maintenance department and to the participating engineering offices. As the result of the discussion in the workshop, two work groups were formed, deliberately focusing on the exploration of the potential of a certain type of IT artifact as well as on problems in existing work practices. The first work group focused on the use of synchronous telecooperation and on methods for the storage of drawings, as it was understood that the discussion of ongoing projects would require references to archived drawings. The second work group dealt with the introduction of 3D CAD and with production-oriented methods of construction. The first work group started by introducing a video-conferencing and application-sharing tool among internal and external maintenance engineers and then derived concepts to extend the functionality of the application (e.g., Jaccuci et al. 1998). Members of the second work group explored 3D CAD but, at the same time, engineers of one of the external engineering offices visited the steel mill's production planning and production department. They found the video-conference system to be better suited for understanding of certain aspects of the production facilities in an ad-hoc manner.

Although the project advanced, after 18 months, which corresponded to half of the envisioned run time of the project, the top management of the steel mill decided to stop outsourcing maintenance engineering work to external offices. The decision seemed to be intended to save costs during a cyclic downturn of the steel market. However, this decision impacted the institutional context of our project in such a way that the change process came to a halt.

With reduced motivation and participation of the organizations involved, we expanded our initial analysis with regard to the knowledge-sharing practices in maintenance engineering (Pipek and Wulf 2003; Hinrichs et al. 2005). Since the central drawing archive played a particular role in maintaining the steel mill, we were able to involve its administrators in the prototyping of an innovative access control mechanism (Stevens and Wulf 2002, 2009).

OrgTech: Reflections

We began with the supposition that an integrated approach to organizational change while exploring opportunities of innovative IT applications was both feasible and desirable. However, when it came to the planning of the different interventions, the different work groups had specific motivations to start either from IT opportunities or from specific organizational problems. It turned out to be easier to start exploring the potential of already-existing IT artifacts, for example, video conferencing and application sharing, than to achieve changes in complex and distributed engineering practices, for example, a better alignment between construction and manufacturing in maintenance engineering. The rollout of video conferencing and application sharing was perceived by the participants to offer new opportunities for external engineers to come into contact with the internal production department.

The broader goals of the project were defined by two middle managers of the steel mill's central maintenance units; they got the research institutes involved and also selected the external engineering offices. However, the analysis and planning for intervention phases was set up in a manner such that these managers had relatively little impact on progress. The organizational culture of the steel mill itself allowed for such an approach but, on the side of the engineering offices, the company owners expected to have considerable involvement in the operative project activities.

This case study gave us some important insights into the importance of institutional conditions when putting the OTD framework into practice. Large organizations and, specifically, the managers initiating such a project, need to be motivated, tolerant, and aware of the fundamental purposes of such interventions, if they are to work. This, in and of itself, implicates the notion of "trust" in project work, and the way in which it does, or does not, emerge. In the case of the steel mill, the establishment of the project was facilitated by the middle managers' earlier linkage with FhG-IGD. Moreover, the culture of the organization seemed to be open enough to experiment with academics on real-world organization-development processes. Additionally, we understood that the middle managers in charge, both still on an upward career trajectory inside the mill, liked to be associated with this type of innovative project. However, they also limited their risk by restricting our project to a focus on the engineering work—and by asking another consultancy to reorganize the manufacturing department. However, from an organization-development perspective, this split in responsibilities was not too helpful.

The external engineering offices were, at least in the beginning, reluctant to let empirical research that was, in their eyes, defined by one of their core clients, happen. However, they accepted the investigation on condition that the steel mill was seen as an important client.

OTD always becomes part of the organizational micropolitics. The resulting changes in work practice may produce winners and losers. The internal actors who have initiated and promoted an OTD project may (implicitly) demand a certain loyalty to their interests. Such an alignment may limit the sphere of potential interventions and become a problem for gaining academic insights. So, a careful and self-reflective analysis of the restrictions resulting from the micropolitical environment is required.

Finally, the sudden end of the originally envisioned OTD process, caused by a top-management decision, made clear how fragile these project settings can be in practice. This fundamental change in the organizational environment disrupted the main line of our research. Given that project funding still existed, we reacted by changing our focus of investigation toward the role of the central archive in the steel mill's maintenance engineering practices. This shift turned out to be academically interesting—but required a certain flexibility and creativity with regard to the originally envisioned research design.

8.3.2 The Iran NGO-CS Project: Development of a Community System for Iranian NGOs

The Iran NGO-CS Project: The Case

During the late 1990s and the early 2000s (under President Chatami), there seemed to be a historic window of opportunity for democratic reform programs in the Islamic Republic of Iran and a possible political opening for Iranian–Western collaboration. This window was closed in 2003, perhaps as a result of the US president G. W. Bush's "axis of evil" rhetoric (2002), the Second Gulf War (2003), and the presidential election of Mahmud Ahmadinedschad (in 2005). However, the project we describe was conducted during the very short period of hope and democratic openness that occurred in Iranian society between 2000 and 2003.

In the beginning of 2000, a study on Iranian NGOs, funded by the Ford Foundation and the Iranian Population Council, showed that the situation for Iranian NGOs was characterized by two broad kinds of problems: (1) conflicts between rural NGOs and urban organizations that were mostly located in Teheran and the (provincial) capitals and (2) significant differences between so-called new NGOs and traditional, community-based, third-sector organizations, which mainly focused on relief work (see Namazi 2000). In 1997 and 2001, two national conferences of Iranian NGOs took place in the cities of Busher and Mashad; more than 120 participants from NGOs, scientists, government delegates, and representatives of the UN attended these conferences (see Hamyaran NGO Resource Center 2001). The meetings were organized by the Hamyaran Iran NGO Resource Center, which was located in Teheran and which at that time, was coordinating the ongoing networking process of Iranian NGOs. As one result, Hamyaran decided to find experts to help Iranian NGOs establish a better networked community and develop an appropriate IT support for this NGO community. In 2002 the "International Institute for Socio-Informatics" (IISI) established a contract with the Department for International Cooperation of Friedrich-Ebert-Stiftung (FES; a foundation aligned with the German Social Democratic Party) for a research-and-development project that aimed to support community building and networking among Iranian NGOs.

The Iran NGO-CS project started with a pre-study that aimed at the analysis of the specific requirements of Iranian NGOs. This analysis was conducted in spring 2002 by means of a detailed questionnaire to be answered by Iranian scientists and NGO experts. This questionnaire included questions concerning the nature of the different Iranian NGOs involved, their ICT infrastructure and Internet connectivity, the computer and language skills of the participants, requirements concerning technical support and training, the current state of the art with regard to socio-organizational networking, and constraints and limitations concerning a potential change process. Based on this analysis, a project plan was set up following the OTD framework.

In 2002, IISI provided the cooperation platform "Basic Support for Cooperative Work" (BSCW), which was developed by Fraunhofer FIT (see Bentley et al. 1997) for Iranian NGOs in order to support their networking processes by technical means. BSCW offered shared workspace functionality via a Web-browser interface. IISI organized the introduction of BSCW to the Iranian NGO network and conducted a train-the-trainer program for members of Iranian NGOs; this program was not only focused on technical training but was also directed toward community building, cooperation training, and project development. The project started in March 2002, included a delegation visit of leading Iranian NGO members and civil-society experts in Germany in December 2002, and ended with a final visit to Iran in September 2003.

The process of socio-organizational networking by and for Iranian NGOs had already been running for several years before our project started. Thus, the planning for NGO-CS (community system) did not start in a social or organizational vacuum but had to cope with requirements that had been articulated before and during the ongoing NGO networking. According to these preconditions, the following strategy for the project was chosen:

Requirements analysis: Based on process documents written by the Iranian NGOs and a pre-study in which Iranian NGO experts were involved, the requirements of the Iranian civil-society organizations concerning technological support were analyzed.

System introduction: In a first expert visit to Teheran, the technical platform BSCW was introduced to a group of leading Iranian NGO members.

System adaptation: In cooperation with Iranian NGO practitioners, a structure for the Iran NGO-CS was developed, BSCW was adapted to the NGOs' needs, and the first content was loaded up to the system. This system was aimed at support for the already-running and ongoing socio-organizational process of NGO networking. A special focus was to bring together people and organizations in the different Iranian provinces, regardless of time and location.

Qualification measures and trainings: In several training measures, Iranian NGO members were trained to use the system and to train other Iranian civil-society practitioners by cascading.

Socio-organizational interventions: In several meetings and workshops, the establishment of a common practice was supported by initializing collaborative projects. Therefore, tools for proposal writing and project management were offered.

Evaluation and redesign: Each measure and intervention was evaluated with questionnaires and expert interviews. Furthermore, the system's usage was also evaluated by means of anonymous log files. During two follow-up visits in Iran, additional training and workshop meetings were conducted in Iranian provinces outside Teheran and the system was redesigned for further use.

International networking: In addition, it was decided to support the international networking of Iranian NGOs by fostering international exchange of experiences, mutual visits, and common research projects.

During the project, all of these technical and socio-organizational measures were carried out in three Iranian provinces, as well as in Teheran itself. The evaluation of all of our activities, based on questionnaires and interviews with stakeholders, was positive, with participants rating the measures to be quite important and helpful. Most stakeholders expected that the established processes of networking, training, and cooperation support would continue and grow throughout the whole of Iranian civil society. Nevertheless, in September 2003, the introduced BSCW community system had only 280 registered users—instead of potentially several thousand, as was originally envisaged. Furthermore, at the project's end there were only a few cooperative project proposals underway. Finally, within a year after the end of the official project in September 2003, the usage of BSCW and the visible cooperation processes among Iranian NGOs significantly decreased and nearly completely stopped. So, the project ultimately failed in achieving a critical mass of participants and thus in being sustainable.

The Iran NGO-CS Project: Reflection

Although our project activities had been evaluated positively, the OTD project as a whole failed with regard to the defined aims and its sustainability. This failure was mainly due to specific political conditions, the organizational structures of NGO networks, and the lack of trust within Iranian civil society.

Our project was planned during a stage of political liberalization, initiated by the Chatami regime, in Iran in the late 1990s. Part of this political liberalization was Chatami's support for Iranian civil society, a necessary precondition for our project. In the wake of this liberalized, domestic policy, the Iranian society seemed to open up for more international cooperation—even the highly conflictual relations between Iran and the United States seemed to be a little less conflictual in 2000. However, in January 2002, the US president G. W. Bush held a speech in which he defined Iran (as well as Iraq and North Korea) as being part of an "axis of evil," blazing the trail for new international rhetoric against Iran. In March 2003, the Second Gulf War started with the US invasion of Iraq. As a consequence, conservative politicians regained influence in Iran, domestic liberalization stopped, and the Iranian regime and society closed up once more against international influences. These political developments were hard to foresee at the start of the project; we were too optimistic in our assumption with regard to the development of the civil society inside Iran.

Another unforeseen internal political issue was the critical relation between governmental organizations and NGOs: while our project started as a close cooperation between international experts and the Hamyaran Iran NGO Resource Center in Teheran, in May 2002 another organization was established: the Iranian Civil Society Organizations Resource Center (ICSORC) started, with the strong support of the Iranian government. At that time, it was somehow unclear, not only to us, as to whether the ICSORC was a real NGO or a sort of government-initiated NGO. Nevertheless, despite the fact that there was supposed to be cooperation between this new organization and our project, with an agreement that we should not hamper each other's activities, there was direct competition between Hamyaran and the ICSORC regarding the support mission for the Iranian civil society. Although ICSORC officials were invited and, indeed, participated in our activities, they started to develop their own technical infrastructure for Iranian NGOs, their own training facilities, and so on. Therefore, in contrast to what was planned, our project activities failed to reach the whole of Iranian civil society but were mainly restricted to the NGOs that were organized around Hamyaran, not the ones that were otherwise addressed by ICSORC.

One main mechanism we based our approach on was the targeted "snowball effect" by train-the-trainer measures. First, a defined group of facilitators within the NGO network was enabled to (tele-)cooperate with each other. Then, these facilitators were meant to be trained as trainers themselves for their colleagues and other NGO members. However, we found that the building of social ties in a community and a successful "snowball effect" were heavily dependent on mutual trustful relations that were rarely freely given in Iranian society. Given the authoritarian nature of (some parts of) society in the postrevolutionary Islamic Republic of Iran, most of the participants in our project had experienced oppression themselves or through affected relatives, friends, and neighbors. More than two decades of oppression and strong governmental surveillance had undermined trustful relations in the Iranian society to a large extent. When setting up our project, we underestimated this widespread lack of trust, a lack that (in addition to the adverse political conditions) hindered the success of our project.

There are at least three differences between the intended application of our original OTD framework and its actual implementation in this particular setting:

1. In contrast to our OTD focus, in the Iranian case study, we did not deal with an already-existing, traditional organization but with a newly emerging network/community structure. Organization development focuses on the organizational change of established organizational structures and processes. In this case study, we faced the challenge of organization development in terms of community building and, therefore, fostering and supporting the emergent and participatory creation of completely new organizational structures and processes. Civil-society networks might be characterized by completely different requirements and constraints then formal organizations are—with regard to group dynamics, membership, ingroup/outgroup mechanisms, motivation, rules and regulations, and so on.
2. Distinct from the "work-system" focus for business organizations, as envisioned in the original OTD framework, the main goal in this case study was the establishment of community learning and collaboration structures within and between very diverse groups, networks, and organizations. Instead of intervening in a more or less well-defined work system of coworkers cooperating on common tasks, the focus in Iran was rather more diffuse, making it difficult to identify common goals and interests, establish shared practices, plan cooperation projects, and so on. Such projects clearly have to start from a different place. There are few clearly articulated goals at anything other than a political level, so the heterogeneous nature of the participating organizations needs to be understood, as does the wider political context. That is, addressing a whole collaboration infrastructure is necessary. The value of understanding infrastructure as a sociotechnical phenomenon was made very clear to us here.
3. While the original OTD framework incorporated awareness of micropolitical impacts and conflicts on organizational levels, our Iranian case study confronted us with much stronger macropolitical conflicts/developments and historical contingencies that could hardly be foreseen, let alone controlled in the process. As mentioned in Section 8.2, OTD projects need a mandate in order to be conducted. In a traditional business organization, the agreement or *votum* of management (and hopefully) a workers' council might do the job—at least until the management changes. In macropolitical structures, multiple players are involved, including governmental organizations (of different countries/states), political parties, voters, secret services, public administrators, and so on. In our project, only two institutions had given us a mandate for the support of sociotechnical and organizational change: FES, which was tolerated by German government, and Hamyaran, which was tolerated by Iranian government. That proved to be not enough.

8.4 Discussion

More than 20 years have passed since the first publication of our OTD framework. The integrated perspective on sociotechnical, organizational, and qualification aspects in practice-oriented ICT design projects has informed our research in many R & D projects, but OTD was very rarely applied in these projects to its full extent. Rather, it has been something of a general conceptual backdrop to implementations that have been realized in various groupware design processes. One needs a fairly broad/general mandate to implement such a complex, integrated program. In industrial projects, this general mandate is often lacking, due to micropolitical decisions and, maybe sometimes, to limited trust in external scientific consultants or resources. A limited mandate for smaller, more clearly defined interventions (e.g., on the technological level, on personal qualification measures, or on controllable managerial changes), in our experience, is more likely to be successful. In this chapter, we analyzed two cases of OTD application. Looking at these two cases, we can sum up our findings about the core concepts of OTD as follows.

The original conception of OTD offered a framework that would allow actors to tackle problems in their social practices, linking technological and organizational change. To establish such an ongoing improvement process, corresponding qualifications, resources, and experiences are required—which again can be built and refined during such a self-reflective change process. In both of the cases observed, we were in a situation to start implementing OTD in fields of applications that had no prior experience with this process model before and were characterized by rather different traditions of cooperative work and experiences with organizational change.

While maintenance in the steel mill was fragmented by structural divides, the mill had a tradition of workers' participation. This tradition helped in setting up the initial steps toward an OTD process. In the case of the Iranian NGOs, only very few prior experiences with collaborative practices across and within institutions existed; instead, a culture of mistrust and suspicion was dominant. Nevertheless, the participating organizations and individuals were quite motivated and hopeful that they might overcome these difficulties and engage in a nationwide civil-society community-building process.

In both cases, OTD was initiated by actors exercising a specific position in the social texture of the fields of application: middle managers, in the case of the steel mill, and a government-supported resource center, in the case of the Iranian NGOs. These actors defined, at least, an initial problem description and project vision. OTD was introduced in the context of an externally funded project, by a state government's innovation program, in the case of the steel mill project, and, in the case of the Iranian NGO, by a foreign foundation. In these constellations, outside academics became the facilitators of integrated change processes. The change processes were enabled in principle but also depended in practice on the availability of external resources. When trying to reach out further with the OTD approach, we found it difficult to convince organizations to start such a process if they had to rely solely on their own resources.

On an institutional level, it turned out to be difficult to find organizations (and especially middle and top managers) willing to partner with an academic institution to pursue integrated and organizational change processes. From our experience, it is much easier to involve them in a research agenda that explores the potential of innovative technologies but does little else. While the appropriation of the resulting artifacts typically leads to changes in practice—a fact of which decision-makers are typically aware—they are unwilling to factor this explicitly into their plans. A focus on technology development in the project setup avoids addressing conflicts that may otherwise be evident immediately. A focus on the development of technology in practice emphasizes the exploratory aspect of these projects and makes them appear, at least, in the initialization phase, to be reversible in their effects on the organization, or less dangerous, as it were. Indeed, we experienced a few cases in which our newly developed IT artifacts were removed from the organization—typically after the funding phase of the research project expired. Finally, overcoming Tayloristic structures has become less of a concern in the recent managerial literature. From the perspective of academic qualification and career building, it turned out to be difficult to find an interested audience and, as a consequence, to position the resulting findings appropriately.

The following reflections on OTD are mainly (but not only) based on the experiences from the two case studies reported in the chapter; it should be noted that these are, by now, quite distant from our accumulated experiences in a wide range of technology-related projects.

8.4.1 *Vis Inertiae*

OTD processes potentially impact work/collaborative practices in a profound manner. While the changes are grounded on the operational level, they are often interwoven and interfere with a strategic level. Most organizations (business companies and social networks/communities) tend to stick to established routines, historically acquired rules and regulations, micro-/macropolitically negotiated strategies, and so on. When asking for a general mandate for OTD understood as organization-wide, sociotechnical change management, many organizations tend to opt for small, easily controllable changes that have no fundamental impact on organizational structure, strategy, or culture. This tendency toward organizational continuity and a stable identity is quite understandable but hinders holistic sociotechnical development programs and leads to half-hearted, insufficient solutions. Without doubt, in our early conceptions of what OTD might offer, we underestimated these needs for stability and identity, and the consequent resistance to deeper organizational changes.

8.4.2 Micropolitics

In traditional, formal organizations, operational affairs are mainly separated from technical, personnel, and organization developmental matters and are in different departments, with their own heads and responsibilities. Although we observed that many organizational (middle) managers are aware of the fact that these different organizational levels are inseparably interdependent, they do not have the organizational mandate to make decisions on a more general level. The organizational division of labor, division of management decisions, and differentiated department structures hinder a more global, general mandate for change processes on an integrated, supradepartmental level. The (expected) impacts of OTD projects affect different departments, heads, and so on, and lead to respective challenges and conflicts. If not overruled by the top management, these interdepartmental conflicts of interest make OTD programs nearly impossible. Even with the mandate of the top management, such micropolitical conflicts have a massive impact on integrated OTD projects. Moreover, the participatory OTD approach needs agreement, consent, and commitment from members of all organizational levels. The top/middle management mandates are necessary but not sufficient conditions for OTD. It needs commitment from members at all organizational levels (although this is true for other OTD projects as well). In this sense, integrated OTD is a fairly ambitious framework.

8.4.3 Macropolitics

OTD did not take macropolitical issues into account. Corporate merger and acquisition activities, political/governmental changes, societal developments, legal reforms, and so on, were not planned for in the original framework. We underestimated micropolitics, but we completely ignored macropolitics. The truth is that the direction of both of the projects described in this chapter was seriously impacted by political and economic developments that were clearly outside the operational scope of the projects (on both micro- and macropolitical levels).

8.5 Conclusion

Besides the lessons we learned from the two projects presented in this chapter, there are some more abstract conceptual considerations with regard to the application of OTD in practice. In the following, we reflect on some potential structural shortcomings of our original framework, not on a primarily empirical basis but rather on a more general basis.

8.5.1 Design-versus-Development Dilemma

In general, the integrated OTD framework followed a sociotechnical understanding, taking technical-design processes as well as socio-organizational development into account. One conceptual misunderstanding of the early work ends in a "design-versus-development dilemma": if dealing with sociotechnical systems, one could probably intentionally design the technical part, but not the social/organizational one—this latter socio-organizational part of the system might be influenced by design, but it develops (mainly) by itself. The development of social systems is emergent, self-organized, and contingent—not intentional, controlled, or deterministic. The original OTD framework showed some awareness of this dilemma but conceptually underestimated its pragmatic significance. While design interventions might be efficient/sufficient in ICT design projects (and even this assumption is critical; see Chapter 1), socio-organizational change might be (positively or negatively) influenced by design interventions but cannot be controlled by designers' aims and intentions. Although this central "design-versus-development dilemma" was already embedded in the original sociotechnical foundation of OTD, its consequences for practical OTD projects have not been elaborated explicitly.

8.5.2 Asynchronicity

OTD conceptualizes organizational, technical, and qualification measures as parallel processes. In practice, these interwoven processes follow different timelines. While a technical-design cycle might last for a specific time (e.g., 6–8 months), the related socio-organizational process might last significantly longer (e.g., 16–24 months). In modifying the original OTD framework publication, this asynchronicity should be taken into account. In practice, OTD projects face the challenge of concurrent but mostly asynchronous development/design processes. Awareness and expectation of this asynchronicity influences planning of OTD projects and probably the decisions of managers to give a mandate for such integrated development processes.

8.5.3 Deepness of Intervention

Our OTD framework plans for technical and socio-organizational changes and developments. Both are interventions into the social practices of organization members affected. Our original framework does not distinguish the depth of intervention with respect to technical versus socio-organizational measures. Based on our empirical experiences, technical versus socio-organizational development cycles might not only rely on different run durations but also imply a different level of depth of engagement. While the implementation of a technical prototype during a pilot study might influence the organizational practice temporarily (and maybe in the first instance) and on a fairly superficial level (and could be extracted if unsuccessful), a socio-organizational intervention (training, business process changes, structural/strategic changes, etc.) could be far more persistent (and not easily rolled back). OTD does not differentiate between any potential consequences of different measures on technical versus socio-organizational levels. Nevertheless, this different depth of intervention might prove to be an obstacle for the establishment of integrated OTD projects.

8.5.4 Output Guarantee

Organization managers usually expect some form of guarantee for development project outcomes. With regard to technical-design solutions, this guarantee could be a contractual matter according to design requirements and technical specifications that have to be met. With respect to socio-organizational changes, the requirements to be met are rather more difficult to define. Given the "design-versus-development dilemma" mentioned in Section 8.5.1, it might be much easier to guarantee the success of design products or artifacts (or, at least, to convince managers with putative guarantees) than to guarantee the success of the results of emergent and contingent socio-organizational development processes. With respect to OTD, managers might be reluctant to give a mandate for integrated technical design, organizational development, and personnel qualification without being guaranteed the output of the whole process. When cooperating with a middle-sized German health insurance company, for example, the management agreed upon our statement that the design of a new e-learning platform would necessarily affect the education and training practices of the company. However, we were only given the limited mandate to design and introduce the new e-learning technology, not the broader mandate to reorganize organizational learning programs. One reason for this limited mandate was—so we were told by some middle managers—that the impact of a new technology would be much easier to foresee and observe than the effects of much more advanced reorganization.

OTD was not published as a recipe or checklist for groupware projects (to fulfill each and every step one by one) but as an orientation framework for action researchers and practitioners, to provide a practice-oriented framework for groupware introduction in organizational settings. Even though the sociotechnical systems approach has been in the public purview for five decades, at the current time, there is still no comprehensive approach to the integration of organization development and technology development at hand—this gap is meant to be bridged by the OTD framework.

In the early days of our research endeavors, the development and exploration of (innovative) IT artifacts in relation to organizational practice was not yet widely accepted. It found a more receptive audience in the computer-supported-cooperative-work and participatory-design communities, and recently also in the human–computer interaction community. Finally, there are very few public-funding bodies that offer support for research into integrated OTD processes. In the current research environment, it is obvious that research agendas promising societal innovation by means of technological progress are much more generously funded than those directed toward the solution—or, at least, the first step of a solution—for problems in workplace practices in individual organizations.

As pointed out, most organization (mainly company) managers do agree in principle on the perception of interwoven technical and socio-organizational aspects with regard to the design of sociotechnical work systems, but many of them avoid giving a general mandate for a fully comprehensive OTD project, perhaps because there are problems of accountability. They prefer a more controllable, smaller-scope approach to sociotechnical change.

Public discourse (and funding) focus solely on social innovation as a result of technology development, pushing for an IT design-oriented research approach. Many managers/organizations either do not see the link between technical and organizational development or are very careful to provide a general mandate (maybe specifically, in the case of universities). On the other hand, OTD looks very much at a planned and facilitated change process. However, IT appropriation and changing practices result often without external facilitation in an emerging manner. Therefore—and based on our empirical experiences so far—we have developed "grounded design," which is a more IT-design-oriented approach to organizational change (Rohde et al. 2017; also see Chapter 1).

This approach, based upon design case studies (Wulf et al. 2011, 2015), offers a more technology- and design-oriented perspective, breaking down theoretically derived principles to some more pragmatic methodological issues and thus envisioning a development cycle that involves a more manageable range of interventions. One could say that this paradigm emerged from the OTD framework by a conventional evolutionary process that led to a better environmental fit. However, there are also considerable differences in the two research paradigms. Typically, OTD processes start from an identified problem with practice. Practitioners, typically supported by certain actors from the organization's hierarchy, assume that the application of innovative technologies could contribute to its solution (without other interventions). In contrast, a design case study starts typically from the idea of exploring the potential of certain technologies or algorithms for social practice, not necessarily with an initial focus on given "problems." It is rather defined by the relationship between a certain technology and the social practice within a specific field of application.

The change process in organizations is typically driven by application-oriented IT professionals. OTD set out, rather ambitiously, to deal with the evident fact that such change is, inevitably, a sociotechnical matter. We continue to have that view. While the main result of a process of OTD is the solution of a real-world problem, however, the result of a design case study is the design of an IT artifact, and the investigation of its appropriation in practice. Pipek (2005) and Stevens (2009) have elaborated on the appropriation of IT artifacts, stating, in effect, that we cannot understand the use of such artifacts as depending entirely on the intentions of the artifacts' designers and, moreover, that potential uses will emerge over time (see Chapter 4). Appropriation, understood as a long-term phenomenon, had not previously, we suggest, been sufficiently investigated empirically. Their implications for (re-)design had not yet been thought out. The results of design case studies indicate that innovative IT artifacts should be designed in a participatory and evolutionary manner, allowing the analysis of changes in practices and organizations over the long term and comparing the results of pre-studies with those of studies of an artifact's appropriation. In contrast, they do not indicate that there should be an initial setting up of a planned process of organization and qualification development, integrated with technology emergence.

These differences in goals have consequences for development methods. As with the OTD framework, after the setup of activities, a pre-study of the given work practices is conducted. However, with design case studies, these empirical investigations are conducted by external actors, such as ethnographers or IT designers. The purpose of this analysis is twofold: (1) to gain new insights about the diversity of given practices, relative to the state of the art, and (2) to ground the design of innovative IT artifacts in this setting. Such an analysis should describe given practices, focusing on those (problematic) aspects that could be improved by means of the IT artifact.

Grounded in the results of the empirical pre-study, evolutionary and participatory-design activities should then be set up under the design case study agenda with at least one field of application—typically, with those from the pre-study. The resulting IT artifacts are, in a third step, rolled out in at least one of the fields of application. Changes in practice related to the appropriation of the artifacts should then be empirically investigated over a longer period of time (Wulf et al. 2011, 2015). While the OTD framework explicitly suggests that planned measures of personal and organizational development should elaborate on given practices, our understanding of the term "appropriation" is rather unspecific as to whether specific measures should be planned and how the organizational learning should be supported (see Chapter 4).

OTD offered an open framework for orientation in sociotechnical change projects, integrating technical-design aspects, socio-organizational development, and qualification issues. Although the basic assumption of interwoven design/development problems on different levels is quite broadly accepted, OTD nevertheless proved to be quite ambitious, complex, and not easily manageable. This complexity led to acceptance problems in practice.

Therefore, we elaborated on design case studies as a more modest instance of OTD philosophy—with a primary focus on technically induced dimensions of change opportunities and a more limited scope. In this way, design case studies could be understood as representing a more technically driven, design-oriented element in a longer-term OTD engagement. They integrate a strong emphasis on appropriation practices but may imply less intervention into organizational practices.

On a fundamental level, our formulation of grounded design as a conceptually derived approach for design science provides a basic theoretical reference frame for OTD, design case studies, and appropriation research (see Chapters 1, 2, and 4). This chorus of theoretical approaches, methodological frameworks, and analytical concepts can be seen as an ensemble geared to enhancing research-and-development projects in practice-oriented computing—and in what we call socio-informatics.

References

Bentley, R., Appelt, W., Busbach, B., Hinrichs, E., Kerr, D., Sickkel, K., Trevor, J., and Wötzel, G. 1997. "Basic support for cooperative work on the World Wide Web." *International Journal of Human Computer Studies* 46: 827–46.

Blomberg, J., Giacomi, J., Mosher, A., and Swenton-Wall, P. 1992. "Ethnographic field methods and their relation to design." In P. Schuler and A. Namioka, eds., *Participatory Design: Principles and Practice.* Hillsdale, NJ: Lawrence Erlbaum Associates, 123–55.

Bødker, K., Kensing, F., and Simonsen, J. 2005. *Participatory IT Design: Designing for Business and Workplace Realities.* Cambridge, MA: MIT Press.

Bourdieu, P. 1986. "The forms of capital." In J. C. Richardson, ed., *Handbook of Theory and Research for the Sociology of Education.* New York: Greenwood Press, 241–58.

Brödner, P. 1986. *Fabrik 2000: Alternative Entwicklungspfade in die Zukunft der Fabrik.* Berlin: Edition Sigma.

Checkland, P., and Holwell, S., 1997. *Information, Systems and Information Systems: Making Sense of the Field.* Chichester: John Wiley & Sons.

Checkland, P. B. 1989. "Soft systems methodology." *Human Systems Management* 8 (4): 273–89.

Cohen, D., and Prusak, L. 2001. *In Good Company: How Social Capital Makes Organizations Work.* Cambridge, MA: Harvard Business School Press.

Coy, W. 1992. "Für eine Theorie der Informatik!" In W. Coy, F. Nake, J.-M. Pflüger, A. Rolf, J. Seetzen, D. Siefkes, and R. Stransfeld, eds., *Sichtweisen der Informatik* Braunschweig: Vieweg, 17–32.

Ehn, P. 1993. "Scandinavian design: On participation and skill." In D. Schuler and A. Namioka, eds., *Participatory Design: Principles and Practices.* Hillsdale, NJ: Lawrence Erlbaum Associates, 41–77.

Fischer, G. 2003. "Meta-design: Beyond user-centered and participatory design." In *HCI'03.* Hillsdale, NJ: Lawrence Erlbaum Associates, 88–92.

Fischer, G., and Ostwald, J. 2002. "Seeding, evolutionary growth, and reseeding: Enriching participatory design with informed participation." In *PDC'02.* New York: ACM, 135–43.

Floyd, C., Reisin, F.-M., and Schmidt, G. 1989. "STEPS to software development with users." In *ESEC'89.* Heidelberg: Springer, 48–64.

Fuchs, P., and Hartmann, E. A. 1993. "Partizipative Softwaregestaltung: Methoden und Instrumente zur Beteiligung der Nutzer." In W. Coy, P. Gorny, I. Kopp, and C. Skarpelis, eds., *Menschengerechte*

Software als Wettbewerbsfaktor: Forschungsansätze und Anwenderergebnisse aus dem Programm "Arbeit und Technik." Stuttgart: Teubner, 361–78.

Greenbaum, J., and Kyng, M. 1991. *Design at Work.* Hillsdale, NJ: Lawrence Erlbaum Associates.

Hacker, W. 1986. *Arbeitspsychologie. Psychische Regulation von Arbeitstätigkeiten.* Berlin: VEB Deutscher Verlag der Wissenschaften.

Hammer, M., and Champy, J. 1993. *Reengeneering the Cooperation.* New York, Harper.

Hamyaran NGO Resource Center. 2001. *Mashad Meeting (Busher+4: Challenges and Approaches).* Final Report. Teheran: Hamyaran Center.

Hartmann, A. 1994. "Integrierte Organisations—und Technikentwicklung—ein Ansatz zur sach—und bedürfnisgerechten Gestaltung der Arbeitswelt." In A. Hartmann, T. Herrmann, M. Rohde, and V. Wulf, eds., *Menschengerechte Groupware—Software-ergonomische Gestaltung und partizipative Umsetzung.* Stuttgart: Teubner, 303–28.

Hartmann, A., and Rohde, M. 1993. "Organisations—und Dispositionsspielräume und ihre Bedeutung für die Gestaltung vernetzter Systeme." In H. Reichel, ed., *Informatik, Wirtschaft, Gesellschaft.* Berlin: Springer, 175–80.

Hartmann, E. A., Fuchs-Frohnhofen, P., Henning, K., and Sell, R. 1994. "Lernen and Fertigen: Ein integriertes Konzept zur Personal-, Organisations- und Technikgestaltung." In K. Henning, V. Volkholz, W. Risch, and W. Hacker, eds., *Moderne Lern-Zeiten—Lernen und Arbeiten in der Neuen Fabrik.* Berlin: Springer, 27–48.

Hinrichs, J., Pipek, V., and Wulf, V. 2005. "Context grabbing: Assigning metadata in large document collections." In *ECSCW'05.* Dordrecht: Springer, 367–86.

Huysman, M., and Wulf, V. 2004. "Social capital and IT: Current debates and research." In M. Huysman and V. Wulf, eds., *Social Capital and Information Technology.* Cambridge, MA: MIT Press, 1–16.

Iacucci, G., Peters, R., Stiemerling, O., and Wulf, V. 1998. "Telecooperation systems in engineering companies supplying the metallurgy." In *PROLAMAT'98.* Dordrecht: Kluwer, 107–19.

Kensing, F., and Blomberg, J. 1998. "Participatory design: Issues and concerns." *Computer Supported Cooperative Work* 7 (3–4): 167–84.

Kensing, F., Simonsen, J., and Bødker, K. 1996. "MUST: A method for participatory design." *Human-Computer Interaction* 13 (2): 167–90.

Kensing, F., Simonsen, J., and Bødker, K. 1998. "Participatory design at a radio station." *Computer Supported Cooperative Work* 7 (3–4): 243–71.

Kuutti, K. 1991. "Activity theory and its application to information system research and development." In H.-E. Nissen, H. K. Klein, and R. Hirschheim, eds., *Information Systems Research: Contemporary Approaches and Emergent Traditions.* North-Holland: Elsevier, 529–49.

Lave, J., and Wenger, E. 1991. *Situated Learning: Legitimate Peripheral Participation.* Cambridge: Cambridge University Press.

Leontjew, A. N. 1974. "The problem of activity in psychology." *Soviet Psychology* 13 (2): 4–33.

Namazi, B. 2000. *Iranian NGOs: Situation Analysis.* Teheran: Hamyaran Center.

Nett, B., Iacucci, G, and Wulf, V. 2000. "Inter-organizational telecooperation: A case study in the German steel industry." In *PDC'00.* New York: ACM, 305–9.

Orlikowski, W. J. 1996. "Evolving with Notes: Organizational change around groupware technology." In C. U. Ciborra, ed., *Groupware and Teamwork.* Chichester: John Wiley & Sons, 23–60.

Pipek, V. 2005. *From Tailoring to Appropriation Support: Negotiating Groupware Usage.* PhD thesis. Oulu: University of Oulu.

Pipek, V., and Wulf, V. 1999. "A groupware's life." In *ECSCW'99.* Dordrecht: Kluwer, 199–218.

Pipek, V., and Wulf, V. 2003. "Pruning the answer garden: Knowledge sharing in maintenance engineering." In *ECSCW'03.* Dordrecht: Kluwer, 1–20.

Rohde, M. 2004. "Find what binds: Building social capital in an Iranian NGO community system." In M. Huysman and V. Wulf, eds., *Social Capital and Information Technology*. Cambridge, MA: MIT Press, 75–112.

Rohde, M. 2007. *Integrated Organization and Technology Development (OTD) and the Impact of Socio-Cultural Concepts: A CSCW Perspective*. PhD thesis. Roskilde: University of Roskilde.

Rohde, M., Brödner, P., Stevens, G., and Wulf, V. 2017. "Grounded design: A praxeological IS research perspective." *Journal of Information Technology* 32 (2): 163–79.

Rönkkö, K., Dittrich, Y., and Randall, D. 2005. "When plans do not work out: How plans are used in software development projects." *Computer Supported Cooperative Work* 14 (5): 433–68.

Schmidt, K., and Bannon, L. J. 1992. "Taking CSCW seriously: Supporting articulation work." *Computer Supported Cooperative Work* 1 (1–2): 7–40.

Stevens, G., and Wulf, V. 2002. "A new dimension in access control: Studying maintenance engineering across organizational boundaries." In *CSCW'02*. New York: ACM, 196–205.

Stevens, G., and Wulf, V. 2009. "Computer-supported access control." *Transactions on Computer Human Interaction* 16 (3): 12.

Stevens, G. 2009. *Understanding and Designing Appropriation Infrastructures: Artifacts as Boundary Objects in Continuous Software Development*. PhD thesis. Siegen: University of Siegen.

Stiemerling, O., Wulf, V., and Rohde, M. 1998. "Integrated organization and technology development: The case of the ORGTech project." In *CE'98*. Johnstown, PA: Concurrent Technologies Corporation, 181–7.

Tajfel, H. 1982. *Social Identity and Intergroup Relations*. Cambridge: Cambridge University Press.

Tajfel, H., and Turner J. C. 1986. "The social identity theory of intergroup behavior." In S. Worchel and W. G. Austin, eds., *Psychology of Intergroup Relations*. Chicago: Nelson-Hall Publishers.

Twidale, M. B. 2005. "Over the shoulder learning: Supporting brief informal learning." *Computer Supported Cooperative Work* 14 (6): 505–47.

Womack, J. P., Jones, D. T., and Roos, D. 1990. *The Machine That Changed the World*. New York: Rawson.

Wulf, V. 1992. "Gruppenorientiertes CAD: Ein Ansatz zur Technikunterstützung teilautonomer Arbeitsgruppen in der Konstruktion." In *CAD'92*. Berlin: Springer, 93–107.

Wulf, V. 1994. "Anpaßbarkeit im Prozeß evolutionärer Systementwicklung." In *GMD-Spiegel* 3 (24): 41–6.

Wulf, V. 2000. "Exploration environments: Supporting users to learn groupware functions." *Interacting with Computers* 13 (2): 265–99.

Wulf, V., Krings, M., Stiemerling, O., Iacucci, G., Fuchs Frohnhofen, P., Hinrichs, J., Maidhof, M., Nett, B., and Peters, R. 1999. "Improving inter-organizational processes with integrated organization and technology development." *Journal of Universal Computer Science* 5 (6): 339–65.

Wulf, V., and Rohde, M. 1995. "Towards an integrated organization and technology development." In *DIS'95*. New York: ACM, 55–65.

Wulf, V., Müller, C., Pipek, V., Randall, D., Rohde, M., and Stevens, G. 2015. "Practice-based computing: Empirical grounded conceptualizations derived from design case studies." In V. Wulf, K. Schmidt, and D. Randall, eds., *Designing Socially Embedded Technologies in the Real-World*. London: Springer-Verlag London 111–50.

Wulf, V., Pipek, V., and Won, M. 2008. "Component-based tailorability: Towards highly flexible software applications." *International Journal on Human-Computer Studies* 66 (1): 1–22.

Wulf, V., Rohde, M., Pipek, V., and Stevens, G. 2011. "Engaging with practices: Design case studies as a research framework in CSCW." In *CSCW'11*. New York: ACM, 505–12.

9 Design, Action, and Practice

Three Branches of the Same Tree

GILLIAN R. HAYES

Action research (AR) is a research approach that involves engaging with a community to address some problem or challenge, and, through this problem-solving, to develop scholarly knowledge. AR is not a method, nor even a suite of methods, but a perspective that makes use of a wide variety of methods. AR is explicitly democratic, collaborative, and interdisciplinary. Thus, AR research focuses on highly contextualized, localized solutions with a greater emphasis on transferability than generalizability. In other words, scholars and community partners work together to develop and learn from solutions that work in a single context; in addition, they collect data that will enable these solutions to be adapted or transferred to other contexts. Most importantly, AR claims that the intervention and the learning, the doing and the knowing, cannot be disentangled.

AR "aims to contribute both to the practical concerns of people" in problematic situations and to the academic goals of science "by joint collaboration within a mutually acceptable ethical framework" (Rapoport 1970, p. 499). Procedurally, AR is "comparative research on the conditions and effects of various forms of social action, and research leading to social action" that uses "a spiral of steps, each of which is composed of a circle of planning, action, and fact-finding about the result of the action" (Lewin 1946, 1948). This approach privileges the local knowledge contributed by community insiders as much as the academic knowledge contributed by community outsiders. In human–computer interaction (HCI), this approach often includes notions of participatory design, both in the traditional Scandinavian sense (Bjerknes and Bratteteig 1995) and more recently adapted views in HCI and computer-supported cooperative work (CSCW; Muller 2003; Foth and Axup 2006) and other co-design methods (Greenbaum and Kyng 1992), to develop novel technologies that address the problematic situations identified through the AR project.

A practice perspective provides action researchers with a way to engage and learn about the world by focusing on everyday practices. In this view, doing and knowing are

Socio-Informatics, Volker Wulf, Volkmar Pipek, Dave Randall, Markus Rohde, Kjeld Schmidt, Gunnar Stevens (Eds). Published 2018 by Oxford University Press.

more important than what is done and what is known, meaning that the practice perspective engages with the world in its becoming rather than with the idea that it "is" at any given point in time (Bourdieu 1977, 1990; Miettinen et al. 2009). Much of the emphasis in HCI and design has been on improving the current state of being, a situation that necessarily requires designers to engage with the products being developed as they are becoming and with the world of users and stakeholders as they change themselves, their situations, and the technologies being used. Both HCI and design take the notion of iterative, cyclical processes seriously and are concerned with the generation of new artifacts (in the case of design) and new scholarly knowledge (in the case of HCI, such as via AR) *through* change and intervention.

AR takes the practice perspective as being inherent. The focus on doing rather than what is done, on generating knowledge *through* action, is fundamental to an AR approach. The practice perspective is therefore embedded in the AR logic, albeit often silently. Only a limited set of action researchers explicitly incorporate practice theory into their writings, and the overlap in the literature is limited. However, as Kemmis notes, AR is a "practice-based practice" (Kemmis 2009). Specifically, AR changes people's practices, their "patterns of 'saying', 'doing,' and 'relating' to form new…ways of life…Action Research is also a practice, composed of sayings, doing, and relating" (Kemmis 2009, p. 463). Thinking of AR as a "meta-practice" allows us to see how the common intellectual traditions of AR and practice theory, the importance of inclusion of nonscientists in scholarly thinking, and a focus on the details of everyday life combine to provide a powerful approach to transformative technological interventions and development of key scholarly knowledge.

Practice theory asserts that through everyday practice, we create and recreate social structure (Bourdieu 1977). Increasingly, everyday practices include technologies that were once the domain of computer scientists, mathematicians, and other "experts." It is time, then, to consider how a practice perspective, which helps us to employ intentionally and explicitly the project of "doing" to understand social behavior and reality, applies to considerations for technology design, a position argued by the editors of this book (e.g., Wulf, Schmidt, and Randall 2015), among others. At the same time, a practice perspective helps us to think about how everyday practices can dissolve existing social structures. In the commercial space, this type of substantial change to existing structures accompanied by a novel technology is often referenced as "disruptive technology," with the implication that the systems themselves are making this change. However, in this work, we examine the ways in which the practices surrounding the action of introducing such technologies provide an important way to examine and consider societal change.

The bulk of this book is concerned with taking a practice perspective in computer science, HCI, and CSCW. In this chapter, I focus on AR as a methodological approach that overlaps and complements these ideas. Although AR can be used in a variety of ways and across a multitude of disciplines, including broad views of computing and information technology (e.g., Baskerville and Pries-Heje 1999), I focus here on its relationship with practice theory within the context of HCI and design.

9.1 Common Historical and Intellectual Traditions

AR has arguably been concerned with practice since its origins, even if the originators did not name it as such. The early pragmatists, like John Dewey, were heavily concerned with the everyday practices and problems of the broad public (Dewey [1927] 1991). Kurt Lewin, who published the first manuscript with the term "action research" (Lewin 1946), argued that knowledge could best be constructed by real-world tests and that "nothing is as practical as a good theory." Although even practice theorists themselves do not always argue for the practicality of this approach, practice theory is, at least arguably, inherently practical (Feldman and Worline 2016), supporting our ability to make and understand change in our world. Lewin's call for AR made intervening in research settings acceptable as a means for scholarly inquiry and therefore made engaging with and changing *practice* acceptable for the generation of new theory.

This approach emerged in part because the scientific culture of the time, led by pragmatists like John Dewey and William James, saw science as relevant and available to everyone, not just the ivory tower elites interested in "esoteric knowledge" (James 1948; Dewey 1976; Greenwood and Levin 2007). Specifically, Dewey advanced the idea that thought and action—or practice—cannot be separated and constitute a cornerstone of AR. Thus, while action researchers asserted that all people can think scientifically, practice theorists began to argue that scientific thinking should necessarily concern itself with the things all people encounter—everyday practices. These two approaches, then, represent two sides of the same coin and lead us to a scientific culture that allows for our topics *and* our collaborators to come from the larger community of people who are not professional scientists and scholars.

Much of AR comes from scholarly fields closely related to the professions (e.g., education) and thus has a particular interest in professional practice. By taking a practice perspective, we see that professional practice is made up of sayings, doings, and relatings (Schatzki 1996, 2002, 2012). These things, in turn, are made possible and are intrinsically shaped by the actions, conditions, and contexts that came before them, what Kemmis and Smith call *mediating preconditions* (Kemmis and Smith 2007).

In this view, an individual's praxis is shaped by three types of mediating preconditions: cultural/discursive, material/economic, and social/political. Cultural/discursive preconditions orient and justify the practices. This is the "saying" or way we talk about our practices, even to ourselves. Material/economic preconditions shape the actual implementation and experience of the practice. Finally, social/political preconditions shape the way we relate the practice to other people and their practices.

A solid understanding of these three types of mediating preconditions is essential for the success of an AR project in two important ways. First, understanding the community and context into which an intervention might be deployed means understanding the preconditions for the existing practices and for the practices surrounding the intervention. This is essentially an issue for intervention design. One cannot design a successful intervention without this understanding. Second, as an intervention unfolds, existing practices change, and new practices emerge. The intervention then becomes a part of the mediating preconditions for these new practices. The development of new scholarly knowledge surrounding the intervention and these practices, fundamental to AR, requires understanding these preconditions.

9.2 The Practice of Change

AR is concerned with generating scholarly knowledge through community-based and community-drive change. It is fundamentally empirical and cyclical, with action and intervention being crafted collaboratively by a democratic team and altered over time in response to emergent evidence.

AR requires researchers and community teams to take action and make change. However, change only happens through engaging people, doing, and everyday becoming in new ways. This reflection and careful consideration of everyday practice is also fundamental to a practice perspective, and a practice perspective is helpful in informing action researchers as they develop new theories based on their AR projects. "Action research aims at changing three things: practitioners' practices, their understandings of their practices, and the conditions in which they practice" (Kemmis 2009, p. 464). None of these practices are stable. AR therefore is and must be critical of the practices and self-critical of the research, change, and intervention around these practices. Action always follows planning and is followed by reflection and review, a cycle Schon (1983) dubbed "reflection-in-action."

Given the limited separation of research and practice in AR, this kind of reflection must consider not only the specific research questions initially posed and those that have evolved from the work but also questions of practice (Dachtera et al. 2014; Hayes 2014). The research team then must ask, what happened? How did the local practice emerge and change through their histories and the intervention? How did the materiality of the technology, the human bodies, and other artifacts involved contribute to the practices observed? What conflicts and politics surrounding the change influenced it, and in what ways did the action surface issues of power and motivation not previously seen?

The practice of doing AR, particularly as it relates to HCI, has been covered elsewhere (Hayes 2011, 2014). It is useful in the context of this book, however, to revisit these practices in light of a practice perspective.

9.2.1 Generation of Research Questions and Problem Statements

AR project teams, comprised of community members and researchers, collaboratively develop research questions and problem statements to launch a new project. Vision statements, typically the first step in this process, enable the AR team to ensure that all voices are heard and issues are named (Stringer 2007). Data, such as from surveys or interviews conducted by the community members, or knowledge from the research literature, can feed such statements, but the inherent expertise of the team in reflecting on their practices can be enough to generate initial visions as well. This is an interesting and important area of difference with respect to other practice-based approaches in HCI. For example, Wulf and colleagues (Müller et al. 2015; Weibert et al. 2015; Wulf et al. 2015) tend to investigate deeply the existing practices prior to developing an intervention, whereas in AR, the intervention itself is a tool for investigation into existing practices. Both are valuable ways to understand the context of potential use, and each allows the researchers to see things that could not be seen otherwise.

As our collaborations move further and further from our own scholarly domains, often into areas of professional practice rather than academic inquiry, it becomes likely that collaborators are not actually interested in traditional academic research questions. Thus, action researchers must learn to develop "research questions" that go beyond what might be publishable and include questions about practice, process, and outcomes of importance to the community partners. These often include questions of quality improvement or local program assessment (Hayes 2014). The pressures of publication, graduation, and even tenure review push against this kind of approach, however. If the HCI community broadly is truly to commit to approaches that take societal change, practices, and community participation at their hearts, it may be time for an open discussion of what is "publishable" work and how we might judge its quality.

A frequent next step for AR teams is to derive operational statements from vision statements. Much more so than vision statements, operational statements are inherently practice focused, as they tend to emphasize how the team members will work together, often in substantial detail (Stringer 2007). For a computing research team, operational statements might include lists of features that must be functional and usable in the resultant technology, but they will also likely include commitments from the community team to adjust policy to support the new technology, and so on. Ultimately, these are all issues of practice, and they are all emergent and likely to evolve throughout an AR project.

Once visions and commitments have been finalized, an AR team can move on to development of research questions and problem statements. It is here, perhaps, that practice theory can be particularly helpful. Given AR's emphasis on the lived experiences and conditions of the community, team members and those who will experience an intervention, drafting scholarly research questions that meet the community's needs can be daunting. Taking a practice perspective encourages us to organize the research around one or multiple practices, adapting and developing methods as needed to trace those practices. This approach can support a research team in limiting scope but brings with it its own, often challenging, new questions. One might then ask how to sample "practices" as the unit of analysis or how to make trade-offs between theoretical and pragmatic logics for choosing particular practices for emphasis. Indeed, one might ask even how we might ever expect to attempt to disentangle practices that are complexly interwoven.

AR has long struggled with these issues (McTaggart 1996). Ultimately, the AR project privileges community needs and interests but requires scholarly contribution. Pragmatically, this means following the lead of the community but with the insights and lenses of a researcher. Over time, a kind of instinct for these trade-offs may develop, but the challenges never disappear entirely. Indeed, with each new community and each new project, the question of which practices, voices, and research questions become central emerges anew. Certainly, a part of this work is to redefine scholarship, an effort that has been happening in a variety of disciplines around community-based participatory research for quite some time. Likewise, the "practice turn" has required segments of the social sciences to reexamine their evaluation of scholarly work, as some argue needs to occur now in HCI and CSCW. However, AR draws our attention explicitly to issues beyond the measurement of scholarly rigor toward issues of community quality and impact. Researchers must think carefully about the coproduction of research questions, to ensure that they are not only doing high-quality academic scholarship but also ensuring that the questions answered are those that are important, meaningful, and impactful for the communities with whom they are working.

9.2.2 Action and Intervention

The cornerstone of an AR project is necessarily the action or, in parlance more familiar to some disciplines, intervention. AR may be concerned with the introduction of new practices or the introduction of a new tool (typically, a novel or innovative technology, in the case of HCI research) that is likely to alter practices. Rather than be an unfortunate side effect or something to be controlled and monitored, AR takes this change as fundamental. It is indeed the goal of the project in many ways. The scholarly knowledge to be generated in an AR project emerges from understanding of how practice is enacted in the face of the action of the project.

To measure, monitor, and understand this change in practice, researchers may combine microlevel, or "zoomed-in" research, with macrolevel, longitudinal, "zoomed-out" research (Nicolini 2013). Again, here, however, we see a slight difference between the requirements of the practice perspective and those of AR. While AR does allow for a "global" view that is long term or enables "transfer" or knowledge from one local case to another (Palen 2010; Hayes 2011), the emphasis is on the local and the now. Although practice theory is often more ambitious in scope, allowing for a true local–global view of a research project, there are examples of practice-based approaches (e.g., Wulf et al. 2015) that take a heavily local perspective. In these projects, as in most AR projects, the researchers can struggle to prepare local, highly contextualized insights for transferability to other related sites or to develop these insights more formally into theory.

9.2.3 Evaluation/Analysis

Evaluation, so central to academic practice, is neither a natural nor a neutral act. The practice of evaluation leads us to other key questions about the setting. Who evaluates? What is being evaluated? What power structures and decision processes led to this evaluation strategy? Evaluation is fundamentally then a value-laden *practice-assessing practice.* AR projects seek to ask and answer questions of interest to both the research community and community partners working on the project (Hayes 2014). Furthermore, AR seeks to "define outcomes in ends that are acceptable to stakeholders, rather than those whose degree of success may be measured against some set of fixed criteria" (Stringer 2007, p. 141). In this model, evaluation is carried out as a joint construction among all the participants. Stakeholder groups are encouraged to air all of their concerns, review data that have been collected about and for the project, resolve any issues they can, and prioritize a list of unresolved items (Guba and Lincoln 1989).

In terms of actually implementing an evaluation strategy, AR is inherently methods agnostic. Action researchers make use of a wide variety of qualitative and quantitative as well as elicitation- and non-elicitation-based methods. However, given the emphasis on local knowledge and change, research tools developed by practice theorists can be helpful for an AR project. As just two examples, discursive genre analysis (Orlikowski and Yates 1994, 2002) and the development of resourcing frameworks (Feldman and Quick 2009) support researchers in thinking clearly and carefully about practice in a way that lends itself to design and action.

Genre analysis focuses on understanding how "socially recognized types of communication actions" (Orlikowski and Yates 1994) produce, reproduce, and change discourse (Levina and Orlikowski 2009). Discursive genres, such as a community town hall or a team design meeting, set expectations for the roles the various participants might play, the timing and location of the communication, and the detailed procedures taking place during that occurrence of the genre (Orlikowski and Yates 2002). Inherently, these kinds of expectations invoke issues of power and accountability, making them relevant to AR in two key ways. First, the leader of an AR project should consider the genres of communication—and their relative familiarity or lack thereof to various participants—when organizing the project. For example, a team meeting that first takes place on a university campus will set a very different tone than one at a community center. The types of invitations and the format of presentation all similarly make an impact on the genre as perceived. Second, during analysis, action researchers must engage with the genres observed at various parts of the AR cycle. Through deep understanding of these communication acts and social templates, each cycle of intervention can be improved, and deep theoretical knowledge might be developed.

Participation, including the sharing of resources, in any community-based project is complex. Feldman and Quick define "resourcing" as a process of connection actions people take, resources they provide, and frameworks and social structured enabled, enacted, and "energized" by this process (Feldman and Quick 2009). In their particular example, Feldman and Quick engaged with the practices of "inclusive management" in city planning to understand the dynamic cycle through which actions, resources, and frameworks interact. Emerging from a combination of a practice perspective and a community-based research site focusing on community-led change, this approach to analysis lends itself well to AR. Again, like in discursive genre analysis, the use of practice in examinations of resourcing in an AR project should be twofold. First, an AR project brings resources in the form of physical and monetary capital as well as human capital and expertise, but an AR project requires resources of the community as well. Careful consideration of the practices around resourcing in the project will help the researchers to proceed ethically and produce higher-quality outcomes—both for the community and academically. Second, when examining the context of the AR project, both before it begins and throughout its cycles, resourcing can be a useful lens through which to see the actors, their needs and interests, and the constraints of the environment. Collectively, these insights can be essential for understanding the impact of the AR intervention and its potential for sustainable change.

Drawing from multiple disciplinary traditions and an assortment of methods can lead to disagreement in some projects, and the risk of "cherry-picking" theoretical and empirical approaches in others. Furthermore, the academic pressures of publishing can privilege certain evaluation approaches over others, even when the community members or the researchers themselves would prefer to use a different approach. In AR, our first duty is to the community with whom we are working. Thus, ensuring all perspectives are represented, even when this means compromising on the evaluation approach, must be a priority. A practice approach to this very struggle, however, can highlight the ways in which the practices around evaluation tell us about the community and context within which we are developing interventions. Likewise, a practice perspective can force researchers out of the comfort zone of published theories that can lead to "model monopoly" (Braten 1973), as the "experts" in an AR team can at times dominate discussion and decision-making.

In particular, a practice perspective can help researchers to be sensitive to the practices "on the ground" both before and after an intervention. The iterative cycle of evaluation and intervention, key to AR, requires careful comparison of the conditions before and after each cycle of intervention. By attending to the practices that existed before an intervention and the ways in which they change or disappear and new ones emerge, one can identify key mechanisms underlying the outcomes of the intervention.

Practice theory also allows for a reconceptualization and alternative study of axiomatic categories (Sandberg and Alvesson 2011). The focus then is on the development of theory through abduction (Weick 1989; Locke et al. 2008; Tavory and Timmermans 2013). Abductive reasoning allows for the discovery of a case in the data for which there is no explanation, the creation of an explanation for that case, and the identification of that case as something that can now be explained. This approach requires explicit engagement with one's own doubts and careful consideration of alternative practices and explanations (Latour 2005), all struggles inherent to the AR perspective.

Ultimately, whatever the evaluation and analysis methods used, AR retains a close tie to practice. These closes ties can be surfaced during analysis by including not only the inherent interest in practice that is "baked in" to the AR epistemology, but also the scholarly thinking inherent in practice theory.

9.2.4 Reporting Research Results

As a means for supporting full community inclusion, AR requires reporting of research results in a variety of venues, with a variety of authors. These materials might take the form of reports written—or presented orally or created through multimedia—for the local community or for practitioner-focused journals of that community. They may also take the form of scholarly works written by and for the traditional researchers on the team.

These reports serve multiple purposes in an AR project, and the acts of generating and presenting these reports are important practices in and of themselves, worthy of study. First, the practices surrounding report creation make space for the entire research team to collectively reflect on the actions they have taken, an important communicative genre (Orlikowski and Yates 1994) inherent in the AR approach. Second, these reports often serve to update local sponsors and gatekeepers (e.g., the board of a community nonprofit organization or elected officials) on the project's progress, the research outcomes, and the results of the action taken. In this style of report, the outcomes of most interest to the community often become focal, with more scholarly interests fading to the background. This kind of report, then, can reward key actors in the project—particularly nonacademic community members—who then have the opportunity to present their activities to a wider public. Reports written in lay terms provide a tangible resource for community partners to then share or adapt for other interested parties (e.g., funding agencies or donors). Finally, the act of making these reports, particularly when they require a variety of types of genre or media, can often shed light on the discourse practices and norms inherent in the organization serving as the community partner (Boczkowski and Orlikowski 2004).

Scholarly writing and academic papers may be more familiar to researchers than the kinds of local reports described above. With careful engagement, community members can be involved in this kind of writing as well. However, scholarly writing in an AR project, particularly one with a practice emphasis, may still be substantively different from other kinds of writing in the field. Here, practice theory again offers support to an AR researcher struggling to report findings in a way that is accessible and informative while making a scholarly contribution. Latour (2005) and Langley and Abdallah (2011) encourage authors to analyze data and present theory by writing out detailed vignettes of evocative examples of practice to reveal and show the underlying dynamic of mutual constitution (Langley and Abdallah 2011; Latour 2005). In an AR project, these vignettes might include information from before, during, or after the action, as all are relevant in consideration of cycles of planning, action, and impact. From these vignettes, one can then model and theorize about the relationships among actors in the setting or between actors and the action taken (Feldman and Orlikowski 2011).

9.2.5 Ensuring Sustainability of Change

AR is concerned with the generation of theory through the creation of change. What sometimes goes unsaid here, however, is that the generation of theory feeds the change, not just the other way around. Well-developed theory should make change sustainable, and sustainable change should make for well-developed theory. Hence, the fundamental nature of AR is cyclical. To create sustainable change, AR teams must engage the world at the level of practice. Thus, a practice perspective is fundamental to AR. The goal is to tweak practices, from the ground up, in a way that enables them to stabilize while helping the researchers to understand the practices, the change, and the means for their stabilization and sustainability.

9.3 AR Views of Practice

AR typically comes in one of three types (Grundy 1988): technical, practical, or critical. Each of these types has a different relationship to practice (Kemmis 2009), as I explore below.

Technical AR (sometimes also called scientific–technical AR) is most often seen in the natural and physical sciences and in engineering. Thus, in some ways, it is a natural fit for computing research. In these domains, truth tends to be thought of as knowable and measurable, with scholarly knowledge intended to be generalizable. In this case, the scientist may take on a stronger leadership role, leaning on the expertise of scientific theory, within the AR project team. Practice, then, is a means to an end. The end goal is to improve outcomes, often on the basis of a preexisting scientific theory. The practice of AR in this case is the way to make those outcomes better, and considerations of the practices surrounding those outcomes are focused on these preexisting theories and the evidence in support of or against them, based on the experience of the intervention.

Practical AR, on the other hand, often called deliberative AR, focuses on the idea that because social realities constantly evolve, they are less knowable, in a positivist sense than the domains addressed by technical AR. Practical AR takes seriously the evolution and definition of reality within a particular situation and surrounding a set of stakeholders. In this case, practitioners often lead or co-lead the research team or, indeed, may be in the process of transitioning out of professional practice and into academia. Practitioners in these projects aim to understand the ends themselves. Are the methods of measuring these outcomes appropriate and just? Are these even the right outcomes to measure in the first place? The majority of my own work has fallen into this category, with projects focused on both improving conditions for the people involved and understanding the larger social phenomena surrounding the projects. For example, in our work with preterm infants (Tang et al. 2012; Hayes et al. 2014), we worked closely with community health partners and parents of children who had been born prematurely, to develop a technological intervention, in the form of a system known as Estrellita, to support the community health workers and the mothers they support. However, from a scholarly standpoint, we were also interested in understanding how patient-generated data is and might be incorporated into clinical workflows (Cheng et al. 2014), the ways in which parents understand health data about themselves and their children (Hayes et al. 2014), and the design constraints and opportunities inherent in this space (Tang et. al. 2012).

Finally, in critical—or emancipatory—AR, the goal is often major disruption of social structure. This approach requires mutual understanding and shared solutions development. Emancipatory AR promotes consciousness raising and criticality, which in turn seek to empower community members to identify and rise up against problems they may not have identified on their own. The role then of the researcher in these projects is often to highlight either practices or mediating preconditions that are in some way unjust or unsustainable. Discursively unsustainable practices tend to originate from irrational thought or to be built on bad data, issues that researchers from the outside can often see more easily than those within. Morally and socially unsustainable practices exclude people in ways that corrode society. Ecologically, materially, and economically unsustainable practices use up too much of the local resources to carry on. Finally, personally unsustainable practices risk harm and suffering or overuse the human resources of time, knowledge, skills, and so on (Kemmis 2009).

9.4 The Evolution of Practice

Practices may be stable, but they are never static. AR is concerned with the evolution of practice in response to explicit intervention, but even AR projects come to a close when funding runs out, students move on, or a relationship turns sour. How then, do we reconcile a world in which the goal is not to reach an end point or to develop a product? This is inherently a practice-based question. Researchers taking a practice perspective can never truly be "done" and thus have much to say to help action researchers who may struggle with the ethical, scientific, and pragmatic challenges of leaving an engagement. AR, at the same time, can push practice theory further, as AR is fundamentally a research practice for assessing, changing, understanding, and developing practice.

The "doing" of any research approach is a practice. In the case of AR, it is a "practice-changing practice" (Kemmis 2009). Like other forms of scholarly research, AR is also a *practice-understanding* practice, one that is focused on the generation of scholarly knowledge. The definition of what constitutes scholarly knowledge in practice-based HCI or in AR within HCI is, to some degree, emergent and changing. Thus, AR is a practice that shapes other practices—what Kemmis calls a "meta-practice."

AR has at its heart the idea that practitioners can, will, and, indeed, *must* become researchers (and therefore theorists). Their expertise lies in their knowledge—often tacit—of practice. AR works best when the practitioners are ready, willing, and able to take on the whole project, by the end, without the professionally trained researchers on their team. Thus, AR is also a *practice-developing practice*, in which practitioners develop new skills, knowledge, and practices around the creation and testing of scientific theory. As one example, in a participatory research project focused on supporting mothers of preterm infants, nurses and case managers worked with us both to develop research questions and protocols and to develop clinical care protocols around using the system (Hayes et al. 2014). In particular, one nurse developed a series of practices around checking the system, providing clinical care, and then hypothesizing about system use in a way that led to scholarly insights. In this way, not only did she develop new skills for working with this kind of clinical data and for working with research data, but she also developed new scholarly knowledge. As an additional example of the development of new practices, in an AR project focused on working with special-education teachers to use technology to support behavior management in their classrooms (Hayes et al. 2008), we worked with one classroom teacher to ensure that the system could continue to be used even after the research project ended. Not only did she develop new academic research practices through her engagement with the project but also, because of the limited IT support available, she developed new IT support practices of her own, following the end of the project. As a final example, we worked with a community partner, initially on a classroom system for children with autism (Hirano et al. 2010) and then an augmented reality system for children with social-skills challenges (Escobedo et al. 2012). Over time, she began to develop her own research questions beyond those we codeveloped in our collaborative projects. This ultimately led to her choosing to leave her career in the K–12 school system to pursue a PhD. Her research and scholarly thinking had developed so strongly that she wanted to engage these pursuits full time.

Although practice theory and AR are both relatively new to HCI research (Palen 2010; Hayes 2011; Light et al. 2011; Hayes 2014; Kuutti and Bannon 2014; Wulf et al. 2015), they are both relevant and useful to empirical, theoretical, and design-based HCI work. By explicitly engaging a practice perspective in AR, we can understand why AR is so powerful, compared to other forms of intervention. AR interventions engage at the level of daily practice. When we do not do this, we often fail in our designs, our interventions, and/or our development of scholarly knowledge.

At the same time, a practice perspective helps action researchers—and designers—to reorient themselves in relation to their definition of success. For AR, success is twofold: the creation of an intervention or change that improves the current state, and the development of scholarly knowledge related to that change (McTaggart 1996). Too often in traditional HCI projects, success is defined by the use, enjoyment, or adoption of a new piece of technology. This paradigm keeps us from understanding how and why some designs fail. Failed designs rarely get published. Both AR and practice theory, however, take a failed design as a stepping point from which one can develop important new scholarship that understands the practices the technology failed to fit (or alter) and from which one might conceive of new designs as part of a cycle of development, practice, and understanding. Success might not be people doing what we ask, following our designs, or using tools the way we think they should. Instead, in this paradigm, success may well be in understanding how things do or do not fit into everyday practice, how people appropriate or abandon tools, and how practices evolve around those tools. This redefinition of success has implications for what we think of in terms of contributions and scholarly knowledge. As others have noted in other contexts, publication of negative results is rare, presenting a major problem for scholarly inquiry (Dickersin 1990; Dickersin and Min 1993; Fanelli 2011; Matosin et al. 2014). It is time for HCI to publish negative results, to understand these results, and to consider what we learn from them to be scholarly knowledge and significant contributions to the community.

9.5 Conclusion

Both AR and practice theory have important roles to play in HCI and CSCW. The focus on local solutions, the details of everyday living, and the inclusion of community partners enables a kind of design solution that other approaches often do not. AR and practice theory are not without their limitations, of course. However, by using a practice lens on AR, we can, in fact, reveal some of the opportunities and challenges associated with using the AR approach in HCI, as discussed in this chapter.

AR is inherently a practice-assessing practice. Before an AR project can launch, current practices must be identified, sampled, and assessed. The emphasis on change and improvement—whether driven by community concerns or scholarly literature—requires at least a minimal sense of what is to be changed or improved and how such change might be measured.

AR is also a practice-changing practice. This is perhaps the most readily obvious way in which AR engages practice. Scholarly knowledge in AR is developed *through* change. The change to practice might be direct or it might occur indirectly through the natural alteration of existing practices, and the emergence of new practices surrounding an intervention.

The requirement not just to change things but to do so in a way that generates new scholarly knowledge makes AR a practice-understanding practice. Beyond just assessment and measurement, understanding practices in an AR project requires the application of existing theory or the development of new theoretical understandings surrounding the project. The change is meant not only to improve the setting in an equitable and socially responsible way for the community of practice but also to generate understanding for the academic community.

Finally, AR often requires community members to develop new scientific practices and academics to develop new community-organization and relationship-building practices. Thus, AR is also a practice-developing practice. Sustainable change is only possible through the development of new capacity in the community around the change. It is not sufficient merely to produce and deliver a piece of technology as requested by or codesigned with the community. The human resources and expertise needed to sustain that change after the researchers leave require the development of new practices within the community.

In summary, practice theory and AR go hand in hand. The logic of practice is fundamental to AR. At the same time, these scholarly traditions provide an inclusive and equitable approach to technology design that would well serve the HCI, CSCW, and larger computing communities.

References

Baskerville, R., and Pries-Heje, J. 1999. "Grounded action research: A method for understanding IT in practice." *Accounting, Management and Information Technology* 9 (1): 1–23.

Bjerknes, G., and Bratteteig, T. 1995. "User participation and democracy: A discussion of Scandinavian research on system development." *Scandinavian Journal of Information Systems* 7 (1): 1.

Boczkowski, P. J., and Orlikowski, W. J. 2004. "Organizational discourse and new media: A practice perspective." In D. Grand, C. Hardy, C. Oswick, and L. Putman, eds., *The SAGE Handbook of Organizational Discourse*. London: Sage, 359–77.

Bourdieu, P. 1977. *Outline of a Theory of Practice*. Vol. 16. Cambridge: Cambridge University Press.

Bourdieu, P. 1990. *The Logic of Practice*. Redwood City: Stanford University Press.

Braten, S. 1973. "Model monopoly and communication: Systems theoretical notes on democratization." *Acta Sociologica* 16 (2): 98–107.

Cheng, K. G., Hayes, G. R., Hirano, S. H., Nagel, M. S., and Baker, D. 2014. "Challenges of integrating patient-centered data into clinical workflow for care of high-risk infants." *Personal and Ubiquitous Computing* 19 (1): 45–57.

Dachtera, J., Randall, D., and Wulf, V. 2014. "Research on research: Design research at the margins: Academia, industry and end-users." In *CHI'14*. New York: ACM, 713–22.

Dewey, J. 1976. *Essays on Logical Theory. 1902–1903*, ed. A. Boydston. Carbondale: Southern Illinois University Press.

Dewey J. (1927) 1991. *The Public and Its Problems*. Athens, OH: Ohio University Press.

Dickersin, K. 1990. "The existence of publication bias and risk factors for its occurrence." *JAMA* 263(10): 1385–9.

Dickersin, K., and Min, Y. I. 1993. "Publication bias: The problem that won't go away." *Annals of the New York Academy of Sciences* 703 (1): 135–48.

Escobedo, L., Nguyen, D. H., Boyd, L. A., Hirano, S. H., Rangel, A., Garcia, D., Tentori, M., and Hayes, G. R. 2012. "MOSOCO: A mobile assistive tool to support children with autism practicing social skills in real-life situations." In *CHI'12*. New York: ACM, 2589–98.

Fanelli, D. 2011. "Negative results are disappearing from most disciplines and countries." *Scientometrics* 90 (3): 891–904.

Feldman, M. S., and Orlikowski, W. J. 2011. "Theorizing practice and practicing theory." *Organization Science* 22 (5): 1240–53.

Feldman, M. S., and Quick, K. S. 2009. "Generating resources and energizing frameworks through inclusive public management." *International Public Management Journal* 12 (2): 137–71.

Feldman, M. S., and Worline, M. 2016. "The practicality of practice theory." *Academy of Management Learning and Education* 15 (2): 304–24.

Foth, M., and Axup, J. 2006. "Participatory design and action research: Identical twins or synergetic pair?" In *PDC'06*. New York: ACM, 93–6.

Greenbaum, J., and Kyng, M. (eds.). 1992. *Design at Work: Cooperative Design of Computer Systems*. Hillsdale, NJ: Lawrence Erlbaum Associates.

Greenwood, D. J., and Levin, M. 2007. *Introduction to Action Research* (2nd edition). Thousand Oaks, CA: Sage.

Grundy, S. 1988. "Three modes of action research." In S. Kemmis and R. McTaggert, eds., *The Action Research Reader* (3rd edition). Geelong: Deakin University Press, 353–64.

Guba, E. G., and Lincoln, Y. S. 1989. "Judging the quality of fourth generation evaluation." In *Fourth Generation Evaluation*,. Newbury Park, CA: Sage, 228–51.

Hayes, G. R. 2011. "The relationship of action research to human-computer interaction." *ACM Transactions on Computer-Human Interaction*, 18(3): 15.

Hayes, G. R. 2014. "Knowing by doing: Action research as an approach to HCI. In J. S. Olson and W. A. Kellogg, eds., *Ways of Knowing in HCI*. New York: Springer, 49–68.

Hayes, G. R., Cheng, K. G., Hirano, S. H., Tang, K. P., Nagel, M. S., and Baker, D. E. 2014. "Estrellita: A mobile capture and access tool for the support of preterm infants and their caregivers." *ACM Transactions on Computer-Human Interaction* 21 (3): 19.

Hayes, G. R., Gardere, L., Abowd, G. D., and Truong, K. N. 2008. "CareLog: A selective archiving tool for behavior management in schools." In *CHI'08*. New York: ACM, 685–94.

Hirano, S., Yeganyan, M., Marcu, G., Nguyen, D., Boyd, L. A., and Hayes, G. R. 2010. "vSked: Evaluation of a system to support classroom activities for children with autism." In *CHI'10*. New York: ACM, 1633–42.

James, W. 1948. *Essays in Pragmatism*. New York: Hafner.

Kemmis, S. 2009. "Action research as a practice based practice." *Educational Action Research* 17 (3): 463–74.

Kemmis, S., and Smith, T. (eds.). 2007. *Enabling Praxis: Challenges for Education*. Rotterdam: Sense.

Kuutti, K., and Bannon, L. J. 2014. "The turn to practice in HCI: Towards a research agenda." In *CHI'14*. New York: ACM, 3543–52.

Langley, A., and Abdallah, C. 2011. "Templates and turns in qualitative studies of strategy and management." In D. D. Bergh, and D. J. Ketchen, eds., *Building Methodological Bridges*. Research Methodology in Strategy and Management. Vol. 6. Bingley: Emerald Group Publishing, 201–35.

Latour, B. 2005. *Reassembling the Social: An Introduction to Actor-Network-Theory*. Oxford: Oxford University Press.

Levina, N., and Orlikowski, W. J. 2009. "Understanding shifting power relations within and across organizations: A critical genre analysis." *Academy of Management Journal* 52 (4): 672–703.

Lewin, K. 1946. "Action research and minority problems." *Journal of Social Issues* 2 (4): 34–46.

Lewin, K. 1948. *Resolving Social Conflicts*. New York: Harper.

Light, A., Egglestone, P., Wakeford, T., and Rogers, J. 2011. "Participant making: Bridging the gulf between community knowledge and academic research." *The Journal of Community Informatics* 7 (3).

Locke, K., Golden-Biddle, K., and Feldman, M. S. 2008. "Perspective-making doubt generative: Rethinking the role of doubt in the research process." *Organization Science* 19 (6): 907–18.

Matosin, N., Frank, E., Engel, M., Lum, J. S., and Newell, K. A. 2014. "Negativity towards negative results: A discussion of the disconnect between scientific worth and scientific culture." *Disease Models and Mechanisms* 7(2): 171–3.

McTaggart, R. 1996. "Issues for participatory action researchers." In O. Zuber-Skerritt, ed., *New Directions in Action Research*. London: Falmer Press, 243–56.

Miettinen, R., Samra-Fredericks, D., and Yanow, D. 2009. "Re-turn to practice: An introductory essay." *Organization Studies* 30 (12): 1309–27.

Müller, C., Hornung, D., Hamm, T., and Wulf, V. 2015. "Practice-based design of a neighborhood portal: Focusing on elderly tenants in a city quarter living lab." In *CHI'15*. New York: ACM, 2295–304.

Muller, M. J. 2003. "Participatory design: The third space in HCI." In A. Sears and J. A. Jacko, eds., *Human-Computer Interaction*. Boca Raton: CRC Press, 165–85.

Nicolini, D. 2013. *Practice Theory, Work, and Organization: An Introduction*. Oxford: Oxford University Press.

Orlikowski, W. J. and Yates, J. 1994. "Genre repertoire: The structuring of communicative practices in organizations." *Administrative Science Quarterly* 39 (4): 541–74.

Orlikowski, W. J. and Yates, J. 2002. "It's about time: Temporal structuring in organizations." *Organization Science* 13 (6): 684–700.

Rapoport, R. 1970. "Three dilemmas in action research." *Stronger Families Learning Exchange Bulleting* 23 (6): 499–513.

Sandberg, J., and Alvesson, M. 2011. "Ways of constructing research questions: Gap-spotting or problematization?" *Organization* 18 (1): 23–44.

Schatzki, T. R. 2012. "A primer on practices." In J. Higgs, R. Barnett, S. Billett, M. Hutchings, and F. Trede, eds., *Practice-Based Education*. Rotterdam: Sense, 13–26.

Schatzki, T. 1996. *Social Practices: A Wittgensteinian Approach to Human Activity and the Social*. New York: Cambridge University Press.

Schatzki, T. 2002. *The Site of the Social: A Philosophical Account of the Constitution of Social Life and Change*. University Park, PA: University of Pennsylvania Press.

Schon, D. A. 1983. *The Reflective Practitioner: How Professionals Think in Action*. New York: Basic Books.

Stringer, E. T. 2007. *Action Research*. Newbury Park, CA: Sage.

Tang, K. P., Hirano, S. H., Cheng, K. C., and Hayes, G. R. 2012. "Balancing caregiver and clinician needs in a mobile health informatics tool for preterm infants." In *PERVASIVE HEALTH'12*. Piscataway: IEEE, 1–8.

Tavory, I., and Timmermans, S. 2013. "A pragmatist approach to causality in ethnography." *American Journal of Sociology* 119 (3): 682–714.

Weibert, A., Aal, K., von Rekowski, T., and Wulf, V. 2015. "'Hey, can we make that, please?': Upon craft as a means for cross-cultural community-building." *The Journal of Community Informatics* 11 (2).

Weick, K. E. 1989. "Theory construction as disciplined imagination." *Academy of Management Review* 14 (4): 516–31.

Wulf, V., Müller, C., Pipek, V., Randall, D., Rohde, M., and Stevens, G. 2015. "Practice-based computing: Empirically grounded conceptualizations derived from design case studies." In V. Wulf, K. Schmidt, and D. Randall, eds., *Designing Socially Embedded Technologies in the Real-World.* London: Springer-Verlag London, 111–50.

Wulf, V., Schmidt, K., and Randall, D. 2015. *Designing Socially Embedded Technologies in the Real-World.* London: Springer-Verlag London.

10 PRAXLABS

A Sustainable Framework for User-Centered Information and Communication Technology Development—Cultivating Research Experiences from Living Labs in the Home

CORINNA OGONOWSKI, TIMO JAKOBI, CLAUDIA MÜLLER, AND JAN HESS

10.1 Researching the Home

During the 1980s, the home became a prominent field for research of human-computer interaction (HCI). Empirical work, especially ethnographically oriented methods like observation, was applied to the understanding of certain aspects of the role of technology within home life. TV and video, especially, played a major role as a focus of research activities. Lull, for example, investigated the social use of TV within families (Lull 1990). With the mass adaptation of PC technologies since the mid-1990s, plenty of new research interests became visible. New devices like interactive TV sets changed the way services were used and also influenced usage practices, for example, those related to an early set-top box trial (O'Brien et al. 1999) or the usage of new services for communication and individual media consumption (e.g., streaming providers like Netflix) on a variety of different devices such as smartphones and tablet PCs (Hess et al. 2012a). Nowadays, smart-home devices, and wearables with smart functions, are further shaping the consumer market and household practices. New devices will continue to impact on usage practices in the long run. Hence, researchers in computer-supported cooperative work and HCI have investigated different dimensions of the home ecosystem.

Socio-Informatics, Volker Wulf, Volkmar Pipek, Dave Randall, Markus Rohde, Kjeld Schmidt, Gunnar Stevens (Eds). Published 2018 by Oxford University Press.

A variety of empirical research work focuses on different aspects of how technology is used and managed within families, for example, computer help at home or technical support (Poole 2012), home networking (Grinter et al. 2009), home automation (Brush et al. 2011), and research on the routine nature of communication (Crabtree and Rodden 2004).

To foster practice-based design in the home, the living lab approach has evolved in the last years (Eriksson et al. 2005), comprising many different methods and tools applied during the diverse research phases. Ethnographic stances and action research-based methods are commonly used during the predesign phase in order to gain a better understanding of the practice contexts and for the construction of a common understanding of the design goals between design teams, end users, and other involved stakeholders (Müller et al. 2012a; Müller et al. 2015b; for an overview of participatory methods, see Muller 2001).

Another pivotal element of living labs is that design and development are informed by continuous feedback from (potential) customers and represented in the form of mock-ups and other intermediate design products that support ongoing negotiation processes between the design team, end-user and stakeholder groups (Ogonowski et al. 2013). To support such processes, self-documentation methods are widely used, for example, in the form of cultural probes (Gaver et al. 1999) or in variations such as playful and creative probes (Bernhaupt et al. 2008) and diary studies (Sohn et al. 2008).

Evaluation of designed products is another important element of living labs. In the ideal case, prototypes are given to households as early as possible, to learn how technology is being appropriated in the real social-practice environment (Stevens et al. 2009).

Methodologically speaking, many different methods are being used to gain empirical insights, often in the form of a mixture of interviews, workshops, observation studies, usability tests, and online questionnaires. However, the approaches of scholars working under the "umbrella" of the living lab approach vary considerably, often because their proximity to real practice contexts varies. Techniques for evaluating the use of IT artifacts in the home, and how such artifacts are appropriated, will be contingent on the degree to which the target group representatives' real-life circumstances are investigated. In addition, little has been done when using living lab approaches, thus far, to systemize research findings so as to build up a scientific corpus, for example, by a systematic comparative approach. That is why we suggest the PRAXLABS framework, one that addresses these shortcomings in living lab research. The PRAXLABS framework is part of a systematic approach to the generation of a scientific corpus of practice-based design work termed "grounded design" (see Chapter 1), which is, in turn, based on the design case study approach by Wulf et al. (2015).

In this chapter, we describe, compare, and analyze the participatory-design processes in three projects aiming at the development of new technologies for domestic contexts: a cross-platform entertainment concept, an energy management system, and an Internet platform aiming at supporting informal help for elderly adults in a local neighborhood. Each project entailed setting up a living lab and included user representatives as well as stakeholders (service providers, industry partners) in a long-term manner, to inform potential design solutions. We discuss the benefits and issues of living labs as an innovation infrastructure and research methodology by focusing on the question of how research experience can be made available in a more sustainable manner and strategically allow future projects to benefit from their predecessors.

In the form of the PRAXLABS framework, we bring our results together to provide a comparative ananlysis of the three differnt living labs studies. To create a systematic understanding of design case studies in living lab environments we develop categories of experiences which may be transferred across living lab projects *within the home* and *across* the borders of the domestic application field.

10.2 Practice-Based Computing

10.2.1 From Participatory Design to Practice-Based Computing

Participatory design aims to involve different stakeholders in the development process to reach a more democratic design (Bjerknes and Bratteteig 1995) and—more generally—to develop software that will successfully be accepted by users. Applying the methods and tools of participatory design aims at fostering a software design process grounded, in some sense, in practice. Traditionally, work in participatory design addresses the context of the workplace (Bødker et al. 2004). Bødker et al. highlight the importance of a design that really is informed by the needs of actual users. Such process requires establishing a *mutual learning process* between designer and users (to address questions such as "What is needed?" and "What is possible?"). Instead of involving users as informants only, *genuine participation* results in a shared understanding of needs, problems, and options toward solutions (see Chapter 7 for a more detailed analysis).

Related to participatory design is the concept of infrastructuring (Pipek and Syrjänen 2006; Pipek and Wulf 2009). Infrastructuring refers to a design process informing the development of an "infrastructure in use" rather than purely focusing on the IT artifact itself. Such a process of infrastructuring needs to include knowledge about the context and the sociotechnical environment. Several aspects become important then, such as, how can the artifact support established practices of group work? How can new tools improve the work of a group and help it to be more successful? How can articulation work be managed more easily? To continuously improve the work environment, infrastructuring can be seen as an ongoing process, including and accompanying the adoption of artifacts and recognizing changes of practices. Thus, the activities of infrastructuring inform a continuous design schedule with respect to existing work culture, tools, and practices. "Points of infrastructure" become visible when infrastructure breakdowns occur and when (socio-) technical innovations are introduced (e.g., when new software is being installed or new practices are being established to support the processes of learning or adapting software).

With the wider distribution of new technologies, domestic contexts have come increasingly into focus for participatory design. In HCI, applying participatory design for the home has become equally popular, for example, in the contexts of home care, aging at home, family interactions around new media, and energy management and sustainability

(Crabtree and Rodden 2004; Palen and Aaløkke 2006). Several concepts have proven successful in providing for transferability from the work context to the home context, such as the design for social awareness (Crabtree et al. 2003), at least to a degree. However, other authors claim that interaction with new research domains beyond the workplace have revealed the need to acknowledge the unique demands of domestic technology appropriation and use. Rather than designing for efficiency and utilitarian pursuits, home technologies aim at fostering sociability, inclusion, and social awareness, thus calling for a taking into account of different underlying design aspects, like designing for recreational or ludic experiences (Gaver 2006).

Design case studies provide a way to structure and learn about practices in and through design (Wulf et al. 2015). Three main phases can be separated within this approach. During the pre-study phase, researchers seek to understand practices so as to then be able to frame a design space. During the technology phase, the design space is mapped onto technologies and transferred onto a design that is believed to address the identified practices. Finally, during the appropriation phase, research aims at understanding how the usage of newly introduced artifacts interferes and interacts in shaping practices. Design case studies thus provide grounds to address a certain context and look into the requirements and impact in close detail, while also affording a basis for comparison. Design and evaluation can take place in different field of practices. The findings can be used to learn how software is being adapted and to gain further insights on how the case (the design solution) might work in similar environments.

10.2.2 The Living-Lab Approach

In the past years, the term "living lab" and its methodological possibilities have attracted increasing attention within the research fields of information and communications technology (ICT) and HCI. The approach is broadly predicated on participatory-design philosophies and practices focusing on the involvement of users in design processes and shared understanding through mutual learning (Greenbaum and Kyng 1991; Kensing and Blomberg 1998; Bødker et al. 2004). According to Eriksson et al. (2005), the term "living lab" was created by Mitchell at the MIT Media Lab and was considered to be an instrument for the careful study of users and their interaction with new IT artifacts in real-life environments, and for longer periods of time. As such, it drew on early insights from product design (as shown by von Hippel 1978, 1986), where the focus was very much on providing a quasi-naturalistic but nevertheless controlled environment. Since then, and depending on the context, the research goal, and the stakeholders involved, the living lab approach has been used with varying emphases. Underpinning all approaches, however, is a common understanding of living labs as research methodology with a strong focus on user-centered research methods, that is, methods that can be applied in real-life environments for "sensing, prototyping, validating and refining complex solutions" (Eriksson et al. 2005). Accordingly, living labs can be also defined as infrastructures where different stakeholders from several sectors—the public, academia, the economy, and citizens—may interact in an open innovative process that takes real-use context (living environments, private households, urban and rural spaces, work environments, etc.)

into account (Niitamo et al. 2006; Almirall 2008). Over the time, four main characteristics have been established around this concept:[1]

- the exploration of user behavior in context, and of market conditions
- the co-creation process between users and designers
- experiments within scenarios
- the evaluation of products and services within real-life environments

Følstad (2008) also emphasizes similar characteristics in his comprehensive literature review. He identifies nine characteristics, four of which are valid for all labs analyzed:

- gaining insights in unexpected ICT uses and new service opportunities
- evaluating or validating new IT artifacts with users
- experiencing and experimenting with such solutions in contexts familiar to the users
- enabling middle- or long-term evaluations with users

In particular, the early and constant involvement of the users into the co-creation processes of IT artifacts is seen as an important characteristic of the approach (Schaffers et al. 2007). Long-term and sustainable collaboration thus enables capturing of both the ideas and the experiences of users in real-usage contexts. Whether this is achieved in practice is another matter and depends on methods chosen by researchers and their training. In this regard, it is important to note that there is no common understanding of the concept as a research framework, something that Schuurman and De Marez (2009) have pointed out.

Living labs with a focus on domestic or private sectors define the notion of a "real-use" environment in different ways. They either are collaborations with users in real-world testbeds or exist in controlled artificial environments within test centers. For example, MIT PlaceLab (Intille et al. 2005), Philips HomeLab (de Ruyter and Aarts 2004), the Georgia Institute of Technology (Abowd et al. 2002), and Fraunhofer Inhouse (Budweg et al. 2012) have conducted short- and medium-term evaluations in large-scale controlled artificial domestic settings by building "typical" apartments or houses in test centers and inviting participants for single-test or short-term studies over several hours or a couple of days. Here, researchers placed great emphasis on the layout of the lab to make "the environment aware of human activity" in the most supportive and least obstructive way (Abowd et al. 2002). In contrast, Bergvall-Kåreborn and Larsson (2008), Müller et al. (2015b), Wan et al. (2014), and Schuurman and De Marez (2009) conducted design studies and evaluations in natural everyday life contexts and collected in-situ feedback on user experience, usability aspects, technology acceptance, and appropriation processes in more longitudinal studies.

[1] See http://www.openlivinglabs.eu.

Our approach for researching domestic contexts is closer to the latter one, as we conduct long-term studies with households in naturalistic settings wherever possible. By collecting context-sensitive data, we seek to gain and contribute to an in-depth understanding of research issues, user groups, and their needs. Longitudinal field research holds, we suggest, a considerable if often unrealized potential for the progressive refinement of design concepts and the evaluation of the artifacts that result.

While living labs have become a common research tool, less work so far has addressed comparative research and reflections on meta- and conceptual levels (Frößler et al. 2007; Følstad 2008; Almirall and Wareham 2009; Hyysalo and Hakkarainen 2014). Ogonowski et al. (2013) for example, have reported varying characteristics in relation to duration and commitment of participants, the role of researchers, the degree of active involvement, and the amount of "structure" in a living lab study. Ley et al. (2015) have compared experiences from two living labs, one in Germany and in the UK, analyzing the dynamics of researcher-user interaction, issues of trust and managing expectations, and the role of mediators between stakeholders for successful research. Schuurman (2015) provides an analytical scheme for describing living labs at a more conceptual level. He extends Almirall and Wareham's (2009, 2011) two perspectives of analysis (macro- and micro-level) with a third one (mesolevel). The macrolevel perspective describes the living lab constellation and/or infrastructure. The living lab project itself, which is conducted on the backdrop of the provided infrastructure and/or constellation, can be described as being at the mesolevel. Single research activities and methods applied in the project can be labeled as being at the microlevel. Although living lab research typically is resource intensive, especially in terms of time spent in the field, we still know too little about whether such costs are associated with real benefits. Ways of making the living lab approach more effective are, we argue, needed.

10.2.3 Limitations of "Disposable" Living-Lab Projects

Given the increasing number of living lab research projects in the home context, it seems reasonable to look for ways of improving the effectiveness of this time-consuming and resource-intensive approach. At first sight, it seems tempting to look into ways of reducing workload and resource input in managing a single living lab project. Important questions arise, such as, for example, how can we gain users and project partners, and how can interactions be managed efficiently? But, in the case where living lab research is not understood as a one-time thing but as a strategic positioning of a research group, it makes sense to see the living lab as a research infrastructure for a series of (future) projects. This raises questions such as the following:

- How can findings be transferred form one project to another?
- How can methodological best practices and experiences be shared and spread effectively among stakeholders?
- What infrastructural places or hardware can be made second use of?

The three cases we describe illustrate the beneficial effects of the PRAXLABS infrastructural and methodological framework when conducting research in the wild. Through these cases, we compare the quality and validity of findings by looking at the transferability of data, concepts, and results within the home domain.

In this chapter, we discuss new ways of making research in the home a source of sustainable experiences. For example, where living lab research typically provides very rich contextual information about user interaction with technology in the home, the research typically also has an expiry date, when the project in question comes to an end. In our experience, at this stage, successful living lab research projects have often amassed an abundance of resources, experiences, and expert knowledge, both topical and methodological. In one-time "disposable" living lab research, the further use of these resources happens, if at all, in a rather disorganized fashion. Therefore, over time, we have come to shape a more systematic and sustained approach to the reuse of findings in living lab research, transcending the boundaries that otherwise exist. In the following, we outline our PRAXLABS approach by describing its infrastructural framework, which consists of a regional network of participants within domestic and industrial contexts; partners, such as companies and associations that have been involved in co-creation processes; locations and resources provided by stakeholders for user interaction and technologies; and devices and prototypes used for the research project in the field. The methodological framework contains a set of methods, experiences, and expertise for study design, as well as best practices for managing stakeholders and projects.

10.3 PRAXLABS: Creating Innovative Technologies in Practice

In previous work, we summarized lessons learned from different living lab studies (Ogonowski et al. 2013; Ley et al. 2014; Wan et al. 2014) and discussed how such insights might be transferred. Our research underwent a transition from single living lab projects to a more holistic and sustained approach. PRAXLABS constitutes an overall framework that basically aims to compare several design case studies, with an emphasis on the participation and co-creation of users in real-use contexts, over longer periods of time, and, at the same time, provides an infrastructural and methodological framework where several stakeholders can pursue their (common) interests.

Research experiences come from different long-term projects in the following topics:

- aging society
- social integration through ICT technologies
- entertainment and social media
- Internet of things and Industry 4.0
- safety-critical systems and crisis management

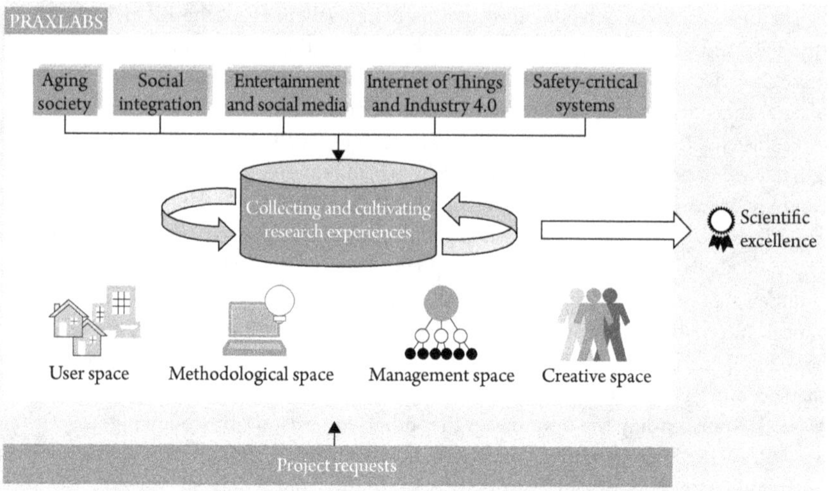

Figure 10.1 Generating and cultivating experiences in the methodological and infrastructural framework of the PRAXLABS approach

By bringing together these research experiences and transferring and cultivating living lab expertise, we found that there are four essential *spaces*, thus extending early definitions of the concept of space (Eriksson et al. 2005; Niitamo et al. 2006; Almirall 2008; Følstad 2008; see Figure 10.1):

- user space
- creative space
- methodological space
- management space

The *infrastructural* framework benefits from this kind of systematization in that a *user space* as a physical regional network of contacts evolves and is mapped in a central database with comprehensive information about potential users in private households. This data is supplemented by contact information regarding regional and national companies and associations that have been involved in co-creation processes or are interested in further cooperation. Having this database connected to a customer-relationship management (CRM) system and maintaining contacts helps to gain new users and further contacts, to select appropriate contacts (users, companies, associations) for new projects and to manage user studies more effectively. Therefore, communication with, and selection of, participants becomes more transparent to other researchers and project managers in the PRAXLABS team and affords communication between different projects. It also helps to reduce overhead in developing communication strategies by providing different established email templates for users according to their technical experience and their commitment to research activities, in order to enhance user participation in different project stages, and by handling technical problems and requests relating to field studies via an integrated ticketing system.

In addition, the user space is characterized by an established IT infrastructure that gradually develops with the projects. This IT infrastructure can be reused and makes it easier to set up new case studies and collaborations. Artifacts like sketches, wireframes, or prototypes can be reused as boundary objects in other settings, or at least at an early stage for informing stakeholders about the design space.

The *creative space* is the second component of PRAXLABS' infrastructural framework. It comprises several physical locations and resources, such as technical equipment, and material for stakeholder interactions. Such spaces were at first associated with academic facilities, like meeting rooms for participants and researchers to create ideas and discuss concepts. Several lab settings originally provided opportunities for usability tests in artificial environments and under controlled conditions. Over time, additional public and semipublic spaces became essential for co-creation processes. Creative spaces are not limited to physical meeting places; virtual platforms such as instant-messaging groups or forums integrated in a software prototype are additional fruitful sources of information and idea creation.

Regarding the *methodological* framework, experiences gained from several living lab projects, transferred and systematized in the PRAXLABS approach, revealed the existence of both a methodological space and a management space. In the *methodological space,* we bring together a selection of established qualitative and quantitative empirical as well as participatory-design methods. The entire design process is covered by our methods toolbox, starting with context studies, the identification of needs, the creation of ideas, and iterative design processes, and ending with long-term evaluations in participants' everyday life (see Figure 10.2). We thus use our extensive experience in user-centered design and reuse effective methods and processes (which are selected according to the research context, the target group, the participating stakeholders, and the outline design requirements of the project) within the creative space when carrying out design case studies.

The *management space* comprises experiences and best practices in coordinating stakeholders and projects. We found that, in living lab projects, successful collaboration could only be realized when the interests and needs of the different partners in the living lab, for example, companies, research institutes, public institutions, and users, were being analyzed and addressed adequately. Therefore, regular meetings and discussions before and during projects are essential. In addition, interdisciplinary projects have to deal with different terminologies. Consequently, mediators are indispensable, as they bridge gaps between stakeholder groups, translate information in a way that keeps individual work processes flowing, and manage any conflicts that may arise either within the consortium or regarding technical decisions or problems. In addition, in order to keep the motivation of participants at a high level and build trust, every project should have a constant contact person. From a management point of view, these are basic positions that every living lab project must fill.

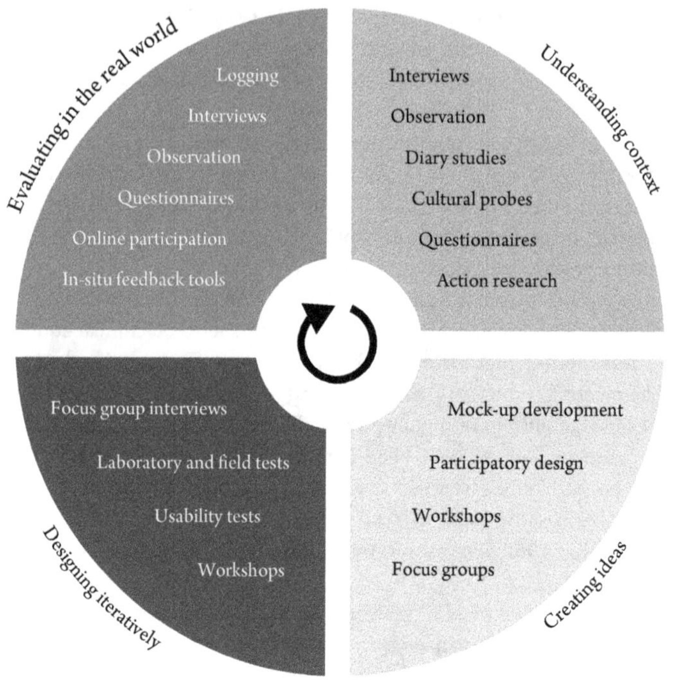

Figure 10.2 Methods and tools of the PRAXLABS approach

10.4 PRAXLABS Projects: Organizational Framing and Setting

In the following section, we outline three design case studies, demonstrating the setup and realization of living labs in domestic contexts. These will provide the basis on which we show the emergence and systematization of the PRAXLABS approach.

10.4.1 SocialMedia: Co-Creating a Cross-Platform Entertainment Concept

SocialMedia was a 4-year research project, running from 2009 till 2013, with a focus on designing multimedia content-related companion services for different stationary and mobile devices. In 2009, when the project started, TV content was primary available on TV sets, and interactive services, such as instant-messenger or social-media activities, were only available on Web-enabled devices like PCs, laptops, tablet PCs, and smartphones. By applying a user-centered design process, we investigated what a more flexible platform with community functionalities might look like. As well as two academic project partners, two industrial partners were involved in this project. One of them co-developed a TV interface, and another was responsible for a mobile application. Industrial partners had a strong interest in the investigation of new social-media technologies. The project focus—the development of a flexible cross-media platform—was seen as highly attractive, as it addressed further market needs. The interest of academic partners lay, as well as in the development of new concepts, in empirical user studies and the collaboration between different stakeholders in a living lab. The project was funded by national public resources.

With a strong focus on user-centered design processes, the project was framed as a local living lab project, where researchers, designers, and end users collaborated. As one of the first activities, participant households were recruited, to explore current media usage practices with state-of-the-art technology (Hess et al. 2011). The recruitment of participants started from scratch and was initiated by advertisements in local newspapers and radio stations. Interested households could apply to the project via an online form. The selection process was informed by initial telephone interviews, to get a better understanding of the households, their structure, their interest in participating in the study, and how self-reflective and communicative applicants were. Minimal requirements for participating in the study were a broadband connection, television reception, an interest in this topic, and willingness to participate actively in co-creation processes and test new prototypes at home, as well as being at a location that was close to the university, to allow regular meetings at the participants' home, and technical support if necessary. For the user sample, sixteen households with twenty-seven participants (fourteen males, thirteen females) were selected to work with a mixed household sample of four single and twelve multiperson households, the latter both with and without children (seven households with children, and five households without children). All participants contributed in different project stages of co-design, including creative workshops, mock-up reflections, user tests, long-term appropriation of prototypes at home, and redesign activities. Figure 10.3 provides an overview of the interventions used, in chronological order.

In this project, we made use of two different locations where interactions with participants could take place. The main research setting built the local test bed in the participants' homes. In this natural home setting, long-term studies of IT appropriation and daily routines were conducted (see Figure 10.4).

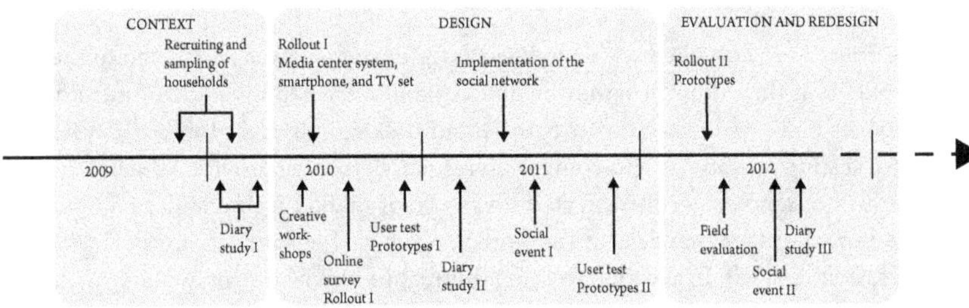

Figure 10.3 Progress of the SocialMedia project (above the timeline: interventions within the field; below: research methods)

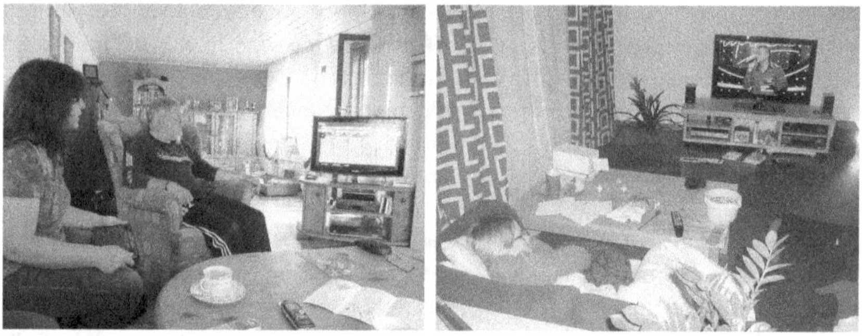

Figure 10.4 Insights into a household's everyday media consumption, self-documented by participants

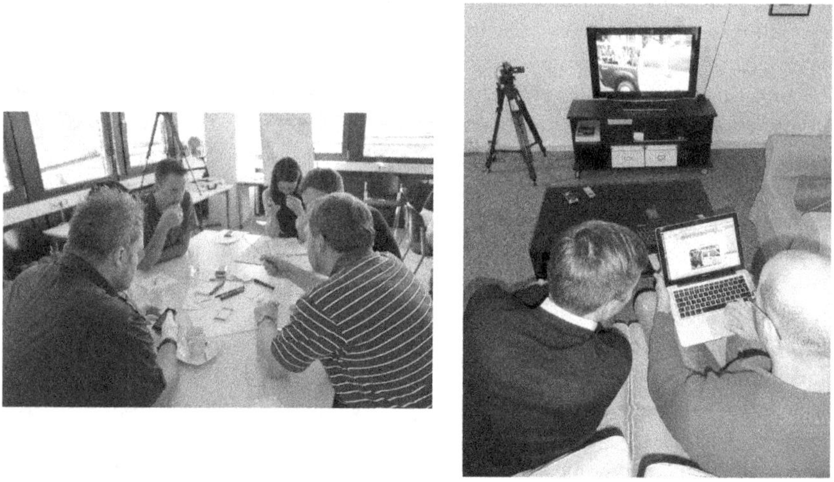

Figure 10.5 (*Left*) Creative workshop and (*right*) usability test, in the living room at the university

Households were equipped with a media center PC, which was connected to the TV set, an HDTV, if they did not have one already, and a smartphone with Android OS. These devices built the basic infrastructure in our user sample and provided a common ground for testing prototypes and comparing results. Before we provided the first prototypes to our households, we investigated how current market technologies and devices influenced media usage practices in the home and during leisure activities (Hess et al. 2011; Hess et al. 2012b). In addition to using this real-life environment, we also made use of an artificial home environment (see Figure 10.5). For this, two offices at the university were rebuilt to create a user-experience lab and were equipped like a living room. The technical setup was the same as the one we provided to the households. We used this physical infrastructure when conducting focus groups, workshops, and short-term evaluations, such as usability tests, for which we invited participants to our "living room" at the university (Hess et al. 2012a). This lab environment also functioned as a place for joint discussion between researchers and users. In early project phases, we discussed, for instance, PowerPoint mock-ups displayed on the TV screen, or paper prototypes for the mobile application.

The project contributed to the state of the art in a technological and empirical way. On the technological side, a cross-platform architecture was developed. TV/video content and related services could be accessed flexibly from different devices such as PCs, laptops, TVs, and smartphones. Services were dynamically implemented, so that the interface for messaging with "chat buddies" could be switched flexibly between the TV and the smartphone (e.g., when someone entered the room, so private conversations would not be shared with others on the "public" TV screen; see Figure 10.6; Hess et al. 2012b). Within the project, different use cases were designed (e.g., to explore scenarios for an interactive coffee table, usage of gesture control, event-based media rules, usage of an in-situ feedback tool, applying photo sharing with location-based references, and ad-hoc group building). During the design stages, privacy concerns came up in almost every discussion with the participants.

To get an in-depth understanding of media usage behavior and media-related challenges within households, long-term investigations with several on-site interviews, physical meetings, and face work with project staff members were undertaken (Ogonowski et al. 2013; Ley et al. 2015). We mainly, and quite deliberately, chose qualitative research methods. Accessing participants' private spaces demands trust relationships between participants, researchers, and other stakeholder groups. Investigating practices of media usage means studying behaviors in very private contexts. Therefore, we made use of self-documentation methods based on cultural probes (Gaver et al. 1999) containing media diaries and photo cameras. Participants were requested to document their watching behavior and media-related practices for 4 weeks before we started an intervention by rolling out new technical devices. The information gained, combined with feedback from the interviews, built the data corpus for our qualitative analysis and a detailed understanding of different usage practices at home (Hess et al. 2011, 2012a). The combination of diary studies and interviews helped participants to better reflect on daily routines and activities. After both technical interventions (Rollout I: current market technology; Rollout II: prototypes), diary studies and interviews were repeated to explore related behavior changes based on new technologies (Hess, Ley, Ogonowski, Reichling, et al. 2012; Ley et al. 2014).

During these project phases, the importance of having a central contact person for participating households, as well as regular informal meetings with participants, became visible. This kind of "artificial" community building—selecting households based on project interests of the consortium—had to be moderated (Ogonowski et al. 2013). For this purpose, we initiated a speed networking event, which allowed participants to get to know each other as well as staff members of the university; a summer BBQ; and, in winter, meetings at the Christmas market. Regarding the co-design process of prototypes, we also became aware that tools were needed to support spontaneous and context-related in-situ feedback. Participants normally used emails to get in contact with us, but a more structured

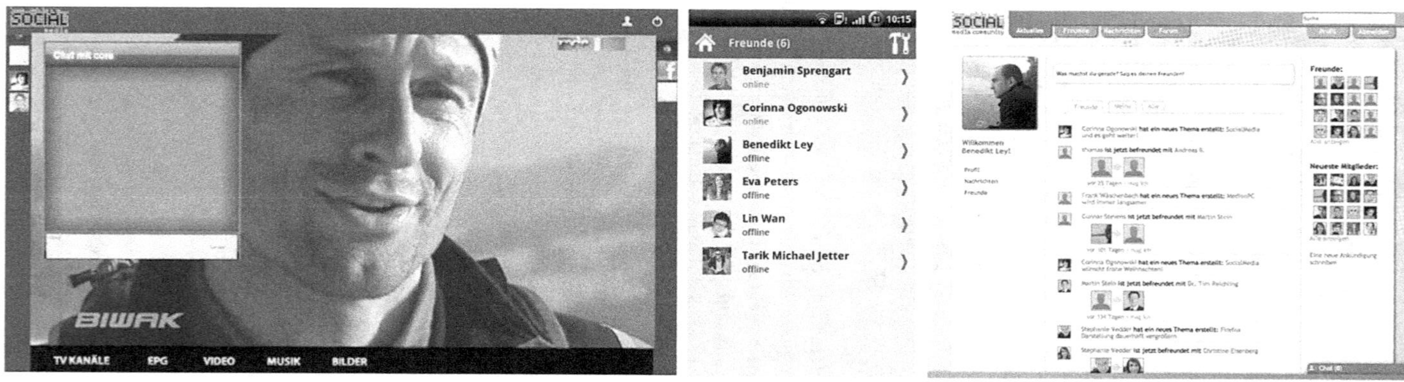

Figure 10.6 (*Left*) TV interface with displayed navigation bars and active chat window; (*middle*) mobile interface with buddy list; (*right*) Web interface

form was necessary. As a solution, we designed an app-based feedback tool that enabled participants to document problems, ideas, or bugs in-situ. In this app, feedback in the form of screenshots, which could be enriched by textual or auditory descriptions, was sent directly to a central repository. The corresponding back-end allowed us to categorize the feedback according to issues and then prioritize these issues for subsequent work packages (Hess, Wan, et al. 2012). The long-term relationship we had with these participating households has shown us how, in addition to technical tools and physical artifacts, social factors, such as having a trustworthy contact person, performing face work, and having informal meetings, are necessary for the success of such living lab projects.

10.4.2 Energy Monitoring: Designing for Energy Practices in the Long Term

Our 3-year energy monitoring (EMON) project started in 2009 as a spin-off from the SocialMedia project, as we found many of the participants in that project were interested in their energy consumption. With both energy demand and prices increasing, we recognized that there was a lack of any effective means (at that time) for consumers to monitor their own energy consumption. Interactive feedback systems are considered crucial for monitoring energy consumption (Burgess and Nye 2008) and have been researched extensively, with a large variety of design approaches mainly in the field of sustainable interaction design (Darby 2001; Mankoff et al. 2007; Fitzpatrick and Smith 2009; DiSalvo et al. 2010). The literature indicates that there can be a potential savings of between 5% and 15% for household energy consumption when such feedback systems are used (Darby 2001, 2006).

When we started the EMON project, however, we were among the first to extend rather simple feedback solutions such as "Kill-A-Watt" and Watt-Lite (Jönsson et al. 2010) to what later was coined a "home energy management system" or "home energy monitoring system" (HEMS), with such applications providing a rich variety of possible interactions and feedback information (Rossello-Busquet and Soler 2012). Our research focused on comparing visualization strategies for such holistic systems, as well as analyzing their long-term impacts on practices around and knowledge of energy consumption. However, we explicitly refrained from using a persuasive-technology lens, which most studies at this time used, as we wanted to understand the appropriation of these technologies into daily practice and its unforeseeable implications for design stemming from these processes (Certeau et al. 1980).

To address the complexity of HEMS use in real-life environments, we applied a living lab approach again. Having no further funding for an independent living lab, we benefited from the ongoing SocialMedia living lab, where we could rely on existing infrastructural and methodological features. Lacking funds, we decided to experiment with the dual use of a living lab participant sample. This relieved us of some of the acquisition work and especially from the need to set up a basic infrastructure for our research within the households. Making a virtue of necessity, we thus integrated our living lab approach into the existing and ongoing SocialMedia project. Although the advantages of this approach, for example, not having to acquire another set of households and their support, were

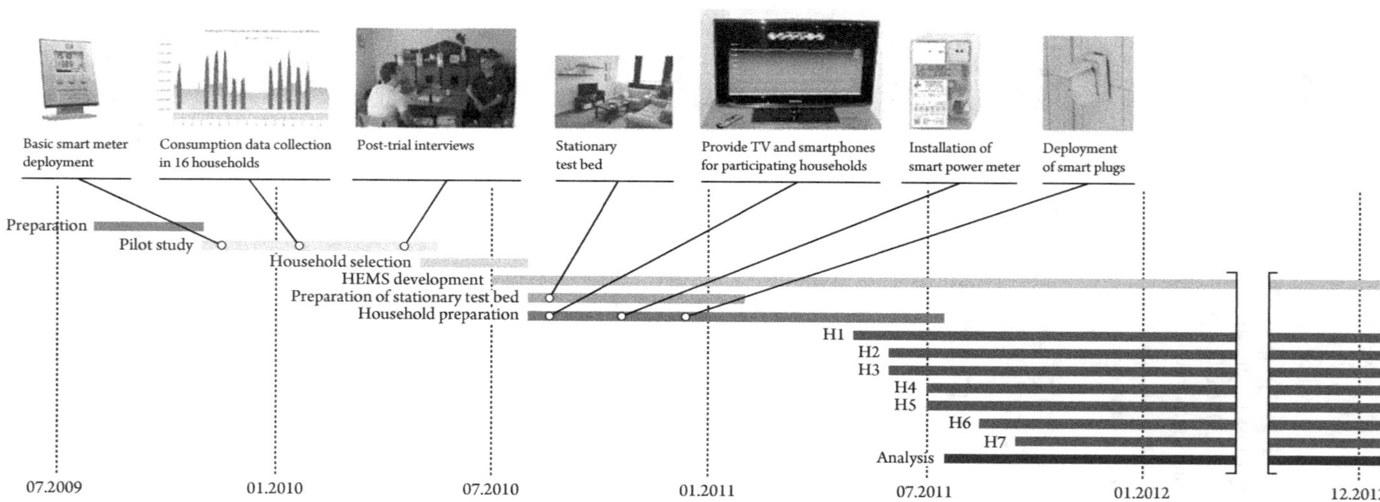

Figure 10.7 Timeline of the different phases of the EMON project

evident, we were also keen to see how households would manage being involved in both projects at the same time.

Figure 10.7 provides an overview of the different phases of the research project. Our acquisition of households therefore started with offering existing participants in the SocialMedia project the opportunity to take part in an energy-monitoring study. Applicants were asked to submit an online questionnaire with basic information concerning their households' infrastructure, their motivation for participation, and their expectations about the project. Additionally, telephone and on-site interviews and interviews with SocialMedia project managers helped in selecting a suitable sample. We ended up choosing a subsample of seven households with sixteen participants, based on the criteria of participants' household size, age, and previous knowledge about energy.

When setting up our research design, we also turned to the SocialMedia researchers, to gain experience about viable methodological choices. The ongoing active exchange covered reports on methods as well as technological or individual peculiarities and constraints; this approach worked well. This methodological expertise and detailed knowledge of the households supported us in choosing appropriately.

In the beginning, our questions centered on the households' initial management of electrical consumption and their attitudes toward resource consumption; we then shifted toward more detailed questions about HEMS use in the participants' daily life. Also, occasional workshops included more specific tasks, such as usability testing and design sessions. Overall, we audiotaped seventy interviews and thirty-four workshops, with a total length of over 200 hours. Several million data points on the energy consumption of households and appliances were gathered over a time span of 36 months.

Our overall approach to households was to introduce new technology and feedback mechanisms incrementally, through multiple rounds of prototyping and field research (Jakobi and Stevens 2013). When we analyze the 3 years of evaluation and development in the project, we can distinguish three main iterations. During this time, the system was a dynamic artifact exposed to continuous development of software and hardware interaction, with research focusing on middleware and especially front ends for desktop, smart TV, and mobile systems. After performing an exploratory interview regarding values in relation to, and understanding of, energy and its consumption for each household, we installed smart meters and a basic feedback device, which allowed users to see their current meter count and their overall household consumption. After letting households use the new features for a couple of weeks, we conducted reflection workshops with each participating household separately, to evaluate responses to this information provision, as well as limitations and emerging demands for better understanding of energy consumption at home. Conducting two further iterations, we successively enriched the energy-monitoring experience with more detailed appliance-based measurements and more nuanced feedback according to user demands explored in reflective workshops described above.

Our workshops typically were conducted in the respective participants' home (see Figure 10.8). This provided the advantage of being able to look over the participants' shoulders, so to speak, when the participants used energy feedback in their everyday environment. During these workshops, we discussed what people did with energy consumption,

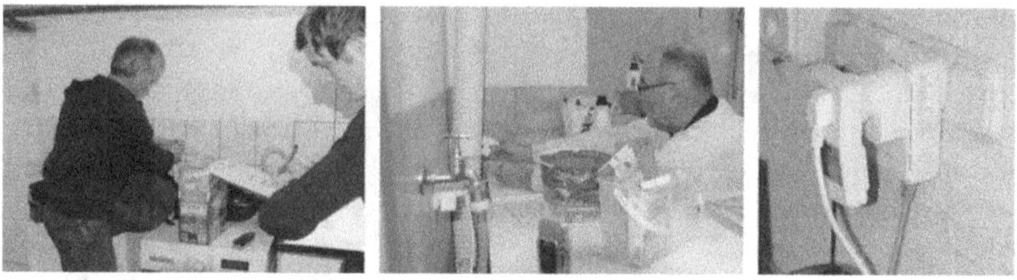

Figure 10.8 Workshops on bringing out appliance-based smart plugs in participating households

to link it with their reflections on what energy meant to them. Overall, users became much more specific in talking about their home energy usage as they learned more about technical features. By observing the development of individual energy practices and their evolution when using our HEMS system, we uncovered several practices for monitoring energy usage and then explicitly designed our front ends to support them:

- In our very first edition, we did not explicitly support mobile use. However, we found that users, while being very curious about energy consumption, were reluctant to use a TV or PC more than occasionally. In-situ feedback on mobile devices, therefore, was critical if HEMS were to impact on everyday practices. At the same time, larger-screen feedback was still important for cooperative reflections, so this was reflected in our choice to include the ability to provide more sophisticated feedback on larger-screen devices.
- We found that households distinguished between base consumption (e.g., the use of routers, phones, and fridges, which were regarded as necessary) and other consumption such as activity-related consumption, which, in principle, was regarded as negotiable.
- We added room- and person-based views on energy consumption, because participants wanted to understand consumption patterns in both ways.
- We added support for building collections of items as "activities"; for example, participants often referred to "watching TV" as a single activity, although it involved using multiple items, including a TV, a receiver, and rooms lights (to provide certain lighting conditions).
- We found that participants also wanted to share consumption information, albeit in limited ways, as open sharing of data carried with it moral implications, and individual participants were wary of being held to account.

Our prototype featured common key design elements related to the representation of data, spatial and temporal aggregation/disaggregation, historical and normative comparison, and the topic of motivation support (Schwartz, Denef, et al. 2013; Schwartz, Stevens, et al. 2013; Schwartz et al. 2014). In addition, we looked into opportunities for end-user development, for tailoring energy feedback to consumer demands (Jakobi and Schwartz 2012; Jakobi et al. 2013).

Since we were using a subsample of the SocialMedia group, we also decided to try to transfer best practices from SocialMedia's management space. For example, we designed EMON kickoff and closing workshops and kept in touch with participants on a regular basis via a single constant contact person. Typical mailings included not only information about activities but also Christmas greetings and acknowledgments of participants' birthdays. Within the project, participants demonstrated continued trust in the researchers and their competences. As with the SocialMedia project, this resulted in us becoming a help desk for, for example, router and general IT-related problems. However, we knew that these "off-topic" efforts were crucial for establishing an open relationship and, subsequently, being able to see and understand household practices. Additionally, this "extra mile" repaid on other levels, too. For example, we were allowed remote access to the households' computers to install software updates, thus making maintenance much more convenient.

During this project, it also became apparent that users had different degrees of flexibility and willingness to experiment with new features. Some technologically savvy participants were very keen on receiving updates as soon as possible and accepted errors as representing a trade-off for being able to test new features. Other participants, however, expected a running system at all times, so that new features and innovation had lower priority. Acknowledging these differences, we explicitly planned some workshops addressing the special capabilities of each user group. Also, keeping in touch with users and building a trustworthy relationship was a major concern, since reflections on energy consumption provided deep insights into the private sphere of participants, and a climate of productive yet open criticism needed to be established in order to get honest feedback regarding usability and requirements of households. Differences in interests and technical knowledge meant that participants adopted distinct roles during the project phases (Ogonowski et al. 2013).

10.4.3 The City-Quarter Living Lab: Development of a Neighborhood Platform for Elderly Tenants

The city-quarter living lab is a project aiming at research and development of ICT-based measures to support elderly tenants in maintaining an autonomous life (Müller et al. 2015b). The project partners include a local housing company, representatives of tenants from 144 dwellings, and a counseling agency that is an expert in participatory change management in housing, as well as HCI university researchers. A software development company is subcontracted to the university.

The aim of the 3-year project lies in the development of a sociotechnical infrastructure for the neighborhood, where the infrastructure contributes to supporting and maintaining information, communication, social interaction, and both formal and informal support. The objectives of the project are as follows:

- to provide support for the maintenance of existing informal support networks in the city quarter as well as enable new channels for communication and interaction

- to provide an interface between the housing company and tenants in order to examine ICT-based possibilities for the company to improve their mutual communication and interaction sphere
- to ensure that all tenants are capable of using the future sociotechnical infrastructure

The initial idea for the technical infrastructure was an Internet portal that could be accessed by both the tenants' individual devices, such as PCs or mobile devices, and displays located in the neighborhood. Consequently, the project involved a multitude of research and design activities:

- deploying a participatory-design process for the neighborhood portal, to align the interests of both end-user groups (i.e., the local tenants and the housing company)
- organizing the selection and decision-making process regarding the hardware and software to be purchased and installed
- setting up a sustainable learning environment for elderly, non-tech-savvy project participants

The housing complex is located in a middle-sized German city and consists of 10 three-story tenements with 144 predominantly small apartments containing 1–3 bedrooms each. The largest proportion of the inhabitants consists of elderly tenants over the age of 60, including both singles and couples. There are also some students from the nearby university, and a few families with young children. The living quarter is situated in one of the town's rather less desirable areas, where the socioeconomic status is predominantly low.

The analysis of this project is based on different sets of data and procedures (see Figure 10.9). The first phase consisted of several meetings and workshops between the housing company and the counselors to gain an understanding of their interests in technology design and future usage visions. Each meeting was documented in the form of

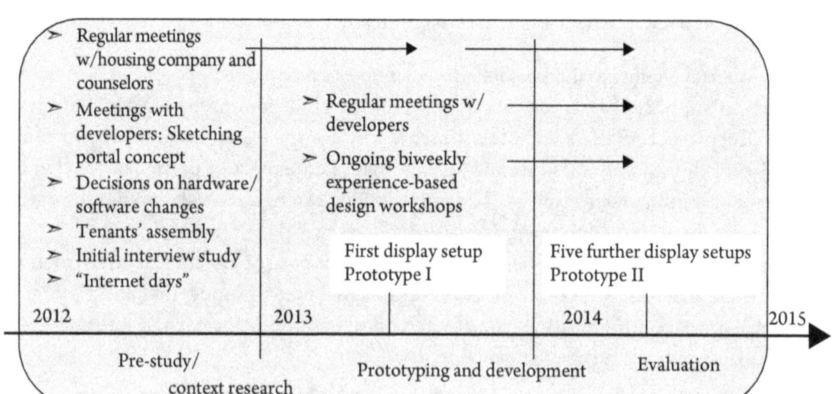

Figure 10.9 Overview of the project activities

common action plans and supplemented by field notes. During this phase, the researchers undertook research on technological components and provided them for discussion with the organizations.

The pre-study interviews focused on the interviewees' everyday lives in the city quarter, their social networks, and their interactions with their neighbors, as well as their attitudes toward and actual usage of new media. The interviews revealed that only a small number of the tenants aged 60+ were familiar with new media. In order to inform them about the possibilities of Internet usage and to provide a space for them to reflect on individual usage options in their individual and collective everyday lives, we started by organizing two "Internet days." These consisted of a 3–4 hour workshop format that we have described elsewhere (Müller, Neufeldt, et al. 2012). The activities and chats with some twenty tenants who accepted the invitation were documented in field notes and photographs.

During the second phase of the project, regular meetings with the organizational partners took place every 3–6 weeks and were conducted either in person or by telephone conferences subsequently complemented by field notes.

The interaction with the tenants intensified when they were offered a mobile device with corresponding introductory sessions from the researchers. We then distributed fifteen tablet PCs and five smart phones to interested tenants, of whom fifteen were 60–86 years old, with the rest being between 30 and 55. Linked to receiving a device was the invitation to join regular *experience-based participatory-design workshops* (Müller et al. 2015a) with the researchers in order to co-create the structure and contents of the neighborhood portal. The workshops were held biweekly and were documented by field notes and photographs. In mid-2013, a first portal prototype was launched, and one public display was set up for test purposes. In order to prepare the elderly, non-tech-savvy tenants to become co-developers, the workshops in the first 9 months served to establish a shared thinking space between developers and the elderly. For this purpose, the workshops at that time (and ongoing today) encompassed two essential features: delivery of the off-the-shelf technology, with support for individual and group-based appropriation, and engagement in concrete participatory-design sessions. The workshops were intended to provide inexperienced participants with a certain level of skills that would enable them to operate the technology in—for them—meaningful ways and to get over their initial skepticism, anxieties, and any negative self-images they had at the start of the project.

The workshops (see Figure 10.10) provided low-threshold activities in order to offer an open, welcoming space where anyone had the chance to form an opinion—on the basis of presentation of, and interaction with, off-the-shelf-technology. We see this as being a prerequisite for participants being able to develop individual sense-making processes around possible ICT usage in their everyday lives. The first steps within the project were to kindle an initial interest and only then to identify further steps to be taken. For the younger and tech-savvy group, we presupposed that they had sufficient knowledge of ICT to make informed decisions about their participation. More information on the concept of experience-based participatory-design workshops to for supporting ICT appropriation for elderly and non-tech affine persons can be found elsewhere (Müller et al. 2015a).

The evaluation of the first portal prototype and the public display happened simultaneously with the ongoing empirical work and requirements elicitation for prototype II. After that,

Figure 10.10 Workshop activities in the community center

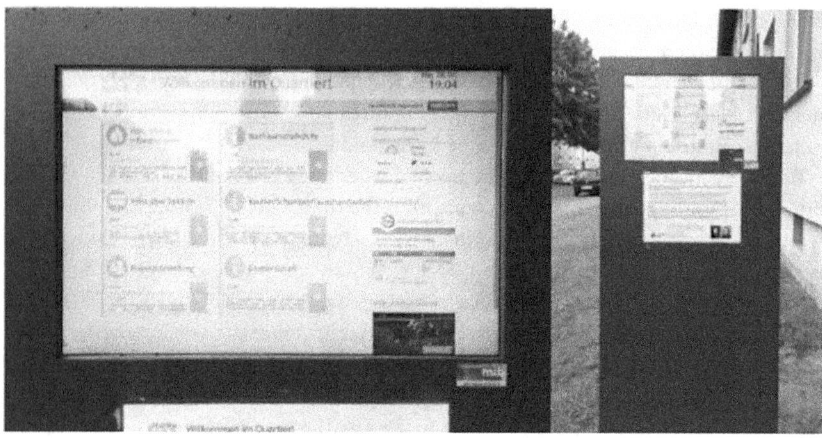

Figure 10.11 Outdoor display: (*left*) starting page for the neighborhood portal (Prototype II); (*right*) actual positioning of the outdoor display

five additional public displays were set up in front of other tenements, and a first version of prototype II has been launched recently (see Figure 10.11).

The division of the project into the three phases is not as strict as depicted in the figure, as all of the phases overlap to a certain degree. For example, the evaluation phase of prototype II and progressive refinements are ongoing. However, we expect only minor refinements to be needed, as the development was predicated on an intense data collection process. For the final months of the project, until spring 2016, a concept development for a sustainable structure after the end of the project has been mapped out in cooperation with the housing company.

The data analysis of interview transcripts and field notes was coupled with the iterative research and design process. The overall methodology combined elements from qualitative data analysis and action research (Hayes 2011; also see Chapter 9). From the beginning, project reflection, activities with stakeholders, and idea generation were framed by means of theoretical sampling regarding data collection, documentation, analysis, reflection, and further planning. The documentation mainly consisted of interview transcripts, field notes, and photos.

The visibility of activities in this project is different from that for the other living lab projects described in this chapter, as, in this project, there are different locations of activities in the public space. First, the workshops are being held in a community room in the quarter provided by the housing company, to support diverse community activities among the tenants. Second, the project is permanently visible in the city quarter, as it is represented by the outdoor monitors in front of the houses. Operating in this "life environment" encompasses certain problems and challenges. For example, the iterative and prototypical approach has led to there being nonworking monitors from time to time, which irritated the tenants and also the housing company, which was concerned about damage to its reputation. In addition, some of the tenants who did not interact with us in the workshops saw the nonworking monitors as project failures and thus lost the motivation to cooperate with us (Müller et al. 2015b).

Having such a high diversity in the target group in terms of age, technical affinity, and interest has also provided a significant challenge for the overall participatory-design approach. As the project was primarily devoted to supporting the elderly generation, we put a lot of effort into developing activities that would get the elderly tenants interested, motivated, and qualified to operate the technology and become co-designers. However, these activities were not very appealing for the younger tenants. For that reason, we had to change the pacing of the project structure, that is, we had to separate the tenant groups and integrated the younger tenants in the evaluation phase.

10.5 Insights into Developing a Sustainable PRAXLABS Concept

In all three living lab projects, artifacts were designed that addressed private households and thus were part of the same domain (i.e., design for the home). In the course of the three studies, we became aware of synergies that emerged, for example, by involving households in different projects or sharing knowledge on best practice. The EMON project, for example, evolved over time from the SocialMedia project, where both an existing user community and existing technical resources were available for reuse.

In this section, we will present our reflections on the user-oriented design process and discuss the unique advantages of using the living lab approach as a methodological framework for single studies in the domestic domain. We will then explicate PRAXLABS, a comparative framework for cultivating experiences and sharing resources.

As for any case study, living lab research faces the challenge of making collected data accessible to a broader research community. Typically, this process focuses on publishing and presenting the main aspects and insights of conducted research. However, some dimensions of experience from the practical project work are less often reported. From our point of view, these aspects may be valuable for subsequent research projects, for example, for tackling practical problems and providing hands-on experience. However, this implicit and accumulated knowledge and experience is seldom discussed explicitly. Although these experiences constitute core competencies for living lab work, they are seldom made available to others in a strategic, coordinated way. We call for more cross-border, practice-based, and critical reflections on the explicit and implicit results of design case studies. Below, we compare the projects presented in this chapter, with respect to how they relied upon and fueled the PRAXLABS pool of expertise, especially in terms of the four spaces that constitute PRAXLABS expertise. For living lab-based research, as for most qualitative studies, questions regarding the transferability of results—due to their strong contextuality—are important on both a methodological and a conceptual level. While it has proven to be the case that methodological practices across living labs can be easily transferred, the potential transferability of research findings and concepts needs elicitation.

10.5.1 Reusing Methodological Best Practices of Living Labs across Projects

On a methodological level, reuse of best practice is very important for choosing valid, reliable, and appropriate research tools. By holding regular meetings, researchers working on living lab projects can exchange thoughts, experiences, and best practices. Our research covers cases of projects that overlap with respect to duration and even homes examined, as in the case of SocialMedia and EMON. However, other instances of PRAXLABS research do not overlap at all. The three projects presented in this chapter, therefore, can provide insights into ways of setting up, running, and conducting research in living labs and the reuse of best practices by transferring them among living lab-based research projects, as Figure 10.12 shows.

Dealing with individual user samples, with their very special attributes, in one sense makes the research process a one-time experience every time. Therefore, no participatory-design process within a PRAXLABS project works in entirely the same way. Each project, application, and context brings up its very specific dependencies and challenges for successful co-design. However, over time, best practices of project maintenance and problem management emerge. We can identify recurring themes to watch out for in order to maintain a PRAXLABS project as an ecosystem for innovation. For example, within a living lab, communication is a key mechanism for paving the way for a successful research process. Finding appropriate and suitable ways of working out the tension between research interests, stakeholder interests, personal sympathies, and methodological

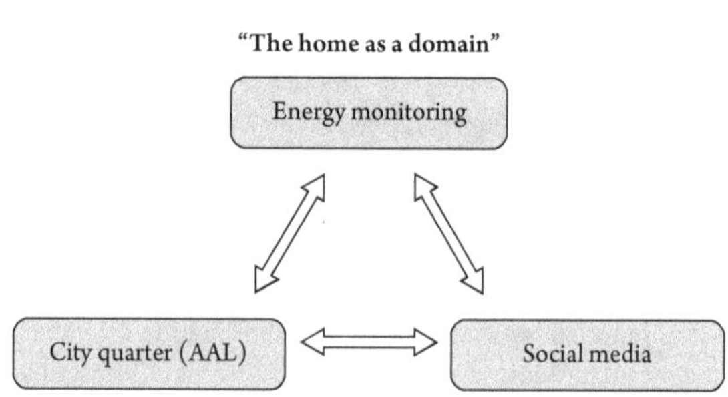

Figure 10.12 Transferring experiences within the home

necessities is time consuming and difficult. In the following subsections, we describe some of the more important factors for developing successful communication strategies, which can be externalized to a certain extent.

Management Space

Mediating among interests of the different stakeholders is an important characteristic of a living lab. Co-designing with (potential) users means much more then collecting requirements and building something that (hopefully) is subsequently appropriated in practice. Depending on the concrete project and the framing, it is often the time available that differentiates partners from academia, industry, and public service. Building a shared perspective on how best to proceed, over what time frame, and with what degree of commitment is one of the most challenging management tasks. Ideally, one might anticipate that agreements around these issues would already be in place in the initial planning phase of the project, but, for this to take place in practice, the subgoals of the partners need to be as concrete as possible (e.g., regarding potential business cases, for the industry partners, and scientific output, for the research partners). Partners also need to understand that, even in these circumstances, the interpretation of goals can be a flexible matter.

Interdisciplinary projects open up room for learning and innovation outside the group. What Fischer (1999) describes as "symmetry of ignorance," or "asymmetry of knowledge," is a reality often underestimated on the management level. When people from different organizations with different backgrounds and work cultures are working together on something new, it can be an opportunity to learn from each other's experience. That means such projects also need, through having regular meetings, to create an atmosphere in which it is possible to learn from each other, to ask the right questions, and also to react more flexibly, and need to transfer knowledge about contracts, available technological support, privacy statements, the timeline of interventions, and a whole host of other relevant matters.

Acquisition. Case study research in the home context may differ from research in the work context, for example, in how one enlists participants in a long-term project. In work-related projects it is often the case that companies are partners in a consortium and as such, the location of research is often predefined, as are the organizational hierarchies and prospective tasks of end users. Home-based living lab projects, in contrast, have first to define their target groups and then assess what might be required of them. In this context, questions of motivation and interest in a long-term engagement in the prospective target group are of high importance.

Further, work-related projects often deal with ICT development in the context of existing technologies in use, such as tools for office workers. This means that, in most cases, a common problem space already exists between target groups and researchers and that, besides this, the technical skills of end users are, in most cases, already there. In contrast, research in home-based contexts often has to deal with a high diversity of households in terms of shared understanding of problem spaces and research visions, as well as technical affinity. It is something of a challenge to find an adequate sample of households matching the criteria set up in the initial research plan, as this heterogeneity has to be dealt with. For example, posting a newspaper advertisement may result in a lot of reaction from interested local households, but this is only a precursor to the serious effort needed to assess the suitability of potential participants and negotiate understandings of the effort and time that may be required.

Sometimes, not enough households can be acquired. That may be because of the varying importance of the topics or also because of the different technologies users get to use. In that case, it has to be shown that contact persons from local associations can support acquisition processes as "door-openers" (Müller, Wan, et al., 2012). This was the case with the housing community research. Because users knew the research group from former projects, and the invitation was sent from a local organizer, several users came to the initial workshop and joined the new project.

Selection of households. It is important to respect specific needs and capabilities. Our experience indicates that it is necessary to have a variety of types of users in order to make up a good living lab sample. In the SocialMedia project, for example, different household structures were acquired, such as singles, couples, and families with kids. Users should be interested in new technologies but do not necessarily have to be "experts" in the domain, as it has proved valuable to involve both technically savvy and less technically savvy users (Ogonowski et al. 2013). More experienced users tolerate and understand technological failure or restrictions better but have more specific demands and ask for more innovative features. At the same time, these users can be intolerant of repeated testing of prototypes and instead seek innovative working solutions. On the other hand, less technologically savvy users are motivated by understanding and learning about technologies. These users, however, typically are not as specific in their need articulation. They expect basic functionalities that work without failures. Living lab projects should include a broad mix of these different types of actors. Additionally, research can be planned accordingly, such that different user subsets can be chosen specifically to deal with different topics of varying complexity. This both adds to the quality of research outcomes and meets the expectations of users, helping to maintain levels of motivation. Thus, it is important to acknowledge the different kinds of capabilities and interests of the user participants, because maintaining levels of motivation over a long-term project's lifetime is an essential task.

There may be good reasons for temporarily separating groups of actors. For example, in the city-quarter project, work was conducted separately within the different target groups (the elderly vs. the young and tech-savvy), and activities were categorized according to time phase.

In sum, while in a work-based context it is important to know the needs of different types of institutional stakeholders (e.g., industry, research, or "users" in general), in a home-based context, knowing the different interests, motivations, capabilities, and competences of the members of the participating households is equally, if not more, important.

Keeping in touch. When starting a living lab and planning supervision of households, establishing a trustworthy relationship has been shown to be essential. Our experience indicates that it is useful to provide participants with a consistent contact person over time. This could be a research associate who regularly communicates and works with participants, as was the case with the SocialMedia and EMON projects, or a local contact person in the community center, in case of the city-quarter project. Having such a contact person is important for various reasons, including keeping participants up to date, introducing new participants, organizing meetings, responding to questions, and dealing with sensitive matters, such as privacy concerns.

A central contact person of this kind is also valuable for building trust. Over time, working in domestic environments means accepting a "guest-like" role—as someone who is interested not only in facts but also as someone who is open for small talk and social exchange. Participants are an essential part of the research project and therefore it is important to give them an understanding of what it means to be part of a larger design team. Thus, it is relevant to think about sharing control between researchers and users and, with that, to reflect about different forms of engagement (Vines et al. 2013).

In a long-term living lab project, it is important to keep the process visible and transparent at all stages. Here, providing awareness is one key aspect for improving acceptance and maintaining motivation. For example, where the deployment of a new systems version is delayed, it helps to provide some basic information from time to time. Especially when departing from existing roadmaps, it is good practice to inform participants and keep them in the loop to maintain feelings of "membership" of the project.

Reflecting about the right forms of information management is of crucial importance, especially in the context of the city-quarter project, where a relatively high number and variety of stakeholders were included and affected by the publicly visible outdoor devices as well as the activities in the community center. Our iterative prototyping approach led to the situation whereby the software frequently needed to be updated and changed and thus did not always run on the outdoor monitors. In the perception of the tenants, the devices did not "run well" and led to skepticism among the group of tenants who did not come to the community center activities and thus did not learn about newer development activities. And for the housing company, the ongoing work on the software and the visible breakdowns even caused fear regarding the company's reputation. Dachtera et al. (2014) showed that there were similar tensions in anticipations and interests between researchers and industry partners in the prototyping process of a navigation support tool for firefighters. This demonstrates the importance not only of regular and widespread public-relations work but also of further articulation work on the specificities of iterative design, in order to improve understanding between all stakeholders.

While keeping in touch with users is one main issue in living lab work, developing and maintaining the collaboration between industrial, academic, and public partners is crucial and can be time consuming and resource intensive. Whereas for academic research, projects themselves are the main focus, other stakeholders often conceive of such projects as being relevant but not important for their daily business. Our experience has shown that every project has to deal with uncertainties with respect to capacities and performance of project partners (Dachtera et al. 2014). Especially when designing and developing new hardware and software prototypes, this should be taken into account when setting up project agendas. In part, these effects can be mitigated by continuous meetings and a high level of communication and exchange. This kind of articulation work can include regular summaries of empirical results and problem-solving strategies (e.g., direct participation of other stakeholder members in the evaluation sessions).

User Space

When setting up living lab infrastructures, there are two main tasks that contribute to the workload: acquiring and selecting users, and bringing hardware and software into the field. In this section, we show how the PRAXLABS framework opens ways of strategically reusing living lab resources, thus managing them more efficiently.

A good example of where infrastructure could be reused and methods transferred between different applications is the interaction that took place between the SocialMedia and the EMON projects. In 2010, the EMON project started without external funding and thus faced the challenge of minimizing resource usage in terms of both manpower and hardware and software supply. Consequently, we looked for ways to conduct valid research while not overly stressing existing resources. Therefore, we decided to ask households already engaged in another PRAXLABS project whether they would be willing to join our new research initiative. Thus, we were able to use an existing living lab infrastructure, adopting its hardware setup and engaging parts of its participants. We analyzed the given labs with regard to their technical setup and the readiness of their participants. As a result, the SocialMedia project was found to be best fitting, in terms of reusing its infrastructure, in relation to two dimensions:

- household structures:
  - household structures participating in the SocialMedia project could be analyzed regarding sociodemographic aspects and interest in the topic and existence of energy-generating appliances such as photovoltaics or thermal power stations
- technical setup:
  - the SocialMedia project involved the use of an interactive TV application, which required installation of a media center PC and getting it to work with existing local infrastructures and different forms of TV reception (DVB-C, DVB-S, and DVB-T), so the project already had equipped households with a media center PC with remote desktop connections and a HDTV
  - this setup matched the needs of the EMON project, which involved collecting and visualizing electricity consumption
  - visualizations of energy consumptions were planned to be made accessible via the TV set
  - as rolled-out hardware was being used, only the metering infrastructure called for an extra investment

We ended up choosing seven out of sixteen households for the EMON study, which ran parallel to the SocialMedia study but lasted longer and finally was converted into a Smart Home PRAXLABS case study in 2014 (Jakobi and Stevens 2013; Jakobi et al. 2013).

Although reusing the infrastructure reduced the effort involved in acquiring new participants and establishing trust, such reuse has several drawbacks. Especially for participants, being involved in parallel projects poses a higher overall workload. On the other hand, for researchers, designing the research studies calls for a more careful planning when other resources are in play. It should be ensured that interventions do not become an actual burden and possibly stress participants (e.g., by an empirical overload based on interviews, observations, self-documentation, or workshops).

The main threat to the success of a PRAXLABS project stems from households losing interest and deciding to drop out. Our experience showed that this danger increases with the time households are involved. The interest in being part of a research project sometimes decreases, and participants lose their motivation to think critically about our prototypes and report on their practices.

Another potential drawback for households is that borders between the projects might blur. For example, participants might confuse appointments or develop interests and practices that are shaped by other projects. Here, a good communication strategy is of high importance for maintaining distance between projects while acknowledging proximity at the same time, for example, by forwarding feedback to relevant stakeholders of other projects.

Acquiring and selecting users for a particular project is a rather complex and time-consuming task. Thus, we began to handle the user recruitment in a more structured way. For our PRAXLABS approach, we set up a CRM system. By using a Web front end, interested households can send in unsolicited applications, independently of currently ongoing project acquisitions. Their contact details and information regarding their household infrastructure, technological infrastructures, habits regarding daily consumption practices, and research interests are saved and managed via an open-source CRM. This way, a database of interested households has emerged that can be easily referred to a first analysis of possible participants. In order to manage the workload for households, the CRM also makes it possible to determine which projects users are currently involved in or have previously been involved in.

Creative Space

Providing room for more informal and creative exchanges is essential for interdisciplinary work among different stakeholders. As stated by Ehn (2008), bottom-up innovations require space and an open culture so that new ideas can evolve in a dynamic and flexible way. In comparison to more traditional forms of innovation processes, as documented in business literature (e.g., those related to lead user theory (von Hippel 1986)), places and structures that enable more free and creative forms of innovation processes become more and more important. The "maker communities" movement currently shows how users with special interest organize themselves, for example, in order to experiment and program in hackathons or reuse existing technologies in contexts other than they were developed for. Such open engagements represent both opportunities and challenges.

Depending on research topics, design cases, and the involved target group, public meeting rooms like the Chamber of Crafts offers opportunities for the formal exchange of information. Informal exchange, multigenerational communication, and co-creation processes can be fostered through semi-public spaces like the community center for the city-quarter project, rooms at the university for creativity sessions, a regulars' table to discuss technical problems, or the fab-lab approach, where everybody can participate in trying out new things with 3D printing. In principle, spaces are essential for fostering blue-sky thinking as well as formal and informal exchange so that experiences can be transferred between stakeholder groups and projects.

Research projects, such as the ones presented here, are based on the ability to redefine requirements as user insights and feedback from field studies, as well as concrete discussions and evaluation of visual concepts, become available. Therefore, we made use of semi-public spaces, where rudimentary concepts and designs in early phases, such as mock-ups and demos, could be iterated as realistically as possible. In the SocialMedia project, for example, we used PowerPoint mock-ups on the TV, and exchangeable paper mock-ups in our artificial living-room setting at the university. The space and the experience made by users stimulated idea generation and reflection in early design phases.

Methodological Space

The methodological space comprises experiences we had with different methods in different contexts during our projects. Some of them proved to be suitable only for specific target groups or contexts; others could be used in nearly every project without changing substantial elements.

In the EMON project, empirical investigations such as individual workshops in front of the TV set at the participants' home, to reflect about ICT-usage, were also helpful for finding ways to collectively evaluate individual energy-consumption data. Based on experience from the SocialMedia project, interviews, workshops, and focus groups were planned. On the other hand, we also needed to reshape methods that were adopted only partly: for example, a diary study was planned based on previous use, but we became aware of the fact that self-documentation about technology use needs to be applied carefully (e.g., it is necessary not to ask too many details or become a burden for the users). Since the relevant data had already been collected in the SocialMedia project, we were able to focus on the visual prototypes and their impact on energy use. The handling of the overall communication behavior remained broadly the same: kickoff and closing workshops were held, and Christmas and birthday cards were sent to keep up relationships with households. These activities were very much appreciated by the participants, and they helped to minimize the overhead involved in preparing users for their involvement and persuading them to continue.

The examples given in this chapter demonstrate that living lab projects addressing home contexts can profit from previously collected experiences. Managing such projects is not only supported, for example, by reusing infrastructures, but also by reusing methods that were previously applied and by learning across project boundaries, for example, by reusing information from households or adapting empirical material such as diaries. With the example of the interaction between the SocialMedia project and the EMON project, we could show that best practices can, to a large extent, be abstracted from a concrete research project and be reused as general knowhow of researching in living lab environments.

Much effort in living lab projects is invested in empirical work. Understanding contexts, needs, and requirements from different stakeholders requires a structured approach. With regard to pre-studies, we obtained value from semi-structured interviews within households. This way, we got to know participants in their homes—thus, we got a solid understanding of how they lived and which technology they already used (e.g., by pointing to or showing certain things). In early project stages, the need for self-documentation methods should not be underestimated. In addition to providing interviews for more detailed empirical insights, they are valuable instruments for making behavior visible to other stakeholders, both to those working on living lab projects and to participants themselves, helping processes of recall and prompting reflection about their own routines. In such cases, we used and adapted, for example, cultural probes with diaries, in which participants could document their usage, consumption, and communication behavior over a defined period of time. As it turned out, documentation periods of 2 weeks were sufficient to get an understanding of established routines and practices.

Later on in our projects, participatory-design workshops and usability evaluations became important. While primary goals of design workshops are collective discussions and reflections of early design mock-ups, usability tests are being applied to evaluate more enhanced and functional prototypes. When prototypes are (partly) working, most valuable feedback can be found when they were rolled out in practice. Valuable insights about whether the application or system prototype is being appropriated in practice and about the way in which it is used are best obtained in this manner. In order to understand the value and drawbacks of prototypes, empirical work needs to be carried on, for example, with feedback interviews, logfile analysis, additional online questionnaires, or in-situ feedback tools that enable participants to document bugs, issues, and potential improvements in context of the use.

Building communities of interest is a challenging endeavor. Formal structures and methods help work processes to progress, but they are not always optimal from the users' point of view. We learned to set up occasions for specific events and informal exchange in order to maintain motivational levels. In order to support community building, for instance, we initiated speed networking activities and offered opportunities to meet up at a regular round table or by inviting participants to the Christmas market to improve relationships.

10.5.2 Limitations of Comparing Case Study Results

In this section, we will describe the limiting factors we had to deal with when comparing case study results and trying to transfer them to another project's context. Not every finding is transferable within the home context, but there are some worth looking at, especially with respect to critical factors like privacy aspects and social practices.

The Home: A Private Sphere

The home is the epitome of the private, at least in Western culture, and we need to respect this when conducting research in such an environment. In many ways, what is considered suitable behavior when researching, interacting, and, in fact, simply being part of this private sphere is not normally part of the researchers' role, but it can simply be thought of as common courtesy.

However, when interactive technology enabling new ways of communication or exchanging information was being introduced, users demanded privacy measures in unanticipated and very individual ways. Handling such demands is always an important challenge for designers and projects' success. This is especially the case when data exchange is at the core of the research agenda, for instance, when investigating the enrichment of media usage with social features or the effects of social comparability in energy feedback.

The difficulty of anticipating privacy concerns for users is often rooted in the phenomenon of the privacy paradox (Norberg et al. 2007), which refers to the fact that there is a gap between what users want to keep private and what they actually keep private in practice. For example, at one point in the project, we discussed the possibility of having remote access to energy-consumption feedback services via cloud computing. Even though, in prior interviews, household users had stated their sensitivity for disclosing private data, nevertheless, they largely did want to have cloud access to their energy data, although this meant permanently providing researchers with access to the households' real-time consumption. Privacy, in other words, tended to be a rather contingent matter.

This is exemplified by our attempt to introduce an Internet-based TV platform that would have enabled users to see the content and channels other users were watching. When we introduced this concept to the participants, it was met with refusal. When we asked users why they did not want to use the system, some of the participants responded that they disliked the feature because they perceived their viewing habits as being very private information that should be kept safe from others, even if this meant not having a potentially desirable service. While, in principle, users would have liked to see information from others—for exploration and comparison—at the same time, they wanted their own personal information to remain private. As a consequence, the idea had to be discarded, and we reduced the visibility of other households' habits by removing information about specific users and the TV programs they watched, thus providing some "privacy by design" (Langheinrich 2001).

Privacy issues also came to prominence in the city-quarter project. Discussing the design of the neighborhood platform with the elderly and non-tech-savvy tenants, we encountered a need to balance a trade-off between the users' visibility in the portal and their privacy. When posting messages on the portal, it became clear that the kind of message posted correlated with the user's wish to be visible to other tenants. Specifically, while they wanted some messages to be visible to the whole neighborhood, some they wanted to be visible only to close neighbors. This need for fine-grained control, as also experienced in the EMON project, is also described in the literature, where the locus of control over data sharing is critical for technology acceptance, especially in smart metering (Kranz et al. 2010; Wunderlich et al. 2012). In the case of the city-quarter project, the task of finding the right balance between privacy and sharing also was linked to the aim of fostering social interaction and awareness between tenants in the city quarter. In regard to these aspects, we discussed possible levels of visibility for messages and introduced three scopes: (a) visibility to all tenants in all ten tenements in the city quarter, (b) visibility to selected houses, and (c) visibility only to direct neighbors in the same house. In the case of the elderly tenants, the importance of "face work" (Goffman 1955) was very strongly visible, as evidenced by comments such as "I do not want all neighbors to think that I am that poor (when trying to sell something)."

Learning about Social Practices

The social behavior of families, and, in particular, their internal relations, affords another basis for comparison. In the SocialMedia project, for example, parents used the TV to schedule the TV consumption of their children. Children were allowed to watch a certain defined set of series for a specified time. In general, parents wanted to be aware of their children's TV watching time and prevent them from spending too many hours in front of the TV set. As such, there are generation-specific appropriation aspects to social TV application, and these need to be considered in design.

Such intergenerational issues also became visible in the city-quarter project. Here, an elderly grandmother who happily participated in our workshops in order to learn to use Internet applications on a tablet PC came one day and reported that she sometimes let her grandson play on her tablet. For her, it was a special situation because she liked to enable her grandson to pursue this activity that he enjoyed so much. However, she was not aware of what kind of games the grandson had downloaded, and she did not see the need to be concerned until one day the boy's mother (her daughter-in-law) grumbled that he was playing games that were not appropriate for his age. After this incident, the elderly lady came to us and asked us to delete the games. Here, another conflict arose that became important for the reflection of our participatory-design work with elderly participants: on the one hand, we strongly encouraged them to share their tablet PC experiences with their family members, but at the same time, such behaviors had to be mediated by moral concerns, which we had to deal with by not only giving the elderly lady guidance about her own appropriation process but also helping her to understand and judge her grandson's activities.

Issues with Transferring Design Concepts

In the case of the EMON project, during our co-design sessions, we found many meaningful dimensions to support the use of energy-consumption feedback information. We specifically designed our home EMON system to support different views on consumption and to provide households with alternatives that optimally suited the way they reflected about energy consumption in their everyday life. These views were crucial for enabling households to gain an understanding of their energy consumption and increasingly allowed them to make informed decisions regarding more sustainable lifestyles. However, the categories we used for monitoring energy were very specific to the energy-monitoring case. Although we discussed possible takeaways for other projects, we hardly found any valuable design implications to apply elsewhere.

Based on this example, it became apparent that when attempting to transfer experiences of design implications across projects situated in the home, we faced a fundamental problem: in order to make further use of our findings, our concepts had to be abstracted to such a degree that their ability to inform design was largely lost. For example, while for EMON, person-, room-, appliance-, and activity-based views on energy consumption were considered to be very helpful, we have not found ways of transferring such concepts into other projects in the home.

This is in stark contrast to our stated ability to reuse methods and best practices in the living lab environments. However, we also found a few cross-cutting schemes that played a major role for the acceptance of our technologies: the need to make trade-offs between privacy and benefits obtained in the use of social features of technologies, for instance, was a recurring theme. While on the one hand, users showed strong interest in receiving community data, such as information regarding what others watched on TV or how much energy other households consumed, on the other hand the willingness to provide data for the community was less evident. Participants did not like to share information about their everyday activities, largely fearing to "lose face," for example, by making transparent how much and what kind of programs they were watching or which kind of messages they were sending.

10.5.3 Reusing Experiences and Concepts across Fields of Application

So far, we have showed the—sometimes—limited possibilities for transferring experiences gathered within living lab-based research from one project to another. While certain methodological approaches can be seen as best practices that most likely will be valid in other projects as well, insights gained are less transferable. What we saw, however, is the need to be able to come to a closer and more detailed comparison of results.

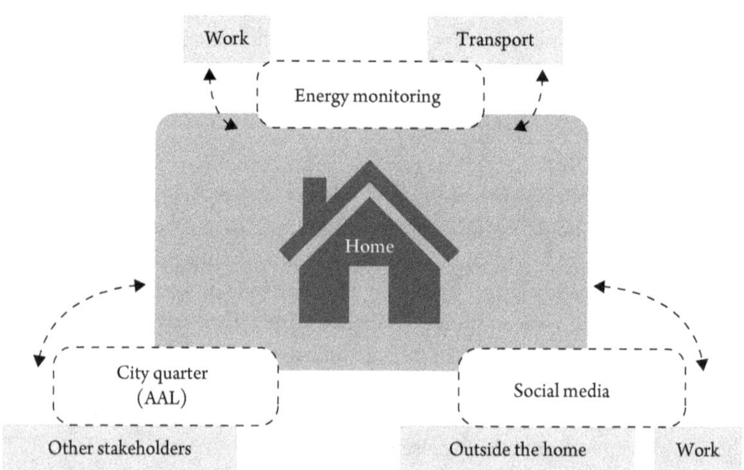

Figure 10.13 Making sustained use of experience along use cases settings by crossing contexts

Here we describe the various ways in which insights from home-based research can be transferred to other contextual settings. Our major insight is that it is a mistake to assume that generalizations are best made within "domains," it is not always clear how a domain is constituted. Thus, we might have imagined at the outset that our point of comparison would be "domestic settings." In fact, where useful comparisons are to be made, it is across similar "use cases." In other words, it is the kind of use to which applications might be put, rather than *where* applications might be used, that turns out to be informative. We will demonstrate the potential of transferring concepts across "classical" boundaries in this section (see Figure 10.13).

Monitoring Energy Consumption (in Different Contexts)

Energy monitoring turned out to be a very specific case, where the transfer of concepts within the home sphere was hardly possible. This may have been due to the special conditions of energy as a resource, being invisible, immaterial, and needing special attention when designing a feedback system under such circumstances. However, we found how peoples' concepts on reflecting about energy consumption in their home provided powerful implications for design in another context.

In the late phase of the EMON project, we conducted an energy-monitoring project in the offices of a local financial service provider (Jakobi and Stevens 2015a, b). We installed workplace-based sensors to inform employees about their energy consumption. Since workplace studies of that kind at that time were rather new and knowledge on how to design for this specific context did not exist, we referred to our experiences from the home domain. Although slightly different, we found many ways in which employees reflected about their energy consumption already supported by our HEMS. For example, room-based energy-consumption visualizations were meaningful to employees. Additionally, distinguishing between a basic energy need (e.g., for fridges and routers) and activity-related consumption (e.g., making coffee or using the microwave) proved a fruitful dimension for energy feedback at the workplace, too. In this regard, while in the home, consumption by printers and the kitchen infrastructure was considered necessary (although it could possibly be reduced by a one-time optimization), in the work environment, consumption by computers and monitors was seen in much the same way. Thus, while there are obvious differences between home and office consumption of energy, the broad distinction between "basic" and "activity-related" needs remained useful. In much the same way, timelines of use proved to provide useful information. The distinction between being "at work" or "not at/doing work" proved fruitful in demonstrating to people where savings could most easily be made. Overall, while being slightly different, many ways of thinking, talking, and acting with respect to energy consumption at the workplace were similar those used at home.

Using Social-Media Tools (in Different Contexts)

In the SocialMedia project, we developed functionalities to make media consumption more flexible (e.g., making it possible to watch videos on different devices in different contexts, or building ad-hoc applications for sharing information). The adoption and usage of such functionalities reached beyond the home, for instance, when these mobile devices were used to manage event visits or when going abroad for vacation. Systems, even when designed for "the home," might well be used in quite different contexts. Within our project, we observed many examples of such flexible usage practices. Facebook, for example, a tool that mainly has been used for leisure activities, has been adopted in work settings as well. Participants often use such applications to get up-to-date information and to communicate with others during working hours (Andreassen et al. 2014). In one participating household, a doctor described situations where Facebook was used by his patients to communicate with him.

The tools developed in the project were used in quite different contexts as well. One of the prototypes enabled users to get up-to-date information from others in relation to specified geographical locations (point of interest). In evaluating the concept with a group of participants, we became aware that such points of interest are rather different for different people and could include, for example, requests for pictures at the workplace, information about shopping opportunities, and where to find the best coffee in town. Put simply, the home is a fluid boundary. Uses cannot be determined merely by reference to it. They extend beyond it. Context "similarity," in other words, is determined by use practices and purposeful interactions with others in and beyond the home.

The Home and the Neighborhood

The city-quarter project aimed at helping elderly persons to stay in their homes as long as possible, through ICT support. However, its vision can be understood as an extension of a classic ambient-assisted-living approach, which, in most cases, is centered only on the home. When looking at activities both in the home and outside, here—in the neighborhood—it is important to also include other interactions with stakeholders around the home of the elderly. There might be neighbors who can be a source of informal help and social interaction, but also the housing company can play (in the future) an important role in the elderly persons' everyday life. The elderly tenant's own apartment can still serve as a place of refuge for the tenant, but their social life also takes place in interactions in the neighborhood, with family members living at other places and in relationships to service providers on a local level.

Comparing our conceptual results to other projects in the field of the aging society, such as, for instance, the project Alzheimer Monitoring (Wan et al. 2014), we see there is a strong tension between "in-home" and "outside-the-home" activities, and this needs to be regarded very carefully for the target group of elderly people. Aspects of face work, that is, how one's face is shown to the outside world, are very important for persons aged 60+. Even though we have seen similar attitudes in the group of younger participants in our other case studies described here, we see a special level of vulnerability in the elderly group, and this may be better compared on a "use case" than on the context dimension "home."

In addition, when reflecting on "helping measures" for the elderly, we immediately encounter the need for autonomy, that is, the ability to lead an independent life, which is not seen in case studies with younger, tech-savvier, and more self-dependent people. Here, social technologies that foster community building per se touch individuals on other levels.

10.6 Conclusion

In developing the PRAXLABS framework through a comparative analysis of three design case studies devoted to different themes in the domestic domain, we have been able to identify both practical procedures that facilitate the working of living labs over extended periods of time and ways to build on the experiences obtained in individual projects by careful comparison. Living labs are made more effective and sustainable in terms of gaining, using, and reusing expertise, ICT resources, and other physical resources and research experiences.

We propose the PRAXLABS framework as a specific approach for the design case study approach by investigating usage practices and balancing ICT design and development among end-user representatives as well as other stakeholders. Although this is best done in naturalistic environments, compromises associated with the living lab are often necessary. In our previous research projects, we initiated and operated living labs to involve end users and stakeholders continuously in the design process and to enable the assessment of the practical value of the developed functionalities. Over time, we became aware that, when strategically using living labs for researching the home, more efficient structures and ways of collecting and cultivating research experiences from different long-term R & D projects might be possible. Our analysis shows that such experiences may provide a more structured access to, and efficient management of, practice-based research. Examples given in this chapter highlight elements that work *within* and *beyond* the domestic context. It is the rationale that people exhibit for using technology in particular ways that determines "similarity."

The PRAXLABS analytical framework encompasses four main elements: *user space, methodological space, management space,* and *creative space,* all of which have proven suitable for systematizing different layers of results and experiences derived in the comparative analysis of the design case studies at hand.

Our work was motivated by the need to structure experiences among a multiplicity of projects. Even if the projects focused on different use cases, we have shown in this work that different elements may be looked at in relation to each other and also reoccur in one way or another. Such elements are not always easy to formalize. However, methodological "lessons learned" may be considered and fixed for further projects and may also constitute "teachable moments" for other researchers engaged in analyses of technology use. In this chapter, we presented a number of such elements from a meta-perspective. Even if transferring experience from one case to another is not a straightforward matter, with the PRAXLABS framework, we demonstrate a means to make both practical reuse and conceptual comparisons possible.

PRAXLABS is a framework through which different viewpoints, experiences, and material may be collected, discussed, and managed systematically. The framework is open for the integration of future design case studies, evolving dynamically with new practice-based projects from other domains and application fields.

Due to the huge variety and high context dependability of research results, it is an important part of the design case study approach that appropriate ways of comparing cases be found. The PRAXLABS framework, we argue, provides a means to do this at the various levels discussed above.

Having said that, we admit that the PRAXLABS framework is an open and evolving structure. Some open questions remain and need to be pursued in future work. Open issues include, for example, questions on how to integrate work (and experiences, lessons learned) accomplished at the point of project acquisition, and how to differentiate user roles and the influence of users in each design phase. Another line for further investigation is the integration of research and teaching in the overall PRAXLABS framework. These and probably many more questions evolving from further comparative analyses of design case studies will have to be addressed in the future and have the potential to further improve and shape PRAXLABS.

References

Abowd, G. D., Bobick, A. F., Essa, I. A., Mynatt, E. D., and Rogers, W. A. 2002. *The Aware Home: A Living Laboratory for Technologies for Successful Aging.* AAAI Technical Report WS-02-02. Available at http://www.aaai.org/Papers/Workshops/2002/WS-02-02/WS02-02-001.pdf (accessed October 16, 2017).

Almirall, E. 2008. "Living labs and open innovation: Roles and applicability." *The Electronic Journal for Virtual Organization and Networks* 10: 21–46.

Almirall, E., and Wareham, J. 2009. "Innovation: A question of fit: The living labs approach." In Mobile Living Labs 09: Methods and Tools for Evaluation in the Wild. Available at http://www.abdoelali.com/pdfs/MLL09_Proceedings.pdf#page=5 (accessed October 16, 2017).

Almirall, E., and Wareham, J. 2011. "Living Labs: Arbiters of mid- and ground-level innovation." *Technology Analysis and Strategic Management* 23 (1): 87–102.

Andreassen, C. S., Torsheim, T., and Pallesen, S. 2014. "Use of online social network sites for personal purposes at work: Does it impair self-reported performance?" *Comprehensive Psychology* 3, 18.

Bergvall-Kåreborn, B., and Larsson, S. 2008. "A case study of real-world testing." In *MUM'08*. New York: ACM, 113–116.

Bernhaupt, R., Obrist, M., Weiss, A., Beck, E., and Tscheligi, M. 2008. "Trends in the living room and beyond: Results from ethnographic studies using creative and playful probing." *Computers in Entertainment* 6 (1): 5.

Bjerknes, G., and Bratteteig, T. 1995. "User participation and democracy: A discussion of Scandinavian research on system development." *Scandinavian Journal of Information Systems* 7 (1): 1.

Bødker, K., Kensing, F., and Simonsen, J. 2004. *Participatory IT Design: Designing for Business and Workplace Realities.* Cambridge, MA: MIT Press.

Brush, A. J. B., Lee, B., Mahajan, R., Agarwal, S., Saroiu, S., and Dixon, C. 2011. "Home automation in the wild." In *CHI'11*. New York: ACM Press, 2115–24.

Budweg, S., Lewkowicz, M., Müller, C., and Schering, S. 2012. "Fostering social interaction in AAL: Methodological reflections on the coupling of real household Living Lab and SmartHome approaches." *i-com Zeitschrift für interaktive und kooperative Medien* 11 (3): 30–5.

Burgess, J., and Nye, M. 2008. "Re-materialising energy use through transparent monitoring systems." *Energy Policy* 36 (12): 4454–9.

Certeau, M. D., Jameson, F., and Lovitt, C. 1980. "On the oppositional practices of everyday life." *Social Text* 3 (1): 3–43.

Crabtree, A., Hemmings, T., Rodden, T., and Mariani, J. 2003. "Informing the development of calendar systems for domestic use." In *ECSCW'03*. Dordrecht: Kluwer, 119–38.

Crabtree, A., and Rodden, T. 2004. "Domestic routines and design for the home." *Computer Supported Cooperative Work* 13 (2): 191–220.

Dachtera, J., Randall, D., and Wulf, V. 2014. "Research on research: Design research at the margins: Academia, industry and end-users." In *CHI'14*. New York: ACM, pp. 713–22.

Darby, S. 2001. "Making it obvious: Designing feedback into energy consumption." In D. P. Bertoldi, D. A. Ricci, and P. A. de Almeida, eds., *Energy Efficiency in Household Appliances and Lighting*. Berlin/Heidelberg: Springer Berlin, Heidelberg, pp. 685–96.

Darby, S. 2006. *The Effectiveness of Feedback on Energy Consumption: A Review for DEFRA of the Literature on Metering, Billing and Direct Displays*. Oxford: Environmental Change Institute, University of Oxford.

de Ruyter, B., and Aarts, E. 2004. "Ambient intelligence." In *AVI'04*. ACM, 203–8.

DiSalvo, C., Sengers, P., and Brynjarsdóttir H. 2010. "Mapping the landscape of sustainable HCI." In *CHI'10*. New York: ACM, 1975–84.

Ehn, P. 2008. "Participation in design things." In *PDC'08*. New York: ACM, 92–101.

Eriksson, M., Niitamo, V., and Kulkki, S. 2005. *State-of-the-Art in Utilizing Living Labs Approach to User-Centric ICT Innovation: A European Approach*. Available at https://pdfs.semanticscholar.org/2edd/5e0fef9f7f9fd0262dea937cb997b3ab8d5f.pdf (accessed October 16, 2017).

Fischer, G. 1999. "Symmetry of ignorance, social creativity, and meta-design." *Knowledge-Based Systems* 13 (7–8): 116–23.

Fitzpatrick, G., and Smith, G. 2009. "Technology-enabled feedback on domestic energy consumption: Articulating a set of design concerns." *IEEE Pervasive Computing* 8 (1): 37–44.

Følstad, A. 2008. "Living Labs for innovation and development of information and communication technology: A literature review." *The Electronic Journal for Virtual Organization and Networks* 10: 99–131.

Frößler, F., Rukanova, B., Higgins, A., and Klein, S. 2007. "Inter-organisational network formation and sense making: Initiation and management of public private collaboration." In *BLED'07*. Atlanta: AIS, 354–71.

Gaver, B., Dunne, T., and Pacenti, E. 1999. "Design: Cultural probes." *Interactions* 6 (1): 21–9.

Gaver, W. W. 2006. "The video window: My life with a ludic system." *Personal and Ubiquitous Computing* 10 (2–3): 60–5.

Goffman, E. 1955. "On face-work: An analysis of ritual elements in social interaction." *Psychiatry* 18 (3): 213–31.

Greenbaum, J., and Kyng, M. 1991. *Design at Work: Cooperative Design of Computer Systems*. Hillsdale, NJ: Lawrence Erlbaum Associates.

Grinter, R. E., Edwards, W. K., Chetty, M., Poole, E. S., Sung, J. Y., Yang, J., Crabtree, A., Tolmie, P., Rodden, T., Greenhalgh, C., and Benford, S. 2009. "The ins and outs of home networking: The case for useful and usable domestic networking." *ACM Transactions on Computer-Human Interaction* 16 (2): 8.

Hayes, G. R. 2011. "The relationship of action research to human-computer interaction." *ACM Transactions on Computer-Human Interaction* 18 (3): 1–20.

Hess, J., Ley, B., Ogonowski, C., Wan, L., and Wulf, V. 2011. "Jumping between devices and services: Towards an integrated concept for social TV." In *EuroITV'11*. New York: ACM, 11–20.

Hess, J., Ley, B., Ogonowski, C., Reichling, T., Wan, L., and Wulf, V. 2012. "New technology@ home: Impacts on usage behavior and social structures." In *EuroITV'12*. New York: ACM, 185–94.

Hess, J., Ley, B., Ogonowski, C., Wan, L., and Wulf, V. 2012a. "Understanding and supporting cross-platform usage in the living room." *Entertainment Computing* 3 (2): 37–47.

Hess, J., Ley, B., Ogonowski, C., Wan, L., and Wulf, V. 2012b. "Flexible Mediennutzung durch die Integration von Geräten und Diensten." In *Mensch und Computer 2012*. Berlin: De Gruyter, 253–62.

Hess, J., Wan, L., Ley, B., and Wulf, V. 2012. "In-situ everywhere: A qualitative feedback infrastructure for cross platform home-IT." In *EuroITV'12*. New York: ACM, 75–8.

Hyysalo, S., and Hakkarainen, L. 2014. "What difference does a living lab make? Comparing two health technology innovation projects." *CoDesign* 10 (3–4): 191–208.

Intille, S. S., Larson, K., Beaudin, J. S., Nawyn, J., Tapia, E. M., and Kaushik, P. 2005. "A living laboratory for the design and evaluation of ubiquitous computing technologies." In *CHI'05*. New York: ACM, 1941–4.

Jakobi, T., and Schwartz, T. 2012. "Putting the user in charge: End user development for eco-feedback technologies." In *SustainIT'12*. Piscataway: IEEE Press, 1–4.

Jakobi, T., and Stevens, G. 2013. "Always beta: Cooperative design in the smart home." In *UbiComp'13 Adjunct*. New York: ACM, 837–44.

Jakobi, T., and Stevens, G. 2015a. *Potentials of Energy Consumption Measurements in Office Environments*. Paris/Amsterdam: Atlantis Press.

Jakobi, T., and Stevens, G. 2015b. *Energy Saving at Work—and When Not Working! Insights from a Comparative Study*. Paris/Amsterdam: Atlantis Press.

Jakobi, T., Stevens, G., and Schwartz, T. 2013. "EUD@Smart Homes: Smart refurbishment of rented apartments to improve energy efficiency." In *IS-EUD 2013*. Dordrecht: Springer, 301.

Jönsson, L., Broms, L., and Katzeff, C. 2010. "Watt-Lite: Energy statistics made tangible." In *DIS'10*. New York: ACM, 240–3.

Kensing, F., and Blomberg, J. 1998. "Participatory design: Issues and concerns." *Computer Supported Cooperative Work* 7 (3–4): 167–85.

Kranz, L. M., Gallenkamp, J., and Picot, A. 2010. "Exploring the role of control: Smart meter acceptance of residential consumers. In *AMCIS'10*. Atlanta: AIS, 315.

Langheinrich M. 2001. "Privacy by design: Principles of privacy-aware ubiquitous systems." In *Ubicomp'01*. Berlin/Heidelberg: Springer, 273–91.

Ley, B., Ogonowski, C., Hess, J., Reichling, T., Wan, L., and Wulf, V. 2014. "Impacts of new technologies on media usage and social behaviour in domestic environments." *Behaviour and Information Technology* 33 (8): 37–41.

Ley, B., Ogonowski, C., Mu M., Hess, J., Race, N., Randall, D., Rouncefield, M., and Wulf, V. 2015. "At home with users: A comparative view of Living Labs." *Interacting with Computers* 27 (1): 21–35.

Lull, J. 1990. *Inside Family Viewing: Ethnographic Research on Television's Audiences*. Abington-on-Thames: Routledge.

Mankoff, J. C., Blevis, E., Borning, A., Friedman, B., Fussell, S.R., Hasbrouck, J., Woodruff, A., and Sengers, P. 2007. "Environmental sustainability and interaction." In *CHI'07*. New York: ACM, 2121–4.

Müller, C., Hornung, D., Hamm, T., and Wulf, V. 2015a. "Measures and tools for supporting ICT appropriation by elderly and non tech-savvy persons in a long-term perspective." In *ECSCW'15*. Cham: Springer, 263–81.

Müller, C., Hornung, D., Hamm, T., and Wulf, V. 2015b. "Practice-based design of a neighborhood portal: Focusing on elderly tenants in a city quarter living lab." In *CHI'15*. New York: ACM, 2295–304.

Müller, C., Neufeldt, C., Randall, D., and Wulf, V. 2012. "ICT-development in residential care settings: Sensitizing design to the life circumstances of the residents of a care home." In *CHI'12*. New York: ACM, 2639–48.

Müller, C., Wan, L., Stein, M., and Neufeldt, C. 2012. *Experience of Giving and Receiving: Living Lab-Based Technology Design with Elderly People*. Available at http://www.ischool.drexel.edu/faculty/jrode/stein.pdf (accessed October 16, 2017).

Muller, M. 2001. "A participatory poster of participatory methods." In *CHI'01*. New York: ACM, 99.

Niitamo, V.-P., Kulkki, S., Eriksson, M., and Hribernik, K. A. 2006. "State-of-the-art and good practice in the field of living labs." In *ICE'06*. Piscataway: IEEE Press, 26–8.

Norberg, P. A., Horne, D. R., and Horne, D. A. 2007. "The privacy paradox: Personal information disclosure intentions versus behaviors." *Journal of Consumer Affairs* 41 (1): 100–26.

O'Brien, J., Rodden, T., Rouncefield, M., and Hughes, J. 1999. "At home with the technology: An ethnographic study of a set-top-box trial." *ACM Transactions on Computer-Human Interaction* 6 (3): 282–308.

Ogonowski, C., Ley, B., and Hess, J. 2013. "Designing for the living room: Long-term user involvement in a living lab." In *CHI'13*. New York: ACM, 1539–48.

Palen, L., and Aaløkke, S. 2006. "Of pill boxes and piano benches: 'Home-made' methods for managing medication." In *CSCW'06*. New York: ACM, 79–88.

Pipek, V., and Syrjänen, A. L. 2006. "Infrastructuring as capturing in-situ design." Available at http://citeseerx.ist.psu.edu/viewdoc/download?doi=10.1.1.84.7596&rep=rep1&type=pdf (accessed October 16, 2017).

Pipek, V., and Wulf, V. 2009. "Infrastructuring: Toward an integrated perspective on the design and use of information technology." *Journal of the Association for Information Systems* 10 (5): 447.

Poole, E. S. 2012. "Interacting with infrastructure." In *CSCW'12*. New York: ACM, 759.

Rossello-Busquet, A., and Soler, J. 2012. "Towards efficient energy management: Defining HEMS and smart grid objectives." *International Journal on Advances in Telecommunications* 4 (3): 249–63.

Schaffers, H., Cordoba, M., Hongisto, P., Kallai, T., Merz, C., and Van Rensburg, J. 2007. "Exploring business models for open innovation in rural living labs." In *ICE'07*. Piscataway: IEEE Press, 1–8.

Schuurman, D. 2015. *Bridging the Gap between Open and User Innovation? Exploring the Value of Living Labs as a Means To Structure User Contribution and Manage Distributed Innovation*. PhD thesis. Ghent: Ghent University.

Schuurman, D., and De Marez, L. 2009. *User-Centered Innovation: Towards a Conceptual Integration of Lead Users and Living Labs*. Available at https://s3.amazonaws.com/academia.edu.documents/45635345/User-Centered_Innovation_Towards_a_Conce20160514-3301-1omehol.pdf?AWSAccessKeyId=AKIAIWOWYYGZ2Y53UL3A&Expires=1508162487&Signature=1N3z3tFsxt3EtR3LlzLzax5NBis%3D&response-content-disposition=inline%3B%20filename%3DUser-centered_innovation_towards_a_conce.pdf (accessed October 16, 2017).

Schwartz, T., Denef, S., Stevens, G., Ramirez, L., and Wulf, V. 2013. "Cultivating energy literacy: Results from a longitudinal living lab study of a home energy management system." In *CHI'13*. New York: ACM, 1193–202.

Schwartz, T., Stevens, G., Jakobi, T., Denef, S., Ramirez, L., Wulf, V., and Randall, D. 2014. "What people do with consumption feedback: A long-term living lab study of a home energy management system." *Interacting with Computers* 27 (6): 551–76.

Schwartz, T., Stevens, G., Ramirez, L., and Wulf, V. 2013. "Uncovering practices of making energy consumption accountable: A phenomenological inquiry." *ACM Transactions on Computer-Human Interaction* 20 (2): 12.

Sohn, T., Li, K. A., Griswold, W. G., and Hollan, J. D. 2008. "A diary study of mobile information needs." In *CHI'08*. New York: ACM, 433.

Stevens, G., Pipek, V., and Wulf, V. 2009. "Appropriation infrastructure: Supporting the design of usages." In *IS-EUD 2009*. Berlin/Heidelberg: Springer, 50–69.

Vines, J., Clarke, R., Wright, P., McCarthy, J., and Olivier, P. 2013. "Configuring participation: On how we involve people in design." In *CHI'13*. New York: ACM, 429–38.

von Hippel, E. 1978. "Successful industrial products from customer ideas." *Journal of Marketing* 42 (1): 39–49.

von Hippel, E. 1986. "Lead users: A source of novel product concepts." *Management Science* 32 (7): 791–805.

Wan, L., Müller, C., Wulf, V., and Randall, D. W. 2014. "Addressing the subtleties in dementia care: Pre-study & evaluation of a GPS monitoring system." In *CHI'14*. New York: ACM, 3987–96.

Wulf, V., Müller, C., Pipek, V., Randall, D., Rohde, M., and Stevens, G. 2015. "Practice-based computing: Empirically grounded conceptualizations derived from design case studies." In V. Wulf, K. Schmidt, and D. Randall, eds., *Designing Socially Embedded Technologies in the Real-World*. London: Springer Verlag London, 111–50.

Wunderlich, P., Veit, D., and Sarker, S. 2012. "Adoption of information systems in the electricity sector: The issue of smart metering." In *AMCIS'2012*. Atlanta, AIS, 16.

Part III

Design Case Studies

11 Information and Communication Technology Design in a Complex Moral Universe

Ethnography-Based Development of a GPS Monitoring System for Persons Who Wander

CLAUDIA MÜLLER AND LIN WAN

11.1 Introduction

Increasing life expectancy and reduced birth rates as results of the recent demographic changes are linked to drastic changes in age structures. The number of persons aged over 80 will double until 2025; at the same time, the availability of care workers in the care sector will be reduced. Consequently, aging societies are facing enormous challenges that are linked to increased age, such as an increase in the number of chronic medical conditions, reduced physical and mental capabilities, and an increased risk of social isolation and reduced autonomy (European Commission 2015).

In order to address these challenges, IT is being given a major role in the development of innovative solutions for preventive and curative measures that may contribute to quality of life and everyday support in informal as well as formal care settings and that may increase the agency of the elderly in their everyday life circumstances (European Commission 2015).

Socio-Informatics, Volker Wulf, Volkmar Pipek, Dave Randall, Markus Rohde, Kjeld Schmidt, Gunnar Stevens (Eds). Published 2018 by Oxford University Press.

A lot of projects and funding schemes in the fields of active aging and ambient assisted living thus focus on information and communication technology (ICT)-based innovations, which aim at developing innovative products as well as services and concepts. However, sustainable implementation of these IT-based innovations fails, because they are not embedded in the everyday practices of elderly people and their surrounding social networks.

We see problematic issues in the following aspects. First, in many cases, IT projects for the aging society are set up under the perspective of "technological innovations." However, IT projects for the aging society need to focus on how technological solutions could be embedded in the real life of elderly people and other relevant stakeholders (e.g., children and spouses as informal caregivers, professional caregivers in homecare/institutional care settings). Here we follow the path of practice-based ICT design and, in terms of methodological thinking, the grounded-design approach (Rohde et al. 2009, 2017; also see Chapter 1). However, we see the need to adapt the methodological and conceptual approaches of grounded design in order for it to be applicable in the field of IT for the aging society, particularly when it comes to research in the everyday contexts of persons who are not tech-savvy. In addition, the agency and autonomy of the persons we strive to design ICT for in this field are issues that need special attention and consideration.

In recent research funding calls, despite the increasing request for user participation in the design process, its realization often remains on a superficial level. Therefore, it is important to sharpen the conceptual and methodical design concepts for the field of IT for an aging society. In this way, research may better recognize the subtle and—on first glance—rather invisible specificities of the everyday life of the elderly and their surrounding and supporting social networks in order to develop IT designs that support sense-making processes and acceptance and appropriation by the target groups (Fitzpatrick and Ellingsen 2013).

The concept of grounded design (Rohde et al. 2017) is being developed as a framework with its instruments of "design case studies" (Müller et al. 2015a; Wulf et al. 2015) and "PRAXLABS" infrastructure (see Chapter 10) and aims at the integration of relevant elements in order to anchor design projects more sustainably in the social practice contexts of the target groups. The approach comprises of an ethnography-based pre-study for a profound understanding of the envisioned field of practice, and a cooperative prototyping phase, as well as a long-term appropriation study that aims to understand changes in social practices through the usage of the technologies introduced and, by this, to be able to measure the success criteria of the project. Through this approach, design ideas may be grounded and carefully explored as well as designed in deep grounding in actual practices.

We would like to contribute to this conceptual framework of grounded design with a specific lens on design and research activities in a project aiming at the development of a locating system for persons who wander, as wandering is a specific symptom in the field of dementia care. To explicate grounded design, Rohde et al. (2017) used case studies on the organizational use of information systems and/or encompassing actors who were younger, relatively tech-savvy, and with a research question that is, from the beginning, put very specifically in a relationship to a current and prospective usage of a ICT tool. We would like to open up discussion on the specificities of ethnography-based design for the field of IT for the aging society and especially for the field of dementia care.

We have described elsewhere (Müller et al. 2012) the challenges of conducting ICT research projects with elderly persons who are not tech-savvy and—this is, in many cases, coupled—with their caregivers (either elderly spouses at home or professional caregivers in institutional contexts), who often are not tech-savvy either. This poses a special challenge to the design team in terms of gaining access to persons who often are initially not very much interested in "our" technical subjective or do not feel comfortable thinking about technological devices in their everyday circumstances. The buildup of trust, motivational aspects, and a common notional frame of reference has proven to be essential. Among others, we have described activity-based research methods to aim these needs (Müller et al. 2012; also see Chapter 10).

ICT research in the field of dementia care, however, illuminates further design challenges beyond an initially lacking common notional frame of reference. In IS research, for example, a common theme or a vision for participatory design projects between a design team and prospective users in a work organization is more easily set up because people already use current technology for their work. Gaver et al. (1999) pinpoint the difficulties that occur when ICT development projects move from the work to the home domain, where everyday settings are less routinized and less "task-oriented" as well as less technology-centered than in work settings.

The field of dementia care poses, on top of this, challenges in the intermingling of the autonomy- and agency-related questions of the target groups, as well as in respect to technology-related attitudes and acceptance (Fitzpatrick et al. 2010; Müller et al. 2010). Our research is inherently contoured by discourses in the field of professional caregiving; these discuss the "right" way to understand and deal with persons suffering from dementia. ICT design projects in this field are inherently interwoven in these discourses and more or less specifically discussed by the design teams in the presentation of their research results.

We would like to present our reflections on IT design in this sensitive setting in respect to practice-based design and grounded design, respectively, and especially emphasize the usage of ethnographic and action-research-based methods to gain a deeper understanding of some specificities of the field of dementia care in Germany.

Therefore, we present a case study aiming at the development of a location system for persons with dementia who wander. After having presented the three steps of the case study (pre-study, prototyping, and evaluation), we will enclose some methodological reflections. We are especially interested in opening up discussion of the tension between the actual practices of the caregivers in the field and their corresponding lines to societal, medial, and medical discourses.

11.2 Related Work

Recent research work on IT for dementia care has demonstrated the need for a deep embedding of technology in everyday practices that implicate the value judgments and attitudes associated with caring for and making decisions for another person (Robinson et al. 2009; Dahl and Holbø 2012a, b). The literature shows the dual nature of surveillance (Essén 2008), which in the field of dementia care produces value conflicts of *awareness versus privacy* and *safety versus autonomy* (Landau et al. 2009; Landau et al. 2010;). Other authors provide a more nuanced picture on the basis of qualitative research results, such as Dahl and Holbø (2012a), who point at the multifaceted nature of stakeholders' views on the dilemmas of GPS tracking patients in professional dementia care. In the same vein, we demonstrate that different aspects of a GPS-based monitoring measure are linked to distinctive and heterogeneous values that range across settings and roles.

For late-phase dementia sufferers, a tracking system could provide a balance between preserving their autonomy and keeping them safe. However, in a first trial of GPS technology used to track dementia sufferers, five out of the eleven respondents dropped out of the study (Miskelly 2005). This is the starting point of our study—a detailed investigation of the sociotechnical factors that make GPS deployment so problematic. As of today, even though there are commercial GPS tracking devices, they are seldom bought and used (Robinson et al. 2009). Our study shows that the take-up of such technologies by either the familial caregivers or the care institutions, in this complicated context, has been underwhelming.

Brodaty et al. (2005) show low take-up of available services by caregivers in general. The reasons for this, the authors suggest, are a perceived lack of need and a lack of knowledge of related services. Stigmatization was given as another reason for the caregivers' reluctance to use services. The low uptake of technological aids in dementia care points at the need for a better understanding of the social/sociotechnical issues in technology usage in dementia care. The social, ethical, and legal universe in which caregivers operate problematizes the deployment of such technologies in a variety of ways, and this chapter aims to detail this.

Here, we present a grounded-design study delivering a holistic documentation covering the full life span of a design case study. This includes (1) a qualitative pre-study on the practices of professional and familial caregiving for dementia patients who wander, (2) design and prototyping of the technology, and (3) an evaluation phase in which the appropriation and usage of the developed technologies in a real-life environment is observed over a long-term period. As such, it is broadly consistent with the grounded-design and design case study approach advocated by Wulf et al. (2011, 2015; Rohde et al. 2017). However, the field offers some specificities that need more reflection, especially in order to gain a thorough understanding of the different discourses in the "application field" and the reflective work needed for ICT designers.

Practice-based design in human–computer interaction (HCI) appears in methodological framings such as participatory design (PD), and living labs in real-life contexts (Carroll and Rosson 2007; Følstad 2008; Ogonowski et al. 2013). These approaches aim at a better understanding of the social fabrics in which future technologies are to be used and how current end-user practices and attitudes may influence the design and appropriation processes of the final product to be developed. In regard to PD with/for the elderly, research has demonstrated the importance of taking elderly persons' attitudes and (self-) images into account. These are often based on a low familiarity with new media, resulting in anxiety and a reluctance to get in touch and hence indicate the type of measures that should be taken in order to develop technology that is meaningful and useful to the elderly (Brandt et al. 2010; Lindsay et al. 2012; Wan et al. 2014). PD work with persons with dementia brings specific challenges with it, as, for example, discussed by Dahl and Holbø (2012a), who worked with persons with early onset dementia and their relatives/familial carers. They show that one potential problem is that the voice of the person with dementia might be suppressed by the caregiver. When working with a person in the later stages of dementia, it may become necessary to rely more on the judgments of their familial or institutional caregivers rather than on the actual person, so the researcher has to evaluate the work via this substitutional interpretation. Thus, the target group incorporates the caring networks in a very close way.

In the literature of ICT support for healthcare, there is a general move toward approaching the design problem from a sociotechnical perspective (Ballegaard et al. 2008; Kaplan and Harris-Salamone 2009; Fitzpatrick and Ellingsen 2013). Themes in the area of home-based healthcare, for instance, evolve around the communication and cooperation needs of various stakeholders in chronic illness treatment (Palen and Aaløkke 2006; Pratt et al. 2006; Mamykina et al. 2008; Pang et al. 2013; Schorch et al. 2016). Research has demonstrated that values and attitudes of each stakeholder play an important role in appropriation and usage of ICT (Christensen and Grönvall 2011).

Other research stresses the social side of healthcare, for example, research into support for social interaction and the sense of belonging for the elderly (Judge et al. 2010; Gaver et al. 2011; Vines et al. 2012; Uzor and Baillie 2013). Such work increasingly focuses on maintaining and boosting the participation and autonomy of older adults so that they can continue living, as much as possible, independently even in circumstances where older people are experiencing cognitive and/or physical decline. Research work in the context of cognitive issues has aimed at key problems such as the role of various stakeholders in the care process and has dealt with such issues as "whereabouts" or "biographical" awareness (Mynatt et al. 2001; Consolvo et al. 2004; Abowd et al. 2006; Wittenberg-Lyles et al. 2010) and monitoring (Morris et al. 2003; Petrakou 2007; Demiris 2009).

This sociotechnical stance is all the more significant in the field of ICT for dementia care. Assistive GPS technology for healthcare, work on the living conditions of older adults with chronic diseases (e.g., dementia), and ICT support options point to the high degree of social embedding of, for example, location-based systems and how different strategies have been applied to minimize the tension between *privacy and awareness* and between *safety and autonomy* (Crabtree et al. 2003; Gowans et al. 2004; Landau et al. 2009; Robinson et al. 2009; Tsai et al. 2009; Landau et al. 2010; Müller et al. 2010; Müller et al. 2013; Wan et al. 2014). This, in turn, has led some researchers to reflect on the appropriateness of research methods, such as the testing of off-the-shelf technologies in real circumstances (Dahl and Holbø 2012b) and to a call for more long-term evaluations of developed prototypes in general (Fitzpatrick and Ellingsen 2013).

Although research indicates that there has been insufficient acceptance of tracking devices in dementia care (Astell 2009), we do not fully understand why the take-up of such technology has been underwhelming. Our review of the literature found no example of previous work that compared different care settings and the moral and ideological world they inhabit. Our study, in contrast, shows that the differences to be found in different contexts are sometimes striking and have a direct impact on the willingness to deploy tracking technology.

Because of the richly situated, continuously evolving, and collaborative nature of healthcare, studies in the field of HCI or computer-supported cooperative work often are carried out with qualitative methods. In the case of dementia care—an example of the "sensitive setting" that Crabtree et al. refer to—research into the problems of dementia sufferers and their families is particularly challenging. Crabtree et al. reported on their experience of adapting cultural probes when developing computer support for former psychiatric patients living in residential care settings, for older members of the community, and for disabled people living at home (Crabtree et al. 2003). Underpinning such work is a concern for "responsibility"—who is responsible for care, and in what circumstances? Can sufferers be relied on to act responsibly in their own interests?

Some authors noted that when conducting PD workshops with both dementia patients and caregivers, it is important to prevent caregivers from becoming the dominant or only voice. Patients may be otherwise unheard (Dahl and Holbø 2012b). Value sensitive design (Friedman 1996), as an information system design methodology, emphasizes how values play out in design and how balancing competing values in various situations plays an important role. Robinson et al. (2009) aim at supporting independent living and involving early onset dementia patients in the design process. We, however, are dealing with late-stage dementia. In fact, we tried to involve the patients in our work but the methodological challenges proved to be insurmountable.

The issue of how to analyze the complex, detailed qualitative data from in-situ studies in healthcare is a further challenge. We align our methodological approach with the practice-based computing research framework of Wulf et al. (2011, 2015). Under this framework, we approach our research in three phases: (1) empirical pre-study, which involves empirically analyzing actual practice in a specific application context; (2) PD, which involves designing ICT artifacts based on the findings of the first phase, with inclusion of the stakeholders; and (3) evaluation, which involves examining the appropriation of the technical artifact over a significant period of time. Our work, then, focuses on presenting the whole design process, which includes building, deploying, and evaluating a system over a long period of time.

11.3 Overview of the Context Study

The aim of the pre-study was to gather data on how conflicting demands and values in dementia care are being dealt with in practice. To do this, we examined practices in domestic as well as in three different institutional care environments, relying mainly on interviews and participant observation for our data. Interviews were only loosely structured, reflecting our general, but initially unfocused, interest in attitudes to and practices with dementia care tools and resources.

The three different care environments in which we found interview partners were care homes, special dementia living groups, and institutional care facilities. In general, it should be pointed out, accessing "users" in these circumstances is difficult. Our first attempts at user contact showed that many dementia-affected families feel reluctant to discuss this sensitive topic with unfamiliar people. It required, as is always the case in such sensitive settings, the development over time of trust in our motives and our ability to behave responsibly over time. To do so, we looked for "gatekeepers" or "door openers" who could help. They were available in the form of organizers of a local self-help organization. These persons had widespread contacts with families as well as institutions, and the willingness of people to be interviewed by us largely depended on their vouchsafing of our good intentions.

We conducted twenty-one semistructured interviews, with six family caregivers (two wives, one husband, two adult daughters, and one adult son of a dementia sufferer) and fifteen professional caregivers (six ward nurses and nine managers) from stationary care facilities. Each interview lasted about 2 hours. All the interviews were audio recorded with approval and were transcribed and anonymized for data analysis. Besides interviews, we have held several meetings with an Alzheimer self-help organization. These meetings have been documented in field notes. Furthermore, we spent some days on participant observation in institutions and families (10 hours in a care home, and 10 hours in a dementia flat share). They were also documented in the form of field notes.

After we readied all the empirical data (interview transcripts, field notes), we started a collective and systematic coding process. As a team, we held data analysis workshops regularly to update the code system, cross-code each other's material, and group discuss on unclear points. This helped to minimize the number of different interpretations among individual team members.

Based on the results of the pre-study, we held regular design workshops with the self-help organization, to test and validate design ideas as soon as possible. As care practice in institutional care strongly suggests the need for a mobile application, we also held two design workshops with nurses in care homes to discuss the mobile application design. In all design sessions with the users, we encouraged them to express their ideas, even very abstract or unrealistic ones. With our help, the participants created paper mock-ups and design sketches.

For the evaluation phase, we remained in contact with most of the interview partners from the pre-study and had hoped to enroll them again for further testing of the system in the long term. However, only one care facility was willing/able to join the long-term evaluation. It was even significantly harder to find participants for the field evaluation than for the pre-study, for three reasons. First, along with the project progress, the problems of the affected persons had also progressed. They were now either not able to walk, or the caregivers were too afraid to let them walk freely. Second, the institutions were very cautious about testing the system in real environment, because of the possible philosophical or legal ramifications associated with technology failure. Third, testing the system in real environments would have brought additional cost to the institutions, including, for example, human resources and time to use the technology, effort to gain a certain amount of expertise with the technology itself, and any additional handling effort if the system malfunctioned. In fact, a lack of available resources was one of the main reasons why many institutions were not willing to participate in our field test.

We finally managed to enroll three environments and tested our prototype there over a time span of 3–5 months. The environments were a hospital ward, an elderly care home, and a family. In all three environments, the caregivers conducted care supervision in an "open" way, which meant that wandering by patients had already been allowed before our IT intervention was introduced, and the caregivers had already developed certain measures to ensure patient safety as much as they could. We handed out user diaries to the caregivers and used them as memory aids for the interview visits we had with them every 2–4 weeks. A more fine-grained description of the three locations is given in Section 11.7.

11.4 Pre-Study: Findings

11.4.1 Understanding the Complexities of Caregiving for Persons with Dementia in Institutions

Patient Admission: Bias in the Bilateral Selection

Taking care of a dementia patient at home is a demanding job for relatives, especially when the patient has a tendency to wander. The physical and mental strain can be overwhelming for family caregivers, who often lack professional insight into care management. When they turn to stationary care institutions, patients and the care institutions can, in theory, choose each other freely and bilaterally. In reality, there is a strongly biased power distribution in this selection. Notably, it is extremely difficult for families to find a suitable institution for the dementia patient with wandering tendencies.

The first issue families consider when prioritizing their choices is the distance of the institution from their home. Very soon they realize that very few of these institutions have a clear care concept for the "wanderer." Their initial choice pool, that is, rapidly diminishes.

One institution, for instance, noted that they would not accept wandering clients because "we cannot take the responsibility for them." This was not, to be clear, because of legal ramifications, but because of a moral concern for the welfare of the wanderer in the absence of a reliable and practical monitoring solution. In contrast, caregivers at another institution, which did accept dementia patients with wandering tendencies, claimed that it was "an open house," as the doors of the care home were not locked and the inhabitants could leave at will. Having said that, they applied a series of precautionary measures, such as using heavy doors that were very difficult to open, hidden door knobs, hidden exits behind curtains, and so on. Again, measures of this kind were not universally accepted among professional caregivers. Some considered these measures to be a legitimate expediency, while others saw them as an affront to human dignity and as manipulative of a group who were not able to distinguish aspects of reality.

Prevention in Practice: Heterogeneity and Controversy

The strategies that institutional care workers use on a daily basis when dealing with the wandering behaviors of dementia patients are highly heterogeneous and contextual. This is partially decided by the complex and volatile situations they face on a daily basis.

Decision-making in such conditions is constantly mediated by legal, ethical, and moral trade-offs. In Germany, detailed legal standards have been institutionalized in such facilities to prevent abuses such as tying patients to beds or chairs. Professionals now routinely refer to "freedom-depriving measures" and told us about their concern that certain preventive actions may be deemed freedom-depriving measures. The standards—although established some years ago—work more as guidelines rather than solutions (although some restrictions on freedom, such as locking the bedroom doors, are clearly illegal). In the absence of an unambiguous definition, there is significant uncertainty and confusion, not to mention a variety of moral positions, on the part of professional caregivers and managers when making decisions.

From our samples, such preventive measures fall into three categories: (1) constructional measures, (2) technical support, and (3) human intervention.

Constructional measures include tricks such as heavy doors and camouflaged (or hidden) exit. Creating "endless corridors" is another commonly used measure. In one dementia flat share we saw, the corridor was built in a circular form around a public area in the middle. This let the patient take walks along the hallway but never reach the exit. Such measures were controversial for care workers and, often, there were quite different perspectives on the acceptability of the measures on view. The "constructional" principle was viewed by some as inhuman: "This is awful to imagine: you are walking and walking and you never arrive. This can make you even more confused!" (female relative).

The second category of preventive measures is using technology to monitor patient behavior. The following monitoring technologies have been (or partially) applied in our samples: video cameras, door safety systems, and sensor mats. The professional caregivers' attitudes toward monitoring technology are more consistent and are characterized as a general reluctance. Their reluctance to use this technology stemmed from the following reasons: (1) fear that it might be categorized as a "freedom-depriving measure," (2) usability issues with the system, and (3) distrust in the reliability of the system.

Third, human intervention describes the way in which some caregivers developed measures to keep patients busy and distracted from the urge to wander. Activities such as reading, chatting with each other, eating together, and going for walks together are the most common ones. Keeping patients busy during the day also helps them sleep better at night, which reduces the danger of patients wandering off. Many caregivers told us that they have to constantly keep an eye on the patients' activities and assess the situation, because "most of the time we don't know whether they have a wandering tendency. Sometimes we can predict it based on the patient's behaviors." This is especially challenging when they are undertaking care routines in patients' rooms. One solution is to put temporary barriers in the way. Commonly used barriers are, for example, the nursing cart or toilet chairs. The nurses told us this is a compromise, because normally they try to keep the hallway barrier-free so that the residents can walk safely but at the same time they have to monitor while coping with staff shortages.

Problems in Finding and Retrieving

Patients can, and do, wander. When a patient is presumed to be lost, members of the care staff will be organized to look for the lost one. The approach is normally ordered as follows: looking inside the building, calling the patient's relatives, looking outside, and finally calling the police. Interviewees told us that some patients have their favorite wandering routes. These routes can be the way home, or a personally favorite path. But there were still many practical problems in coordinating the search and finally bringing back the patient. How to bring the patient back to the institution is another challenge, especially when the patient does not recognize the care staff and is reluctant to return to the home with them. Some professionals reflected that they sometimes use "white lies" to trick the found patients to come back with them, such as, for example, "Your daughter has just called." They mentioned that for each patient there are several "key words" that typically work well. But these "key words" are highly individual for each patient. And it requires deep understanding of the patient so that one can apply them appropriately in a challenging situation.

Attitudes of Care Institutions toward GPS Monitoring Systems

None of the institutions we interviewed used a GPS tracking system to monitor patients. Despite the fact that they have a need for such as a system (as care staff are overburdened), the sheer heterogeneity of care concepts/practices makes commercial products unsatisfactory. Inappropriate merchandizing of providers to users who are not technologically savvy is another reason given by caregivers for the reluctance to deal with the technology. Inconsistent attitudes inside institutions also inhibit unanimous acceptance of such technology. At the macrolevel, legal and ethical standards are vague and subjective, and guidelines are in short supply.

However, all the institutional care managers who were asked for an interview did invite us to get information on the state of the art in this area. All of the interviews with managers—and many of the interviews with relatives caring at home—thus had the form of an informal information-and-experience-exchange space. In many cases, during the interview, we used the Internet to look up information on state-of-the-art systems and then discussed them with our interview partners in regard to their perceived needs. This way—as with the activity- and technology-based procedures with elderly and non-tech-savvy persons (Müller et al. 2012)—we could build up a common thinking space and help managers/relatives rethink their attitudes and ideas about the possible benefit or harm the monitoring technology might have for them and the persons they cared for.

11.4.2 Understanding the Complexities of Caregiving for Persons with Dementia at Home

Autonomy versus Safety: Two Entirely Opposite Cases

The analysis of the interviews with family caregivers—husbands, wives, sons, and daughters—offers very different perspectives on the evaluation and discussion of the autonomy and freedom needs of the affected family member. The difference can be significant. In one case, where care took place in the home, a husband reported that he allowed very little freedom of movement to his wife. While in their home, he would not allow her to be alone in another floor—for fear that she might hurt herself. Being a retired engineer, he developed coping mechanisms for their everyday life: he "engineered" her eating, sleeping, and bathroom times with medication. In his understanding, autonomy was not relevant for his wife, as she was "no longer here" with her mind.

In contrast, the daughter of a woman with medium-stage dementia built a social network to collaboratively take care of her mother, so that her mother can live independently in her home and conduct everyday tasks—even go to the city—on her own. For the daughter, it is vital that her mother feels that she is autonomous—and she has adopted many measures to "artificially" achieve this, such as asking shop clerks and bank officers to give the mother what she wants, but up to a certain level. Sometimes the daughter "shadows" her mother on her way to town. For the daughter, her mother's ability to maintain a public and independent "face" is of primary importance.

For many of the relatives we interviewed, the classic value trade-off between safety and autonomy is of minor relevance in their decision-making, especially when the disease advances. Many relatives report primarily on the overwhelming burden of concern for the dementia-suffering family member. So for them, keeping the loved ones safe is much more important than preserving their autonomy. As the disease progresses, the patient's mental existence is normally perceived as "fading away," and autonomy becomes less and less important for them (although this is not universal; it is a feature of such relationships that they engender a great deal of reflexive concern, contingently negotiated).

Impact of Preexisting Family Patterns on Care Concepts

In the home context, families tailor care strategies to fit local conditions and needs. Each family has its own habitual familial pattern, determined by the family's structure and hierarchy, balancing between genders, and children/parent roles. Our empirical analysis indicates that preexisting roles can have completely different effects on the care concept when dementia occurs. For example, in one case, a daughter and her mother who took care of the father who suffers from dementia at home reported that the father had always had a dominant role in the family and a strongly independent attitude. Even with the onset of dementia, he continued to assert this dominance. He still took long walks on his own, leaving his family in a self-confessed position of helplessness: "We cannot hold him" (Mrs. C.). This, we discovered, is quite common in situations where female relatives have to cope with male dementia sufferers. In contrast, in the case of the husband who "engineered" the behavior of her wife, his preexisting and continuing dominance in the family had actually "helped" him manage his wife's life with less resistance.

Thus, dementia care is mediated by prior family patterns and the role expectations contained therein. How to design a universal technical support that will work in all familial situations is, unsurprisingly, challenging. Technology support in the family context needs somehow to balance the continuities and changes experienced by both patients and their caregivers.

Attitudes of Family Caregivers toward GPS Monitoring Systems

Family caregivers tend to be more open about the possibilities of a GPS-based monitoring system. However, the degree to which such a system is required depends very much on the progression of the disease and the coping strategies adopted by caregivers.

As in the institutional context, the interviewed families had a need for technological support and were aware of its existence, but none had bought a commercial product. Some of our users made the frustration with their experience of searching for a GPS solution very clear, stating that there was a lack of reliable information channels about such products, or that insufficient information was provided by the product websites that, in addition, were perceived as addressing technological specialists only.

11.4.3 Design Implications

From the empirical results of the pre-study, we were able to identify the following design implications. Clearly, heterogeneous assumptions demand flexible solutions. Tailorability (Henderson and Kyng 1991; Wulf et al. 2008) and end-user development (Lieberman et al. 2006; also see Chapter 13) in this case are of great importance. The system should provide as much flexibility as possible to allow for divergent attitudes, ethical/legal concerns, and care routines to find their footing in it. Consequently, there are the following implications for design:

- *reliability*: reliability is an important requirement for all IT systems but is critical in this context; tolerance of system failure is very low, especially in the institutional context
- *history of paths*: almost all caregivers, no matter whether professional or familial, told us that patients have their favorite wandering routes, and in large degree are predictable, so keeping a history of the wandering routes in system could help identify such favorite routes and thus help in the search for patient; more importantly, when provided with such a history, caregivers might be able to identify the patients' motives behind the wandering and their reasons for choosing these routes
- *high flexibility of system configuration*: the constant value trade-off between safety and autonomy requires the system to provide options for the user to tailor the system according to temporal and spatial evaluation of the situation; for instance,
  - it should be possible to set up safety areas (or *digital fences*) on the map and receive prompt notification when the patient leaves those areas
  - the caregiver should be able to configure the tracker to update the positions either automatically or manually (pulling or polling mode)
  - the position update interval should be adjustable
  - information on the patient needs to be anonymized, in order to meet the privacy requirements of certain institutions
- *support for cooperative monitoring*: caregivers already cooperate with each other to manage the care work in practice, and cooperation also happens between professional and familial caregivers; the system should therefore support communication, coordination, and negotiation between them

For the mobile application, we had the following design implications:

- *elderly-friendly user interaction*: the design of the mobile application should supply simple design and straightforward user interaction; many caregivers are themselves elderly and have difficulty in reading small screens and understanding smartphone operations
- *navigation function*: it is essential to provide a navigation function in the mobile application to locate the wandering patient and navigate the caregiver to him/her
- *"key words" and integrated contact lists*: the caregiver should be able to access some "hint" information to help persuade the patient to come back, such as the "key words" mentioned in Section 11.4.1; in addition, a contact list should be added so that the caregiver can order help via the mobile if needed

The design decision to use a Web portal in combination with a mobile application allowed a distribution of functions. On one hand, this made it possible to use functions at their most suitable screen size. The Web portal functionality was designed for the PC screen, which provides enough space for location monitoring, system configuration, and jobs that are easier done with mouse and keyboard, such as drawing a safety area. The mobile application suited situations that require mobility, such as the navigation function in a patient searching. Having said that, flexibility of access turned out to be extremely important.

11.5 Prototype Development

In the institutional context of this research, the actual development of the prototype was the responsibility of a software company who formed part of the project consortium from the start. We conducted regular project meetings every 3–4 weeks with the developers from the company, to transfer our results and design. As a research institute, we also developed an iPhone application, which had not been envisioned in the draft of the project plan.

The final prototype was a complete GPS-based location monitoring system to help caregivers better manage the wandering behavior of dementia patients. The system consisted of GPS trackers to be carried by the patients, a Web portal for monitoring the patient's position and adjusting settings (e.g., configuring trackers and defining safety areas on the map), and an iPhone app for mobile monitoring (see Figure 11.1).

The prototype featured all of the features mentioned in Section 11.4.3, save one: the cooperative monitoring feature. Given that we were partnered with a commercial organization, our design ideas had to be filtered through their interests, and this was the main reason why the cooperative monitoring feature was not implemented. Nevertheless, we were able to refine our part (the iPhone app) in multiple design cycles based on several PD workshops together with the caregivers. We experienced, we should say, significant difficulties in working with commercial interests alongside our own research objectives. However, a detailed analysis of such organizational issues is not within the scope of this chapter (but see Chapter 16).

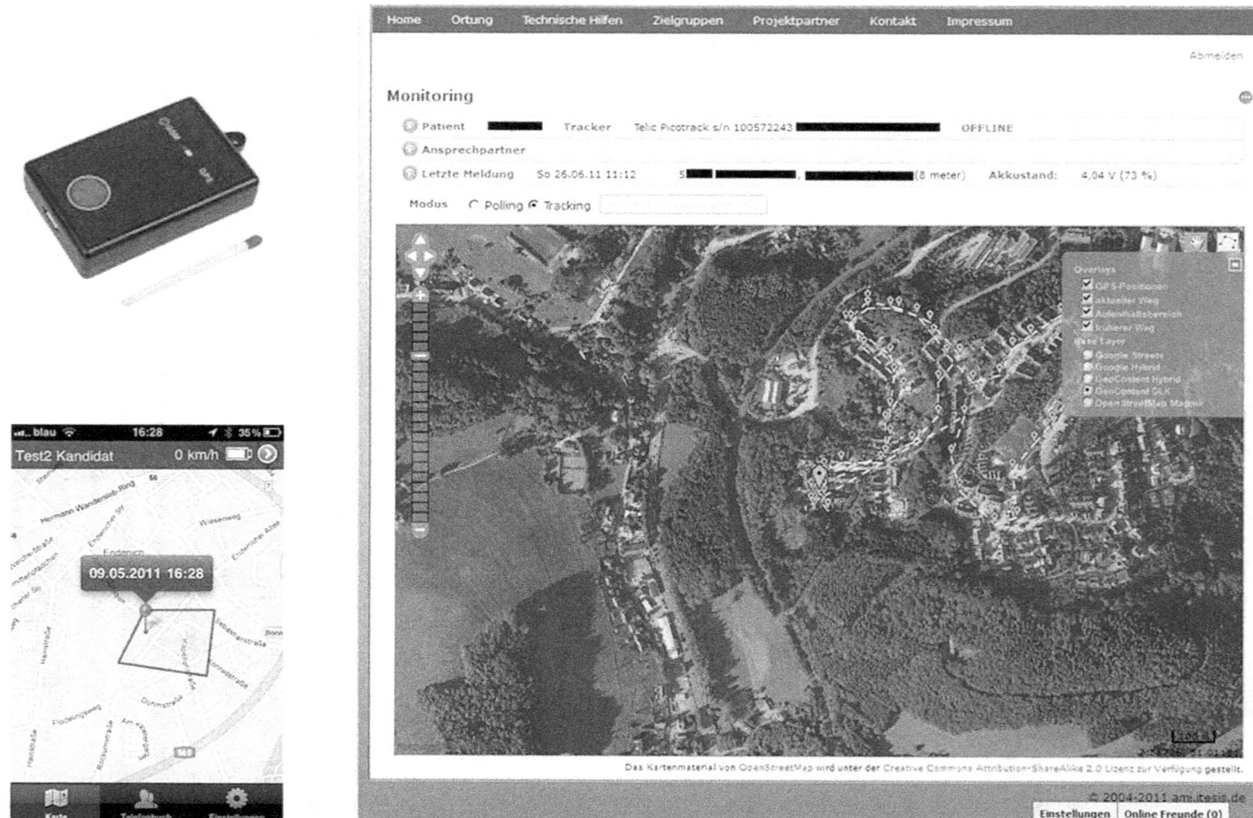

Figure 11.1 Screenshots of the prototype

11.6 Evaluation: Methodology

We rolled out the prototype in three different locations and tested it in real-life situations over a time span of 3–5 months. The locations included a household in which the husband is suffering from dementia (age 55), a care home with a focus on dementia care, and a special ward of a hospital.

Deploying the technology was anything but straightforward. Prior to the actual deployment, we conducted several semistructured interviews in each setting in order to obtain a detailed overview of their technology infrastructure and any specific conditions, so that we could make a customized deployment plan for each setting. In the institutions, we had at least two on-site meetings to inform management and ward nurses about the evaluation plan. Prior to our visits, all evaluation partners had tried to get information on GPS support technology on the Internet, but all had given up because of the poor quality of the provider websites in terms of providing information about the technical issues. The on-site visits were audio recorded, and field notes were taken.

Despite our detailed preparation, we still faced unexpected difficulties during the technology installation in each location. We had to be very flexible and creative to fine-tune the prototype so that it could be integrated into daily practice. For example, for the special ward in the hospital, we had to deliver an iPad that had a 3G connection, in order to access the monitoring website, because the Internet speed in that hospital was too slow to allow for serious roll-out of the prototype.

We visited the family and the institutions regularly every 2–4 weeks and were available 24/7 by phone in case of questions and problems. Altogether, we conducted twelve on-site visits and six telephone interviews, with the interviews typically lasting 1.5–2.0 hours. All the interview sessions were audio recorded with consent and later transcribed. During the evaluation, we kept in close contact with our testers, and all the emails and phone calls were documented in field notes. Furthermore, we asked the testers to fill in a media diary of their daily experience with the system. The diaries also worked as a basis for discussion in the on-site interviews. The data analysis was approached in the same as in the pre-study. We started with an open code system and regularly held internal analysis workshops.

11.7 Evaluation: Findings

11.7.1 The Settings: Two Institutions and a Family

The prototype system was evaluated in three locations, which were chosen because they enabled "real-world" evaluation without endangering patients: a hospital ward, an elderly care home for dementia care, and a family. The study thus had three different scenarios of use, where different experiences were reported.

11.7.2 Institution A: A Dementia Care Home

Institution A is a dementia care institution in a rural area. The care home is committed to following new dementia care philosophies, including giving the residents as much space as possible to be mobile on their own. Around the care home, there is large protected area in which the residents are allowed to walk freely. There is an alarm system attached to the main entrance, and patients with a special wristband, passing through the entrance, will trigger a phone call to the care staff. The manager of the care home is of the view that patients should be able to leave the area if they wish to, although care workers at the home are less liberal in their views.

Three young male volunteers, to whom the head nurse had handed the prototypes, tested our system. Interestingly, these young men were all IT familiar but saw older professional caregivers as "lay" users of such technology. The head nurse shared this view, saying: "older persons [meaning her colleagues] could not use this system, because in this institution they have only low experiences with technology and computers." She emphasized this with reference to her colleagues' general problems with care documentation work at the computer: "my colleagues already have problems with simply clicking the right things in our records."

11.7.3 Institution B: A Hospital Ward

Institution B is located in a big city and is a big hospital and care complex. The ward in which we tested the system has a special focus on long-term care for persons with cranial–cerebral trauma and comorbidities such as dementia. Here, location-tracking services were welcomed, but worries were also raised because of the high mobility of the patient. In this case, a relatively young man, who used to be a marathon runner, suffered from severe dementia as consequence of a car accident. The ward is an "open ward," which means that locking the doors is forbidden. This patient "escapes" regularly and is very difficult to manage as a result of his level of physical fitness. A specific limitation of the tracker was its low precision in indoor positioning, and this patient was often "lost" in the ward (e.g., once he was found in the basement, having spent hours in a disoriented state).

On the day we brought our prototype to the ward, we noticed that the Internet connection in the hospital was too slow for a sensible field test. As an alternative, we bought an iPad with a 3G data tariff so that the staff could use the iPad to access the Web portal. Two days later, when we visited the ward again, they told us that "the iPad is safely locked in the cabinet [so that nobody will steal it]." Because of the high mobility of patients and relatives in the hospital in general, they were extremely afraid of losing the costly device, and it was initially locked away unused. We then bought a protection case and a lock for the iPad so it could be securely attached to a desk.

The staff then started to use the system. Several days later, we received a phone call from our contact person—a nurse in the house—telling us that a patient had been lost for 20 hours and had been found the next day 30 km away from the ward. She told us that before this accident had happened, the patient had been carrying the tracker 24 hours a day but that the battery life of the tracker was inadequate. Although she had tried to keep the

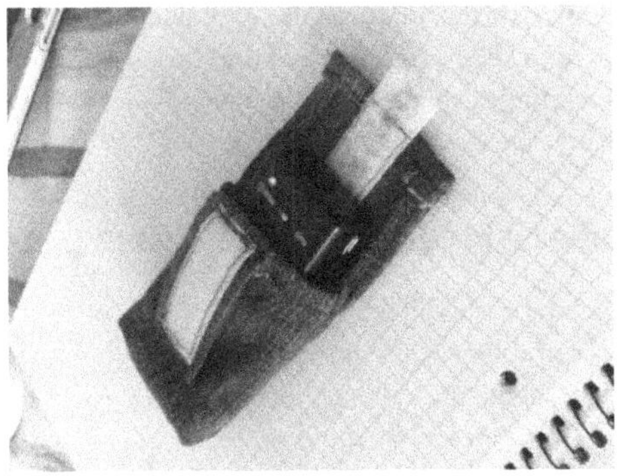

Figure 11.2 Self-made textile bag to carry the tracker around the belt

tracker charged, she had no idea how the patient went out without triggering an alarm; she went on to say that "in this form we cannot trust the system." After investigating the system, together with the nurse, we found out that the battery had died within the safety area, right before the patient left the house. What we learned from this case is that the system should send a notification when the tracker battery is low. After discussion with the ward, we deployed another tracker for the patient, so that the trackers could simply be exchanged, with there always being one fully charged. After this incident, the system has been used 24 hours per day; our contact person in the ward has reported several successful instances where the system has been helpful, and the staff members have started to trust the system more and more. The relatives of the patient also started to trust the system and grew dependent on it. The wife of the patient even made a carrying case for the device so that her husband can attach it to his belt and thus carry the tracker around more easily (see Figure 11.2).

11.7.4 A Family Setting

In this setting, the sufferer is cared for at home by a spouse. He, a former doctor, lives with his wife and three children aged between 15 and 20. Mr. C. walks the dog several times a day on short routes in the nearby neighborhood. The routes he walks along are well known to the family and are, according to his wife, "routinized." Before he leaves the house, he tells his wife or children where he intends to go. They then estimate roughly the time he should return. It has already happened several times that the man was not able to return home on his own. That is why a volunteer from a local charity organization now comes three times a week to take him and the dog for a long walk. Mr. C., however, very much dislikes the company of the volunteer, because he considers himself to be still autonomous enough to walk on his own.

In our interviews with Mrs. C., she told us that our system has been extremely helpful for her. She began, she said, to rely strongly on the technology after only a few weeks. She used the system not only at home but also at work. She said that the system gives her peace of mind, as she can see on the map that her husband is walking on the regular route. But she appropriated the system in a way that preserves as much privacy as possible for the husband. For example, she had not used the digital fence at all, as it felt too intrusive to her. And she slightly reduced the frequency of the tracker's position report. She did not want to constantly track her husband; for her, being able to look into the system and know that he was safe was already a great relief.

11.7.5 Some General Findings across Cases

We identified some general issues affecting the acceptance of trackers. First, the size of the tracker was seen as a problem by the interviewees. Although the device is quite small (the size of a match box), dementia sufferers often dislike devices of any size attached to their body or clothes. Thus, caregivers would prefer to use something very small, like a thin bracelet, or something in the form of wristwatch or necklace, which—as a known artifact to the sufferers—would be better accepted by them. Given the need for battery size, that is, in current years, difficult to realize.

Given the demand for autonomy, "open house" philosophies mean that caregivers negotiate the freedoms of patients, where possible, to maximize them. "Digital fences" are, in principle, extremely useful in this respect. Professional caregivers, however, suggested an additional structuring of the feature into three zones: a green zone, a yellow zone ("be alerted, person has left the safe area"), and a red zone ("act immediately, he/she is in danger"). The family carers, unlike those in institutional settings, scarcely used the digital fence function at all.

The system was viewed as extremely useful in the institutional context even when it could not locate accurately indoors, because it helped refine search strategies. Thus, for instance, in the case of the former marathon runner, although the system could not tell the exact position in the building, it nevertheless indicated that the patient was not outside, which greatly reduced the search area, and thus made the search more targeted.

A similar benefit of the technology was perceived by Mrs. C., who argued that because the system allowed her to retrace routes her husband had taken, she was able to get a better sense of why her husband deviated from his normal route, thus reducing her anxiety. For example, one time her husband's decreasing cognitive capability had led to a situation where he had ended up on a highway (Autobahn) construction site but had been unable to explain how he had found himself there. As Mrs. C. said: "We do not know even today why he had gone to this Autobahn construction site... Something must be happened that made him leave the normal route. It can drive you crazy that you do not know the reason why." Now, with the technology, there is the option to at least to reflect on possible reasons for new path choices.

11.8 Discussion

11.8.1 Discussion of Design Implications

Overall, our proposed solutions have had a positive effect on the experiences of dementia sufferers, their families, and professional caregivers. Particularly, in two of our three test sites, the professional and familial caregivers have grown dependent on the prototype and have shown active appropriation of the technological artifact. Having said that, the sheer complexity of the different situations that occasion concern, the heterogeneous nature of organizational and family routines, and the different moral/ideological commitments expressed by different parties underpin the need for solutions that are both very flexible and practical to implement. In the organizational context, it is clear that these complexities mean that support for collaborative searching and for the flexible definition of "boundaries" needs to be better implemented. Professional management of issues of autonomy, privacy, and safety are constantly negotiated and arranged in accordance with specific and local definitions of patient condition. Solutions must allow tailoring to meet these conditions. Another aspect our long-term and practice-based study shows is the significance of the shape and size of the tracker, as well as compromises that have to be made and discussed when deploying a practice-based evaluation study. The study also demonstrates that there is a great need for individual customization of the tracking devices in the form of jewelry, wristwatches, and so on.

In addition, technical support must fit with the established routines of family and institutional life. Constant monitoring from fixed positions is extremely difficult in many care institutions, where there are constant demands on time, and the need to be available in different locations. In family contexts, demands include the fact that carers themselves are sometimes elderly, or have other family or work commitments. Even professional caregivers can have problems learning new technologies, especially older caregivers. This was exemplified in the case of Institution A, where the prototype was not actively used because of this technology barrier. The relationship between technology appropriation and the low IT affinity of some caregivers had already been described, for example, in the article by Pot et al. 2012. Our study augments this problem sphere by describing additional aspects impacting appropriation, such as the high heterogeneity in care concepts and moral and legal standpoints, which also may cause a reluctance in the willingness to use IT in dementia care.

Nevertheless, it would be naive to imagine that technical solutions can solve all problems. As Rogers has argued,

> while most projects are sensitive to the privacy and ethical problems surrounding the monitoring of people, they are not easy to solve and have ended up overwhelming UbiComp research. Indeed, much of the discussion about the human aspects in the field has been primarily about the trade-offs between security and privacy, convenience and privacy, and informedness and privacy. This focus has often been at the expense of other human concerns receiving less airing, such as how recording, tracking and re-representing movements and other information can be used to facilitate social and cognitive processes. (Rogers 2006, p. 410)

Our long-term field test shows several impacts of the monitoring technology on the cooperative and social processes of dementia care. For example, it allows the "lines of conflict" to be renegotiated. Concerns such as awareness vs. privacy and safety vs. autonomy can be differently managed given location-awareness support. To a large degree, the management of these concerns is a function of varying institutional and familial arrangements. This is compounded by the evident fact that policy, especially in the institutional context, around "freedom deprivation" is often ambiguous.

The constant renegotiation of care philosophies is a complicating factor. With Dahl and Holbø (2012a, b) we see that new care philosophies, such as person-centered care (Kitwood 2001), are being used in many care institutions. However, the related practices are not clear-cut. Therefore, we—in a manner slightly different to that of Sugihara et al. (2013), who promote patient-centered care as "appropriate for applying the norm of human-centered design"—recommend looking more deeply at the different ways in which care theories are being applied in situated practices.

Thus, autonomy is not a fixed metric. On the one hand, as indicated, this points at the need for flexibility in design technologies in its functionalities and settings. Just as importantly, however, it points to ethical issues in respect of how the researcher positions his/herself in these developing ideologies. If we support changing views of patient care in organizational settings, are we not bound to have a view of how patients are treated in family settings? Can we be comfortable supporting highly "engineered" solutions like the one described above?

Having to work with a software company in the consortium caused further difficulties in conducting this research project. It was especially hard for us to transfer qualitative empirical results and design suggestions to the company. This discrepancy in design philosophies brought some friction to the interaction (see Wan et al. 2016). It is our view that agile development processes are much more suitable for environments of this kind. This insight is not always fitting with design approaches of industrial partners who are still strongly influences by traditional approaches in software engineering (Dachtera et al. 2014).

The need to customize artifacts as well as the need to take aesthetic aspects into consideration when designing products for the elderly, especially those in dementia care, has been stressed elsewhere (Wallace et al. 2012; Angelini et al. 2013). Similarly, our inability to extend the tracker to cope with "indoor" situations limited its perceived value in this design case study.

In conclusion, we set out to contribute to a better understanding of the subtleties and complexities entailed in the familial and institutional management of dementia sufferers with wandering tendencies. With a full description of a design case study (investigative pre-study, design, and long-term evaluation) we have established, we feel, a fine-grained basis for understanding how lines of conflict may occur for these patients and how a suitably flexible GPS locating system can aid in the resolution of such conflict. It is clear to us that technology alone does not provide a full assistive solution, and it is always mediated by varied ideological and practical considerations in different contexts. The heterogeneity of caregiving contexts means assistive solutions (both the technology and service around it) must be very flexible and creative, adapting to differing users' needs in each specific context. Caregivers in our study found these things in very short supply.

Besides technological features, we also contribute to promoting a new ethos surrounding IT support for dementia management. A planned market roll-out of assistive technology in this sector requires detailed consideration of support for installation, education, legal matters, after-sales service (counseling, adaptation), and so on. The business model of such a product needs careful thought since service before, at, and after sale is at least as important as the technology itself. Again, any recognition of the need to provide other forms of support to caregivers is almost entirely, absent from the philosophy of technology providers in this challenging context.

11.8.2 Methodological Reflections

In this section, we will discuss the investigation of care practices and sociotechnical design in the field of dementia care in relation to the theme of this book: practice-based design, its research framework, and grounded design (Wulf et al. 2015; Rohde et al. 2017; also see Chapter 1).

We conducted our project under the methodological lens of grounded design, which is based on design case studies and typically comprises an extensive empirical pre-study, a prototyping phase, and a long-term evaluation and appropriation phase. The field of IT for the aging society, and specifically dementia care, shows some specificities that we would like to emphasize for the pre-study and appropriation phases.

First, the grounded-design framework builds in its first phase on data gathering techniques such as semistandardized interviews or participant observation of practices for the formulation of initial design ideas. Under a practice-oriented research paradigm, the data to be collected is linked to the situated practices (Suchman 1987) of the target group (in this case, the persons with dementia, and when the disease progressed, the familial and institutional caregivers). In Reckwitz's (2002) argumentation (also see Chapter 16), practice theory is a specific form of cultural theory, together with cultural mentalism, textualism, and intersubjectivism. In his view, these approaches differ according to the way in which they define the smallest unit of social theory: "minds, discourses, interactions, and 'practices'" (Reckwitz 2002, p. 244). Reckwitz confesses that his heuristic concept may not satisfy the rich works of the practice theoreticians he refers to, such as Bourdieu (1977), Giddens (1984), and Schatzki et al. (2001); in addition, his heuristic differentiation between the cultural theory approaches is perhaps not entirely helpful for framing research and design work in the IT field for the aging society, and especially in dementia care. In particular, we do not see imposing a strict separation between practice and textuality, or between practice and discourse, as being helpful. We would suggest using a stronger link between discourse analytic approaches, which focus on symbolic representations, and a practice-theoretical lens, as this would favor the analysis of everyday practices, which comprise aspects of embodiment and materiality (Baumann et al. 2015).

Our study, as well as other studies in the field of IT for the aging society (Müller et al. 2015a, b; Schorch et al. 2016), demonstrate this in the following aspects. Beginning with the issue of access to the target groups (including primary end users ("the elderly"), secondary end users (relatives, familial caregivers, professional caregivers, care homes, etc.), and tertiary end users (e.g., welfare associations), researchers are often confronted with huge problems in communicating their research objectives and in getting the target groups interested. This is essentially due to the fact that all groups have a low familiarity with new media, as well as the fact that the design projects take place in a highly discursive field, with different images of aging and with varying attitudes concerning the potential benefits of the use of new technology, as one measure among others, to assist the elderly in their activities of daily living. Our project in the field of dementia care makes these discourses highly visible: there are different (medical, sociopsychological) approaches and attitudes toward the concept of dementia and what the best treatment of persons suffering from dementia would be (Cantley 2001). The medical and psychological perspectives on dementia care have undergone a radical shift over the last three decades. The concept of personhood (inter alia, and prominently developed by Kitwood 2001) and the accompanying theory of dementia have had a profound influence on the development of new care concepts, by providing a philosophical base for the change in therapeutic approaches (Cantley 2001).

Looking at the care practices, our study shows that former approaches in dementia care, based on biomedical concepts, are still present, together with newer approaches such as person-centered care (Kitwood 2001), at least in the German context. The concurrency of the different care concepts has concrete manifestations in the attitudes and practices of the caregivers, which we found in both familial as well as institutional contexts. The strongest manifestation is visible in the concurrent usage of two different terms to describe wandering behavior in German: *Weglauftendenz* (the tendency to run away) and *Hinlauftendenz* (the tendency to run toward something). These two terms are strongly linked to ideological ascriptions and accompanying care measures (as well as in the estimation of the benefit or harm of an IT-support system), with the first being influenced by biomedical thinking, and the second by newer, personhood-oriented approaches. In our pre-study, we found similar differences in the attitudes and practices of caregivers.

This shows that actual practices are deeply rooted in educational programs—both the professional education of caregivers as well as in educational offers for familial caregivers at home—and their availability and acceptance.

This also means that these care practices, both in home care and in institutional care, are deeply rooted in questions of how the policy affects service developments, based on general conceptions of how a society treats persons with dementia and, accordingly, defines basic concepts such as autonomy, personhood, inclusion, and so on. Comparative studies on national levels pinpoint differences at societal levels: "Attitudes to dementia held by the general public, health and social care professionals, policy makers, relatives and others can influence the ways in which people view this set of conditions, their willingness to pay for medical treatments, and their willingness to see scarce tax or social insurance funds allocated to the support and care of people with dementia" (Knapp et al. 2007, p. 17).

Against the background of a deep entanglement of situated care practices in a highly discursive field, we would suggest not viewing the theoretical approaches of discourse analysis and practice theory as being mutually exclusive (as in Reckwitz's heuristic), because neglecting the discursive field would lead to there being blind spots in the empirical analyses.

A second aspect of the pre-study phase in the design case study, specific for IT for the aging society, is a methodological problem that occurs in the beginning of a project. The low tech-savviness of our target groups (in the case of the dementia care project, this was true for a large proportion of the caregivers, both in familial as well as in institutional, professional settings) urged us to think about methods that leveraged access to potential research partners to gain their willingness and motivation to give us interviews or let us participate in their everyday circumstances. We thus had to think about anchor points that would help them decide to cooperate with us—that is, to build up a common notional space of possibilities between the design team and the research participants. This led us to complement field study methods, such as interviews and participant observation, with action-research-based methods. In other settings in the field of IT for the aging society, action-research-based methods had proven helpful in developing such anchor points, via the early introduction of off-the-shelf products and engaging in common activities (such as experience-based PD workshops) to help develop device practices that would be meaningful and linked to individual interests and needs (see Müller et al. 2012, 2015a, b). In the study at hand, we were not able to use such an approach with our target group, people with dementia; however, it was equally important to help caregivers reflect on and discuss possible usage scenarios for a monitoring device. In the initial interviews, we discussed other off-the-shelf monitoring devices, and this discussion often led to deeper discussions. In the interviews with institutional carers, legal and ethical aspects opened up as themes that were further reflected upon. Thus, we found that our first inquiry for an interview or participant observation sparked further interest in a deeper reflection of the possible benefits, as well as the possible harm, our technology might provide.

Concerning G. Hayes's ideas in Chapter 9, our approach to data collection in the pre-study phase is somewhat between that used in action-research projects and that used in the approach described by Wulf et al. (2015) for the design case study concept. In the field of IT for the aging society, it is important to use additional measures to gain access to the field and to interest and motivate potential research partners for project participation (see also Chapter 10). These measures aim at collaboratively identifying anchor points that then influence interest and motivation (in the best case) for a long-term participation. However, we would not say that these measures set the stage for a fully collaborative start of the project (e.g., with co-developing research questions, such as in action research). In our work on IT for the aging society, the first steps are often slow and careful in order to be not too overwhelming for the elderly (or younger but non-tech-savvy) persons.

A third aspect that shows some specificity for the field of dementia care in the context of data collection and (participatory) design is the challenge of communicating with representatives of the target group. Dahl and Holbø (2012b) discuss some strategies for how to involve persons with mild forms of dementia in interview settings, to give them a voice and prevent the caregivers from dominating the interview. The authors relate their work to newer care philosophies such as person-centered care (Kitwood 2001) as also do Sugihara et al. (2013), who say that this concept is "appropriate for applying the norm of human-centered design." However, as we said in Section 11.8.1, it might not be enough for researchers to follow these philosophies, as they are not applied in all care practices and by all caregivers.

The case of the couple where the husband suffered from dementia, discussed in Section 11.7.4, illustrates the complexity of such interview settings. We performed all interviews and meetings together with the couple. The husband suffered from only mild dementia, so we were able to ask him some questions. However, we only could ask him very simple questions and had to rely on his wife to fully understand the management of their everyday life, their routines, and their support needs. Even though we tried to integrate the husband very carefully into the interview situation, we had to accept that the wife was the one carrying all responsibility for both. Thus, even though we tried to give him a voice in the situation, we had to give more space to his wife, as she was the one who organized their everyday life and carried the huge responsibility that we were addressing with the technology. In addition, finally, the caregiver has to decide whether to cooperate with us, and this means that the researcher must negotiate the situation in a very careful and flexible way.

However, when working with families or professional caregivers of persons with dementia in progressed states where oral communication is no longer possible, researchers have to rely on substitutional interpretations. This may put the researcher in delicate and complex situations, as he or she must supplement what is being said with his or her own observations (if possible) and has to guess at what is really being said. In the case of the woman whose husband "engineered" her everyday life, the researcher felt awkward about the way this man treated his wife. This caused some difficulty for the researcher, as the question then arose as to whether there was a need to take additional action (e.g., to try to educate the husband about personhood-oriented ways of caring, or even to inform a local authority). In other interviews, relatives started crying, which also put an emotional burden on the researcher.

These examples demonstrate the need for further reflection on how to be well prepared for settings involving the care of chronically ill persons. This is especially important against the background of research projects that integrate university education.

11.9 Conclusion

In this chapter, we presented a practice-based design process of a GPS-based monitoring system to be used by persons with dementia and with a tendency to wander. GPS tracking, although a well-established technology, is rarely used in dementia care in practice. We investigated current care practices, IT design options, and the appropriation of GPS technology in dementia care and assessed the practical and ideological issues surrounding care to understand why. The design case study consisted of three phases: (1) a qualitative, empirical pre-study, (2) a PD and prototyping process, and (3) a long-term field evaluation and appropriation study in three environments. What comes to the fore is the need for IT design to reflect upon complex ideological and practical issues that form part of a moral universe where sensitivity is crucial.

Methodologically speaking, we propose some adjustments to the design case study approach by Wulf et al. (2015) in order to accommodate some specificities of design in the field of IT for the aging society and especially for the field of dementia care.

Acknowledgments

Our thanks to the persons who unhesitatingly provided us with insights of their challenging everyday and working lives and discussed their concerns, attitudes, and ideas in regard of technical aids with us. Special thanks to the self-help organization Alzheimer Selbsthilfe e. V. Köln.

References

Abowd, G. D., Hayes, G. R., Kientz, J. A., Mamykina, L., and Mynatt, E. D. 2006. *Challenges and Opportunities for Collaboration Technologies for Chronic Care Management.* Available at http://pdfs.semanticscholar.org/7e7d/1a985a86697f9027b09c993121d6eb3c54ce.pdf (accessed October 16, 2017).

Angelini, L., Caon, M., Carrino, S., Bergeron, L., Nyffeler, N., Jean-Mairet, M., and Mugellini, E. 2013. "Designing a desirable smart bracelet for older adults." In *UbiComp'13 Adjunct.* New York: ACM, 425–34.

Astell, A. 2009. *REAFF: A Framework for Developing Technology To Address the Needs of People with Dementia.* Available at http://pdfs.semanticscholar.org/bcea/11c67f947bc94b42641f35eb48aff498f8cd.pdf (accessed October 16, 2017).

Ballegaard, S. A., Hansen, T. R., and Kyng, M. 2008. "Healthcare in everyday life: Designing healthcare services for daily life." In *CHI'08.* New York: ACM, 1807–16.

Baumann, C., Tijé-Dra, A., and Winkler, J. 2015. "Geographien zwischen Diskurs und Praxis—Mit Wittgenstein Anknüpfungspunkte von Diskurs—und Praxistheorie denken." *Geographica Helvetica* 70 (3): 225–37.

Bourdieu, P. 1977. *Outline of a Theory of Practice.* Vol. 16. Cambridge: Cambridge University Press.

Brandt, E., Binder, T., Malmborg, L., and Sokoler, T. 2010. "Communities of everyday practice and situated elderliness as an approach to co-design for senior interaction." In *OzCHI'10.* New York: ACM, 400–3.

Brodaty, H., Thomson, C., Thompson, C., and Fine, M. 2005. "Why caregivers of people with dementia and memory loss don't use services." *International Journal of Geriatric Psychiatry* 20 (6): 537–46.

Cantley, C. 2001. *A Handbook of Dementia Care.* Buckingham: Open University.

Carroll, J. M., and Rosson, M. B. 2007. "Participatory design in community informatics." *Design Studies* 28 (3): 243–61.

Christensen, L., and Grönvall, E. 2011. "Challenges and opportunities for collaborative technologies for home care work." In *ECSCW'11.* London: Springer-Verlag London, 61–80.

Consolvo, S., Roessler, P., Shelton, B. E., LaMarca, A., Schilit, B., and Bly, S. 2004. "Technology for care networks of elders." *IEEE Pervasive Computing* 3 (2): 22–9.

Crabtree A, Hemmings T, Rodden T, Cheverst, K., Clarke, K., Dewsbury, G., Hughes, J., and Rouncefield, M. 2003. "Designing with care: Adapting cultural probes to inform design in sensitive settings." In *OzCHI'04.* New York: ACM, 4–13.

Dachtera, J., Randall, D., and Wulf, V. 2014. "Research on research: Design research at the margins: Academia, industry and end-users." *CHI'14.* New York: ACM, 713–22.

Dahl, Y., and Holbø, K. 2012a. "There are no secrets here!": Professional stakeholders' views on the use of GPS for tracking dementia patients." In *MobileHCI'12.* New York: ACM, 133–42.

Dahl, Y., and Holbø, K. 2012b. "Value biases of sensor-based assistive technology: Case study of a GPS tracking system used in dementia care." In *DIS'12*. New York: ACM, 572–81.

Demiris, G. 2009. "Independence and shared decision making: The role of smart home technology in empowering older adults." In *EMBC'09*. Piscataway: IEEE Press, 6432–6.

Essén, A. 2008. "The two facets of electronic care surveillance: An exploration of the views of older people who live with monitoring devices." *Social Science and Medicine* 67 (1): 128–36.

European Commission. 2015. *Growing the European Silver Economy*. Available at http://ec.europa.eu/research/innovation-union/pdf/active-healthy-ageing/silvereco.pdf (accessed October 16, 2017).

Fitzpatrick, G., Balaam, M., Axelrod, L., Harris, E., McAllister, G., Hughes, A. M., Burridge, J., Nind, T., Ricketts, I., Wilkinson, A., and Mawson, S. 2010. "Designing for rehabilitation at home." In G. R. Hayes and D. S. Tan, eds., *Proceedings of the First International Workshop on Interactive Systems in Healthcare*, 49–52. Available at https://eprints.soton.ac.uk/272084/1/WISH2010Proceedings.pdf (accessed November 21, 2017).

Fitzpatrick, G., and Ellingsen, G. 2013. "A review of 25 years of CSCW research in healthcare: Contributions, challenges and future agendas." *Computer Supported Cooperative Work* 22 (4–6): 609–65.

Følstad, A. 2008. "Living labs for innovation and development of information and communication technology: A literature review." *Electronic Journal of Organizational Virtualness* 10: 99–131.

Friedman, B. "Value-sensitive design." *Interactions* 3 (6): 16–23.

Gaver, B., Dunne, T., and Pacenti, E. 1999. "Design: Cultural probes." *Interactions* 6 (1): 21–9.

Gaver, W., Wright, P., Boucher, A., Blythe, M., Jarvis, N., Cameron, D., Kerridge, T., Wilkie, A., Phillips, R., and Wright, P. 2011. "The photostroller: Supporting diverse care home residents in engaging with the world." In *CHI'11*. New York: ACM, 1757–66.

Giddens, A. 1984. *The Constitution of Society: Outline of the Theory of Structuration*. Oakland: University of California Press.

Gowans, G., Campbell, J., Alm, N., Dye, R., Astell, A., and Ellis, M. 2004. "Designing a multimedia conversation aid for reminiscence therapy in dementia care environments." In *CHI EA'04*. New York: ACM, 825–36.

Henderson, A., and Kyng, M. 1991. "There's no place like home: Continuing design in use." In J. Greenbaum and M. Kyng, eds., *Design At Work: Cooperative Design of Computer Artefacts*. Hillsdale, NJ: Lawrence Erlbaum Associates, 219–40.

Judge, T. K., Neustaedter, C., and Kurtz, A. F. 2010. "The family window: The design and evaluation of a domestic media space." In *CHI'10*. New York: ACM, 2361–70.

Kaplan, B., and Harris-Salamone, K. D. 2009. "Health IT success and failure: Recommendations from literature and an AMIA workshop." *Journal of the American Medical Informatics Association* 16 (3): 291–9.

Kitwood, T. 2001. *Dementia Reconsidered: The Person Comes First*. Buckingham: Open University Press.

Knapp, M., Comas-Herrera, A., Somani, A., and Banerjee, S. 2007. "Dementia: International comparisons." Summary report for the National Audit Office. London: Personal Social Services Research Unit, London School of Economics and Political Science and the Institute of Psychiatry, King's College.

Landau, R., Auslander, G. K., Werner, S., Shoval, N., and Heinik, J. 2010. "Families' and professional caregivers' views of using advanced technology to track people with dementia." *Qualitative Health Research* 20 (3): 409–19.

Landau, R., Werner, S., Auslander, G. K., Shoval, N., and Heinik, J. 2009. "Attitudes of family and professional care-givers towards the use of GPS for tracking patients with dementia: An exploratory study. *British Journal of Social Work* 39 (4): 670–92.

Lieberman, L., Paternó, F., and Wulf, V. (eds). 2006. *End User Development*. Dordrecht: Springer.
Lindsay, S., Jackson, D., Ladha, C., Ladha, K., Brittain, K., and Olivier, P. 2012. "Empathy, participatory design and people with dementia." In *CHI'12*. New York: ACM, 521–30.
Mamykina, L., Mynatt, E., Davidson, P., and Greenblatt, D. 2008. "MAHI: Investigation of social scaffolding for reflective thinking in diabetes management." In *CHI'08*, New York: ACM, 477–86.
Miskelly, F. 2005. "Electronic tracking of patients with dementia and wandering using mobile phone technology." *Age and Ageing*. 43 (5): 497–9.
Morris, M., Lundell, J., Dishman, E., and Needham, B. 2003. "New perspectives on ubiquitous computing from ethnographic study of elders with cognitive decline." In *UbiComp'03*. Berlin/Heidelberg: Springer, 227–42.
Müller, C., Hornung, D., Hamm, T., and Wulf, V. 2015a. "Measures and tools for supporting ICT appropriation by elderly and non tech-savvy persons in a long-term perspective." In *ECSCW'15*. Cham: Springer, 263–81.
Müller, C., Hornung, D., Hamm, T., and Wulf, V. 2015b. "Practice-based design of a neighborhood portal: Focusing on elderly tenants in a city quarter living lab." In *CHI'15*. New York: ACM, 2295–304.
Müller, C., Neufeldt, C., Randall, D., and Wulf, V. 2012. "ICT-development in residential care settings: Sensitizing design to the life circumstances of the residents of a care home." In *CHI'12*. New York: ACM, 2639–48.
Müller, C., Wan, L., and Hrg, D. 2010. "Dealing with wandering: A case study on caregivers' attitudes towards privacy and autonomy when reflecting the use of LBS." In *GROUP'10*. New York: ACM, 75–84.
Müller, C., Wan, L., and Wulf, V. 2013. "Dealing with wandering in institutional care: Exploring the field." In *PervasiveHealth'13*. Piscataway: IEEE Press, 101–4.
Mynatt, E. D., Rowan, J., Craighill, S., and Jacobs, A. 2001. "Digital family portraits: Supporting peace of mind for extended family members." In *CHI'01*. New York: ACM, 333–40.
Ogonowski, C., Ley, B., Hess, J., Wan, L., and Wulf, V. 2013. "Designing for the living room: Long-term user involvement in a living lab." In *CHI'13*. New York: ACM, 1539–48.
Palen, L., and Aaløkke, S. 2006. "Of pill boxes and piano benches: 'Home-made' methods for managing medication." In *CSCW'06*. New York: ACM, 79–88.
Pang, C. E., Neustaedter, C., Riecke, B. E., Oduor, E., and Hillman, S. 2013. "Technology preferences and routines for sharing health information during the treatment of a chronic illness." In *CHI'13*. New York: ACM, 1759–68.
Petrakou A. 2007. "Exploring cooperation through a binder: A context for IT tools in elderly care at home." *ECSCW'07*. London: Springer, 271–90.
Pot, A. M., Willemse, B. M., and Horjus, S. 2012. "A pilot study on the use of tracking technology: Feasibility, acceptability, and benefits for people in early stages of dementia and their informal caregivers." *Aging and Mental Health* 16 (1): 127–34.
Pratt, W., Unruh, K., Civan, A., and Skeels, M. 2006. "Personal health information management." *Communications of the ACM* 49 (1): 51–5.
Robinson, L., Brittain, K., Lindsay, S., Jackson, D., and Olivier, P. 2009. "Keeping In Touch Everyday (KITE) project: Developing assistive technologies with people with dementia and their carers to promote independence." *International Psychogeriatrics* 21 (3): 494–502.
Rogers, Y. 2006. "Moving on from Weiser's vision of calm computing: Engaging UbiComp experiences." In *UbiComp 2006*. Berlin/Heidelberg: Springer, 404–21.
Rohde, M., Brödner, P., Stevens, G., Betz, M., and Wulf, V. 2017. "Grounded design: A praxeological IS research perspective." *Journal of Information Technology* 32 (2): 163–79.

Rohde, M., Stevens, G., Brödner, P., and Wulf, V. 2009. "Towards a paradigmatic shift in IS: Designing for social practice." In *DESRIST'09*. New York: ACM, 15.

Schatzki, T. R., Knorr-Cetina, K., and Savigny, E. von. 2001. *The Practice Turn in Contemporary Theory*. London: Routledge.

Schorch, M., Wan, L., Randall, D., and Wulf, V. 2016. "Designing for those who are overlooked: Insider perspectives on care practices and cooperative work of elderly informal caregivers." In *CSCW'16*. New York: ACM, 787–99.

Suchman, L. 1987. *Plans and Situated Actions: The Problem of Human-Machine Communication*. Cambridge: Cambridge University Press.

Sugihara, T., Fujinami, T., Phaal, R., and Ikawa, Y. 2013. "A technology roadmap of assistive technologies for dementia care in Japan." *Dementia*, 14 (1): 80–103.

Tsai, J. Y., Kelley, P., Drielsma, P., Cranor, L. F., Hong, J., and Sadeh, N. 2009. "Who's viewed you? The impact of feedback in a mobile location-sharing application." In *CHI'09*. New York: ACM, 2003–12.

Uzor, S., and Baillie, L. 2013. "Exploring and designing tools to enhance falls rehabilitation in the home." In *CHI'13*. New York: ACM, 1233–42.

Vines, J., Blythe, M., Lindsay, S., Dunphy, P., Monk, A., and Olivier, P. 2012. "Questionable concepts: Critique as resource for designing with eighty somethings." In *CHI'12*. New York: ACM, 1169–78.

Wallace, J., Thieme, A., Wood, G., Schofield, G., and Olivier, P. 2012. "Enabling self, intimacy and a sense of home in dementia: An enquiry into design in a hospital setting." In *CHI'12*. New York: ACM, 2629–38.

Wan, L., Müller, C., Wulf, V., and Randall, D. W. 2014. "Addressing the subtleties in dementia care: Pre-study & evaluation of a GPS monitoring system." In *CHI'14*. New York: ACM, 3987–96.

Wan, L., Müller, C., Randall, D., and Wulf, V. 2016. "Design of a GPS monitoring system for dementia care and its challenges in academia-industry project." *ACM Transactions on Computer-Human Interaction* 23 (5): 31.

Wittenberg-Lyles, E., Oliver, D. P., Demiris, G., and Baldwin, P. 2010. "The ACTive intervention in hospice interdisciplinary team meetings: Exploring family caregiver and hospice team communication." *Journal of Computer-Mediated Communication* 15 (3): 465–81.

Wulf, V., Müller, C., Pipek, V., Randall, D., Rohde, M., and Stevens, G. 2015. "Practice-based computing: Empirically grounded conceptualizations derived from design case studies." In V. Wulf, K. Schmidt, and D. Randall, eds., *Designing Socially Embedded Technologies in the Real-World*. London: Springer-Verlag London 111–50.

Wulf, V., Pipek, V., and Won, M. 2008. "Component-based tailorability: Towards highly flexible software applications." *International Journal on Human-Computer Studies* 66 (1): 1–22.

Wulf, V., Rohde, M., Pipek, V., and Stevens, G. 2011. "Engaging with practices: Design case studies as a research framework in CSCW." In *CSCW'11*. New York: ACM, 505–12.

12 come_NET

Connecting Computer Clubs with a Community Platform

KONSTANTIN AAL, ANNE WEIBERT, KAI SCHUBERT, MARY-ANN SPRENGER, AND THOMAS VON REKOWSKI

12.1 Introduction

The come_IN initiative of intercultural computer clubs aims to foster and support understanding and respect across cultures and generations by means of collaborative project work with computers and modern media. With this, come_IN contributes to societal efforts to come to terms with migration and an increasingly socially and culturally diverse population on the most basic level of local neighborhood communities. It is here where come_IN translates the general ambition of cultural integration—which is concerned with the creation of a common basis for living, involving an agreement on a common language, core values, common rules, and mutual respect for and knowledge of social and cultural differences (Berry 1984, 1992)—as well as structural integration, being concerned with equal access to all parts of societal life (Schuck and Münz 1998), into weekly project activity involving information and communication technology (ICT; Stevens et al. 2005; Weibert and Schubert 2010; Weibert and Wulf 2010; Schubert et al. 2011; Aal et al. 2014; Weibert et al. 2014).

Mostly located in schools in socially and culturally diverse neighborhoods, the come_IN computer clubs bring together people of different migration backgrounds and different ages. In the clubs' weekly meetings, children as well as adults work on joint projects, study, and play.

This speaks to the social dimension of integration in that it fosters intercultural as well as intergenerational discussion, negotiation of opinions and perspectives, and the acquiring and refining of language skills. It tends the structural dimension of integration in that

Socio-Informatics, Volker Wulf, Volkmar Pipek, Dave Randall, Markus Rohde, Kjeld Schmidt, Gunnar Stevens (Eds). © Oxford University Press 2018. Published 2018 by Oxford University Press.

it contributes to the bridging of the so-called digital divide—the unequal access of immigrant communities, as compared to mainstream society, to computer infrastructure (e.g., Norris 2001; Wagner et al. 2002; Witte and Mannon 2010), providing open, yet guided access to modern information and computer technology. In addition, come_IN computer clubs follow a decidedly open structure. Participation in the clubs is voluntary and free; topics for project work are developed by the participants (both children and adults) themselves and then jointly agreed upon; tutors and a teacher provide help and guidance but do not set up a predefined schedule to follow for the clubs' weekly meetings.

As come_IN has grown into a network of several clubs in Germany (as well as in Palestine; e.g., Aal et al. 2014, more recently), it became necessary to develop a tool that would allow sharing of ideas and experiences across distances, foster collaboration, and make skills and expertise accessible in a sustainable way. Although there are numerous social-media and sharing platforms already available, the collaborative nature of computer club activity, and the young age of most of the participants, required the development of a specific, new platform. Thus, the online platform *come_NET* was designed in close cooperation with the computer club participants, to best meet their skills and needs. The work we describe in this chapter took place within the general context of the "design case study" (Wulf et al. 2015) and the associated notion of "grounded design," but carried with it some specific challenges: those associated with working with children, and those associated with working across a range of cross-cultural values, which can sometimes be in conflict.

12.2 Background

12.2.1 come_IN Computer Clubs

In intercultural neighborhoods in Germany, the structure of the come_IN computer clubs supports integration at the level of the local neighborhood (Stevens et al. 2005; Weibert and Wulf 2010; Schubert et al. 2011): designed as an open space for computer-related project work, the clubs bring together children and adults from the respective neighborhoods to work on topics of their own choice. In addition, a teacher from the neighborhood school participates in the computer club (Weibert et al. 2011). Tutors provide technical help and support the club participants in the translation of their ideas into computer- and media-related projects. The club's neighborhood often has a large impact on the types of projects that club participants decide to work on (see, e.g., Weibert and Schubert 2010). Examples of such projects include "Neighborhood Stories", which is a series of brochures containing information about interesting, nice, or ugly places in the neighborhood around one club; a stop-motion film about friendship, created by another club; and a video about the breakfast-for-children initiative in one of the elementary schools.

Computer clubhouses have been established in numerous cities in the United States and around the world to serve the disadvantaged inner city youth and open up opportunities by helping youth to increase their technological fluency and creativity. Their success is well documented in research (e.g., Resnick and Rusk 1996; Resnick et al. 1998; Michalchik et al. 2008; Kafai et al. 2009). The come_IN network has built upon this concept and adapted it to meet the needs of the German setting.

12.2.2 Sharing Tools

Sützl et al. describe sharing to be "one of the most unexpected developments of the early 21st century" (Sützl et al. 2012), resulting from easy and almost omnipresent access to advanced ICT for sharing and communicating. Platforms like Facebook, Snapchat, Twitter, Instagram, and so on are very popular, and there are numerous platforms that have been designed and set up to address specific sharing needs (e.g., for photographs, video, animations, programming, written stories, cartoons, or artwork). One particular aspect of sharing is "knowledge sharing," or "expertise sharing," which is about using the practical knowledge and expertise of members to solve problems or get work done (Ackerman et al. 2013). Research in computer-supported cooperative work and human–computer interaction (HCI) has followed this development closely, exploring sharing practices, and designing tools and software to meet specific requirements (e.g., Ames and Manguy 2006; Maloney et al. 2010; Mathur et al. 2012; Weilenmann et al. 2013).

Children have specific needs with regard to online sharing: as their analytical as well as their reading and writing skills are still developing, they cannot yet fully anticipate the consequences of their working online, or grasp the often complex structures, for example, of privacy settings. Thus, social-media and sharing tools designed for them need to fulfill specific, age-related requirements. Numerous studies have examined this, exploring how social-media and sharing tools can contribute to child learning (e.g., Ahn et al. 2015) and support creativity (e.g., Revelle et al. 2010) as well as an interest in science (e.g., Ahn et al. 2012; Yip et al. 2014).

Sharing tools have also gained attention as a means to support distributed communities and their activities. One popular example is the Intel network of computer clubhouses in the United States with clubhouses located in various other countries around the world: these clubhouses are connected via a shared intranet called "The Village."[1] This online platform enables clubhouse participants to network, collaborate, share and discuss their projects (e.g., Freidus and Hlubinka 2002; Sylvan 2006, 2007).

12.2.3 Children as Technology Users/Design Partners

It is clear that, today, media and technology are omnipresent in children's lives. Children grow up in close contact with video games, television, and "touch technology." Thus, it is necessary for them to have a complex media competence. Baacke (1996) emphasizes the need for youth work to offer children other and more access to new media than schools can otherwise do. Media use in activity-oriented media education includes production as well as reception. Therefore, children need to evolve from being mere consumers of

[1] See http://www.clubhousevillage.org.

media to being "prosumers" (Toffler et al. 1981), which means that they need to learn how to adapt and actively produce media content as well as consume it.

Children are experts at being kids (Druin 1999). So, it can be argued, they probably are the most qualified to say what it is that children want, need, and are able to handle. HCI research has found that the following three design methodologies are most productive when working with children: (1) contextual inquiry (Holtzblatt and Jones 1993), that is, gathering field data from users within their normal context; (2) technology immersion (Boltman and Druin 1998), that is, applying the observation techniques of contextual inquiry in a decidedly technology-rich environment; and (3) participatory design (Druin et al 1997; Druin 1999; Muller 2003), which entails users and designers viewing each other as equals, and relies on techniques that can support intergenerational design teams involving children.

The design and implementation of the online community platform come_NET builds on these approaches, in that it relies on cooperative and contextual inquiry in order to design techniques that view children as equals in the design process and involve them within their usual settings and contexts. It speaks to related works on sharing practices and tools in that it applies them to the specific local setting of intercultural computer clubs and the needs of children as users within that context. In this case, a platform was needed that was able to (1) cater for the specific needs of younger children with regard to privacy issues as well as their developing literacy and cognitive skills, and (2) foster the sharing of ideas and knowledge in a specific local, intercultural setting. As existing platform solutions fell short on one or both of these requirements, there was a clear need for the design of a platform that met the specific needs of the computer clubs and their participants.

12.3 Case Study: come_IN Computer Clubs

12.3.1 Research Setting

Over the course of the last decade, the come_IN project has established a network of seven computer clubs in Germany (see Figure 12.1 and Table 12.1). The first "come_IN" computer club was opened in Bonn Nordstadt in 2004. In Siegen, the transferability of the concept was tested in 2006 with the establishment of a second club. The experience gathered in Bonn helped to refine social and technical aspects of the concept. The "come_IN" initiative grew into a network when four clubs were founded in summer 2009. A school complex in Bonn Tannenbusch with a primary school, a secondary modern school, and a grammar school on one site brings together children, teenagers, and their parents in two clubs. A neighborhood initiative in the Nordstadt of Dortmund established a club in a primary school. Senior citizens in Kreuztal adapted the "come_IN" concept for their idea of a computer-project with teenagers in a youth center. In summer 2010, another club followed in a comprehensive school in Kreuztal.

Even though it is decidedly open, the project work in the computer club follows a few set structures. First among them are the opening and closing joint discussion rounds that

Figure 12.1 Computer club locations within the German state of North Rhine-Westfalia

begin and end every one of the weekly 90-minute club sessions. This is the place where ideas for club projects are developed and decided upon, where all activities are planned, and where problems are solved. When it became apparent that children and adults were not equally capable of letting their voices and opinions be heard in a circle like this, it was decided that the discussion rounds would have a moderator team of a child and an adult—thus ensuring that no one would be left behind. Another fixed part of the weekly session is the free time at the beginning for individual activity, followed by the main working time devoted to the project. Furthermore, an important aspect of project work in the club is the aim to involve several generations. From the start, a parent–child rule had been established, stating that children could only participate in come_IN together when they were with one of their parents. Later, this rule was changed, when it became apparent that it meant that the children who would benefit most from the club would be excluded. Children participating in the club are still asked to bring an adult, wherever possible, but the adult can be a family friend, an older brother, or a grandparent, for

Table 12.1 Overview of computer clubs and their characteristics

Club	Type of School	Year of Foundation	Participation	Cultural Backgrounds	Specific Features
Bonn Nordstadt	Elementary school	2004	2 adults and about 10 children	German, Turkish	Temporally parallel to all-day school Currently not running
Bonn Tannenbusch	Secondary school	2009	One complete class (6th grade), which does not focus on sports or music; parents are invited but not all of them participate	Polish, Russian, German, Turkish, Iraqi, Iranian	Obligatory for the children, and part of their regular lesson plan
Bonn Tannenbusch	Elementary and middle school in combination	2009	2–3 mothers and 6–7 children High fluctuation among the participants	Polish, Russian, German, Turkish, Iraqi, Iranian	Managed by elementary school and middle school teachers Currently not running
Dortmund Nordstadt	Elementary school	2009	5–7 parents (mostly mothers) and about 10 children	Turkish, German, Russian, Macedonian, Moroccan	Formation supported by neighborhood managers, local residents, and a local community organization Meets in parallel with all-day school
Kreuztal	Comprehensive school	2011	About 20 children from the 6th grade	Turkish, Moroccan, German, Russian	Part of the optional course plan of this school
Kreuztal	Community center	2009	Older adults and teenagers	German, Serbian	Senior citizens and teenager collaboratively developed a concept for the club Previous experiences showed that the two groups work separately Meets in late afternoons
Siegen	Elementary school	2006	7 children and 4 parents or older siblings	Turkish, Russian, German	The club has established "its own" computer room Temporally parallel with the all-day school

example. Thus, the clubs aim to foster intergenerational learning that may find its continuation in family contexts long after the computer club session is over.

12.3.2 Method

Wulf et al. (2015) have emphasized how, in order to be able to achieve appropriate design, it is necessary to understand the relationship between specific instances of social practices, and the design space for IT artifacts in their support. The design of IT artifacts needs to take the given social practices, including the already-existing IT infrastructures, into account (Wulf et al. 2015), allowing context-sensitive "grounded design" (Rohde et al. 2017; also see Chapter 1) to emerge. However, when these artifacts are rolled out "in the wild," these practices undergo changes during the appropriation process. We need to understand the interaction between the IT design and the appropriation activities over a longer period of time (Pipek and Wulf 1999; Rohde et al. 2009; Wulf et al. 2011; Wulf et al. 2015). Thus, in order to assess the field of application, the pivotal actors, and their practices, the design case study in our come_IN computer clubs consisted of three phases:

- an empirical pre-study
- prototyping, or (participatory) IT design
- evaluation, and study of appropriation

Empirical Pre-Study

The empirical pre-study involved assessing social practices prior to the intervention, describing already-existing tools, media, and their usage, as well as capturing the development from a technological, organizational, and social perspective (Wulf et al. 2015). Against this backdrop, the first phase of our case study was conducted while building the computer clubs. We studied common practices in the clubs over 3 years, thus identifying recurring patterns and challenges that would then be addressed by the platform design.

We adopted a participant action research approach (McTaggart and Kemmis 1988): the members of the come_IN research team are active members of the computer clubs, where they act as tutors on a regular basis. They document the weekly sessions in the form of brief notes that are later written out as more extensive field notes (Wolfinger 2002; Emerson et al. 2011). Their focus in very general terms lies on the interactions of children and adults during computer club project work, their observable collaborations, and on children's and adult's appropriation of media and computer technology, as well as associated processes of learning. Over the period of 4 years, weekly field notes (all in all, around 300 pages) were collected and analyzed using a qualitative content analysis approach.

Prototyping/(Participatory) IT Design

In this phase, we described the innovative IT artifact from a product as well as from a process perspective. This included a description of the specific design process, the involved stakeholders, the applied design methods, and the emerging design concepts.

It also included the changes in social practices the stakeholders anticipated and aim for, how these considerations influenced the design of the IT artifact, and how they should be documented (Wulf et al. 2015). Methodologically, we applied a combination of qualitative methods and context-specific research approaches, focusing on incorporating end users immediately in the software development process, while taking into account their specific needs and the contexts of their ICT appropriation, as well as the interaction going on between the IT design and the appropriation process. Accordingly, a first prototype of the platform was developed, which then was tested with several children (around thirty younger children and ten older ones) in usability tests. These were conducted during the weekly club sessions in several computer clubs. We applied a participatory-design process (Muller 2003), engaging the end users, that is, children, as design partners in the development process of "their" online community platform come_NET. In the beginning of this process, several planning sessions in the computer clubs involved children and tutors in the assessment of crucial features and functions, thus, in principle, ensuring design according to children's needs (Druin 1999), alleviating several recurring problems, such as difficulties in retrieving personal files in the network storage, and making the sharing of personal digital creations possible in a secure online environment, as well as allowing safe online networking and communication among the immature club participants.

Evaluation/Appropriation Study

In this phase, the introduction, appropriation, and potential redesign of the IT artifact in its respective domain of practice was documented (Wulf et al. 2015). As well as our observation of participants in the computer clubs, additional qualitative interviews with the children of the clubs in Bonn, Dortmund, and Siegen over the course of a year (see Section 12.4.4) enabled us to assess the appropriation of the platform and inform the iterative redevelopment and refinement of its design and features.

12.4 The Empirical Pre-Study for come_NET: Identifying Recurring Challenges in Computer Club Work

Over the course of almost 10 years of project work on the come_IN computer clubs, several recurring challenges became evident. In our pre-study, we collated the most central issues, which we describe in this section. These issues emanated from the nature of the overall project work and the activities of the children and adults in the computer clubs.

Many of these issues are concerned with material aspects related to the project work in the clubs. Due to the fact that most come_IN clubs are conducted in the premises of cooperating schools and are dependent on the participation of the tutors and teachers, participants' engagement in project work is usually limited to a single 90-minute meeting per week. But large or time-consuming projects, such as those that require video editing or the creation of large Scratch projects, may at times demand work efforts that exceed regular club times (Resnick et al. 2009). As a result, participants have repeatedly displayed their wish for the ability to work on projects outside regular club hours and access and process their project data at home. "Time's up," the teacher and tutors would regularly say, announcing the end of the club session; the children in the club would receive this with disappointment, protesting "But I'm not finished!" and asking whether they would be able to continue the activity from home as well. When this was not possible, children would sometimes return to the club in the following session with a project creation of their own—thematically related to the overall project theme, but made on their own. For example, one time, the project in the Dortmund computer club had been the creation of a trickfilm (a kind of animated cartoon [Seeber and Schobert 1979] that is popular among children and youth in Germany), and two of the boys at the club had sought a way to be able to pursue this topic further at home. They subsequently returned having taken hundreds of photographs of their Lego figures performing the story of a police chase that the boys had observed in their neighborhood, (as well as their very own cover version of a game of "Super Mario").

Our field notes repeatedly document how the securing and sharing of artifacts, as well as the retrieval of project data, is a problem in the clubs, especially for the children. The children frequently lose track of where they have stored their data when they attempt to continue their project work in the club the following week. The following scene from the computer club in Bonn illustrates this issue:

Girl: "Oh no. My work! It's all gone!"

Tutor: "Did you save it?"

Girl: "Yes! But now it's not there... "

Tutor (*looks*): "See—there it is. You were looking into the wrong folder."

Many children face problems retrieving their project data from the local storage drives; this is usually because the children are not able to memorize the file's name or location over a week's course, but it occasionally happens because their data has been moved or deleted by other users. As a result, children (and tutors) have to spend time searching for the data, thereby losing considerable parts of their already limited time for progressing with actual project work. This was an irritating and time-consuming issue for all parties concerned and also caused projects to take longer than originally anticipated. Also, children frequently have problems completing up- or downloading processes.

Furthermore, the clubs face problems related to privacy issues: some computer clubs did not have a secured drive at first, or all participants could access all of the club data—with loss of data frequently occurring because someone had accidentally deleted something.

With regard to the project work itself, all computer clubs shared the requirement that expertise among the participants should easily be identified and made use of. Especially in those clubs where not all children were initially known to each other, they were often not aware of mutual interests and relative skills. As a result, they sometimes found progressing with a project task to be difficult, as they did not know whom to ask (besides the tutor or teacher) in order to overcome a problem. "Ok, who can help," teacher and tutors were frequently heard to say whenever a problem occurred during club work, thus fostering an atmosphere where the participants could help each other master difficult tasks. Identifying the social distribution of expertise, with different individuals having different skills, and "knowing who knows" potential solutions (e.g., how to perform a certain programming task or draw well) are problems to be overcome. Joint discussion rounds at the beginnings and endings of the club session, therefore, were established in the clubs, to plan upcoming project work and find solutions for unresolved problems that may have occurred during the session.

In addition, the computer clubs also share challenges on the social level. On a basic level is the challenge to come up with an idea for a new computer club project. Where does one find inspiration? The following scene from the computer club in Dortmund illustrates the issue:

(*A boy is sitting in front of his computer, undecidedly clicking around.*)

Boy: "Now what? I'm done."

Teacher: "Let me see."

(*The boy demonstrates and explains the project he has just finished.*)

Teacher: "This is cool. Great job!"

(*Boy looks around.*)

Boy: "Now...?"

(*He wanders around the room, looking at the activities of others, and then sits down near a bookshelf in the corner of the room, flipping through various books. After a while, he returns to the computer.*)

Boy: "I'll do a shark. Those are my favorite."

Another challenge is related to turning an inspiring, but perhaps not well formulated, idea into an interesting project in the computer club, ideally spanning a broad range of competences, skills, and interests. It is especially challenging for the participants to predict what challenges may occur when a project idea is implemented. This was the case, for example, when the computer clubs in Dortmund and Siegen decided to do an audio play, with the children and adults "learning by doing" about the complexity of audio recording and editing. These challenges fed the computer clubs' demand for networking, as it led to the participants exchanging knowledge derived from their respective experiences with past projects.

The population of children who participate in the computer clubs changes regularly, especially when the children finish elementary school and have to leave for secondary school. Often the children, especially those who have spent a long time in "their" computer club, voice a desire to stay in contact with the computer club. "Can I come back?" a girl in Dortmund asked at her last day of computer club before she left for secondary school. And one boy from the computer club in Bonn later became a computer club tutor when he was a teenager in a secondary school. Another boy from the club in Bonn was seen to return to the club week after week, long after he had left elementary school.

Also, we found that many of the children wanted to spend more time together than simply at the weekly club session. Some already knew each other from class; others had discovered in the club that they shared an interest or a hobby, like playing soccer or dancing. Furthermore, our field notes reveal that children are always curious about the network nature of the computer clubs: they like the idea that there are other children in other computer clubs engaged in projects similar to their own. Our field notes documented that the children would occasionally ask the tutors about the participants in the other clubs (e.g., who they were, what they did, and what their projects were). This interest was triggered, for example, by project activities where tutors tell about experiences with similar activities in another club. An annual joint computer club meeting called "*Aktionstag*," which brings children and adults from all clubs in the network together in one place, fuels this demand for further exchange and communication. Consequently, the teachers and parents in the computer clubs were always concerned that this communication and contact was enabled in a safe manner.

12.5 The Participatory Design of come_NET

Based on the challenges and patterns that we observed in the pre-study, we found that there was a need for a safe communication tool that would allow participants to stay in touch after club sessions, share and manage own digital projects, and find expertise and inspiration from other. As a result of parent's concerns regarding open online community websites and after several requests by participants, the development of a closed community platform was initialized. Since children were the target audience for the new system, great attention was paid to privacy issues and, due to the young age of the users, as well as their low levels of experience in general, special requirements had to be taken into account. In order to meet those requirements best, the young end users were regarded as crucial stakeholders and design partners in the participatory-development process. The technology used had also a vast impact on the development of the platform: for example, one initial choice that had to be made was whether to use an already-existing customizable content management system or to design a platform from scratch. However, while the content management system was easy to install and configure, it could not be adjusted for the specific needs of the younger participants of the computer clubs.

To achieve a successful interface design, end users should be incorporated in usability tests in the development process early on. In addition, over the whole course of the development process, iterative testing with children and their feedback suggestions often provided a basis for discussing suitable design metaphors for the interface. The children from the clubs in Dortmund and Siegen were usually the first ones to be involved in testing of new versions, since these clubs had the youngest participants. Developing for and with this user group requires special techniques on the part of the developers. For instance, the weak reading skills of the young users had to be taken into account, and various functions had to be represented via child-appropriate design, for example, using icons that would allow users who were not (fully) literate to navigate the platform. This approach helped to create a colorful and child-oriented platform (see Figure 12.2). Different colors were

Figure 12.2 come_NET

used for different menus: yellow menu items were used for personal topics (e.g., profile page, pictures, friends), orange menu items were used for club topics (e.g., those posted on the club blackboard), and purple menu items were used for platform topics (e.g., those posted on a pinboard accessible to everyone). Nearly every week, a new version of the design was presented to the children; their feedback and interactions were then recorded (audio and the screen capture), and these led to another iteration of the design. Additionally, observations by the tutors and researchers helped us to understand the emerging challenges of the platform and informed the design of the next iteration of the platform.

Recurring privacy concerns and discussions in the club, for instance, regarding children's careless online behavior, led to a demand for easy and adjustable privacy options for come_NET users. Participants had to be made aware of the security settings of their artifacts and adjust who could see and download the artifacts. In addition, this concept had to be made understandable for children. As one of the first steps in the development of come_NET, three security levels were created: "for me," "for us," and "for all." With these levels, the user could adjust the artifact to be visible just to him or her, to everybody in the club, or to every user on the platform.

Next, we implemented a drag-and-drop upload function, so that a user could upload any artifact (e.g., games, animations, sound, and pictures) by dropping it into a special area on the website. We did this because a "drag-and-drop" procedure is easier to use than the Windows dialog mode, which involves first clicking on the upload button on the platform, then using the Windows Explorer function to search for the artifact while navigating through the whole folder structure of the computer, and finally selecting the artifact and clicking on the upload button. It is then possible to find these artifacts, via a sitewide search, and then download them.

During the first few weeks of using the platform, participants needed some guidance on exploring the new functions and how to use them. Based on these insights, we developed two additional components of the platform: a playful component, which let the participants interact with each other, and a guidance component, which helped new participants explore the platform while solving riddles. These functions were developed in close collaboration with the participants: every week, a new version of the function was prepared and tested, and the participants' feedback was then incorporated into the next version of the function.

In the following section, we provide a detailed overview of the development of the platform, and the design process that led to its different features.

12.5.1 The Development Process for come_NET

The development process consisted of four consecutive phases (Figure 12.3). The first prototype (Phase 1) was built on a regular content management system (Joomla![2]) and had only a few functions (e.g., messaging, profile), based on a requirement analysis that was conducted via interviews in four different computer clubs (Bonn Tannenbusch, Bonn Nordstadt, Dortmund, and Siegen). But the content management system had a lot of limitations with respect to adjusting the design of the platform and extending the existing functions to meet the requirements of the children (e.g., to be able to download artifacts).

Therefore, in Phase 2 (Figure 12.3), come_NET was redesigned; it is now based on a PHP framework. In a participatory-design process, children from two clubs (Siegen and

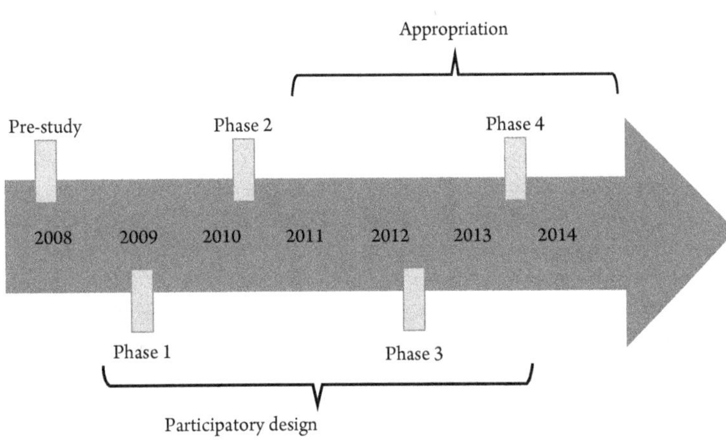

Figure 12.3 Timeline of the development

[2] See http://www.joomla.org.

Bonn Tannenbusch) were involved during the development and provided feedback on a weekly basis: new ideas from the children were implemented (as functioning mock-ups) and evaluated the week after (e.g., via messaging or the blackboard). This iterative development approach led to a more advanced version, which was tailored to fit the demands of children and parents in come_IN computer clubs.

Phases 3 and 4 extended the existing platform to address issues observed during the weekly sessions by the tutors. In Phase 3, the goal was to develop a child-oriented artifact exchange; children should be able to upload their artifacts to come_NET as easy as possible. The drag-and-drop upload function was developed, with children in Dortmund and Siegen acting as codesigners, informing the look and feel of the implemented feature. The objective of Phase 4 was to enable the children to get familiar with navigating the platform; to achieve this goal, a gamification element was designed in an iterative development process: different game concepts were presented to the children, and their feedback and ideas influenced further development. Detailed bottom-up documentation will enable newly arriving developers to come to terms with the system.

12.5.2 Design of the Communication Function

During the iterative development process, children were faced with various design suggestions made by the technical designer to incorporate their feedback as future users. However, occasionally, the designer's ideas were dismissed by the young testers, and the children's alternative design ideas were taken up instead.

The start page of the platform is the platform's entry point (see Figure 12.2); it shows the latest actions of the participants' friends, in order to create awareness and foster interactions. Participants can see who uploaded new artifacts (e.g., pictures), who wrote on the pinboard or blackboard, and who messaged them. Also, they can see which friends have accepted their friendship requests, and they can send a message to the newly acquired friend. The view created provides friends the opportunity to upload pictures, allows individuals to upload their own ideas, and, in general, aims to support and motivate children to share the different views and projects.

Every club has its own blackboard in order to communicate interclub-related topics, collect ideas for future projects, talk about current challenges, and discuss upcoming events (e.g., the annual computer club meeting; Figure 12.4, left). Since all the children are already attending school, the blackboard was chosen as metaphor for this kind of interaction by the designer and was approved by the children's feedback. The built-in pinboard is a place for short messages and greetings to other members or just for the generation of quick idea (Figure 12.4, right). Participants used this communication tool to create yellow post-its with their thoughts on it to share with everybody else.

12.5.3 Design of the Artifact-Sharing Function

Simplicity was key in the design of the upload section for artifacts (Figure 12.5). The buttons are bigger than usual, have different colors representing the different security levels

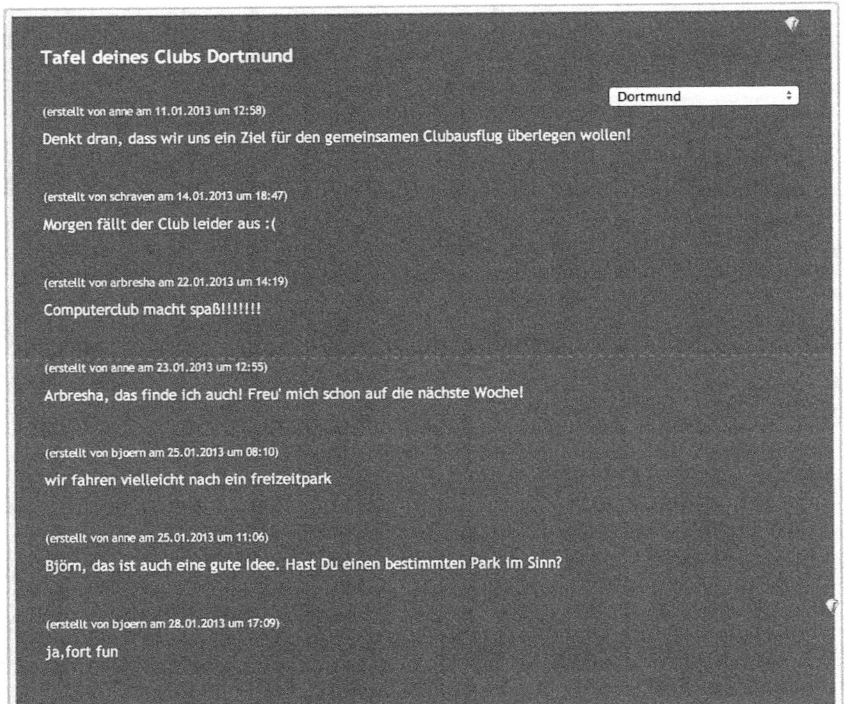

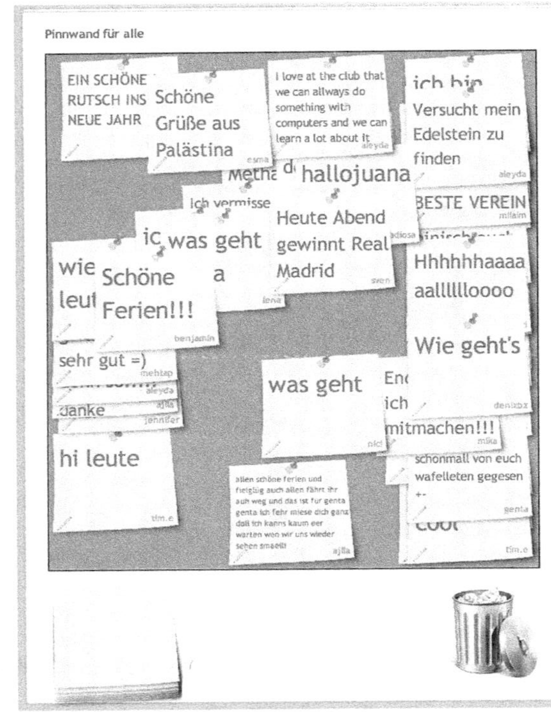

Figure 12.4 *(Left)* The club blackboard; *(right)* the club pinboard

Figure 12.5 The artifact upload section

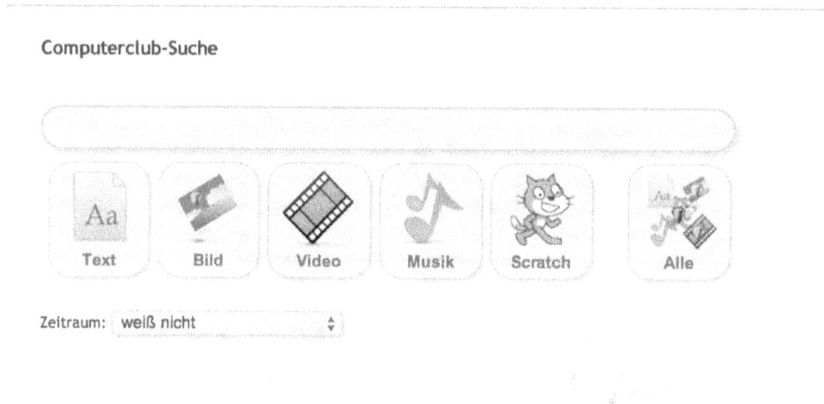

Figure 12.6 The computer club search

(based on the overall come_NET menu), and are easy to handle; in addition, the section has a large field with a drag-and-drop option, to make it easy for creative members to share their self-made projects. The field needed to be big since children have limited motor skills; our observations of computer club project work revealed that children often have difficulties with clicking small buttons or using the mouse to navigate to a small area. Once uploaded, the artifact is available both for the children (e.g., to download it at home) and for other participants of come_NET.

To address the children's problem with safely storing and locating their project data, as well as to encourage collaboration and the exchange of ideas, a computer club search function (Figure 12.6) was implemented. Here, the user can select different data types and artifacts to search for (e.g., Scratch projects or videos). Besides enabling participants to browse the projects of community members, this functionality makes it possible to archive projects, instructional material, and best practice recommendations. In this way, the networking and exchange of data is supported, and its purpose in sharing expertise encouraged. The design of the search function is plain and easy to understand—the participant can start a search for a specific artifact with a click on one button; also, a time frame for the search can be set. There is a button to search for Scratch projects, one to search for pictures, one to search for texts, one to search for videos, and one to search for music, as based on our observations, the vast majority of shared digital projects could be subsumed under those five categories. There is also a button that will allow the user to search in all of these categories at once. In addition, as our observations indicated that the search function was also often used to get inspiration for new projects, the search tool allows also "blind" searches, that is, searches of file types without inputting a keyword.

12.5.4 Design of the Networking Function

On the profile page, participants can provide information about themselves (e.g., where they live, their favorite movies, their best friends), change their password, play a game, and see those with whom they became friends (Figure 12.7). Completing the profile page was one of the first activities participants did; they spent a lot of time thinking about the different questions they might want to address until they finally found a satisfying answer. Every week, participants verified their current answers and modified some of the answers if their preferences changed.

The main communication tool for participants was the messaging function. Received messages, sent messages, deleted messages, and message composition were all indicated by different icons (Figure 12.8). The size of all the icons was bigger than usual in order to simplify the usage. Participants could write a message to every other member of come_NET without having to become friends. In addition, an auto-complete extension for the username was incorporated: participants could write down the first letters of the recipient's name, and the extension would suggest members whose name started with these letters.

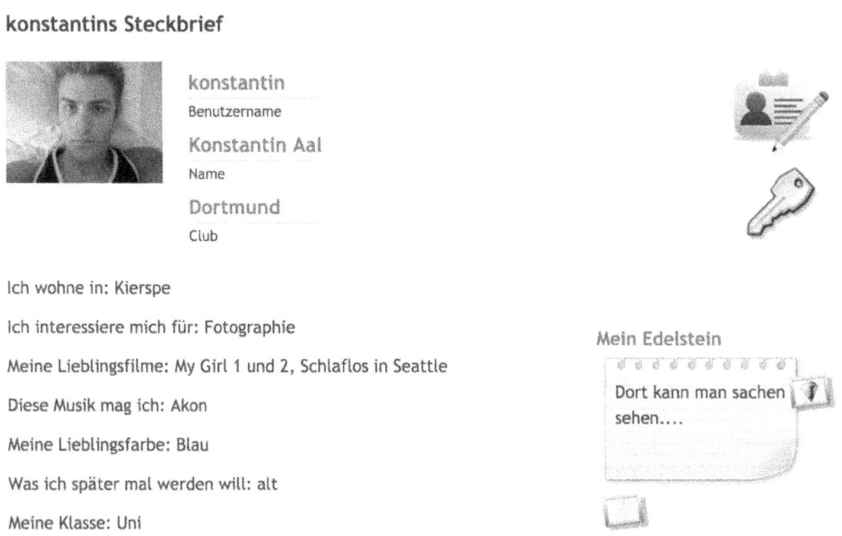

Figure 12.7 The profile page

Figure 12.8 The mailbox for messages

Figure 12.9 The artifact upload, with privacy settings

12.5.5 Design of the Privacy Settings

Privacy was a concern, not only for many parents in the clubs but also for the tutors. One important factor is that come_NET is a closed platform where only computer club members can participate. That means an account can only be obtained by asking a tutor or the teacher to set one up. If a case of harassment were to happen, the tutors would know the participant and could talk with him or her privately about the issue.

The artifact upload function has three different levels of privacy settings (see Figure 12.9):

- "for me" (indicated by yellow): when this setting is used, the artifact can only be seen by the user who uploaded the artifact (the owner); this function can be used to store the artifact on come_NET and then download it later at a different place

- "for us" (indicated by orange): the artifact can only be seen by the artifact owner's club; club participants can download the artifact and ask the owner questions in real life, if they want
- "for all" (indicated by purple): the artifact can be seen by everybody who is part of come_NET; the name and club of the owner is noted on the artifact, and other come_NET participants can write him or her a message if they have questions

Come_NET aims to raise the awareness for privacy issues by creating a safe environment. Especially for children, the simplicity of the artifact upload function helps children to learn the responsible handling of private information and artifacts using an online platform.

12.5.6 Design of the Gamification Function

At the beginning, participants in the club asked continuously for help in operating the platform. Most of the young users were inexperienced in using a social-media platform. To overcome this hurdle and enable the children to get familiar with navigating the platform, a gamification feature was implemented (see Figure 12.10). As our experience from the computer club sessions showed, browser games fascinate children, who never have to be asked twice to play. Against this backdrop, the gamification element of the platform was developed as a tutorial to motivate the clubs' participants to explore and make use of the platform on their own. In the feature, an avatar asks children to fulfill different tasks (e.g., upload your first artifact, send your first friendship request); while doing so, the participants investigate the platform and learn how to use the different functions. After the successful completion of one task, the next task is ready to be addressed. The system also tracks those participants who have already solved the different tasks; if children struggle with their current task, they have a person whom they can ask for help (either by using the platform messaging tool or by communicating in real life).

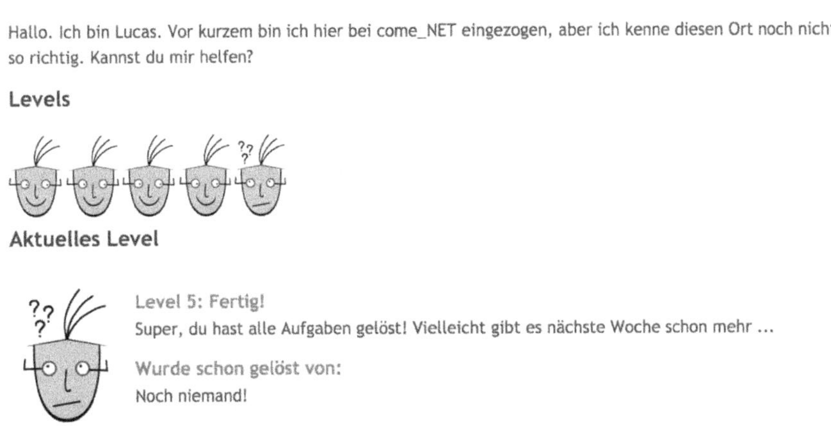

Figure 12.10 The gamification menu

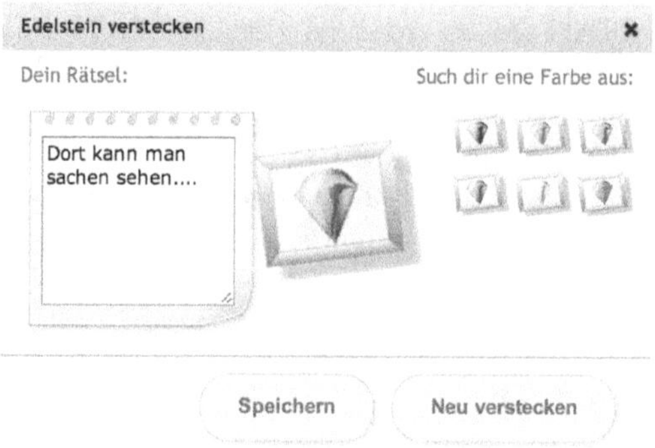

Figure 12.11 Screenshot of the gem search game

Another element of the platform is a gem-search game, to motivate the participants to use come_NET. Members can search for the gems of other users (see Figure 12.11). By clicking on them, they can collect these gems, which come in a variety of colors, and they can also set a riddle and choose a color for their own gem when they "hide it" by placing it somewhere on the platform for other users to find.

12.6 The Appropriation of come_NET

12.6.1 The Use of come_NET in the Club Sessions

Once the online platform come_NET was ready for the clubs to use, it was received in the clubs in different ways, depending on the different needs and prerequisites of the respective clubs.

The computer club in Dortmund absorbed the new platform in a rather lively manner. Children adopted it as an addition that would provide them with entertainment during the initial free time for individual play and work during the club session. After some time, we found that come_NET even replaced the educational game "*Lernwerkstatt*," which is what the children usually spent all their free time playing during the club session. "Can I do the platform now?" children would immediately demand when entering the computer room; this rather technical wording may indicate these children's involvement with the development of come_NET. Others would demand: "I want to do come_NET." And still others would seek to use come_NET by naming their favorite activity on the platform: "Let's go on our page and write messages!" Regularly, the children were seen to write messages to each other on the platform during club session time. They enjoyed writing these, and then watching how their friends in the club receive and read them.

The computer club at the elementary school in Siegen joined come_NET more than a year after the platform had first been launched for the general use in the clubs. The Siegen club maintains very restricted exposure to the Internet; thus, its participants did not feel the initial need to engage in come_NET. After the tutors had explained the platform in the club, the participants who were present registered on come_NET, but no activity from that club has yet been recorded; since there is no particular culture of Internet use in this club, the come_NET platform is effectively unused, although it has remained available in the background. This may be because the Siegen club is much smaller than the Dortmund club, fluctuation among the children participants is relatively high, and many of the project activities (e.g., a stop-motion film project or an outdoor photo activity) can take place offline and do not involve the Internet.

The elementary school club in Bonn has seen preliminary versions of the platform and children participated in the testing of the platform early on, but they did not engage in the fully launched platform because the club was closed at that time, due to a fundamental change in the school's after-school program.

A computer club at a secondary school in Bonn Tannenbusch participated in the development of the platform but did not engage much in its use after the platform was launched. As many of the participating teenagers had already created profile pages on other social-media sites, such as Facebook, and had developed a regular habit of using those, they considered it interesting to be involved in the development of the platform and thus learn something about the design process first hand. However, they did not see much need to create yet another online profile for themselves. Plus, the come_NET platform lacked features such as online games that the teenagers were used to playing with their peers.

The computer club in Kreuztal is affiliated with a secondary school and included in the lower grades' curriculum. For this club, come_NET was introduced in the club's first year, when fifth graders participated in the computer club. The children were granted a quarter of an hour of free online time in the beginning and the regular pattern of usage was to log in to the come_NET platform as soon as the lesson started and then to check for new messages that other come_IN members might have sent over the week. The next activity usually was to "update" the personal profile page, especially the profile picture, which was not necessarily a picture of the user but rather on associated with the "currently most hyped topic," often a picture of the latest smartphone or coolest-looking car. Currently, come_NET is not used on a regular basis in this club. Unlike groups in prior years in this school and in other come_IN clubs, the present group of participating children is comparatively older, aged 13–15 years, and so already have Facebook profiles. Therefore, they see come_NET as lacking several features and elements they were already used to, such as online games and an instant messenger or chat tool. Most importantly, they miss the option of being connected to peers and contacts who are not in the come_IN club, so the closed nature of the platform is not well received. However, former participants in this club appreciated this "parent-approved" online community, especially its message function.

The annual joint come_IN meeting (*Aktionstag*) triggered the use of come_NET more noticeably, as children from different clubs contacted each other via come_NET after they had met in person at the event. Our field notes document how the children engaged in writing messages to the children they had met at the joint gathering, and how the writing and receiving of these messages were accompanied by giggles and laughter whenever the communication went across genders. Notably, before come_NET, there had not been any forms of cooperation among the different clubs.

None of the clubs used the platform as a tool for collaboration. This was mainly due to the fact that, as yet, no project activities have been conducted that reached beyond a single club.

Given the ways the different clubs used come_NET, our subsequent presentation of the usage of the different platform features focuses mainly on its usage in the computer clubs in Dortmund and Kreuztal. These two clubs mainly engaged in using the platform after its launch.

12.6.2 The Appropriation of the Artifact-Sharing Function

By the time the platform was introduced to the club in Dortmund, participants had completed a number of project activities using MIT's programming environment, Scratch. Accordingly, the first projects that the children uploaded to their profiles in come_NET were Scratch projects that they had completed. However, this did not result in major data sharing on the side of the children. Rather, sharing activities that occurred were directly linked to the actual production process (e.g., when one child in the club was seen to create a new project in Scratch, another child observed this, was impressed by a detail of its design or programming logic, and would then ask for permission to use this in a project of his or her own). Almost always, this resulted not in the sharing of actual artifacts but rather in the sharing of the knowledge about how to make them. The children preferred to create something of their own, so their main interest was in the knowledge of the production process, rather than on reusing someone else's creation.

In the club in Kreuztal, only on rare occasions was come_NET used to share user-created content. In most cases, the shared artifacts were Scratch projects, which were uploaded just for testing, to explore how the sharing works, and, in some cases, after tutors encouraged participating children to "share their cool project also with the other clubs," but it was usually not as a result of any personal incentive of the children. This may be due to the fact that online sharing at that time and at their age was not as common a practice as it seems to have become today, with messenger services like WhatsApp,[3] and numerous smart phone applications also used by children.

12.6.3 The Appropriation of the Communication Function

Children in the club in Dortmund initially liked the message feature of come_NET. They enjoyed writing messages with their friends. Surprisingly, they were mainly engaging with this during club time, writing messages to other children in the club. Since the children they were writing to were often sitting at the computer right next to them, the children were frequently seen to turn their computer screens and keyboards, typing in rather awkward positions, so their friends would not be able to see the message before it was sent. Also—once the message was ready and sent—children were frequently seen to run across the room to the computer of the child that was the receiver of the message.

[3] See http://www.whatsapp.com.

Child 1: "Did you get my message?"

Child 2 (*engaged in something else*): "No?"

Child 1: "Quick! Have a look! I sent it just now!"

In the computer club in Kreuztal, the text chat tool was used mainly for instant messaging other peers in the same computer club location, posting ideas and questions, broadcasting updates on current activity, and informing others to check self-created come_NET content, such as blackboard entries or profile changes, this way allowing the children to communicate while the pursuing project-associated activities, so they would not lose time by leaving their own computers and current activity.

It may appear trivial, but as the weekly club meeting time was usually limited to just 1.5 hours, children in the club in Bonn Marienschule, as well as in Dortmund, were often observed to avoid the slightest delay in their project work, and any delay "caused by others" (e.g., when a tutor could not solve a hardware issue immediately) resulted in harsh criticism for "losing track of the others' project progress" (i.e., losing the "leading developer" role).

12.6.4 The Appropriation of the Networking Function

In Dortmund, come_NET was initially received as an ideal instrument for children who had left elementary school, and, with it, the computer club, to still keep in contact with their peers from the computer club. Several children also wrote messages to the teacher and the tutors in the club, asking about project activities and whether they could visit the club again.

Also, the club's blackboard turned out to be an important feature for networking. Children would post messages there outside of club times, greeting others and trying to prompt responses from other children in their club.

Interclub networking was noticeably triggered by the clubs' joint meetings. For example, after participants returned from a joint trip to a working-world exhibition, the event was addressed on the come_NET platform in various ways. For instance, the shared experience was used afterwards as a common reference (e.g., in the description of the gems: "My gem is nearby a girl who was in my group at DASA Dortmund.")

12.6.5 The Appropriation of the Privacy Settings

Awareness for privacy settings was fostered in the club in Dortmund in close relation to the upload function in come_NET. While at first, children did not really spend much time thinking about whether they wanted the upload of an artifact to be "for me," "for us," or "for all," over time, this became an issue, and children were seen to discuss with their best friends in the club whether the artifact they wanted to upload was of shareable quality.

This awareness of privacy settings was further deepened when one of the girls in the computer club lost her account password and it was used by an unknown person. After this, the club held a special session on password security and privacy online, where the children, teacher, and tutor jointly discussed the topic and developed guiding principles for the children to keep in mind (e.g., asking whether everyone in the club network should know one's personal address or see personal pictures, or if one's best friend should know login data).

Since data sharing via come_NET did not constitute a regular practice in Kreuztal, children in this club were not much concerned with the available privacy settings. On the rare occasions the sharing function was utilized, sharing was always used to publish a project for as big an audience as possible; therefore, the privacy option was always set to "for all."

12.6.6 The Appropriation of the Gamification Function

All children in Dortmund were seemed especially entertained by searching for images to upload on their profile pages on the platform. To them, this was a playful way of getting to know the features of the platform and individualizing their own appearance in it.

Gamification elements were well appreciated by the children in the computer club at the comprehensive school in Kreuztal as well, and just as much by the older participants. For instance, one of the implemented gamification elements let players hide and seek little gem icons on the come_NET pages, triggering usage with notifications on who found the hidden gems. Older kids, around the age of 13, were observed laughing and making fun of engaging in these "childish" hide-and-seek activities but, nevertheless, engaging in this activity regularly. One of the reasons for that may be the fact that gems "hidden" on one's personal profile page were easily noticed by the page's owner who, just by clicking, could "clean" the page. Also, some children tried to get a huge collection of gems (found gems would be displayed in a nice collection on the profile page), while others were eager to find the best stash for the little gem icons (e.g., on the site notice page, which rarely would be accessed by any of the children).

12.7 Discussion

The online community platform come_NET has been in use in the computer club network for more than a year now, and our detailed analysis of the reception of its features in the club routines in the various clubs reveals three main factors determining a sustainable implementation. These are (1) a reliable *social structure* within the club and beyond, (2) a close structural connection to, and awareness of, the general *(social-)media and computer-use habits* of the prospective child and youth users, and (3) the employment of *gamification* to motivate usage.

12.7.1 Social Setting

Since come_NET is an online platform designed to support the offline activity of computer clubs, our findings showed that having a dependable social setting within the club, as well as beyond, was an important prerequisite for the lively usage of come_NET. Platform usage in the computer club in Dortmund illustrates this—here, strong friendship ties had already developed among the children in the club, and come_NET bore features (e.g., messaging) that were able to support and intensify these online. Indicative of this might also be the fact that computer club alumni greeted the platform as a means to stay in contact with "their" club after they had left elementary school and came to visit whenever possible.

12.7.2 Interacting with Given IT Infrastructures

Especially among the older children and youth participants in our computer clubs, there was relatively little interest in engaging in platform usage and maintaining an account there. Especially among the youth computer club participants, this was attributable to general social-media and computer-use habits: most of the girls and boys already kept Facebook accounts and engaged in the use of instant-messaging services like WhatsApp, so the closed, intranet-like appearance of come_NET was of little appeal to them. This finding supports earlier work by Pipek and Wulf (2009), who showed how "the strength of use patterns coined in practice and conventions may equal the strength of use patterns enforced through technology" (Pipek and Wulf 2009, p. 466). Among the younger children, who were not yet "settled" with regard to their use habits for social-media and related computer technology, come_NET bore features that were obviously of great interest to the children—most prominently among them the messaging feature, as well as photo-related features like the ability to create albums with the user's favorite images, and the option to personalize the account with a profile picture.

It became apparent that whenever come_NET was able to create a close connection to the general social-media and computer-use practices of the children and youth participants in the computer clubs, this resulted in a lively and sustainable platform usage. The usage also included elements of guidance, for example, with regard to privacy, and an awareness of data security and sharing online, as could be seen in the club in Dortmund, where a special session on password security was held in the club after one of the girls had lost her password. Here, it was the social setting of the club that allowed for a safe and thus sustainable reception of the online platform: the guidance by tutors and the teacher as well as guiding features implemented (e.g., explanations about what makes for a safe password) made the children feel secure—lost passwords could always be restored at a club session, and insecurities (e.g., in the managing of personal data in account profiles) could also be discussed and fixed there. This observation is in agreement with insights presented by Ahn et al. (2015) on how social-media and sharing tools can contribute to child learning. In line with Revelle et al.'s (2010) work on prosocial media for children, the platform was seen to be able to trigger creativity and the exchange of knowledge, for example, when children in the club in Dortmund exchanged knowledge about the creation of a specific artifact, rather than sharing and reusing the artifacts themselves.

12.7.3 Gamification

The computer club is decidedly separate from conventional school activities, offering guidance but not teaching in a traditional manner. The design of come_NET follows this open yet guiding structure by using elements of gamification to trigger usage of the platform among the child participants in the computer clubs. Overall, elements like the hide-and-seek game with little gems, as well as the tutorial with the avatar, showed promise in that they triggered playful exploration of the platform among the younger children and even entertained the more media-experienced youth participants in the computer clubs.

12.8 Conclusion

The younger participants in the come_IN computer clubs were not used to maintaining a personal online appearance in form of a website or a personal profile in an online social community. Their parents sometimes exhibited reservations regarding their children's engagement in openly accessible online communities. Against this backdrop, the closed online community platform come_NET was well received by children and parents, as well as by teachers. The participatory-design process, closely involving the participants in the computer clubs and paying special attention to the needs of the children, fostered a profound understanding of the platform structure and its functionalities. It thus inspired trust and supported the appropriation of the platform among the computer club participants. Younger children were particularly able to benefit, as the platform enabled them to gather experience as users of social media, but in a safe and guided manner. However, the intranet-like structure of come_NET entailed limitations to its targeted user group: come_NET was found to not be appealing to teenagers, who had already gathered some experience as social-media users and preferred engaging in open communities.

Future work will involve the extension of the come_NET platform to newly established computer clubs in Palestine (Aal et al. 2014). This will potentially trigger international collaborations among come_IN clubs, as well as an increased application of come_NET, eventually leading to redesign and new features.

References

Aal, K., Yerousis, G., Schubert, K., Hornung, D., Stickel, O., and Wulf, V. 2014. "Come_in@palestine: Adapting a German computer club concept to a Palestinian refugee camp." In *CABS'14*. New York: ACM, 111–20.

Ackerman, M. S., Dachtera, J., Pipek, V., and Wulf, V. 2013. "Sharing knowledge and expertise: The CSCW view of knowledge management." *Computer Supported Cooperative Work* 22 (4–6): 531–73.

Ahn, J., Clegg, T., Yip, J., Bonsignore, E., and Rick, J. 2015. "Innovations in interaction design learning." In *IDC'15*. New York: ACM, 462–5.

Ahn, J., Gubbels, M., Kim, J., and Wu, J. 2012. *SINQ: Scientific INQuiry Learning using Social Media*. New York: ACM Press.

Ames, M., and Manguy, L. 2006. "PhotoArcs: A tool for creating and sharing photo-narratives." In *CHI EA'06*. New York: ACM, 466–71.

Baacke, D. 1996. "Medienkompetenz–Begrifflichkeit und sozialer Wandel." 1996. In A. von Rein, ed., *Medienkompetenz als Schlüsselbegriff*. Bad Heilbrunn: Julius Klinkhardt, 112–24.

Berry, J. 1992. "Acculturation and adaptation in a new society." *International Migration* 30 (S1): 69–85.

Berry, J. W. 1984. "Cultural relations in plural societies: Alternatives to segregation and their sociopsychological implications." In N. Miller and M. B. Brewer, eds., *Groups in Contact: The Psychology of Desegregation*. New York: Academic Press, 11–27.

Boltman, A., and Druin, A. 1998. "What children can tell us about technology: The CHIkids model of technology immersion." In *CHI'98*. New York: ACM, 135–6.

Druin, A. 1999. *The Design of Children's Technology*. San Francisco: Morgan Kaufmann Publishers.

Druin, A., Stewart, J., Proft, D., Bederson, B., and Hollan, J. 1997. "KidPad: A design collaboration between children, technologists, and educators." In *CHI'97*. New York: ACM, 463–70.

Emerson, R. M., Fretz, R. I., and Shaw, L. L. 2001. *Writing Ethnographic Fieldnotes*. Chicago: University of Chicago Press.

Freidus, N., and Hlubinka, M. 2002. "Digital storytelling for reflective practice in communities of learners." *ACM SIGGROUP Bulletin* 23 (2): 24–6.

Holtzblatt, K., and Jones, S. 1993. "Contextual inquiry: A participatory technique for system design." In D. Schuler, A. Namioka, eds., *Participatory Design: Principles and Practices*. Boca Raton: CRC Press, 177–210.

Kafai, Y. B., Peppler, K. A., and Chapman, R. N. (eds.). 2009. *The Computer Clubhouse: Constructionism and Creativity in Youth Communities*. New York: Teachers College Press.

Maloney, J., Resnick, M., Rusk, N., Silverman, B., and Eastmond, E. 2010. "The Scratch programming language and environment." *ACM Transactions on Computing Education* 10 (4): 16.

Mathur, A., Majumder, A., Datta, S., Menon, S., Malhotra, S., and Dahiya, A. 2012. "LifeView: A lifelog visualization tool for supporting sentimental recall and sharing." In *OzCHI'12*. New York: ACM, 371–80.

McTaggart, R., and Kemmis, S. 1988. *The Action Research Planner*. Victoria: Deakin University.

Michalchik, V., Llorente, C., Lundh, P., and Remold, J. 2008. *A Place to be Your Best: Youth Outcomes in the Computer Clubhouse*. Available at http://www.computerclubhouse.org/sites/default/files/A%20Place%20to%20Be%20Your%20Best%20FINAL%207-25.pdf (accessed October 8, 2017).

Muller, M. J. 2003. "Participatory design: The third space in HCI." In A. Sears and J. A. Jacko, eds., *Human-Computer Interaction: Development Process*. Boca Raton: CRC Press, 165–85.

Norris, P. 2001. *Digital Divide: Civic Engagement, Information Poverty, and the Internet Worldwide*. Cambridge: Cambridge University Press.

Pipek, V., and Wulf, V. 1999. "A groupware's life." In *ECSCW'99*. Dordrecht: Springer, 199–218.

Pipek, V., and Wulf, V. 2009. "Infrastructuring: Toward an integrated perspective on the design and use of information technology." *Journal of the Association for Information Systems* 10 (5) 447.

Resnick, M., and Rusk, N. 1996. "The computer clubhouse: Helping youth develop fluency with new media." In *ICLS'96*. International Society of the Learning Sciences, 285–91.

Resnick, M., Rusk, N., and Cooke, S. 1998. "The computer clubhouse: Technological fluency in the inner city." In D. Schön, B. Sanyal, and W. Mitchell, eds., *High Technology and Low-Income Communities: Prospects for the Positive Use of Advanced Information Technology*. Cambridge, MA: MIT Press, 263–86.

Resnick, M., Maloney, J., Monroy-Hernández, A., Rusk, N., Eastmond, E., Brennan, K., Millner, A., Rosenbaum, E., Silver, J., Silverman, B., and Kafai Y. 2009. "Scratch: Programming for all." *Communications of the ACM* 52 (11): 60–7.

Revelle, G., Fenwick-Naditch, A., Kronenberger, L., and Mays-Green, M. 2010. "CHI 2010 special interest group: Creating prosocial media for children." In *CHI EA'10*. New York: ACM Press, 3185–8.

Rohde, M., Brödner, P., Stevens, G., Betz, M., and Wulf, V. 2017. "Grounded design: A praxeological IS research perspective." *Journal of Information Technology* 32 (2): 163–79.

Rohde, M., Stevens, G., Brödner, P., and Wulf, V. 2009. "Towards a paradigmatic shift in IS: Designing for social practice." In *DESRIST'09*. New York: ACM, 15.

Schubert, K., Weibert, A., and Wulf, V. 2011. "Locating computer clubs in multicultural neighborhoods: How collaborative project work fosters integration processes." *International Journal of Human-Computer Studies* 69 (10): 669–78.

Schuck, P. H. and Münz, R. 1998. *Paths to Inclusion: The Integration of Migrants in the United States and Germany*. New York: Berghahn Books.

Seeber, G. and Schobert, W. 1979. *Der Trickfilm in seinen grundsätzlichen Möglichkeiten*. Frankfurt am Main: Deutsches Filmmuseum.

Stevens, G., Veith, M., and Wulf, V. 2005. "Bridging among ethnic communities by cross-cultural communities of practice." In P. Van Den Besselaar, G. de Michelis, J. Preece, and C. Simone, eds., *Communities and Technologies 2005*. Dordrecht: Springer, 377–96.

Sützl, W., Stalder, F., Maier, R., and Hug, T. 2012. *Media, Knowledge and Education: Cultures and Ethics of Sharing: Medien-Wissen-Bildung: Kulturen und Ethiken des Teilens*. Innsbruck: Innsbruck University Press.

Sylvan, E. 2006. "Who knows whom in a virtual learning network? Applying social network analysis to communities of learners at the computer clubhouse." In *ICLS'06*. International Society of the Learning Sciences, 758–64.

Sylvan, E. 2007a. "Network models of online communities of creators." In *CSCL'07*. International Society of the Learning Sciences, 868–70.

Sylvan, E. 2007b. *The Sharing of Wonderful Ideas: Influence and Interaction in Online Communities of Creators*. PhD thesis. Cambridge, MA: MIT.

Toffler, A., Longul, W., and Forbes, H. 1981. *The Third Wave*. New York: Bantam Books.

Wagner, G. G., Pischner, R., and Haisken-DeNew, J. P. 2002. "The changing digital divide in Germany." In B. Wellman and C. Haythornthwaite, eds., *The Internet in Everyday Life*. New York: John Wiley & Sons, 164–85.

Weibert, A., Marshall, A., Aal, K., Schubert, K., and Rode, J. 2014. "Sewing interest in E-textiles: Analyzing making from a gendered perspective." In *DIS'14*. New York: ACM, 15–24.

Weibert, A., Sander, B., and Schubert, K. 2011. "Upon the role of the teacher in the informal learning setting of an intercultural computer club." In *CSCL'11*. International Society of the Learning Sicences, 950–1.

Weibert, A. and Schubert, K. 2010. "How the social structure of intercultural computer clubs fosters interactive storytelling." In *IDC'10*. New York: ACM, 368–71.

Weibert, A. and Wulf, V. 2010. "'All of a sudden we had this dialogue…' : Intercultural computer clubs' contribution to sustainable integration." In *ICIC'10*. New York: ACM, 93–102.

Weilenmann, A., Hillman, T., and Jungselius, B. 2013. "Instagram at the museum: Communicating the museum experience through social photo sharing." In *CHI'13*. New York: ACM, 1843–52.

Witte, J. C., and Mannon, S. E. 2010. *The Internet and Social Inequalitites*. Abingdon-on-Thames: Routledge.

Wolfinger, N. H. 2002. "On writing fieldnotes: Collection strategies and background expectancies." *Qualitative Research* 2 (1): 85–93.

Wulf, V., Müller, C., Pipek, V., Randall, D., Rohde, M., and Stevens, G. 2015. "Practice-based computing: Empirically grounded conceptualizations derived from design case studies." In V. Wulf, K. Schmidt, and D. Randall, eds., *Designing Socially Embedded Technologies in the Real-World*. London: Springer-Verlag London, 111–50.

Wulf, V., Rohde, M., Pipek, V., and Stevens, G. 2011. "Engaging with practices: Design case studies as a research framework in CSCW." In *CSCW'11*. New York: ACM, 505–12.

Yip, J., Ahn, J., Clegg, T., Bonsignore, E., Pauw, D., and Gubbels, M. 2014. "'It helped me do my science.': A case of designing social media technologies for children in science learning." In *IDC'14*. New York: ACM, 155–64.

13 Enabling Users of Enterprise Systems to Mash Up Resources and Develop Widgets

MICHAEL SPAHN, JULIAN DAX,
FAHRI YETIM, AND VOLKMAR PIPEK

13.1 Introduction

Many companies use enterprise software systems like enterprise resource planning (ERP) systems to support and facilitate their business. Companies operating in dynamic environments need to continuously adapt their information systems to changing business processes and practices as well as their associated information needs (MacKay 1990; Henderson and Kyng 1991; Wulf and Rohde 1995). Small and medium-sized enterprises (SMEs) in particular often suffer from their inability to adapt enterprise software to their needs, due to a lack of resources and expertise (Roth and Scheidl 2006; Yetim et al. 2010; Dörner et al. 2011). As a consequence, they are often forced to adapt their work processes and practices to the possibilities offered by the used enterprise software or to delegate configurations to IT professionals. This adaptation process is both lengthy and costly (Markus and Tanis 2000; Brehm et al. 2001; Wulf and Jarke 2004) and often has adverse consequences for businesses competitiveness.

One possible way to deal with this challenge is to enable end users of ERP systems, from now on referred to as business users, to tailor systems to their needs, since they are managing and executing business processes on a daily basis and thus know best about changing requirements and the consequent need for adaptations. Usually, ERP systems allow users to access relevant business data directly via the user interface, or to extract data using queries and reports. However, in many cases, users need to create custom queries and build tools consuming and processing information in a way uniquely tailored

Socio-Informatics, Volker Wulf, Volkmar Pipek, Dave Randall, Markus Rohde, Kjeld Schmidt, Gunnar Stevens (Eds). © Oxford University Press 2018. Published 2018 by Oxford University Press.

to their needs (Spahn, Dörner, et al. 2008b; Dörner et al. 2011). The complexity of ERP systems and available tools remains, it seems, challenging for business users with less technical knowledge.

Enabling users to adapt systems on their own, without the need for specialized technical knowledge, is one of the main concerns of approaches to tailorability and end-user development (Henderson and Kyng 1989; Fischer et al. 2004; Lieberman et al. 2006; Wulf et al. 2008; Spahn, Dörner, et al. 2008a; Dörner et al. 2009). The aim is to do rather more than design systems that are flexible and easy to adapt. It is, above all, a call for sociotechnical infrastructures to enable users to participate in their work contexts through the use of their application systems (Pipek 2005; Pipek and Wulf 2009; Stevens et al. 2010; Yetim et al. 2012). End-user oriented approaches emphasize both the flexibility of systems for adaptability in a technical sense, and the methods to leverage this flexibility at the hands of end users. Achieving these goals may require the integration of several technologies (Dörner et al. 2011; Hess et al. 2012; Boden et al. 2014). For example, service-oriented architectures (Erl 2005) provide increased flexibility and rich possibilities for IT professionals. However, technical flexibility cannot be leveraged by end users alone, as they typically lack the IT expertise to make use of these complex standards. In contrast, Web-based applications such as mash-ups (e.g., Microsoft Popfly, Yahoo! Pipes, and IFTT) embody lightweight design principles and allow users to mash up data from different resources into a single integrated tool and thereby create new and distinct services. These mash-ups and composite applications were considered one of the top ten strategic technologies of recent years (Gartner 2007).

The goal of the research described in this chapter is to develop methods and tools to enable business users to create individual information artifacts tailored to their individual information needs and work practices. In order to archive this, we followed a design case study approach. In a design case study, there are three phases (Wulf et al. 2011, 2015):

1. Empirical investigation of the practices in a specific field
2. Development of a hard- or software prototype based on the findings of the first phase
3. Empirical investigation of the appropriation of the hard- or software prototype over a longer period of time

This translates to the following three phases in our study:

First, we conducted empirical investigations into the work practices of users in SMEs to identify datacentric adaptation problems that business users face in their work context. We analyzed the results on a meta-level to identify existing processes for creating information artifacts, and the building blocks used in them. As such artifacts need to be created by users in an intuitive and lightweight way, we also conducted a participatory design workshop (PDW) to get insights into how users create information artifacts using a simple box-and-wire design technique.

Second, to address some of the identified problems and needs, we developed a prototypical design environment that allowed business users to create widgets. Widgets are small interactive applications for displaying data, packaged in a way so that they can be executable on a user's machine (Caceres 2008). By using a very lightweight mash-up design technique and encapsulating mash-ups as widgets, we aimed to enable business users to develop small, interactive applications using enterprise resources and deploy these applications directly to their machine, without the need for any programming knowledge. In this way, the whole process of developing building blocks and combining them to create widgets is put in the hands of SMEs.

Finally, we deployed the prototype in three German SMEs, evaluated its usability and usefulness, and investigated its appropriation. We were interested in how business users could create widgets using the lightweight design approach, and which practical problems could be addressed by using simple applications such as widgets.

In the following sections, we present each of the steps and their results and also provide some conclusions.

13.2 Background

There are many definitions of the term "mash-up." Depending on the perspective and context of the researchers, they define mash-ups according to technological or economic criteria. Some have attempted to find an overarching definition that encompasses all these factors. Koschmider et al. (2009), for example, define a mash-up as "a Web-based application that is created by combining and processing online third party resources, that contribute with data, presentation or functionality." In this chapter, we adopt the definition of enterprise mash-ups from Hoyer and Stanoevska-Slabeva: "An Enterprise Mashup is a Web-based resource that combines existing resources, be it content, data or application functionality, from more than one resource in enterprise environments by empowering the actual end-users to create and adapt individual information centric and situational applications" (Hoyer and Stanoevska-Slabeva 2008, p. 149). When we discuss mash-ups in this chapter, we always refer to enterprise mash-ups in this way.

Several tools and approaches allow end users to create mash-ups (e.g., Yu et al. 2008). In this chapter, we will focus on those that are most closely related to our work and served as an inspiration for it. We categorize these approaches and tools according to whether they support resource integration, resource transformation, or widget orchestration.

13.2.1 Resource Integration Tools

Resource integration tools encapsulate resources and provide access to them. They do this in a way that allows other components to use them. This needs to be done in a seamless, substantial, and appropriate fashion. Examples of resource integration tools are Dapper (http://www.dapper.net/open/) and OpenKapow (http://openkapow.com). These tools allow users to define rules to extract structured data from unstructured HTML files. The research prototype, Karma (Tuchinda et al. 2008), uses this approach and extends it by allowing users to specify examples of how the extracted data should look and automatically generate transformation rules from these examples. Another research prototype, called Marmite (Wong 2007), allows end users to combine existing Web content and services from multiple Web sites into new applications that had not been envisaged by the websites' designers. Marmite uses a dataflow architecture that is similar to Unix pipes. It supports the extraction of content from websites (e.g., names, addresses, and dates), which can be processed in different ways, such as by filtering values or adding metadata. Its output can be directed to different sinks, such as databases, map services, and Web pages. However, Marmite cannot use data sources other than websites and hence cannot be utilized in an ERP context.

13.2.2 Resource Transformation Tools

Resource transformation tools support the creation of newly configured software by recombining and transforming resources and then providing the result as a single resource. Examples of such tools are Yahoo! Pipes, JackBe Presto Wires, and IBM Damia. Users can use these tools to combine parameterizable function blocks from a predefined catalog. Yahoo! Pipes uses a user-interface design that is similar to the one used by Marmite. It allows end users to manipulate, integrate, and visualize data using a box-and-wire structure. Users can share the "pipes" they create with other users on the platform. The research prototype DERI Pipes (Le-Phuoc et al. 2009) is similar to Yahoo! Pipes but extends its approach to the usage of semantic Web technologies. All of these approaches are arguably not well suited to the ERP context, however.

13.2.3 Widget Orchestration Tools

Widget orchestration tools allow the creation of widgets from the resource transformation and resource integration tools provided. We classify the created mash-ups into presentation mash-ups and application mash-ups.

Presentation mash-ups combine different widgets into one user interface without interconnecting these widgets. Often, users can simply choose from a collection of predefined widgets (e.g., widgets for stock prices, weather, or news) and add them to the mash-up interface. After that, the selected widgets can be customized. Examples of tools that do this are MyYahoo (https://my.yahoo.com/), Netvibes (http://www.netvibes.com/), and uStart (http://www.ustart.org/).

Application mash-ups are also created by combining different widgets in an integrated user interface, but, in contrast, they also allow the definition of application logic. Widgets can be connected to create reactive and interactive applications. One example for this is IBM QEDWiki, a prototype that lets users create portal pages out of widgets. Intel MashMaker (Ennals and Garofalakis 2007), for instance, is a browser plug-in which allows the manipulation of existing Web pages. Another system in this category is Enterprise Mashup Application Platform (EMAP), which enables users to create mash-ups of enterprise applications (Gurram et al. 2008). Like many such systems, EMAP comes with predefined widget components that can be combined and parameterized. Unlike Yahoo! Pipes and Marmite, it uses events to communicate between widgets. It is one of the few systems focused on the business domain. Ardito et al. (2014) present an integrated, general-purpose mash-up environment that allows the creation of so-called personal information spaces. In these spaces, users can gather, integrate, and visualize data from different Web services and application programming interfaces (APIs). This environment was then developed further into the EFESTO platform (Desolda et al. 2016), which also supports other data sources like Linked Open Data.

More reviews of mash-up technologies can be found in the work by Hoyer and Fischer (2008), Koschmider et al. (2009), Albinola et al. (2009), Aumüller and Thor (2008), and Yu et al. (2008).

13.2.4 Research Gaps

Currently, there is something of a lack of empirical studies in the area of enterprise mash-ups. Most research is focused on technology and tools. Papers discussing the use of mash-ups in companies (e.g., Soriano et al. 2007; Hoyer and Stanoevska-Slabeva 2008) are based mainly on theoretical considerations and explorations of general trends. There are some empirical studies, but they only deal with the usability aspect of mash-up tools (e.g., Wong 2007). Evaluation is not typically done in the field. In this chapter, we provide insight into how these tools are used in real work environments and investigate the utility of mash-up approaches in the organizational contexts for information access.

13.3 Empirical Investigations in Practice

13.3.1 Exploration of Users' Problems and Needs in Practice

To understand the problems experienced and requirements for the design of practically relevant tools, we conducted fourteen semistructured interviews based on qualitative research methods (Kvale 1996) in three German midsized companies that use the SAP ERP system to support their business.

Company A is a producer of bags, backpacks, suitcases, and similar items, with 140 staff members. A partnering company in Asia procures most of the raw materials and manufactures subassemblies. Final assembly, marketing, and sales of the products take place in Germany. Company A does not sell directly to retail customers but uses resellers. Company B is a software company that develops and sells its software products but also develops software on commission. It has 500 employees. Company C produces custom textiles for the automobile industry and employs 137 people. So, two of the companies we investigated were from the production industry (137 and 140 employees), and one was a larger software vendor (500 employees). In all three companies, the IT department manages the introduction or modification of software, together with technically adept employees from the affected department. These so-called key users help to disperse the knowledge about the new system in the company and serve as local counterparts of the IT staff, for other users who experience problems or have questions about the software. Every department has one key user. In some cases, external consultants are also involved in the introduction process.

We conducted semistructured face-to-face interviews in an exploratory way to get insights into operational tasks and existing work practices. This investigation revealed that users face two classes of problems associated with information display:

- information related to a particular task is scattered around the ERP application, hard to find, or only available in several different applications
- information cannot be filtered, accumulated, combined, or displayed in a way suitable to a specific task

As an example of the first category of problems, one interviewee who was in charge of reviewing customers credit lines reported the following: "I occasionally have the problem that I need to access four or five things in one row in order to get what I need... for example, when I do the annual review of credit lines. I need master data, data from SD [SAP's ERP module for sales and distribution] and some data from accounting." An example related to finding information was given by another interviewee: "When it is about master data, then I know that I can jump to the field in most cases and press F1 for help, where the data is saved.... But there are things which you cannot find this way, not even X from the IT department."[1]

As an example of the second category of problems, an IT manager described the following case: "[the ERP system] sums up the revenue numbers on a monthly basis. To calculate the daily revenue, we access the revenue numbers every morning at the same time and manually enter them in an Excel sheet. By subtracting the collected sums, we then calculate the daily revenue numbers."

We found several cases in which Excel sheets were used to deal with problems in the second category. These Excel sheets can get quite sophisticated, as one user describes: "To plan how much to order, I separate the year into several time periods based on experience.... I can estimate when demand is going to be high or low, which colors sell the best and if a product introduction causes additional demand." The user created his own individual, complex solution, which he has to update manually at regular intervals, to carry out this planning and forecasting task. More concrete examples of problems in the two categories can be found in the work by Spahn (2010).

Due to the complexity of the data model used by the ERP system, and the complexity of the tools for query creation provided by the ERP system, most users were not able to create custom queries on their own in order to get data out of the ERP system in the way they desired. Additionally, business users were not able to create any custom information artifact providing interaction on live data with the ERP system. Many users have to access a particular set of data relevant to their individual working tasks from the ERP system many times a day. In many cases, this data cannot be accessed from a single location within the graphical user interface (GUI) of the ERP systems, thus forcing users to access multiple locations and collect the needed data in an unnecessarily cumbersome fashion. As the users are not able to create any customized GUI or interactive application that would provide access to relevant data at a glance, many working tasks can only be executed

[1] All names are anonymized to protect participant's privacy.

in an inefficient and cumbersome manner. More details of this study are documented in the article by Spahn, Dörner, et al. (2008b).

13.3.2 Observing the Users' Design

A prerequisite for building lightweight design environments for composition is the identification of a straightforward and easy-to-use design technique for composition. We therefore investigated the effects of confronting users with a simple design metaphor like boxes and wires (e.g., employed by mash-up tools like Yahoo! Pipes). We chose the boxes-and-wires technique because it enables visual modeling while using a minimum of different design entities. To get initial insights into how users interact with a fairly elementary modeling approach, we complemented our interview study with a PDW, putting users in the role of designers (Muller 2003).

In the PDW business, users had to design an information artifact representing a tool that could support users in an analytic task that participants took from their work context. To create the solution, the users could add boxes to the design space that represent data or functionality. Boxes had output ports and input ports, and users could connect these ports by drawing lines to define data or control flow between the boxes. The boxes-and-wires model was left underspecified. We gave no concrete instructions to the users on how to formally specify the meaning of the used design elements. The underspecified semantics enabled us to observe users' natural design behavior while they were using the design elements (Pane et al. 2001) more or less intuitively. The design behaviors and the artifacts created by the users were then analyzed to get a better understanding of how users approached this design task.

The PDW (for a visual concept, see Figure 13.1) revealed that users intuitively thought of boxes as a representation of tabular data, organizing data in rows and columns.

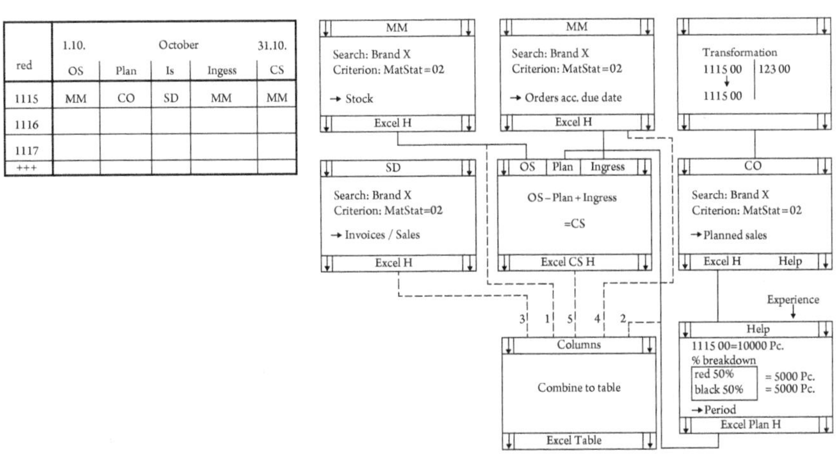

Figure 13.1 (*Left*) Visual concept of the desired output of the system; (*right*) visual concept of the user interface designed in the PDW

By connecting boxes, business users related data from different boxes and defined the data flow of the solution. The users had no problems using the boxes-and-wires design paradigm itself to specify a solution but had problems expressing what data a box should represent. The users decided to describe the data by giving a short description on how they would access the data in their used ERP system. Details of this study are presented in the articles by Spahn, Dörner, et al. (2008b) and by Dörner et al. (2011).

13.4 Design and Development of the Widget Composition Platform

13.4.1 Motivation and Preliminary Remarks

To address the problems and needs identified in the empirical investigations, we subsequently developed two prototypes for supporting business users. These tools solve two main problems. First, business users create custom spreadsheets and rely on getting relevant data from the ERP system by using queries but face considerable challenges when trying to define custom queries for their individual information needs. The first application, called "Semantic Query Designer" (SQD), provides sophisticated visualization, navigation, search, and query building abilities and enables business users to create custom queries. A detailed description of this application is provided in the article by Spahn, Kleb, et al. (2008).

The second central problem concerns the fact that business users needed to access the same set of data within the GUI of the ERP system over and over again in a cumbersome manner and were not able to create custom interactive applications that provide the information relevant to individual working tasks at a glance. In response to this problem, we developed a Web-based environment called the "Widget Composition Platform" (WCP), to enable business users to mash-up enterprise resources in a visual-design environment in a very lightweight way and to deploy the created mash-ups in the form of widgets to their local machines.

In this section, we will describe the functionalities and architectural components of the WCP. In response to the positive results of the PDW on the usefulness of the box-and-wire technique, we decided to implement this metaphor in the WCP for offering a very lightweight visual mash-up design environment. Boxes represent services that provide enterprise data that is, in most cases rendered, in a table. As the empirical investigations revealed, business users were able to use such a format in an intuitive way for designing software artifacts.

For the realization of a visual mash-up design environment, we were able to build on an early internal prototype developed by SAP, who was one of the partners in the consortium, and modify and extend it to suit our needs. Despite this, we faced considerable challenges in realizing a solution that could be deployed and used within SMEs, for two main reasons. First, SMEs often use ERP systems that are not (yet) service enabled and thus cannot provide enterprise resources as services that are accessible using standard Web protocols, which is an essential precondition for deploying developed mash-ups as a widget on standard widget runtimes. Second, even if enterprise systems were exposing a fixed set of resources as services, this set could not be extended without programming skills and thus would limit the creatable solutions to combinations of predefined services. To address these challenges, we implemented middleware that could wrap resources from not previously service-enabled ERP systems and provided these as services that were accessible using standard Web protocols. SMEs must be able to create new services using existing knowledge and without any programming skills, since some of their members, at least, do not possess the requisite skills. There are SMEs that can build queries within the existing ERP system, so we enabled the implemented middleware to wrap queries stored within the ERP system and then provide them as services. Using the existing skills of query creation to allow the creation of new building blocks for widget creation has several advantages. It limits entry barriers, enabling users to utilize the new technology in a flexible way. It can also be seen as a kind of gentle slope of complexity approach (MacLean et al. 1990; Spahn, Dörner, et al. 2008a; Wulf et al. 2008) that puts the whole chain of widget creation in the hand of SMEs. Additionally, by enabling the use of queries as services, a relation between the SQD and WCP prototypes is established, as end users can use the SQD for easy query creation, and the WCP to mash up these queries to widgets.

In the following subsections, we describe the system prototype in detail. We first describe the basic conceptual layers that are implemented by the WCP environment and then explain the architectural components of the WCP environment and their interaction. Finally, we describe the user-interface aspects of this system and explain how business users can create widgets by mashing up enterprise services.

13.4.2 Conceptual Layers

On a conceptual level, the WCP and the widgets it is used to create are based on a layered architecture. Significant components of this conceptual architecture are classified and structured in the widget stack depicted in Figure 13.2. The widget stack consists of five primary layers: the resource layer, the API layer, the wrapper layer, the service layer, and

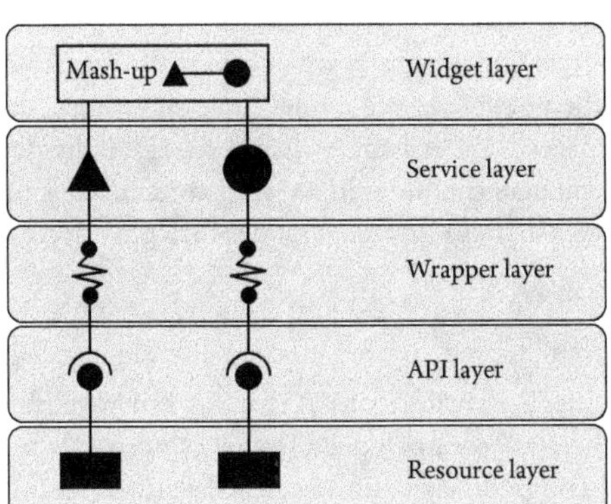

Figure 13.2 The conceptual layers of the widget stack in the WCP environment

the mash-up/widget layer. We will describe the layers in Figure 13.2 by starting with the bottom layer and ending with the top layer, as each layer requires the functionality provided by the layer below it (Spahn and Wulf 2009; Spahn 2010).

The Resource Layer

The resource layer consists of all the resources that can be integrated into mash-ups. Resources can be data, such as customer master data stored in an ERP system, or functionality, such as locating an address and returning the corresponding image of a map, which would be provided by a map application. Resources are managed and provided by systems that can be internal or external to an organization. Internal systems might be various enterprise systems, like ERP systems, customer-relationship-management systems, or general-purpose relational database management systems (RDBMs). External resources might be provided by systems accessible to a closed user group, including systems of suppliers, customers, or B2B marketplaces, or by systems publicly available over the Internet (e.g., map services or stock quotes).

The API Layer

The API layer consists of well-defined interfaces provided by the systems managing the resources. Depending on these systems, different formats and protocols may be needed to call the APIs and access the resources. APIs of modern service-enabled systems may be provided as Web services that can be called using standard Web protocols, while legacy systems may provide APIs only as libraries that can be linked into source code and communicate with the system using proprietary protocols. Required formats of input parameters and formats of returned results vary accordingly and range from XML structures to proprietary binary formats.

The Wrapper Layer

The wrapper layer provides a unified service model. The service model is consumable by the service layer and abstracts from the heterogeneity of APIs, protocols, and formats. More specifically, wrapper components transform abstract requests to the abstract service model to concrete requests using the respective API, protocol, and parameter format of the addressed resource. These components convert the raw results received from the API to a format that the unified service model can process (e.g., data structures storing tables, lists, or even images). The resources do not require individualized wrapper components, as generic wrappers can be used to wrap certain types of resources, like SAP ERP queries or RSS feeds. These generic wrappers are provided as service types in the service layer.

The Service Layer

The service layer provides a repository of services that can be mashed up in the mash-up environment. All services are parameterized instances of service types, relating services to a certain wrapper component in the wrapper layer. For example, a service called "Customer Data" and that provides data from an SAP ERP query is an instance of the service type "SAP ERP Query," which relates the service to an appropriate wrapper component. The service instance uses parameters to specify the concrete query inside the SAP ERP system, which the wrapper component can access. Services provide further configuration possibilities that vary depending on the type of service. For example, the desired type of data visualization (e.g., rendering data as a table or a list), or the set of available data filters that the GUI provides in the mash-up environment, can be configured. Services can be further described by adding information like name and description text.

The Mash-up/Widget Layer

The mash-up and widget layer adds mash-up functionality to the unified service model of the service layer and provides the functionality to deploy mash-ups as widgets. Users can define mash-ups by specifying a wiring of design elements, interconnecting design elements, and defining the desired data flow. Design elements can be services or additional user-interface elements (e.g., text boxes). The wiring defines how data from one design element is used to parameterize calls to other (dependent) design elements. Dependent design elements react on data updates of connected design elements and update their data accordingly. Mash-ups can be encapsulated as widgets and deployed as self-contained applications to individual runtimes (e.g., the Yahoo! Widget engine [http://widgets.yahoo.com]). The mash-up creation and widget deployment functionality are provided by the mash-up and widget layer to end users by an integrated end-user development environment.

Relevant business data needs to be available as services in the service layer to enable business users to create custom widgets supporting their individual working tasks. Therefore, wrapper components and service types need to be implemented to be able to wrap resources from relevant enterprise systems.

13.4.3 Architectural Components

Our prototype instantiates the conceptual widget stack (Spahn and Wulf 2009; Spahn 2010). Figure 13.3 provides an overview of the system components. The central component of the prototype is the WCP, a Web application that is implemented using Java technology and runs inside a Web application server. The WCP provides an integrated, Web-based, graphical end-user development environment for widget creation. A service repository manages all services that users can mash up within a widget. A widget deployment component within the WCP is responsible for creating source code, encoding the currently created widget for multiple runtime environments. During the process of widget composition within the WCP user interface, this component generates code for the WCP browser runtime libraries, so that the widget is fully functional within the user interface that the browser renders. If the user decides to deploy the developed widget to a widget runtime engine, the component generates code tailored to that engine. It also packages the widget to a file that has the corresponding structure and format. To persist data stores, like the service repository, the personal repository of end users' created widgets, or the login and access right information, the WCP uses an RDBM.

On the client side, end users access the user interface of the WCP by using a Web browser to call a certain URL. This simplified access to the WCP makes it very easy for

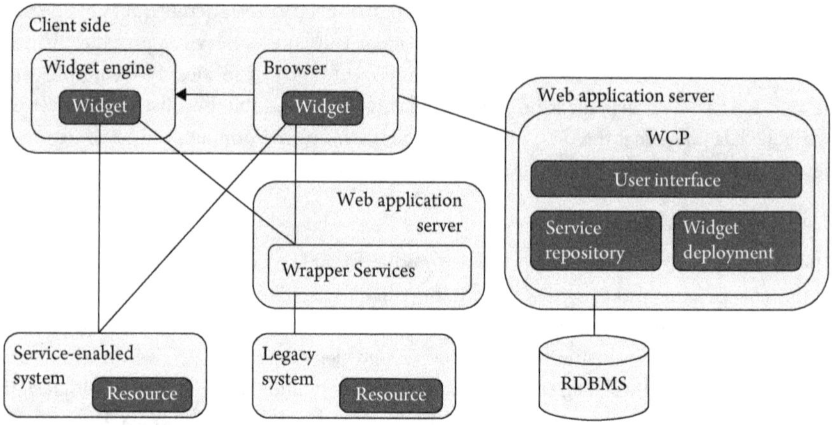

Figure 13.3 Architectural components of the WCP

end users to start with the development of individual widgets. Within the browser, widgets run via a WCP runtime library implemented in JavaScript using common Web standards. This enables rendering of the widget and provides full widget functionality inside the browser during the development process. For deployment, the WCP is delivering a single file that contains the widget packaged in the specific format required by the runtime environment.

As described in Section 13.4.2, widgets access the resources that are mashed up within the widget via wrapper components. If service-enabled systems manage resources, wrapper components can address the resources directly by using standard Web protocols. If the resources are managed by legacy systems that do not provide an API that is addressable using standard Web protocols, the wrapper components are assisted by wrapper services. Wrapper services are deployed to a dedicated Web application server and provide access to legacy systems. In our particular setup, we implemented wrapper services to access queries within non-service-enabled versions of SAP ERP systems by encapsulating SAP remote function calls via the SAP Java Connector and executed SQL queries to RDBMs or Excel files by using Java Database Connectivity. This approach enabled wrapper components to access resources within such systems by using simple Web protocols, keeping the technology needed on the client side as straightforward and lightweight as possible.

13.4.4 The WCP User Interface

The WCP provides a browser-based user interface representing an integrated development environment that enables the visual development of widgets without requiring the user to have any programming knowledge. Figure 13.4 shows a screenshot of the user interface.

We separated the user interface into several panes. On the left side, a list of all services contained in the service repository is provided. The list groups services according to

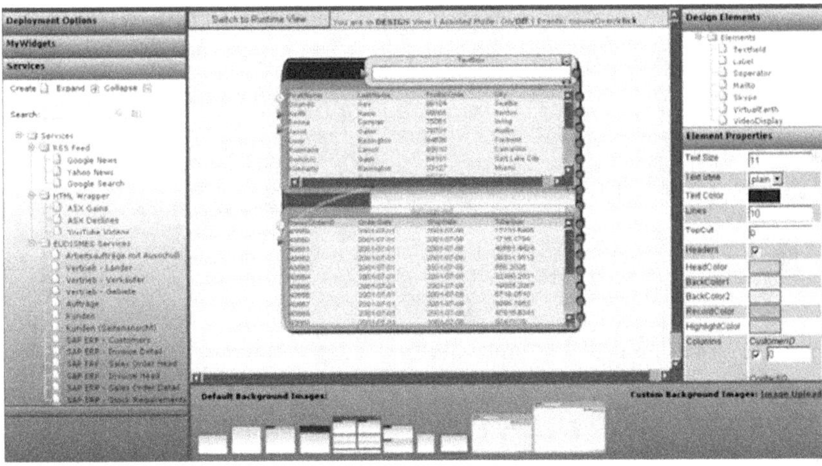

Figure 13.4 The WCP user interface

their service types. Users can add services to a mash-up simply by dragging and dropping the service to the design pane, which is located in the middle of the interface. Besides services, additional design elements, like text boxes, can be dragged from the upper right of the interface into the design pane. If a user-interface element in the design pane is selected, its properties become visible and modifiable in a properties pane on the right. Properties that can be modified include not only visual properties (such as color or font faces) but also—more importantly—the structural properties of services. From the background pane at the bottom of the user interface, the user can select a background image, enhancing the visual appearance of the created widget. After services or design elements are added to the design pane, they are immediately populated with live data and provide runtime interaction possibilities. All design decisions create immediate effects, thus blurring design time and runtime and enabling development close to a WYSIWYG manner, increasing the confidence of the user in creating the desired results.

In order to mash up services, a wiring has to be defined using a simple box-and-wire design. As depicted in Figure 13.5, services and other design elements offer input ports and output ports that can be connected in order to define the wiring. Users can connect elements by drawing a line that goes from the output port of a source element to the input port of a target element. Whenever data in the source element changes, the new data is pushed as input to the target element, which updates itself accordingly. The update of data in target elements might again push new information to dependent elements, which in turn might trigger updates. In the example shown in Figure 13.5, a service providing customer master data is connected to a service providing sales order data. When selecting a customer in the customer table, the connected sales order service is automatically updated to show only the sales orders of the selected customer. In the case of the depicted services, input ports correspond to filters on table columns, and output ports correspond

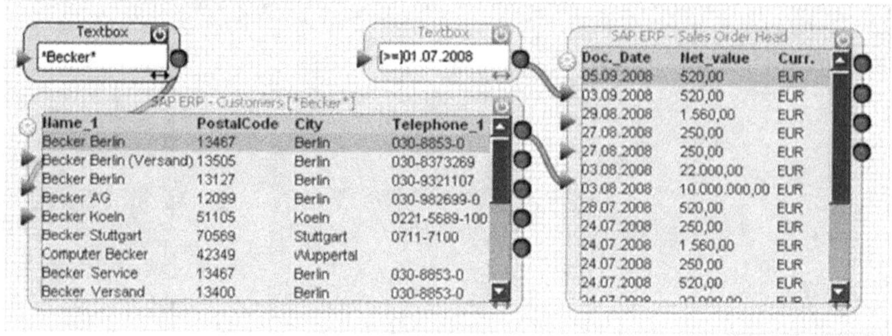

Figure 13.5 Wiring of services and design elements

to the column values of the currently selected row. In this example, two text boxes are used to enable the user to interactively define values that are pushed to services as input. The text box connected to the customer data service restricts the customers shown according to the given name pattern. The text box joined to the sales order service restricts the sales orders shown to those sales orders that have been received at or after a specific date. In addition to text boxes, other design elements exist that provide additional functionality. Examples are design elements that use email addresses or Skype names as input and provide the ability to send an email or establish a Skype call by clicking on an envelope or telephone symbol.

If a resource for the current mash-up is missing in the service repository during the creation process, an appropriate service can be defined using the "Create" option of the service pane. To define a service, the user needs to select the service type (e.g., SAP ERP query) and then the resource that the service should encapsulate (e.g., by providing the SAP ERP system storing the query, and the name of the query). After the service is saved to the repository, it can instantly be used in the mash-up process.

At any point in time, the user can switch from the design mode to the runtime mode (the design principle of direct activation; see Wulf and Golombek 2001). Although the widget is fully functional even in the design mode, the runtime mode hides all the visual elements that users only otherwise need in the design mode, like input ports, output ports, and connections, and prevents modifications to the widget. In this way, the widget is presented as it would appear if deployed to an external widget engine. Widgets can be saved to and loaded from a personal widget repository managed by the WCP. This functionality is accessible through the "MyWidgets" pane on the left of the user interface. Using the "Deployments Option" pane, the system can deploy the widget to multiple widget runtime environments, like Yahoo! Widget Engine (http://widgets.yahoo.com) or Microsoft Windows Vista Sidebar (Lal 2008).

When deployment is selected, the WCP returns a single file that can either be directly opened and thereby be deployed to the client-side widget engine or can be saved as a file that can easily be sent via email or moved to a file share in order to share the widget with colleagues. Widgets that are deployed to a client-side widget engine run independently of the WCP and are small, self-contained, interactive applications.

13.5 The Appropriation Study

13.5.1 Goals and Methods

The WCP environment, which was designed to enable business users to create custom widgets, was introduced in practice to explore whether business users in SMEs would create widgets using the WCP and how they might appropriate the widgets for addressing practical problems in real work contexts.

To determine this, we conducted two complementary studies in the three German midsized companies in which we conducted the pre-study. The first study considered use cases in practice. Its goal was to observe how users adopted and used the WCP to create widgets and services. The second study conducted a questionnaire-based survey among the employees as potential users of the WCP to get feedback from a broader user base on the proposed WCP-based solution. In the following, we briefly present the qualitative study.

13.5.2 Evaluation through Use Cases in Practice

In this section, we first describe the setup of the practical evaluation of the WCP and then described the results of the use within SMEs, through example use cases.

Setup of the Evaluation in Practice

We deployed the WCP environment in the three German SMEs. Among those, 50, 70, and 116 employees have access to the SAP ERP system; 18, 60, and 70 employees use the SAP ERP system on a regular base. In two of the three companies, the WCP was initially installed in cooperation with the IT department, and in the third business, it was installed in collaboration with the person responsible for IT concerns, as no dedicated IT department existed. After installation, the WCP could be used by every employee with access to the internal network of the company.

In every business, one advanced end user was nominated to be the contact person, who was responsible for all concerns about the WCP. This person, in principle, acted as an evangelist to promote the usage of the new technology, as well as provide support to users if questions arose. In the first phase, the contact person was given an introduction to the WCP and then asked to experiment with it to get more familiar with its concepts and usage. We defined five distinct services encapsulating SAP ERP data, as a starting point for experiments. The services provided ordinary data related to customers, sales orders, and invoices. To increase the motivation for experimentation, we included some appealing external services that users could access, like a service for visualizing addresses on a map, a YouTube video service, Google news, and a stock quote service. In the second phase, we discussed any problem that might have arisen in the first phase and provided help to solve these problems. We also discussed potential use cases of widgets within the company. In the third phase, we encouraged the contact person to act as an evangelist and promote the usage of the WCP by approaching employees who might be interested in the discussed usages, giving them an introduction to the WCP, and motivating them to explore it. We also conducted interviews with employees who were using the WCP. Our aim was to investigate the appropriation of the WCP and how end users use the WCP and widgets to address practical problems.

Appropriating the WCP and the Widgets in Practice

In the following section, we discuss four examples of cases that show how business users appropriate widgets.

Case 1: A sales-support widget A staff member in the sales department of Company A is in charge of answering questions from customers. Customers contact the employee by phone to get information related to the content and status of their orders. Inquiries resulting from such calls might be questions as to whether or not certain goods have been bought to fulfill a specific sales order, or what the current state of the order's processing is, for example. To be able to answer such questions, the sales officer has to access multiple locations inside the GUI of the SAP ERP system. In the first step, the user needs to access the customer's master data to identify him or her. In the second step, the user accesses sales order header data to filter the sales orders of the respective customer and the sales order in question. In the third step, the individual items of the sales order are accessed to track the ordered goods, their quantity, and their status. If the customer enquiries about items on multiple sales orders, the user needs to switch back and forth between the different sales order list and their details. The sales employee we talked to considered incrementally gathering required information via the GUI by accessing multiple reports and switching back and forth between them to be rather cumbersome, especially since he had to access the information many times a day for different calls.

After the evangelist approached the sales employee and introduced the WCP to him, the employee started to experiment with the WCP. Using the services we had defined as standard demo services during installation, the employee was able to create a suitable widget for his needs. The widget shows customer master data, sales order header data, and sales order details as three distinct tables. Using text-box user-interface elements, the sales employee added filters for customers by name or customer number, and filters for the order dates of sales orders. He deployed the widget to his desktop to make it readily available when customers required information. Via the filters in the widget, a client can be uniquely identified in a rapid and convenient way. By clicking on a customer in the table, all of the sales orders of the buyer come up in another table, directly beneath the customer table. The user then can restrict the visible sales orders to the ones ordered at or after a specified date. When the user clicks on a sales order, all the relevant details are shown in a third table. The employee in question configured the tables to only show data relevant to him, resulting in a compact overview providing required data at a glance. To view details of other sales orders in question, the employee can now simply click on the sales order in the sales order table.

The widget this employee created is now used by the sales staff some forty times per day to answer standard customer questions related to orders. As the user does not need to access multiple tables/reports within the complicated GUI of the SAP ERP system but instead gets all the relevant data at a glance, he or she can answer standard customer inquiries in approximately half the time, compared to when using the GUI of the SAP

ERP system. Because of this, the sales staff decided to send the widget via email to a colleague who needed to access the same data occasionally. This employee had no programming skills and was able to create a custom widget for supporting his individual working task within 3 hours after having seen the WCP for the first time. He explained to us that experimenting with the WCP was fun for him. He thought that the WCP had an appealing user interface and that the creation of widgets was simple, comprehensible, and easy to learn.

Case 2: A material-lookup widget An employee in the procurement department of Company A needs to access certain information related to material many times a day. For instance, she needs to identify a specific spare part by its material number and then find out how much is currently in stock and how much is already scheduled for production. To get a first overview of the status of the spare part, she could determine a rather fixed set of information that she considers to be highly relevant for her work context. As in the previous case, this information is widely spread within the GUI of the SAP ERP application, and users have to gather it in a cumbersome manner.

When the evangelist introduced this employee to the WCP, she immediately thought of building a widget to tailor her standard data set of related information. As predefined services that might deliver relevant data did not exist, the evangelist discussed with the employee which data was needed. Then he searched for possible data sources like tables and queries within the ERP system. Building on a larger query, the evangelist managed to create a SAP query joining five distinct tables and providing most of the requested data. The query was wrapped as a service for the WCP and was used by the user to create a suitable widget.

The widget is rather simply structured and consists simply of a text box and the created service (see Figure 13.6). The text box defines a filter for the material number to the service. As the service just returns a single record, the results are not rendered as a table with a single row but as a list, showing all attributes of the record with according values as rows. The user in this case configured the service to show only the most relevant data and arranged all the design elements neatly to create an appealing widget. We also deployed the same widget on the PC of an employee who worked in the raw material storage facility and did not have direct access to live data from the SAP ERP system (due to SAP's license fees). By using the widget, he was able to access the most critical data related to material in a very easy way, without needing to learn about and understand a complex enterprise system.

Case 3: An address-book widget All three businesses keep Excel sheets of employee information and contact data, like telephone, fax, and cell phone numbers, email addresses, and departmental affiliation. Employees distribute these sheets via email among themselves. To have this list readily available, employees tend to keep the latest version of it in designated folders on their PCs or print it out.

To improve on this process, the WCP evangelists in all three firms independently developed an address-book widget. The evangelists took the data from the existing Excel sheets, which they copied onto network shares and integrated into the WCP as a service. Figure 13.7 shows two examples of address-book widgets from two different companies.

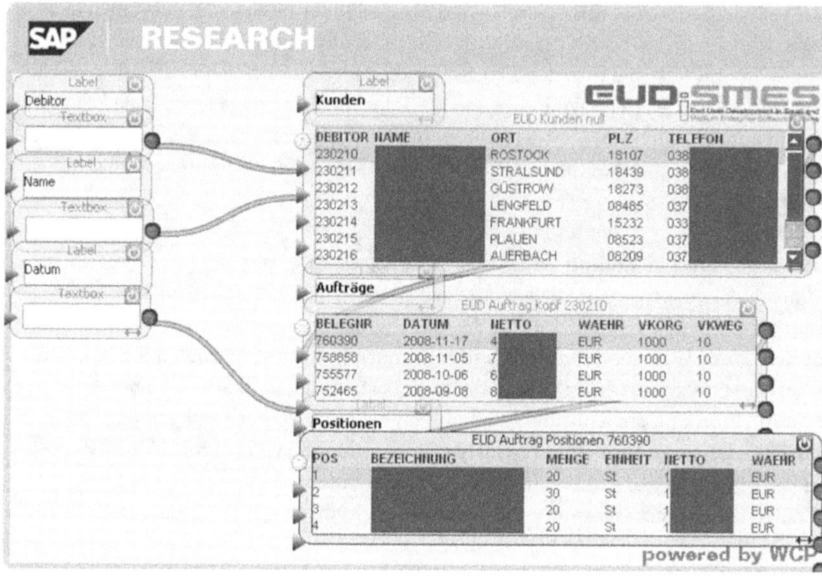

Figure 13.6 Screenshot of the material lookup widget in design mode

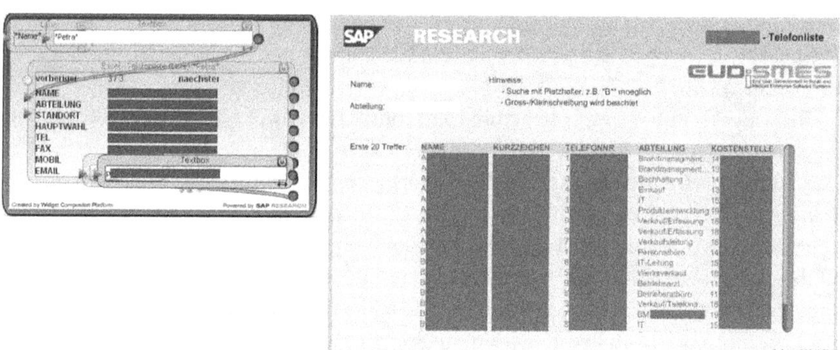

Figure 13.7 Screenshots of two of the three address book widgets

The widget shown on the left allows users to search for employees by name. The search results are presented one at a time and can be navigated by using a "back" button and a "forward" button. Email addresses are clickable links. The widget shown on the right uses a table to display the first twenty search results. In this widget, employees can be searched for not only by name but also by departmental affiliation. The WCP evangelist shared the widgets using email. These emails also contained links to the Yahoo! Widget Engine, which allowed employees to use the widget directly on their desktops, without a Web browser. The Yahoo! Widget Engine also enabled users to set a hotkey for the widget.

The widget was adopted quickly in all three firms, and the users liked its handiness. An employee in Company A remarked: "The address list was a good idea; it is something practical.... Everyone can make good use of that.... Otherwise, I would have to look for slips of paper."

The address-book widget was widely used and distributed in all three businesses and therefore was the first contact many employees had with the WCP and with widgets in general. It stirred interest in the WCP and introduced employees to the idea of widgets that can be created, modified, and used by end users.

Case 4: A birthday widget The birthday widget shows how users can appropriate widgets to their needs through modification and adaptation. Employee X in the quality assurance department of Company B received the address-book widget via email. He then asked the local WCP evangelist about creating such widgets himself. The local evangelist then introduced the WCP to Employee X. As Employee X kept a list of his colleagues' birthdays in an Excel sheet, he decided to adopt the address-book widget so it could be used to keep track of his colleagues' birthdays. To archive this, the employee copied the existing address-book Excel sheet and added a column with the birthday information. Employee X then made this copy available in the WCP, thus creating a service. He completed this task without problem by using the existing address-book service as a guide. Then he made a copy of the address-book widget and modified it. The employee changed the data source for the newly created service and then added a text field for filtering the list by the date or date range. He also changed the layout and added labels to the new user-interface element. The resulting widget is shown in Figure 13.8.

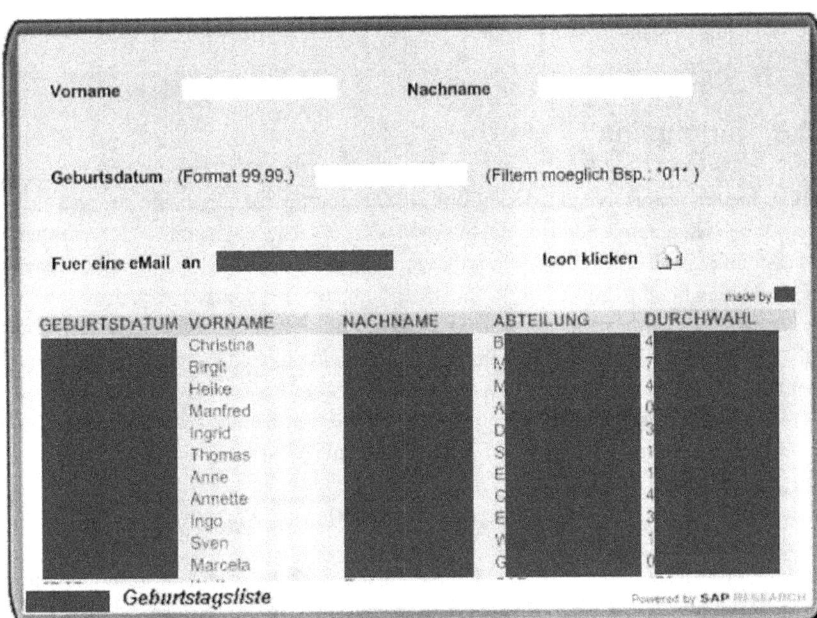

Figure 13.8 Screenshot of the birthday widget

Employee X sent his widget to about ten of his colleagues, who, in turn, sent it to more coworkers. The widget became quite popular in the company and is jokingly referred to as the "lunch optimizer," as many employees use it to check if there is a birthday celebration with some snacks or cake, in which case they hold back on lunch.

Collaboration

In the evaluation, we identified three main types of users who collaborated in different ways:

1. Very advanced users
    - mainly evangelists who had the technical knowledge to create data sources and services
    - helped other users to understand and use the application
2. Key users
    - identified fields of application where the use of widgets would make sense
    - came up with ideas for new widgets and implemented them by combining existing services
    - created new services in collaboration with advanced users
    - distributed the widgets to other end users
3. Other users
    - mainly widget consumers, who only used and shared widgets
    - did not create or modify widgets but gave suggestions for improvements to the widget creators

13.6 Conclusion

In this chapter, we presented a design case study from the domain of end-user development. The WCP environment enables business users to create enterprise widgets for their personal information needs. The design approach, that is, the Web-based environment WCP, enables business users to (1) mash up enterprise resources in a visual-design environment in a lightweight way by using a simple box-and-wires configuration technique and (2) deploy the created mash-ups in the form of widgets to their local machines. In our case, these new functionalities for creating custom widgets allowed business staff to create small, interactive applications to display relevant data in a fast and convenient way, without the need for heavyweight and complex enterprise systems and cumbersomely collecting data from multiple locations. Additionally, advanced users can now create new services to be mashed up within the WCP by creating and wrapping related resources within enterprise systems.

Our approach to the development of the WCP follows the design case study approach. We first presented the results of empirical investigations in real enterprise contexts; these investigations were conducted in order to understand the practical problems and the pressing needs of users when working with ERP systems. Next, we described the prototyping leading to the WCP. We explained its basic concepts, the architectural components, and how they work together. We also explained how business users can create individual mash-ups of enterprise resources by using the box-and-wires design, and how the tailored mash-ups can be deployed and exchanged as widgets on the local computers of the users. Finally, we described how end users appropriated the WCP in three German SMEs. Supported by a local expert, the office workers were able to build mash-ups that assembled tables in such a manner that the search for data from the ERP system was made considerably easier. So, the WCP enabled business users to tailor custom widgets that would support their individual work tasks.

Beyond this, we have learned from our observation of the widgets' use in three different organizational contexts that the appropriation of WCP is a collective endeavor (cf. Nardi 1983; Wulf 1999; Kahler 2001; Pipek and Kahler 2006). Based on our observations, it makes sense to distinguish between three different types of users: widget consumers, widget creators, and service creators.

Widget consumers use widgets but do not create them. These users are typically less familiar with IT in general or show less of a willingness, at least at the moment, to engage in tailoring. They receive widgets from more experienced colleagues and use them to access data in an easy and comfortable way without needing to learn or understand complex information systems (Nardi 1993; Wulf 1999; Kahler 2001; Wulf et al 2008). The value of widgets for this type of users is that they allow users to efficiently access relevant information without needing to ask colleagues.

Widget creators are users who create widgets for themselves or others to support individual working tasks. They are motivated by multiple reasons, including the need to simplify data access for their working tasks or to provide others with specially tailored widgets. This improves data supply to others engaged in the same business processes. Providing better tools in support of their work practice is especially relevant for employees that are responsible for certain processes, so they are motivated to act as widget creators to optimize these processes and improve process performance.

Service creators are advanced users who can create new resources that can be wrapped and added to the service repository, from where they can be used for widget creation. By extending the service repository with new services, service creators enable widget creators to address more use cases and create more and more precisely tailored widgets. Without service creators, widget creators would be limited to a certain set of predefined services, so the number of creatable solutions would be limited. Concerning the WCP environment, service creators are end users who have the skills of creating, modifying, or at least locating suitable queries inside the SAP ERP system to match the existing information needs of widget creators.

Overall, our research has contributed to the field of end-user development by providing the WCP environment, which enables business users to create simple software artifacts like widgets and to address practical problems in real enterprise work contexts. The study has also shown how the design case study approach can be used to design and develop a usable and useful end-user development environment. The approach allowed us to (1) analyze and document the work practices in the three companies, (2) develop a software system that supports these practices, and (3) observe use, appropriation, and tailoring of this application in the different companies through various users. Our data suggests that by enabling SMEs to create enterprise resources through using existing knowledge and then wrapping these resources as building blocks, the whole development chain of software artifacts can be put in the hands of SMEs. This shift would reduce the need for external IT professionals and, at the same time, increase flexibility in adapting the currently used software infrastructure to emerging individual needs.

Acknowledgments

The research presented here was funded by the German Federal Ministry of Education and Research (BMBF) as part of the project EUDISMES (Number 01ISE03C).

References

Albinola, M., Baresi, L., Carcano, M., and Guinea, S. 2009. *Mashlight: A Lightweight Mashup Framework for Everyone*. Available at http://www.ra.ethz.ch/CDstore/www2009/integror.net/mem2009/papers/paper9.pdf (accessed October 17, 2017).

Ardito, C., Costabile, M., Desolda, G., Lanzilotti, R., Matera, M., Piccinno, A., and Picozzi, M. 2014. "User-driven visual composition of service-based interactive spaces." *Journal of Visual Languages and Computing* 25 (4): 278–96.

Aumüller, D., and Thor, A. 2008. "Mashup-Werkzeuge zur Ad-hoc Datenintegration im Web." *Datenbank-Spektrum* 8 (26): 4–10.

Boden, A., Dörner, C., Draxler, S., Pipek, S., Stevens, G., and Wulf, V. 2014. "Tangible and screen-based interfaces for end-user workflow modeling." *IEEE Software* 31 (4): 65–71.

Brehm, L., Heinzl, A., and Markus, M. L. 2001. "Tailoring ERP systems: A spectrum of choices and their implications." In *HICSS'01*. Piscataway: IEEE Press, 9.

Caceres, M. 2008. "Widgets 1.0 Requirements." W3C working draft. W3C.

Desolda, G., Ardito, C., and Matera, M. 2016. "EFESTO: A Platform for the end-user development of interactive workspaces for data exploration." In F. Daniel and C. Pautasso, eds., *Rapid Mashup Development Tools*. Cham: Springer, 63–81.

Dörner, C., Draxler, S., Pipek, V., and Wulf, V. 2009. "End-users at the bazaar: Designing the next generation of ERP systems." *IEEE Software* 26 (5): 45–51.

Dörner, C., Yetim, F., Pipek, V., and Wulf, V. 2011. "Supporting business users in tailoring business processes." *Interacting with Computers* 23 (3): 226–38.

Ennals, R. J., and Garofalakis, M. N. 2007. "MashMaker: Mashups for the masses." In *SIGMOD'07*. New York: ACM, 1116–18.

Erl, T. 2005. *Service-Oriented Architecture: Concepts, Technology, and Design*. Upper Saddle River, NJ: Prentice Hall.

Fischer, G., Giaccardi, E., Ye, Y., Sutcliffe, A. G., and Mehandjiev, N. 2004. "Meta-design: A manifesto for end-user development." *Communications of the ACM* 47 (9): 33–7.

Gartner. 2007. *Gartner Identifies the Top 10 Strategic Technologies for 2008*. Available at http://www.gartner.com/newsroom/id/530109 (accessed October 17, 2017).

Gurram, R., Mo, B., and Gueldemeister, R. 2008. "A web based mashup platform for enterprise 2.0." In *WISE'08*. Berlin/Heidelberg: Springer, 144–51.

Henderson, A., and Kyng, M. 1991. "There's no place like home: Continuing design in use." In J. Greenbaum and M. Kyng, eds., *Design At Work: Cooperative Design of Computer Artefacts*. Hillsdale, NJ: Lawrence Erlbaum Associates, pp. 219–40.

Hess, J., Reuter, C., Pipek, V., and Wulf, V. 2012. "Supporting end-user articulations in evolving business processes: A case study to explore intuitive notations and interaction designs." *International Journal on Cooperative Information Systems* 21 (4): 263–96.

Hoyer, V., and Fischer, M. 2008. "Market overview of enterprise mashup tools." In *ICSOC'08*. Berlin/Heidelberg: Springer, 708–21.

Hoyer, V., and Stanoevska-Slabeva, K. 2008. "The changing role of IT departments in enterprise mashup environments." In *ICSOC'08*. Berlin/Heidelberg: Springer, 148–54.

Kahler, H. 2001. *Supporting Collaborative Tailoring*. Ph.D. thesis. Roskilde: Roskilde University.

Koschmider, A., Torres, V., and Pelechano, V. 2009. *Elucidating the Mashup Hype: Definition, Challenges, Methodical Guide and Tools for Mashups*. Available at http://mashup.pubs.dbs.uni-leipzig.de/files/paper14[1].pdf (accessed October 17, 2017).

Kvale, S. 1996. *Interviews: An Introduction to Qualitative Research Interviewing*. Thousand Oaks, CA: Sage.

Lal, R. 2008. *Creating Vista Gadgets*. Indianapolis: Sams.

Le-Phuoc, D., Polleres, A., Hauswirth, M., Tummarello, G., and Morbidoni, C. 2009. "Rapid prototyping of semantic mash-ups through semantic web pipes." In *WWW'09*. New York: ACM, 581–90.

Lieberman, H., Paternò, F., and Wulf, V. (eds.). 2006. *End User Development*. Dordrecht: Springer.

Mackay, W. E. 1990. *Users and Customizable Software: A Co-Adaptive Phenomenon*. PhD thesis. Cambridge, MA: MIT.

MacLean, A., Carter, K., Lövstrand, L., and Moran, T. 1990. "User-tailorable systems: Pressing the issues with buttons." In *CHI'90*. New York: ACM, 175–82.

Markus, M. L., and Tanis, C. 2000. "The enterprise system experience: From adoption to success." In Zmud, R. W., ed., *Framing the Domains of IT Research: Glimpsing the Future through the Past*. Cincinnati: Pinnaflex, 173–207.

Muller, M. J. 2003. "Participatory design: The third space in HCI." In A. Sears and J. A. Jacko, eds., *The Human-Computer Interaction Handbook: Fundamentals, Evolving Technologies and Emerging Applications*. Hilldale, NJ: Lawrence Erlbaum Associates, 1051–68.

Nardi, B. 1993. *A Small Matter of Programming: Perspectives of End User Computing*. Cambridge, MA: MIT Press.

Pane, J. F., Ratanamahatana, C. A., and Myers, B. A. 2001. "Studying the language and structure in non-programmers' solutions to programming problems." *International Journal of Human-Computer Studies* 54 (2), 237–64.

Pipek, V. 2005. *From Tailoring to Appropriation Support: Negotiating Groupware Usage*. PhD thesis. Oulu: University of Oulu.

Pipek, V., and Kahler, H. 2006. "Supporting collaborative tailoring." In H. Lieberman, F. Paterno, and V. Wulf, eds., *End User Development*. Dordrecht: Springer, 315–346.

Pipek, V., and Wulf, V. 2009. "Infrastructuring: Towards an integrated perspective on the design and use of information technology." *Journal of the Association for Information Systems* 10 (5): 306–32.

Roth, A., and Scheidl, S. 2006. "End-user development for enterprise resource planning systems." In *Informatik 2006*. Bonn: Gesellschaft für Informatik, 596–9.

Soriano, J., Lizcano, D., Cañas, M., Reyes, M., and Hierro, J. 2007. "Foster innovation in a mashup-oriented Enterprise 2.0 collaboration environment." *System and Information Sciences Notes* 1 (1): 62–8.

Spahn, M. 2010. *Flexibilisierung und Individualisierung des betrieblichen Informationsmanagements durch End-User Development.* PhD thesis. Siegen: University of Siegen.

Spahn, M., Dörner, C., and Wulf, V. 2008a. "End user development: Approaches towards a flexible software design." In *ECIS'08.* Atlanta: AIS, 303–14.

Spahn, M., Dörner, C., and Wulf, V. 2008b. "End user development of information artefacts: A design challenge for enterprise systems." In *ECIS'08.* Atlanta: AIS, 482–93.

Spahn, M., Kleb, J., Grimm, S., and Scheidl, S. 2008. "Supporting business intelligence by providing ontology-based end-user information self-service." In *OBI'08.* New York: ACM, 10.

Spahn, M., and Wulf, V. 2009. "End-user development of enterprise widgets." In *IS-EUD'09.* Berlin/Heidelberg: Springer, 106–25.

Stevens, G., Pipek, V., and Wulf, V. 2010. "Appropriation infrastructure: Mediating appropriation and production work." *Journal of Organizational and End User Computing* 22 (2): 58–81.

Tuchinda, R., Szekely, P., and Knoblock, C. A. 2008. "Building mashups by example." In *IUI'08.* New York: ACM, 139–48.

Wong, J. 2007. "Marmite: Towards end-user programming for the web." In *VL/HCC'07.* Piscataway: IEEE Press, 270–1.

Wulf, V. 1999. "'Let's see your Search-Tool!': Collaborative use of tailored artifacts in groupware." In *GROUP'99.* New York: ACM, 50–60.

Wulf, V., and Golombek, B. 2001. "Direct activation: A concept to encourage tailoring activities". *Behaviour and Information Technology* 20 (4): 249–63.

Wulf, V., and Jarke, M. 2004. "The economics of end user development." *Communications of the ACM* 47 (9): 41–2.

Wulf, V., Pipek, V., and Won, M. 2005. "Component-based tailorability: Towards highly flexible software applications." *International Journal of Human-Computer Studies* 66 (1): 1–22.

Wulf, V., and Rohde, M. 1995. "Towards an integrated organization and technology development." In *DIS'95*, New York: ACM, 55–64.

Wulf, V., Rohde, M., Pipek, V., and Stevens, G. 2011. "Engaging with practices: Design case studies as a research framework in CSCW." In *ACM'11.* New York: ACM, 505–12.

Yetim, F., Dörner, C., and Pipek, V. 2010. "Unterstützung von Softwareanpassungen in Kleinen und Mittelständischen Unternehmen: Wege zu einer Anpassungskultur." *i-Com Zeitschrift für interaktive und Kooperative Medien* 9 (2): 31–7.

Yetim, F., Draxler, S., Stevens, G., and Wulf, V. 2012. "Fostering continuous user participation by embedding a communication support tool in user interfaces." *AIS Transactions on Human-Computer Interaction* 4 (2): 152–67.

Yu, J., Benatallah, B., Casati, F., and Daniel, F. 2008. "Understanding mashup development." *IEEE Internet Computing* 12 (5): 44–52.

14 A Fitting Solution

KAORI KASHIMURA,
TAKAFUMI KAWASAKI JR.,
NOZOMI IKEYA, AND DAVE RANDALL

14.1 Introduction

In this chapter, we describe an ethnography of a complex scenario involving the construction of a power plant and, in so doing, try to show the importance of a practice-based approach to the problem of technical and organizational change. The term "practice based," in keeping with much of what has been said in this book, refers to the "real-world" character of working and social life, and to the features of it that can be held to be consequential for development and change. These may cover, as is suggested elsewhere in this book, attention to a number of things, including an orientation to ongoing practices in complex domains, and a reflexive attitude to the relationship between description and design. The ethnography described here covers three sites and describes and analyses their interlocking dependencies. We analyze the difficulties encountered at each location and the way in which the delays that result cascade through the different sites. The sites are as follows:

1. The construction site itself; here, the building of a power plant facility involves the scheduling of work months in advance of the work activities themselves, and the need to order parts and equipment in accordance with work schedules
2. The subcontractor site, where pipes and other equipment are manufactured in accordance with the work orders received
3. The storage site, where part and materials are delivered by the subcontractor and stored until they can be delivered to the construction site

Socio-Informatics, Volker Wulf, Volkmar Pipek, Dave Randall, Markus Rohde, Kjeld Schmidt, Gunnar Stevens (Eds). © Oxford University Press 2018. Published 2018 by Oxford University Press.

14.2 Method

The fieldwork team was responsible for the conduct of fieldwork designed to elicit why delays appeared to be endemic in the construction process. The team, consisting of around ten people, contains individuals with a background, variously, in psychology, sociology, user experience, HCI, interaction design, and so on. The individual responsible for most of the data we describe in this paper is an experienced fieldworker. The team is responsible not only for the conduct of fieldwork and its analysis but also for the representation of results to design teams and participation in design workshops. The fieldwork took place over several months and involved visits to all three of the sites described. Data collection took the form of observation, unstructured interviews, and the collection of video and photographic data. An obvious feature of the work we describe is that it took place under commercial auspices. As such, the relative luxury of "innocence," as described by Hughes et al. (1992), was not available to us. It should also be said that, regardless of the various positions that ethnographers and others in computer-supported cooperative work (CSCW) have taken concerning the relationship between fieldwork and design, the fieldwork in this instance is pragmatically driven. That is, even though a manufacturing control system for plant construction was used in this setting, delays were commonly occurring. So, we were tasked to identify the causes of these delays in construction and identify ways in which these delays could be resolved. Having said that, no view as to the likely reasons for delay were expressed in advance of the enquiry, and we had considerable freedom to visit sites as and when it was felt necessary. No theoretical or analytic lens of the kind we normally associate with CSCW or human–computer interaction (HCI), such as, for instance, distributed cognition, activity theory, grounded theory, ethnomethodology, and so on, was used. Although the fieldworker was familiar with the "contextual enquiry" framework (Beyer and Holzblatt 1998), the framework was used primarily as a means to organize data into representational forms. The issue of how best to represent data to designers formed a constant backdrop to this and other work done by fieldworkers. That is, workflow records, diagrams of physical layout, and so on, were produced as recommended by contextual design. In large part, this was because the analytic work that was done needed to be structured in such a way that it could be used to communicate with design teams, and early on in the research, decisions had not been made as to how this would best be done. The sheer complexity of the relationships between the different sites, the existence of time pressures, and the existence of a professional in-house design division tasked to provide technical and organizational solutions also precluded anything that we might ordinarily think of as participatory design. Instead, the representational process took the form of regular meetings with designers; in these meetings, rough "storyboarding" techniques were used to describe the workflow across all three sites, and the "breakdowns" that sometimes occurred in and between those sites. In addition, vignettes were provided to exemplify both the type of problem witnessed and the reasons for it. A complication here is that design work in this context takes place at a relatively generic level. It makes no sense to invest resources in a project that results in a system that can only be used in this location. Rather, we were interested in finding a solution that could be applied to other, similar settings.

14.3 Background: Plant Construction and Maintenance

Plant construction and maintenance are often treated as similar themes in what we will call the standard literature. For the most part, this literature is either framed around engineering issues and the quality, design, and technical matters that surround them or is specifically related to such matters as safety, accident, failure, and cost (see, e.g., Niskanen 1994; Assaf et al. 1995; Hudson et al. 1997; Stevens and Wulf 2002; Antaki 2003; Chan and Chan 2004; Haslam et al. 2005). Perhaps the most telling intervention over the past 20 years has been the notion of "lean construction." Here, the perception that substantial resources are put into the planning process, detailing what *should* happen (see Ballard and Howell 1997; Howell and Ballard 1998) is not always matched by *control processes* to ensure that it does. The main critique of standard construction methods is that "coordination between organizations or crews is primarily controlled from a central plan that establishes sequence and determines when an activity will start" (Howell and Ballard 1998, p. 3). As the authors put it, "everything works fine until someone drops the ball, then a chain reaction takes place" (Ballard and Howell 1997, p. 107). They estimate that what does happen diverges from what should happen approximately one-third of the time in construction projects and that some 80% of that is accounted for by lack of materials, drawings, and so on. Lean construction aims to solve these problems by implementing procedures for instant delivery, so that there is "nothing in stores" (Howell and Ballard 1998). More specifically, they go on to suggest that

> the rule to synchronise and align applies more easily and directly to construction. Consider two broad types of application. The first is the flow of materials from suppliers and fabricators to the site. Synchronising the sequence and rate of delivery with the sequence and rate of installation is obviously valuable. Failing to do so causes both installation inefficiency and large inventories of materials on site... [the second broad type] "transparency" means that the state of the system is made visible to people making decisions throughout the production system so that they will take decisions locally in support of systems objectives. (Howell and Ballard 1998, p. 6)

There is an obvious similarity with "just-in-time" procedure in manufacturing, although the suggestion here is that the dynamic nature of construction projects makes implementation somewhat different (see Ballard and Howell 2000.) What we have here is a fairly generic description of the kinds of problem that typically arise on construction sites, aligned with proposals for a more efficient "flow of work" through lean construction. As we will argue, however, in a context where possible technical solutions to these problems have become appreciably more sophisticated in the intervening period, a more detailed understanding of how the flow of materials is interrupted, along with a better view of what causes lack of transparency, is needed.

There is, of course, a more qualitatively oriented literature, some of which will be more familiar to a CSCW and HCI audience. Phelps and Horman (2010) provide a useful summary of such studies and their methodologies. Rooke et al. (2004) have looked at tendering claims in the building industry through an ethnographic lens. Pink et al. (2010) focus on communication practices between workers and management on construction sites, while Demian and Fruchter (2006) focus on the knowledge networks that inform knowledge reuse in architecture, engineering, and construction. Christensen (2012) has conducted one of the few studies of a construction site in the CSCW arena, focusing on the network of actors and the "taskscapes" involved in the relationship between design and construction, and the sequential traces that lead from one element to the next. The importance of this work lies in its commitment to the close analysis of the relationship between plans, practices, and artifacts in the building industry, developing the work of Schmidt and Wagner (2004). Schmidt and Wagner, in their study of an architectural practice, argue that CSCW has had a tendency to spend too little time investigating real-world cooperative and coordinative work settings. As they put it,

> cooperative work is characterized by an infinite variety of non-discursive interactions. That is, for example, in doing his or her individual work one actor changes the state of an object (a machine part, a drawing, a piece of software code), not for the purpose of conveying a message, but for the purpose of simply doing the job; noticing the result of this, another actor, perhaps at another location, perhaps at a later stage, makes other changes to the state of the object or other objects, and so on. All kinds of variation of this pattern are at play. Parts, materials, documents, etc. may pass from actor to actor, in the sequential pattern of a "work flow"; or the responsibility of undertaking certain tasks may pass on from actor to actor, in a sequential "task flow"... In fact, cooperative work may involve any mixture of concurrent, sequential, and reciprocal action and interaction. (Schmidt and Wagner 2004, p. 350)

They assert, in our view, with some justification, that too little research has focused on the way in which real-world activities in complex work environments entail the ordering of both practices and artifacts. Charles Perrow, in a somewhat different (and more theoretical) fashion, has reached similar conclusions in his work on catastrophic failure. Perrow (1999) argues that two factors—"interactive complexity" and "tight coupling"—mean that, in some contexts, accidents are more or less inevitable. "Tight coupling" refers to the strong causal link between one action or event and the next, while "interactive complexity" refers, fairly obviously, to the many and varied ways in which people and systems can interact in complex organizations. Perrow is particularly interesting insofar as, when he points to failure, he identifies several individual factors that are relevant, including human error, mechanical failure, the environment, the design of the system, and the procedures used, but argues forcefully that catastrophic failure is never produced by any one of these factors but by the interaction of them all. While the work we rehearse is not concerned with catastrophic failure, the insistence that coupling and complexity are vital to our understanding of work in organizational environments is something we are sympathetic to. Julian Orr's (1996) study of photocopier repair also directs our attention to relevant matters, including the fact that *work is heterogeneous*, meaning that problems are much more varied and unpredictable than we might assume. This turns out to be especially true in the case we report.

14.4 The Setting(s)

The context we describe is the construction of a power plant in Japan. As such, it is a specific case of construction work. Construction work, as we can see from the literature outlined in Section 14.3, is highly complex insofar as it is characterized by a number of distinctive features. Most importantly, construction work is often done by discrete teams, which are usually subcontracted. Traditionally, the work is executed in accordance with an overall plan that is constituted as an architectural "design," and work schedules—at least in theory—are organized around that design. The flow of the work takes place across a number of sites, so, for instance, the parts and materials necessary for construction work to take place are normally manufactured/extracted elsewhere. It is a domain where work activities are circumscribed by health and safety issues, since the site contains heavy, often moving, equipment, can be poorly lit, and can entail maneuvering in constrained spaces. It is also highly dynamic since, by definition, conditions on the site will vary daily for a number of reasons, including factors such as the weather. It is, lastly, a domain where the organization of space is critically important, since it makes no sense to have materials and parts stored too far from the construction site—ideally, they should be readily available.

14.5 The Construction Site

The construction site, as already mentioned, is where a new power plant in Japan was being built. The order in which work is to be done, unsurprisingly, is based on architectural design (see Schmidt and Wagner 2004; Christensen 2012), which, in this case, is a construction plan. That is, an order for the work is instantiated in the database. Certain parts of the plant ought to, in principle, be built at certain points in the process and thus the requisite materials need to be produced and delivered on time. Having said that, overall redesign of the proposed build takes place approximately once every 2 months, reflecting a very tight construction schedule and the fact that endless contingencies arise (a common feature of construction work, as weather and other factors intervene in what can be done, and in what order). This entails, for instance, the reordering of processes. As the build progresses, work orders sheets (WOSs) and delivery slips (which contain lists of materials) are produced by admin staff. Each WOS and delivery slip can take up to some 30 minutes to prepare, often because the necessary information is not in the system (the database, which contains all relevant documentation), or the data is found to contain errors. The admin staff need to check that the system data and the drawings they are working from contain the same information. If the information from the system data does not match that from the drawings, it is sometimes necessary for staff members to phone the design department to establish what the correct version should be. It is not uncommon, for instance, to find that information about bore diameters or construction materials are missing from drawings. WOSs are produced on site, on request from the subcontractor manager, who inspects the work, records work progress on a laptop when a task is completed, and decides what work needs to be done and in what order. WOSs are normally produced 3 days before they are required. They are produced so as to allow the just-in-time delivery of construction materials from other sites. The 3-day turnaround gives enough time for equipment, such as trucks or cranes for moving pipes around, to be booked and for fit-up teams, who will assemble the materials, to be assigned to the upcoming task. "Groove-aligning" work, which basically makes spaces manageable, is done by a small team from a second-tier subcontractor. The WOSs detail the materials and dimensions of the construction materials that will be used; this information is needed in order for the work is to proceed as anticipated (a large part of which involves pipes through which water and steam will pass). At the same time that the WOS is produced, a delivery slip is generated; this slip details the date on which the construction material is needed, and the person who ordered it. Both the WOS and the delivery slip are then sent to a delivery operator, who organizes the construction materials for delivery. Of course, what is described here is an ideal state; in practice, the need to deal with various contingencies that arise as the work proceeds means that parts and materials are sometimes needed immediately. One example of such a contingency is the occurrence of unexpected weather conditions, which happens at almost all construction sites. Other common interruptions to planned work include pipe failure, changes to inspection dates, a lack of necessary tools, and inadequate preparation of the work environment (with respect to scaffolding, lighting, etc.). Rather than have workers sit idly, alternative work is found for the fit-up teams. Negotiation takes place between team leaders and managers as to how schedules might reasonably be altered, and managers then organize for delivery slips to be produced (either by themselves or by the admin staff). Of course, the various parties responsible for scaffolding, lighting, and so on, need to be informed of such schedule changes. Such rescheduling also means, of course, that the timescale for the delivery of parts and materials will need to be shorter than the 3 days normally mandated.

In addition, different subcontractors work at the construction site at various times (a commonplace feature of construction sites), so it is necessary to coordinate them as well. This means that, although subcontract workers can be assumed to be knowledgeable about the technical work they are doing, they may be less knowledgeable about conditions on the site itself and about required procedures, since, in some circumstances, they may not be there for very long. Interviews with fit-up team leaders and workers made it clear to us that they felt burdened by what they perceived to be cumbersome and time-consuming documentation processes, which, they felt, intruded on their primary task.

14.6 The Pipe-Manufacturing Subcontractor

The pipe-manufacturing subcontractor manufactures pipes according to a master operation schedule, which is, in turn, drawn from the construction plan. The master operation schedule states what pipes are to be worked on and what the expected completion dates are. At the subcontractor, there are four teams at work. The first of these teams, the production engineering group, develops the master operation schedule. The second, the arrangement team, develops specifications for work to be done, including cutting instructions for each pipe, from that schedule. The third, the cutting group, cuts pipes to the dimensions required in accordance with the master schedule and the work specifications. The fourth, the bending group, receives cut pipes from the cutting group and bends the pipes to the shapes required. The manufacturing process can take up to 6 months. Strict quality control procedures are in operation, given the intended destination of the pipes.

Problems can arise, first, as a result of redesign at the construction site. This means that work instructions have to be changed, so the work has to be rescheduled. As one member of the arrangement group put it, "There was a design change due to the plant construction's issues, and we were asked to revise the work instructions, so we ask the cutting group to please go ahead with the work for the next pipe." However, changes to the schedule mean that it is not always easy to find the pipe to be worked on. This happens because pipes, which in theory are arranged by bore size, become mixed up as unscheduled work is carried out. As a member of the cutting team said, "It sometimes takes a few hours to find a pipe. Sometimes, where possible, we give up and find another pipe on the work schedule instead, and work on that."

The site at which this work takes place is over 100 km distant from the construction site; hence, heavy trucks are used for transport. Fit-up workers at the construction site are responsible for cutting and connecting the pipes in accordance with the design. The distance involved means there is a considerable cost overhead for the subcontractor, one which is partially reduced by ensuring as far as possible that every truck leaves the manufacturing site full. Once the pipes are manufactured, deliveries take place in accordance with the WOSs and delivery slips (i.e., the pipes are delivered 3 days after they are initially ordered). Drivers carry with them both the delivery schedule (which states what is theoretically supposed to be delivered) and a load list (which lists the items that are actually on the truck).

14.7 The Storage Site

Pipes, upon manufacture, are delivered to the storage site, where, in theory, they are delivered for construction on demand. One feature of this site is that space is constrained. Parts and materials need to be kept in reasonable proximity to each other and to the construction site so as to minimize the time taken for transportation. The dimensions of the site are approximately 300 meters by 250 meters and the site has room for both indoor and outdoor storage. At any one time, there are several thousand pipes on site, and they can remain there for periods of time ranging from a week to more than a month. Having said that, materials are being brought to the site from the subcontractor in large number every day; to complicate matters, these materials are, in the main, of nonstandard shapes and sizes. Materials, notably the pipes, are delivered to the storage site in advance of their supposed use, in accordance with design schedules. Given their size, pipes are delivered by trucks, which are unloaded by receiving operators, who often use heavy equipment. A team consisting of receiving operators, store operators, and delivery operators is responsible for organizing storage. It is often the case that there is a line of trucks waiting to be unloaded. Speedy unloading reduces turnaround time and thus reduces delivery costs (as drivers are paid by the hour), so operators are under some pressure to unload quickly. Receiving operators need to (1) check delivery schedules and load lists to ensure they correspond, (2) determine where they can store the pipes being delivered, and (3) identify what kind of equipment will be needed for unloading and transportation around the facility, all the while dealing with a constant stream of truck deliveries to the site. Having checked that what has been delivered corresponds to what is on the shipment manifest, the delivery operator uploads this information into an inventory database and then determines where on the site pipes and other equipment will actually be placed. Pipes are stored with RFID tags, and their locations are recorded there and then on a laptop. In theory, then, there is a record of the nature of the pipes and the places where they are stored. As we have indicated, that turns out not always to be the case.

Requests for pipes are submitted by construction site workers 3 days before they are needed. These requests are recorded on delivery slips, which are sent to delivery operators. A typical delivery slip would have requests for between five and thirty pipes or other pieces of equipment. Each request details the pipe bore size, its length, and its spool number (although not its shape). Pieces of white tape with delivery dates and the name of the individual who requested the delivery are attached to the pipes upon request for delivery to the construction site. It is the responsibility of delivery operators to instruct fit-up workers at the construction site that pipes are ready and to find the pipes that are to be delivered. To give some idea of the scale of this storage operation, the storage manager told us that, for a single project, approximately 150 km of pipes would be stored and used. Once delivery has been organized, delivery slips are then passed to a data-entry operator, who inputs information into the system and files the physical slips in binders.

Problems occur because both storing and finding pipes and other materials turns out not to be straightforward. First, cost pressures for the subcontractor mean that pipes are often delivered that are not on the load list (effectively, they are delivered early). Space has to be found for these unanticipated items. Second, the sheer range of dimensions and shapes means that pipes cannot always be easily stored in their allocated spaces, as the following vignette demonstrates:

> F: "They won't fit in this space. They are more bent than I thought."
>
> Y: "We could put them here... but we will need to move those [pipes]... we will need the crane."
>
> (*The crane is brought over [other work halts while it is being used], and the two pipes are relocated. F and Y continue to supervise unloading. The relocation of the two pipes [which had previously stored in a recorded location for weeks] goes unrecorded.*)

Third, there is a difference between the 6-month manufacturing cycle, which leads to the delivery of the pipes to the storage site, and the 2-month redesign schedule. This means that sometimes pipes are delivered that are not immediately needed because the design has altered in the interim. However, there is limited physical space available to store the pipes. The fact that pipes and other materials thus have to be frequently moved around hinders the search for materials when delivery slips are received from the construction site. Fourth, workers from the construction site sometimes come to search for and collect pipes themselves in order to meet the tight deadlines they are working to (and, as mentioned in Section 14.5, when unexpected contingencies mean that they need materials at very short notice). The following vignette shows what can happen in these situations:

> *(A and B, who work for a subcontractor at the construction site, arrive at the storage site. They have a delivery slip, but the delivery date on the slip is more than the standard 3 days ahead, so no material has been assembled for delivery (i.e., A and B will have to find the materials themselves.)*
>
> A: "Our team leader has asked if we can find the materials now as we want to be ahead of time."
>
> *(The delivery operator gives them permission to look for the materials.)*
>
> B: "The delivery slip has more material on it than we requested. It's the first time I've been in this storage yard. We only came to the construction site two weeks ago. I don't know where we are going to put all these things when we take them there."
>
> *A and B split up to search for the different materials. When they find what they are looking for, they place green tape around the material to indicate where it should be placed at the construction site. They then both go to an area of the storage site where the delivery slip indicates a particular part should be. Unable to find the part, they also search the adjacent area. The delivery slip indicates that the part they are looking for begins with the designation "SA x x x"; after 20 minutes of searching, they discover that there are in fact a number of similar [but not identical] pieces of material that begin with that designation. Thus, they begin to suspect that the part number on the delivery slip may be incorrect. When a store manager passes by, they stop him to ask whether he can shed light on their difficulties.)*
>
> A: "There are parts in this yard with similar numbers to the one we are looking for. Is the designation maybe incorrect?"
>
> *(The store manager looks at delivery slip.)*
>
> Store manager: "No, it's right…"
>
> *(He helps in the search, but they are still unable to find the material. The store manager then returns to his office to print out a drawing of the part [the delivery slip contains information about the dimensions of the pipe but not the shape]. In the interim, B loads other parts and materials into his car and takes them off to the construction site. A waits 20 minutes for the drawing, which is eventually given to him by an operative. Fifteen minutes after that, he finds the part they are looking for.)*

While searching for the things they need, workers are likely to move pipes and other materials around, further compounding the problem. In addition, the contingencies that necessitate changes to work orders can mean that materials organized by delivery operators in accordance with delivery slips sometimes go uncollected. Delivery operators confirm that situations of this kind occur "almost every day" and that it is often the case that they will spend 3 hours looking for a single pipe. It is, we are told, very common for operators to search for images of the requested pipes (mostly, drawings) in order to facilitate their searches.

14.8 Conclusion

We make no comment as to whether "lean construction" as a philosophy is either new or effective (although see Green 1999 for a critique). We content ourselves with the observation that some part of what Ballard and Howell (2000) suggest are typical problems in the construction industry appear to be commonplace in our setting as well. That is, the existence of a "plan" to which all parties are supposed to adhere is compromised by necessary redesign and rescheduling, causing problems to cascade along the supply chain. Such conclusions are very much in keeping with the arguments presented in Chapters 2 and 6 concerning the way in which "practices" might be characterized as having some common elements, both in terms of routines followed and in terms of normative expectations. This takes place in a context that, while probably not unique to construction, nevertheless has a critical importance, to whit, that work is being done to very tight schedules. Slippage is very costly. Nevertheless, at various points, we see slippages in smooth operation happening and, in large part, this is a product of failures in the way information is recorded, stored, and transmitted, despite the fact that a standard database is being used. The primary reason for this is that tight schedules are not matched with up-to-date and accurate information, nor do they reflect the practical need to order work in keeping with the (sometimes unexpected) flow of materials from elsewhere. At the manufacturing site, workers spend more time dealing with "bureaucratic" elements of the work than they wish to and have some difficulty matching procedural requirements to their ongoing need to "do work while they can." There are holdups at the pipe-manufacturing site as a result of inadequate communication and distinctive priorities between different groups. Upon delivery to the storage site, large amounts of parts and material are often stored for lengthy periods of time and regularly "go missing" for periods of time. Contingencies that arise at the construction site mean that deliveries of parts and materials are frequently rescheduled. The point here is that what we see is a complex chain of activities in which problems that occur at different points have the overall effect of causing delay and inefficiency.

As we have indicated, the aspects of the research we described were from real-world experience and were commercially driven. The relationship between the fieldwork and the design was circumscribed by a number of features. One, perhaps the most salient, is that (and we should not be surprised by this) proposed design solutions are intended to be integrated in order to (1) address a variety of problems seen across the work sites, and (2) be useful in other environments, not just the site of this power plant. That is, the main design objective was to produce an improved version of a general integrated plant construction system, which is intended to support various aspects of the work. The fieldwork was geared toward the production of explicit and implicit requirements for the improved system. This is no mean task, and it would be naive in the extreme to imagine that the results of these enquiries led directly to design solutions. The process of relating ethnographic results to design requirements is one where a considerable amount of time, in the first instance, is spent in organizing materials so as to make them relevant to design considerations. This entails, inter alia, the development of a standard way of representing results, in and through the "patterning" of these results (Alexander 1977; Martin et al.

2001; also see Kashimura et al. 2015), to provide, ultimately, a searchable database of results in order to enable the comparison of different settings that exist within an identifiable domain (in this case, defined by us as being to do with "construction and maintenance practices") and, hence, provide a degree of generalization, which is predicated on some low-level questions related to particular kinds of problems we were able to identify via literature searches and the examination of other cases (Alexander 1977; Martin et al. 2001; Kashimura et al. 2015). Regular meetings are, nevertheless, held at which emerging results are presented and designs do emerge in response to the insights gathered during the fieldwork. In this instance, a number of proposals have been or are being implemented for the next generation of the system. These include using tablet displays to provide a better solution for workers at the construction site, allowing them to do their work with less administrative overhead. Functionalities include zoomable layouts of the construction site, with one-touch zooms to individual buildings, floor layouts, and the specific locations of work in progress. Touching one of these locations produces a pop-up WOS. A single touch will bring up relevant drawings, allowing for more immediate comparison between the two documents and substantially reducing the amount of paper documentation that fit-up team leaders and workers have to carry around in a constrained and sometimes poorly lit environment. The tablet will also allow for dedicated video conference calls with the design office, with support for shared images and documentation. The newest versions, yet to be fully implemented, will support augmented reality applications with a "point-and-tag" functionality that will allow the matching of virtual models of layouts, buildings, parts, materials, and so on, to real images; this ought to lessen the search time for pipes and materials, in keeping with our observation that delivery operators often have to refer to printouts of drawings to help them in their searches.

Augmented reality devices are developing in sophistication and are being applied in a number of domains. They include functionalities that provide 3D location finding (see, e.g., Rekimoto and Ayatsuka 2000), to support a variety of work environments and meeting room scenarios (see, e.g., Lahlou 2009). Wagner and Schmalstieg (2003) and Wagner et al. (2005) outline procedures for augmented reality on handheld devices. Webster et al. (1996) detail an augmented reality device specifically for construction and similar environments

Overall, the case described in this chapter raises a number of questions about the relationship between ethnography and design in circumstances where the following characteristics pertain:

1. The fieldwork takes place in a real-world commercial context, where more exploratory work is not possible, so fieldworkers must perform a detailed examination of known problems in order to ascertain a more nuanced view of the reasons for those problems
2. The fieldwork takes place in complex settings where there is a constant time pressure and some kind of supply chain across different commercial stakeholders and/or interests
3. The design considerations are not restricted to one particular setting but are intended to have a more generic application; that is, there is an existing system that

does not seem to be dealing adequately with problems that arise, so redesign is felt to be necessary

In some ways, our study answers a question posed by Plowman et al. (1995), to whit, "What are workplace studies for?" Plowman et al.'s paper pointed to the absence of (or at least very limited number of) studies that could be shown to lead directly to a design prototype and suggested that the reason for this may lie in a mismatch between the kinds of accounts provided by social scientists, and the more specific problem-solution-oriented needs of designers. While the work we have been involved in, and which this study forms part of, has entailed grappling with representational issues and the problem of translating complex narratives about work into problem/solution frameworks, the reality here is, arguably, that the range of technological possibilities and the need for organizations to engage in a cost–benefit calculus introduces complicating factors that ethnographic results, on their own, can resolve. Workplace studies of this kind do not always translate directly to design prototypes because the range of possible outcomes, given the possibilities inherent in near-future technologies, is substantial. First, the situation we describe involves a number of quite discrete problems that are manifested across different sites but are consequential across all the sites. Second, there is an evident problem of scope, a problem that cannot be determined by fieldworkers alone. Solutions, in principle, could involve technologies that address each problem individually or could be systematic solutions that deal with problems arising across the whole supply chain. Moreover, the problem of scope involves deciding questions such as the degree of generalizability associated with envisaged systems. Commercial systems, after all, may stand or fall on the degree to which they can be tailored for various settings in (and possibly beyond) given domains. Moreover, developments could entail procedural rather than (or in addition to) technological changes (see Chapter 2).

Of course, there is no reason to presume that ethnography has any determinate relationship to design. After all, such a relationship must depend on any number of possible variables. Schmidt has, for instance, posed two distinct possibilities—the role of workplace studies in contributing to the design of specific artifacts, and the role of workplace studies in contributing to the conceptual foundations that underpin such designs. In a context where CSCW technologies are immature at best, specific design recommendations (the "murky prehistory" as Schmidt terms it [Schmidt 2008, p. 154]) are unlikely to be realized. Of course, arriving at a design solution is not the point. Arriving at a design solution that, in all important respects, meets the needs of those who work in complex environments, where problems commonly arise, most certainly is. It is difficult to see how solutions might ultimately be derived without understanding what those problems might be. Even so, the relationship between setting-specific features and the general characteristics of a domain remains a critical problem, and not just for CSCW and other human-centered design researchers. Design case studies of the kind advanced in this book represent, we feel, a way forward. It is in the investigation of practice, we suggest, where both the problems that are specific to a given site and the ways in which they might relate to more generic, perhaps tailorable, solutions can best be examined.

References

Alexander, C. 1977. *A Pattern Language: Towns, Buildings, Construction*. Oxford: Oxford University Press.

Antaki, G. A. 2003. *Piping and Pipeline Engineering: Design Construction, Maintenance, Integrity and Repair*. London: Taylor and Francis.

Assaf, S. A., Al-Khalil, M., and Al-Hazmi, M. 1995. "Causes of delay in large building construction projects." *Journal of Management in Engineering* 11 (2): 45–50.

Ballard, G., and Howell, G. 1997. "Implementing lean construction: Stabilizing work flow." In L. Alarcón, ed., *Lean Construction*. Rotterdam: A. A. Balkema. pp. 105–14.

Beyer, H., and Holzblatt, K. 1998. *Contextual Design: Defining Customer-Centered Systems*. London: Academic Press.

Chan, A. P. C., and Chan, A. P. L. 2004. "Key performance indicators for measuring construction success." *Benchmarking* 11 (2): 203–21.

Christensen, L. R. 2012. *Coordinative Practices in the Building Process: An Ethnographic Perspective*. London: Springer-Verlag London.

Demian, P., and Fruchter, R. 2006. "An ethnographic study of design knowledge reuse in the architecture, engineering and construction industry." *Research in Engineering Design* 16 (4): 184–95.

Green, S. D. 1999. "The missing arguments of lean construction." *Construction Management and Economics* 17 (2): 133–7.

Haslam, R. Hide, S., Gibb, A., Gyi, D., Pavitt, T., Atkinson, S., and Duff, R. 2005. "Contributing factors in construction accidents." *Applied Ergonomics* 36 (4): 401–15.

Howell, G., and Ballard, G. 1998. *Implementing Lean Construction: Understanding and Action*. Available at http://www.researchgate.net/profile/Glenn_Ballard/publication/228960283_Implementing_Lean_Construction_Understanding_and_Action/links/0fcfd509c29f29f7f7000000/Implementing-Lean-Construction-Understanding-and-Action.pdf (accessed October 17, 2017).

Hudson, W. R., Haas, R., and Udin, W. 1997. *Infrastructure Management: Design, Construction, Maintenance, Rehabilitation, and Renovation*. New York: McGraw-Hill Education.

Hughes, J. A., Randall, D., and Shapiro, D. 1992. "Faltering from ethnography to design." In *CSCW'92*. New York: ACM, 115–22.

Kashimura, K., Hara, Y., Ikeya, N., and Randall, D. 2015. "Patterns of work: A pragmatic approach." In V. Wulf, K. Schmidt, and D. Randall, eds., *Designing Socially Embedded Technologies in the Real-World*, London: Springer-Verlag London, 35–62.

Lahlou, S. (ed.). 2009. *Designing User Friendly Augmented Work Environments*. London: Springer-Verlag London.

Martin, D., Rodden, T., Rouncefield, M., Sommerville, I., and Viller, S. 2001. "Finding patterns in the fieldwork." In *ECSCW'01*. Dordrecht: Springer, 39–58.

Niskanen, T. 1994. "Assessing the safety environment in work organization of road maintenance jobs." *Accident Analysis and Prevention* 26 (1): 27–39.

Orr, J. 1996. *Talking about Machines: An Ethnography of a Modern Job*. Ithaca, NY: Cornell University Press.

Perrow, C. 1999. *Normal Accidents: Living with High-Risk Technologies*. Princeton, NJ: Princeton University Press.

Phelps, A., and Horman, M. J. 2010. "Ethnographic theory-building research in construction." *Journal of Construction Engineering and Management* 136 (1): 58–65.

Pink, S., Tutt, D., Dainty, A., and Gibb, A. 2010. "Ethnographic methodologies for construction research: Knowing, practice and interventions." *Building Research and Information* 38 (6): 647–59.

Plowman, L., Rogers, Y., and Ramage, M. 1995. "What are workplace studies for?" In *ECSCW'95*. Dordrecht: Kluwer, 309–24.

Rekimoto, J., and Ayatsuka, Y. 2000. "CyberCode: Designing augmented reality environments with visual tags." In *DARE'00*. New York: ACM, 1–10.

Rooke, J., Seymour, D., and Fellows, R. 2004. "Planning for claims: An ethnography of industry culture." *Construction, Management and Economics* 22 (6): 655–62.

Schmidt, K., and Wagner, I. 2004. "Ordering systems: Coordinative practices and artefacts in architectural desin and planning." *Computer Supported Cooperative Work* 13 (5): 349–408.

Wagner, D., Pintaric, T., Ledermann, F., and Schmalstieg, D. 2005. "Towards massively multi-user augmented reality on handheld devices." In *Pervasive'05*. Springer, 208–19.

Wagner, D., and Schmalstieg, D. 2003. *First Steps towards Handheld Augmented Reality*. Available at http://data.icg.tugraz.at/~dieter/publications/Schmalstieg_067.pdf (accessed October 17, 2017).

Webster, A., Feiner, S., MacIntyre, B., Massie, W., and Krueger, T. 1996. *Augmented Reality in Architectural Construction, Inspection, and Renovation*. Available at http://www.columbia.edu/cu/gsapp/BT/RESEARCH/PAPERS/ar-asce.html (accessed October 17, 2017).

15 Toward Transferability in Grounded Design

Comparing Two Design Case Studies in Firefighting

MATTHIAS BETZ AND VOLKER WULF

15.1 Introduction

Grounded design is a particular design-research approach applied in case studies. The approach aims to investigate social practices with the purpose of identifying and unveiling problematic aspects of that practice. The investigation is not autotelic but is targeted to inform the design of IT artifacts that are expected to mitigate the identified problems by providing features to enable practitioners to originate changed or new practices. In addition, there is an explicit aspiration to develop context-specific artifacts that enable the users of such artifacts to develop their practices further; the grounded-design approach designates such endeavors "design case studies" (Wulf et al. 2011, 2015). In research contexts, design case studies are conducted by applying established research methods such as ethnographic field studies, participatory design, and action research. However, conducting design case studies generates situated knowledge and often situated technical solutions. As a research approach, grounded design claims to contribute to scientific knowledge by creating a collection of documented cases that is accessible for a further comprehensive and overarching analysis. This contribution provides an example of such a study by comparing two design case studies in the field of civil security research. This comparative analysis generates bottom-up concepts that are conducive to scientific discourses. However, conducting design case studies is a practice itself that is embedded in cooperative and institutional contexts that need to be further reflected upon (see Chapters 1 and 16).

Socio-Informatics, Volker Wulf, Volkmar Pipek, Dave Randall, Markus Rohde, Kjeld Schmidt, Gunnar Stevens (Eds). © Oxford University Press 2018. Published 2018 by Oxford University Press.

15.1.1 Grounded Design, and Design Case Studies

Design case studies are epistemologically rooted in pragmatism (Wulf et al. 2011; Goldkuhl 2012; Kuutti and Bannon 2014) and practice theory (Mead and Morris 1972; Bourdieu, 1990; Reckwitz 2002; Garfinkel 2011). Design case studies embrace the situatedness and particularity of social practices and thus stand in contradistinction to positions of positivism or interpretivism (Braa and Vidgen 1999; Goles and Hirschheim 2000; Becker and Niehaves 2007). Wulf et al. (2015) provide a detailed and in-depth positioning of design case studies in the different scientific and epistemological traditions. Methodologically, design case studies are structured in three phases:

1. *Empirical pre-study*: The pre-study aims to provide a profound understanding of the situated practice in the addressed field. It should provide a detailed description of the existing social practices in terms of roles, organizational structures, regulatory constraints, appropriation, tools and media (including their usage), and trends, all from technological, organizational, and social perspectives. In order to provide profound and deep insights, appropriate methods have to be applied to ensure an accurate documentation of the addressed subject matter. Methods from qualitative social research, such as participatory observation and open or semistructured interviews, are typical for that first phase. The pre-study should conclude with a set of problem statements or need statements, to inform the construction of a further research design. The problem-oriented documentation of the addressed social practice underpins the "pre"-character of the study by providing insights to inform design activities "after the 'pre.'" That is, a pre-study in the context of grounded design is not simply an empirical documentation of existing practices and cultures, as an ethnography is in sociology; it is, rather, a problem-oriented description of existing relationships between practices and technological artifacts, with a broad set of technological opportunities in mind.
2. *IT artifact design*: Based on the identified problems and needs in the pre-study phase, a design process is set up. It ideally involves the practitioners who participated in the pre-study. To contribute to the design case study, this phase should document participative design decisions, bounding technological and organizational constraints, applied design methods, actual design processes, main influences of relevant stakeholders and negotiations of conflicts. The documentation should demonstrate the potential influences of the artifact design on the existing social practices aimed at or anticipated by the participants in the design process. The resulting artifacts should be functional in the sense that practitioners are able to introduce them into practice for evaluation purposes.
3. *Evaluation and appropriation*: In this phase, the designed artifacts should be introduced into the addressed practice, to allow the practitioners to experience the features of the artifact, its practical impact, and the resulting changes in existing practices. Evaluative activities address the quality of the design regarding user experience and usability. Evaluation methods are applied in dedicated settings to

assess the state of a prototypical design in a certain point in time. Those methods mostly come from the human–computer interaction (HCI) discipline, which addresses, in particular, usability and has roots in cognitive psychology. The other part of this phase is the investigation of appropriation phenomena, by observing the autonomous usage of the functionally designed IT artifacts in real or at least realistic social contexts. The methods applied in this phase should capture longer periods of use and so often require tool support for monitoring and capturing usage in the absence of researchers and designers. Appropriation research is particularly interested in changes of existing practices, and deviations from the initially intended usage of the designed artifacts.

The phases should be conducted in several loops to refine and complete the pre-study, with insights acquired in the participatory design and the appropriation phases, and to further inform the design with these insights. All phases finally contribute to the documentation of a holistic design case study, by answering the question, "Why does the designed artifact work in the investigated context?" By explicitly documenting the circumstances under which the answer of this question is given, the insights of the design case study can be revealed (see Figure 15.1).

Design case studies represent knowledge derived from situated social practices, including research, development, and design. From a scientific perspective, one important question is how to make the generated situated knowledge arising from the design case studies transferable to other contexts. One way to do this is to compare different design cases studies with each other to identify similarities and differences between them (see Figure 15.2). As stated by Rohde et al., "This type of interpretative [design research]

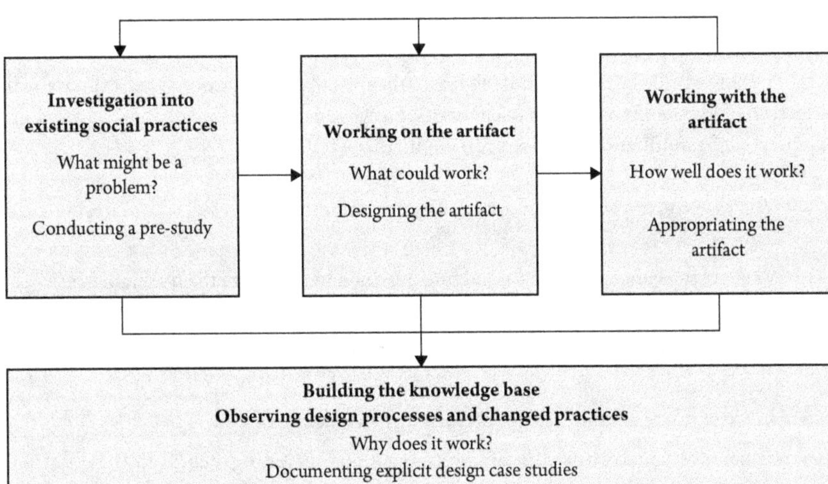

Figure 15.1 Structure and perspectives of design case studies (from Rohde et al. 2016)

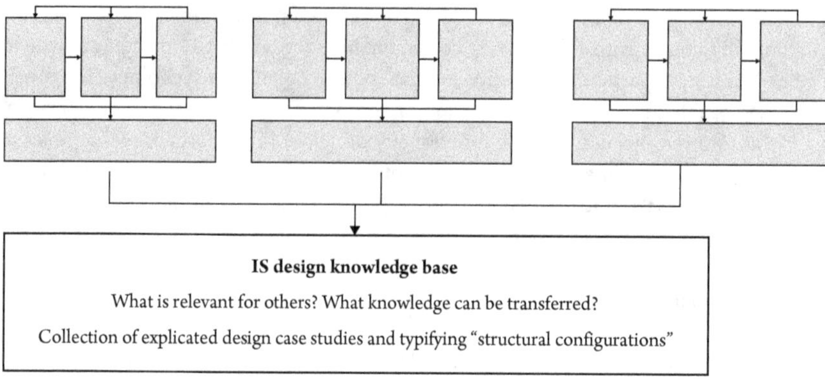

Figure 15.2 Illustration of the grounded design principals (from Rohde et al. 2016)

may offer transferable knowledge for other design cases by typifying common 'structural configurations' in the IT design space and the social practices at stake" (Rohde et al. 2016, p. 173). Comparing unique design case studies seems to be a valid approach to generate more abstract knowledge from a meta-perspective. However, by providing an epistemological foundation of this approach, Wulf et al. (2015) and Rohde et al. (2016) remain unspecific as to how such a comparison should be applied and what common features each design case study has to provide to make such a comparative meta study possible.

15.1.2 The Transferability of Design Case Studies

Rohde et al. (2016) claim that grounded design contributes to the information system (IS) knowledge base by providing in-depth design case studies as a basis for further comparative meta-studies. Grounded design is conceptually deeply rooted in a theoretical reflection of IS paradigms and practice theory. However, from the perspective of "research as a practice," a number of questions remain unanswered:

- What are the appropriate methods for documenting the results from design case studies?
- What are the general criteria for judging the documentation of the qualitative research conducted in grounded design?
- Which methods of knowledge sharing exist within the science and research community?
- How can nonacademic designers learn from academic designers?
- What are archival formats for design case studies, including records from field studies, interim results, developed categories, design drafts, discarded design variants, prototypes, code versions, and so on?
- What is an appropriate methodology for conducting comparative meta-studies?

Table 15.1 Four criteria for judging qualitative research, and the analogous positivistic criteria

Positivistic Criteria for Judging Quantitative Research	Phenomenological Criteria for Judging Qualitative Research
Internal validity	Credibility
External validity	Transferability
Reliability	Dependability
Objectivity	Confirmability

In this chapter, we compare and discuss two consecutive design case studies, the "Landmarke" and the "Koordinator" projects, and propose ways that such studies could be documented that would enable other researchers to comprehend the results of the studies and the contexts from which they originated, and to relate them to other design case studies.

Lincoln and Guba (1990) proposed four criteria for judging the results of qualitative research; these criteria are analogous to the four central positivistic criteria used to judge results from research in the natural sciences and engineering (see Table 15.1).

Credibility means that, from the perspective of the participants in the research context, the results are believable, that is, the phenomena of interest should be described from the perspective of the participant, or, vice versa, the credibility of the results can only be legitimately judged by them. Thus, participants should be actively involved in the process of reflective appropriation to enhance the credibility of the results of a design case study.

Transferability determines the degree to which the results of qualitative research are relevant for other contexts or settings. Transferability can be supported by a thorough documentation of the circumstances under which the results were generated. This includes the research context, the applied methods, and the underlying assumptions. The transferring person must be enabled to judge the transferability into another context. Thus, the documentation has to comprise all relevant information to allow for this assessment.

Qualitative research takes place in ever-changing social contexts. *Dependability* supports the traceability of changes in the research context and the impact of such changes on further research. Other than the criteria of reliability in the positivistic research paradigm, dependability embraces context changes by making them understandable to others—rather than trying to achieve replicability.

Qualitative research results that can be corroborated by others follow the criterion of *confirmability*. One strategy to enhance confirmability, according to Lincoln and Guba (1990), is to share the documentation of the analysis of the qualitative data. Confirmability can be reached by enhancing the backward traceability of qualitative results. Data audits are another possibility for ensuring the confirmability of the results of the analysis of qualitative data.

Since the volume and relevance of interpretive research has markedly increased in recent years (Goles and Hirschheim 2000; Walsham 2006), it appears reasonable to perform cross-sectional investigations across a number of design case studies, looking for context similarities or patterns and basic "structural configurations" in the design and appropriation processes of different IT design case studies (Rodon and Sese Muniategui 2008). Such similarities, patterns, or structural configurations may constitute an a posteriori typification of IS design contexts and procedures. These efforts need to be complemented by the search for an adequate organization of the knowledge base for improving its accessibility.

This chapter will reflect on the grounded-design approach by giving an example of a comparative analysis across two design case studies in the domain of first response.

15.2 Design Case Studies in the Domain of Firefighting

The research experience in developing IT-based support for firefighters operating indoors may serve as a suitable series of design cases to illustrate the significance and application of the grounded-design principles for complex IS projects. The research effort comprises almost 7 years of work in participatory design based on "ubiquitous computing" technology (Weiser 1999) involving four different fire brigades in France and Germany. In the course of two consecutive research projects, the practice-centered perspective shifted the design focus. Based on a thorough observation of the firefighting routines, the design focus shifted from automatic location detection to technical support for computer-enhanced way-finding practices in reconnaissance missions. As a result, we realigned the way-finding platform by adding functionality for a structured text-based communication channel. In the following sections, we provide an overview of the two design case studies conducted in this research and development context. Due to our focus on a comparative analysis, we will not provide technical or practical details. For further reading, we refer to the detailed documentation of both design case studies in the work by Ramirez and Dyrks (2010), Ramirez et al. (2012), Betz and Wulf (2014), and Betz et al. (2014). However, the basic structure of these sections is kept as a narrative for better comprehensibility.

15.2.1 The Landmarke Project: Navigation and Orientation Support for Firefighters

In fire incidents, indoor reconnaissance missions are an essential part of the work of firefighters. In such missions, a team of firefighters must enter an unknown building in order to systematically inspect and assess the situation, to look for victims, report their progress, and, eventually, attack fire sources. Due to heat and fumes, firefighters have to wear special protective suits and breathing protection equipment that provide support for restricted periods of time only. Moreover, they have to drag along heavy fire hoses when attacking possible fire sources, both for self-protection and for guiding their way out.

Inspection is complex cooperative work that requires a lot of training and experience. It imposes a high work load with additional impediments caused by severely restricted agility, due to the need for protective and firefighting equipment. In particular, safely finding a way out before exhausting the air supply is of vital importance, as getting lost is a frequent cause of serious accidents. Longer-lasting reconnaissance missions require alternating inspection teams and so calls for space-related communication between the teams and the operation controllers. To ensure a reliable backup of indoor-working firefighters and a quick provision of help should an accident occur, it is important to communicate the mission's progress to the leaders outside the building.

The Pre-Study Phase: Investigating Existing Practices

The pre-study research investigated existing firefighting practices. On the one hand, it drew on psychological knowledge about way finding and, on the other hand, it was based on a thorough ethnographical study (participatory observation and interviews) of existing social practices for indoor tactics in firefighting. The study revealed the following complex and partly non-obvious inspection and way-finding practices.

The interactive exploratory teamwork based on distributed tasks has to be done under difficult environmental and sensorial conditions due to heat, fumes, and heavy protective equipment, forcing the team members to interact and to keep in touch mainly through body contact, lifelines, and fire hoses carried with them. To maintain orientation, the firefighters follow the "right-hand rule," a systematic approach comparable with "depth-first" traverse algorithms as basic exploration strategy. While in this way exploring the actual situation and the spatial structure, the firefighters build situated cognitive maps based on meaningful "landmarks" (such as walls, aisles, doors, or windows) as the core result of their mission. To enable leaders in front of the building to participate in the construction of such a cognitive representation of the incident place, indoor-working firefighters have to report important milestones and decisions of their progress to their leader outside via radio devices. Landmarks and milestones may be actively augmented with additional signs to denote specific results of their exploration, (e.g., standing for "already inspected" or "an alternative way out"). The situation-specific cognitive maps thus provide them with a shared collection of reference for keeping them aware of the environment, for orientation and communication, for finding the way out, and for instructing follow-up or rescuing safety teams in case of an accident. Consequently, the researchers' original understanding of the underlying problem as being a standard navigation problem, and the original design proposal of providing the firefighters with navigation software for position determination, were inappropriate or, in the worst case, harmful, as firefighters are afraid of losing their navigational skills and competences by using maps and positioning-based navigation tools.

The in-depth study of existing social practices produced an enriched and empathic comprehension of the firefighters' world. As such, it offered valuable insights for guiding design ideas. In particular, the idea of intentionally launching artificial "landmarks" on-site was inspired by the existing practices we identified.

The Design and Appropriation Phases: Working on and with the Artifact

The main design and appropriation phase of the research project built upon the results of the pre-study phase and followed a participatory and evolutionary process organization. It was based on a sequence of specification and prototyping workshops with firefighters and firefighting instructors in order to generate design ideas for technical artifacts supposed to improve their demanding work situation, in this case, small, embedded ubiquitous computing device.

During the workshops, participating and contributing with their own experience and the perspective of improving the situation proved to be a sound motivation for practitioners. Reflecting their own practices and discursively confronting them with functional offers of suitable artifacts presented by the researchers (or designers) turned out to be an important source for generating new design ideas. In this way, a number of sound, emergent design ideas were contributed by firefighters. Moreover, such participatory procedures help to solve signification and legitimation problems, particularly acknowledging firefighters' requirements in this regard.

Inspired by the firefighters' use of different forms of marking and annotating spatial objects and structures, artificial "landmarks" with sufficient functionality for use in electronic networks were proposed. The core idea is to successively build an on-site, ad-hoc reference system, which is in continuous construction during firefighting missions. The system is progressively built up and augmented by deploying an electronic grid of small, networked tokens that serve, when deployed, as reference points representing tactical information about the site and the progress. They support spatial orientation and space-related communication among the firefighting teams and the outside coordinators as well. When equipped with suitable sensors, they further enrich the emerging cognitive maps with situational and environmental information (see Figure 15.3).

As envisaged by an evolutionary project organization, several variations of the electronic "landmark" tokens with different functional complexity have been designed and appropriated step by step for practical use in reconnaissance missions in a training center where emerging practices can be observed and evaluated. Each of these prototype versions

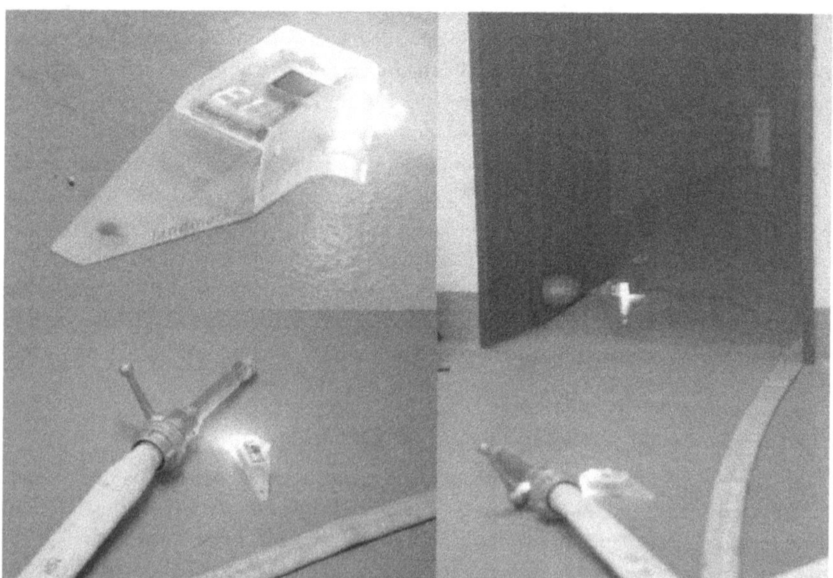

Figure 15.3 Building an electronic grid to support orientation and space-related communication

has been tested and evaluated in practical use in this way, which has led to new design ideas being generated. The evolutionary approach also allows for a step-by-step introduction of very early and less mature "sketches" to allow for the documentation of user experiences that provide essential contrasts for the review of existing practices.

A paramount result of this overall procedure is that, by the intentional deployment of the tokens, the firefighters are enabled to construct richer cognitive maps of the site than before: the numbered sequence of electronic landmarks not only indicates locations but provides additional context information coded by color. With this sort of artifact at hand, firefighters can partially abstain from the burden of dragging along heavy fire hoses, and at the same time they can improve their spatial orientation and navigation due to the enriched context information. This further enables them to substantially shorten the retreat path, as shown in Figure 15.4, which compares old and new practices.

Close to the end of the Landmarke research project, the professional firefighters from Cologne stated that up to this point they found the electronic landmarks useful for navigation purposes but they doubted that the advantages of this functionality would justify the introduction of such a platform into real firefighting practices.

During the appropriation of the Landmarke infrastructure, the participating firefighters step by step learned to understand the technical capabilities of the system. They identified patterns and similarities of the infrastructure with other well-known artifacts in their day-to-day practice; for example, the network infrastructure of the Landmarke platform provides a multi-hop mesh network, which enables applications to pass messages via changing routes over large radio distances. After understanding the technical feasibilities, the firefighters mapped them to the constraints of their familiar voice radios. They envisioned a possible use of the Landmarke platform to enhance the range of their voice radio devices.

Based on the experiences they gained during the participatory design and appropriation process, by the end of the project, the firefighters were able to judge the strengths

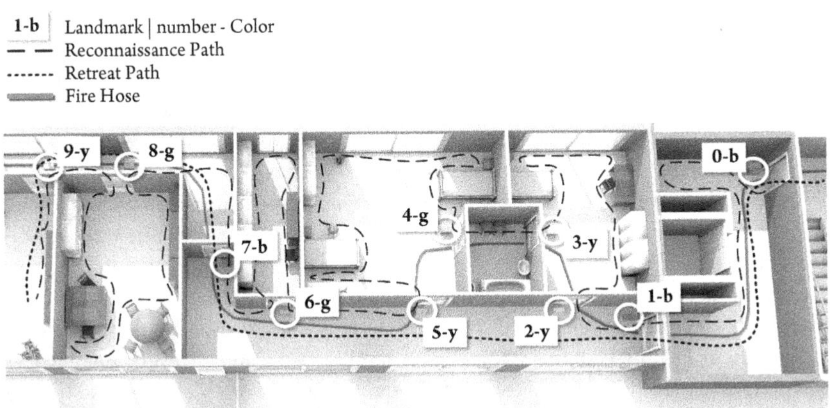

Figure 15.4 Analysis of a trial reconnaissance mission

and weaknesses of their own practices. While they highly appreciated the mutual learning and reflection process, they expressed concerns whether the Landmarke platform offered enough "added value" compared to the additional effort caused by the deployment of the beacons. However, we observed the firefighters appropriating the beacon's color codes to deal with the problem of unstable connectivity on their voice-over-radio communication between indoor-working teams and their commanders outside the building. We observed how they used the feature to remotely set the color of each beacon to articulate simple questions such as "Everything ok?" and their responses, like "yes" or "no."

Thus, the appropriation of the platform for navigation support led to the disclosure of other, probably even more immediate problems in indoor firefighting. The reflection on the current case formed a *knowledge base* that served as a platform for further investigations in other aspects of the observed and addressed social practice. In our case, we extended the ethnographic work toward communication and coordination between indoor-working firefighter teams and their commanders outside the building. Identified patterns in the presented Landmarke case study represent important findings for the investigation of communication and coordination practices.

15.2.2 The Koordinator Project: Coordination and Communication Support for Firefighters

A second project, called "Koordinator," was developed based on the design knowledge base built in the Landmarke project to create a design case study to work on artifacts for communication and coordination support and to investigate the appropriation of these artifacts. This design case study was documented in the work by Betz and Wulf (2014); Betz et al. (2014).

The Pre-Study Phase: Investigating Existing Practices

As in most countries, firefighters in Germany utilize radio sets to establish voice communication between indoor operating units and the command structure outside. Based on knowledge built in the Landmarke design case study and a complementary pre-study in cooperation with different German volunteer fire brigades over a time span of more than 3 years, the advantages and disadvantages of the current voice-over-radio communication tactics and techniques have been analyzed. The methods of inquiry of the Landmarke design case study were extended by "map exercises" and quantitative measures to extend the number of evaluative dimensions. Map exercises allowed for a turn-by-turn simulation of fictional fire scenarios. Map exercises enabled both researchers and practitioners to walk through a scenario in slow motion and to pause the ongoing fictional mission to allow for in-depth reflections and discussions about regulatory aspects and their in-situ appropriation. It turned out that navigation, communication, and coordination practices are interwoven across many dimensions. Requirements from regulatory constraints, historically evolved systematic reconnaissance approaches, and routinized and partly formalized patterns of communication and coordination form a web of issues that can, to some degree, be anticipated.

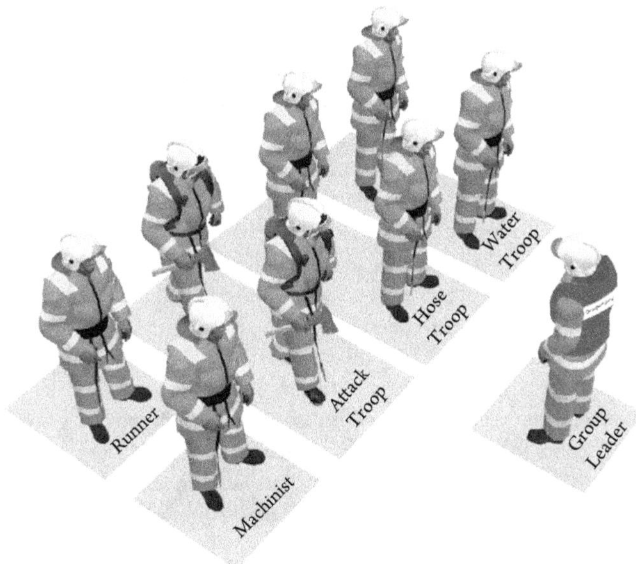

Figure 15.5 A "group" as the smallest operational unit in fire runs

Communication and coordination is necessary due to the dislocated actions of the members of the core operational unit of German fire brigades; this unit is called a "group" (see Figure 15.5). A group is the crew of a fire engine. It contains all relevant roles and expertise to be able to act in a fire after arriving on-site. This is also reflected in firefighting regulation, where a group is defined as the smallest unit that has the legal capacity to act.

A "group" consists of a machinist, who is the driver of the fire engine and the operator of the pump; a runner, who acts as a supportive resource; and three teams called "troops," who are responsible for dedicated tasks. The "attacking troop" is responsible for finding and for fighting the source of a fire. The "attacking troop" is equipped with self-contained breathing apparatuses (SCBAs) and is able to enter burning and smoking buildings for reconnaissance and rescuing purposes. The "hose troop" is responsible for establishing an infrastructure of fire hoses to provide water supply for the "attacking troop." This includes repositioning fire hoses inside a building. The "water troop" searches for water supplies in the surroundings of an affected building. It connects the fire engine with an appropriate water supply. After the establishment of a stable water supply for the fire engine, the "water troop" is equipped with SCBAs and stands by as a backup for rescuing the attacking troop. The designed artifacts in the Koordinator design case study focus on the communication between the "group leader" and the "attacking troop" on its reconnaissance and rescue missions inside the affected building.

The Design and Appropriation Phases: Working on and with the Artifact

The Koordinator design case study builds upon the network infrastructure implemented in the Landmarke design case study. The communication and technical constraints of the deployable Landmark infrastructure indicated that there should be a shift from voice-based to text-based communication; so, for the Koordinator project, the Landmarke remote control was completely redesigned to provide text-based communication features. The resulting device and its appropriation were then evaluated in a total of fifty full-scale training missions including extensive debriefings. In particular, the debriefing sessions offered an opportunity for intensive participation and steering by the participating firefighters. Mainly volunteer firefighters from different levels of responsibility were invited to participate in the Koordinator project, to complement the professional perspective from the career firefighters participating in the Landmarke project.

When communication features were added to the original Landmarke platform, the "added value" of the resulting artifact designed for the Koordinator case study was assessed as significant enough to justify its introduction as official firefighting equipment. The main reason for the change of mind lay in the improved cost–benefit balance regarding the addition of a further piece of equipment, as well as the effort already involved in the manual deployment of the "landmarks." In particular, it was found that appropriation of the Koordinator IT artifacts reduced both the firefighters' work load and the overall inspection time of the site (see Betz and Wulf 2014 and Betz et al. 2014 for more detailed results).

15.2.3 Building and Extending the Knowledge Base

These two design case studies are examples of how to analyze and design IT artifacts when confronted with complex organizational practices, and they demonstrate the application of grounded-design principles. Existing research efforts mainly focus on exceptional large-scale incidents by supporting command and control structures of multi-agency efforts to cope with disaster situations. Research on emergency response and crisis management tends to focus on the "exceptional in the exceptional," that is, it is grounded in the assumption that innovative information technology support is needed particularly in situations where emergency response agencies are faced with emergent and overwhelming situations. The design case studies presented here follow a different approach: Grounded in practice theory, the research efforts aim to methodically unveil everyday practices and their often indiscernible problematic aspects.

To begin with, by investigating existing firefighting practices, it was discovered that the real underlying problem in firefighting reconnaissance missions is not the mere determination of locations for spatial navigation , but rather the proper formation and communication of cognitive maps of the site, with sufficiently rich context information as a shared reference system, for both individual navigation and collective coordination. However, this fact is not obvious and could only be disclosed through a sound ethnographic investigation based on participatory and empathic, highly reflective observation. The studies confirmed underlying insights, as derived from practice theory, that actors are often not fully aware of their current existing practices. The map exercise in particular enabled practitioners to make internalized routines explicit and accessible for reflection.

The insights from the pre-study had a great impact on which technical functions were searched for in design discourses with the practitioners: automatically dropping artificial location-tracking devices following the inspection paths, as developed and applied in previous attempts (Klann 2009; Liu et al. 2010), is seen as not sufficiently supportive for the firefighters to actively construct the inner situated operational picture of the site; rather, it would appear to be more suitable to look out for artificial devices that can be enriched by social and environmental context information in the course of the inspection process. The second design case study revealed further insights and findings regarding the practice in the field of first responding. By focusing on the practice of firefighting in the first line of intervention, it transpired that the successful coordination of "groups" of firefighters as the smallest operational units is crucial for successful performance in reconnaissance missions in the early phases of fire incidents.

15.3 Comparative Analysis: Results and Findings

A sound analysis of existing social practices and IT artifacts developed in their support can orientate and inspire the design discourse. Such an analysis provides insights into *what could work* when coming up with promising prototypes in real use. *Appropriating* the prototypes for use is again a creative effort, the results of which are not predictable. The proof of their usefulness and usability depends on the emerging social practices in which the artifacts are being used. Reflecting on the experiences with new social practices using IT artifacts can answer questions such as *how does it impact* and *how well does it work?* These findings can serve as a fruitful source for creating further design ideas. Ethnographical observation of the design and appropriation processes, and conceptual reconstruction of the whole design case, as shown with the Landmarke and Koordinator projects, delivers a set of design case studies that can be integrated into an IS design knowledge base, as shown in Figure 15.2. In the context of the Landmarke design case study, an innovative method of communicating during indoor reconnaissance missions evolved from the study. The realization then led into a completely new feature set being added to the platform, thus increasing the "value" of the existing artifacts. The design and development of the communication functionality thus led into a second design case study and consequently extended the knowledge base and allowed for additional, comparative studies.

A comparative analysis of these design case studies reveals categories and "structural configurations" which contribute to the generation of additional insights. Regarding the state of the art, a description of firefighters' mundane practices is not generally the focus of civil security research in academia. The emphasis on supporting large command and control structures underestimates the relevancy of the social practices of smaller operational units. The design case studies presented here unveil the informational interdependencies between incident commanders and operational forces. These interdependencies underline the perception that the top-down approaches prevalent in crisis management (e.g., the use of large command posts and centralized crisis management teams) have to be complemented by bottom-up perspectives from the first line.

In this section, we first summarize the results of our meta-analysis by identifying common structural configurations from the selected design case studies. We discuss the identified common aspects by pairing counterparts together due to the conspicuous dialectic tension between them. The pairs underpin the interdependencies of certain technical features and their impact on practice.

To begin with, the analysis of the relationship between the *autonomy* of the indoor firefighting teams and the *monitoring* commander outside the building revealed interesting insights (Denef et al. 2011; Betz and Wulf 2014). The impression of a strongly hierarchical paramilitary structure of order and obedience may belie the fact that the commander outside the building heavily relies on the observations of the indoor-working teams and that his decisions are firmly interwoven with or even determined by the autonomous decisions of the teams indoors. This autonomy requires a synchronization of the operational picture. Tools to support the monitoring of the indoor-working teams allow for more autonomy inside the building. Contrary to the implicit assumption of vast *uncertainty* in early incident phases, an in-depth analysis of existing practices showed that there is also a large element of *routine* and trained discipline in the practical handling of emergency cases. Thus, actions, such as those in typical fire incidents, are to some extent predictable, and therefore allow for *anticipation* and *predefinition*. On the other hand, predefinition of actions supports discipline and creates space for *safe improvisational action*.

It is important to understand that the autonomy of operational units is a key feature of firefighting organizational structures. As such, it should be considered when designing useful and supportive IT artifacts for emergency response. The relationship between *standardization* and *expressiveness* provides another interesting focus when analyzing (multimodal) communication practices in hierarchical organizational structures. Other emerging categories are the tensions between *anticipation* and *unpredictability*; *addressability* and *awareness*; and *complementation* and *substitution* with regard to the design of multimodal communication support (cf. Betz and Wulf 2014). Another interesting aspect of the cooperation and the communication in safety-critical settings such as firefighting is the practice of *periodically reducing uncertainty*, and the relationship between *communicative effort* and *risk* in safety-critical dislocated cooperative work settings.

All these concepts emerged from our design case studies and contributed significantly to a better understanding of cooperation, coordination, and communication aspects to be found in firefighting and its technical support. We outline these concepts in the following sections in a contrasting dialectic form.

15.3.1 Autonomy and Monitoring

Existing scientific literature suggests that first responding in general, and firefighting in particular, are organized in a strong hierarchical manner with rigid organizational structures. Terms like "command post," "command centers," "decision makers," "common operational picture," "disaster management," and so on, dominate wide parts of research publications and often set the agenda for design research. In the course of our investigations, it turned out that within the rigid organizational structures, there is a vast amount of space for autonomous actions, especially by members of the lower ranks.

Autonomy needs structures to enable others to anticipate the implemented actions. On an organizational level, service regulations are the basis for autonomous but reliable cooperation within operational units. The service regulations are a set of legal instructions in form of a handbook that describes permitted and not-permitted practices of firefighting. Regulations also define the role definitions, boundaries, and responsibilities of each actor. It is also the basis for the training, education, and evaluation of firefighting practice. In that sense, each firefighting unit, from two-man troops to groups or even whole brigades, are, to some extent, free to make their own decisions. The regulatory framework ensures not only the safety but also the predictability of such autonomous actions. In our design case studies, troops are responsible for the performance of the mission, in the sense that their actions are directed at expediting mission goals. Group leaders are responsible for observing, assessing, and guiding the performative actions of a troop. Monitoring is essential for binding the performative and the observative aspects toward a safe and targeted coordinated action, at least in safety-critical contexts. From the perspective of a troop member inside the building, being monitored by the group leader unburdens him from the responsibility of correlating his own actions with those of other units. This is an important basis for autonomous and situated action.

From the perspective of the group leader, monitoring allows for autonomous actions to be secured by reacting to emergent events that are relevant, for example, for the troop inside the building. To support the performance of autonomous local action, technical artifacts have to enable the coordinating actors to monitor these actions and the circumstances under which they take place.

These insights are mainly gleaned from the Koordinator design case study, in which we focused on coordinative and cooperative aspects of the investigated practice of indoor firefighting. For that project, we designed a mobile software application for the group leader to monitor the following:

- the deployment of Landmarke nodes
- the node colors set by the troop
- the sensor data gathered by the Landmarke nodes
- the results from an activity recognition device attached to the firefighters
- the fill levels of the SCBAs
- the reported operational progress (Betz and Wulf 2014)

By incrementally introducing these monitoring features, we observed a quantifiable reduction of voice-over-radio communication between the group leader and his attacking troop. So, the appropriation of these features led to a less obstructive way to ensure the securitization of the troop advancing in the burning building. The troops stated that the monitoring features provided a much better underlying feeling of security and that this then enabled them to perform their tasks with considerably less disturbance from voice-over-radio communication and, consequently, faster.

15.3.2 Anticipation and Unpredictability

From an external perspective, firefighting deals with exceptional situations when extinguishing fire and rescuing people from smoking, toxic, and unknown buildings.

Regarding the rarity of such events for non-firefighters, such incidents give the impression of uniqueness and unpredictability. From a domain-internal perspective, however, incidents such as a fire in a building are perceived as non-exceptional events that are expected and for which firefighters are well prepared. The following quote from a volunteer firefighter participating in the Koordinator research project illustrates his perception of his role:

> Fighting fire or rescuing people is the essence of being a firefighter. Simply put, you can say it like this: A fire alarm is the most normal thing for a firefighter. Every hour of training, education, and qualification is aimed towards mastering such a situation. For affected people on-site the situation may look chaotic and uncontrollable but there is a well-defined and trained routine that takes place. If these routines fail, or if something happens that seriously affects that routine, first responders would call it a critical incident. Until then, it's basically normal work. Dangerous, but normal work.

An important basis for establishing a well-defined routine is set by the prescribed regulations of indoor firefighting, and firefighting in general. Actions are principled and rooted in strict guidelines that form the foundation of the organization, education, training, and practice of firefighters. There may be discussions about single topics in the regulatory framework but, in general, the framework is well accepted and taken seriously.

Due to the pervasive character of such a standard, there is a high level of predictability in the practice of indoor firefighting. Therefore, a huge number of actions in firefighting or rescuing reconnaissance missions can be anticipated, and this has an effect on higher-level steps, from the initial alarm until the first troop enters the building. However, actions on a micro level as well, like the route a troop takes inside a building, or the way the progress of the mission is reported via the radio channel, can be anticipated to some extent.

On the other hand, there is still a significant potential for the emergence of unforeseeable and unpredictable events and occasions firefighters have to cope with. These emergent events may not have a disruptive character but they sometimes require deviance from the predefined procedures. These deviances are decided locally and so explicit communication is needed to enable others to assess them regarding potential individual risks and the consequences for the whole operation. One example is the deviation from the "right-/left-hand rule" on a reconnaissance trail inside a building. Particularities in the floor plan of a house or apartment can make it necessary to switch from the right-hand to the left-hand-rule, or vice versa. To find a troop affected by an accident, it is crucial to reliably communicate such an alternation in the reconnaissance tactics to enable the backup troop to find and rescue the affected troop. Another example is the tactics used by the attacking troop on leaving a building. The regulations state that firefighters should leave a building by following the fire hose back to the entry point. However, sometimes it is safer and more appropriate to leave a building from some other point (e.g., from the rear). If this change in behavior is not communicated to the group leader—as happens regularly—it is mandatory for the group leader to assume that an accident has befallen the attacking troop, after a predefined lapse of time of perceived continuance in the danger zone inside the building.

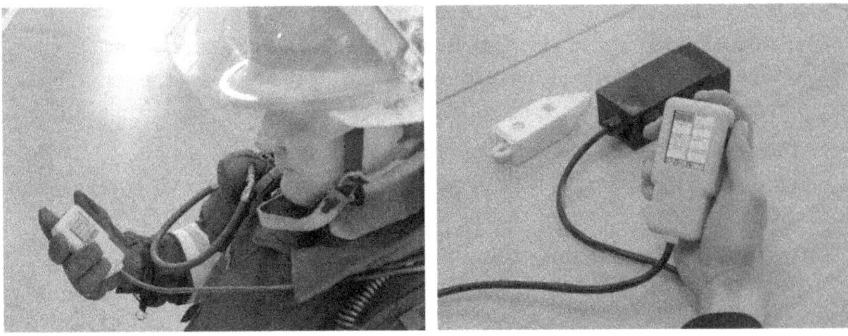

Figure 15.6 (*Left*) A firefighter using the EmergencyMessenger messaging device for indoor firefighting troops; (*right*) from left to right: the final version of the Landmarke beacon (with a wedge form factor), the activity recognition device, and the EmergencyMessenger messaging device

The Landmarke platform, as a tool to support way finding in unknown buildings, was designed to support the practice of routinized and well-defined rules of reconnaissance tactics. On the one hand, the color codes for marking the reconnaissance path are explicit enough to support the established cooperative practice by matching particular colors to particular actions or decisions (cf. Ramirez and Dyrks 2010). On the other hand, the codes are open enough to be appropriated in unusual situations. Thus, the technical artifact called the EmergencyMessenger was designed to support the communication and monitoring of anticipated action (see Figure 15.6). It was built specifically to efficiently support the regulated and therefore to some extent predictable task of the indoor-working attacking troop to report the progress of the reconnaissance mission. Moreover, it supports the outdoor group leader in his monitoring task. However, due to a lack of features that would allow for expressing complex deviances from routines, we never observed the appropriation of the EmergencyMessenger to cope with unforeseen situations. On these occasions, the firefighters preferred the voice-over-radio communication.

15.3.3 Standardization and Expressiveness

As mentioned in Section 15.3.2, the degree of anticipation of action during a reconnaissance mission is high enough to introduce a standardized navigation, orientation, and communication framework that enables indoor-working firefighters to improve their performance in a significant way. The Landmarke artifact is an example of where the framework is deliberately vague and open enough to support both standardized routines and appropriation to cope with emergent situations (cf. Ramirez and Dyrks 2010). The communication framework developed in the Koordinator design case study followed a different approach. The framework deliberately forces the usage of a fixed catalog of simple textual "speech acts," that is, a set of predefined requests that include a fixed and predefined set of responses. Such a high level of standardization in the available acts of communication had several rationales:

1. The communication framework of the EmergencyMessenger supports the highly routinized practice of indoor firefighting and reconnaissance work. It makes it possible to shift the routinized communication from the shared voice-over-radio channel into another channel that is optimized for speed, clearance, and documentation.
2. The catalog of textual "speech acts" is ordered sequentially at the interface, following the messages' temporal structure during the mission. The currently relevant message can be found quickly to be sent to the receiver's device.
3. The catalog provides a guideline for the indoor-working firefighter to avoid missing the next relevant report in the ongoing tactical proceedings.

However, the high level of standardization and the restriction of the communication channel to using short text messages provided far too little expressiveness for communicating unforeseen and unpredictable circumstances during an ongoing mission. It was also impossible for another firefighter to "read between the lines" of statements sent by a well-known comrade.

15.3.4 Complementation and Substitution

In total, we observed over fifty full-featured training missions. The training missions took place in one of the largest training facilities for firefighting in Germany. The standard training mission scenario was a fire in an apartment on the first or second floor of an apartment building or a single-family home. The work of the group leader outside the building was observed with conventional video cameras while the indoor-working troops were observed with a thermal imaging camera, owing to the darkened environment caused by the use of artificial smoke (see Figure 15.7). The training center allowed for the simulation of a complete fire run, including the arrival of the fire engine, the provision of

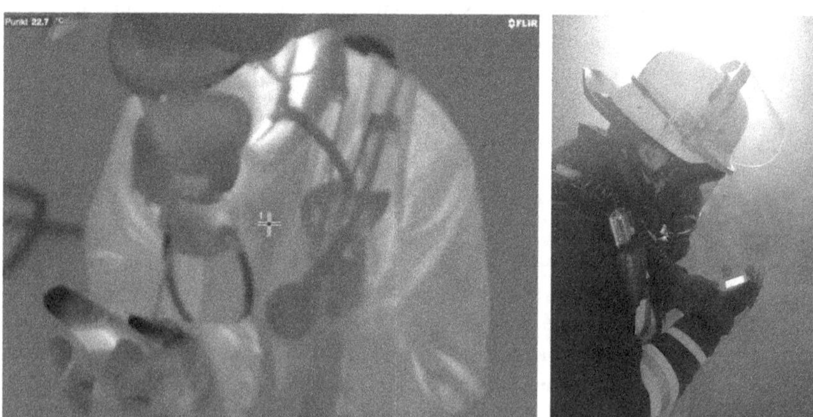

Figure 15.7 *(Left)* Picture from a thermal-imaging video camera in a darkened and smoky indoor environment; *(right)* a firefighter with a SCBA in a lightly smoky indoor environment

a fully functional water supply infrastructure, and the enrichment of the scenarios with optical fire indicators and screaming remote-controlled puppets inside the building. Thus, the training facility provided the most realistic conditions possible. The use and evaluation of the prototype technical artifacts in real fire runs was not allowed, owing to regulatory constraints and the lack of necessary technical security standards. In addition, real fire runs would not have allowed for such thorough documentation.

First, we find evidence that the conventional voice-over-radio communication is error prone and time consuming: While using radios, we observed that, on average, there were twelve acts of verbal communication, per training mission, between the group leader and one indoor troop. Even without there being any other disturbing traffic from other firefighting units, as often happened on the shared radio channel, we observed communication problems, such as bad link quality, no responses from the addressee, or difficulties in understanding concrete information (like SCBA filling levels). Problems that needed further attention, like repetition requests, occurred in at least three and up to eight acts of verbal radio communication in each training mission. Indoor troops needed 12–14 minutes on average to find a missing person and to hand him/her over to the medical services. On average, 04:33 minutes of this time were spent with radio communication, which means 27 seconds on average for each act of verbal radio communication.

The textual messaging technique introduced by the EmergencyMessenger enabled group and troop leaders to communicate significantly faster than by voice-over-radio communication. We also observed that the introduction of the EmergencyMessenger led to a more detailed level of reporting and monitoring: when the EmergencyMessenger was being used, we counted seventeen acts of communication, on average, between the group leader and one indoor attacking troop member, in a typical scenario. The ad-hoc deployed network provided 100% coverage in an apartment with a kitchen, a bathroom, and four other rooms on the second floor. We observed no problems in communication that needed further attention. Attacking troops spent 2:37 minutes on average for communication with the EmergencyMessenger, which meant 9 seconds, on average, for each act of text-based communication. In summary, the EmergencyMessenger communication framework helped to unburden the voice-over-radio channel by shifting routine communication to another medium. This allowed for a much more reliable communication via conventional channels.

Based on these facts, it may seem appropriate to substitute the existing voice-over-radio practice with the new text-based approach, due to the obviously better performance of the latter. However, the firefighters involved in the study put their positive experience with the newly introduced technical artifact in an overall context, stating that and using the text-based messenger was no better or worse than using the voice-over-radio channel:

> The pager is not better than the radio. It's more like, um, the one contributes to the other. By shifting the routine communication to the pager we have finally found a way to clean up the on-site radio channel. Now, the radio becomes what it's meant to be, a way to express complex things like unforeseen situations, gut instincts, etc. We shouldn't substitute the radio. We should keep it and leverage from the newly created space.

Consequently, while designing technical support for an existing cooperative practice, the interplay of the new artifact with already existing ones has to be taken into account. The value of one artifact can be strongly interdependent with that of others. To go further, the features of a newly introduced artifact can trigger the reappropriation—in the sense of changes in use—of already existing artifacts.

15.3.5 Addressability and Awareness

In the Landmarke project, the main feature of the deployable nodes were its exterior attributes, which were perceivable by "whomever it may concern," that is, all firefighters who cooperatively appropriated the color codes in a particular way were able to read the landscape of the deployed mark-ups inside the building when passing by. That is, the question of the identity of the addressee of a certain piece of information is avoided by focusing on the common appropriation of the intentionally introduced ambiguity of the encoded meaning and its public nature(cf. Ramirez and Dyrks 2010). The conventional voice-over-radio communication on-site basically follows the same approach. Most incidents require the establishment of only one radio channel; that is, all firefighters on-site share this one public radio channel. To address a certain receiver of a voice message, the firefighters conduct a rigid protocol to guarantee the successful transmission of a message. In technical words, the conventional on-site radio communication works in a half-duplex and broadcasting mode of operation.

In the Koordinator design case study, the focus shifted toward a communication approach with stronger organizational mapping. Regarding the structure of fire brigades and the regulatory framing in Germany, the main addressee of reports issued by troops operating inside a building is the superordinated group leader outside the building. In an early phase of the Koordinator project, the IT design addressed these circumstances by utilizing the typical technical characteristics of the underlying network infrastructure by routing the information of the Landmarke nodes, colors set by the troops, the sensor data gathered by the nodes, the results from the activity recognition device attached to the firefighters, the reported fill levels of the SCBAs, and the operational proceedings reported with the EmergencyMessenger to a certain recipient in the communication network. In the EmergencyMessenger case, the group leader gathers all this information, undertakes a continuous assessment, makes decisions, and reports up the hierarchy, for example, to the head of the section or the officer overall in charge.

Both approaches—broadcasting, and the exclusive addressing of messages in a cooperative context of work—raises the aspect of awareness, which is central in many IS and compute-supported cooperative work (CSCW) discourses (Schmidt 2002; Gross 2013; Schmidt and Randall 2016). As already discussed, the Koordinator messaging approach moves messages from a public to a private channel, which means excluding a large number of recipients. The design of this technical feature was a catalyst of many controversial discussions about the side effects, both negative and positive.

On the one hand, particularly those firefighters who are on standby as a so-called backup troop are not able to follow the reported progress of the reconnaissance mission while standing outside the building. Some firefighters tend to listen to the verbal reports of the foregoing attacking troop inside the building by following the voice-over-radio broadcast. They construct their personal operational picture to be ready in case they need to jump in to help or to rescue their comrades. On the other hand, it is exactly this broadcasting feature of the voice-over-radio channel that is considered harmful by many group leaders, as the following statement made by a group leader shows:

> To be honest, I really appreciate the effect of keeping them out of the communication between myself and the attacking troop. I know they try to help and they try to be prepared in case they are deployed, but their operational picture is often incomplete. I just have more information about the whole context, the building, the missing person, the characteristics of the apartment or the house. From my experience, their operational picture is, um, how should I put it, um, scrappy. And it is often plain wrong. In case they are deployed, I would prefer not to have a discussion about the situation, which has actually happened to me several times.

It seems that in the investigated context of first responding, the awareness provided by the technical artifact of voice-over-radio does not perfectly enable "cooperating actors [to] align and integrate their activities with those of their colleagues in a seemingly 'seamless' manner; that is, without interrupting each other, for instance by asking, suggesting, requesting, ordering, reminding, etc. others of this or that" (Schmidt 2002, p. 285). Rather, it may disturb a rigid structure and culture of information gathering, situation assessment, and decision-making in the context of strongly limited time and safety-critical actions. This insight should be seen as a dedicated contribution to the refinement of the concept of "awareness" in the CSCW domain (cf. Schmidt and Randall 2016).

15.3.6 Communicative Effort and Risk

As previously mentioned, a reconnaissance mission inside a burning building requires a continuous monitoring of the attacking troop working indoors by the group leader working outside the building. The term "continuous" in the context of a cooperative but dislocated work setting is shaped by several aspects:

1. What are the available technical resources that enable the group leader to monitor the assigned troops?
2. In which phase of an incident does a group leader have the ability to monitor his troops, and to what extent?
3. What effort does it take to monitor the troops, that is, for the group leader and for the troops themselves?
4. What is the intensity of the incident, that is, are troops imperiled and, if so, to what extent?
5. What is the personal risk preference of the group leader, that is, is the group leader self-confident? What experiences have been gathered in the past? Does he trust his group members? How does he assess the capabilities of the indoor-working attacking troop?

The firefighters participating in the Landmarke and Koordinator projects explained the monitoring and communication behavior of a group leader by using a simple model. When the attacking troop enters the danger zone inside the building, the uncertainty immediately begins to grow, dependent on the intensity of the given incident situation. Every group leader has an individual risk preference, a "threshold" at which he decides that it is necessary to contact the troop to request their status. After the troop responds, the level of uncertainty is significantly reduced but when the communication ends, the uncertainty starts to grow again until the risk threshold is again reached. Figure 15.8 illustrates four different communication patterns. The combination of a perceived incident intensity and the individual risk preference results in the number of communicative acts.

From the perspective of the troop leader, communication for monitoring purposes is perceived as a burden while working inside the burning building; it is a necessity for their own safety but, at the same time, it is also something of a disturbance. Troop leaders appreciate group leaders with a higher risk-preference level, because this leads to less attempts at communication and therefore to faster mission progress. So, monitoring activities in the work of firefighters should be understood less as a continuous flow of information and more as a rhythmic process of periodically reducing uncertainty and where the resulting communication behavior is dependent on external factor and personal preferences.

The real-time streaming of results from an activity recognition feature to monitor the indoor-working troops tries to overcome this pattern by providing a seamless picture of the reconnaissance progress. Further research on this shift from a periodical toward a streaming concept of monitoring dislocated cooperative activities is, we suggest, an important feature of the way we consider "awareness" in CSCW and IS.

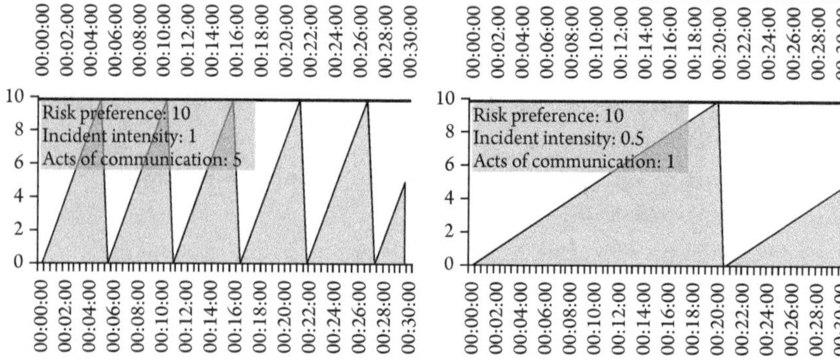

Figure 15.8 Four examples of the communication behavior of group leaders dependent on the personal risk preference and the incident intensity

15.4 Discussion

In this section, we present a discussion of the grounded-design research approach, based on the findings of and practical experiences in the Landmarke and Koordinator research projects. In the article by Rohde et al. (2016), the grounded-design approach is discussed with a certain focus on the *processes* of doing research through proposing a tripartite methodology of conducting pre-studies on practices, designing artifacts, and then investigating their appropriation. In the following section, we focus on the *products* of the approach in terms of documenting and presenting study findings, design implications, and prototypes.

We present practical configurations in the context of scientific research organized in projects, which is the default format in public funding nowadays (see Chapter 16). We discuss the impact of such contextual patterns on the application of grounded design, with the aim of developing the approach. Finally, we propose a set of criteria for judging the qualitative research results in general and design case studies in particular. We then highlight some organizational characteristics of our analysis of the design case studies conducted in the Landmarke and Koordinator projects.

15.4.1 Historicity in Lines of Research

The research projects presented in this chapter form part of a sequence of at least four projects in the context of first responding and firefighting. The first project in this context ("wearIT@work," founded by the European Union in the sixth framework program [WearIT@Work, n.d.]) started in 2004 and followed a human-centered design approach by trying to introduce a given technology into an already existing practice. Driven by experiences made in technology evaluation workshops in "wearIT@work," parts of the research team developed an alternative approach for designing ubiquitous computing support for reconnaissance missions in burning buildings. In 2008 the team was awarded 3 years of funding to follow that approach in the context of the Landmarke project (Fraunhofer-Institut für Angewandte Informationstechnik 2011). In 2011, motivated by questions raised in the course of the Landmarke project, newly joined team members solicited 3 years of funding for the Koordinator project. Each of these externally funded projects consisted mainly of one design case study that had its own motivations, objectives, challenges, and partners. However, the shape of each project and the resulting design case studies were mainly determined by the results achieved, experiences made, and questions raised by its predecessor. This is a case of a rather successful establishment of a coherent line of research in an environment strongly driven by external funding. This is, however, an ex-post perspective—since each project had to be acquired in a competitive manner, it was not particularly easy to establish a long-term research agenda.

The grounded-design approach described in the work by Wulf et al. (2011, 2015) and Rohde et al. (2016) implies the coexistence of individual, well-documented design case studies that form the basis for meta-analysis at a higher level. Actually, in the context of a longer line of consecutive research efforts, which may fill the timespan of a decade, there is often a historicity in developing design concepts in related fields of application carried out in a context of overlapping generations of researcher, overlapping constellations of project partners, and overlapping project durations.

15.4.2 Accumulation of Knowledge

The historicity of (partly) consecutive design case studies is an important factor for comparative analysis. Besides there being an opportunity for generating knowledge by analyzing design case studies across different domains and fields, there is also an accumulation of knowledge within a "track" of chronologically conducted design case studies. This implicit accumulation should be made more explicit, to sensitize researchers for the assumptions made by others in the past, as these assumptions may guide their own course of action or even dominate it. To highlight this aspect, Figure 15.2 should be complemented with a time dimension, as sketched in Figure 15.9. In addition, the implicit flow of knowledge between consecutive design case studies should be made visible.

15.4.3 Personal (Dis-)Continuity

The focus on appropriation phenomena is an important and unique feature of the grounded-design approach. Appropriation takes time and usually takes place when the pre-study in the consecutive design case study has already begun. From our experience, the appropriation of artifacts from prior design case studies often influences the pre-studies of the following ones, especially when there is an overlap of participating researchers or partners in the field of application. This personal continuity has both advantages and disadvantages. Knowledge from the past can be assumed, and time for the re-contextualization of new participants can be saved. On the other hand, if both researchers and actors in the field take part in design case studies over a span of multiple design case studies, their open-mindedness could ease with the time. It is also observable that actors begin to develop their own hidden agenda that they also try to enforce.

Academia is a working context with an (intentional) fluctuation of personnel. Working on design case studies in projects goes in parallel with the typical young researchers' qualification goal of reaching an MA or a PhD degree. This being so, there is often not enough time left to explicate, document, and analyze design-relevant insights beyond writing traditional academic publications (see Chapter 1). However, without personal continuity, the tacit knowledge passed on by overlapping generations of actors tends to get lost.

15.4.4 Architectural Heritage

Design case studies as a central element of the grounded-design approach are focused on the design of IT artifacts, which include hardware and software. In the context of a series of consecutive design case studies, software and hardware developers tend to reuse existing artifacts and try to extend them with additional features. As an example, in the Landmarke

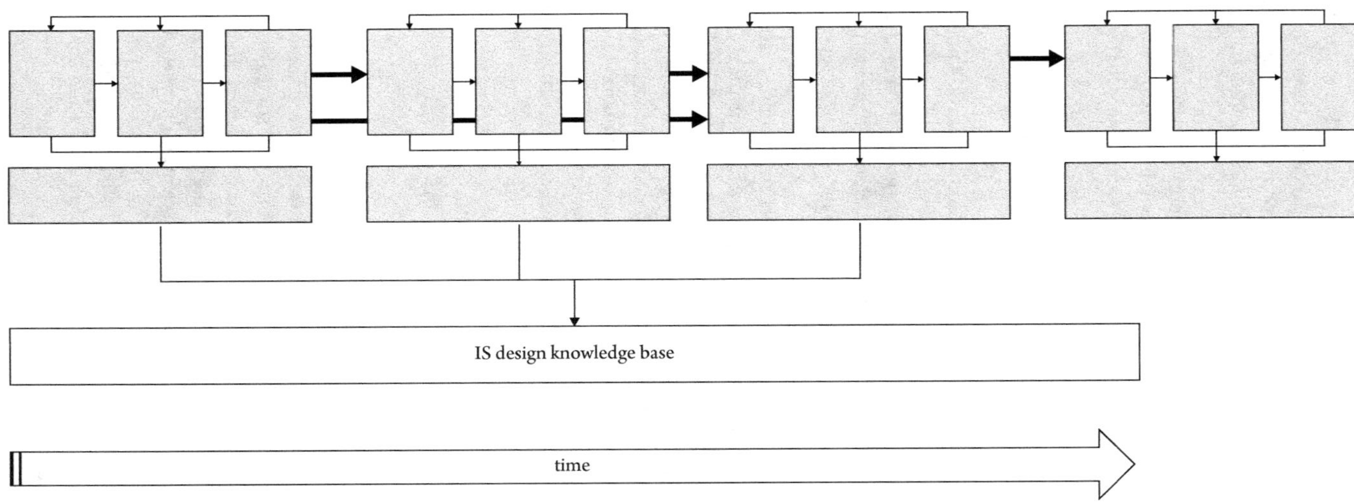

Figure 15.9 Introducing time as a dimension in grounded design

project, the participating firefighters appropriated the introduced color beacons to encode messages in a sequence of color changes to use the navigation support features of the electronic wedges for communication purposes, especially in those situations where the voice-over-radio was not available. In the Koordinator project that followed, the technical infrastructure was kept and extended by a dedicated communication feature. This approach had many advantages but also many disadvantages. In later phases of the Koordinator project, while the navigation and orientation features of the nodes were partly abandoned, the technological infrastructure was retained unchanged. However, it was only after a dedicated review of the suitable and available technologies for the communication use case that this architectural heritage became visible.

15.4.5 Barriers of Appropriation

Firefighting is a safety-critical and highly regulated domain. It was therefore not possible to observe the appropriation of the designed and introduced artifacts in real fire incidents. The quality of the technical artifacts was sufficient to use them in training missions under realistic conditions but the absence of certifications and the high standards regarding the robustness of official firefighting equipment hindered any observation of long-term appropriation phenomena. Such limitations should be considered both at the beginning of a design case study and later on, when the results are examined. There may be other domains with similar limitations, such as policing tactics, medical contexts, geriatric nursing, and so on. Crisis management is an example whereby the infrequence of usage hinders the appropriation of introduced artifacts. For each case, the responsible researcher has to consider alternative ways of investigating artifact appropriation. In the context of the Koordinator design case study, we ran—in addition to a large number of realistic training missions—several workshops to recall real fire incidents from the past to create and document "what-if-I-had-this-artifact" scenarios, which turned out to be very useful in filling the appropriation gap.

15.5 Conclusion

As discussed in this volume, common formats of scientific publication are journal papers and conference contributions. Text-based publication media, with its hard constraints of paper-based printing, and with its common limitations regarding the extent of each contribution, does not support the documentation of design case studies very well, especially with regard to the criteria for qualitative research usually accepted. Thus, contributing to the IS, HCI, or CSCW knowledge base by documenting complete design case studies can be challenging with regard to the current dominant scientific documentation culture. The documentation of complete design case studies in such scientific formats, it transpires, is challenging with regard to the epistemological assumptions and expectations of the communities we address. Due to epistemological differences and cultural mismatches, reviewers often do not appreciate an in-depth analysis of existing practices as a starting point for the articulation of research questions or as grounding for the design of interactive systems. One reason for conflicts in this area could be, for example, the lack of technological novelty due to the focus on identifying and addressing practical problems. A related way of documenting existing practices with the purpose of informing design is shown by Denef et al. (2011). They propose the identification of *patterns* derived from ethnographic studies of a domain practice as a way to ground design. The questions of "What could work?", "How well does it work?", and "Why does it work?" still remain unanswered due to the lack of concrete appropriable artifacts. Here, we provide both a summary of several concluded design case studies and a comparative analysis.

In order to make meaningful use of this type of design knowledge base in future design cases, it is necessary to acknowledge the unescapable fact that social practices in organizations widely differ in each case. Design and appropriation ideas and procedures working in one social context therefore need not be successful in another social context. Frequently, even the underlying problems of existing, but dissatisfying, social practices are not obvious and often need first to be disclosed by extensive observation and analysis to be able to envisage suitable measures for improving the efficiency of the practices or to make use of knowledge from other cases. In this respect, the grounded-design approach goes beyond action design research as proposed by Sein et al. (2011), as it avoids addressing a typified problem class in early stages of the intervention.

Similarly, with its emphasis on evolutionary design and knowledge formation procedures, the grounded-design approach is closely related to multigrounded design (Goldkuhl and Lind 2010) and soft design science methodology (Baskerville et al. 2009). However, due to the contingency of creative design and appropriation processes, we suggest that using transferability of design solutions as the a priori determination of whether a class of artifacts offers solutions to a problem class is normally not possible. We therefore accept the necessity of building the transfer of knowledge on previously completed conceptual reconstructions of design cases as specific solutions to specific social practices in the form of design case studies. Based on detected similarities, such knowledge can guide the new design efforts.

Relevant research communities—IS, CSCW, HCI, and so on—are currently bound by specific formats for the presentation and publication of results. This mitigates against the documentation and presentation of complete design case studies. Gaver and Bowers (2012) propose an interesting approach on how to share the genesis of an artifact in a particular design context within an interested community. To unfold the potential of the grounded-design approach, scientific communities involved in design processes need to develop alternative holistic formats for the publication of design-centered research process outcomes, to enable others to reconstruct the design path, including the back tracing of relevant crossroads and the abandoned routes. Recipients of such contents need navigation support to benefit from the results and experiences shared by others. During the application of the grounded-design approach, researches have to keep the documentation of pre-study, design, and appropriation in mind. Similarly, having minimum standards and criteria regarding the quality of such documentation would improve the reflection of the design case study later on.

References

Baskerville, R., Pries-Heje, J., and Venable, J. 2009. "Soft design science methodology." In *DESRIST'09*. New York: ACM, 9.

Becker, J., and Niehaves, B. 2007. "Epistemological perspectives on IS research: A framework for analysing and systematizing epistemological assumptions." *Information Systems Journal* 17 (2): 197–214.

Betz, M., Dyrks, T., and Wulf, V. 2014. "Emergency Messenger als Kommunikationskonzept für Notfallarbeit/EmergencyMessenger as a communication concept for emergency response work." *i-com* 13 (1): 4–11.

Betz, M., and Wulf, V. 2014. "EmergencyMessenger: A text based communication concept for indoor firefighting." In *CHI'14*. New York: ACM, 1515–24.

Bourdieu, P. 1990. *The Logic Of Practice*. Cambridge: Polity Press.

Braa, K., and Vidgen, R. 1999. "Interpretation, intervention, and reduction in the organizational laboratory: A framework for in-context information system research." *Accounting, Management and Information Technologies* 9 (1): 25–47.

Denef, S., Keyson, D., and Oppermann, R. 2011. "Rigid structures, independent units, monitoring: Organizing patterns in frontline firefighting." In *CHI'11*. New York: ACM, 1949–58.

Fraunhofer-Institut für Angewandte Informationstechnik. 2011. "landmarke." Available at http://www.fit.fraunhofer.de/de/fb/ucc/projects/landmarke.html (accessed October 7, 2017).

Garfinkel, H. 2011. *Studies in Ethnomethodology*. Cambridge: Polity Press.

Gaver, B., and Bowers, J. 2012. "Annotated portfolios." *Interactions* 19 (4): 40–9.

Goldkuhl, G. 2012. "Pragmatism vs interpretivism in qualitative information systems research." *European Journal of Information Systems* 21 (2): 135–46.

Goldkuhl, G., and Lind, M. 2010. "A multi-grounded design research process." In *DESRIST'10*. Berlin/Heidelberg: Springer, 45–60.

Goles, T., and Hirschheim, R. 2000. "The paradigm is dead, the paradigm is dead…long live the paradigm: The legacy of Burrell and Morgan." *Omega* 28 (3): 249–68.

Gross, T. 2013. "Supporting effortless coordination: 25 years of awareness research." *Computer Supported Cooperative Work* 22 (4–6): 425–74.

Klann, M. 2009. "Tactical navigation support for firefighters: The LifeNet ad-hoc sensor-network and wearable system." In *Mobile Response 2008*. Berlin/Heidelberg: Springer, 41–56.

Kuutti, K., and Bannon, L. J. 2014. "The turn to practice in HCI." In *CHI'14*. New York: ACM, 3543–52.

Lincoln, Y. S., and Guba, E. G. 1990. "Judging the quality of case study reports." *International Journal of Qualitative Studies in Education* 3 (1): 53–9.

Liu, H., Li, J., Xie, Z., Lin, S., Whitehouse, K., Stankovic, J. A., and Siu, D. 2010. "Automatic and robust breadcrumb system deployment for indoor firefighter applications." In *MobiSys'10*. New York: ACM, 21–34.

Mead, G. H., and Morris, C. W. 1972. *Mind, Self, and Society: From the Standpoint of a Social Behaviorist*. Chicago: University of Chicago Press.

Ramirez, L., and Dyrks, T. 2010. "Designing for high expectations: balancing ambiguity and thorough specification in the design of a wayfinding tool for firefighters." In *DIS'10*. New York: ACM, 390–99.

Ramirez, L., Dyrks, T., Gerwinski, J., Betz, M., Scholz, M., and Wulf, V. 2012. "Landmarke: An ad hoc deployable ubicomp infrastructure to support indoor navigation of firefighters." *Personal and Ubiquitous Computing* 16 (8): 1025–38.

Reckwitz, A. 2002. "Toward a theory of social practices: A development in culturalist theorizing." *European Journal of Social Theory* 5 (2): 243–63.

Rodon, J., and Sese Muniategui, F. 2008. "Structural configurations: An explanation for iois implementation failure." In *ECIS'08*. Atlanta: AIS, 83.

Rohde, M., Brödner, P., Stevens, G., Betz, M., and Wulf, V. 2016. "Grounded design: A praxeological IS research perspective." *Journal of Information Technology* 32 (2): 163–79.

Schmidt, K. 2002. "The problem with 'awareness': Introductory remarks on 'awareness in CSCW.' " *Computer Supported Cooperative Work* 11 (3–4): 285–98.

Schmidt, K., and Randall, D. 2016. "Preface to the special issue on 'Reconsidering "Awareness" in CSCW.' " *Computer Supported Cooperative Work* 25 (4–5): 229–33.

Sein, M. K., Henfridsson, O., Purao, S., Rossi, M., and Lindgren, R. 2011. "Action design research." *MIS Quarterly* 35 (1): 37–56.

Walsham, G. 2006. "Doing interpretive research." *European Journal of Information Systems* 15 (3): 320–30.

WearIT@Work. n.d. *Emergency Response: A wearIT@work Application Field.* Available at http://cordis.europa.eu/docs/projects/cnect/6/004216/080/publishing/readmore/www-Emergency-Flyer.pdf (accessed October 17, 2017).

Weiser, M. 1999. "The computer for the 21st century." *Mobile Computing and Communications Review* 3 (3): 3–11.

Wulf, V., Müller, C., Pipek, V., Randall, D., Rohde, M., and Stevens, G. 2015. "Practice-based computing: Empirically grounded conceptualizations derived from design case studies." In V. Wulf, K. Schmidt, and D. Randall, eds., *Computer Supported Cooperative Work: Designing Socially Embedded Technologies in the Real-World.* London: Springer-Verlag London, 111–50.

Wulf, V., Rohde, M., Pipek, V., and Stevens, G. 2011. "Engaging with practices: Design case studies as a research framework in CSCW." In *CSCW'11*. New York: ACM, 505–12.

Part IV

Meta-Research

16

Research into Design-Research Practices

Supporting an Agenda toward Self-Reflectivity and Transferability

DAVE RANDALL, TOBIAS DYRKS, BERNHARD NETT, VOLKMAR PIPEK, LEONARDO RAMIREZ, GUNNAR STEVENS, INA WAGNER, AND VOLKER WULF

16.1 Introduction

In the introduction to this book, the view was expressed that any "practice-based" approach to computing would necessarily entail reflection about whose practices we might be concerned with. It is one thing to examine the practices of a group of workers or indeed any other group of people engaged in certain practices that we feel might require empirical analysis to ground design—if computing is to be improved. It is equally true that any such examination requires us to investigate to the same extent the ways in which organizations manage IT design in practice. In particular, as design researchers we should be examining our own practices.

A practice-based research approach is based on case studies that are shaped by the particularity of the individual field of application, as well as by the specific design (research) team. While the individual cases are particular, an overall research agenda should document these cases to allow for a comparative analysis (e.g., see Chapter 1). To this end, we suggest introducing a specific genre of empirical studies to investigate the particularities of individual design case studies that typically follow project organization. In a practice-based research paradigm, such a genre of study should

Socio-Informatics, Volker Wulf, Volkmar Pipek, Dave Randall, Markus Rohde, Kjeld Schmidt, Gunnar Stevens (Eds). Published 2018 by Oxford University Press.

- encourage the reflexivity of IT designers and contribute to the improvement of a particular design (research) team's practices,
- document the particular setting of individual design cases, thus fostering the transferability of design-relevant insights across different settings, and
- be fundamental to the building tools of to support a practice-based design paradigm (e.g., the ePortfolio; see Chapter 1).

Moreover, as any intervention into social practices may be confronted with the question of its legitimacy, research into the design practices of individual projects may offer an empirical basis for both reflexivity and normative discourses.

Empirical investigation can deal with many different aspects of a design (research) project and can apply various methods. At the University of Siegen, for instance, research projects typically follow the grounded-design paradigm. These projects are mostly funded by public sources and follow a specific (Central) European approach to the institutionalization of research. The European Commission, the German Federal Government, and other government agencies at the German state level try to foster IT-induced social innovation by funding research projects in which academia, IT industries, and, often, application partners submit joint proposals in a competitive manner. In case of success, research is often conducted in consortia of partners representing different interests and perspectives. These funding schemes are quite distinct from the institutionalization that is required, for instance, to apply for funding from the National Science Foundation in the United States. These schemes try to incentivize IT-induced innovations that tackle societal problems. In principle, they can facilitate practice-based design research, but in practice, they can lead to a complex institutionalizations of research that requires critical reflection on the research practices that they result in (see Dachtera et al. 2014).

The aim of this chapter is to outline a research agenda. We have termed this "meta-research into practice-based computing" and use our own work to exemplify elements of it. Such an agenda requires coherent framing and needs to be conducted in sufficient breadth and depth. We are still evolving this research agenda. Our first step was to introduce a distinction between levels on which investigations into practice-based design research might be positioned. Consortia settings may vary in terms of the number of participating partners and the heterogeneity of interests and perspectives. In any case, design research needs to bridge the different practices of the participating IT professionals, whether they are from academia or from IT industries. Moreover, there is a need for techniques to be developed to align with the social practices to be supported in the fields of application. The kind of meta-research we propose can focus on different entities:

1. *A design case study that is conducted by a research consortium:* We have started to investigate the emerging practices of IT professionals in different design case studies using an ethnographic approach. Methodologically, we suggest ethnographical investigations into the design practices of specific research projects. Some studies of this kind already exist. Dachtera et al. (2014) for instance, examined the

cooperation between academic, application, and industry partners during participatory-design activities in the firefighting domain. Wan et al. (2016) conducted a similar study looking at a project in which a GPS tracker was designed for elderly dementia patients suffering from "wandering syndrome."

2. *A research group that runs different practice-based design projects in parallel over a longer period of time*: Some of the authors of this chapter have begun an ethnographic study of the research practices of our own group (WiNeMe). To extend these insights, we follow up by looking specifically at the subgroup working on IT for the aging society. We are particularly interested in patterns of knowledge sharing and cooperation, as well as the use of IT tools. As a result of the internal presentation of the empirical findings of this study, a workshop process was set up to deal with critical issues that had not been visible before. The results of this project, it is argued, should ground the design of IT tools in supporting recurrent research practices (e.g., the ePortfolio; see Chapter 1).
3. *Commercial companies that work on design projects from a practice-based angle (IT industries as well as application partners)*: When Nett et al. (2008) conducted action research to understand user-centered development practices at a particular software company, they found that the company had, for various reasons, difficulties in incorporating user perspectives into the design process. To analyze these difficulties, the authors used the conceptual lens of transferring, translating, and transforming knowledge across boundaries and concluded by suggesting that one should distinguish between user-centered design as an espoused theory (which has become quite popular in recent years), and user-centered design in practice. Providing practitioners with a blueprint for the "right" method was judged to be insufficient. Instead, one has to take their given constraints and work practices seriously in developing a solution that fits the context (Stevens et al. 2009).
4. *A practice-based academic IT design community*: Initial investigations have begun into the practices of our two international reference communities, the European Society of Socially Embedded Technologies (EUSSET) and ACM SIG-CHI. One of our researchers has observed program-committee meetings and interviewed senior members of these academic communities. Here again, opportunities for IT support were a key issue. The redesign of the EUSSET Web site and its digital library were based on elements of the empirical findings.

In the field of human-centered computing, the research program outlined here is quite novel—to the best of our knowledge. Post-disciplinary research, whether within a project, a research group, a business organization, or an academic community, depends on and deals with a complex constellation of interests, motivations, and historically grown practices. We need to understand these design activities better—and also to support them better. A corresponding research program needs to be outlined in more detail.

This is done in three steps. First, we present some of the driving forces behind "post-normal" interdisciplinary science carried out in research consortia, as well as our methodological approach to performing ethnographies on research projects. We then describe two examples of meta-research performed by the Siegen group. Finally, the concluding part of this chapter highlights the main insights from these projects, outlining a more detailed research agenda.

16.2 The State of the Art

Our research agenda reflects a historic development in the ways research has been practiced and theorized. It is influenced by a set of concepts and approaches that emerged as a result of this debate. While the research programs that inspire our approach range from social studies of science (e.g., science and technology studies [STS]), to action research and participatory design, to newer developments in the field of human–computer interaction (HCI), the notion of practice and a commitment to ethnographic studies of practices are key to our approach. In the field of design, the notion of "reflective practice," which is associated with the writings of John Dewey and Donald Schön, is of particular relevance (see Chapter 1).

16.2.1 New Forms of Research Collaboration

Some time ago, it was recognized that the production of scientific knowledge was undergoing a structural change—one that involved stronger participation by nonacademic social actors, with a consequent focus on knowledge production as contributing to socially relevant problems (Funtowicz and Ravetz 1993; Gibbons et al. 1994). In passing, we should acknowledge that the direction of this change was not endorsed by some, nor was it always accepted that it was, in fact, taking place. It was suggested that this "scientification" of society and its correlate, the "politicization of science" (Weingart 1997), might lead to increasing populism and commercialization and might possibly culminate in the erosion of scientific reliability and "neutrality." The increasing demand for practical relevance in research has also stimulated a discourse about the commercialization of research, and the role of the university as a business actor in the knowledge society (e.g., Slaughter and Leslie 1997; Carrier and Nordmann 2011). Authors such as these investigate the consequences that arise from the increasing pressure for practically relevant results for different disciplines. Often, these contributors adopt a critical approach toward the demands placed on science.

Regardless, Weingart (1997) explains these changes in the role of science in society as follows:

> The university has lost its monopoly on knowledge production. Research centers, government agencies, industrial laboratories, think-tanks, consulting firms are also producing new knowledge. Through their interrelations in networks, contexts are created which replace the traditional disciplines.... Knowledge production becomes socially accountable and reflexive. Research comes under new pressures of legitimation. (Weingart 1997, p. 596)

This new mode of involving social actors in scientific knowledge production, also referred to as "Mode 2" (Weingart 1997; Bartunek 2011), offers new opportunities for transdisciplinary research; these are understood as representing an attempt to go beyond interdisciplinary collaboration among disciplines to develop approaches that transcend not only the different academic disciplines but also the different interests of commercial, academic, and other partners, thereby providing a foundation for solutions to socially relevant problems (Pohl and Hirsch Hadorn 2007; Hirsch Hadorn et al. 2008).

The different ways in which scientific research is "contextualized" (Nowotny et al. 2001) is one of the main focuses of STS. On the one hand, ethnomethodologists have produced close descriptions of scientists' shop work, revealing the local, situated rationalities of everyday scientific practice (e.g., Lynch, 1993), while on the other the famous "Laboratory Studies" (Latour and Woolgar 1979; Knorr-Cetina 1981) also focused on how science was practiced in the laboratory. Among other things, these studies demonstrated that the world of science "is rife with political passions, contestations of power, ever-changing definitions of logic and proof" (Doing 2008, p. 286). Other STS researchers looked at the kind of "consortium research" we are interested in. For example, Michel Callon, one of the founders of actor–network theory, carried out a study on a French electric car project from 1960 to 1977. In "*L'État face à l'innovation technique: le cas du véhicule électrique*" (Callon Michel 1979), he describes how the different actors (the most powerful among them being EDF, Renault, and the state) shaped the research agenda of the electric car. While these (and other) studies focused on the collaborative nature of research and its framing by networks of researchers, funding agencies, industrial partners, and so on, there was also an "engaged program" of STS (Sismondo 2008) that promoted the social responsibility of science. On a practical–political level, this engagement, which also went under the label "democratization of science," was reflected in various initiatives. Among these were consensus conferences, the first of which was held in Denmark, and so-called science shops, which provided technical advice to citizens, associations, and nonprofit organizations and also carried out small-scale research projects. Reflecting on steps toward bringing science into the "public arena," making it more democratic, Callon (1999) stated:

> Since science produced in laboratories is at best incomplete, at worst unrealistic and, in any event, incapable of accounting for the complexity of the specific problems to which it is applied, it is advisable to open the forum for discussion and deliberation so as to create the conditions of its enrichment. (Callon 1999, p. 86)

For several reasons, such endeavors have become much more common in design-oriented research cooperatives. Some research methodologies postulate the need for cooperation with practitioners during the evaluation of innovative artifacts to address stakeholder-relevant problems (Hevner et al. 2004; Otto and Österle 2010; Wulf et al. 2011, 2015; Rohde et al. 2017). The explicit aim of early Scandinavian participatory design was to foster workplace democracy by involving workers in learning about new technologies and participating in their design (see Chapter 7). Furthermore, as a precondition for the approval of joint research projects, specifically in Europe, publicly funded research typically requires the involvement of entrepreneurs, end users, or experts of a specific social domain to ensure application-oriented results through the emergence of innovative products or services (Laudel 2006; The Federal Ministry of Education and Research 2009; EU 2013).

Even so, and intertwined with the changes in funding policies, a problem-solving perspective on scientific knowledge production has arguably become more prevalent in the research discourses and methodologies of several scientific disciplines (Van De Ven 2007; Mathiassen and Nielsen 2008). The emergence of a "relevance gap," or a need to identify and tackle practice-relevant problems, was promptly diagnosed in several disciplines (Rosemann and Vessey 2008). For information systems research, the "relevance gap" translates into research on how specific nonacademic stakeholders can be involved in design activities and the evaluation of design artifacts (Rohde et al. 2009; Otto and Österle 2010).

Nevertheless, we argue that analytic approaches to research activity have thus far paid too little attention to the problems of interorganizational collaboration, having typically focused on disciplinary perspectives and their internal mechanisms of stabilization. In these latter studies, socialization into a research community goes hand in hand with the acquisition of a certain world view and way of life (Stichweh 1992). Weingart (1997) looks specifically at interdisciplinary research and distinguishes between the level of the funding agencies' rhetoric and the level of actual research work. He finds that on the rhetoric level, interdisciplinarity is discursively connected with dynamics, flexibility, and liberality, while the level of actual interdisciplinary research as yet remains only an ambition. That is, interdisciplinary collaboration may be challenging in a variety of ways, although we currently have relatively little empirical evidence to demonstrate how, in practice, outcomes are realized. There are some exceptions. In an empirical study, Mansilla et al. (2015) found that "shared socio-emotional-cognitive platforms" decisively contribute to the success of interdisciplinary synthesis. In a similar vein, McCallin and Bamford (2007), in a grounded-theoretical study, highlight the importance of emotional intelligence in interdisciplinary teamwork. There is, nonetheless, a pressing need for a "practice" orientation to the processes of interdisciplinary enquiry.

16.2.2 Why "Meta-Research" into "Practice-Based Computing"?

Two methodological problems make a reflexive practice-based approach attractive. The first is that many engineering conceptions are focusing more on the application of formalistic knowledge to known products, rather than on the analysis of applied solutions for individual cases. This partly has to do with the established form of industrial technology development. However, the historical relation between engineering and mass production has become threatened by mass customization on the one hand and the rise of the "information economy" on another. The invention of "software" has made value enhancement by the individualization of products much easier and thus has motivated business concepts in which such individualization plays a larger role. A substantial part of commercial software development is about custom-built products, which are poorly supported by (mass-production) engineering conceptions.

A second motivation for conducting reflexive project ethnographies is that assessment of the value of technology products is often conducted by stakeholders with heterogeneous expertise. This complicated problem is scarcely solved by naive consensus building, since unexpected inputs can dramatically affect one's plans (see Fischer and Giaccardi 2006; Stevens and Nett 2009).

A more recent proposal, emanating from the fields of computer-supported cooperative work (CSCW) and HCI, comes from Jackson et al. (2013), who have suggested that science policy should build on the manifold experiences and insights from the discourse on "cyberinfrastructure" within CSCW. They argue that as "we are likely to see interdisciplinary and translational mechanisms and mandates expand," research will in the future "need many of the things that cyberinfrastructure promises to deliver—collaboration, interdisciplinarity, larger and multiple perspectives on problems of public import, etc." (Jackson et al. 2013, p. 1118). Publications in this tradition, as well as in the areas of e-research and e-science, have particularly emphasized the human aspects of "infrastructuring" as an activity in collaborative research work (Lee et al. 2006; Pipek and Wulf 2009; Barkhuus and Brown 2012). These studies have deployed a practice-oriented perspective on the research activities of different scientific fields.

The need for such a "meta-analytic" view is arguably becoming more pressing as our vambitions in respect of the analysis of practice develop. For instance, it is evident in the abovementioned interest in sociotechnical infrastructures and, closely related to it, our interest in the ebb and flow of relations inherent in technological development, organizational and infrastructural change, and work practice (e.g., Lee et al. 2006; Ribes 2014). Given that the outcomes associated with design are inevitably uncertain, it makes sense that some investigation of the processes in and through which design outcomes are arrived at should take place and that empirical materials concerning those different outcomes might be a source of material for our reflections. However, it remains the case that such enquiries remain, at the time of writing, relatively unusual (but see Dachtera et al. 2014). We need, we would argue, empirical knowledge to inform how the claim of cooperation can be concretely operationalized in research (Rosemann and Vessey 2008; Österle and Otto 2010). Particularly for the practice-oriented approach presented in this book, the analysis of adequate collaborative project cases can help researchers focus on critical moments of the process, which are significant for building a profound knowledge base from design studies (Krohn 2008). This implies, of course, an appeal to a certain kind of reflexivity, and this bears some examination.

16.2.3 The Notion of "Reflective Practice"

As stated before, the notion of "reflective practice" goes back to John Dewey, who considered reflection to be essential to the development of practices. Dewey defined reflective thinking as a number of phases in thinking: "(a) a state of perplexity, hesitation, doubt; and (b) an act of search or investigation directed toward bringing to light further facts which serve to corroborate or to nullify the suggested belief" (Dewey 1910, p. 9). Schön (1983) took up this notion, using it in describing design as a reflective process, with designers engaging in two modes of reflection: while performing and evaluating a particular design move ("reflection in action") and when looking back at a project, evaluating the approach s/he has taken ("reflection on action"). Both Dewey and Schön focused on the individual designer and, at the time, did not think of the complex constellations of research and design today.

Reflexivity has become a much used, and much abused, term that is often associated with sociological output. However, it can imply a number of different things. It implies some interrogation of the concepts and theories one deploys, and one's reasons for doing so; some critical reflection on one's behavior in relation to the people one studies; a degree of self-awareness; and an awareness of the institutional forms that construct one's thinking. As indicated at various points throughout this book, however, a concern for sociological concepts and theories is not part of our project here. Rather, we are interested in the way in which a specific project produces certain outcomes, the way in which these outcomes are managed and negotiated, how partners in projects might learn from such examinations, and how we might make a more generic sense of, and document, the organizational processes that influence these outcomes.

Reflection is one of the cornerstones of action research. Action research is a framework for inquiry that "seeks to bring together action and reflection, theory and practice, in participation with others, in the pursuit of practical solutions to issues of pressing concern to people" (Bradbury and Reason 2001, p. 1). While not design oriented as such, it postulates a strong link between inquiry and action and "the credibility and validity of [action research] knowledge is measured to a large degree by the 'workability' of solutions—that is, their ability to address real problems in the lives of the participants" (Hayes 2011, p. 158). One of the aims of action research is to make the research part more participatory. Reaching mutual understanding in such a process requires a high degree of reflexivity—to reflect on one's own positions, on the research situation, and on the research process. Bergold and Thomas (2012) suggest several types of reflection: reflection on participants' "personal and biographical attributes and dispositions," reflection on the social relationships between partners, "structural reflection on the social field of the research project," and reflection on the research process itself (Bergold and Thomas 2012, p. 205 f.) In this tradition, Bjørn and Boulus demonstrate how "reflection on our own assumptions, thoughts, and beliefs" (Bjørn and Boulus 2011, p. 283) in two ethnographic studies in the field of healthcare, as well as on "the work that went into constructing the project, making it function as a coherent whole" (Bjørn and Boulus 2011, p. 285), provided an important opportunity for learning. There was a reflection "ex post" when they came together to conduct a conversation about their projects, challenging each other's views.

Participatory design also advocates reflection as an important principle. For example, Bødker and Iversen state that "professionalism is dependent on an ongoing reflection and off-loop reflection among practitioners in the [participatory design] process" (Bødker and Iversen 2002, p. 11). However, there are few examples of more in-depth studies of participatory-design practitioners systematically reflecting on their practices. This does not mean that the practice of participatory design is "unreflective"—there are fine examples of participatory-design practitioners critically examining their practices, as for example, that by Winschiers-Theophilus et al. (2010), who analyzed some of the problems they encountered when working with communities in Namibia. While these personal reflections of a research team are valuable, they are selective and partial. For example, Bratteteig and Wagner (2014, 2016) went back to several of their own participatory-design projects, attempting to reconstruct the important moments in the design process.

Revisiting project diaries and other documents helped them piece together the stories of these different projects, including moments of conflict in the project teams. Even so, their analysis is limited to what they were able to reconstruct from their own perspective (and with a view to decision-making) on the design ideas that were put forward and how some of them were selected and further developed.

One exception is the work of Pedersen (2007), who, referring to his own participatory-design project in the area of maintenance work, critically examined his (and his coresearcher's) efforts at making this work "public" and "demonstrating promising results" to the participating stakeholders. For example, he describes how the fieldwork itself had to be formatted for different uses, and the constraints of having to avoid conflict with the people under study. In his analysis, which is influenced by actor–network theory literature, he suggests a distinction between "representatives" and "constituencies," arguing that partners in a design project not only bring their own knowledge and commitments into a project but are also accountable to the communities to which they belong.

CSCW researchers have studied how designers, including IT professionals, work. But these studies do not necessarily look inside large and complex projects with multiple stakeholders. Again, an exception here is an ethnographic study by Martin et al. (2009) of the introduction of electronic patient records within all hospitals of the National Health Service in England and Wales. They, for example, point at the difficulty of understanding the work practices of all the different user groups and taking account of them, how healthcare policies set targets the project could not afford to fail, and how a myriad of organizational issues made it difficult to coordinate work. While, in some respects, these studies come close to what we think doing ethnography on projects is or should be, their aim is not necessarily to feed observations back into the project team in order to help them improve their practices and build a corpus of knowledge with a view not only into a particular research group but the whole community of practice-based research.

16.2.4 Doing Ethnography on Projects: The Approach

The first, and perhaps most obvious, complication to deal with is how best to conceptualize the relationship between observation of practice and subsequent design interventions. As Dourish (2006) has argued, the idea that there is, or can be, any direct and determinate relationship between the two is an oversimplification, to say the least. First, and most clearly, observations of practice cannot eliminate all the various possibilities that are inherent in design decisions. There are cost–benefit considerations that implicate, at best, estimates concerning the future. There are decisions to be made concerning the generic applicability of new technologies across settings (or domains), about the degree of modularity that might be required, or about the limits to be placed on deployment. There are constellations of interests, ethics, and commitment to be considered. As Schmidt has pointed out, when discussing the impact of ethnography for CSCW, the term "shared goals" in respect of project outcomes is somewhat misleading: "the 'shared goal' is not there in advance. It is constructed by the members in the course of the project, and it is in the course of agreeing to a 'shared goal' that the designers arrive at an agreed-to design.

When the designers "have a 'shared goal' they have—for all practical purposes—finished the design task" (Schmidt 2011, p. 151 f.). Schmidt goes on, citing Bucciarelli (1988), to argue that "a design decision in this instance is best seen as an overlay of interests rather than their synthesis within some flat, cognitive domain" (Bucciarelli 1988, p. 164). This is exactly the reason why documenting design decisions, who contributed to them, how priorities were set, which kinds of resources were available, and so on, is crucial for an understanding of design practices and why a particular design result has been achieved (Bratteteig and Wagner 2016).

Gaver and Bowers have put forward the idea of creating "annotated portfolios" that bring together design artifacts "as a systematic body of work," with annotations capturing "family resemblances between designs in a mesh of similarities and differences" (Gaver and Bowers 2012, p. 46). Through this work, they seek to identify "conceptual schemes" that may lend themselves to some generalization. Our approach is different, insofar as we aim to investigate the practices of our own community in line with the practice-based perspective rehearsed throughout this book, and, perhaps most importantly, do not see this as something that is done after the serious business of design is finished but as something that should take place simultaneously with the design process. It is, put simply, constituted as an ongoing reflection about what we do and how we do it. The need for this is reflected in the fact that a community dedicated toward analyzing and supporting practices has, to date, provided very few empirical accounts of their own research practices (but see Dachtera et al. 2014). It would be naive in the extreme to imagine that the move toward any kind of model of heterogeneous collaboration comes without challenges, and empirical work ought to reveal something of what those challenges look like. It is to be hoped that, eventually, such accounts of research and development practice might serve both to design supporting IT artifacts and to inform research policy.

It makes sense to think of these aims in terms of organizational (or rather interorganizational) learning (Argyris and Schön 1996) and, more specifically, second-loop learning (Argyris et al. 1985). As such, it would have something in common with organization and technology development, as first suggested by Wulf and Rohde (1995), but with a more explicit ethnographic focus, one that addresses the meaning of a project for the participants. Institutional ethnography (e.g., Smith 2006) is one approach to organizational learning that "encompasses participant observation…and an encouragement of people to 'tell their story'" (Bell and Morse 2007, p. 100).

We also may take inspiration for doing ethnographies of projects from recent work in other fields, such as sustainable development, or in large-scale interventions in third-world countries. Looking back at a project about implementing community interventions for HIV prevention, Evans and Lambert (2008) make a distinction between a project's internal documentation, and the donor agencies' insistence on ordering and systematizing practice by creating models, manuals, and guidelines. This represents two aspects of what we call "public accounts of practice" (Evans and Lambert 2008, p. 475) and "insider accounts" that are written to understand the more subtle aspects of project collaborations. The authors use ethnographic material from one particular intervention project in India to demonstrate that "observation of actual intervention practices can reveal insights that may be hard for project staff to articulate or difficult to pinpoint…and can highlight important points of divergence and convergence from intervention theory or planning documents" (Evans and Lambert 2008, p. 477).

Pottier (1993) reflects on the possibilities of "project appraisal through ethnography" to improve the management of development projects. He makes his case by referring, among other things, to a study by Moris and Hatfield (1982), who demonstrated how a project introducing Western technology clashed with the pastoralism of the Maasai. An important argument for doing ethnography on projects is made by Mosse (2007), who examines how expertise is constructed in international development. He argues that project work in development is driven by "global policies," which he characterizes as "'travelling rationalities' with general applicability that assert the technical over the political, the formal over the substantive…, the categorical over the relational" (Mosse 2007, p. 4). Mosse suggests conducting ethnographies of how development work is practiced in different contexts by different types of experts in collaboration with local participants—work that, in some respects, may be considered similar to an IT R & D project. While the idea of "meta-research into practice-based computing" is about learning across projects for future work, project ethnographies in international development seem more intended to deconstruct the dominance of "global policies" that do not sufficiently take account of local practices.

When we examine what can be learned from different approaches to doing ethnographies of projects in different contexts, three points stand out:

- the issue of "positionality" that action research addresses: from whose perspective are these ethnographies written, as reflected in the differences and potential tensions between "insider accounts" and accounts by an external observer?
- the "focus" on data collection: is it on the actual practices of collaborative design as they unfold in everyday project work or are these observed with a particular lens onto, for example, decision-making, situations of conflict, how these are handled, and with which result?
- the main objectives of such studies: is it to improve collaboration in a particular project, to learn across projects, to develop guidelines, an analytical framework, and so on?

The meta-research program outlined in the introductory remarks of this chapter is quite comprehensive. However, so far we have elaborated only on a small part of the themes brought up there (Dachtera et al. 2014; Wan et al. 2016). In the following, we want to clarify the research program, with examples.

We first examine the Landmarke project in detail, focusing on the way in which a successful design outcome is reached and what kinds of activity produce that outcome. Here, the role of experience, communication across professional boundaries, and an explicit focus on the exchange of ideas is apparent. Then we investigate the collaborative practices of WiNeMe, a research group conducting projects that follow the practice-based research paradigm of grounded design. Yet another under-rehearsed aspect of meta-research is to understand research groups, specifically, the roles of collaboration, knowledge sharing, and their interactions with a wider academic community.

16.3 Ethnographies of Design Case Studies and Projects

We want to start by outlining a methodological framework to investigate specific design (research) case studies and projects. This framework is inspired by an approach called business ethnography (Nett and Stevens 2008; Nett 2010). Ethnographies of IT projects do not refer to any specific set of commitments but can be understood as reflexive activity within design case studies, as discussed in Section 16.2.4. The reflexive ethnographer needs (and generally has) some practical understanding of what the project in question is about and what role he/she is undertaking. While the role of the ethnographer as producer of data about, and communication of, practitioner practices in interdisciplinary work is by now (at least arguably) well understood, his/her potential role as a communicator of data about practices within a given project is not. To undertake such an activity, of course, requires explicit commitment from partners, and a clear understanding of the meta-process involved and its implications.

While, from an analytical point of view, development and documentation have to be separated, this is not done ex ante in project ethnography. Instead, the project ethnographer acts as a project partner who, at the same time, continues to communicate and discuss his/her role throughout. In doing so, he/she opens his/her own separation of development and documentation to critique from the project partners. The project ethnographer may even take a position on his/her own, but this must be done transparently, with the reasons documented and an analysis provided of how this conflicts with the task of mediation (Alexander et al. 2006) and how the reactions of project partners might be negotiated. As such, an ethnography of an IT design project can be thought of as a form of action research. The concept of action research was first developed by the psychologist and field theoretician Kurt Lewin 1946, who was critical of the ignorance in his discipline of its own sociohistorical framing. Instead of reflecting on its impact on the understanding of the task to be accomplished, psychology would simply focus on the impact of the individual psyche on society, thus reducing the interplay between the individual mind and its sociohistorical conditions to unidirectional causation. In order to contrast his action research against mainstream psychology, Lewin borrowed overtly interventionist terms (from medicine) to describe a process that starts with the examination of the status quo ("diagnosis"), continues with the identification of a change strategy ("treatment"), and is studied in the "evaluation" of the intervention's impact upon the situation. The evaluation can become a new "diagnosis," and the process repeated. Action research was thus essentially critical, especially of disciplinary assumptions, if they limited the space for solutions to be considered.

While Lewin has been credited as having been one of the founders of action research, a similar approach was developed at the Tavistock Institute (Emery and Trist 1969). It was in the perspective of achieving social change and therapeutic action that the method was suggested and probed, starting with a "diagnostic stage," which included a collaborative analysis of the social situation by the researcher and the subjects of research. The "therapeutic stage" involved collaborative change experiments. Moreover, although members of the target community were considered important collaborators from the beginning, in early action research, the researcher remained in control of the scientific investigation itself, directing the research design, the definition of key concepts and variables, data collection and analysis, and the interpretation of results. Various forms of action research have been developed in different disciplines such as social science (Moser 1980), organizational development, pedagogics (Moser 1978, 1980; Kemmis and McTaggart 1988; Altrichter and Posch 1990), and humanities (Bortz and Döring 2002). It was also—and this is central to the need for an ethnography of project processes—transdisciplinary. Thus, it sought precisely to overcome the limitations of disciplinary thinking (and, at least by implication, other sources of heterogeneity [see Davison et al. 2004]) and to refocus disciplinary approaches from a more general perspective. In effect, this necessitates a move from a conception of ethnographic work as observational in its early stages, and interventionist in some (still rather undecided) sense, to a conception that sees observation and intervention as closely tied together. The intervention, equally, will be rather more than simply providing some kind of support to design decision-making but will entail assistance in the management of its evolution. Again, it is necessary to recognize the fact that project practices are underdetermined by formal organizational roles and initial estimates of how the division of labor is constituted.

16.4 Critical Moments: Understanding Collaborative Exchanges within an IT Design Project

We exemplify our argument by investigating the practice of design research in the Landmarke project, which is described in Chapter 15. Here, however, our focus is on research processes rather than research outcomes.

The Landmarke project, involving collaboration between researchers at the University of Siegen and a consortium including practitioners, industries, and domain-specific experts, was concerned with the work of firefighting. In total, it involved collaboration between nine different partners:

1. The University of Siegen Department of Information Systems, which coordinated the project
2. The Fraunhofer Institute for Applied Information Technology
3. A research institute focusing on mobile sensor networks and ubiquitous computing
4. A research institute focusing on manufacturing science and rapid prototyping
5. A small-enterprise business specializing in technical systems for logistics support
6. A small-enterprise business area specializing in wearable electronics
7. A large-enterprise business providing protective equipment for firefighters
8. The Cologne professional fire service, which attends 55,000 incidents per year
9. The firefighting training institution in Münster, the Institut der Feuerwehr Nordrhein–Westfalen (IDF), which has 15,000 students per year

The observations we make in this chapter about the working of the research project are founded on 60 hours of audio and video recordings, a personal research diary, and two series of interviews with actors in the consortium. The first series was conducted in project workshops between 2008 and 2011. The interviews provide access to the inner workings of workshops in which actors from a wide range of professional backgrounds and including academic researchers, practitioners, and entrepreneurs from both small and large companies participated. Here, we are particularly interested in what we will call "critical moments" in the collaboration among partners, as these seem to be critical in identifying and developing technical innovations with the intention of producing significant practical benefits for a specific social domain. An analysis of these "critical moments" shed some light on how we might bridge the "relevance gap" (Hodgkinson and Rousseau 2009; Kieser and Leiner 2009) and how we could improve grounded design from an interactional perspective.

The Landmarke project was predicated on what is assumed to be a critical need in the work of firefighters: to need to perform a reliable assessment of an incident in a timely fashion. This is, for fairly obvious reasons, particularly crucial during indoor reconnaissance missions (see, e.g., Ramirez et al. 2007; Denef et al. 2008; Ramirez et al. 2012). "Getting lost" on a mission inside an unknown building is one of the most frequent causes of accidents in firefighting (Fahy 2002). The project we discuss here leveraged the idea of an ad-hoc reference system that would be laid down during the firefighting itself. The envisaged system involved a mesh of small deployable tokens that, once dropped, worked as reference points to support the spatial decision processes of firefighters, creating a rich layer of information (Ramirez et al. 2012). Tokens might communicate with each other or with the firefighters. Analysis of work practices thus focused on the identification and definition of problems relevant to the reconnaissance work of firefighters, the invention of possible improvements through the design of artifacts, and the evaluation of their possible benefits and any difficulties to be addressed.

In this section, however, we focus on the collaboration within the research consortia and on the themes that emerged among participating actors. In so doing, we examine the dialogic processes that led to an emerging understanding of the various issues that underpinned the research, the agreements and disagreements that reflected distinct interests and understandings, and the resulting changes in project direction. As Table 16.1 shows, these issues became salient during the conduct of various collaborative activities.

As Table 16.1 shows, four generic types of collaboration activities were identified as being predominant in the project between 2008 and 2011. Even though this analysis is rather sketchy and incomplete, it facilitates a focus on collaborative activities, explaining how the designs of technical artifacts emerge from un(der?) specified ideas and how design decisions are linked to the analysis of firefighting work practice.

16.4.1 Dialogs and Discussions

After identifying the activities being carried out by the principal actors, analysis focused on the contents of the various dialogs emerging in the conduct of those

Table 16.1 Collaborative activities in the Landmarke project

Activities in Collaboration	Examples	
Administration and planning	Negotiation of roles Coordination and planning of subsidiary tasks among technical developers Budget planning for purchasing technical equipment Negotiating a common understanding of public relations work	Bilateral meetings and multilateral workshops Conference calls Email
Explaining firefighting work, including practical demonstrations	Conducting firefighting exercises to demonstrate current work practices and tactics with regard to reconnaissance in danger zones and extensive areas Recounting anecdotes with in-depth descriptions of personal experiences gathered in real firefighting missions "Empathic workshops": professional firefighters guide scientists and industrial partners in simplified firefighting exercises as a means to presenting a first-person perspective on their work (Dyrks et al. 2009)	Workshops at the IDF training center Bilateral and multilateral meetings at the Cologne professional fire service as well as at the IDF training center
Technical development of the Landmarke platform	Specification of user and system requirements, using agile approaches Specification of system interfaces, protocols, and system behavior	Email Chat clients Microsoft Word documents
Collaborative research, "dialog process"	Joint preparation and observation of experiments of Landmarke components in specially designed firefighting exercises Joint analysis of experiments using Landmarke components with consideration of various observers with contrasting perspectives (e.g., mission leader vs. members of different reconnaissance teams vs. outside observers)	Workshops at the IDF training center Bilateral and multilateral meetings at the Cologne professional fire service, and the IDF training center

activities. Table 16.2 provides a list of identified topics. We discuss three of them in this section.

The first topic identified was the question of technical and tactical feasibility. Discussions on technical feasibility explored the "opportunity space" of design ideas and whether concepts were technically feasible for implementation. Restrictions to the feasibility of designs could arise from limitations of the technology platform chosen in the beginning of the project (with the platform consisting of specific hardware and software components). A good example of one restriction was the limitation on the wireless range between two tokens;

Table 16.2 Topics addressed in the Landmarke dialog during Project months 1 to 36

Project Months	Topics	Actors Involved	Remarks
4–30	Technical feasibility of design ideas with regard to restrictions of the technology platform chosen at the beginning of the project	Industrial partners Scientists	Considered in 60% of the workshops Became clear in the course of the technical development process, in particular concerning problems with hardware platforms selected to become the technology basis for the project
3–18	Tactical feasibility of Landmarke-based reconnaissance tactics with regard to tactical firefighting procedures and obligatory safety regulations	Firefighting working group (actors from the Cologne professional fire service and from IDF) Scientists	Considered in all workshops Assessments on this aspect might be supported by a large number of experiments with experience prototypes
1–24	Good working practice of firefighting Behavior of officers-in-charge when quickly assessing a situation Cooperation of reconnaissance teams working in the danger zone and under limited visibility	In particular, firefighters who frequently act as brokers between the firefighting working group and scientists as well as industrial partners	In particular, the importance of preparation in workshops when experiments and exercises are planned with regard to research objectives and evaluations of Landmarke artifacts Supported by storytelling from individual knowledge from operational experience
10–24	Performance of current firefighting tactics for reconnaissance in terms of accuracy, quickness, and safety	Firefighting working group Scientists	Discussed in 10%–20% of the workshops Supported by experiments specially designed to provoke disorientation
3–30	Economic value of the Landmarke design and estimated development costs	Industrial partners Scientists	Discussed in 30%–40% of the workshops, in particular when discussing hardware designs
10–36	Value of Landmarke in everyday missions and established as obligatory safety equipment	Firefighting working group Scientists	Considered in all workshops
27–36	Further potential of the Landmarke platform beyond navigation support	Some members of the firefighting working group Scientists	The availability of the stable wireless network connection among landmarks in the last quarter of the project duration triggered a reflection on the relevance of communication breakdowns for firefighting practice The "Koordinator" project (2011–14) explored the practical benefit of using landmarks as infrastructure for communication and support (Betz and Wulf 2014; also see Chapter 15)

this arose because of the use of commercial off-the-shelf hardware components. Therefore, a minimum number of tokens required for reliable connectivity had to be taken into account in the theoretical exploration of ideas for reconnaissance tactics based on the tokens.

The second topic consisted of the explanations and reflections around the work practices of professional firefighting and its potential risks. There were two sets of reflections on the work practice: an internal dialog among members of the firefighting practitioners group, characterized by an exchange of knowledge and experience between experts in the topic of firefighting, and a dialog that took place with scientists and industrial partners and that centered on how and why an expert firefighter would likely behave in a certain situation. The internal dialog among firefighters was characterized by assessments of risks and considerations of improvements motivated by changes in the reconnaissance procedures created by the use of the tokens as a means for navigation. Over the course of the project, these dialogs moved from an exchange of opinions toward evaluations of tactical changes informed by experimental exercises conducted in the project.

The third topic area we were able to identify comprised assessments on the value of the emerging technology—the tokens as a navigation tool or as a commercial product. This reflection went beyond viewing the token as a technical artifact and considered it, in the first instance, to be a navigation tool that offered support to its users. In Month 27 of the Landmarke project, however, we found dialogs, which had been initiated by a member of the firefighting working group, about potential uses of the Landmarke platform, where these uses went beyond its use as a navigation support tool (e.g., whether it could help during communication breakdowns by providing a second communication channel during reconnaissance).

16.4.2 Leading and Facilitating Discussions

Workshops were, in the main, hosted at the IDF firefighting training center. As part of these workshops, IDF trainers and lecturers hosted discussions, in particular before and after exercises, experiments, technical evaluations, or training missions were conducted, recapitulated, and analyzed.

The substantial experience of the lecturers in hosting discussions in large groups of people became visible particularly when discussions began to drift into unproductive controversies which hindered a deeper exchange of arguments. Some of the trainers applied different techniques to overcome this kind of situation. For example, as a means of overcoming controversies, some trainers demanded an opinion-forming process from discussion partners via majority decision-making; opinions defeated by the majority were explicitly acknowledged as "important opinions showing aspects not to be forgotten in future work." Questions were raised in order to foster an exchange of opinions, or to focus the discussion on a specific aspect. Professional firefighters as well as IDF trainers recounted anecdotes from their personal experience, illustrating how they experienced critical situations in real incidents; these anecdotes had the effect not only of underpinning opinions by experiences from real life but also of focusing and informing debates on a specific aspect. In addition, trainers supported the negotiation of meaning between the discussion partners as they hosted discussions handling both unexplored and undecided design alternatives. For example at one point, the term "programming" was used by the participants to reflect on the decision as to whether the color shown in a token could be changed by a firefighter team in life-threatening situations (e.g., when firefighters need to act to rescue a person). The subject of the discussion was whether, in this situation, a firefighting team should be able to change the color of a token (which is referred to in the discussion as a "Landmark") in order to leave information for other supporting teams in their reconnaissance:

> Professional firefighter: "A [firefighting] team finds a person and grabs them to take them out. This is now an 'uncritical' situation. But—and I'm willing to bet on this—the team won't *reprogram* the Landmarks."
>
> IDF trainer: "So the team explores the room, and then Landmark Number 4 is reprogrammed to the color green, 'room has been inspected', this is uncritical now. According to our *new terminology*, Landmarks *are not being reprogrammed* anymore, because the information on directions is programmed automatically by the Landmarks as they are removed from the carrying container."
>
> (*Note: The color green on the token represents the tactical information "the room has been checked; nobody is inside." A token showing the color blue at a specific location means "the firefighting team passed this location."*)

By using the expression "new terminology" with the term "programming," the host changed the meaning of "programming" explicitly and thus changed a decision on the design: tokens should not need to be changed manually to blue to indicate that a firefighting team passed the marked location, but they should reprogram themselves to blue when they are removed from the carrying container.

In another case, a trainer used written scenarios to guide a 2-hour discussion that resulted in *a deepening of the discussion,* so that a topic was thoroughly reflected from multiple perspectives. He prepared a 2D floor plan on paper, including markings showing the locations of tokens that had been deployed. The position, color, and number of deployed tokens corresponded to a deployment tactic that had been collaboratively defined in a previous workshop. By *thinking aloud,* the participants were able to explore from an imaginary first-person perspective whether the deployment strategies would work as a systematic approach for any possible cases. The deep reach of the dialog was possible because controversial opinions on feasibility and possible modifications to the deployment tactics had to be justified concretely on the deployment situation described on the floorplans. The discussion produced revised versions of the deployment tactics.

16.4.3 The Role of Emerging Expectations in the Dialog Process

We expanded our analysis by considering the question of how actors produce and react to specific workshop situations. Taking the dual perspective of human actions proposed by Lofland (1995) helped us to understand how the dialog process in Landmarke was shaped over time. The following transcript reveals how eight participants from six different partner institutions exchange ideas on how the components of the platform could be specified and what functionalities would make sense for its intended users.

The data comes from a technical workshop that took place in the sixth month of the project, shortly after the development of a tactical concept by a team of firefighters participating in the project. The concept proposed the use of colored tokens to codify information relevant to supporting collaboration among different firefighter teams performing reconnaissance.

In Month 5 of the project, the tactical concept had been explored practically in a training mission. We should note that the participants in this dialog—"L" and "S," who are from the Fraunhofer Institute for Applied Information Technology, "I," who is from a research institute focusing on manufacturing science and rapid prototyping, and "M," who is from a large-enterprise business providing protective equipment for firefighters—come from industrial/scientific partners and therefore have no background in firefighting.

L: "And how do I choose a color?"

(*This question triggers a rough description of the expected use of the tokens.*)

M: "It is only about activating [tokens]. Just blue."

L: "As default, Landmarks are blue?"

(*The second question is for clarification.*)

M: "Blue is default. [...] This is the requirement: the default setting is what we currently call 'mode blue'. Landmarks only have the function of a beacon. This would be a requirement for the specification."

S: "Right!!"

I: "This means that we always see 'blue' on all [tokens]?"

S: "No, we don't."

M: "We see blue, at least."

L: "So blue codifies the presence of a Landmark?"

S: "Yes."

(*The dialog continues, with further refinement of the anticipated use of the tokens, with the following characteristics: (1) the tokens always carry location-related information, by their presence alone, and (2) this attribution is described as the "blue" mode in the conversation.*)

16.4.4 The Role of Anticipation and Speculation in Dialogs

Such speculative descriptions of the use of technical artifacts were very common in Landmarke workshops. Regardless of whether firefighters were involved or not, anticipation was often used to argue for or against statements. These speculations can be characterized as follows:

- *anticipation was often speculative*: actors in the project expressed views that were frequently speculative descriptions of a specific subject
- *such speculations were sometimes made spontaneously*: when new possibilities were suggested by participants in the course of the conversation in workshops, they seemed to be developed spontaneously as the result of creative thinking and were not always well informed by expert knowledge
- *anticipation and speculation also came from "less expert" sources*: suggestions were often made as a first-person narration, as if one were directly confronted with the situation described in the anticipation (e.g., "the display shows me the number of deployed landmarks") and were made by actors even if those actors were not experts in a related field; hence, the remarks allowed actors to participate in dialogs, even if the actors came from a different professional background
- *suggestions included a context*: anticipatory narrations included the dimensions of time and place and, more importantly, a concrete situation that was used to motivate the idea (e.g., a firefighting team having an accident during reconnaissance, creating the need to guide a rescue team to the incident location); in the case of discussing possibilities of the future use of technical artifacts, these narratives were based on previous experience from real use, even if the artifact was nothing more than a vague idea

Types of Speculation

We were able to identify four types of anticipation of development, based on the subject to which anticipation was related:

1. *Speculations referring to an artifact in use*: We observed suggestions about the technical artifact, including artifacts that were sometimes nothing more than a vague idea. This type of speculation is highly relevant for innovative-oriented project work, because it plays the role of a metaphorical placeholder, storing ideas of characteristics or features that can be modified over time by dialog among partners. The following comment by S, a scientist from the Fraunhofer Institute for Applied Information Technology, on whether the color of tokens should be changed remotely over a wireless connection is an example:

   > The question is whether [the tokens] can be remotely controlled at all. [...] Until now, we have been talking about one change of status only, from yellow to green. [The question is] whether *I can make this change* of status using my remote device, *when the thing is lying in the corner over there.*" (*He points with his hand.*)

2. *Speculations referring to feasibility*: We observed anticipation focused on assessments of technical or tactical feasibility or whether landmark tokens as a technical concept might or could be further developed to a marketable product. For example, see the dialog below, which a continuation of the discussion in which the comment

above was made. In it, S refers to problems with the feasibility of remote color change and articulates the problem of designing an HCI concept that would be usable by firefighters under harsh conditions:

> S: "And therefore we don't need to change the status remotely."
>
> B (*from a research institute focusing on mobile sensor networks and ubiquitous computing*): "But we have a radio connection!"
>
> S: "We need interaction. The problem is interaction in a wearable system, which we would need."

3. *Reflection on work practice, including speculations referring to problems:* Firefighters often reflected on their own experience and speculated on possible problems emerging from confronting dangerous situations. This speculation was strongly based on experience; for example, H, who is a professional firefighter, stated the following:

> There are three [situations] that happen very often. The first is the power is out on the radio device and you've forgotten to bring a spare battery. [...] The second is that you can't get a radio connection to the outside of the building due to its structure, and the third is that somebody is pressing the pushbutton of the radio while they're crawling, and you can hear how they are breathing, but no one else is able to talk on the radio.

4. *Speculations on the relevance of problems*: In the following dialog, a group of participants speculate on the potential for work improvement enabled by using the tokens. The firefighting domain finds this speculation on relevance very difficult because they have to take into account two types of situations: (1) improvements for day-to-day situations being predictable for well-experienced firefighters, and (2) situations that evolve from routine situations into dangerous incidents in which even well-trained firefighters are under threat:

> MS (*from a research institute focusing on mobile sensor networks and ubiquitous computing*): "Think differently. Suppose we are able to produce this added value that we talked about [...]. Then it would be amazing if we could do the same as we do today with the thermal imaging camera. [...] I have a system that could perhaps replace the thermal imaging camera someday."
>
> JH (*from the IDF*): "No, this system will always be worse than the thermal imaging camera. With the thermal imaging camera, I can find people with certainty."

16.4.5 How Suggestions Emerged in Dialogs

Weakly Substantiated or Purely Fictional Suggestions

We classify suggestions as weakly substantiated when it is not plausible to consider them as being based on any robust external reference. They are, thus, highly speculative. They emerge as moments of inspiration and typically spark a dialog, in particular at the beginning of the design process. We classify suggestions as fictional when they describe what could theoretically happen but are grounded neither in informed opinion nor in experiences articulated.

By way of example, in the sixth month of the project, and with no functional artifact yet developed, S, who is not a firefighter but a scientist, anticipated how a firefighter could be faced with a number of tokens already deployed in a building:

> *You could have* a radio connection to the last Landmark. *You could have* a radio connection with the *last one.* [...] Then they go into a room [..] and set the yellow one, go to the next, to the next [and turn it to] green, to the next [and turn it to] green, then they eventually come back and complete this room then.

This anticipation of an artifact in use is rather imprecise and hardly referenced to intersubjective accessible facts that could be verified by the other peers taking part in the dialog. Why a token should be deployed and what the last deployed token should be for are important points that should be determined by a firefighting team. Furthermore, the need for the tokens to be switched to different colors is not explained by S and remains unclear. Later on in this workshop, technical developers shared initial ideas on how the "last token" should be properly visualized on a mobile user interface, even in cases when up to ten tokens would be in range. At that time, the value of the design idea of having a mobile interface had not been discussed with the professional firefighters.

Informed Opinion

In Month 24 of the Landmarke project, an IDF trainer and a professional firefighter had a discussion about what scenarios could be used to provide evidence of whether the designers could modify the Landmarke system could to support more than just navigation during reconnaissance, thus creating added value by providing support for other aspects of delicate operating conditions. In the following, we see one of the exchanges between the IDF trainer JH and T, a professional firefighter with years of operational experience:

> JH: "The second one is a scenario which *has no practical benefit* for the fire service. Because such systems are already available. For example, the system developed by [Company A] provides this..."
>
> (*The conversation pauses for a moment while the men look at the device.*)
>
> T: "[It's a] dead-man's handle!"
>
> (*A dead-man's handle is a small device that can be mounted firmly to the safety equipment and produces noise when a firefighter has not made any movements for a certain span of time, indicating a critical situation.*)

These observations were made on the basis of knowledge held by both participants, knowledge that came from the performance and evaluation of experiments with technology but was confirmed by T, who had extensive experience of firefighting practice. Thus, information from experiments and from real-world experience can provide the basis for an emerging consensus. Incident analyses also prompt reflection. In Month 19 of the project, Firefighter U described a situation he experienced in an incident:

> We checked a floor. The mission was quite normal until we found the burning area, where we found a woman sitting in front of a bed. At this point there was obviously a shift in the mission. To make matters worse, a colleague tried to get the woman out of the building, but he fell down with her sitting on his lap, and hurt himself. Of course the situation changed, they started out quite relaxed, checking every flat, and then all of a sudden there were problems at several locations, and all at once more task forces were required.

Firefighter U then described a possible use for the tokens:

> It *would have been helpful* to have *Landmarks at hand*, because we were withdrawn to support our colleagues and no one knew which areas had already been checked. The smoke spread through open doors because we had to open all the doors that had previously been closed.

This shows a reflection on work practice, with clear implications for the design of the tokens. On the one hand, Firefighter U reflected on his individual experience of being confronted with a critical situation and the lack of information about which apartments had already been checked for people. On the other hand, the narrative implies the value of a technical tool for marking the doors of the apartments already checked by a reconnaissance team. We called such narratives *anticipations modified by reflected experience.*[1] The use of the tokens in this specific mission was fictional (as they were not yet available when the mission took place). However, since it was informed by real-life experience, this anticipation, as a sort of thought experiment, pointed to a clear practical value for the tokens in support of cooperation in reconnaissance missions.

16.4.6 Supporting Arguments in Dialogs

The kinds of anticipation we have referred to play an important role in producing qualitative assessments of the value of technical artifacts in supporting work practices. In the next lengthy example, we see a discussion of the value of providing a remote-control functionality to change the colors of the markings on the tokens; this discussion illustrates the role of anticipated value. The discussion is from a workshop with eight participants from the scientific and industrial partners of the Landmarke project:

> S (*from the Fraunhofer Institute for Applied Information Technology*): "What is your argument for the remote control?"
>
> M (*from a large-enterprise business providing protective equipment for firefighters*): "What can we do with it that we couldn't do before without it?"
>
> I (*from a research institute focusing on manufacturing science and rapid prototyping*): "I no longer need to go to the Landmark."

[1] A sort of "alienation effect" used as a resource to reflect on project work (Stevens and Nett 2009).

S: "You could be connected [by radio] to the last Landmark. You could have a radio connection with the last one. But this is not the case; for example, for the scenarios that we had, the last Landmark is not always the one that got set [to another color]. They enter a room [...], they set a yellow one, go to the next and the next [and turn it to] green, green, until they eventually come back to the first room and they complete this new room ..."

(*S wants to change the color of a specific landmark. He goes on to argue that firefighters may not be able to remember the exact numbers of landmarks as well as the places where firefighters have deployed them in the course of a reconnaissance.*)

S: "Whether they still remember how many they have deployed in this room is rather questionable."

(*Here, then, an argument against remote control is being made. M supports this view.*)

M: "They are not able to remember a number, they don't care. You cannot request a firefighter to shout [speaking loudly] 'I've placed Number 3 at the door, 2 is in the bathroom and over there is something like a gas cooker, that is where 4 is then.'"

S: "It could indeed happen that they do just that."

M: "Oh no!"

S: "When I find [Landmark number] 3 again, I need a reference in my mind, of course it is linked to the surroundings, so that I link the moment now to the moment before. This is important for me!"

M: "That is quite true."

S: "So, knowing the number would help!"

M: "Yes, of course the number helps! But do we want to force them to remember the number? [...]"

L (*from the Fraunhofer Institute for Applied Information Technology*): "It could strongly be recommended to them, but you couldn't force them. We cannot make further assumptions at this point."

(*That is, it is uncertain whether firefighters would remember the numbers and their locations.*)

M: "That's my point!"

S: "But then we cannot operate them remotely."

L: "Unless you could perform actions in some kind of generic way: For example, switching off all landmarks in range."

Although S and M argue against the idea of having a remote control, L utilizes this argument not to disagree with the assumptions but to provide some closure for the discussion by suggesting that remote control might still be a possibility in situations where reliability is less crucial. What we see here is a careful assessment of the feasibility of an idea, done by examining a variety of scenarios in which it might be useful or, conversely, cause problems. The uncertainty about whether firefighters will be able to remember deployment numbers in combination with information about their surroundings leads to the conclusion that the tokens cannot be selected and then changed remotely. L makes the uncertainty explicit (we cannot make further assumptions on the idea of forcing firefighters to remember deployment numbers). It is worth noting that at this point, the discussion partners could have decided to involve the firefighting group on this question but do not. We can assume that their combined experience and knowledge is deemed sufficient for them to examine all realistic possibilities and reach a determination.

16.4.7 Discussion

The rehearsal of the dialog involved in reaching design decisions, and the various interests and experiences that go into the reaching of those decisions, serve to flesh out observations already made about reflexive ethnography. By focusing on deliberations in project workshops, we develop a deeper understanding of how stakeholders in a collaborative project react when confronted with technical artifacts while being involved in design activities informed by analytical reflections on firefighting practice. Our analysis identified several issues as being relevant to the value of anticipation, speculation, and suggestion in informing decisions in the design of technical artifacts. In the case of the Landmarke project, artifacts functioned not only as boundary objects (Star and Griesemer 1989; Stevens 2010) but also as a context from which anticipation, speculation, and suggestion emerged. Such technical "prompts," which have something in common with the PRAXLABS approach discussed in Chapter 10, not only allow for creative thinking (Kensing and Madsen 1991) but also allow for actors to contribute to the construction of meaning for the central concepts that emerge. Coyne and Snodgrass (1995), when considering the role of metaphors in design thinking and in communicating while solving design problems, remarked that

> The emphasis is on design as a collaborative enterprise.... The power of metaphors to define problem regimes suggests a particular approach to design practice. The practitioner does not come to a situation with fixed, pre-defined problem statements, but undertakes an investigation and engages in dialogue through which appropriate metaphors emerge. These metaphors are arrived at by both the practitioner and the client in the specific situation. Problems are presented and addressed through such exchanges and collaborations. (Coyne and Snodgrass 1995, p. 61)

Anticipations in the Landmarke project emerged from creative thinking and were informed by individual experiences from real incidents or by practical evaluations in training missions. They were intersubjectively reflected upon and served as a means to support or reject arguments on the practical value of landmarks. Through observing these anticipations and how they were embedded in the Landmarke dialog, we developed hypotheses that explain how the concept of landmark tokens evolved and, hopefully, provide a more general understanding of how technical artifacts come to be designed. The result of all these interactions represented a form of innovation across professional boundaries (Kimble et al. 2010). In this particular case, reflection on navigation practices conducted in the dialog was extremely complex. Some of the issues that concerned the actors in the consortium were as follows:

- anticipations of problems in real-life reconnaissance missions and in the dynamics of emergency situations, such as how firefighters might respond to specific situations, what tactical considerations are relevant to resolve critical situations, and so on
- assessments on the relevance of problems for work practice, including estimations of the likelihood of a certain problem to occur
- standard firefighting practices
- specification of the Landmarke concept both as a technical component and as a set of services
- learning about Landmarke features and services and how they could support reconnaissance work (e.g., the practical benefits of having an ad-hoc network that would allow transferring relevant tactical information between firefighters)
- assessments on the impact of having a token as a navigation tool for ordinary missions
- assessments on the impact of having a token as a navigation tool in the case of rare but very dangerous situations

An important consequence that we can draw for research practice is that anticipations need to be primarily substantiated by knowledge from experience in order to check whether the assumptions made can be confirmed. Real-world experiments are essential in coping with uncertainty (Klinke and Renn 2002) and, in particular, to reveal unexpected effects (Groß et al. 2005). In the case of firefighting, the latter aspect was very important. Decisions about the feasibility of new reconnaissance tactics were very difficult to make and rather uncertain. Firefighting tactics are procedures conducted in cooperation, which makes them dynamically complex. They have emerged from years of experience in coping with critical incidents in firefighting operations. Furthermore, emergency situations can change in very unexpected ways, and these changes always have an impact on the chosen firefighting tactics. Speculation and anticipation, then, are grounded in existing practice but just as much entail reflection on the degree to which existing practices can change. As we have discussed, anticipations on possible problems in reconnaissance missions, on the practical value of tokens, and so on, were not only supported by experiences (e.g., by working with Landmarke artifacts and by analyzing critical incidents in real missions) but also involved speculation. More specifically, actors oriented toward a specific set of questions, such as the following:

- Which problematic situations are likely to occur during reconnaissance?
- What technical option could solve the situation that an anticipation is uncovering?
- What functions of the artifact are really useful in improving navigation practices, and in what kind of situations (e.g., rare but critical situations, day-to-day missions, or both)?

Particularly critical were the assessments of whether a certain problem was worth being researched. As Volkema argues,

> Problem formulation plays a crucial role in conducting research and potentially affects succeeding phases, including theory building, research design and conduct, and conclusions. Yet problem formulation is often rushed or taken for granted. People tend to be solution-minded, rather than problem-minded. When problem formulation is rushed or taken for granted, in all likelihood important dimensions of the problem go undetected and opportunities are missed. (Volkema 1995, p. 28)

In this case, the problems of reconnaissance teams in navigation were formulated during the setup of the project, which started from a set of pre-studies conducted with the Paris fire brigade (Denef et al. 2008; Ramirez et al. 2009).

An essential tool for exploring anticipation and confirmation was, in our case, provided by prototyping, a form of the working-with-the-artifact stream proposed by grounded design (see Chapter 1). A good example of the dynamics between anticipation and confirmation can be found in the original assumption that the last deployed token would be highly relevant for improving the navigation capabilities of a firefighting team. This anticipation emerged as a speculation but was confirmed by a number of training missions with firefighters using appropriate mobile user-interface prototypes (Ramirez et al. 2012).

The Landmarke project, as we have seen, allowed us to study research-oriented project work with actors from different professions and with varied experiences. The funding model of the civil security research program of the German Federal Government encourages project proposals aimed at having practical benefits and improving civil security. This design results in a strong involvement of stakeholders coming both from industry and from civil security authorities. This made a good fit with the practice-based research philosophy that provided the foundation of the researchers leading the project.

We have shown how design emerged not only from technical artifacts created as visions of future navigation practices but also from reflection on existing navigation practices as described and embodied by professional practitioners. This served as the argument to explore feasible changes in reconnaissance tactics. Decisions were informed by reflection on experiences coming from real firefighting missions, as well as from practical evaluations of technical artifacts in safe training exercises. What is important about the use of experience in assessing the potential value of artifacts is the fact of communication. Whereas, in other cases, experience is used on an individual basis to provide justification for decisions that went unchallenged in the organization, in this case, the constant exchange of ideas was central to the success of the project. Collaborative reflections on navigation practice justified technical designs to support navigation.

Collaborative evaluations of artifacts allowed firefighting practitioners to reflect on possible problems in relation to navigation tactics. This was critical for progress in the project and helped industry partners, scientists, instructors, and firefighters as a group to identify the potential of the Landmarke technology as a promising tool that could go way beyond simply supporting navigation.

16.5 Historically Grown: Understanding the Design Practices of an IT Research Group

A second ethnography investigates the research practice of our group at the University of Siegen (WiNeMe) and, to some extent, its linkage with EUSSET, its academic reference community at European level. On both levels, the ethnographies deal with community formation and knowledge sharing beyond individual (design) case studies. One of the relatively unexamined set of relationships we have alluded to is that of those that exist above and beyond the ones entailed in a specific case study. Here, then, we outline some features of an ongoing attempt to generate community participation on a more permanent basis.

As we suggested early on in this chapter, so-called post-normal or "Mode 2" research may constitute something of a new paradigm for research activity. One of the less frequently discussed aspects of this putative shift, however, is the degree to which the kinds of disciplinary and organizational heterogeneity that result may well require collaboration and engagement over time. We engage in some early reflections on our own activities with a view to a better understanding of the way in which both an individual research group, WiNeMe, and an academic communities' research group, EUSSET, operate. EUSSET, comprised of actors from both academia and industry, aims to foster academic and practical exchange between its members, end users, and other practitioners. Ironically, little is known at present about the work practices of these participants engaged in practice-based computing.

Here then, we take early steps as part of a continuing "research about research" to identify how design case studies would be influenced by factors external to the project. Stakeholders coming together in a case study have, as we have already seen, heterogeneous expectations about project work, expectations which are shaped by the traditions, routines, and expectations of their home institutions (Dachtera et al. 2014).

With regard to our investigation of WiNeMe, the specific focus was on the everyday work of interdisciplinary, practice-oriented design activity by (mainly) PhD researchers. While becoming acquainted with their role, practice-oriented researchers developed their own set of practices, which, given the increasing demand for practice-oriented research, deserve to be described in detail.

We will start by introducing EUSSET. It was funded in response to newly emerging European funding schemes that focus on practice-oriented research. European actors (mainly) from the fields of participatory design, CSCW, and HCI found that their voices were not well enough represented in Brussels. Moreover, parts of the European CSCW community did not feel very well treated by ACM SIG-CHI when this US organization moved to rearrange its respective conference schedules. EUSSET, founded in 2011, relies on an infrastructure of personal relations, conferences, and publication venues, most of which existed before, but, it was felt, were too little interconnected to deal with the abovementioned challenges.

EUSSET was founded as a community of mainly university-related actors who were oriented toward practically relevant research and who recognized some of the difficulties entailed in managing collaboration across different institutions and with heterogeneous actors. Most of the early participants work at universities. Those who do not still usually have a university background and, often, a PhD degree. Furthermore, their professional positions are often research related (e.g., innovation manager in a company). The community aims to integrate perspectives on empirical research (mainly qualitative, with methods from the social sciences) with technical knowledge and design-related approaches. By aiming to be practically relevant, the community concentrates on the practices of other groups of people ("practitioners" or "end users") by studying them, publishing empirical material about them, and designing and evaluating IT artifacts together with them in support of their practices. The practices of the community are quite diverse; this is, along with other factors, a function of the differences in national science systems. While there are efforts to integrate these different steps into coherent frameworks, such as "design case studies" (Wulf et al. 2011, 2015), in fact most individual actors have a focus on the particular steps that their disciplines and commitments orient them toward. Relating to and negotiating these concerns with others is a large part of their work.

Much of what is reported here is the work of one of the authors, who, in the course of his PhD research, undertook a lengthy qualitative study. This involved, as is typically the case in such work, an ad-hoc mixture of interview and observation and was made more complex by the very heterogeneity and geographic dispersal we have already referred to. Considerable parts of the research were conducted by the researcher through involvement in project work, project acquisition, university politics, and bureaucracy, along with attendance at international conferences and program-committee meetings (as an observer). Field notes, memos, and group discussions involving other authors played a crucial role in the development of the analysis; they were used to triangulate the interview statements with the results from participant observations and with preexisting knowledge from a literature review. While generally the study had an exploratory character, it was conducted with an eye on the design of IT support and can hence be seen as representing the first step of a "design case study" (cf. Randall et al. 2007; Wulf et al. 2011, 2015). Finally, since EUSSET is an organization in the process of establishing itself, we were interested in how it was constructed by the interview partners. Hence, the method of "ethnography of scaling" proved to be a valuable sensitizing concept for analysis (cf. Ribes 2014). We begin here, however, with an account of WiNeMe. Compared to research into individual design case studies, research into larger research groups or academic communities is still less well understood.

16.5.1 WiNeMe: A Practice-Based Group of' Design Researchers

The research group in question is based in Siegen, at a midsized German university. Universities typically rely on formal role definitions, such as student, PhD student, professor, administrator, research manager, and so on. These roles entail a certain positioning on the academic career ladder and carry assumptions about the next step to which the holder might aspire. In this manner, master's students, for example, strive for their master's degree, and PhD students aim to complete their theses. How such matters are managed in practice forms part of our enquiry. WiNeMe, at the time of writing, comprises approximately thirty PhD students, eight postdocs, four faculty members (two with tenure), and thirty-three student researchers. Most of the staff are financed through soft-money projects funded by German government agencies or European institutions. Only the most senior staff hold tenured positions. Most of the external funding comes from project calls, as is typical of the European funding model. Hence, the projects usually run in consortia comprising academic, industry, and end-user partners. Project topics are dependent on the current calls of the funding agencies; at the moment, they are mainly in the fields of IT for the aging society, civil security, energy efficiency, and sustainability.

Members of the senior staff have worked together for approximately 20 years, even though changing academic institutions. One of the senior researchers, whom we shall refer to as Sen2, recalled the days when they started to build the group (still at a different university):

> WiNeMe was one of seven areas at [one chair in computer science at the University of Bonn]. [...] *We had to acquire our positions ourselves.* Basically, we acquired our asses off... [...] The *only thing* we could rely on from [the chair] was that when there was money on the horizon, *we could sometimes get interim financing* from the institute for, say, 3 months.

When the senior researchers started to work in academia as PhD students, they were based at an institute where human-centered or even practice-oriented research was only tolerated at best—if it financed itself from external sources. The institute's chair was not particularly interested in financing the then emerging senior researchers' research agenda from his university budget. Hence, the researchers had to rely on third-party funds in order to secure their own positions. On the one hand, the orientation toward project-based funding schemes grew out of a necessity. On the other hand, relying on them also enabled the now-senior researchers to build a research group in an environment that pursued a completely different research agenda (see Wulf et al. 2011). Today, this ambiguity is still reflected in the daily work routines of the researchers, as can be seen by one PhD student, whom we shall call PhD1, when he described his tasks:

> So, my practice, what I do is, my *work basically consists of project work, publishing and writing project proposals* again. What comes into play with the publications is supervising students and teaching, a job which is on the one side [...] a bit laborious, but on the other side of course *one gets input from the students,* who often undertake a lot of project- and practice-related implementations or research work. You can get a lot of input for publications from there.

The daily work practice in the research group is mainly defined by the three interrelated themes of writing proposals, "doing projects," and writing publications. Furthermore, students are involved in all three themes. This mode of working sustains the group both financially and academically. In Section 16.5.2, we will explore how senior researchers, students, and PhD students accomplish these tasks together, and which work steps are involved therein.

16.5.2 Project Acquisition and Project Work

As mentioned in Section 16.5.1, research projects in WiNeMe are conducted in a variety of thematic areas. The concrete tasks of such research projects vary, but in general, the goals are related to studying the practices of (IT-)users, designing technology for them, or both. These research projects usually combine stakeholders from different research areas with industry partners and end users for a certain period of time (2–4 years). Financing of staff who do not have a tenured position (e.g., PhD students and some postdocs) is hence always for fixed periods of time; the ongoing acquisition of projects is a practical necessity. When asked about how he perceives project acquisition, PhD1, who was in his second year at the time, replied:

> Well, writing proposals. I more or less came into my first project because other people had got money in, more or less for me, so that I could get my position. And, because of that, I think *it is only fair to take care of the generation after me by getting in money for them.* I see it as a cycle [...] And thus, for me, writing proposals is just a fixed part of my work. [...] And, actually, *I personally enjoy writing proposals, especially in a team* [. . .] Of course, I particularly include things in them which I personally would like to do—for instance exploring new technologies, if I would like to take a step towards industry [...] I also do it *because I am personally interested in the results, or in the projects in general* [...], although it is clear that I will not work in all of them.

Here, the work of writing proposals is portrayed in two ways: on the one hand, for the PhD student, it is morally justified to spend a considerable part of his working time on acquiring projects. He accepts the necessity of doing this work because he also profits from the work of others. On the other hand, he also enjoys this kind of work and sees it in a positive light, as it allows him to participate in decisions about the research topics. The projects are typically acquired in response to funding agencies' calls for proposals; these calls are structured according to topics that are deemed "societally relevant." The fact that financing mainly comes from these third-party funds forces WiNeMe members to address the topics that the funding agencies deem relevant, and they have to adhere to the project structure required in order to obtain the funding money.

16.5.3 Acquiring a Research Project

Another PhD student, PhD3 reflected on how the process works in general and refers to a recent experience:

> So, there is the set target [to acquire projects], which stands at the beginning and then *research opportunities appear*, possibilities to research, like the call from the BMBF [German Ministry for Research], Civil Security [...] And then [...] you start reflecting about it. [...] You have to say, [Sen2] *has a lot of ideas* [...] And then he says, write something down and we talk in passing [...] and then you talk to other colleagues [...] talk to this person and that person, because there once was an application which was rejected but maybe we can still make something out of it.

This PhD student is an experienced researcher, having worked in the group for some 8 years and is now in the final phase of his PhD thesis. He has been involved in both successful and unsuccessful project acquisition processes. Here it becomes clear that project acquisition is always a team process, where reflecting about possible research ideas takes place among many different actors in the group. Furthermore, in this reflection process, previous proposal documents with related ideas are taken into account. While PhD3 locates the actual writing work on the level of the PhD students, the more coordinative and strategic work is attributed to the senior researchers:

> Mostly it just works out somehow with regard to who is involved in the project acquisition; these are "magical forces" to me, *which I have not yet fully understood*, because [I am just asked]: [...] can you do this and that? [...] And it just happens that [Colleague 1] and [Colleague 2] and [Colleague 3] join, which is wonderful, great.

This student is not concerned with the more strategic management work and states he is not entirely aware of the criteria used for selecting colleagues in the division of labor. The PhD student PhD2 held a similar view:

> *Faculty, then, think much more strategically*, also in the long term, which reaches beyond my time as a PhD student, for example. And... where they want to place themselves, where they want to get money from. [...] I think *I take their advice* because they think in terms of the chair's strategy, I don't do this myself. [...] *I [would] rather concentrate on my own work.*

Senior researchers thus organize the acquisition process, set the agenda in terms of selecting relevant research calls, and represent their respective teams at the official meetings. It is mainly the quality of their political network that determines the quality of the project team. When it comes to serious issues, they take over the negotiations, and they have to sign the official documents. The main work of writing the proposal document and contacting partners for the first time is, however, mainly done by PhD students, who are motivated by, inter alia, prolonging their work contracts. The exact division of labor and the distribution of competences thus varies considerably. Section 16.5.4 sheds some more light on how a proposal document comes into being.

16.5.4 Writing a Proposal Document

A completed project proposal mainly consists of a single text document. PhD3 explained how this document grows over time:

> It is about the *project sketch at first* [...] because besides the project idea and everything concerned with that, *you need a consortium* [...] well, cold calling, well, somebody usually knows somebody [...] it is not really cold [. . .] Well. Sometimes it is [...] but somehow we have the contacts from somewhere [previously] [...] So, what we did before is to *develop a one-pager* about the project goal, the call, briefly [...] what the idea is and how to go about achieving these goals.

As can be seen, the first step in getting funding is to assemble a project team according to the criteria put forward by the funding agency. This process is inherently political since it involves negotiating not only the research topic but also the distribution of financial means and tasks, the research approach, and the duties and responsibilities of each of the prospective project partners. Hence, the personal network(s) of the applicant(s) plays a crucial role. Often, partners know each other from previous cooperation, be it from a project or from, for example, jointly authored publications. Acquiring partners completely "cold" is therefore the exception rather than the rule. When assembling a project team, it seems it is crucial to align the requirements from the funding side (e.g., desired research perspectives on the problem, types of partners, distribution of results) with the possibilities allowed by the personal network. This is also the initial spark for the proposal document, which typically emerges as a "one pager" and grows subsequently to eventually become a fully fledged proposal.

The document circulates among the prospective project partners as an internal plan for how to distribute financial means among the project partners and as a convincing research outline for the duration of the project (usually 2–3 years). While writing the document is a team activity, usually the prospective project-leading institution coordinates the process. Building a practice-oriented project means that, besides stakeholders from a variety of scientific disciplines and industry partners, "practitioners" from "society" plays a key role. PhD3 reported on the tension that frequently occurs when negotiating with other partners:

> The development and practice partners of course *want a rather precise account of what will happen*, what they have to do and also, if they come in with a product, have an interest in [...] further developing their product. We, however, don't want to tie ourselves down too much [...] *rather look at how it will develop* [...] *because it contradicts our approach a bit, because I first want to look at what the practice yields.* [...] One has to find a way [...] concrete enough, but also with enough leeway.

The proposal document is separated into several sections, including a justification as to why the proposed research is societally and scientifically important, a report on the state of the art of the respective area, and a work plan laying down the prospective division of labor. Furthermore, cooperation between the different partners is divided up into discrete tasks, such as empirical studies and knowledge transfer from the end users to the researchers; technical development work for prototypes; evaluation; and others. It is a challenge to account for the openness of the research process on the one hand and to provide enough detail so that a commonly shared idea becomes clear on the other. Even if the idea is clear to all project partners, the project holder still requires a precise account of what will be done during the funding phase. Unsurprisingly, this is done by means of a detailed work plan describing the division of labor in the prospective project on a formal level.

Project acquisition also requires communication with the funding agency or the project holder. Some aspects of this are obvious. The success of a project proposal becomes more likely the more it matches the expectations of the funding agency (and of reviewers).

While calls already contain a number of requirements for proposals, applicants can fine-tune their project in all respects and hence increase their opportunities of actually obtaining funding by talking personally to the agency's employees. The political dimension of proposal writing is more complex, as the interests of the participants are often not openly debated, with discussion rather taking place on an ideological and rhetorical level. Following a certain rhetoric or adhering to a particular research tradition may be beneficial for some participants while being problematic for others, as we have previously seen. In addition, the funding agency may also expect a particular rhetoric, for instance, relating the research topic to a particular "societal problem" that it is deemed politically feasible, although not to say desirable, to tackle.

Besides the traditions and interests of the respective institutions, individual researchers also have preferences regarding research traditions, methods, and the topic to be followed in the project. In addition, there may be diverging conceptions of how to involve end users in the proposed cooperation. All these differences need to be mediated in the process of writing the proposal document. The end result is a document that is, in principle, accepted by all partners and that is uploaded in time on the funding agency's Web portal.

16.5.5 Project Work

Once the acquisition process has been successfully mastered and the project is accepted for funding, the actual project work begins. While, in the proposal document, the project work practices are described on a formal level, it will come as no surprise to experienced researchers that the actual project work may substantially deviate from this description. One reason for this is the *legitimation character* of the project proposal. After all, the purpose of an application is to get funding money—and its content is designed accordingly. The actual project work may require a different distribution of labor for various reasons and, again, as we have seen, regardless of formal commitments, practical understanding of what these commitments may mean often varies. WiNeMe projects are particularly prone to such changes, because what is to be developed technically is a function of the empirical work that precedes it. As PhD1 said,

> So, we are dominated by coordinative meetings and telephone conferences, simply to check the current state of the deliverables or work packages [...] Which result documents will be sent where and when? The *actual project work is really accomplished together with students*; we have employed three or four student assistants who do investigations for us, and we often just finalize and put together the students' work. And *we do the administrative part; that is, the work with other project partners, the writing of the final deliverables.* [...] Our actual project work is very much coordinative, administrative activity.

WiNeMe frequently takes over the role of the project coordinator and is therefore located at the interface between the other partners. It also typically acts as the expert for end-user research within the consortia. A crucial part of the work hence concerns coordinating activities within the project, organizing meetings, and writing reports.

Furthermore, student assistants are actively involved in the projects and contribute with implementations and research, often in the context of their BA or MA thesis, to the projects. In addition to this work, a lot of other things have to be done, as PhD2 remarked:

> Then all these things crop up that you also need to do, like *teaching*, small things, *organizational stuff* like filling out forms for travel expenses, collecting bills, searching for hotels [...] or [somebody asks you] can you write a short paragraph on this and that, *which doesn't actually have anything to do with the projects.*

University life also includes dealing with the university administration as well as with other bureaucratic and teaching duties. PhD2 found getting acquainted with these procedures particularly irksome. In addition, the culture within the group also includes helping out other colleagues with their work. Although employees are assigned to individual projects, there is a substantial amount of cooperation between them, which in turn requires coordination activities. As PhD2 said,

> You prioritize things internally with yourself. [...] I have a piece of paper and *actually prioritize the tasks and clarify with the relevant persons what the greatest priority is.*

Formally, individual researchers are responsible for their own project; in fact, a culture of mutual learning from others' experiences exists among WiNeMe researchers. Prioritizing tasks is thus a team process in which colleagues synchronize and negotiate prioritization of joint activities.

Even if the work practice within a project deviates from the work plan previously outlined, there are still formal requirements that need to be met throughout the course of the project. These involve regular reports and milestone meetings with the project holder, with these serving to account for the project's progress. Additionally, bearing in mind the limited financing period of the research project, researchers need to start preparing further applications in order to ensure their continuing employment after the project has ended. It is important to understand this context when considering how the practice-oriented knowledge particular to WiNeMe is produced. Research is always a compromise between the funding agency's agenda, the necessities within the project, the demands of the end users, and the individual researcher's personal interests.

16.5.6 Knowledge Creation and Publishing

Publications in WiNeMe usually cover one of the steps of a design case study (Wulf et al. 2011, 2015): a pre-study of the field, or the design and/or evaluation of an IT artifact. Publication venues tend to be decided depending on which step is salient. For WiNeMe PhD researchers, publications usually stem from work related to their respective third-party-funded projects. A complicating issue that constrains practice-oriented research is the disciplinary structure of publication venues. WiNeMe results are typically published outside these mainstream venues. The journals and conferences mentioned by the interviewees are not within the usual scope of any individual discipline. CHI, the best-known conference outlet for human-centered computing, may well be the "the premier international conference" of HCI, but HCI is not a well-established or well-understood discipline in the German (or European) academic system as of yet.

16.5.7 Publications as a Part of the Dissertation Process

In order to understand the role of research publications in WiNeMe, it is important to know how the process of acquiring a PhD degree is organized at the University of Siegen, where WiNeMe is based. Faculty guidelines require a thesis including, inter alia, material from two top-tier publications, before the PhD process can officially start. The most important publications for WiNeMe are either ACM CHI conference publications or publications in journals with an International Scientific Indexing impact factor higher than 1. From the perspective of individual PhD researchers, the main role of their publications is to serve as part of their dissertation thesis. The following quotation illustrates how PhD2 saw his publication strategy:

> Well, *because I want to go back into practice one day, into industry, I don't have endless time* [to complete the PhD]. I would say... *if I had a CHI publication sometime soon I would feel much better and would be more relaxed about it*... Because you just don't know... if it doesn't work out now... you don't know if it will work out next year either... Of course there's always the possibility of publishing in journals... but *if I had one, let's say, top-level publication already, I would be more relaxed and I would be able to say, ok, I might publish somewhere else as well* [at ACM CSCW, for instance].

Here, PhD2 referred to the annual CHI conference, which, for him, represented an opportunity to take another step toward his PhD degree by having a full paper accepted there. This view was confirmed by other PhD students in many informal interviews. It became clear that among other things, the relevance of CHI papers for the dissertation process represents a major incentive for PhD students to invest time in publishing there. For this reason, it is very important which papers count for the degree at faculty level and which do not. Another relevant issue is that publications also carry politics within the group. The reason behind this is that each paper can only be used by one PhD student for the dissertation. Usually, however, writing is a team process and, hence, authorial rights have to be negotiated. At this point, the distribution of labor within a project becomes relevant, as mentioned in Section 16.5.6. It matters whether researchers mainly spend their time with publications or with other types of work, such as administration or management.

16.5.8 Publication Policy of the Project Holder/Funding Agency

Publications are usually also part of the contract agreement with the funding agencies or the project holder. The writing of several project acquisition processes entails detailing a publication strategy as an explicit work package within a project proposal. In addition, it needs to be borne in mind that different funding authorities follow different policies with regard to the venues in which publishing is appreciated. PhD2 mentioned several German agencies, some of which are more oriented toward scientific venues. Others put more emphasis on publication media related to the respective impact on IT industries or practitioners. Students also engage in publishing to satisfy the funding agency's demands.

16.5.9 IT Media Use in WiNeMe

A range of different IT tools support the described practices. However, a general policy for particular tools does not exist within WiNeMe, as described by one senior researcher:

> It has to do with the culture [...] *there is no tool except email, which is used throughout the entire group* [...] there are no formalities and also no traditions of use, which leads to a kind of uncontrolled growth.

However, within smaller groups and project teams, a multitude of different tools are used. When Sen2 reflects about his own usage patterns, he argues that he adapts to different audiences with regard to the tools he uses:

> I have an account on ResearchGate, [...], Facebook, [...] Twitter, [..., and] Google+, *but I don't use them actively.* I was invited several times by my employees to build Mendeley groups, which I have accepted [to do] although I haven't done anything actively yet. As *for the future,* [...] *I have planned to work on my infrastructure a bit* [...] With regards to content, if I work together *with Americans, we mainly hold video conferences using Google+ Hangouts and Skype,* for instance and I have Dropbox, Skydrive, and other cloud folders in which I store research-related stuff.
>
> Interviewer: "So you do this when working internationally, but with your own employees, with people from our group, you don't...?"
>
> Sen2: "Yes, I do! With [Colleague 1] and [Colleague 2], I regularly collaborate on Skydrive [...] For years I *used Endnote as a database,* but don't do it anymore; [reports on technical problems]. What else? Ok, *for investigations I use the ACM Digital Library, Google Scholar, and stuff like this...* My own Google Scholar page is not published yet, because [...] it needed to be cleaned up first. And besides that, I do an awful lot via email.

The quoted passage makes clear that tool use is heavily dependent on personal preferences and on the concrete social situation with specific individuals. Sen2 uses different tools with different people, but in general he is, at the moment, still mostly reliant on email communication, since it represents the lowest common denominator inside and outside the group; as he says, "It is *difficult to change customs* and this here has to do with customs."

16.5.10 Emotional Tensions in Practice-Oriented Work

The previous sections described the circumstances under which publicly funded practice-oriented research takes place. It has been made clear that the position of PhD students is characterized by tension. This tension originates from the multitude of tasks that they are confronted with and need to become acquainted with. As PhD2 said,

> You are *thrown in at the deep end* sometimes, you don't know these things as a student. But it is interesting, *you also grow into it.* [...] But there really is a lot of work which has nothing to do with the concrete research work. It is a lot of networking [...] it is also work, because it *costs you quite an effort,* you have to develop strategies for yourself, you have to learn that for yourself. It is not like: you read it and then you know it, but it has *very much to do with personality and personality development,* being in this field.

PhD2 described his personal learning process as being, to an extent, painful—and as one in which he had to develop strategies to deal with situations he was not prepared for during his studies. A crucial yet underestimated aspect of work in general, and of interdisciplinary, practice-oriented research work in particular, is the role of emotions. In the process of becoming acquainted with WiNeMe, PhD2 had to learn the aforementioned practices—and not just in a formal and superficial sense. Rather, learning took place *in practice,* which meant that he was "thrown in at the deep end." One strategy for dealing with this challenge is for students to concentrate on their respective strengths. This has, however, certain disadvantages as may be seen in the following statement by PhD3:

> Then somebody asks you: *'Why don't you write publications?'* And I am like 'Wait a second, I do the project management.' [...] And then, there are all these other things, like teaching, which you cannot skip [...] then something has to be dropped and this is usually publishing [...] your own research endeavor [...] and then again the question: 'Why don't you publish?' And I'm like: *Well, if I am working on two project proposals, how should I publish?* [...] and, well, writing papers is also relevant for one's cumulative doctorate. *So, what counts at the end of the day are publications.*

Here, PhD3 mentions the fact that if one solely concentrates on the project management and on writing project proposals, it becomes difficult to work on publications at the same time. This can become a problem, insofar as publications are the basis for the cumulative dissertation model, as explained before. PhD3 hence sees a disadvantage for those researchers mainly concerned with the project management, as they lack the relevant publications in the end.

In a similar manner, other PhD students doing more analytic work expressed the desire to have more control over the practicalities of project work. Since they were less involved in the management decisions of the project work, they felt somewhat marginalized from the course of the projects and felt a lack of control over their own work conditions and about the direction of the work with end users. There is an evident balancing act to be performed, and the balance has to entail both a collective and an individual perspective.

As we have indicated, researchers are usually trained in a particular field, with particular expectations about professional work in that field. Furthermore, the academic cultures in which students are educated during their studies not only consist of a body of knowledge but also carry a certain "habitus" (Bourdieu 1977). When comparing the discussions of more "academically" oriented researchers with those of design-oriented researchers, it appeared that this is especially true with regard to issues of *understanding* and *intervention*. Empirically oriented subdisciplines from the humanities and the social sciences tend to focus on qualitative fieldwork, with explicit reservations about intervention. Intervention-oriented fields, such as business management, information systems, or design, in turn, usually base their intervention decisions not on extensive and systematic empirical work but rather on models of the world, and these models do not necessarily correspond to the situation at hand. Given that such things are also acquired largely through osmosis, negotiating them entails self-reflection. In addition, the process of socialization into the WiNeMe community of practice goes in hand with learning about one's own unconscious presuppositions about the science system in general and about related career options in particular.

New members of staff face the project reality with little knowledge about what is actually going to happen. Students educated in academic fields such as informatics, sociology, interaction design, media studies, or other areas, which go in hand with images of particular professional roles, are subjected to interdisciplinary practices with the other project stakeholders from the outset. As previously explained, solely focusing on one's strengths is not a viable option over time. In addition, as mentioned, tasks are sometimes ambiguously distributed, and participants are irritated by the fact that they have to take on tasks for which they were not prepared for in their academic education. Being confronted with the requirement to carry out such tasks while at the same time maintaining a professional attitude may lead to feelings of stress. As PhD2 said,

> And sometimes when the weekend comes, I say I cannot really take a weekend, somehow. And this creates stress and I *take the stress with me into the weekend* and it happens that I wake up at night and think "Oh dear, I still have to do this and this." And that is a tendency which is getting stronger at the moment and I actually want to work against it... otherwise the quality of my work declines.

Given this demanding work situation, the PhD degree assumes the function of a *reward* after a while. As PhD2 said,

> Well, at first not really... but then I realized that it doesn't actually make sense, to take all this [...] well, this scientific method, there is an intrinsic motivation, but I think, if you spent so much time doing this, then in the end you also want the PhD degree as an appreciation [...] I think *intrinsic motivation alone is not enough* [...] It needs to be compensated and that is *the doctoral degree as a reward in the end.*

PhD2 is intrinsically well motivated. He is interested in the topics he investigates and is positive about his personal learning process in the group. When he started working in the group, attaining a PhD degree did not have a high priority for him. In the course of his studies, this changed, due to the compensatory nature of the degree. Other interviewees shared this view; it was also mentioned that, in contrast to industry positions, which are often characterized by a high amount of stress as well, being a PhD student had the advantage that the degree represented a challenge as well as a personal benefit.

16.5.11 A Comparative Perspective toward Other EUSSET Groups

Our empirical study included not only actors from WiNeMe but also other researchers related to the European network EUSSET, as previously described. When comparing the insights gained about WiNeMe practices to those gained about other actors, it became obvious that the insights were only transferable to a limited degree. This is the consequence partly of the radically different circumstances under which researchers work, as well as of different epistemological preconditions. The German academic system carries certain particularities that do not necessarily translate to other European countries. While our data concerning different institutions is limited and hence it would be wrong to overgeneralize from our presentation of WiNeMe's research practices to the whole of EUSSET, it became clear that there are certain similarities and differences. The following findings should stimulate further investigation in the future:

- As already mentioned, EUSSET members are at the intersection between different scientific disciplines. One feature shared by most EUSSET actors is thus that they pursue a publishing strategy in interdisciplinary venues. Within their home discipline, or the one to which they are formally assigned, EUSSET actors thus frequently experience a problematic relationship vis-à-vis other interests.
- WiNeMe is probably one of the largest EUSSET-related groups in Europe and has grown considerably during the last decade by means of third-party funding. As previously outlined, this has certain implications concerning project acquisition, project work, and publishing. In our study, it became clear that other EUSSET groups have different ideas about, for instance, their PhD students' education, and the relationship between senior researchers and PhD students.
- WiNeMe's financial base heavily relies on public funding, and this has implications with regard to project length. EUSSET actors differ with regard to a project's typical duration, since some of them (especially those with a strong tradition in participatory design) can build on a culture of long-term involvement with practitioners, especially in the public sector.
- While the majority of EUSSET actors are based at universities, the community also includes practitioners from industry. Since these actors' organizations do not solely rely on public funding to be sustained financially, their daily work practices differ significantly from those of the researchers at universities. An idea of these differences is given in Section 16.5.4.

16.5.12 Discussion

This section has described in some depth the research practices of WiNeMe, one of the German research groups in the EUSSET network. The empirical findings testify to the very particular conditions under which WiNeMe emerged within the German academic system. Without strong governmental funding programs, the origins of the research group could not have been established—in an otherwise rather hostile academic environment. The empirical data also indicates how the conditions of WiNeMe's emergence have shaped the research practices of the group: acquisition and soft-money orientation have become major factors of the group's identity, since the senior researchers survived in academia in this manner. Thus, WiNeMe has developed elaborated practices of acquiring and working in soft-money projects, which are handed over from generation to generation of PhD students. Interestingly, the group has only a rather basic common IT infrastructure, while subgroups can be rather sophisticated in their technology appropriation. So, IT infrastructures following the CSCW design paradigm could be of value within the group.

WiNeMe is characterized by a certain normative consensus, at least among the group's senior researchers, that research should be directed toward societal ends, with the goal of contributing to "a better world." Standing in the tradition of the European CSCW community, the group's design agenda is directed toward IT support for human activities rather than toward full automatization. There is, then, a somewhat vague but still important consensus that creates a normative grounding and is an important element of group identity. The positioning toward societal ends corresponds often with governments' funding agenda in the sense that they address societal problems as well.

To understand knowledge sharing within WiNeMe, the concept of "communities of practice" comes to mind (Lave and Wenger 1991; Wenger 1998). About two-thirds of the PhD students and postdocs have been recruited internally—from a wide range of disciplinary backgrounds such as computer science, information systems, anthropology, psychology, sociology, journalism, and design. Being hired as students, they typically are already working in research projects—often writing their master's thesis and starting to coauthor academic papers. Those who do a good job as a student and want to stay for a PhD degree get hired—in cases where the financial conditions permit.[2] There is quite a long process of enculturation into WiNeMe's community of practice (Wenger 1998). However, the members' different disciplinary backgrounds, identities, and job trajectories tend to create tensions and insecurities at times and prevent certain actors from full enculturation.

To make a practice-based research paradigm work, one needs an established network of partners in the IT industry as well as among the relevant fields of application. Such a network requires acting, at least in part, on a regional basis, because such a design-research practice and the related knowledge-sharing practices require some level of local proximity (Fischer et al. 2007; Rohde et al. 2007).

The empirical findings make it clear that it is hard work to establish a new interdisciplinary research paradigm in a landscape of traditional academic fields. Occasionally, the senior researchers in the group joke that they would never have started that endeavor if they had known how difficult it would have been and how unlikely final success was at the beginning in the 1990s. In particular, when in the process of conducting the research

[2] PhD students are rather well paid in the German academic system. In computer science, they typically get a full position at an annual gross salary of some €40,000.

(since the group is only somewhat institutionally settled), the PhD students suffer occasionally from challenging working conditions. This is due to the triple demand of having to acquire externally funded projects, work in those projects, and, at the same time, publish the results at top venues. It is due to the personal structure of the group that, at times, even rather inexperienced PhD students are responsible for managing complex research consortia in a practice-based design paradigm (Dachtera et al. 2014). At the same time, the financial resources enable WiNeMe to invite senior researchers who consult with PhD students in their research and specifically support them in framing high-end publications.

So, the very particular funding situation made the emergence and institutionalization of WiNeMe possible—within the German academic system. It took a long time—from the mid-nineties until now—to elaborate on the practice-based design paradigm documented in this volume. It also demanded, and still demands, quite a bit of effort to position this paradigm in the international academic community of human-centered computing, specifically inside ACM SIG-CHI. The creation of EUSSET was a major step in this direction on the European level. These challenges rest mainly with the group's senior researchers and other researchers affiliated with WiNeMe and its research paradigm.

16.6 Conclusion

This chapter has presented two ethnographies on design-research practices. We focused on the aspects of how IT design projects are developed and how they are carried out in practice. Each of these studies has a particular focus and style of meta-research. Together, these studies seek to contribute to a better understanding of the domain of practice-based computing.

In so doing, we provide a reflexive account of our own practices. In some ways, our descriptions will appear rather familiar to experienced practitioners in HCI and similar communities. We should remember, however, that the same would be true of any group of people subject to a broadly ethnographic enquiry. Our "subjects" are supposed to be familiar with their own practices. Not all people working in the domain of human-centered computing have that degree of experience with practice-based research, however; and not all of them are university employees. We hope our work will help to familiarize those in more distant situations with the day-to-day reality of this kind of work. Our analysis contributes to the existing literature with regard to "constraints on practice orientation" and "management of practice orientation."

Ample attention has already been paid in HCI literature to bridging the gap between users and researchers, specifically in the field of participatory IT design. However, given the circumstances in which researchers work, managing end-user involvement in a project context still remains a challenge. Our main point, then, is that practice-oriented research, as a subset of a broader agenda in human-centered computing, remains an even more challenging activity for all participants.

As we have seen, one of the means of achieving practice orientation is, in principle, combining researchers from different disciplines to investigate and intervene in social practices. When these "lifeworlds" (Stichweh 1992), "ecological niches" (Lenoir 1997), and "communities of practice" (Lave and Wenger 1991; Wenger 1998) are combined, it is supposed to foster creativity (Fischer 2000) and lead to innovation (Weingart 1997). What is clear, however, is that the learning process implicated in this is problematic across organizations, across disciplines, and between individuals. The observation by one of the PhD students at WiNeMe that felt he had been "thrown in at the deep end" would appear to be characteristic of many experiences at different levels.

We have tried to show that the learning that takes place often has an informal and non-explicit character and, as we saw in our first example, is not always realized. In the light of our examples, it is perhaps useful to distinguish between self-management, collaborative management, and the management of others. With regard to the former and in line with Mansilla et al. (2015) and McCallin and Bamford (2007), we find that heterogeneous work involves a high degree of what Hochschild (2003) calls "emotional labour" and Strauss et al. (1985) describe as "sentimental work." Both have pointed to the competent handling of emotions as an important dimension of work practices—of flight attendants in the case of Hochschild's study, and of clinical staff in the case of Strauss et al. This aspect of negotiated academic outcomes is often neglected. The social situation of interdisciplinary work does not encourage the expression of "negative" feelings, given that certain "commitments" are required. This aspect may deserve to be investigated in further research, since recent studies suggest that emotions may play a far greater role for the social structure than has been assumed in the past.

Collaborative management and the management of others involve a range of skills, interests, and practices that we make visible through the reflexive approach we discuss. As we argued in the introduction to this chapter, both practices and the assumptions behind them are heterodox. Consequently, identifying the locus of decision-making in respect of design is not straightforward. Moreover, practices and assumptions originate from a complex network of personal relations, rules, regulations, instructions from external bodies, and so on. In the examination of our own work in the context of the two different studies, we begin to see what those complexities look like and perhaps provide the teachable moments we have recommended.

From a methodological perspective, investigations into research practices often have an auto-ethnographical character—in the sense that the researchers are part of the institutional framing of the research project, group, or community. This is also the case for the two studies presented in this chapter. In the case of the study on "critical moments," the study was conducted by the coordinator of the Landmarke project as part of his PhD work. In the case of the WiNeMe study, the main researcher—also a PhD student—was part of the group, although not working on any of the design-oriented projects. In the Wan et al. (2016) study, the meta-research was also part of the research activities of the design team, whereas in other cases we created the role of a specific outsider to conduct this type of meta-study (Dachtera et al. 2014). Indeed, the complexity of practice-based research endeavors requires deep and long-term engagement. Investigations into research practices need a culture of openness if an external researcher is working with a design team, and of honesty if the study is conducted by members of the design team themselves.

Carrying out ethnographies and communicating their results can be painful and full of conflicts—particularly whenever they try to strengthen reflection and learning within a research team. The meta-researcher may come to grapple with what he might believe to be recurring problems, structural inefficiencies, elements of incompetency, or personal conflicts. If this is the case, the researchers' analysis is likely to criticize the given practices; some actors may not agree this criticism and might even construe it as personal criticism. In a constellation such as this, the researcher may lose access to the field or even his/her peace of mind, because of the conflicts. From the point of view of the practice-based designer as the object of meta-studies, being challenged or criticized while conducting complex design interventions can be quite stressful. Finally, meta-research can create conflicts for the project coordinators as well as for the group's management, whose positioning and conduct may be subject to critical analysis and challenged as a result. We have seen instances of all these painful phenomena when setting up a meta-research agenda inside our own research group.

Interestingly, there is little institutional recognition of the necessity of such a meta-research program. In publicly funded research schemes, there are typically not any resources designated for the role of a "meta-researcher." However, such research findings would be very helpful for improving the performance of practice-based research consortia. Honest and self-reflective empirical analysis could also be a permanent trigger for improving the mechanisms applied within the Central European approach to research funding. The practice-based design community should, however, try to avoid the pitfalls from which the international community of development cooperation suffers—namely, the ongoing creation of sugar-coated evaluation reports.

This paper offers a first outline of a potential meta-research program in practice-based computing. Yet, it is not fully conceptualized and has not been even half carried out. So far, the main focus has been on self-reflectivity and refinement in the field of practice-based computing. Moreover, we need to tackle one of the central challenges in the field: how can meta-research contribute to a comparative analysis of design case studies and thus help the transferability of design-relevant insights? Finally, it is also possible for meta-research to be directly relevant to the design of IT in support of the analyzed research practice. In this sense, the two studies presented so far can also be understood as context studies for the design of IT tools to support practice-based design research. Thus, we are engaged in something we might call "computer-supported cooperative research,"[3] the self-application of the CSCW paradigm.

References

Alexander, N., Gottwald, W., and Trenczek, T. 2006. "Mediation in Germany." In N. Alexander, ed., *Global Trends in Mediation* (2nd edition). Köln: Otto Schmidt, pp. 179–212.

Altrichter, H., and Posch, P. 1990. *Lehrer erforschen ihren Unterricht: Einführung in die Methode der Aktionsforschung*. Bad Heilbrunn: Julius Klinkhardt.

[3] We owe this term our dear and invaluable colleague Erhard Schüttpelz.

Argyris, C., Putnam, R., and Smith, D. M. 1985. *Action Science: Concepts, Methods and Skills for Research and Intervention*. San Francisco: Jossey-Bass.

Argyris, C., and Schön, D. A. 1996. *Organizational Learning II*. Boston: Addison-Wesley.

Barkhuus, L., and Brown, B. 2012. "The sociality of fieldwork: Designing for social science research practice and collaboration." In *GROUP'12*. New York: ACM, 35–44.

Bartunek, J. M. 2011. "What has happened to Mode 2?" *British Journal of Management* 22 (3): 555–8.

Bell, S., and Morse, S. 2007. "Story telling in sustainable development projects." *Sustainable Development* 15 (2): 97–110.

Bergold, J., and Stephan, T. 2012. "Participatory research methods: A methodological approach in motion." *Historical Social Research/Historische Sozialforschung* 37 (4): 191–222.

Betz, M., and Wulf, V. 2014. "EmergencyMessenger: A text based communication concept for indoor firefighting." In *CHI'14*. New York: ACM, 1515–24.

Bjørn, P., and Boulus, N. 2011. "Dissenting in reflective conversations: Critical components of doing action research." *Action Research* 9 (3): 282–302.

Bødker, S., and Iversen, O. S. 2002. "Staging a professional participatory design practice: Moving PD beyond the initial fascination of user involvement." *NordiCHI'02*. New York: ACM, 11–18.

Bortz, J., and Döring, N. 2002. *Forschungsmethoden und Evaluation für Human—und Sozialwissenschaftler*. Heidelberg: Springer.

Bourdieu, P. 1977. *Outline of a Theory of Practice*. Cambridge: Cambridge University Press.

Bradbury, H., and Reason, P. 2001. "Introduction: Inquiry and participation in search of a world worthy of human aspiration." In P. Reason and H. Bradbury, eds., *Handbook of Action Research: Participative Inquiry and Practice*. London: Sage, 1–14.

Bratteteig, T., and Wagner, I. 2014. *Disentangling Participation: Power and Decision-Making in Participatory Design*. Cham: Springer International.

Bratteteig, T., and Wagner, I. 2016. "Unpacking the notion of participation in Participatory Design." *Computer Supported Cooperative Work* 25 (6): 425–75.

Bucciarelli, L. L. 1988. "An ethnographic perspective on engineering design." *Design Studies* 9 (3): 159–68.

Callon, M. 1979. "L'État face à l'innovation technique: le cas du véhicule électrique." *Revue française de science politique* 29 (3): 426–47.

Callon, M. 1999. "The role of lay people in the production and dissemination of scientific knowledge." *Science, Technology and Society* 4 (1): 81–94.

Carrier, M., and Nordmann, A. 2011. "Science in the context of application: Methodological change, conceptual transformation, cultural reorientation." In M. Carrier and A. Nordman, eds., *Science in the Context of Application*. Dordrecht: Springer, 1–7.

Coyne, R., and Snodgrass, A. 1995. "Problem setting within prevalent metaphors of design." *Design Issues* 11 (2): 31–61.

Dachtera, J., Randall, D., and Wulf, V. 2014. "Research on research: Design research at the margins: Academia, industry and end-users." In *CHI'14*. New York: ACM, 713–22.

Davison, R., Martinsons, M., and Kock, N. 2004. "Principles of canonical action research." *Information Systems Journal* 14 (1): 65–86.

Denef, S., Ramirez, L., Dyrks, T., and Stevens, G. 2008. "Handy navigation in ever-changing spaces: An ethnographic study of firefighting practices." In *DIS'08*. New York: ACM, 184–92.

Dewey, J. 1910. *What Is Thought? How We Think*. Columbia University Press.

Doing, P. 2008. "Give me a laboratory and I will raise a discipline: The past, present, and future politics of laboratory studies in STS." In E. J. Hackett, O. Amsterdamska, M. Lynch, and J. Wajcman, eds., *The Handbook of Science and Technology Studies* (3rd edition). Cambridge, MA: MIT Press, pp. 279–95.

Dourish, P. 2006. "Implications for design." In *CHI'06*. New York: ACM, 541–50.

Dyrks, T., Ramirez, L., Denef, S., Meyer, D., and Penkert, B. 2009. "Designing for firefighters: Building empathy through live action role-playing." Available at http://pdfs.semanticscholar.org/e9ca/8cf8f28bdaf66b73162434a139b191885f64.pdf (accessed October 17, 2017).

Emery, F. E., and Trist, E. 1969. *Form and Content in Industrial Democracy*. London: Tavistock.

EU. 2013. *FP7-COOPERATION: Specific Programme "Cooperation" Implementing the Seventh Framework Programme of the European Community for Research, Technological Development and Demonstration Activities*. Available at http://cordis.europa.eu/programme/rcn/846_en.html (accessed October 17, 2017).

Evans, C., and Lambert, H. 2008. "Implementing community interventions for HIV prevention: Insights from project ethnography." *Social Science and Medicine* 66 (2): 467–78.

Fahy, R. 2002. *US Fire Service Fatalities in Structure Fires, 1997-2009*. Available at http://tkolb.net/FireReports/2011/US_FatalitiesInStructures77-09.pdf (accessed October 17, 2017).

Fischer, G. 2000. "Symmetry of ignorance, social creativity, and meta-design." *Knowledge-Based Systems* 13 (7): 527–37.

Fischer, G., and Giaccardi, E. 2006. "Meta-design: A framework for the future of end-user development." In H. Lieberman, F. Paternò, and V. Wulf, eds., *End User Development*, Dordrecht: Springer, 427–57.

Fischer, G., Rohde, M., and Wulf, V. 2007. "Community-based learning: The core competency of residential, research-based universities." *International Journal of Computer Supported Collaborative Learning* 2 (1): 9–40.

Funtowicz, S. O., and Ravetz, J. R. 1993. "Science for the post-normal age." *Futures* 25 (7): 739–55.

Gaver, W., and Bowers, J. 2012. "Annotated portfolios." *Interactions* 19 (4): 40–9.

Gibbons, M., Limoges, C., Nowotny, H., Schwartzman, S., Scott, P., and Trow, M. 1994. *The New Production of Knowledge: The Dynamics of Science and Research in Contemporary Societies*. London: Sage.

Groß, M., Hoffmann-Riem, H., and Krohn, W. 2005. *Realexperimente: Ökologische Gestaltungsprozesse in Der Wissensgesellschaft*. Bielefeld: transcript Verlag.

Hayes, G. R. 2011. "The relationship of action research to human-computer interaction." *ACM Transactions on Computer-Human Interaction* 18 (3): 15.

Hevner, A. R., March, S. T., Park, J., and Ram, S. 2004. "Design science in information systems research." *MIS Quarterly* 28 (1): 75–105.

Hirsch Hadorn, G., Hoffmann-Riem, H., Biber-Klemm, S., Grossenbacher-Mansuy, W., Joye, D., Pohl, C., Wiesmann, U., and Zemp, E. 2008. *Handbook of Transdisciplinary Research*. Dordrecht: Springer.

Hochschild, A. R. 2003. *The Managed Heart: Commercialization of Human Feeling*. Oakland: University of California Press.

Hodgkinson, G. P., and Rousseau, D. M. 2009. "Bridging the rigour-relevance gap in management research: It's already happening!" *Journal of Management Studies* 46 (3): 534–46.

Jackson, S. J., Steinhardt, S. B., and Buyuktur, A. 2013. "Why CSCW needs science policy (and vice versa)." In *CSCW'13*. New York: ACM, 1113–24.

Kemmis, S., and McTaggart, R. 1988. *The Action Research Planner*. Victoria: Deakin University Press.

Kensing, F., and Halskov Madsen, K. 1991. "Generating visions: Future workshops and metaphorical design." In J. Greenbaum and M. Kyng, eds., *Design at Work Cooperative Design of Computer Systems*. Hillsdale, NJ: Lawrence Erlbaum Associates, 155–68.

Kieser, A., and Leiner, L. 2009. "Why the rigour–relevance gap in management research is unbridgeable." *Journal of Management Studies* 46 (3): 516–33.

Kimble, C., Grenier, C., and Goglio-Primard, K. 2010 "Innovation and knowledge sharing across professional boundaries: Political interplay between boundary objects and brokers." *International Journal of Information Management* 30 (5): 437–44.

Klinke, A., and Renn, O. 2002. "A new approach to risk evaluation and management: risk-based, precaution-based, and discourse-based strategies." *Risk Analysis an Official Publication of the Society for Risk Analysis* 22 (6): 1071–94.

Knorr-Cetina, K. D. 1981. *The Manufacture of Knowledge: An Essay on the Constructivist and Contextual Nature of Science*. Oxford: Pergamon Press.

Krohn, W. 2008. "Epistemische Qualitäten Transdisziplinärer Forschung." In M. Bergmann and E. Schramm, eds., *Transdisziplinäre Forschung : Integrative Forschungsprozesse Verstehen Und Bewerten*. Frankfurt am Main: Campus Verlag.

Latour, B., and Woolgar, S. 1979. *Laboratory Life: The Social Construction of Scientific Facts*. London:Sage.

Laudel, G. 2006. "The art of getting funded: How scientists adapt to their funding conditions." *Science and Public Policy* 33 (7): 489–504.

Lave, J., and Wenger, E. 1991. *Situated Learning: Legitimate Peripheral Participation*. Cambridge: Cambridge University Press.

Lee, C., Dourish, P., and Mark, G. 2006. "The human infrastructure of cyberinfrastructure." In *CSCW'06*. New York: ACM, 483–92.

Lenoir, T. 1997. "The discipline of nature and the nature of disciplines." In *Instituting Science: The Cultural Production of Scientific Disciplines*. Redwood City: Stanford University Press, 45–74.

Lewin, K. 1946. "Action research and minority problems." *Journal of Social Issues* 2 (4): 34–46.

Lofland, J. 1995. "Analytic ethnography, features, failings, and futures." *Journal of Contemporary Ethnography* 24 (1): 30–67.

Lynch, M. 1993. *Scientific Practice and Ordinary Action: Ethnomethodology and Social Studies of Science*. Cambridge: Cambridge University Press.

Mansilla, V. B., Lamont, M., and Sato, K. 2015. "Shared cognitive–emotional–interactional platforms markers and conditions for successful interdisciplinary collaborations." *Science, Technology, & Human Values* 41 (4): 571–612.

Martin, D., Mariani, J., and Rouncefield, M. 2009. "Practicalities of participation: Stakeholder involvement in an electronic patient records project." In M. Büscher, R. Slack, M. Rouncefield, R. Procter, M. Hartswood, and A. Voss, eds., *Configuring User-Designer Relations*. London: Springer-Verlag London, 133–55.

Mathiassen, L., and Nielsen, P. A. 2008. "Engaged scholarship in IS research." *Scandinavian Journal of Information Systems* 20 (2): 3–20.

McCallin, A., and Bamford, A. 2007. "Interdisciplinary teamwork: Is the influence of emotional intelligence fully appreciated?" *Journal of Nursing Management* 15 (4): 386–91.

Moris, J., and Hatfield, C. 1982. "A new reality: Western technology faces pastoralism in the Maasai Project." In International Rice Research Institute, ed., *The Role of Anthropologists and Other Social Scientists in Interdisciplinary Teams Developing Improved Food Production Technology*. Manila: International Rice Research Institute, 43–61.

Mosse, D. 2007. *Notes on the Ethnography of Expertise and Professionals in International Development*. Available at http://ceas.iscte.pt/ethnografeast/papers/david_mosse.pdf (accessed October 17, 2017).

Moser, H. 1978. *Didaktisches Planen und Handeln*. München: Kösel.

Moser, H. 1980. *Aktionsforschung als Sozialforschung*. Hagen: Studienbrief der Fernuniversität Hagen.

Nett, B., and Stevens, G. 2008. "Business ethnography: Aktionsforschung als Beitrag zu einer reflexiven Technikgestaltung." In J. Becker, H. Krcmar, and B. Niehaves, *Wissenschaftstheorie und gestaltungsorientierte Wirtschaftsinformatik*. Dordrecht: Springer, 43–67.

Nett, B. 2010. *Konstruktion und Rekonstruktion von Technik. Business Ethnography als reflexives Forschungsdesign für Technikentwicklungsprojekte*. Habilitation thesis. Siegen: University of Siegen.

Nett, B., Meurer, J., and Stevens, G. 2008. "Knowledge management-in-action in an EUD-oriented software enterprise." In M. Ackerman, R. Dieng-Kuntz, C. Simone, and V. Wulf, eds., *Knowledge Management in Action*. Dordrecht: Springer, 139–49.

Nowotny, H., Scott, P., and Gibbons, M. 2001. *Re-Thinking Science: Knowledge and the Public in an Age of Uncertainty*. Cambridge: Polity Press.

Pedersen, J. 2007. *Protocols of Research and Design. Reflections on a Participatory Design Project (Sort of)*. PhD thesis. Copenhagen: IT University of Copenhagen.

Pipek, V., and Wulf, V. 2009. "Infrastructuring: Towards an integrated perspective on the design and use of information technology." In *Journal of the Association of Information System* 10 (5): 306–32.

Pohl, C., and Hirsch Hadorn, G. 2007. *Principles for Designing Transdisciplinary Research*. München: Oekom Verlag.

Pottier, J. 1993. "The role of ethnography in project appraisal." In J. Pottier, ed., *Practicing Development: Social Science Perspectives*. London/New York: Routledge, 13–33.

Österle, H., and Otto, B. 2010. "Konsortialforschung." *Wirtschaftsinformatik* 52 (5): 273–85.

Otto, B., and Österle, H. 2010. "Relevance through consortium research? Findings from an expert interview study." In *DESRIST'10*. Berlin/Heidelberg: Springer, 16–30.

Ramirez, L., Denef, S., and Dyrks, T. 2009. "Towards human-centered support for indoor navigation." *CHI'09*. New York: ACM Press, 1279–82.

Ramirez, L., Dyrks, T., Denef, S., and Stevens, G. 2007. *Context as a Resource for Diagnostic Work*. Available at http://s3.amazonaws.com/academia.edu.documents/36235316/ecscw07-diagnosing-Ramirez.pdf?AWSAccessKeyId=AKIAIWOWYYGZ2Y53UL3A&Expires=1508270374&Signature=ujY9L%2BWzMOm9nY8ReE0Cz7eB3Ng%3D&response-content-disposition=inline%3B%20filename%3DContext_as_a_resource_for_diagnostic_wor.pdf (accessed October 17, 2017).

Ramirez, L., Dyrks, T., Gerwinski, J., Betz, M., Scholz, M., and Wulf, V. 2012. "Landmarke: An ad hoc deployable ubicomp infrastructure to support indoor navigation of firefighters." *Personal and Ubiquitous Computing* 16 (8): 1025–38.

Randall, D., Harper, R., and Roundefield, M. 2007. *Fieldwork for Design*. Berlin: Springer.

Ribes, D. 2014. "Ethnography of scaling, or, how to a fit a national research infrastructure in the room." In *CSCW'14*. New York: ACM, 158–70.

Rohde, M., Klamma, R., Jarke, M., and Wulf, V. 2007. "Reality is our laboratory: Communities of practice in applied computer science." *Behaviour and Information Technology* 26 (1): 81–94.

Rohde, M., Stevens, G., Brödner, P., and Wulf, V. 2009. "Towards a paradigmatic shift in IS: Designing for social practice." In *DESRIST'09*. New York: ACM, 15.

Rohde, M., Brödner, P., Stevens, G., and Wulf, V. 2017. "Grounded design: A praxeological IS research perspective." *Journal of Information Technology* 32 (2): 163–79.

Rosemann, M., and Vessey, I. 2008. "Toward improving the relevance of information systems research to practice: The role of applicability checks." *MIS Quarterly* 32 (1): 1–22.

Schmidt, K. 2011. *Cooperative Work and Coordinative Practices: Contributions to the Conceptual Foundations of Computer Supported Cooperative Work*. London: Springer-Verlag London.

Schön, D. A. 1983. *The Reflective Practitioner*. New York: Harper Collins.

Sismondo, S. 2008. "Science and technology studies and engaged program." In E. J. Hackett, O. Amsterdamska, M. Lynch, and J. Wajcman, eds., *The Handbook of Science and Technology Studies* (3rd edition). Cambridge, MA: MIT Press, 13–31.

Slaughter, S., and Leslie, L. L. 1997. *Academic Capitalism: Politics, Policies, and the Entrepreneurial University*. Baltimore: Johns Hopkins University Press.

Smith, D. E. 2006. *Institutional Ethnography as Practice*. Lanham: Rowman & Littlefield.

Star, S. L., and Griesemer, J. R. 1989. "Institutional ecology, 'translations' and boundary objects: Amateurs and professionals in Berkeley's Museum of Vertebrate Zoology, 1907–39." *Social Studies of Science* 19 (3): 387–420.

Stevens, G., and Nett, B. 2009. *Business Ethnography as a Research Method To Support Evolutionary Design*. http://s3.amazonaws.com/academia.edu.documents/8809932/stevens-nett_ethnography_evolutionary-design_2009.pdf?AWSAccessKeyId=AKIAIWOWYYGZ2Y53UL3A&Expires=1508271397&Signature=Y0%2BqNnOoVrivSdA4BHyhQRKGB%2F8%3D&response-content-disposition=inline%3B%20filename%3DBusiness_Ethnography_as_a_research_metho.pdf (accessed October 17, 2017).

Stevens, G. 2010. *Understanding and Designing Appropriation Infrastructures: Artifacts as Boundary Objects in the Continuous Software Development*. Available at http://dokumentix.ub.uni-siegen.de/opus/volltexte/2010/433/ (accessed October 17, 2017).

Stevens, G., Schwartz, T., and Meurer, J. 2009. "A dialectic view on Open Innovation." In *AMCIS'09*. Atlanta: AIS, 668.

Stichweh, R., 1992. "The sociology of scientific disciplines: On the genesis and stability of the disciplinary structure of modern science." *Science in Context* 5 (1): 3–15.

Strauss, A., Fagerhaugh, S., Suczek, B., and Wiener, C. 1985. *Social Organization of Medical Work*. Chicago:University of Chicago Press.

The Federal Ministry of Education and Research. 2009. *Research for Civil Security: Protection Systems for Security and Emergency Services*. Available at www.straz.gov.pl/download/1133 (accessed October 17, 2017).

Van De Ven, A. H. 2007. *Engaged Scholarship: A Guide for Organizational and Social Research*. Oxford: Oxford University Press.

Volkema, R. J. 1995. "Managing the problem formulation process: Guidelines for team leaders and facilitators." *Human Systems Management* 16 (1): 27–34.

Wan, L., Müller, C., Randall, D., and Wulf, V. 2016. "Design of a GPS monitoring system for dementia care and its challenges in academia–industry project." *ACM Transactions on Computer Human Interaction* 23 (5): 31.

Weingart, P. 1997. "From 'finalization' to 'Mode 2': Old wine in new bottles?" *Social Science Information* 36 (4): 591–613.

Wenger, E. 1998. *Communities of Practice: Learning, Meaning, and Identity*. Cambridge: Cambridge University Press.

Winschiers-Theophilus, H., Chivuno-Kuria, S., Kapuire, G. K., Bidwell, N. J., and Blake, E. 2010. "Being participated: A community approach." In *PDC'10*. New York: ACM, 1–10.

Wulf, V. and Rohde, M. 1995. "Towards an integrated organization and technology development." In *DIS'95*. New York: ACM, 55–64.

Wulf, V., Rohde, M., Pipek, V., and Stevens, G. 2011. "Engaging with practices: Design case studies as a research framework in CSCW." In *CSCW'11*. New York: ACM, 505–12.

Wulf, V., Müller, C., Pipek, V., Randall, D., Rohde, M., and Stevens, G. 2015. "Practice-based computing: Empirical grounded conceptualizations derived from design case studies." In V. Wulf, K. Schmidt, and D. Randall, eds., *Designing Socially Embedded Technologies in the Real-World*. London: Springer-Verlag London, 111–50.

Epilogue

Socio-Informatics: Intertwining Analytical and Design-Oriented Research into Social Practices

VOLKMAR PIPEK, DAVE RANDALL, AND VOLKER WULF

The various investigations in this book can be characterized as putting forward an argument for a nondeterministic relationship between investigation and design for social practices in which IT artifacts have an acknowledged relevance or a potential. The term "practice," it is clear, provides a focus for careful analysis of the ways in which people orient to the use of technology over time, the way in which technology mediates behaviors, and the various constraints, technological and otherwise, under which people operate. Nevertheless, it has been argued throughout this book that very little purchase on "practice" is provided by naive recourse to sociological theorizing. To varying degrees, all the authors in this book recognize the need for concept development that specifically orients to the problem of design and development. This has never been more relevant, given the rapid technological changes evident almost everywhere we look.

The computer-supported cooperative work (CSCW) research community, in particular, has long sought to examine the relationship between technology and "work" in relation to the support one can provide for the other. Such a position is in sharp contrast with approaches that aim to automate work, in the sense of fully replacing human activities by machines, for example, in the traditional mainstream of the artificial intelligence community. However, supporting, in our sense, typically means engaging with and often accepting these practices may change—at least on a microlevel. As part of a practice-based design agenda, the term "support" needs, then, to be developed more carefully, since it may well include the formalization and even the automation of certain elements of human activities (Christiansen and Harper 2016). The critical issue here, as always, is to understand more completely just how change might ramify, rather than crossing one's fingers, hoping for the best, and ignoring possible ramifications.

Socio-Informatics, Volker Wulf, Volkmar Pipek, Dave Randall, Markus Rohde, Kjeld Schmidt, Gunnar Stevens (Eds). © Oxford University Press 2018. Published 2018 by Oxford University Press.

This volume brings together contributions from authors with different foci but with a passion for a shared endeavor to come to more accountable, transparent, empowering, and sustainable ways to foster technology-related practice improvements. This epilogue aims at setting out an agenda, or at least a number of questions and milestones that illustrate potential pathways in our effort, while considering technological trends as well as current and future working conditions of practitioners and researchers. We would like to think of an agenda of "practice-based computing" as forming a discourse on what we would call "socio-informatics," although that term has been widely used to mean a number of different things.

The term "socio-informatics" was first used by some of the editors around the year 2000. Having worked during the 1990s at a traditional computer science department, they came to the conclusion that applied computing suffers from some rather fundamental incoherencies and deficits, which are deeply ingrained in the historically grown identity of the field (see Rohde and Wulf 2011; Schmidt 2011). These include the following:

- limitations with regard to research methods, notably focusing on "top-down" approaches to design, and process models that emphasized the "formal" character of the organization; in sum, focusing on the technical in the sociotechnical equation
- a limited understanding of the field's theoretical foundations, with a primary focus on mathematical or formal theorems
- a problematic epistemological positioning that judges the validity of insights independently of the (social) context of application

CSCW, at its inception, and specifically in its European instantiation, aimed to identify a new research paradigm, one that might overcome the given deficiencies and (re)introduce some notion of the "social" in computing. Our point, however, is that we are a long way from producing a coherent alternative. While without question rooted within a CSCW community, many practitioners have identified a variety of interests that may require new ways of thinking about the investigation/design relationship, for instance when examining "nonwork" environments like the home, games, or IT systems with a general role in society (e.g., technology affording an "electronic" democracy) or when trying to understand how principles such as participatory design might be worked out in practice in these new conditions. Not least, making sense of more long-term shifts in the way IT systems are embedded and used in different contexts seemed to be a complex and unresolved problem. Information systems (IS) discourses around notions of "sociotechnical systems" can seem both arbitrary and argued at such a rarified theoretical level as to be useless for practical design and development work. Finally, the technology landscape underwent revisions at a faster pace than theory-led researchers could work. These deficits have been alleviated by a number of approaches, some of which are discussed in this book. It remains the case, however, that making sense of "practice" and its ramifications across settings and domains is a radically unfinished project.

Balancing investigation and design work remains, we would argue, a central objective of CSCW and cognate disciplines. Our use of the term "informatics" (which is used in

German synonymously for "computer science" but also has connotations of applied mathematics and the information-processing sciences) thus remains a useful way of reminding us that design is still an integral feature, while we remaining committed to ways of overcoming the limitations stated above. In our understanding, socio-informatics is still a field of informatics—it remains our ambition to build innovative IT artifacts and to inform the work of programmers and others involved in technology-development processes. Investigation into practice, however, may entail investigations into a gamut of interests, including those of (sometimes ill-defined) users (as "customers" of technology development), designers (as "manufacturers" of IT artifacts to be developed), and, of course, ourselves as researchers trying to understand and improve the landscape defining the relation between technology production and technology use. Moreover, we felt the need to establish a language and conceptualizations that did not prioritize one practice as given (e.g., information and communications technology [ICT] development) while other practices are under reconsideration (e.g., practices of potential ICT "users"). We have outlined a number of concepts and approaches in this book to foster (self-)reflection among different practitioners who are concerned with or affected by new technological developments.

Some part of the objectives rehearsed above can be seen as a reaction to an epistemological monoculture, one where science and engineering models, the logic of process modeling, or the presumed efficiencies of new programming techniques all act in roughly the same direction. A "practice" perspective, it can be argued, entails a certain methodological and normative pluralism, such that careful comparison of cases, where similarity and difference are acknowledged at levels appropriate to the different interests in play, might result in a genuine transferability.

In this volume, we aimed to give a stronger foundation to these practice-oriented approaches around IT development. We can distinguish two rather different accounts of "practice" here: (1) a conceptual–historical one developed by K. Schmidt in Chapter 2 and (2) a practice–theoretical one, outlined by, among others, A. Reckwitz. Schmidt provides an analysis of the twisted history of the concept of "practices," spanning over the last 2,000 years. When it comes to the account's relevancy for IT design, he points to the importance of the interplay between rules, principles, and situated activities—a topos already deeply engrained in the CSCW discourse. Reckwitz (2002) develops his "practice" term out of a meta-analysis of current sociological theorizing—a pattern of academic work that Schmidt, in a second contribution to this book, harshly criticizes. It is evident that the various contributors to this book do not always agree on what might be entailed in the characterization and use of the term "practice." Some have found that Reckwitz's meta-analysis offered some stimulation to their design work (see Wulf et al. 2011, 2015). However, both of these distinctive accounts, whatever position one takes, are sensitive toward the developmental trajectories of social practices due to the introduction and design of IT artifacts. From a design point of view, however, in and of themselves, they lack a strong empirical foundation—an argument Schmidt puts forward when criticizing the practice theorists. The issue, then, has to do with the role of theory, and what kind of theory is likely to prove most useful for the purposes we designate. As indicated repeatedly in this book, useful theories must orient to both analytic investigation and design and need to do so while recognizing the longer-term transformations that occur as new technology is designed, introduced, used, and, in some cases, appropriated. These theories can, of course, be used in a variety of ways, including to determine what kind of analytic work should be done (a role we reject) or in that "sensitizing" or "illuminating" way that Herbert Blumer famously recommended. At this point, we believe that Randall et al. (2007) still offer a very decent and yet flexible set of suggestions as to how we might go about the empirical investigations implied.

A design-oriented account needs, then, to provide the detailed contextual descriptions that the "practice turn" has always implied, but it needs as well to engage with potentialities. Analytical accounts of existing or potential practices are not sufficient; they have a target they aim to inform and engage: technologically knowledgeable designers on the one hand and, on the other hand, (potential) users who find enough reason and motivation to reconsider their practices based on a recognition of possible improvements and perhaps become actively involved in redesign processes. As researchers in this arena, on the given assumption that we are engaged in both investigation and design, we are required to reflect upon our own practices as well, not least because, at some point, we will be involved in decisions about how, and to what extent, we can legitimately generalize from our findings and, just as much, what elements of the designs that result can also be reused, form part of modular constructions, or support end-user development.

Design case studies, recommended by the Siegen school in this book, can be understood in the tradition of a (participatory) action research paradigm (Whyte 1991; also see Chapter 9), using technological interventions to understand the dynamics of evolving practices in the domain at hand. In doing so, they lead to the design of innovative IT artifacts and accounts on their long-term appropriation, going at least some way to providing guidelines for the conceptual and building work that forms the core of our discipline. Aside from an intensified reflection on the practices involved in this kind of endeavor, the methodological foundations of IT development need to be constantly challenged. Where classic accounts of these methods in computer science focus on the completed product (hardware, software, or both), we can choose to look at a (successfully) established usage as the anchor point in technology development. Stevens and Pipek (in Chapter 4), in this way, reflect on technology appropriation studies and their consequences for design, also discussing a potential theoretical framework based on Bowker and Star's (1999) notion of infrastructuring. "Grounded design" is the umbrella term used here to organize the generative effort of developing IT artifacts together with technologically enhanced practices and is aligned with the idea of the "PRAXLABS" framework and other flexible approaches to the issue of "method," aimed at sustaining connections between development and use practices beyond traditional project-based structures. The focus is essentially pragmatic, rejecting any deterministic view of appropriate methodology in favor of general analytic commitments, which are reflected on in separate chapters—Chapter 6 on "ethnography and design," Chapter 7 on "participatory design," and Chapter 9 on "action research"—but all in varying degrees reflecting on the kind of involvement that one might expect and encourage from users.

To this end, the notion of end-user development is considered as an arm of this kind of thinking. The aim here is to provide flexibility over longer periods of use and across several use situations, to support technology management by actors whose primary goal is not building the application at hand. End-user development typically provides a "gentle slope of complexity" that allows users to make an active choice on how far they want to immerse themselves in technological details of their infrastructure (Lieberman et al. 2006; Wulf et al. 2008). Chapter 4 usefully elaborates on the social and collaborative notion of end-user development.

The final chapter on meta-research aims to elaborate on means to foster self-reflectivity among researchers, and its consequences for a research discourse in general (including the issue of comparability of results) and on the feasibility of methodological approaches for consideration of the possibility of practice improvement.

Socio-Informatics: Establishing a Research Discourse for Practice-Based Computing

The practice-oriented perspective, it has been argued above, can foster a closer relation between development and use practices—and has the merit of providing the flexibility required for understanding new technological affordances (e.g., ubiquitous computing, and the Internet of things) in a rapidly changing social and organizational context. Continued work on such practice-oriented perspectives could entail technological challenges, methodological challenges, and epistemological positioning.

Technological Challenges

The technological challenges emerging from a practice-based research paradigm span from better support of appropriation activities to fundamental issues of software architecture and development.

Appropriation Infrastructures

Pipek (2005) suggested a new direction of technological development in supporting appropriation activities, specifically from the perspective of user–user cooperation. Stevens (2010) extended this line of thinking by suggesting appropriation infrastructures are to be understood as communication channels via which practitioners of the technology-development domain can interact with those from the use domain. The technological connection between these practice spheres still needs to be further explored as new technological ecosystems emerge (see Draxler and Stevens 2011 for a related study into the Eclipse ecosystem).

Designing Sociable Technologies

Sociable technologies (Ludwig et al. 2014) describe an important extension of software artifacts being equipped with appropriation infrastructures for addressing the emerging world of physical artifacts in the realm of phenomena such as ubiquitous computing or the Internet of things. Sociable technologies suggest the design of physical (and software) artifacts in ways that allow and actively support the sharing of use stories and configurations and suggest integrating additional sensors, actuators, and communication channels that relate not only to the functional purpose of a technology but also to a discourse on how to use it.

Supporting Communities of Developers

To make practice-based computing more effective and efficient, there should be some reuse of components of newly developed and given IT artifacts. Therefore, it would make sense to have an open-source repository, maybe connected to the documentation of the individual design case studies. That way, a community of practice-based designers could draw not only on each other's design ideas but also on each other's code. Such elements of code sharing would be obviously also beneficial in implementing appropriation infrastructures or sociable technologies.

IT Architectures

An approach to reuse can be supported by appropriately designed IT architectures. The design of IT architectures could take the results of different design case studies into account to compare the differences in requirements. Based on such a comparative analysis of design case studies, the software architects could decide on a module structure that would make it easy to change the more differentiated aspects of the artifact while ingraining other architectonical decisions more deeply.

End-User Development

We have suggested that applications should be built in a way that end users, typically not being professional software developers, can modify these applications according to their changing needs (Lieberman et al. 2006; see also Chapter 13). This is important in supporting the appropriation of IT artifacts because, with changing practices, the artifacts may need to be tailored accordingly.

Methodological Challenges

Challenges when conducting individual design case studies have already been extensively discussed in this volume. In the following, we want to focus on infrastructural and methodological challenges resulting from a comparative approach dealing with a set of individual design case studies.

Networks of PRAXLABS Projects

The PRAXLABS framework has been introduced in this book (see Chapter 10) as a research and development infrastructure that allows connecting to practice domains beyond the scope of a single design case study or project. Taking this approach seriously, we envision building a network of PRAXLABS projects that cover various domains. The connection of neighboring domains will not only become a resource for innovating practices and an ecology to allow technology manufacturers to develop their products but also a research environment to look comparatively at the frictions of similar or competing practices.

Understanding Appropriation

We already have a large variety of methods that structure the work of developing IT artifacts. These methods reach out into the practice domains that an IT development aims to support. However, there is not any complementary conceptualization of the creativity that happens in these practice domains when IT artifacts get appropriated. Following Donald Schöns's groundbreaking work on the "reflective practitioner," one could imagine trying to understand the IT users' craftsmanship on a level of theoretical reflection that IT design methodologies have reached.

The Comparative Approach

We have still little experience with bottom-up concept building when comparing different design case studies. Wulf et al. (2015) and Betz and Wulf (in Chapter 15) make first attempts in this direction. However, we need to better explore how to establish a creative environment in which researchers with backgrounds in different case studies can be supported in finding conceptual similarities. We also need to explore how sensitizing concepts need to be framed and described to become meaningful in different contexts.

Portfolio of Design Case Studies

To support the building of design-related concepts and to make the insights manifested in individual concept better accessible over time, we need to learn the best way to document individual cases. Working on each case typically creates a multitude of materials that are rarely preserved and shared beyond the individual research project.

Meta-research

An agenda for research into grounded design-research practices is still to be elaborated upon. So far, we have looked into the emergence of new design ideas and the cooperation within research consortia and research groups (Dachtera et al. 2014; Wan et al. 2016; also see Chapter 16). We still need to better understand the particularity of the relevant design practices in order to allow other actors to draw on these experiences and insights. Another issue will be to decide how far meta-research might become embedded in the institutional environments of design research.

Epistemological Positioning

It remains difficult to foster an epistemological research position that emancipates itself from the origins of our societies' traditional conception of "science" as aiming at deriving factual knowledge and universally applicable operational descriptions of observable phenomena. In fact, the speed of development that came with the phenomena of "digitalization" throughout all spheres of modern lives makes tangible, in a single lifetime, changes that took centuries before, together with the potential of "digitalization" to transcend and connect these spheres. These developments make a bottom-up approach to concept building and a stronger integration of reflective spheres not only possible but necessary. In this sense, this volume has tried to formulate a post-objectivist research paradigm in the domain of human-centered computing.

We discussed grounded design, design case studies, and ePortfolio ideas in this book to generate an integrated perspective on the development of practices as well as IT artifacts, to be complemented by a level of self-reflectivity in design research. We started a design-oriented discourse on the concepts of "appropriation" and "infrastructuring" (Pipek and Wulf 2009; Stevens et al. 2010; also see Chapter 4) to develop a new terminology to describe these phenomena in a more accurate and integrated way. There are alternative conceptualizations (e.g., Engeström 2005) that aim to address a similar level of integration (but were not able to foresee the phenomena and opportunities that "digitalization" provides today), and there may be additional ideas to come.

We point out that the arenas sketched above along a scale from the local and immediate to the global and reflective are a significant extension to traditional discourses in computer science and IS. In their claim to universality, these discourses resemble the approaches to system theory and cybernetics that ran through these disciplines in the fifties and sixties of the last century. Socio-informatics remains concerned with the concrete spheres of practice improvement, technology innovation, and scientific reflection when discussing its rigor. Socio-informatics aims to provide a roadmap for the investigation/design problematic, signposted by our running theme, the appeal to practice-based design.

References

Bowker, G. C., and Star, S. L. 1999. *Sorting Things Out: Classification and Its Consequences.* Cambridge, MA: MIT Press.

Christiansen, L. R., and Harper, R. 2016. "The many faces of computational artifacts." In *COOP'16.* Cham: Springer, 93–106.

Dachtera, J., Randall, D., and Wulf, V. 2014. "Research on research: Design research at the margins: Academia, industry and end-users." In *CHI'14.* New York: ACM, 713–22.

Draxler, S., and Stevens, G. 2011. "Supporting the collaborative appropriation of an open software ecosystem." *Computer Supported Cooperative Work* 20 (4–5): 403–48.

Engeström, Y. 2005. *Developmental Work Research: Expanding Activity Theory in Practice.* Berlin: Lehmanns Media.

Lieberman, H., Pateró, F., and Wulf, V. (eds.). 2006. *End User Development.* London: Springer-Verlag London.

Ludwig, T., Stickel, O., Boden, A., and Pipek, V. 2014. "Towards sociable technologies: An empirical study on designing appropriation infrastructures for 3D printing." In *DIS'14.* New York: ACM, 835–44.

Pipek, V. 2005. *From Tailoring to Appropriation Support: Negotiating Groupware Usage.* PhD thesis. Oulu: University of Oulu.

Pipek, V., and Wulf, V. 2009. "Infrastructuring: Towards an integrated perspective on the design and use of information technology." *Journal of the Association of Information System* 10 (5): 306–32.

Randall, D., Rouncefield, M., and Harper, R. 2007. *Fieldwork in Design.* Berlin: Springer.

Reckwitz, A. 2002. "Toward a theory of social practices: A development in culturalist theorizing." *European Journal of Social Theory* 5 (2): 243–63.

Rohde, M., and Wulf, V. 2011. "Aktuelles Schlagwort: Sozio-Informatik." *Informatik-Spektrum* 34 (2): 210–13.

Schmidt, K. 2011. *Cooperative Work and Coordinative Practices: Contributions to the Conceptual Foundations of Computer-Supported Cooperative Work.* London: Springer-Verlag London.

Stevens, G. 2010. *Understanding and Designing Appropriation Infrastructures: Artifacts as Boundary Objects in the Continuous Software Development.* PhD thesis. Siegen: University of Siegen.

Stevens, G., Pipek, V., and Wulf, V. 2010. "Appropriation infrastructure: Mediating appropriation and production work." *Journal of Organizational and End User Computing* 22 (2): 58–81.

Wan, L., Müller, C., Randall, D., and Wulf, V. 2016. "Design of A GPS monitoring system for dementia care and its challenges in academia–industry project." *ACM Transactions on Computer Human Interaction* 23 (5): 31.

Whyte, W. F. (ed.). 1991. *Participatory Action Research.* Newbury Park, CA: Sage.

Wulf, V., Pipek, V., and Won, M. 2008. "Component-based tailorability: Towards highly flexible software applications. *International Journal on Human-Computer Studies* 66 (1): 1–22.

Wulf, V., Rohde, M., Pipek, V., and Stevens, G. "Engaging with practices: Design case studies as a research framework in CSCW." In *CSCW'11*. New York: ACM, 505–12.

Wulf, V., Müller, C., Pipek, V., Randall, D., Rohde, M., and Stevens, G. 2015. "Practice-based computing: Empirically grounded conceptualizations derived from design case studies." In V. Wulf, K., Schmidt, and D. Randall, eds., *Designing Socially Embedded Technologies in the Real-World.* London: Springer-Verlag London, 111–50.

Index

The manufacturer's authorised representative in the EU for product safety is Oxford University Press España S.A. of el Parque Empresarial San Fernando de Henares, Avenida de Castilla, 2 – 28830 Madrid (www.oup.es/en or product.safety@oup.com). OUP España S.A. also acts as importer into Spain of products made by the manufacturer.

www.ingramcontent.com/pod-product-compliance
Lightning Source LLC
LaVergne TN
LVHW011856200926
848484LV00002B/463
* 9 7 8 0 1 9 8 7 3 3 2 4 9 *